"We Thank God and England..."

A documentary book consisting, principally, of a wide selection of memorabilia about the evacuation of the Gibraltar civilian population 1940 -1951

By

J. Gingell

This documentary book was first published in Gibraltar by J.Gingell in October 2011.
Reprinted in January 2012.

A catalogue record of this book is available from the British Library.

ISBN 978-0-9569756-0-7

Front and back covers designed by J.Gingell.

CONTENTS

CHAPTER

ACKNOWLEDGEMENTS

First and foremost I wish to express my sincere personal appreciation and gratitude to every person who has in anyway very kindly supported this charitable project. Without their contribution it would have been utterly impossible to fulfil my two aims; to raise moneys towards cancer related charities and also make my own humble personal contribution about the evacuation of the Gibraltar civilian population.
The help I have received, in term of information, to complete this document has ranged from very casual conversations to that of more detailed written and pictorial material from various organisations, institutions, associations, historical studies offices, archives, libraries, museums and newspapers in Gibraltar, the UK and in the USA. Acknowledging every person or place individually would be totally impossible and I would certainly run the risk of omitting or erroneously naming people and places. I also wish to acknowledge that I found it very helpful for my research to consult the following books and other sources of information:

Sir Winston Churchill's	- The Second World War
Sir William Jackson's	- The Rock of the Gibraltarians
Sir Kenelm Creighton's	- Convoy Commodore
Mr George Hill's	- The Rock of Contention
Mr Tommy Finlayson's	- The Fortress Came First
Mr Anthony Beevor's	- The Battle for Spain
Mr Manolo Rodriguez's	- I, Remember
Mrs Lourdes Galliano's	- A Rocky Passage to Exile
Mr Albert Pizzarello's	- Sus Poesias
Messrs E.G.Archer's & A.A.Traverso's	- Education in Gibraltar 1704 -2004
Mrs Mariola Summerfield's	- A Woman's Place
Strait Vision Productions'	- Evacuation: Cause and Effect
Mr Dennis Beiso's	- Talks on the following subjects: 1. The Effects of the Spanish Civil War in Gibraltar 2. The Jose Luis Diez Incident 3. 300 years of Constitutional Developments
Mr Tito Vallejo's	Collection of photographs and written material

The names of the persons that appear in the captions related to all the family photographs are as I understood them to be when they were given to me by the respective families. There are names which I was unable to obtain after many enquiries and are shown either with question marks or left blank. In this respect, I apologise for any omissions or errors but would only be too pleased to correct them for any future editions of this documentary book.

Foreword

It gives me enormous pleasure to be asked to write a foreword to Mr.Joe Gingell's excellent book on the evacuation of the civilian population of Gibraltar. The evacuation was a central event in our history, one which had a lasting impact and which affected our people in many different ways.

Many historians have pointed to the importance of the evacuation to the development of Gibraltarians as a people and indeed other excellent books exist which document those effects on our identity in a very detailed manner.

Mr.Gingell's book is, however, a human story. The many images contained herein (many of which have not been seen publicly before as they come from private family collections) are a testament to the human experiences of Gibraltarian families during the war years. His words provide an account not just of the history of this seminal event, but also an account of a very personal experience and yet one shared by so many individuals and so many families in Gibraltar.

Mr.Gingell's has been a labour of love, one born out of the tragic passing away of his daughter Michelle (to whom the book is dedicated) and one which he has seen through to completion through sheer determination, hard work, and not a little personal sacrifice. I know every Gibraltarian will identify with the words and images contained in these pages. The book represents history at its best – in its most personal and emotive form.

I know you will enjoy reading this book as much as I did.

The Hon Steven Linares

Minister for Culture

INTRODUCTION

This is documentary book which consists mainly of a collection of memorabilia about the evacuation of the Gibraltar civilian population. The information contained has come principally from persons who have donated photographs, written or verbal information, newspaper cuttings and from consultations from those who were knowledgeable about the evacuation. The dates and other statistical information quoted relating to the different events are those obtained from sources, which, to the best of my knowledge, are reliable and correct.

When I initiated my research, my intensions were to prepare a documentary book exclusively about the Whitelands College. I suppose, like many of those who were evacuated, I always had a desire of one day visiting the place where my family were accommodated during the evacuation. Although I had visited London on many occasions, I was unable to fulfil this desire until the summer of 2001. On that occasion I went to see my daughter who was convalescing after receiving treatment for breast cancer at the Royal Marsden Hospital. It was then that I thought about the idea of visiting the Whitelands Training College with my daughter, as she was also very keen to visit the place where my family was living during the war. As soon as we entered Whitelands and walked around and inside the building, very vivid memories of my childhood began to come back from the time when I used to play around with other children in the beautiful surroundings of the College. During this visit I obtained some information about Whitelands but the only reference that I could find about this centre was a brief mention in the book, **I, Remember** by the late Mr Manolo Rodriguez. After reading this book, other publications and documents, I was somehow prompted with the idea of carrying out a research about the evacuees at Whitelands.

My daughter and I at Portobello when we talked about the idea of compiling a document about the Whitelands College in aid of the Cancer Charities.

With the aim of appealing for information I wrote stories in the Gibraltar Chronicle, the Insight Magazine, the Wandsworth Museum Newsletter, the Evacuees Reunion Association's Newsletter, the Wandsworth South News and some websites.

The exhibition held at The John Mackintosh Hall in November 2002 to launch my research about Whitelands.

I also held an exhibition at the John Mackintosh Hall in November 2002 to afford me with the opportunity of being able to meet with some of those who had some personal knowledge to contribute towards the intended documentary. Equipped with much more information, I visited the College on two more occasions in February 2004. Once accompanied by daughter and the other by my son. Incidentally, these visits coincided exactly with the sixtieth anniversary of the bombing of Whiteland on the 19th February 1944.

After these visits I decided to go ahead with the preparation of a draft documentary book which served me in becoming much more knowledgeable and intrigued about the whole period of the evacuation. With these thoughts in mind, I held an exhibition at the John Mackintosh Hall in October 2005 which included the entire period of the evacuation with the aim of acquiring more information.

At the exhibition held in 2005 with Mr Lionel Massetti who served on the Resettlement Board at the time of the repatriation.

The response was excellent and I also received much encouragement from visitors to go ahead with researching further the subject of the evacuation in order raise more funds for cancer charities. I was convinced too that the best method to acquire further information was by holding another similar exhibition. After some planning I held my final exhibition in September 2006 by displaying double the number of photographs displayed in 2005.

Mrs Maria Guilliano who as many other evacuees of her time who visited the exhibition provided me with a fountain of knowledge about her experiences during the evacuation

The response to this exhibition was still much better and obviously I obtained many more photographs and much more information in the form of written and verbal materials. It could be said that the book has been written by those who experienced that period in the history of Gibraltar. As a lay author I have narrated and presented all this information to the best of my knowledge and ability.

DEDICATIONS

Dedicated in loving memory of my daughter Michelle whose inspiration and advice encouraged me always, even in her last days, with the realization of this documentary book, which unfortunately she did not live to see complete.

Michelle posing for the Bosom Buddies Calendar 2007 to raise money towards breast cancer awareness. Photograph by Mark Montovio.

In memory of those women
Who we miss since they departed

Women who were diagnosed
With a disease that can't be forgotten!

As well wishers we must pray
For the souls that have long left
But we must never forget
Living souls need prayers as well

Breast cancer is a disease
That hits one in every 9
Some are women, some are men
Could be daughters, sons or wives
solidarity must be shown
to eradicate this malady
by obtaining funds for research
like this book intends to try it…

Dedicated to Michelle
For her strength
throughout this odyssey
is a father who supports
others living his same story…

"Early detection equals survival!" Do not leave for tomorrow what you HAVE to do today!

Sonia Golt (Breast Cancer Survivor)

REASONS FOR PROJECT IN AID OF CANCER RELATED CHARITIES

As mentioned in my introduction, I went to visit my daughter after she had been treated for breast cancer at the Royal Marsden Hospital. While convalescing, we visited the Whitelands Training College. There we found out that one of the students' charitable activities included donating money for Breakthrough in Breast Cancer. After pondering for a few days it occurred to us to compile and publish documentary book about the Whitelands College as an evacuation centre to raise funds for cancer research. Since then we set on this project and up to her very last few days Michelle was constantly inspiring and advising me, despite her own struggle with cancer, to complete this documentary which encompasses the whole subject of the evacuation.

Although she has not been physically present to see its completion, I know for certain, that she continued guiding me to fulfil our promised task of donating all the proceeds from this book towards cancer related charities.

Michelle and I at Fulham Road near the Royal Marsden Hospital.

NOTES ON INDEXES TO CHAPTERS

The bulk of the photographs displayed in this documentary book were donated by many families who did their best to find the names of their relatives in the photographs. Considering that these photographs are about seventy years old it was undoubtedly one of the most arduous tasks with regard to the compilation of information for this documentary book. Many photographs appear without names or just with a few names as it was impossible to trace all the names of the person that appear in the photographs despite many efforts and enquiries. In the case of females, the same person may appear in some photographs with their maiden names while in other photographs with their respective married names. There could be cases where the same persons appear in different photographs and could be recorded in the indexes as if they were different persons. Whilst every possible effort has been made to record the names as accurately as it is possible there could be some genuine errors and omissions for which I very sincerely apologise. In this respect, I would appreciate very much to be informed of any errors or omissions for any possible subsequent edition of this documentary book.

CHAPTER ONE

CIVILIANS IN A FORTRESS

When Britain captured Gibraltar there were about 4,000 Spanish civilians living in what was already a fortress. They all fled except for about 70 who decided to stay behind. After about twenty years from its capture and in accordance with the 1725 census there were 1,113 civilians who were already made up of several nationalities. The strength of the garrison was then 1,200 plus families. At the start of the 1727 siege the garrison stood at about 3,200 but the number of civilians was reduced to nearly 700 mainly as a result of the 400 Spanish residents, who according to some historians, were ordered to leave. The census held in March of 1753 showed that the population was made up of a garrison of 4,426, including families and the civilians living in the fortress then stood at 1,816, and as in the previous census, it was also made up of different nationalities, including 185 Spaniards.

During Britain's imperial rivalry with France, Gibraltar became strategically important for Britain and consequently brought about an increase in strength of its garrison and the renovation of its defences. To carry out the necessary work on the defences, there was a need to hire a regular civilian labour force. The military authorities needed at the same time to deal with different traders for the supply of essential goods and materials. This, inevitably, brought more civilians seeking to reside within the confines of the fortress.

Just before the Great Siege of 1779-83, the civilian population stood at 3,201 and at the start of hostilities the garrison was 5,400 strong but increased to 7,000 during the siege.

A plan of the Fortress of Gibraltar during the siege of 1727. As can be seen most of the defences shown in the map were built during the Spanish occupation of Gibraltar. Map London Illustrated News.

After the Great Siege, the civilian population was reduced to less than 1,000. There were two main contributing factors to this reduction in the number of civilians. Some civilians were killed due to hostilities and others left of their own volition for safer places before the blockade and hostilities started.

It took a few years for the number of civilians to get to the level of just over 3,000 that existed before the siege. The delay in the recovery of the pre-Great Siege levels of the civilian population was mainly due to the fact that many buildings were destroyed during the bombardment and those civilians who wished to return could not do so because of the lack of actual living accommodation. As from the beginning of the 19th century the civilian population started to increase very quickly in comparison to the previous 100 years. In 1804 the number of civilians residing within the fortress was about 6,000. Taking into account that the civilian population was almost negligible when Gibraltar was captured in 1704, this figure of 6,000 civilians represented nearly the net-increase during the first 100 years of British occupation.

As a result of an epidemic of malignant fever thousands of people died. This obviously had had a negative effect in the increase of the civilian population during that period. Judging from the ratio of civilians to that of the garrison it seems that it remained adequately enough to meet the needs of the fortress. I could find no mention in the history books of any forced evacuation of the civilian population during the two sieges mentioned. The rapid growth in the civilian population from then on, particularly during the period of the Napoleonic Wars, was mainly as a result of many people who were fleeing from the immediate surrounding Mediterranean countries to take refuge and trade in Gibraltar. After this came another period of relative peace in Europe during which Britain was then able to control most of the key trade routes, by enjoying an era of unchallenged sea power.

Observing the trend in the growth of the civilian population in Gibraltar in just over 50 years, that is, from 1807 to 1860, it reveals that there was a very significant increase from about 7,500 to 17,647 civilians.

During this period and for the first time since 1704, the number of civilians overtook that of the military garrison. It was at this point, that the then Governor, Sir Hew Dalrymple, considered it to be too large a civilian population for the size of the fortress.

The period of "Pax Britannica" brought further increases in the civilian population. This was due to more people wishing to settle in Gibraltar for reasons of prosperity and security. There were also notable increases in civilians by natural means. This in fact gave rise, at the time, to the pertinent military authorities to consider how to manage the civilian population in a conflict involving the fortress of Gibraltar. An inter dependence between the needs of the military garrison and the interests of the civilian population had already began to be recognised. During the Victorian era Britain was at the height of her imperial power achieving economic strength and also her largest ever territorial expansion. The retention of this status had to be maintained by having military posts around the world. When the Suez Canal was opened in 1869, Gibraltar was the first military post defending Britain's interests from the Mediterranean to the Far East. In line with this policy, the defences and military installations at Gibraltar had to be modernised.

Then at the turn of the 19th century there was a challenge posed by Germany's imperial expansion. Britain responded to this new challenge by modernising her fleet and her dockyards. In Gibraltar dry docks, workshops, barracks and hospitals were built, which a few years later proved very useful.

The maintenance of these military requirements meant that there was still more need for skilled workers with the majority having to be imported from Britain and Malta. Due to this increase in military activities, more businesses and traders were attracted resulting in yet a larger civilian population.

By the late 19th century Gibraltar was not only a fortress but had also become an important trading post. By then there were about 19,000 civilians residing within the fortress. This rapid growth gave rise to the introduction of residential permits and other legislations in order to curb further the increase in the civilian population within the fortress. At the beginning of the 20th century, the Kaiser Wilhelm II, of the Imperial Germany created by Bismark, began to build a high seas fleet to back her colonial demands

Modernisation of Gibraltar defences at turn of the 19th Century. Photo Mr J Chiara

This policy brought about a deterioration of relations between Britain and Germany and consequently plans were laid down to counteract this with the expansion and improvement of defences in Gibraltar.

The construction of the dockyard with the dry dock. Photo Mr M Bruzon

At that time, diplomatic relations between Britain and Spain were considerably improved as a result of the marriage of Alfonso XIII to Ena of Battenburg - Queen Victoria's granddaughter.

A German High Seas Fleet battleship. Old Ship Gallery

War ships in the harbour about the turn of the of the 19th century. Photo MrJ Chiara

These relations were further improved after an agreement between France, Britain and Spain in 1907. In this agreement Britain confirmed Spain's title to the Balearic Island, Ceuta and Melilla. Spain for its part confirmed Britain's possession of Gibraltar giving Britain much comfort in her control of the Mediterranean Sea, which was vital to her possessions in the Far East. It also placed Gibraltar at a great advantage as a trading post for ships going either via the Cape of Good Hope, the Suez or even to the American continent. As a result of these new understandings more entrepreneurs were attracted to settle in Gibraltar in order to establish businesses.

When the Great War broke out in 1914 there were no difficulties posed by the civilian population within the confines of the fortress. Although Britain was at war, Gibraltar was not strictly in the front line of hostilities. Gibraltar's role was that of providing facilities for allied warships, which were controlling the vicinity of the Straits and was also used as a convoy assembly point.

The recently built dry docks provided essential repairing facilities for the ships damaged by enemy submarines in the approaches to Gibraltar. Much of the needed labour force to work in the docks and as coal heavers came across the frontier from the nearby Spanish towns. This obviously served to help the economy in the region, which was then in a bad shape. Apart from two occasions when German submarines were detected and fired upon, there were very few war incidents in which Gibraltar participated directly in the Great War. In this context the need for an evacuation of the civilian population did not arise at all. In fact during the war years Gibraltar's economy prospered and those of the Spanish neighbouring towns benefited as well. Just a few days before the First World War ended, the then famous battleship **HMS Britannia** was sunk off Cape Trafalgar with a great loss of life. Many of the injured were brought to Gibraltar, some of whom later died at the Royal Naval Hospital. One of the many sailors who died was Officer's cook J.Vassallo (of Maltese origin and related to the Gibraltar Vassallo family) buried at the North Front Cemetery.

HMS Britannia. Old Ship Gallery

J.Vassallo's resting place. Photo by J.Gingell

By this time a large proportion of the working civilian population were either employed directly or indirectly by the British military authorities. Although business was flourishing, Gibraltar was strictly a fortress in every sense.

A parade in the 20s (where the Alameda Estate is presently) as an indication of the strength of the military presence in Gibraltar. Photo J.Gingell

Accommodation in Gibraltar became scarce, relatively expensive and very difficult to obtain. There were also many people living in overcrowded conditions and with very poor sanitation. Strict controls on residential permits were being introduced to halt the increase in the civilian population. These strict measures forced many civilians, even British ex-servicemen, who had decided to settle in Gibraltar, to find accommodation in the nearby towns of the Spanish hinterland. Between the two great wars it has been reckoned that there were about 4,000 civilians from Gibraltar living in the Campo area and thus easing by that much the growth of the civilian population within the actual confines of the fortress.

Children of British subjects born in Spain were normally registered in the nearby British Consuls. The First World War, which had been called the war to end all wars, led to the creation of the League of Nations. Britain, in pursuing a policy to secure world peace, reduced armament spending worldwide affecting as a result the local economy, which was overwhelmingly oriented to the military needs. By this time, however, Gibraltar had become an important port of call for many luxury liners and other maritime trades which helped to cushion the effects of the reduction in military spending. In those days the decisions in the running of Gibraltar's administration was very much in the hands of the military authorities. By 1921 a City Council was created, albeit, with a very minor say in the running of Gibraltar's domestic affairs. The world recession of the late twenties and early thirties was bound to affect Gibraltar's economy as well. However, trade soon recovered and started to grow gradually. Life in Gibraltar between the war years was very peaceful and with a standard of living which was relatively better than that of the Spanish hinterland. At that time Britain's relations with Spain vis-à-vis Gibraltar was good, save for the occasional rhetorical speeches made by dictator General Miguel Primo de Rivera to promote the recovery of Gibraltar by Spain. Amidst all these rhetorical speeches there was an incident, which I think deserves mentioning, as it seemed to me like a blessing in disguise, serving to help relations between Britain and Spain over Gibraltar.

The incident occurred in July 1929 when the aircraft piloted by Major Ramon Franco, then a famous aviator and brother of General Franco,got lost in the Atlantic after some navigational errors. The seaplane had been missing for a few days when the Royal Navy was requested by the Spanish navy through the naval authorities in Gibraltar to assist with the search. **HMS Eagle** which was then precisely on its way from the UK to Gibraltar was signalled to look for the seaplane. When **HMS Eagle** arrived at Gibraltar with the rescued Spanish crew and plane there were people, including many from Spain, waiting along the sea front to welcome both the lost crew and rescuers. The then Governor of Gibraltar, Sir Alexander Godley invited the rescued Spanish crew and the officers of **HMS Eagle** to appear at the balcony of his residence to acknowledge the tumultuous welcoming crowd as seen in the photograph below:

The crowd outside the Convent welcoming the rescued crew. Photo Royal Gibraltar Police

The officers of **HMS Eagle** were also invited to Madrid to be received by none other than General Miguel Primo de Rivera and were later decorated by him with the Grand Cross of the Order of Naval Merit (First Class). The Royal Navy and Britain were highly praised by the Spanish people, including Alfonso XIII, King of Spain, for having rescued the sea-plane which had been lost for a number of days. The Governor of Algeciras also thanked the Governor of Gibraltar for the rescue via the Gibraltar Chronicle.

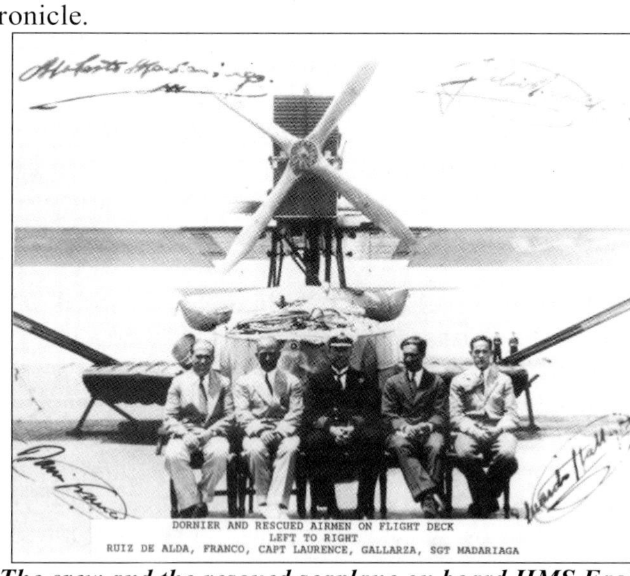

The crew and the rescued seaplane on board HMS Eagle. Photo Mr E Vallejo

As we look at the international political situation, two events added further fuel to the inevitable conflagration. The first was the defection of the United States from the League of Nations. The second was that this defection made this organisation almost ineffectual and rendered it unable to promote peace in a world already very close to a world wide conflict.

The Home and Mediterranean Fleets in 1932. Photo Mr C. Ellul

At that time Germany, Italy and Japan were anxious to increase their world power and all three were eventually governed by dictatorships wanting to expand at the expense of their neighbouring countries. Britain and France on the other hand whished to secure a peaceful world but did not prepare militarily for a possible world of conflict. The world's economic depression then served to increase fear and mistrust that resulted in national rivalries. There were treaty violations and acts of aggressions, which paved the way for nations like Germany, Italy and Japan to prepare for a war of conquest. Examples of these policies were the Sino-Japanese war in 1931, the remilitarisation of the Rhineland in 1936, the annexations of Austria, the Sudetenland and part of Czechoslovakia in 1938 and the conquest of Ethiopia by Italy in 1936.

When Germany had occupied the whole of Czechoslovakia and Italy seized Albania in 1939, Britain and France were compelled to abandon their policy of appeasement and thus created a pact with other nations, including Poland, to stop further aggressions.

The Ethiopian conflict compelled the deposed Emperor Helei Salassi to leave his country and sail on **HMS Capetown** to Gibraltar where after very a short stay he went to live in exile in the UK until his return to Ethiopia in May 1941.

Prior to World War Two, Britain had the largest navy in the world. This gave the people of Gibraltar a sense of security in the approaching world conflicts. But the effects that these conflicts were going to have in Gibraltar were bound to be completely different to that of the First World War.

At that time, in Spain too, there were growing divisions between the ruling and working classes which split the country both geographically and ideologically. In July 1936 Spain's internal conflicts led to the awaited civil war, which many analysts saw as a prelude to the Second World War.

Both Germany and Italy helped the Nationalist forces of General Franco to overthrow the democratically elected Republican Government.

Ethiopian Emperor Helei Salassie in Gibraltar Onboard the cruiser HMS Capetown. PhotoMr E.Gilbert

Helei Salassi leaving the Rock Hotel accompanied by police inspector E.Gilbert. Photo Mr E. Gilbert

During the Spanish conflict there were a few nearby incidents that affected Gibraltar directly and which I think are worth mentioning.

At the very outset of the war ships of the Republican Spanish Government consisting of the battleship **Jaime Primero**, the cruisers, **Libertad, Miguel de Cervantes**, the destroyer **Almirante Churruca** and other naval units were tasked to stop Franco's forces from crossing the Strait of Gibraltar to reach the towns of Algeciras and La Linea. Many of the officers serving in these ships were not loyal to the Government. However the crew who sympathised with the Government mutinied against their officers in their determination to carry out the orders of the Government to stop the rebel forces from sailing from Ceuta. These ships were in need of replenishments but were unable to do so from nearby Spanish ports, which by then were in the hands of the Nationalist forces.

Franco's Moroccan Troops at the old neutral ground between Gibraltar and Spain. Photo Mr J Chiara

In view of this, the ships sailed for the nearest neutral port of Gibraltar. They anchored in the bay in the hope of obtaining, badly needed, fuel, water and other provisions. The Gibraltar military authorities in keeping with Britain's non-intervention policy refused the request from the ships. The situation was very complex for Britain, which could not be seen as supporting one side or the other in the conflict. All the diplomatic channels were tried to solve this delicate situation at Gibraltar's doorstep. Whilst the ships were waiting in the bay they fired at a Nationalist aircraft, which had attempted to bomb the ships. The shells fired from the Spanish ships fell in Gibraltar but luckily there were no casualties and no actions were taken. After a few days the ships raised anchors and whilst sailing out of the Bay of Gibraltar they bombarded the Spanish neighbouring towns of La Linea and Algeciras where some of Franco's forces had already landed. The policy of neutrality by Britain throughout the whole conflict was strictly maintained although some historians have argued, with some evidence that it only served to help the Nationalists. On the other hand both Germany and Italy were assisting Franco to overthrow the Republican Spanish Government.

The Republican battleship Jaime Primero. Photo Mr E Vallejo

When the Spanish Civil War flared up about 4,000 Spanish nationals found refuge in Gibraltar. They were temporarily accommodated in what was known as the neutral ground on the Spanish side of the frontier at North Front.

The port of Algeciras bombarded by Republican ships in July 1936. Photo Mr E Vallejo

About 1,500 of these refugees sought political asylum in Gibraltar for fear of reprisals from Franco's regime.

Spanish refugees at the Gibraltar frontier. Photo Mr J Chiara

Most of the Gibraltar families who were living in Spain also came over initially to Gibraltar and were temporarily billeted in what was then the Victoria Gardens, which is now the area where the air terminal is built.

Spanish refugees onboard HMS Hood. Photo Mr Stephan Oeller HMS Hood Association

This sudden influx of people naturally augmented the civilian population by about 2,000 at a time when accommodation was already extremely scarce with serious overcrowding. The people in Gibraltar were, in someway, divided in to two groups: the pro-republicans and the pro-nationalist. As a result of these groupings, there were tides of demonstrations coming from one group or the other. These demonstrations sometimes caused feelings to run high, leading in some instances, to riots that suggested that there was a much divided population in Gibraltar as a result of the Spanish Civil War.

At the end of May 1937 the German pocket battleship **Deutschland** was anchored at the Balearic Islands, already in control of the Nationalist forces, when two Republican aircraft, which according to some historians were flown by Russian pilots, bombed the **Deutschland.**

The Deutschland with the markings used during the Spanish Civil War. Photo Mr M Emmerich – German Navy History.

The Republican air force pilots' version was that they had mistaken the **Deutschland** for the Nationalist ship **Canarias**.

The Nationalist cruiser Canarias. Photo Old Ship Gallery

Many sailors were killed and wounded. The **Deutschland** unable to cope with the casualties sailed for Gibraltar where on arrival the wounded were taken to the Military Hospital.

The number of injured sailors was such that help was sought for nurses to be flown from UK to assist. The dead were buried with full military honours with coffins draped with the Nazi German flags. The cortege, which started from the Dockyard's North Gate, went along the sea front roads up to the North Front Cemetery. A detachment from **HMS Despatch** provided the saluting shots. The **Deutschland** returned to Gibraltar by mid June 1937 to collect the sailors that were fit for duty and the exhumed bodies of the sailors to be returned to Germany on Hitler's personal orders. As a result of this incident, Germany took reprisals by bombarding the Republican held port of Almeria by the pocket battleship **Admiral Scheer** and other German naval units causing many deaths amongst the civilian population of Almeria. There was also an international political upheaval which both Germany and Italy found opportune to leave the meetings of the Non-Intervention Committee.

The cortege along what is now Sir Winston Churchill Avenue. Photo Mr E Vallejo.

This incident also brought home the thought that Gibraltar could be similarly attacked by air, sea and land.

The German pocket battleship Admiral Scheer, with special markings, at Gibraltar. Photo Mr T Smith

A couple of weeks before the **Deutschland** incident, **HMS Hunter** was mined when patrolling off the Spanish coast near Almeria. She was engaged on this task in accordance with the League of Nations non-intervention policy. Eight of her crew were killed and the ship managed to stay afloat until she was towed by the cruiser **HMS Arethusa** to Gibraltar for repairs. Within the context of the Spanish Civil War, this incident was seen in contrast to the use of Gibraltar as a base by German and Italian ships to intervene in the war whilst the Royal Navy was patrolling in order to avoid the intervention of other countries.

The last incident of the Spanish Civil War to affect Gibraltar more directly than the two others previously mentioned was that of the Republican Spanish warship the **Jose Luis Diez**.

HMS Arethusa towing HMS Hunter.
PhotoOld Ship Gallery

When the **Jose Luis Diez** passed through the Straits on its route to Cartagena in August 1938, shells were fired from the Nationalist cruiser **Canarias** hitting the **Jose Luis Diez** in the bow. She was badly damaged and made for the nearest neutral port – Gibraltar. The damages were extensive and had to be carried out before putting to sea again. The repairs, because of the non-intervention policy, had to be carried by the ship's crew which took them until mid of December 1938 to complete.

The damaged bow of the Jose Luis Diez.
Photo Mr E Vallejo

In the very early hours of the 30th December the **Jose Luis Diez** slipped anchor with the intentions of evading the Nationalist warships, waiting in the Straits. Apparently, flares were fired from Gibraltar alerting the Nationalist ships. The Republican ship's intentions were to sail to Cartagena but was chased and fired on sustaining damages that compelled her to run aground at Catalan Bay to avoid being sunk or captured. Some shells from the Nationalist ships hit Catalan Bay houses. Police Constable Joseph Baglietto was injured by shrapnel and members of the Stagno family were injured when the roof of their house collapsed. The crew of the **Jose Luis Diez** were later taken to Republican held port of Almeria by two Royal Navy destroyers. The **Jose Luis Diez** was towed to Algeciras in March 1939, just before the Civil war ended. Britain's appeasement policy, had no doubt, influenced her handling of the **Jose Luis Diez** incident at Gibraltar. While Spain was engulfed in a civil war, the British Prime Minister Mr Neville Chamberlain was hopeful of securing a peace treaty with Hitler when he met him at Munich. It was after this meeting that Mr Chamberlain made his famous speech of ".... a peace in our time."

The Republican warship Jose Luis Diez grounded at Catalan Bay. Photo Mr J Piris

The damaged roof of the Stagno's house.
Photo Mr E Vallejo

This peace agreement, as is well known, did not last very long. Britain's policy, which Churchill was so critical about, only managed to delay the world conflict for about a year. When Britain came into the war in September 1939, the population of Gibraltar was about 22,000. Experts then foresaw Gibraltar's military role similar to that of the First World War.

It was then thought by military strategists that the main theatre of conflict would take place in northwest Europe and therefore very light defences were installed at Gibraltar. Despite this policy, some administrative and logistical preparations were made in case there was a need to evacuate the bulk of the civilian population.

Studies were also being made as to where to take the civilian population in case of an evacuation. These preparations, however, remained dormant for about six months until April 1940.

The war in Europe until then had been labelled the "phoney war" with very little impact on Gibraltar's role in it. But as from April onwards the war was spreading rapidly to other areas of conflict that was bound to affect Gibraltar significantly, especially after Italy took sides with Germany and Spain showed sympathy towards the Axis powers.

On the 8th April Denmark was overrun, on the 10th May the Low Countries were invaded and after four days Holland surrendered.

Mr Neville Chamberlain waving his peace agreement reached with Hitler at Munich. Photo Wikipedia Free Encyclopedia

Although Spain was officially neutral, there was no guarantee about her intentions with regard to Gibraltar. Both Germany's and Italy's involvement in helping the Nationalists during the Spanish Civil War, made Gibraltar's position potentially vulnerable to an attack. In anticipation of such a likely event, Gibraltar was preparing for the worst. Shelters were being built which altogether had capacity for about 8,000 people. The Gibraltar defences were updated and the dry docks were made larger to accommodate the new line of battleships and aircraft carriers. The Gibraltar Defence Force was instituted and many volunteers were enlisted. Other civilians volunteered to serve in various other capacities like the Police Force to assist in duties connected with the war situation.

One of the shelters built at the beginning of the war. Photo taken by J.Gingell

The military authorities then perceived that if Spain became hostile, Gibraltar could easily be bombarded from the Spanish mainland and also from the Spanish enclaves of Ceuta, Melilla and Tetuan on the other side of the Straits. Given that possible military scenario, hasty preparations were made for the evacuation of the civilian population. These preparations were carried out amidst some misunderstanding between London and Gibraltar with regard to the timing of the evacuation. The question of where to evacuate the population to, however, still then remained to be decided. Many places were considered including the West Indies, the then Union of South Africa, and Canada. Even Spain was approached but Franco turned down the idea to take the Gibraltar evacuees. The UK was the last option. In the end it was finally decided to take the evacuees to French Morocco for reasons of its proximity. A delegation from Gibraltar went across to French Morocco to assess the facilities being prepared for the Gibraltar evacuees. There were conflicting evaluations by the officials about the accommodation facilities in French Morocco. Some officials assessed the accommodation offered as adequate for Gibraltar standards whilst others reckoned that the facilities left a lot to be desired. By that time the war was taking a turn for the worse for both Britain and France. The Germans were advancing at a very fast pace with their blitzkrieg tactics, pushing both the French and British armies towards Dunkirk. On Thursday 16th May 1940, British troops withdrew from Louvain, west of Brussels as troops of the German 6th Army broke through the Allied Dyle line in Belgium. By the 17th May 1940 Germans attacked further into N-E France. General Maurice Gustave Gamelin, who had put much hope on the Maginot Line, gave allied troops 'conquer or die' orders but failed dismally. Charles de Gaulle with his newly raised 4th armoured division launched a counter-attack near Laon, which was easily repulsed by the German forces.

CHAPTER TWO

EVACUATION TO MOROCCO

Since early May there were very strong rumours creeping within the Gibraltar's population about an imminent evacuation. Very indicative of a war like situation was the voluntary distribution of gas masks around town by the Boy and Sea Scouts.

A Government notice No.73 dated 16 May 1940 published in the Gibraltar Chronicle on the 17 May 1940 confirmed that the rumours of a possible evacuation were well founded. The notice, as can be seen from the copy reproduced below, advised the general public to prepare for an eventual evacuation but without being very specific about the destination in the likely event.

GOVERNMENT NOTICE No. 73.

It is generally known that the Gibraltar Government has in preparation a scheme for the evacuation of women and children and aged and infirm men in certain eventualities.

2. Circumstances may arise which may necessitate His Excellency the Governor ordering such evacuation and making it compulsory.

3. In the meantime, however, there is no objection whatsoever to individuals who are in a position to do so making their own arrangements for their families. In fact, the prior departure of a number of families under their own arrangements would greatly facilitate the work of the authorities particularly in connection with housing and food problems whilst undoubtedly the journey in such circumstances would be under better conditions for the individuals than might prove to be the case at a later stage.

4. The public are advised, however, to arrange in the above circumstances for their families to go to a British Empire or allied country if possible in view of financial restrictions. In the case of neutral countries it will be necessary to restrict drastically the transfer of money and credits.

Colonial Secretary's Office, Gibraltar, 16th May, 1940. (M.P. No. 14/39).

By Command, ALEXR. E. BEATTIE, Colonial Secretary.

On the 18th May another official notice No.75 was published in the Gibraltar Chronicle with reference to the application for passport visas to French Morocco obtainable from the French Consulate in Scud Hill. This notice seemed to imply that the most possible likely place for the evacuation was French Morocco.

GOVERNMENT NOTICE No. 75.

With reference to Government Notice No. 55 of the 13th of April regarding passport visas for French Morocco, the public are again reminded that applications MUST be made on the prescribed form in duplicate and be accompanied by two photographs.

2. Forms are obtainable at the French Consulate, Scud Hill, and the Consul for France has kindly promised to deal with them with the least possible delay and if practicable within 48 hours.

Colonial Secretary's Office, Gibraltar, 18th May, 1940. (M.P. No. 378/39).

By Command, ALEXR. E. BEATTIE, Colonial Secretary.

On the 21st May another official notice No 78 was published in the Gibraltar Chronicle confirming that the evacuation would take place forthwith. This notice applied to families in category A, who were required to make their way with their embarkation cards to the Egyptian vessel **Mohamed Ali el-Kebir.**

GOVERNMENT NOTICE No. 78.

With reference to Government Notice No. 73 of the 16th of May regarding the evacuation of women and children it is hereby notified for information that His Excellency the Governor has received instructions from the War Cabinet that owing to the international situation this evacuation should take place forthwith upon shipping becoming available.

2. His Excellency has issued an Order under the Defence Regulations making this evacuation compulsory at his discretion.

3. The evacuation will take place under the scheme prepared by the City Council, and under which arrangements have been made in all districts through their respective Air Raid Wardens.

4. His Excellency has ordered that in the first instance all families within Group A of the scheme, with the exception of families in which there are no children below the age of 14 years shall be evacuated by the "Mohamed-Ali-Kebir" which has been chartered by His Majesty's Government for the purpose. With the kind cooperation of our gallant Allies arrangements have been made for their reception and accommodation in French Morocco. Further instructions will be issued by the City Council through the Air Raid Wardens.

5. His Excellency fully realises that these steps will cause a great deal of anxiety and inconvenience, but they are being taken in the interests of the persons concerned and in those of the Fortress. He feels sure that all citizens will abide loyally by his instructions, and cheerfully endure such sacrifices as they are called upon to make towards the successful prosecution of the War.

Colonial Secretary's Office, Gibraltar, 20th May, 1940. (M.P. No. 14/39).

By Command, ALEXR. E. BEATTIE, Colonial Secretary.

Government notice confirming the evacuation orders.

When preparation for the evacuation was under way, a story about the war situation in France appeared in the Gibraltar Chronicle on the 18th May 1940. This news items, one assumes, must have been very worrying for those making their way to French Morocco and also for the families who had to stay behind.

ALLIES WITHDRAW TO WEST OF BRUSSELS

Massed Tank Attacks On Sedan Front

(*Through Reuters Agency*)

London, May 17.

Reuter learns from authoritative quarters in London on Friday afternoon that the position continues grave, and that German armoured divisions have broken through the French lines and penetrated some distance into French territory.

The place where they have broken through was not the real Maginot Line, but was an extension covering the Belgian frontier, which has been built during the last twelve months.

The dent in the line has now become a bulge.

The German success is mainly due to the new technique of clearing the ground by heavy tank attacks supported by low diving-bombing.

It is believed that the Germans are employing some 1,200 tanks in these operations, including, it is understood, a new type of heavy tank which has not been seen before. Heavy tanks are followed by infantry and mechanised troops. Considerable use has also been made of parachutists. When the advance of the tanks is checked they withdraw until a new wave of bombing has confused and incapacitated the defence.

They then renew the advance. The tanks and armoured cars are not supported by any great numbers of infantry.

Gibraltar Chronicle story about war situation.

The arrangements for the evacuation were carried without any further delay. The first group consisting of 494 civilians left Gibraltar for French Morocco on the **Gibel Dersa II** on the 21st May 1940.

This group of evacuees although under the auspices of the evacuation arrangements paid for their own passages. It was being suggested, that if possible, boys should travel dressed with their Sea or Boy Scout uniforms, as it was thought that it would help their reception in Casablanca. The families of servicemen in Gibraltar were evacuated to the UK on 21 and 22 May on the troopships the **Empress of Australia** and the **Devonshire** respectively.

The Gibel Dersa II. Photo MH Blands

The **Gibel Dersa II** made another trip with 544 voluntary evacuees on the 19th June 1940. The rest of the evacuees amounting to over 12,000 civilians had to leave Gibraltar compulsorily within the official scheme on the Egyptian vessel **Mohamed Ali el-Kebir.**

The SS Mohamed Ali el-Kebir. Photo Mr P Smith

The first trip on this 7,000 tons vessel was made on 22 May 1940. The details of the trip were published in the Gibraltar Chronicle as shown in the next column. The report of the trip seemed to have been intended to encourage further evacuations as opposed to the different explanation given of the same journey by the Medical Officer on board, Dr James Giraldi. Dr Giraldi stated in his report that the majority of the passengers were tired and in a low state of morale after waiting many hours in the quay before embarking.

He also said that the passengers became seasick and had vomited on the decks giving the ship a very unpleasant odour. He furthermore stated that some of the passengers became very emotionally upset and hysterical after leaving behind their loved ones.

FIRST EVACUEES LEAVE FOR CASABLANCA

Over 900 evacuees belonging to Group A of the City Council Scheme, consisting of women and children under 14 years of age, and a few elderly and infirm persons left Gibraltar on Wednesday evening for Casablanca by the S.S. Mohamed-Ali-Kebir, which had been chartered by His Majesty's Government for that purpose. The Mohamed-Ali-Kebir arrived at Casablanca early on Thursday morning.

Cheers and greetings were exchanged between those on the ship and friends ashore as the steamer left the wharf.

Certainly the younger element regarded the evacuation as a great adventure and for many of them it was their first experience of travel.

Lorries were provided by the City Council for the conveyance of the belongings of evacuees from convenient points to the wharf in the Dockyard.

The evacuees appeared to have carried out the instructions issued by the A.R.P. organisation to whom the detailed work was delegated, and embarkation arrangements worked satisfactorily.

It should be remembered that in the carrying out of a large scheme of this nature, some hardship to individuals cannot be avoided, particularly in view of the short time available. A few of the inconveniences of the first day will doubtless be averted in the light of experience gained in the initial stages.

Report of the first trip made by Mohammed Ali el-Kebir.

The vessel **Mohamed Ali el-Kebir** left in the evenings from its allocated berth at the Gun Warf. Before embarking the evacuees were assembled at the bottom of Ragged Staff. They carried their luggage and some bedding. Some evacuees when embarking on the **Mohamed Ali el-Kebir** found that all the cabins had been previously booked for the relatives and acquaintances of the officials in charge of the evacuation procedures. Those evacuees who spent the whole trip on the decks were very critical of those who had made the arrangements. Below are the details of the journeys made by the **Mohamed-Ali el-Kebir** to French Morocco.

Date	No of evacuees
22 May	950
24 May	850
26 May	908
30 May	920
1 June	1,111
3 June	1,279
6 June	1,183
9 June	1,020
12 June	1,410
17 June	896
19 June	924
24 June	593
Total	**12,044**

On the 25th May 1940, a report was published in the Gibraltar Chronicle commenting about the initial arrangements being made in French Morocco for the first contingent of evacuees. On that same day, as if wanting to boost people's morale and remind everyone of the many atrocities which had been committed by the Germans during the First World War, a film about the story of the British Nurse Edith Cavell, condemned to death by the Germans, was shown at the Rialto Cinema.

Below the Gibraltar Chronicle announcing the film at the Rialto Cinema.

RIALTO CINEMA
(ENTERTAINMENTS LIMITED)

SATURDAY, 25th MAY
3 Houses: 6.30, 8.30 & 10.15 p.m.
ENGLISH TALKING
BY SPECIAL REQUEST
Nurse Edith Cavell
with Anna Neagle, Edna May Oliver, George Sanders and May Robson

TO-MORROW, SUNDAY
LET'M HAVE IT
with Richard Arlen, Virginia Bruce, Alice Brady & Bruce Cabot
Stalls 9d. Dress Circle 1/3

Tickets booked in advance must be taken up one hour before each house

The evacuation to French Morocco went on so fast that there was concerned expressed by those who making the necessary arrangements at the receiving centres in Casablanca. On arrival the evacuees had to go through the normal formalities of entry requirements and customs procedures. After the normal entry clearance, they were then directed to the awaiting buses to take them to their respective booked accommodations where they were received by the appointed officials as described in the cutting from the Gibraltar Chronicle of 25th May 1940 shown below.

EVACUATION FROM GIBRALTAR

The evacuation scheme which had to be implemented as a precautionary measure immediately and somewhat unexpectedly after the whole question had received the careful consideration of the War Cabinet is now in full operation.

A 7,000-ton ship sent to Gibraltar by the Ministry of Shipping specially for the purpose is proceeding at regular intervals to Casablanca, and will continue to do so until, for the present, all mothers of families with their children under the age of 14 years have been transported.

According to those in a position to judge the first embarkations went off most satisfactorily, and the greatest credit is due to the City Council and its A.R.P. organisation, and others responsible, not overlooking the evacuees themselves for their orderly and cheerful behaviour.

Commendable work was performed, too, by the Police and Special Constabulary, members of St. John's Ambulance Association (male and female), and many others. In the light of experience now gained the machinery will undoubtedly work in even still smoother fashion in future.

It is understood that a number of the first contingent, whose first experience it was of being at sea, or for that matter, of being off their native Rock at all, did not altogether enjoy the journey owing to sea-sickness, but all reached their destination without mishap after a 13 hours' passage.

At Casablanca, the French Red Cross Society provided hot drinks and other refreshments on arrival—this greatly appreciated service having been organised by Mrs. Day, sister of our esteemed French Consul, Monsieur René Neuville.

Here too, the "advance guard" sent from Gibraltar under Mr. Charles Gaggero and Mr. L. J. Imossi, aided by a number of Gibraltarians resident at Casablanca, set about their duties in an admirable manner in getting the passengers disembarked and allotting them temporary accommodation, whilst at the same time assisting them in complying with the various necessary French formalities. Thanks to helpful cooperation on the part of the French authorities, these formalities have now been reduced to a minimum.

It has to be realised that the accommodation available for a large number of evacuees, such as the Colony is sending in circumstances demanded by the situation, cannot be expected to be of the highest standard, but as time goes on and opportunity permits, every effort will be made to improve the conditions.

It is hoped that all concerned will exercise patience and understanding, for it is the endeavour of the authorities that Gibraltar evacuees should be spared the hardships and sufferings being endured by the many thousands of evacuees in various parts of Europe, due to the present serious world crisis brought about by Hitler and his followers in their attack upon liberty and civilisation.

The authorities in French Morocco are giving all possible assistance, as are also His Majesty's Consul-General at Rabat and His Majesty's Consul at Casablanca, and we are deeply grateful to them all. Mr. Gaggero and his loyal assistants are working extremely hard at a task which all will appreciate is not an easy one.

Dr. James Durante has been sent by the Gibraltar Government to report upon medical arrangements, and has now been given the assistance of Dr. Giraldi, whilst financial arrangements are in the hands of Mr. Horatio Bacarisas of the Colonial Treasury, who also has been transferred temporarily to Morocco.

Report published in the Gibraltar Chronicle on 25th May 1940

A postcard of the port of Casablanca. Photo Miss A Pardo

Despite the reports about the difficulties being experienced with accommodation, nearly 10,800 evacuees were still to be evacuated to French Morocco. While the evacuation was proceeding, the war situation was getting far worse with Allied troops being evacuated from Dunkirk on the 26th May 1940.

All the disembarkations in French Morocco were carried out at Casablanca but the first contingent of evacuees were still required to travel for about another hour by train to Rabat where they were found accommodation which consisted mainly of the old hotels like the Transatlantique, the Guessous and a few others. Other evacuees were taken to apartments situated on the outskirts of Rabat. Many of evacuees had to buy essential items such as bedding materials, cooking utensils, crockery and cutlery. Some evacuees were visited in Casablanca by relatives in Gibraltar to assist with the accommodation arrangements like Mr J Sacramento seen in the photograph below.

Kneeling in front is Mr John A Sacramento when he visited his family in Casablanca. Photo Mr Henry Sacramento

With regard to the type accommodation, there were many cases of evacuees who were living in conditions, which were described as truly appalling. The main reasons for these deficiencies were due to the rapid arrival of evacuees and the short time given to make the places habitable.

Olivares children Maruja, Mariluz, John, Emily, Lourdes, Doris, Gladys and Carmelia in Rabat Photo Mrs Latter nee Olivares

While the evacuation continued, some Italian ships attempted to scuttle themselves unsuccessfully near the Gibraltar harbour on the 10th June 1940. That same day, Italy declared war on France and Britain. On the 12th June Spain changed its policy from strict neutrality to that of non-belligerency.

Evacuees at 40 Rue de Tanger, Rabat. From left to right: Millie Barea, Rosario Martinez, Mercedes Barea, John S T Barea and Mr J S T Neale. Photo Mr John S T Barea

The Lopez family arriving in Rabat. Both this and the photo below by Mr S Lopez

The second group of evacuees who arrived at Casablanca had to be billeted in communal dwellings in areas of Casablanca known as Ocean Plage, Luna Park, Park Beaulieu and Guingnette Fleurie. In these places the sanitary and health facilities were not much better than that provided for the first group of evacuees. It was said that in fact they were still worse.

Antonio and Salvador Lopez in Rabat.

Below the Gibraltar Chronicle communiqué of the 24th May 1940 warning evacuees of accommodation shortage in Casablanca.

ACCOMMODATION AT CASABLANCA

The Colonial Secretary has received a communication from His Britannic Majesty's Consul at Casablanca intimating that unless they have friends in that town who can arrange accommodation for them, voluntary evacuées proceeding to French Morocco under their own arrangements should be encouraged to go to some other town, as there is a shortage of suitable accommodation in Casablanca.

My family was accommodated at Luna Park with no privacy at all. After a few days my mother and my aunt managed to find alternative private accommodation within Casablanca.

The medical officer in charge was very critical of the way the evacuees were living from the point of view of health and sanitation. Again part of the blame for this situation was being pointed at the fact that there was very little time to cater for the rapid influx of evacuees and that in the circumstances everything possible was being done to make conditions generally acceptable. Some evacuees were also taken to other main towns like Mogador and Meknes etc where the problems of accommodation and other associated conditions were very bad.

The Gonzalez family in Casablanca. Photo Mr V Gonzalez

By the 14th June 10,700 civilians had already been evacuated to French Morocco when the Germans entered Paris.

The French weep seeing German troops marching into Paris. Photo History Place

The last group of 593 evacuees left for Casablanca on the 24th June 1940 – the same day that France had officially capitulated. With this last group, there were about 13,500 evacuees living in French Morocco. At that time, majority of the civilian population had never travelled far from Gibraltar. Despite the lack of knowledge and experience with regard to travelling abroad the evacuees tried to settle as best as they possibly could, particularly, when taking into account the war situation. The first priority in trying to settle was to find adequate accommodation and food. There was a consensus of opinion among the evacuees that the cost of living was much cheaper than in Gibraltar. I believe that the weekly subsistence allowance per person amounted to about 70 Moroccan Francs. I also found out that at the time the rate of exchange to the pound was approximately 175 Moroccan Francs. This rate of exchange was said to have favoured the evacuees when they went shopping for their basic necessities. The food, to my understanding of conversations with those knowledgeable, was generally plentiful and consisting mainly of fresh country produce.

Mr John A Sacramento when visiting his family in Casablanca. Photo Mr H Sacramento

As can be seen from the photographs taken in Morocco, the evacuees made their best, unaware that their stay in French Morocco was going to be of a very short duration. On the 28th June Reuters was reporting through the Gibraltar Chronicle the presence of German troops at the Spanish border along the Pyrenees.

GERMAN TROOPS ON SPANISH FRONTIER

(Through Reuters Agency)

Madrid, June 27.

German troops have arrived on the Franco-Spanish border at Hendaye.

Cutting from Gibraltar Chronicle reporting presence of German troops Spanish/French border.

There were also reports that the International Zone of Tangier had been occupied by Spain with 3,500 troops. By then, according to some historians, Franco had also secret plans to prevent the Royal Navy ships from entering the Strait of Gibraltar from the approaches of Spain's south western coastal areas. These plans according to the same source were to coincide with Germany's plans to invade Britain - Operation Sea Lion.

The armistice arrangements, made the presence of the Gibraltar evacuees in Vichy French Morocco unsustainable. One evacuee recalled that the place where the Gibraltar families were billeted was pelted with stones and consequently, they had to stay indoors for a whole day. Others said that by then some French nationals were also giving the Gibraltar evacuees a cold shoulder. In fact by the 1st July there were rumours that the evacuees could not stay much longer in French Morocco.

Mrs Mariola Summerfield (Nee Benvenuto) in Rabat. Photos above and below Mrs Summerfield

Children enjoying a day at the beach.

While the evacuees were trying to make the best of a tense situation, they were completely unaware of the serious drama that was awaiting them.

Mr John A Sacramento visiting his family in Casablanca. Photo Mr H Sacramento

The Benvenuto family enjoying a day at the beach in Rabat. Photo Mrs M Summerfield

On the 30th June 1940 amidst these happenings a Free French aircraft was shot down by machine gun fire from the Spanish frontier when it was attempting to land at Gibraltar. The plane crashed into the sea near Western beach and all four crew were killed. It appeared that it was trying to make an emergency landing at Gibraltar. Other French pilots made similar attempts but apparently, also crashed. The Gibraltar Chronicle reported that both the pilot and co-pilot were killed when it crashed in sea. After a funeral service they were buried at the North Front Cemetery with coffins covered with the French flag. It is believed that they were seeking political asylum for their disagreement with the armistice arrangements made by the Vichy Government with the Germans.

The funeral was attended by the Governor and other authorities. In recent years a ceremony was held to pay homage to the crew who were killed in this incident.

On the left photo of resting place of one of the Free French Air Force crew at the North Front cemetery.
Photo J.Gingell

Britain not being fully acquainted with the terms of the agreement that France had reached with the Germans over the French warships, took the decision not to allow the possibility of the French ships to fall into German hands. The Admiralty therefore instructed Vice-Admiral Sir James Somerville, who was stationed at Gibraltar, to deploy a task force to the port of Oran. The ships in this task force were **HMS Hood, Resolution, Ark Royal, Valiant** and about eleven destroyers. On the 3rd July the task force approached Oran to await the latest instructions from the Admiralty. A series of proposals were made to Admiral Gensoul who was in command of the French ships berthed at the military port of Mers el-Kebir in Oran.

The Battlecruiser HMS Hood.
Photo HMS Hood Association

The Battleship HMS Valiant.
Photo Old Ship Gallery

The proposals made to Admiral Gensoul at Oran were basically for the ships to join the British fleet and fight the Germans, to be escorted to a British port, have them disarmed under the supervision of the Royal Navy, or scuttle them at Mers-el-Kebir's French naval base. When all these proposals were rejected, there were tense talks between the French and British commanders but the situation escalated when the entrance to Oran was mined by planes from **HMS Ark Royal.** In retaliation, Admiral of the French Fleet Darlan ordered the French warships in the Mediterranean ports to assist Admiral Gensoul. In view of this tense situation, Vice Admiral Somerville was instructed to put into effect Operation Catapult and destroy the French warships at Oran. Many French sailors were killed or injured in the action and ships like the **Dunkerque** and **Bretagne**, which were the pride of the French Navy, were either sunk or severely damaged.

The Battleship HMS Resolution.
Photo Old Ship Gallery

The aircraft carrier **HMS Hermes** was also deployed to bomb the modern French battleship **Richelieu** stationed in Dakar. As a result this action, the Vichy Government broke diplomatic relations immediately with Britain.

The Aircraft Carrier HMS Ark Royal.
Photo Royal Naval Museum

This was obviously bound to make matters very difficult for the Gibraltar evacuees living in French Morocco. The Vichy French Government in retaliation for the destruction of their fleet and the killing of their sailors sent their aircraft to bomb Gibraltar resulting in the first bombardments of the Second World War.

HMS Hood and Valiant in action during Operation Catapult. Photo HMS Hood Association

Vichy French Aircraft operating from French Morocco carried out a few raids on the 5th July with very little success as all the bombs fell into the sea. Gibraltar was then called to play the vital role of defending the entrance to the Mediterranean and the approaches to the Atlantic.

French warships at Mers-El-Kebir.
Photo HMS Hood Association

Coinciding with these serious happenings, 15,000 French Troops arrived at Casablanca on 8th and 9th onboard British merchant ships. They had sailed from Liverpool and arrived at Casablanca not knowing about the Mers-El-Kebir incident as they had been kept out of the ships' radio rooms. These troops had given up their fight against Germany and wanted to be returned to join their families in French Morocco. The French and Moroccan nationals who felt humiliated turned their hate on the Gibraltar evacuees and demanded their immediate expulsion. The French Vichy Government's version of these happenings was that they ordered the leaving of the evacuees from French Morocco as a protective measure from the anger felt by the French nationals. The British interpretation was that the evacuees were exchanged for the French sailors in order to humiliate the British Government for having ordered the destruction of the French fleet and the killing of sailors. The evacuees who had been given 24 hours notice to leave French Morocco had no choice but to make their way to Casablanca to await any further orders.

The French Fleet under attack at Mers-El-Kebir.
Photo HMS Hood Association

There are accounts that the evacuees were insulted and even spat at as they walked along the streets of Casablanca. Many evacuees who had bought items of basic necessity had to leave everything behind. But the main crunch came when the French authorities demanded that the ships, which were arriving at Casablanca with the French troops, were to be used to take away the Gibraltar evacuees. The Admiralty instructions to Commodore Creighton were to disembark the French troops and then leave Casablanca as quickly as possible. Contrary to these planned arrangements,Commodore Creighton was threatened on arrival to embark the evacuees on the ships once emptied or else have the ships impounded. These ships, which had carried troops on a long journey, were obviously not ready to take the evacuees. The stinking odour in the ships, which had been vacated by the French troops after spending two weeks in the them, was unbearable. Commodore Creighton pleaded that the ships had to be cleaned and replenished before taking on board any evacuees in view of the fact that they consisted mostly of women, children, elderly and infirm people. This request was flatly refused and it was pointed out to Commodore Creighton that failing to take the evacuees immediately would result in the arrest of all the ships. The evacuees who had suffered tremendous insults as they made their way to the ships were made to wait in the heat , typical of the month of July in that part of the World.

As a result of this long wait without food or water many elderly people collapsed. Mothers tried to shield babies from the burning sun. Then they were hurdled into the ships, and in some cases, pushed with the rifle butts as they climbed up the gangways. This, inevitably, caused many scenes of panic among the evacuees as they boarded the ships. Other evacuees protested and yelped at the treatment they were receiving from the French troops. Some evacuees when they were boarding the ships at Casablanca believe that the onlookers, who were French and Moroccan nationals, made threatening gestures with their hands implying that the ships were going to be sunk. Commodore Creighton in his book "Convoy Commodore" stated that he could understand the fears of the French troops who wanted to join their families. However, he said he could never forgive them for their callous behaviour in having the helpless evacuees driven like cattle through the streets to rot in the sun.

Faced with this dilemma, Commodore Creighton signalled Admiral North explaining the situation and that he intended to sail to Gibraltar with the evacuees. The reply he received from Admiral North read: "For Heaven's sake don't - we have had enough trouble getting them out." Commodore Creighton, who had no option but to accept the demands of the French authorities set sail for Gibraltar and ignored the instructions from Admiral North. On the 10th July the ships carrying approximately 13,000 evacuees sailed for Gibraltar. In view of the stinking state of the ships the evacuees were advised to remain on the upper decks throughout the journey. The **SS Balfe** with Commodore Creighton in command was the last ship to leave after the convoy had spent two days in Casablanca. The perplexing situation facing these evacuees was further worsened when the Governor of Gibraltar issued a communiqué on the 10th July 1940 stating that the evacuees would not be allowed to disembark on their return to Gibraltar. As the ships were heading for Gibraltar there was an immediate reaction to this communiqué giving rise to a spontaneous demonstration on the next day. Early in the morning, while the shops remained closed many people began to assemble at the John Mackintosh Square and other places in the centre of the town.

Officials addressing the demonstrators told them that they were arranging to make some representations to the Governor. Shortly after, a delegation, composed of Messrs Baldorino, Benady and Serfaty left the John Mackintosh Square to seek a meeting with the then Governor Sir Clive Liddell.

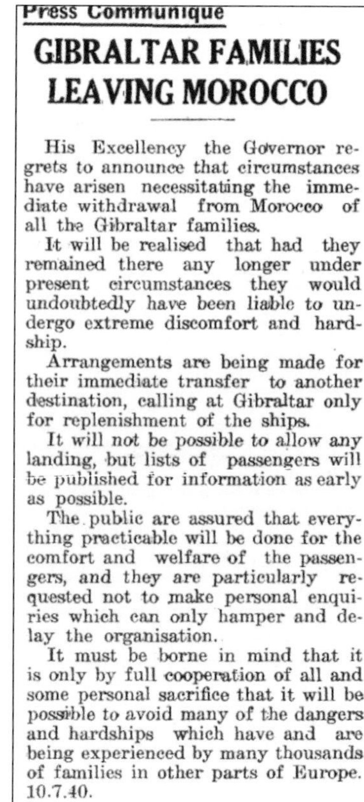

Press Communique

GIBRALTAR FAMILIES LEAVING MOROCCO

His Excellency the Governor regrets to announce that circumstances have arisen necessitating the immediate withdrawal from Morocco of all the Gibraltar families.

It will be realised that had they remained there any longer under present circumstances they would undoubtedly have been liable to undergo extreme discomfort and hardship.

Arrangements are being made for their immediate transfer to another destination, calling at Gibraltar only for replenishment of the ships.

It will not be possible to allow any landing, but lists of passengers will be published for information as early as possible.

The public are assured that everything practicable will be done for the comfort and welfare of the passengers, and they are particularly requested not to make personal enquiries which can only hamper and delay the organisation.

It must be borne in mind that it is only by full cooperation of all and some personal sacrifice that it will be possible to avoid many of the dangers and hardships which have and are being experienced by many thousands of families in other parts of Europe.
10.7.40.

Copy of communiqué dated 10th July 1940 which appeared in the Gibraltar Chronicle on the 11th July 1940.

The same day that the above communiqué appeared in Gibraltar Chronicle and as result of the meeting with the Governor a press release appeared stating that the evacuees were going to be allowed to land. Admitting that the ships had to be made ready for what was going to be a very long journey, the evacuees were also allowed to spend a few days of grace with their families. All the available means of transport were put at the disposal of the evacuees to take them home. Other groups of volunteers helped with accommodation, food and clothing.

Demonstrators at the John Mackintosh Square. Photo Mrs Wood

CHAPTER THREE

THE RETURN FROM FRENCH MOROCCO

An evacuee recalled that when the ships arrived in Gibraltar from French Morocco a woman who was travelling in the same ship with this evacuee collapsed and died. This evacuee believed that her collapse was probably due to the anxiety felt among many evacuees.

Gibraltar Evacuees Back From Morocco

There was some excitement in the centre of the town on Wednesday night when it became known that the Gibraltarian evacuees from French Morocco could not be allowed to land at Gibraltar and that their destination was not yet known.

Yesterday morning nearly all shops were closed and many workmen did not go to their employment in the expectation of more definite information.

Crowds assembled in Mackintosh Square where several speakers expressed their views, but there was no disorder.

Shortly before 11 a.m. a deputation, consisting of Mr. A. J. Baldorino and Mr. S. Benady, City Councillors, and Mr. A. B. M. Serfaty, Acting President of the Exchange and Commercial Library, went to Government House where they were informed that His Excellency would allow the evacuees to land and remain in Gibraltar for two, three or four days prior to re-embarkation for the United Kingdom, and that an official notification to that effect would be issued as soon as possible.

When this was announced from the City Hall the tension was relieved and the crowds quickly dispersed after cheers had been given for His Majesty the King and His Excellency.

Early in the afternoon the landing of evacuees by tender from the ships in the Bay commenced. Prior to this food had been sent by the authorities on board the various ships which were not provisioned for this unexpected evacuation.

Numerous buses, taxicabs, private motor-cars and gharries were placed at the disposal of the evacuees who showed the effects of their enforced journey and shortage of food and sleep.

Hundreds of relatives waited at Waterport Wharf entrance and in Casemates to greet their families.

Gibraltar's evacuees were landed up to a late hour last night, when it was estimated that nearly half had returned.

As we go to press more ships from Morocco are entering the harbour, and it is anticipated that the disembarkation will be completed to-day.

It is inexpedient for the present to publish any account of their experiences or of the reasons for the hurried departure from Morocco.

But it may be said that Nazi poison by way of propaganda has been widely spread among the people of Morocco who are in ignorance of the truth concerning recent happenings.

A cutting from the Gibraltar Chronicle Reporting on the demonstration.

The Bloch MB 174 Light bomber reconnaissance aircraft with Vichy French markings flew frequently over Gibraltar. Photo the Probert Encyclopaedia in aid of Multiple Sclerosis

Below is a copy of the official notice stating that the evacuees were being allowed to land on the understanding that the evacuation to the United Kingdom was compulsory.

GOVERNMENT NOTICE No. 136.

CIVILIAN EVACUATION.

With reference to the official communique issued yesterday His Excellency the Governor has now been notified by His Majesty's Government that evacuees from Gibraltar should proceed to the United Kingdom. Arrangements are being made accordingly.

2. Gibraltarians from Morocco are now arriving in various ships.

3. As soon as practicable they will be permitted to land **temporarily** but on the clear understanding that they will be reembarked as soon as ships are ready for the further journey. This will be in the course of the next few days. For those who have not their own accommodation temporary accommodation will be provided as far as is possible and they will be notified of this on disembarkation.

4. It is hereby impressed upon all concerned that **the evacuation to the United Kingdom is now compulsory for all those persons in Categories A and B, including those who did not go to Morocco.**

(Category A.

Mothers (or guardians) and children under 14 years of age.

Category B.

All females.

Males over 60 years of age or who are physically unfit).

5. Any persons in the above categories employed in an essential service or willing to undertake such essential service, must apply to the Evacuation Committee at the City Hall to be placed in a new evacuation Category C. The numbers in this new category will be kept to an absolute minimum.

6. His Excellency in announcing these revised arrangements calls upon the citizens of Gibraltar to do everything in their power to assist the authorities in carrying out these orders, and feels sure that he can rely on their patriotism and loyal co-operation.

Colonial Secretary's Office, Gibraltar, 11th July, 1940. (M.P. No. 14/39 (4)).

By Command, ALEXR. E. BEATTIE, Colonial Secretary.

Compulsory notice of evacuation to UK compulsory.

When the ships were entering the Bay of Gibraltar an aircraft was seen flying very high and the Rock's anti-aircraft guns started firing at this aircraft. This aircraft used by the Vichy Government for military reconnaissance. After some regular appearances become known locally as "El Chivato"- the informer.

During the few weeks that the Gibraltar evacuees were in French Morocco some children were born. Among these children were Eddie Hammond and Joseph Reyes.

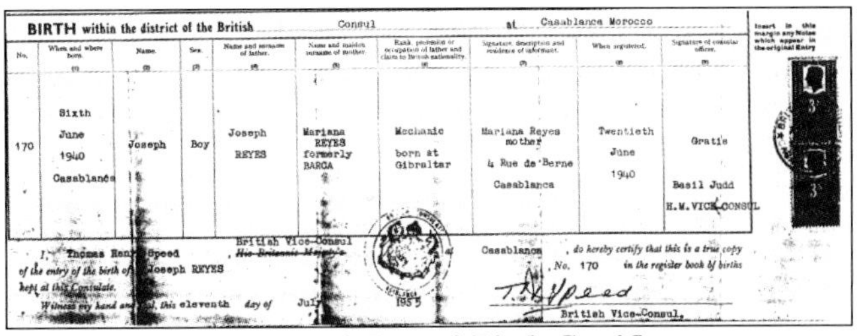

BIRTH within the district of the British Consul at Casablanca Morocco

No.	When and where born.	Name.	Sex.	Name and surname of father.	Name and maiden surname of mother.	Rank, profession or occupation of father and claim to British nationality.	Signature, description and residence of informant.	When registered.	Signature of consular officer.
(1)	(2)	(3)	(4)	(5)	(6)	(7)	(8)	(9)	
170	Sixth June 1940 Casablanca	Joseph	Boy	Joseph REYES	Mariana REYES formerly BARCA	Mechanic born at Gibraltar	Mariana Reyes mother 4 Rue de Berne Casablanca	Twentieth June 1940	Gratis Basil Judd H.M. VICE CONSUL

Insert in this margin any Notes which appear in the original Entry

I, Thomas Henry Speed, British Vice-Consul ~~His Britannic Majesty's~~ at Casablanca, do hereby certify that this is a true copy of the entry of the birth of Joseph REYES No. 170 in the register book of births kept at this Consulate.

Witness my hand and seal, this eleventh day of July 1955

T.H. Speed
British Vice-Consul.

Copy of Joseph Reyes' Birth Certificate.

Other children like Alex Pizzarello were born on board the ships when sailing back to Gibraltar as described in the poem below by Alex Pizzarello's uncle.

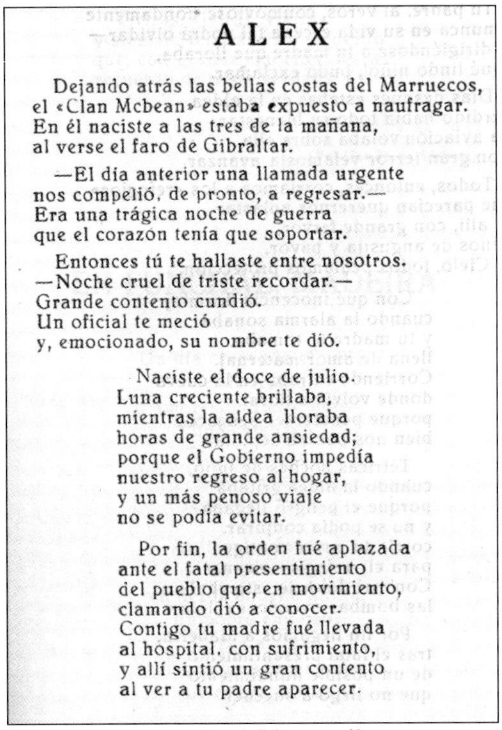

ALEX

Dejando atrás las bellas costas del Marruecos,
el «Clan Mcbean» estaba expuesto a naufragar.
En él naciste a las tres de la mañana,
al verse el faro de Gibraltar.

—El día anterior una llamada urgente
nos compelió, de pronto, a regresar.—
Era una trágica noche de guerra
que el corazón tenía que soportar.

Entonces tú te hallaste entre nosotros.
—Noche cruel de triste recordar.—
Grande contento cundió.
Un oficial te meció
y, emocionado, su nombre te dió.

Naciste el doce de julio.
Luna creciente brillaba,
mientras la aldea lloraba
horas de grande ansiedad;
porque el Gobierno impedía
nuestro regreso al hogar,
y un más penoso viaje
no se podía evitar.

Por fin, la orden fué aplazada
ante el fatal presentimiento
del pueblo que, en movimiento,
clamando dió a conocer.
Contigo tu madre fué llevada
al hospital, con sufrimiento,
y allí sintió un gran contento
al ver a tu padre aparecer.

Poem by A.Pizzarello.
(Mrs Martin)

Since the evacuation started, the number of guns in Gibraltar had been doubled from 8 light anti-craft guns to 16 heavy anti-aircraft guns. There were other reinforcements of Gibraltar defences which are mentioned in more detail in Chapter Ten **"Gibraltar During the War."**

Anti-aircraft guns at the south end of the Rock.
Photo Mr Ferrary

The return from French Morocco was completed on 13th July 1940 and all the fifteen ships that had brought the evacuees back to Gibraltar were awaiting orders in the bay. There were other ships also arriving to assist with the task of carrying out another compulsory evacuation of civilians. The ships, in the meantime, were refuelled, cleaned and replenished with food and water. Because these ships were designed to carry just cargo, some basic alternations and additions were made in order to carry people instead of cargo in their holds.
The only two destinations envisaged for the re-evacuation at that moment were Madeira and the United Kingdom. The evacuation to Madeira had been agreed at the very last moment with the Portuguese authorities, which had stated that the Madeira authorities could accept up to 2,500 evacuees.

One of the heavy guns at the top of the Rock.
PhotoMr J Chiara

Admiral Sir Dudley North, Governor Lt General Sir Clive Liddell and Deputy Governor Major General Sir Noel Mason-MacFarlane. Photo Mr E Vallejo

But the British Government stated that the number of evacuees to Madeira should be limited to not more than 2,000 evacuees who could afford their passage and maintenance in the island.

The decision to take 11,500 evacuees to the United Kingdom was agreed very reluctantly at the very last moment by British Government. By then there were still over 3,000 civilians who were earmarked as potential evacuees. The only civilians who were allowed to remain behind consisted mainly of about 4,000 men, who were required to work on essential services for the war effort. The number of civilians for this purpose was kept to an absolute minimum.

Within a week from the arrival of the expelled evacuees from French Morocco, preparations were completed to evacuate the women, the children, the elderly and infirm to London. By then the Battle of Britain had already started. Germany with a very much superior air force and its blitzkrieg tactics was preparing to launch "Operation Sea Lion" to invade Britain. There were reasons to believe that discussions were taking place between Spanish and German officials to agree a combined invasion to capture Gibraltar. I learned from a very reliable source that the wife of a Spanish military officer, with acquaintances in Gibraltar, came over from Algeciras, very discreetly, to inform high ranking military officials in Gibraltar, including the Governor, that she had overheard discussions in military circles about an imminent plan to capture Gibraltar. See page 345 about Spain's own plan to capture Gibraltar. In the meantime, the people of Gibraltar were getting ready to comply with the evacuation orders which effectively entailed leaving their homes at very short notice. For the 11,500 who were going to be taken to UK, it meant embarking on a long and perilous journey across the Atlantic Ocean with very little or no protection from possible attacks by enemy submarines. Their destination, unknown to them at the time, because of war secrecy, was going to be to the heart of London. At that time the British merchant navy was suffering from heavy losses of men and ships in the Atlantic and thus threatening Britain's lifeline.

As if to vindicate the military authorities' view of an impending attack, Gibraltar suffered the first casualties of the Second World War. As reported in the Gibraltar Chronicle, three civilians and a soldier were killed on the 18th July 1940. The civilians were Sister Lorcan O'Connor, Mr Luis Dallia, employed as gardener at the Loreto Convent, and his wife Maria.

The soldier was Leonard Percival, a Royal Artillery gunner at 4 H/ Battery. The names of the victims were obtained with the kind help of Mr Alfred Ryan, Superintendent of the Gibraltar Cemetery.

During air raids most people made it to the newly constructed shelters in different parts of the town.

Others while waiting to be called for re-embarkation and in anticipation of any air raids opted to spend most of their waiting time in the shelters.

Below copy of Gibraltar Chronicle report referring to bombing.

Press Communique

THREE CIVILIANS KILLED IN AIR RAID

The following communique was issued by the Military Authorities this morning:

"Several bombs were dropped on Gibraltar during the early hours of this morning, but little damage was done.

"There were a few civilian casualties, including three killed.

"A.-A. fire was opened, and the aeroplane, illuminated by searchlights, was seen by several people who were in the open and ought to have been under cover."

Loreto Convent damaged by bomb which killed Sister Lorcan O'Connor, caretaker Mr Dallia and his wife.
Photo Miss D Prior

Notice in Gibraltar Chronicles of the 16th July 1940 in connection with the evacuation.

GOVERNMENT NOTICE No. 142.

CIVILIAN EVACUATION.

With reference to Government Notice No. 136 of the 11th July His Excellency the Governor directs that the following persons be evacuated from Gibraltar within the next few days.

(a) All children of both sexes under the age of 17 years on the 1st August, 1940.

(b) All women except those who, on the recommendation of the Controller of Man Power, are considered by the Gibraltar Evacuation Committee to be in an essential service.

(c) All men who are physically unfit.

(d) All men above the age of 45 years except those who on the recommendation of the Controller of Man Power are considered by the Gibraltar Evacuation Committee to be in an essential service.

2. All men between the ages of 17 and 45 on the 1st August 1940 may apply to the Committee to be evacuated. Applicants will be evacuated if not engaged in essential services and not required for such services.

Colonial Secretary's Office, Gibraltar, 15th July, 1940. (M.P. 14/39 (4)).

By Command,
ALEXR. E. BEATTIE,
Colonial Secretary.

Many marriages took place during that waiting period, mainly in the cases were the husband-to-be had to stay behind.

Below copies of the follow up notices in relation to Government notice 142 detailing instructions to the civilian population with regard to the evacuation procedures.

NOTICE

GIBRALTAR EVACUATION SCHEME.

With reference to paragraph 2 of Government Notice No. 142, forms of application for evacuation from men between the ages of 17 and 45 may be obtained at the entrance hall, City Hall.

T. E. PENNINGTON,
Secretary,
Gibraltar Evacuation Committee.

City Hall, Gibraltar,
July 18th, 1940.

NOTICE

Gibraltar Evacuation Committee

Females

1. **With reference to Government Notice No. 142 regarding, inter alia, the compulsory evacuation of all females, applicants, other than persons engaged in any of the medical services, military laundresses, cooks, and charwomen and canteen workers, (who are being dealt with separately) may obtain a form of application for exemption from the scheme at the entrance hall, City Hall.**
2. **These forms when completed should be forwarded to the undersigned not later than Saturday, the 20th instant. They will then be sent to the Controller of Man Power for his scrutiny and recommendation prior to consideration by the Evacuation Committee.**
3. **It may be pointed out that it is considered that very few classes of female labour, other than those mentioned above, can be considered essential at this stage and the request is made that the time of the Evacuation Committee will not be wasted by having to consider unnecessary applications.**

T. E. PENNINGTON,
Secretary,
Gibraltar Evacuation Committee.

City Hall, Gibraltar,
July 18th, 1940.

NOTICE

Gibraltar Evacuation Committee

Men over 45

1. **With reference to Government Notice No. 142 regarding, inter alia, the compulsory evacuation of men over 45, Employers, other than H.M. Dockyard, War Department, Colonial Government and City Council (who are being dealt with separately) are requested to submit to the undersigned on or before Saturday, the 20th instant, a list of their employees over that age, whom they consider essential. Lists should show the full names, address, age and occupation of the employee.**
2. **In the case of small or one-man businesses, a form of application for exemption from the scheme may be obtained at the entrance hall, City Hall, and should be similarly forwarded, after completion, to the undersigned.**
3. **Such lists or applications will then be forwarded to the Controller of Man Power for his scrutiny and recommendation, prior to consideration by the Evacuation Committee.**

T. E. PENNINGTON,
Secretary,
Gibraltar Evacuation Committee.

City Hall, Gibraltar,
July 18th, 1940.

Boarding cards were issued and with them all the necessary instructions with regard to assembly points and ships to embark on. The ships that were scheduled to take the bulk of the evacuees to UK were essentially cargo vessels which had also by then undergone the necessary basic modifications to carry passengers. The alterations consisted of the simplest type of lavatory facilities like buckets and washbasins. Very basic cooking utensils were also provided. As the evacuees were later to experience at first hand, the facilities provided in these ships were not in the least adequate for human transportation. Government notices, as those at the top of this column, continued to appear in the local newspapers warning the civilian population of the legal implications of non-compliance with these notices.

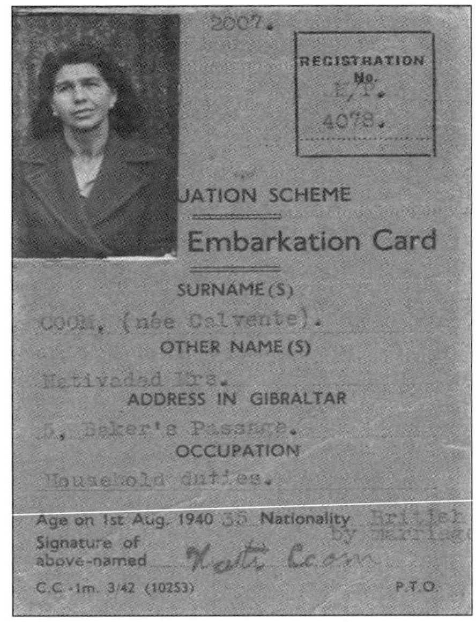

An example of an Embarkation Card.
Card. Mr C Coom

Taking heed of these Government notices the evacuees prepared their luggage which consisted mainly of bedding items like blankets, pillows and mattress as none of these were provided on board the ships. All luggages had to be carefully marked with the names of the evacuees and the ship in which they had been assigned to travel on. Other ships arriving were the **Royal Ulsterman**, the **Ulster Monarch**, the **Royal Scotsman** and the **Athlone Castle**.

Coinciding with the evacuation preparations, there was some breaking news by Reuters Agency in Madrid about a possible peace offer by Hitler to Britain as shown in the next column.

MORE RUMOURS OF PEACE OFFERS

(Through Reuters Agency)

Madrid, July 17.

Despatches from Spanish correspondents in Berlin coincide in the view that Herr Hitler will make a peace offer at the week-end.

The rejection of the offer will probably be followed immediately by an attack against Britain.

The talk about a peace offer was apparently started by an article by Signor Gayda in Rome, but the idea has evidently been fostered in Germany, where the authorities "neither confirm nor deny" the rumours.

HITLER'S TIME TABLE UPSET BY BRITAIN'S FIRMNESS

Istanbul, July 17.

Hitler's time table in the present war appears to be upset by Britain's firm stand.

German diplomats in Turkey who predicted with reasonable accuracy the date of the German entry into Paris and the French capitulation were last week giving Monday as the date for the initial occupation of a portion of Britain by German troops.

Now this date has passed with no sign of Hitler's invasion.

The Germans here are now talking instead of the Fuehrer's peace plans.

A cutting from the Gibraltar Chronicle of the 19th July 1940 referring to a possible peace treaty.

When the evacuation to French Morocco was taking place, about 30 members of the Hindu community in Gibraltar opted to be evacuated to India in order to join their families. However, their last chance for their preferred destination was on Saturday the 8th June 1940 on the British liner the **SS Kemmendine.** She had been initially scheduled to sail to India via the Suez Canal but was instead diverted to sail round the Cape of Good Hope as it was considered safer for the reasons that it was expected that by then Italy would have entered the war against Britain.

The SS Kemmendine. The Old Ship Gallery

On the 26th June they reached Cape Town where they disembarked for a few hours. During their short stay, many passengers decided to send telegrams to their relatives without realising that they were giving away the position and route of the **Kemmendine**. The next day it sailed for Colombo on its onward journey to Rangoon with passengers feeling that they had already travelled through the most risky part of their journey.

The Goldenfels before converting to the German raider Atlantis. The Old Ship Gallery

On the 13th July within a couple of days sailing from Colombo, the **Kemmendine** was intercepted by the German raider **Atlantis.** After some firing it ordered the transfer of passengers and crew by life boats to the **Atlantis**. Fortunately there were no casualties but the prisoners witnessed how the **Kemmendine** was sunk with two torpedoes. Once onboard, the prisoners were treated to refreshments. On the 1st August the **Atlantis** captured the Norwegian vessel **Tirranna** in the south of the Indian Ocean. Most of the prisoners on the **Atlantis** were transferred to the **Tirranna** which was then ordered to sail to France via South Africa.

The Norwegian Vessel Tirranna. The Old Ship Gallery

The **Tirranna** was carrying about 270 prisoners and after fifty days at sea she reached the Bay of Biscay flying the German flag. On Sunday 22nd September when near the Gironde Estuary the British submarine **HMS Tuna** spotted the **Tirranna** and fired three torpedoes.

HMS Triton same class as HMS Tuna. The Old Ship Gallery

Many of the prisoners were watching the scenery on the upper deck when three bangs at short intervals were heard. Within minutes the **Tirranna** began to list and very shortly afterwards it started to sink very fast taking 87 lives. The survivors spent a few hours clinging to debris before they were eventually rescued by German vessels. Among the survivors was 8 year old Krishna Khubchand, who was placed on a raft by the family cook who was also evacuated from Gibraltar. Mr Khubchand's parents, three sisters and two brothers were among the Indian community evacuees who lost their lives in this very tragic incident. Other survivors from Gibraltar were Mr Hotu Khemchand Mahtani and his expecting wife who gave birth in German occupied France. The baby was named Monica after the doctor's wife. They were later sent to a concentration camp in Germany where they remained until liberated by Allied troops in 1945. Krishna Khubchand was looked after for a year by a friend of his father in France and then they crossed into Spain travelling to Algeciras to join other relatives there. Because they could not come back to Gibraltar they went to Tangier where they stayed until repatriated at the end of the war.

CHAPTER FOUR

EVACUATION TO MADEIRA

After the return from French Morocco, the first evacuees to leave Gibraltar were the ones who sailed to Madeira on the **Royal Ulsterman** on Friday 19th July 1940 with 449 passengers.

The MV Royal Ulsterman. Photo Old Ship Gallery

The MV Ulster Monarch. PhotoOld Ship Gallery

NOTICE

Messrs. Smith, Imossi & Co. announce that, with the approval of the Government, they are in a position to arrange passages to Madeira for persons and families prepared to furnish a guarantee that whilst in Madeira they will be responsible for the cost of their own accommodation and maintenance.

2. Passage tickets will not be issued in respect of persons who are not eligible for evacuation under the Civil Evacuation Scheme to the United Kingdom.

3. It is essential that early application should be made for these passages as the ship will sail within a few days.

4. Passage rates will be: £6 First Class; £4 Tourist Class; £2 Third Class. Children from three years to twelve years of age, half rate. One child under three years of age free. Additional children under three years of age, one-quarter fare.

Copy of advert in the Gibraltar Chronicle offering passages to Madeira.

The second group of evacuees left also for Madeira on 21 July 1940 on board the **Ulster Monarch** with 282 evacuees. As mentioned in a previous page, these two groups of evacuees consisted of families who were able to pay privately for their passage and give an undertaking to be responsible for their maintenance during their stay in Madeira.

Evacuees on the Royal Ulsterman.

A local shipping company placed an advertisement (see previous column) in the Gibraltar Chronicle offering passages, specifically for the evacuees who wished to travel privately to Madeira. The evacuees who travelled privately to Madeira were categorised as group A. Both journeys took a couple of days to get to Madeira. On board, with the first group of evacuees, were the wife of the then Governor of Gibraltar Sir Clive Liddell and her son. Below a notice warning of non-compliance with civilian evacuation.

Government Notice No. 149

Civilian Evacuation

1. It is hereby notified for information that the embarkation of evacuees will commence on Thursday the 25th of July. Details and times will be notified as soon as possible by the Evacuation Committee.

2. All concerned are hereby warned that unless they register by 12 noon on Wednesday 24th July they render themselves liable to be embarked in any ship available and without previous notice.

3. They are reminded also that failure to comply with any of the Orders made under the Defence Regulations renders the offender liable on summary conviction to a fine of £100 as well as imprisonment for a term of three months.

By Command,
ALEXR. E. BEATTIE
Colonial Secretary.

Colonial Secretary's Office,
Gibraltar, 22nd July, 1940.
(M. P. No. 14/39 (4)).

The SS Neuralia. Photo Old Ship Gallery

HMS Gallant. Photo Old Ship Gallery

Below is copy of the customs certificate issued on the arrival of the SS Neuralia with 1248 Evacuees. Copy Mr L Pereira

ALFÂNDEGA DO FUNCHAL

ENTRADA DO NAVIO

Contra-marca n.º 261/940

ALFÂNDEGA DO FUNCHAL 13 AGO 1940 PIQUETE

Gr. A — Modêlo n.º 40

DECLARAÇÃO FEITA PELO CAPITÃO		DOCUMENTOS E OBJECTOS ENTREGUES	
Qualidade do navio	Vapor	Manifesto de carga para êste pôrto	
Nacionalidade	Inglesa	Manifesto de carga para outros portos	1
Nome do navio	NEURALIA	Declaração adicional ao minifesto	
Nome do Capitão	A.A.KAY	Relação dos passageiros e bagagens	1
Procedência	MAR ALTO	Relação dos tabacos da tripulação	1
Dias de viagem	2	Relação de mantimentos e sobrecelentes	1
Tripulantes	241	Relação dos volumes de amostras	
Tonelagem bruta	9182	Certidão de lastro	
Tonelagem liquida	5624	Declaração ou protestos de avarias	
Passageiros para êste pôrto	1248	Malas do correio	
Ditos em trânsito	nil	Ofícios avulsos	
Consignatario	BLANDY BROTHERS & CO. LDA	Cartas avulsas	
Representante do capitão ou seu agente na Alfândega	M. LUIZ NUNES	Impressos	
Qualidade da carga para êste pôrto	NIL	Documentos diversos	
		Volumes de amostras	
Idem para outros portos	NIL	Pólvora (para ser depositada)	
Motivo da entrada	PASSAGEIROS	Lista de Tripulantes	1

O capitão de navio, acima designado, ficou sciente das prescrições dos regulamentos fiscais que lhe dizem respeito, e, em cumprimento delas, entregou os documentos e mais objectos acima designados declarando que nada mais tinha a bordo além da carga constante dos mesmos documentos, e que se sujeitava às penas das leis por qualquer infracção dos mesmos regulamentos. E, dando-lhe licença para começar a descarga, obrigou-se a participar a conclusão daquela, logo que electivamente seja concluida.

Bordo, 13 de AGOSTO de 1940

O capitão,

REGISTADO

O Representante da agencia.

The third party of evacuees destined for Madeira, numbering 1,248 evacuees, sailed on the **Neuralia** on the 10th August 1940. The destroyer **HMS Gallant** escorted this group of evacuees among which included many residents from the village of Catalan Bay.

The evacuees on this journey were those in categories B and C. They arrived at Funchal on the 13 August with nothing significantly to report with regard to the journey. The category B evacuees disembarked at the main harbour but the evacuees in category C were transhipped and disembarked on a small quay near the cliffs by the Lazareto Buildings. This is something, which many of these evacuees disliked as they felt that they had been discriminated.

Local poet Albert Pizzarello, residing at Catalan Bay, dedicated one of his poems to the occasion when the people of Catalan Bay were evacuated.

Nuestro buen Gobernador,
de moral tan conocida,
fijó, para el 10 de agosto,
nuestra forzosa salida.

Se sucederán los años,
y este rasgo conocido
lo retendrá en su memoria
quien se estime agradecido.

Dejando nuestros hogares,
en tal fecha de ese mes,
afligidos embarcamos
en un lindo buque inglés.

¡Qué frases tan conmovente
proferidas por amor!
¡Y qué lágrimas caían
causadas por el dolor!

Mientras, el destructor Gallant,
a la hora crepuscular,
trasmitía, al Neuralia,
la orden dada de zarpar.

Siguiendo a esta unidad,
de nuestra potente armada,
partimos de la bahía
con la mente lacerada.

Descendiendo iba la luna
con pálido resplandor,
y, ante la terrible idea...
temblábamos de pavor.

Poem by Albert Pizzarello.
Copy Mrs Martin

CHAPTER FIVE

EVACUATION TO THE UK

A series of Government notices appeared almost daily in the Gibraltar Chronicle and other newspapers giving detailed instructions about the implications of the planned evacuation.

The SS Avoceta. Photo Old Ship Gallery

The SS Bactria Photo. Old Ship Gallery

The SS Clan Macbean. Photo Old Ship Gallery

In accordance with these notices, the first evacuees to leave for the United Kingdom were those who left on the 21st July 1940. They sailed in a convoy code named HG39 made up of 21 ships including the **Avoceta, Bactria** and **Clan Macbean** which carried 146, 140 and 213 evacuees respectively.

The elderly, the infirm and the mentally incapacitated evacuees who arrived on the **Bactria** from French Morocco, were not allowed to disembark and therefore remained on board until they arrived in the UK. During the journey these evacuees were escorted by nurses and other caring staff. In addition to the Gibraltar evacuees, the **Avoceta** was also carried about 100 refugees made up of different nationalities who were already on board when the ship arrived at Gibraltar from Lisbon. On this ship was Mr Dryburgh, who had been involved with the control of the evacuees in French Morocco. He was also given responsibilities by both London and Gibraltar for the administrative arrangements concerning the evacuees travelling in this convoy to the UK. The ships were escorted by the anti-submarine trawler **HMS Artic Ranger** until the 24th July.

Crew of HMS Artic Ranger in Gibraltar before leaving to escort Convoy HG39. Photo Mr C Mamo.

The whole journey took sixteen days arriving safely in the UK on the 5th August without anything significantly to report apart from the very long journey.

The evacuees disembarked at the ships' assigned ports as follows: **Avoceta** – Swansea, **Bactria** – Avonmouth and **Clan Macbean** – Cardiff.

The convoy's only escort for the whole journey was provided by the sloop **HMS Scarborough.**

HMS Scarborough. Photo Old Ship Gallery

The other ships which made up the entire convoy, each carrying different types of cargo, including explosives, were the British vessels: Britannic, Baron Tweedmouth, Palomares, Bruyere, Lisbon, Baron Renfrew, Erato, Cortes, Alcora, David Livingstone, Alpera Garston, Cara, the Irish vessel City of Bremen, the Norwegian vessel Evviva and French vessel Le Rhin Barry, all berthing at different ports.

Despite the anxiety brought about by the developments of the war and its impact, there were also some moments for entertainment. The Gibraltar Chronicle on the day of the departure of the first group of evacuees to UK announced a dance which was held at the Royal Hotel to the music of the Tarik Band.

The Tarik Band
At the back J.L.Diaz
Middle row: L to R. C.Carter F.Grau A.J.Palmer W.Scott A.E.Howes
In front J.T.Noguera J.J.Bado H.Teuma. Photo by Mr A.Palmer

Gibraltar Chronicle dance advert of the 21st July 1940

ROYAL HOTEL BAR PHONE No. 520

THE MANAGEMENT OF THE ROYAL HOTEL BAR INFORM THEIR DISTINGUISHED CLIENTELE THAT THEY HAVE NOW REOPENED THEIR PREMISES. DANCING FROM 7.30 P.M. TO 9.45 P.M. TO THE **TARIK DANCE BAND.**

The Athlone Castle. Photo Old Ship Gallery

The second contingent of nearly 1,600 evacuees left for the UK on the 26th July 1940 by sailing on the 25,000 tons Union Castle liner **Athlone Castle** with designation letter D. In charge of the evacuees on this ship was Mr Haynes assisted by his support staff. The composition of the evacuees onboard the **Athlone Castle** consisted mainly of elderly, disabled persons, families with toddlers and maternity cases.

As the evacuees were embarking, some Vichy French aircraft carried out an air raid which did not last very long with about 30 bombs falling on various places. Two civilians were killed during this enemy action: Encarnacion Ressa aged 30 and Charles Neale aged 2.

An inquest was held, and in both cases the Coroner returned a verdict of death as the result of wounds caused by enemy actions. About 40 other persons were injured during the bombing. On the night of that same day there was another air raid warning but no bombs were dropped.

The journey on the **Athlone Castle** took nearly a week with the evacuees arriving safely at Liverpool on the 1st August 1940 with additional evacuees born on the trip. One of those born on this trip was a girl named Athlone Angeles Lopes. Her family recollect that the ship's crew celebrated the baby girl's arrival by drinking to the health of both the child and her mother. They presented the baby's mother with many of the old three-penny coins which they considered to be a sign of good luck.

Once on land, the baby and mother were carried to the nearest maternity hospital.

When the ship arrived, Liverpool like many other British cities had already been bombarded as part of the ongoing German campaign to bring the British public into submission.

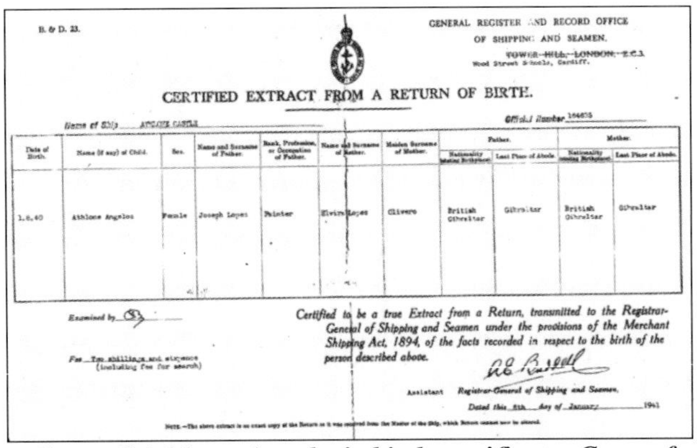

B. & D. 23.

GENERAL REGISTER AND RECORD OFFICE OF SHIPPING AND SEAMEN.
~~TOWER HILL, LONDON, E.C.3~~
Wood Street Schools, Cardiff.

CERTIFIED EXTRACT FROM A RETURN OF BIRTH.

Name of Ship ... Official Number ...

Date of Birth	Name (if any) of Child	Sex	Name and Surname of Father	Rank, Profession, or Occupation of Father	Name and Surname of Mother	Maiden Surname of Mother	Father: Nationality (stating Birthplace)	Father: Last Place of Abode	Mother: Nationality (stating Birthplace)	Mother: Last Place of Abode
1.8.40	Athlone Angeles	Female	Joseph Lopez	Painter	Elvira Lopez	Olivero	British Gibraltar	Gibraltar	British Gibraltar	Gibraltar

Examined by ...

Fee Two shillings and sixpence (including fee for search)

Certified to be a true Extract from a Return, transmitted to the Registrar-General of Shipping and Seamen under the provisions of the Merchant Shipping Act, 1894, of the facts recorded in respect to the birth of the person described above.

Assistant Registrar-General of Shipping and Seamen.

Dated this 8th day of January 1941

Copy of Athlone Angeles's birth certificate. Copy of Certificate Mrs Parody

Throughout the whole journey the **Athlone Castle** was being escorted by the destroyer **HMS Velox**

Destroyer HMS Velox. Photo Old Ship Gallery

When both the **Royal Ulsterman** and the **Ulster Monarch** returned from taking evacuees to Madeira they were again tasked with taking the third group of evacuees to the UK. The **Royal Scotsman** was also commissioned to join these two vessels. The distribution of the evacuees on board these ships were as follows:

Ulster Monarch - 640
Royal Scotsman - 633
And **Royal Ulsterman** - 650.

All the three ships left for the UK on the evening of the 27th July 1940 with a total of over 1,900 evacuees within convoy HG.40F. Their respective designation letters were E, F and G. On that same day there was an accident, as a result of which three soldiers from the Black Watch Regiment were killed. The soldiers killed in this mysterious explosion were L/Cpls William Baird, Charles Marr and Corpl. Robert Cor. All the soldiers were stationed at the 4 Battery.

The names of all the soldiers killed were very kindly supplied by Mr Alfred Ryan, Superintendent of the Gibraltar Cemeteries.

Royal Scotsman. Photo Old Ship Gallery

Evacuees about to embark on the Royal Scotsman. In the photo are Mrs Catania and her sons Victor and Adolfo. Photo Mr A Catania

After 10 days, they reached Liverpool safely on the 3rd August. The convoy was escorted partly by destroyers **HMS Vidette and MacKay**

Scene in Liverpool after a bombing raid. Photo Liverpool Records Office

Following the departure of this third group of evacuees, there were two more air raids on the 28th and 29th July.

The forth contingent of evacuees to leave for the UK embarked on a convoy, code named GH40. This was the largest of all the convoys and consisted of 24 ships including many of the ships that had brought back the evacuees from French Morocco.

The following is an extract from an official notice which appeared in the Gibraltar Chronicle on Monday 29th July 1940 giving specific instructions to be followed in connection with the evacuees embarking in ships with designation letters L, P, H and T.

It is most important that evacuees deposit their baggage at the Collecting Posts against the appropriate ship's letter, which will be indicated on boards, otherwise it is quite possible that baggage may be inadvertently placed on the wrong Ship. Baggage for ships "P" and "T" **must not** be left at Collecting Posts before 10.30 a.m. and 12.30 p.m. respectively.

5. Mattresses and blankets must be packed separately from other baggage as they will be required on the voyage. Knife, fork, spoon, plate, cup or mug, towel and soap must be carried in hand baggage. Sufficient food should be carried to last until supper which will be the first meal on board. It is necessary that evacuees should try to arrange themselves into small family groups for feeding purposes and have available with them some simple cooking utensils, to assist the ship's staff.

6. Evacuees will be conveyed by bus to Waterport and the conveyance of baggage will take place at the same time by lorry. Loading of baggage and assistance generally at the collecting places mentioned above will be given by Military personnel. **No private cars will be allowed to take evacuees to Waterport separately.** Applications for the use of an ambulance for the conveyance of an infirm person must be made to the Medical Officer of Health's Department (Telephone A. 778) not later than 5 p.m. on Monday, the 29th instant.

7. Embarkation will take place immediately on arrival at Waterport and proceed until completed.

8. All assistance at Waterport will be provided by Naval and Military personnel only and no member of the public will be allowed on the Wharf.

9. **All evacuees detailed for these ships must embark.** Non-compliance with any of the above instructions will make the delinquent liable to penalties under the Defence Regulations.

10. The date and destination of any further embarkation are not known but as much advance information as possible will be given, if shipping becomes available. The registration office in Commercial Square will close on Tuesday evening. Those persons who come within the limits of the compulsory Evacuation Order and have not yet obeyed the various orders which have been given regarding registration, must do so forthwith.

At the time I was two years old and because of my age I would have been entitled to sail on the **Athlone Castle**, which was much larger than any of the ships in this convoy. However, my mother for the sake of travelling in the same ship as my aunt and our three cousins opted to travel with them. As a result, all eight of us, embarked on the **Brittany**, which carried the largest number of evacuees –718 but was the second smallest ship in the whole convoy.

We left our home at Serfaty's Passage on Sunday 28th July 1940 and were taken to Waterport where we showed our documents. Our embarkation registration card number was 6906. From Waterport all the evacuees were then taken by tender boats to embark on their respective assigned ships that were anchored in the bay.

Serfaty's Passage Where My Family lived before the Evacuation. Photo J.Gingell

We spent a couple of days on board until the convoy finally left at sunset on Tuesday 30th July. The convoy was escorted locally by the destroyer **HMS Wishart** and the anti-submarine trawler **HMS Leyland** but on the 3rd August they were detached from the convoy.

The destroyer HMS Wishart. Photo Old Ship Gallery

Some of the evacuees who remember the journey explained that most of the ships were more ready for the scrap yard than for anything else. The convoy sailed under the command of Commodore Creighton who travelled onboard the **SS Balfe** and the Vice Commodore Captain Wood on the **SS Brittany**. Looking after the welfare of the evacuees on the **Brittany** was Mr L Bruzon. The only escort ship provided for the whole convoy was the corvette **HMS Wellington.**

Despite the war trauma, there were still moments for relaxation at the Theatre Royal on Monday 29th July 1940.

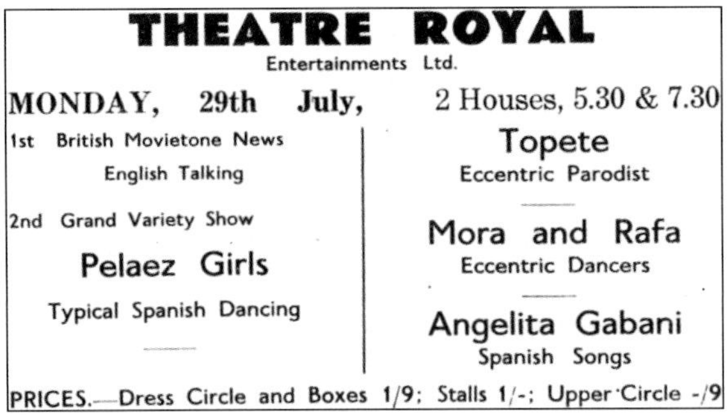

For those who left on the next convoy there were many emotional scenes as they saw the Rock from the distance for a very long time before sailing out of the Strait of Gibraltar and into the Atlantic Ocean.

A view of the Rock from one of the ships in convoy GH40. Photo Gibraltar Museum

Referring to the shortage of escort vessels, Commodore Creighton explained that they were needed for more vital prosecution of the war at a time when Britain's fate was on the balance. There was hardly any life saving gear and no doctors in any of the ships in the convoy. And as to the evacuees, Commodore Creighton commented that taking these evacuees into exile separated from their husbands and loved ones, to be taken to a strange land was a tragic affair but that in war necessity knew no law.

The hygienic facilities made available on this convoy were truly appalling. The **Brittany**, for example, had six lavatories for about 718 evacuees. As there were no doctors available, the evacuees had to attend to the sick with no medical facilities and no nursing experience. All they had in the way of medical equipment was a first aid box in each ship. One of the many cases attended to by the evacuees was that of a ten-year-old girl Elena Bagna. She had sustained severe injuries to her head from a piece of shrapnel as a result of an air raid a few days before embarking on the **City of Evansville**.

The corvette HMS Wellington. Photo Old Ship Gallery

Elena required daily attention to her very serious wound which had to be cleaned every day for fear of infection. This was done by the evacuees with very little or no experience at all but who did everything possible to ameliorate her painful injuries – for two weeks!

When Elena arrived in London she underwent immediate surgery resulting in having a piece of special metal implanted permanently to her skull just above the area of the left hand side of her forehead.

Elena Bagna. Photo Mrs Alman

There were also cases of the evacuees having to attend to births without any experience at all. Twelve children were born during the journey. Five of these children were Alfonso Duncan Alvarez on the **John Duncan**, James Balfe Gomez on the **Balfe** and Marina Bagna sister to Elena Bagna on the **City of Evansville**, a boy on the **City of Windsor** and another boy on the **Dromore Castle** but who later died. The **Baharistan** developed some engine problems which required that the rest of the ships in the convoy had to slow down their speed. But the most tragic of all the experiences were those related to the evacuees who died during the journey.

No doubt due to the anxiety and stress of the voyage, five elderly persons and a boy had to be buried at sea - one on the **Strategist**, another on the **Baharistan** and another three on other ships.
There were many cases of the elderly and infirm that had to remain in the holds for the entirety of the journey. The ladders in the ship had being built for able people but obviously the majority of the evacuees were unable to climb these steep ladders. As a result many of the evacuees spent most of the journey in holds and unable to get some fresh air.

The Calumet. Photo Old Ship Gallery

The City Of Windsor. Photo Old Ship Gallery

The evacuees had to do their own cooking and in each ship there were volunteers who did the cooking for the rest of the evacuees.

The Dromore Castle. Photo Old Ship Gallery

Considering that it was summer, the air in the holds must have been quite stale. Some of the evacuees I spoke with assured me of the presence of cockroaches and rats. My mother used to tell me that she had been sea sick for most of the duration of the journey and my two elder brothers had to go to the galley to fetch our daily food.
Below is a detailed account of the journey written by an evacuee girl on the **SS Dromore Castle** which was nicked named by the evacuees as "El Cigarron."

After spending all day and night packing, we were due at 7.30 a.m. at the War Memorial, where military lorries were ready to take us to the tender in Waterport Wharf—and so to the ship. Everybody was very sorry to leave, as nearly every family was leaving some relative behind. My father and uncles were among the latter.

Once inside the "Drumore Castle" which was a cargo ship, we all hoped the journey wouldn't take too long. We were divided into four groups, each in one hold beneath the deck with about one hundred to one hundred and fifty persons in each. The only ventilation was an opening where an improvised wooden ladder gave access to the deck. There was nothing comfortable about the ship, I don't think it was meant for human beings at all. The only alteration made was a large wooden table in the middle of each of the holds, and we passengers laid our mattresses on the floor round it to sleep at night.

We had to wait 48 hours in the harbour, and on the second evening at 6.00 p.m. we sailed in a convoy with 36 other ships, mostly cargo vessels, and nearly all of them carrying evacuees.

On leaving the Rock most of the people were on deck, and now our only hope was to be safe from any raid at sea, and to reach our destination (which we didn't know at first) soon. Little did we imagine that there were 17 more days at sea lying ahead of us.

The sailors were all very nice to us, always playing about with the children and telling them tales. It was nice to see a group of youngsters with some sailors giving them chocolates or sweets, and explaining the different parts of the ship. But what they all wanted to see was the engine room, and that was a prohibited area.

Once a week, we were given a ration of sugar, tea and coffee, but after ten days there was no more bread left, so we were given a limited number of hard water biscuits. Each family had to cook their own food and sometimes it was trying as there was only one coal stove for each group.

By now we were getting tired of just seeing sea and sky, and on asking any sailor when we would reach land his reply was always the same, "In a few days' time."

SEA TRAGEDY

One evening, a little boy was taken very ill and as there was no doctor or even a nurse in our ship, a doctor had to be called from another, but the sea was too rough for him to cross. That night, the boy died, and he was buried at sea the next morning.

Early every morning I used to be the first up on deck to see if there were any sign of land, but what I usually saw were big patches of oil on top of the water.

Above script by Mrs M E Russo

Throughout the remaining part of the journey, the evacuees had to feed, in some cases with just potatoes and in others with just rice full of weevils. The master and crew of the ships had no responsibility for the evacuees. The local persons who had been appointed to accompany the evacuees were made responsible for their well being.

The SS Baharistan. Photo Old Ship Gallery

The SS Beckenham. Photo Old Ship Gallery

Although I cannot remember anything that transpired on the journey, from what I have heard the food was not very appetising. After about a week at sea most of the ships in the convoy had practically no food left.

The SS Swinburne. Photo Mr N Sene

It was reported that most of the ships had also run out of bread and the evacuees had to do with very hard biscuits that they came to call "galletas de perros"- dogs' biscuits. There was also in almost every ship shortage of fresh water which had to be rationed. The very young children, who obviously were not aware of what was going on, played on the upper decks if the weather or circumstances permitted.

Throughout most of the journey the weather had been good, which helped to make things easier from the point of view of seasickness, as most of the time the evacuees were travelling in the holds. When the convoy entered the North Sea it met with rough seas. Throughout the whole journey there was also the obvious constant fear of the high risk of being attacked by enemy submarines during that period of the war. One evacuee recollects having seen an enemy aircraft followed by some firing from one of the ships in the convoy. In fact reports from official sources mention that an aircraft approached the convoy on the 10th August machine-gunning the **SS Libano** but without causing any damage. Another aircraft was sighted on the 11th August about 50 miles off Tory Island. It flew over the convoy and was chased off by **HMS Wellington** with gunfire until the aircraft disappeared. While this firing was going on, many were conscious of the danger that this meant for their safety. The incident naturally, gave rise to the obvious concern that these same enemy aircraft could alert any enemy submarines in the vicinity as to the convoy's position and make it vulnerable to being attacked.

Commodore Creighton stated in his book "Convoy Commodore" that the thing that worried him most was the lack of life-saving gear which were designed for normal able seamen but could not go very far among a thousand persons. He stated that if the convoy had been attacked it could have resulted in one of the worst maritime disasters in history. This he said in the knowledge that the composition of the evacuees was such that they were expected to panic in any emergency situation. He further remarked that the majority of the evacuees, who were travelling in the holds, would have been drowned before they could manage to get out of the type of ships that would have sunk in a matter of seconds.

During the 9th and 10th August when approaching the northwest coast of Ireland, there was much danger from submarine activities and the Admiralty changed the convoy's route. Many emergency turns were also made, both during the day and during the night, because of reports received during that part of the journey. At that stage of the journey the weather condition was getting worse with the sea becoming rough making it difficult for those not used to travel by sea, particularly the women and children. Strong north-westerly winds with heavy seas and thick rain squalls were prevailing at the time. Before entering the North Channel rendezvous was made with convoy OG.40 which deployed the destroyer **HMS Westcott** and provided additional escort as from the morning of the 10th August to the 14th August.

The destroyer HMS Westcott. PhotoOld Ship Gallery

From then on some ships in the convoy began to diverge. Some ships proceeded to the Firth of Clyde area and others continued sailing southward into the Irish Sea to make for the different ports along the established route.

Rear Admiral Sir Kenelm Creighton.
Photo "Convoy Commodore"

When passing near the Isle of Man the masters of the **Brittany** and the **City of Windsor,** which were carrying diabetics, requested permission to berth at Liverpool as they were in desperate need of food with sugar content for the diabetics. They both berthed at Liverpool on the 13 August 1940 amidst air raids.

Isaac Abensur who was then 8 years old described his recollection of his arrival at Liverpool as follows: "The port was strewn with ships sank by the German bombers and at least one German fighter plane was sank with a dead pilot inside.

The impact on children was dramatic. On landing we were transported by bus, a double decker seen, for the first time by many, to a basement where we got a meal - boiled carrots with sugar! Then we were taken to a place with many bath tubs and given a scrubbing with large brushes and disinfectant followed by painting our bodies with an anti scurvy liquid." Other evacuees who have described similar experiences of their arrival recall the long penetrating mournful sound made by the air raid sirens. Shortly after arriving at Liverpool the evacuees were transferred by train to London. What is interesting to know from this is that although the ships arrived at Liverpool, the expectant mothers for unknown reasons were taken to give birth at Glasgow. The children who were born in Glasgow were Joe Felices, also baptised at Glasgow, Charles Cartwright and Lydia Pozo. She unfortunately died soon after arriving in London. I could not find out the reasons why it was decided that the births of these children should have been carried out at Glasgow and not at Liverpool. I can only assume that the hospitals at Liverpool must have been fully saturated with casualties from the bombing which at the time was affecting many of the British cities. A few days later both mothers and babies were taken back to Liverpool and then to London. As an anecdote, Joe was registered in the UK as Felices although the rest of his family are registered as Felice. It is possible that these children were the first evacuees to be born on UK soil.

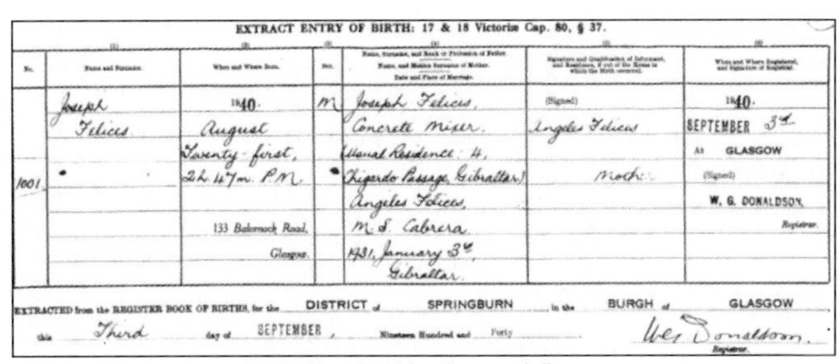

EXTRACT ENTRY OF BIRTH: 17 & 18 Victoriæ Cap. 80, § 37.

No.	Name and Surname.	When and Where Born.	Sex.	Name, Surname, and Rank or Profession of Father. Name, and Maiden Surname of Mother. Date and Place of Marriage.	Signature and Qualification of Informant	When and Where Registered, and Signature of Registrar.
1001	Joseph Felices	1940. August Twenty-first, 2h. 47m. P.M. 133 Balornock Road, Glasgow.	M	Joseph Felices, Concrete mixer. (Usual Residence: 4, Riguardo Passage, Gibraltar) Angeles Felices, M.S. Cabrera 1931, January 3rd, Gibraltar	(Signed) Angeles Felices Mother.	1940. September 3rd At Glasgow (Signed) W. G. Donaldson Registrar.

EXTRACTED from the REGISTER BOOK OF BIRTHS, for the DISTRICT of SPRINGBURN in the BURGH of GLASGOW

this Third day of SEPTEMBER, Nineteen Hundred and Forty

W. G. Donaldson, Registrar.

J.Felice's birth certificate

The SS Brittany. Photo Old Ship Gallery

The rest of the ships that made for the Bristol Channel arrived off Milford Haven at 10.30 am on the 13th August but owing to the port being closed because of mines, the ships had to wait until onward routing orders were sent off by boat and then proceeded independently.

Balfe, **Baharistan** and **Calumet** entered Milford Haven at 2.30 pm. The **Strategist, Euryades** and the **City of Evansville** were sent to Swansea where evacuees disembarked on the 14th August.

The SS City Of Evansville. Photo Old Ship Gallery

The SS Belgravian. Photo Old Ship Gallery

A scene of Liverpool after a bombing raid.
Photo Liverpool Records Office

The **Swinburne, Belgravian, Dromore Castle** and **Beckenham** went to Cardiff where the evacuees were able to disembark safely on the 15th August.

In addition to the ships that were carrying the evacuees there were other ships in the same convoy, which carried all types of cargo ranging from sardines, onions, iron ore, wine and many other types of merchandise

These general cargo vessels were of the following nationality: British – the Courland, Balmore, Libano, Heminge and Fidra. Swedish – the Bifrost, Magne, Urd, Veronica, Taberg and Calabria. Greek - Aghia Eirini.

The SS Strategist. Photo Old Ship Gallery

The SS Euryades. Photo Old Ship Gallery

At the end of the journey lasting fifteen days, Commodore Creighton wrote to the Admiralty in the following terms:

"The Officers and crews of many of the ships of this Convoy had taken 13,500 French soldiers and sailors to Casablanca from England.

The SS Balfe. Photo Old Ship Gallery

They then brought 13,300 evacuees, women, children etc. from Casablanca to Gibraltar by order of the French authorities, and subsequently have brought 5,800 women and children evacuees from Gibraltar to England. In these three voyages it was recognised that in view of the lack of boats for the numbers carried, there would be little chance for the officers and crews in the event of accident. It is submitted for consideration that a letter of appreciation of their service from Their Lordships is forwarded to the Masters for promulgation to the officers and crews concerned."

During my research I was able to contact via the British Merchant Navy website one of the seamen who served on one of the ships in the convoy. Below is an extract from what he wrote about his recollections in the following terms:

"When the war broke out, the civilian population of Gibraltar had been evacuated to Casablanca because of the expected Italian air raids. They now had King George's subjects eating their heads off so we were released to take them away. We youngsters were more than pleased to have a big proportion of pretty girls as passengers. Here again my choice of European languages at school paid dividends and my Spanish improved as much as my French had. We put them all ashore in Gibraltar and after three weeks joined a convoy of a dozen ships taking the civilians back to the UK. Here again they were nearly all women, children and girls. To keep themselves occupied during the voyage they did all our washing and ironing for us. I can remember the astonishment of my mother when I came home on leave with a trunk full of clean, beautifully ironed clothes. The voyage home took three weeks and we were lucky not to be attacked, as our only escort was an armed tug."

Newport Road, Cardiff after and air raid.
Photo Cardiff Libraries and Information Services

These ships, like the two which berthed at Liverpool a couple of days before, arrived amidst sirens and enemy planes flying low to shoot ships in the area. There were several bomb blasts and flares in the sky, which was witnessed by evacuees who remembered seeing it all from aboard the **Beckenham** the night before the evacuees started to disembark.

Evacuees after disembarking from SS Beckenham at Cardiff on the 15th August 1940. In the photo are Monolo and Tony Rodriguez. Photo Mr M Rodriguez

The following is an account of how an evacuee recalls the moments when she arrived at Cardiff.

"Nineteen days after leaving Gibraltar we reached Cardiff but we couldn't land until the next day, and the same evening the raids started. The alarms sounded twice that very night. When we landed, we had to wait nearly all morning to be medically examined, and after that we were taken to an institute where we were given some food. From there we were taken by buses, which were waiting at the door. We had to leave the buses two or three times to take shelter, and in one of them, some workers gave us tea and something to eat. On the train and on the outskirts of Cardiff, we thought ourselves more or less safe. Although it was about 10 pm it was still light and I enjoyed looking out of the carriage window."

Swansea docks destroyed by bombs.
Photo Swansea Libraries and Information Services

Like with the previous two groups of evacuees, this group was taken to portable clinics at the different ports of disembarkation for medical examination and delousing treatment. From then onwards they were taken by train to London.

The next largest party of evacuees to sail for the UK went onboard the **Neuralia** after she had taken about 1,250 evacuees to the island of Madeira on 10th August. When the **Neuralia** sailed it carried nearly 1,800 evacuees on the 20th August 1940 and arrived in Liverpool on the 4th September. I was told that on this ship, the cooking arrangements for the evacuees were looked after by the Galia brothers. The menu consisted mainly of boiled potatoes, carrots, vegetables and some meat.

The ship which was originally scheduled to take these evacuees to the UK was the **Mohamed Ali el –Kebir.** She left Avonmouth on the 5th August for Gibraltar but after two days at sea she was sunk by an enemy torpedo with the loss of 120 lives. In view of this, the **Neuralia** was commissioned instead. By then there were still over 3,000 civilians who were categorised as evacuees. Spain by then was sympathetic towards the Axis powers with the conviction that England would be invaded and that the Allies would lose the war. The menace of an invasion with the involvement of Spain was seen as very possible and Gibraltar was busy turning into a fully-fledged fortress. The military authorities in Gibraltar assessed that it was necessary to evacuate these remaining civilians as the policy was still, that non-combatant civilians had to leave the fortress as they would become a hindrance in any military operation to defend the fortress. The Governor was, therefore, still urging the British Government to give the utmost priority to the need of evacuating these remaining non-combatant civilians. It was even suggested that if necessary the British Government should look into the possibility of arranging for some civilians to be evacuated to Argentina because of the language and the fact that there were already some Gibraltarians who had emigrated there some years back.

After the evacuation to Jamaica, there were still over 1,000 civilians in Gibraltar and the Governor remained adamant that they, too, should be evacuated. However, the first group of these remaining 1,000 civilians did not leave for the UK until the middle of the following year.

In the next column is a copy of the notice which appeared in the Gibraltar Chronicle in connection with the departure 340 civilians who left on the Union Castle Line ship the **SS Arundel Castle** on the 23rd May 1941 escorted by the cruiser **HMS London** but which later half way the journey was ordered to leave the escort and join the task force in the chase to sink the German pocket battleship **Bismark**. During the journey on the **Arundel Castle** one of the evacuees, Mrs Ines Roca gave birth to a baby girl. The **Arundel Castle** reached Avonmouth on the 15 June 1941.

GIBRALTAR EVACUATION SCHEME

1. Embarkation of evacuees whose names have appeared on the lists published by the Controller of Man-Power on the 20th instant will take place on Thursday next, the 22nd May, 1941, at 8 a.m.

2. Heavy baggage must be deposited at either of the two collecting places, viz., CASEMATES or LINE WALL, opposite the City Hall, by 7-30 a.m. on the 22nd May, 1941.

3. Evacuees must assemble for transport at any of the two collecting places by 8 a.m. on the 22nd instant.

4. All baggage should be marked with the names and EMBARKATION NUMBER of the evacuee.

5. The allotment of accommodation on the ship will be done arbitrarily by the ship's officers and no application for individual preference will be considered.

6. All evacuees detailed for this ship **MUST EMBARK.** Proceedings under the Defence Regulations will be instituted against any person who does not comply with the above instructions.

For and on behalf of the Evacuation Committee.

Man-Power Office,
Gibraltar, 20th May, 1941.

J. H. S. Lacey,
Major R.E.
Controller of Man-Power.

CIVILIAN EVACUATION

All persons being evacuated are reminded that not more than £10 in sterling notes can be taken out of the Colony by any individual.

Arrangements will be made by the Command Paymaster to exchange local currency notes into sterling at the place of embarkation before going on board ship.

Cutting of notice in the Gibraltar Chronicle ordering the embarkation of a determined list of evacuees.

The Arundel Castle. Photo Old Ship Gallery

Another group consisting of 500 civilians left a few days later for the UK on the Greek ship **Nea Hellas** on the 30th May 1941.

The evacuation notice in connection with the departure of this group of evacuees on the **Nea Hellas,** which is shown in the next in the page, appeared in the Gibraltar Chronicle on the 29th May 1941, a day before these selected evacuees were due to leave.

The Nea Hellas. Photo Jim Kalafatis

GIBRALTAR EVACUATION SCHEME

1. The embarkation of all British Families from Tangier and La Linea at present in Gibraltar awaiting evacuation and all persons whose names have appeared on lists published by the Controller of Man-Power will take place on Friday next, 30th May, 1941.

2. Heavy baggage not wanted on voyage must be deposited at either of the two collecting places, viz., **CASEMATES** or **LINE WALL**, opposite the City Hall, by 7-30 a.m., 30th May, 1941. This baggage, which must not include articles of furniture or household effects, will be clearly marked with name and Registration Number of the owner, and will be limited to two packages per person. No package will exceed 3 ft. x 3 ft. x 2 ft. in size. Mattresses will **NOT** be required on the voyage.

3. Evacuees will assemble at the times mentioned below at either of the two Collecting Places.

(a) British Subjects ... ... at 8-00 a.m.
(b) Aliens ... ... at 10-00 a.m.

4. The hand baggage required on the voyage will be brought to the Collecting Places by the evacuees. This baggage will also be clearly marked with the name and Registration Number of the owner and must be limited to two suit cases or their equivalent. A knife, fork, plate and cup or mug should be included and spare blankets or rugs may be taken in addition to this hand baggage.

5. The allotment of accommodation on the ship will be done arbitrarily by the ship's Officers and no application for individual consideration will be entertained.

6. All evacuees detailed for this ship **MUST EMBARK.** Proceedings under the Defence Regulations will be instituted against any person who does not comply with the above instructions.

Man-Power Office, Gibraltar, 28th May, 1941.

J. H. S. Lacey, Major R.E. Controller of Man-Power.

Amidst the evacuation of the remaining civilians, it is interesting to note that the then Governor General Lord Gort paid an official call on the Military Governor of the Camp de Gibraltar, General Agustin Muñoz Grandes* at Algeciras on the 19th May 1941. Shortly after, on the 22nd June 1941 Hitler launched Operation Barbarrosa.

**** General Muñoz Grandes became Commander of the Blue Division that fought alongside the Germans in the Eastern Front against the Russians from 1941 to 1943.***

The last party consisting of 152 evacuees left for the UK on the 4th July 1941 on board the **Pasteur.**

Reading the foregoing notices it seems that they were mainly intended for the evacuation of those families who were living either in Tangier or La Linea but who still, as British families, had to abide with the evacuation orders, as otherwise, they would not have been able to enter Gibraltar.

The notice in connection with the departure of this last party of evacuees on the **Pasteur** appeared in the Gibraltar Chronicle as shown in the next column.

GIBRALTAR EVACUATION SCHEME

In pursuance of the Order made by the Governor under Regulations 56(1) (b) of the Defence Regulations 1939.

1. All persons in possession of an Embarkation Card issued to them by the Controller of Man-Power and all British families from LA LINEA and TANGIER now in Gibraltar awaiting evacuation will embark on Tuesday, 1st July, 1941.
2. Heavy baggage, not wanted on voyage, must be deposited at the Collecting Point at LINE WALL opposite the City Hall by 7-30 a.m., 1st July, 1941. This baggage, which must not include articles of household furniture, must be clearly marked with the name and Registration Number of the owner. Mattresses will NOT be required on the voyage.
3. Evacuees will assemble at the Collecting Point at LINE WALL at 8-00 a.m.
4. Hand baggage required on the voyage will be brought to the Collecting Point by the evacuees. This baggage will also be clearly marked with the name and Registration Number of the owner, and will be limited to 2 suit cases or their equivalent. A knife, fork, spoon, plate and cup or mug should be included and spare blankets or rugs may be taken in addition to this hand baggage.
5. The allotment of accommodation on the ship will be done arbitrarily by the Ship's Officers and no application for individual consideration will be entertained.
6. All evacuees detailed for this ship MUST embark. Proceedings under the Defence Regulations will be instituted against any person who does not comply with these instructions.

Man-Power Office, Gibraltar 27th June, 1941.

J. H. S. Lacey, Major, R.E. Controller of Man-Power.

The Pasteur. Photo Old Ship Gallery

There were other evacuees like the Harper family who were living in Tangier and decided to join their relatives who had been evacuated previously to the UK. There were others who had been declared medically unfit or were considered to be over-aged and therefore were deemed to be evacuated. The Harpers travelled with this group of evacuees on the Polish freighter the **Sobieski** berthed at the Detached Mole for about a week and from where she sailed escorted on the 4th March and reached the Clyde on the 11th March 1942.

The Sobieski. Photo Mr A Harper

CHAPTER SIX

EVACUATION TO JAMAICA

The idea to evacuate the civilian population to the West Indies was one of the considered options when the initial evacuation plans were drawn. After the return of the evacuees from French Morocco it became one of the few available alternatives. Indeed, on the 25th July 1940 the go ahead was given to build two evacuation camps in Jamaica. Since the camps were going to take at least a couple months to complete, there was no other alternative at the time but to take the evacuees initially to UK, as a temporary measure, until the camps were ready. After two months of intensive work, the first camp in Jamaica was ready by end of September to accommodate about 4,000 evacuees. The British Government then put in motion the procedures to take the evacuees from the UK to Jamaica and gave notice of its intentions to all the authorities concerned by means of the following a memorandum:

> His Majesty's Government greatly regret that it has been necessary for you to leave your homes in Gibraltar, on account of the threat of enemy action, and they have given very careful consideration to the arrangements, which should be made for your safety and welfare. It is their desire and intention that you and your children should be able to live comfortably and safely for the remainder of the war, under conditions as similar as possible to those to which you have been accustomed in Gibraltar.
> These conditions are unfortunately not available in England where danger from enemy action will persist. The winter is damp and cold and the accommodation is limited. But in the British West Indies, the Governments of Trinidad, Jamaica and St. Lucia have generously offered to provide temporary homes for you while the war lasts. Some of you may be reluctant to undertake another journey, but in the West Indies the climate is warm and sunny like the climate of Gibraltar. Suitable accommodation with greater privacy for each family can be provided and facilities will be available for the education of your children.
> His Majesty's Government are fully satisfied that it will be in your best interests to go to the West Indies and that you will be assured of a warm welcome from the people of the loyal British Colonies to which you are sent.
> Arrangements for your journey to the West In dies are being made and will be notified to you later. Suitable ships will be provided and you may be sure that you will not be called upon to endure the hardships of your previous journeys.
> The organisation for the transfer of more than 10,000 people is a complicated matter and his Majesty's Government feel certain that you will all do your best to assist the authorities and to comply with the instructions, which will be issued to you from time to time.

The above memorandum was displayed at all the evacuation centres in the UK. Instructions were also given on the 15th September to build a second camp to house another 5,000 evacuees.

The memorandum, as can be seen, advised the evacuees that it was in their best interest to be transferred to the West Indies and asked for their cooperation with the authorities.

The evacuation advisory committee in the UK headed by Major J Patron was supportive of this policy. Meetings were held in many of the evacuation centres where very firm arguments were put against the arrangements. The evacuees in the UK and the families in Gibraltar feared the perils involved in crossing the Atlantic once again. Both Cardinal Hinsley and Archbishop Amigo appealed to Mr MacDonald, Minister of Health, not to proceed with the plans. Amongst the many others who opposed the idea was Fr Thomas Smith. He looked after the welfare of about 800 evacuees at the Anerley Receiving Centre and kept Archbishop Amigo, posted regularly with their sentiments expressed by the evacuees of having to sail to the West Indies. He offered to go with the evacuees if they were forced to do so. According to the British Government one of the main consideration was on health grounds as it was thought that many evacuees could die as a result of not being unaccustomed to the cold and damp English weather. The doctors in Gibraltar, who knew most of the evacuees personally, did not share this view. The Governor in Gibraltar also conveyed the fears expressed by families in Gibraltar against the re-evacuation to the West Indies.

On the 18th September, coinciding with this notice and the attempts to persuade the evacuees to move to Jamaica, the **SS City of Benares** was sunk with a loss of many lives, including, 77 British children who had been evacuated to Canada. 105 survivors were saved but due to some misunderstanding, one of the life boats carrying 46 survivors, including six children, went mistakenly adrift in the Atlantic and were not spotted until eight days later by an RAF Sunderland flying boat.

The City Of Benares. Photo Old Ship Gallery

The City of Benares' tragedy no doubt vindicated the main fears of the Gibraltar evacuees who, as a result mounted further opposition to cancel the planned re-evacuation to Jamaica. The press in the UK also urged the British Government to discontinue the evacuation of British children.

Surviving children from the City Of Bernares. Photo Mr Mackenzie J Gregory

During the autumn and winter of 1940, Britain was suffering the greatest losses of her merchant navy ships in the Atlantic Ocean. It seems that upon considering these hard facts and on the advice of the Admiralty, the British Government cancelled its plans and postponed indefinitely the idea of evacuating British children by sea passage. However, the British Government still maintained that the Gibraltar evacuees should be sent to the West Indies. On the 15th November 1940 all new works on Camp Two were discontinued. On the 30th November 1940 Archbishop Amigo was informed by Mr MacDonald that the plans had been abandoned but those who wished to go voluntarily to Jamaica could do so. However, for the 1,500 civilians of the 2,500 remaining in Gibraltar who had been categorised as evacuees no choice was given and consequently the decision was taken to evacuate them to the newly completed camp in Jamaica.

In view of the urgency, it was decided by the British Government that the troopship **Neuralia** would sail from the UK to Gibraltar to take evacuees to Jamaica. Before arriving in Gibraltar from the UK, the **Neuralia** called at Lisbon to collect Polish and Jewish refugees.

The evacuation from Gibraltar to Jamaica proceeded with the first contingent of evacuees sailing on the 9th October 1940 within a convoy. According to an evacuee, during the first few days the sea became very rough and many, including the captain, became sea sick. After four days at sea, the convoy diverged and the **Neuralia** proceeded on its own as from Sunday 13th October. When only a few days of sailing were left to reach Jamaica, the **Neuralia** began to ziz zag after observing a large vessel in the distance. Apparently this vessel began to zig zag as well and then disappeared completely with the evacuees becoming naturally very concerned. The evacuees numbered 1,104 made up of 185 men, 673 women and 248 children. They arrived at Port Royal in Jamaica on Friday 25th October with an addition from Mrs Maria Hall who gave birth to a boy named Arthur Andrew after the ship's captain.

A second party consisting of nearly 400 evacuees embarked on the 8,176 tons Belgian ship **SS Thysville** on the 31st October. She left on the following day within a convoy but after the first two days, she proceeded on its own towards Jamaica.

A few days before reaching Jamaica there was a scary incident with another ship. This ship, then unidentified, was approaching the **Thysville** from the starboard side. Her guns began to be trained in the direction of **Thysville**. Meanwhile, the **Thysville** hoisted the Belgian and the British flags. There was also an exchange of visual signals. As the mystery ship came nearer, a boarding party was lowered on a small boat. By then it was not yet clear whether the ship was friendly or foe.

The troop ship SS Thysville. Photo Old Ship Gallery

The waiting to find out was endless. Once alongside the **Thysville,** there was a heartfelt relief when it was found that the ship was certainly British but the boarding of the **Thysville** nevertheless still went ahead to make sure that everything was in order. After checking the **Thysville**, the boarding party returned to its ship which by then was known to be a Royal Navy corvette and then sailed away. The evacuees waved their hands and wish her and the crew God speed. The rest of the journey to Jamaica went on without any further incidents with the evacuees arriving at Jamaica on the 15TH November. With regard to the ship itself, the remarks from the evacuees were that the accommodation provided during the journey was comfortable and the crew very helpful and sociable.

CHAPTER SEVEN

EVACUEES IN MADEIRA

Madeira as is well known is a beautiful island in the Atlantic with a mild subtropical climate. However, for the Gibraltar evacuees, the separation from the loved ones, the lack employment opportunities, particularly, for the young evacuees, and the uncertainty imposed by war itself was only made bearable by the island's natural beauty and the hospitality afforded by the people of Madeira.

An old view of the Bay Of Funchal. Photo Mr F Chincotta

Writing about her recollections during the evacuation, this is how an evacuee described her experience when she was a young girl in Madeira.

"There were plenty of flowers everywhere. Most of the houses had their own garden. The mountains in the background were so green with many small farms scattered all over making the place very pleasant but my heart was in Gibraltar all the time............"

Conversely, I think it is also true to say that many Gibraltarian hearts and minds have remained for always in Madeira. As prophesised by the Madeira 1940 newspaper clipping, shown on the right hand column, the ties of friendship between the people of Gibraltar and Madeira still last.

View of the main squares in Funchal at time of the evacuation. Photo Mr L Pereira

A Newspaper in Funchal reporting on the arrival of the Gibraltar Evacuees

Os evacuados de Gibraltar

Estão na Madeira cêrca de dois mil evacuados de Gibraltar, em virtude da anormalidade que a guerra impôs áquela poderosa base militar inglesa.

A vinda para esta ilha de numero tão importante de subditos estrangeiros, numa ocasião em que estava por completo paralisado o movimento de turismo, não deixa de ter para a Madeira um alto e evidente interesse.

São duas mil pessoas que aqui se encontram, gastando, consumindo, fazendo entrar e girar na vida comercial da Madeira uma avultada verba diaria com evidente vantagem para a economia geral da ilha.

Independentemente dessa circunstancia de ordem material uma razão de natureza moral faz com que olhemos com a maior simpatia estes hospedes da Madeira durante o tempo de guerra. Antes de tudo habitam perto de Portugal, vivem na mesma Peninsula onde se edificou e progrediu a nação a que nos orgulhamos de pertencer. Além disso são subditos dum imperio que se acha ligado a Portugal por fundos laços de amizade e por uma aliança politica que é das mais antigas do mundo.

A natureza da actual guerra, a necessidade de condicionar toda a vida de Gibraltar aos imperativos da defeza militar, fez com que uma parte importante dos seus habitantes viessem até nós. Tiveram de deixar as suas casas, o seu lar, os lugares que mais diletamente falavam á sua alma e ao seu coração. Entre as contrariedades duma tal mudança, imposta pelas circunstancias, não deixará de ser grato aos subditos britanicos constatarem o ambiente acolhedor que aqui os aguardava. O mesmo mar azul da sua cidade mediterranea, o mesmo ceu de sol maravilhoso, a mesma alma e o mesmo afecto da gente do sul.

Estão aqui, ha algumas semanas já, sem ninguem quasi dar por eles, entregues á sua vida, mas fazendo já parte do aspecto habitual da cidade. E, com certeza, vão por aqui ficar enquanto durar a guerra e a defeza de Gibraltar não fôr compativel com a volta da sua população civil.

Estamos certos de que deste convivio das populações do Funchal e de Gibraltar vão nascer laços perduraveis de amizade entre as duas cidades e que, mais uma vez, a boa gente da Madeira vai dar provas do seu cavalheirismo e do seu espirito de hospitalidade.

A view of the Savoy Hotel during the evacuation - the lido is in the forefront of the photograph. Photo Mr J Chincotta

As explained in the pages about the evacuation to Madeira, the policy for selecting those who wished to be evacuated to Madeira was applied to families who were prepared to pay for their passage and their upkeep during their stay on the island. The total number of evacuees which could be absorbed in the island with the agreement of the Portuguese and British Governments was 2,000. But the total number of evacuees who were able to maintain themselves was much less than 2,000. In fact the total number of evacuees who could maintain themselves and who had been categorised as group A was slightly less than 1000. In view of this shortfall and to fill up the agreed complement, the option to be evacuated to Madeira was offered to other evacuees. This other group of evacuees was again divided into two further categories, which were known as category B and C. Those in category B had to make some contribution towards their upkeep by an agreed scheme. The evacuees categorised as group C and who had no means of maintaining themselves were required to make some contribution via related wage earners in Gibraltar in accordance with a means testing method.

The evacuees who formed part of categories A and B were initially placed in hotels where special rates had been previously arranged and negotiated by the authorities concerned, that is, the British Consul in Madeira.

The class and type of accommodation provided was in line with the financial status of individual families. The main hotels were the Savoy, the New England, the Victoria, the Camacha, the Quinta Esperanza, the Belmonte and a few others. As soon as they could manage, many of these evacuees in the category A group moved to other private accommodations in the form of boarding houses at more economic rates than those being paid at the hotel although many of the category B group evacuees remained in the initial hotels. The evacuees in category C, numbering about 350 were accommodated in buildings called the Lazareto and in another separate building in a place named Quinta Das Cruzes. One of the largest hotels occupied by the evacuees was the Savoy Hotel which remained full to capacity throughout the whole period of the evacuation. The photographs on the next column were donated by Mr L Pereira.

As can be appreciated from the photographs the Savoy Hotel was situated near the centre of Funchal. The evacuees in this hotel belonged to those in categories A and B.

The Savoy Hotel dinning room.

The Lounge.

At the entrance of The Savoy At the back L to R: H.Chichon and Luis Pereira. In front: Joseph Warne and Desmond Baker

The Catering Staff at the Savoy.

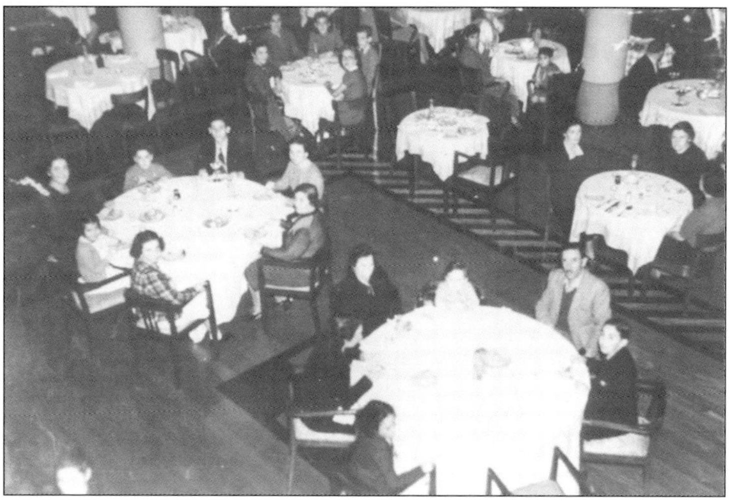

Evacuees in the Savoy Hotel dinning room.
In the photo are the Pereira, the Nunez and Dalmedo Families.

At the terrace of the Savoy.
From L to R: J.Capurro L.Codali E.Pearce L.Pereira L.Olivero A.Brooks W.Pisani J.Ramirez W.LDarby

Mainly due to the continual rise in the cost of living in Madeira and the unforeseen prolonged stay, some evacuees were eventually forced to move down in categories.

The entrance to the Savoy.

The lounge at the Savoy

All the photographs on this page were donated by Mr L Pereira.

Taking part in a fancy dress ball held at the Savoy Hotel. Chef L.Pereira
Waitress Maribel Correa

Evacuees in Madeira

At the entrance of the Savoy in the photo are
L.Pereira J.Warne D.Baker H.Chichon Dolly Chichon Cassaglia Sisters, L.Goldwin, Julie Dobinson and Macedo Sisters.

The Golden Gate Hotel as can be appreciated from the photographs was situated near the sea front. This hotel, like the Savoy, was also fully occupied during the period of the evacuation. All the photos on this page were donated by Mr L Pereira.

Evacuees at the entrance to the Golden Gate Hotel.

At the terrace of the Savoy Hotel.

A close look of the entrance to the Golden Gate Hotel.

The Golden Gate Hotel by The Tourist Office.

Evacuees at the Golden Gate.

The Gilbert family at The Golden Gate Hotel.

The Golden Gate Hotel.

All the photos on this page were donated by Mr L Pereira.

The Belmonte Hotel was about 8 kilometres away from Funchal and as can be seen from the postcard below it offered a spectacular view of the bay. All the photos on this page, except the ones below were donated by Mr and Mrs Brittenden

A *view from Grand Hotel Belmonte during the evacuation. Photo J Gingell*

The Grand Hotel Belmonte. Photo Mr Brittenden

A more recent view of the Belmonte Hotel.

Alfred Brittenden with his family in the garden of the Grand Hotel Belmonte.

A recent view of the entrance to the Belmonte Hotel.

Families getting together in the garden in front of the picture is Alfred Brittenden.

The photographs in this page show the New English Hotel, which was much further away from the centre of Funchal. The other hotels were the Quinta Esperanza, the Victoria, the Camacha and the Monte Palace Hotel.

Evacuees at the New English Hotel
At the back L to R: E.Debono M.Bugeja M.Santos M.DebonoIn front: J.Bugeja O.Chichon J.Morello L.Debono manager's daughter and nanny. Photos abovge and below Mr L Pereira

At the garden of the New English Hotel.
In the photo are Luis Bosano and Mariluz Debono

The New English Hotel. Mr L Pereira

The Victoria Hotel. Mr L Pereira

Mrs Maruja Hook (nee Dalmedo) at Victoria Hotel. Garden. Photo Mrs Hook

The Camacha Hotel. Photo Mrs Clark

The Quinta Esperanza Hotel. Mr L Pereira

The Monte Palace Hotel. Photo Mr J Chincotta

This page shows photographs of the communal accommodation at the Lazaretto Building and Quinta das Cruzes.

A recent photograph of thebuilding at Quinta Das Cruzes now a museum. Photo Mrs R.Field

As mentioned earlier, the evacuees in group C were accommodated in the Lazareto area. Accommodation in this place consisted of two large buildings and two other smaller ones where a total of about 270 evacuees were billeted. Another group of about 80 evacuees were accommodated in another building in a place called Quinta Das Cruzes. In both places all the buildings had to have many alterations made in order to make them habitable for the evacuees.

The alterations mainly consisted in converting the existing rooms into dormitories, toilets, dining rooms, kitchens, bathrooms and all the necessary sanitary installations required for the need of a communal dwelling including laundering and other communal facilities. There was also an infirmary where a doctor attended daily to the health needs of the evacuees. As explained in the section about education, one of these buildings was converted into classrooms to provide schooling for the children in the Lazareto area. Most of the evacuees in the Lazareto were those who had been selected from the Catalan Bay Village.

Evacuees by the Lazaretto building. Photo Mrs Martin

Women from Lazaretto building.
In the photo are M.Stagno Juana Parody L.Stagno M.Robba (Nee Macarri) Photo by Mr M Robba

A more recent view of the Lazareto buildings. Photo Mr M Robba

As mentioned in the introductory page many evacuees moved out of the hotels and found private accommodation at cheaper rates. Below is a photograph of the private accommodation where the Eddings family used to live during most of the time in Madeira.

The house where the Eddings family used to live during the evacuation. Photo Mrs M Lima

Some members of the Jewish Community in their private accommodation in Madeira. Photo Mr M Belilo

I think it is interesting to mention that evacuees had to have, apparently, a residential permit to be able to stay in Madeira. The family of Mr P Davis still retains the permit card which shows a record of Mr Davis's monthly registration.

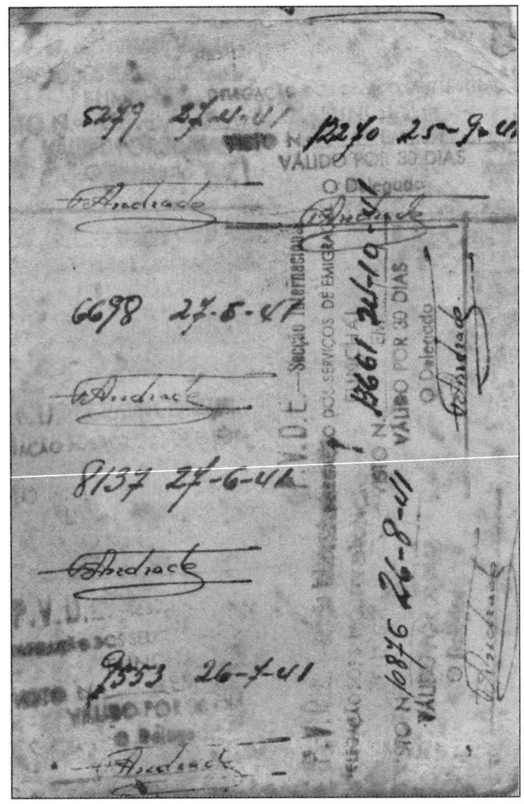

5249 27-11-41
8240 25-9-41
VÁLIDO POR 30 DIAS
O Delegado
6698 27-8-41
8661 26-10-41
VÁLIDO POR 30 DIAS
O Delegado
8137 27-6-41
6876 26-8-41
9353 26-7-41

Copy of 30 days permit issued to Mr Davis.

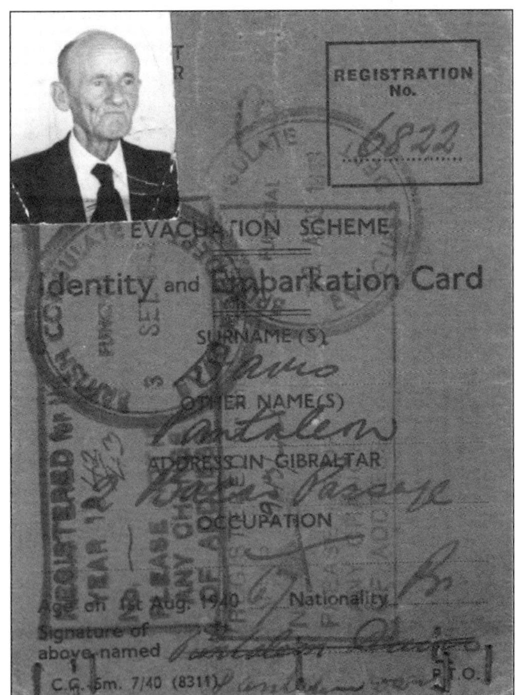

REGISTRATION No. 6822

EVACUATION SCHEME

Identity and Embarkation Card

SURNAME(S) Davis

OTHER NAME(S) Pantaleon

ADDRESS IN GIBRALTAR

OCCUPATION

Age on 1st Aug. 1940 Nationality Br

Signature of above-named

C.G. 6m. 7/40 (8311) P.T.O.

Mr Davis Identity Card. Photo Mrs Prior (nee Davis)

In Madeira there were over 400 children of school age. Schooling was arranged and started reasonably soon. In fact by the 1st October 1940 all the children were already attending the newly opened schools. Below is a cutting from the Gibraltar Chronicle reporting on schooling for the evacuees.

MADEIRA

The British Consul at Funchal, with th assistance of an advisory committee, ha completed arrangements for the provisio of school facilities for the 438 evacue children from Gibraltar.

A large house on a healthy site wa rented with ample play-ground and garde accommodation. School furniture wa bought and made locally, and transpor arrangements provided for those livin far away from the school. Classes hav been opened in the hostel where they re side for 50 or 60 children who live too fa away to attend the school.

The headmaster is a local British re sident who has had many years' experi ence of such work. Seventeen assista teachers were selected from among th evacuees who have had teaching experi ence in Gibraltar schools.

Local British residents are responsib for religious instruction, physical trainin and for music. The courses of stud follow the lines of the preliminary Junio and Senior Cambridge School Certificate Special importance is being attached t the teaching of English and to the pre servation of the British atmosphere. Th School is supplied with appropriate Briti periodicals.

By December, 1940, 168 boys and 14 girls had been enrolled. The average at tendance is 278 and health is reported t be excellent. The rate of fees range fro £2.8.0 to £4.8,0 per year. Fees are no charged to those who cannot afford t pay. The estimated annual net cost o the school is £2,400.

The children who belonged to categories A and B totalling about 250 pupils attended the main British School for Gibraltar children in Funchal. The remaining children totalling about 50 to 60 who belonged to category C, attended classes in the Lazareto building. The schools had been opened largely at the expense of the British Government and the curriculum was very much in line with the British system of education. A lot of work had to be done in turning the building into an adequate school premises.

Many items of school furniture like desks, benches, blackboards and other type of school items had to be obtained from manufacturers and dealers in Madeira. Some evacuees with office and administrative experience offered to assist the British Consulate staff with the running of the schools. One of these evacuees was Mr Mèndoza. The emphasis in the selection of teaching staff was fluency in English rather than knowledge of the subjects being taught or teaching experience. The level of teaching was the same in both schools. In upholding the policy of fluency in English in the schools, much emphasis was given to the speaking of English in every subject, including during religious instructions.

British School for Gibraltar children main building in Funchal during the evacuation. Photo Mr J Chincotta

A recent photo of the former British School for Gibraltar Children in Funchal. Photo Mrs Field.

“ We Thank God and England..”

The Lazareto School Children.

1.J.Baglietto 2.J.Osborne 3. J.L.Robba 4.S.Robba 5.J.Robba 6.D.Pisharello 7.J.Calamaro 8.P.Gaetto 9.S.Gustavino 10.C.Osborne 11.P.Yome 12. P.Stagno 13.H.Robba 14.A.Bonfiglio 15.C.Odo 16.M.Pisharello 17.V.Yome 18.E.Lopez 19. O.Perera 20.P.Chincotta(Calamaro) 21.M.Walker 22. Estella 23.L.Pisharello 24.B.Calamaro 25.C.Yome 26.M.Robba 27.K.Martin (Pisarello) 28.J.Bonfiglio 29. L.Martin (Revagliatte) 30.A.Milan 31.V.Yome 32.A.Baglietto 33.A.Baglietto 34.R.Yeats 35.H.Robba 36.L.Calamaro 37.Miss L.Parody (teacher) 38. Mr.A.Milan (teacher) 39.Mr N. Power(Headmaster) 40.Mr S Macarri (teacher) 41.C.Robba 42.E.Odo 43.A.Riddle(Martin) 44.A.Baglietto 45.J.Stagno 46.L.Gustavino 47.J.Yome 48.M.Parody 49.S.Stagno 50.S.Lopez 51.C.Milan 52.H.Stagno 53.V.Tracey 54.T.Redman 55.F.Parody 56. ?

The above photograph was donated by Mr A Traverso

School rules were obviously set up to institute a form of discipline. The speaking of Spanish within the school environment was strictly forbidden. Children who disobeyed this rule were severely reprimanded or even punished.

Copies of bus tickets Photo Mr J Chincotta

School girls in the play ground during a school break. Photo Mr L Pereira

One of the school's classrooms. Photo Mr L Pereira

Below copy of school rules

THE BRITISH SCHOOL FOR GIRBALTAR CHILDREN SCHOOL RULES

School will begin daily at 9 am sharp. All pupils must be in their places in their class room before the hour.
Each pupil must learn and remember his or her School number, and upon entering the School must first of all hand hat, cap or coat on the peg bearing that number.
A bell will ring one minute before the time marked for each lesson on your time-table, and immediately this signal is given pupils must go immediately to their places.
A break of a quarter of an hour will be given from 11 o'clock to 11.15.
During the break boys must go to the playground at the back of the building: girls can play on the terrace in the front and at the side of the building.
At the end of the break each class must fall in the line and walk quietly with the teacher to the respective class-room.
No talking is allowed in the class-rooms. Attention and respect must be paid to the teachers.
It is strictly forbidden for pupils to touch any of the electric bells. Offenders will be punished.
Special care must be taken not to damage or deface any of the School furniture or the walls or floors of the building.
English is the only language allowed to be spoken in the School. Those who speak Spanish may be punished.
It is strictly forbidden for pupils to touch the taps in the garden, and the water from those taps must never on any account be brought to the mouth nor drunk.
The water laid on in the house is drinking water.
At the close of school pupils travelling by the special buses must without delay get their things together and go to their respective bus, according to the number on their ticket which they must keep from previous journey to school that morning.
Only those who show their tickets will be allowed to enter the bus.
Those intending to come to school by bus the following day must get a book of tickets from their teacher before they leave school today.

The schools' headmaster was Mr Nigel Power and his teaching staff, who were mostly recruited from among the Gibraltar evacuees in Madeira, were Miss M Attias, Miss V Baker, Miss M Carboni, Mr F Cabutto, Miss M Canessa, Miss T Coelho, Miss A Imossi, Miss T Imossi, Mr E Pons, Mrs Q Richardson, Miss E Romero, Miss F Ross, Miss E Teuma, Miss L Warne and Mr Cunha from Madeira.

Physical education, which formed part of the school curriculum, was taken care of by Miss P Porrall at the school in Funchal. Apparently, for some reasons this subject was not taught at the Lazareto School.

The teachers engaged in religious instructions were Miss H King and Mrs F de C Keogh. The singing in English, to help with its practice,was introduced as part of the schools curriculum. Appointed to take care of this aspect of the school teaching policy was Miss Majorie Discombe.

There was a club for the boys' football team and another club for the girls' netball team. The main aim of these clubs was also intended for the purpose of encouraging the use of English. The schools opened only in the mornings. The reason for this was mainly to avoid the transportation hassles and the additional transport expenses that would have been entailed by having to make the same trips again in the afternoons.

Parents in the categories A and B had to pay the school fees.

The amount of fees paid by parents, which ranged from 20 to 40 escudos a month, depended on the level of teaching. Those parents in the category C and who could demonstrate that they could not afford the fees had their children taught free. This policy was also applied to school transport fees. Those parents who could afford it had to pay for school transport fees. Samples of bus tickets, issued in books of twenty, for school transport during the evacuation can be seen in the previous page. The photographs below were donated by Mr L Pereira.

Miss Elsie Teuma with school children outside the British School. Among the children is Pepe Morello.

Students in the photograph with Miss Ellen Romero. Amongst the students are J.Capurro, L.Montegriffo, J.Ferrary, J.Ramirez, W.Darby, J.Baglietto, A.Dalmedo and W.Pissani

In this page the photographs show the students and teachers at the start and ending of the academic years in the British School for Gibraltar Children. The photographs on this page were donated by Mr L Pereira.

Mr Francis Cabutto with his students at the school entrance

Students gathered to receive their school certificates.

Students with teachers at the entrance to the school.

Some of the school teachers. in the photograph are Miss E.Romero and Miss E.Teuma

Students collecting certificates. In the photo are J.Warne and S.Seruya

During their schooling in Madeira many Gibraltar students obtained certificates which were considered to be equivalent to the General Certificates in Education which in some cases served as recognition for a place in further education and eventually to university entry. Some of the photographs show the students waiting to receive their school certificates.

“We Thank God and England..”

The British School for Gibraltar Children Funchal, Madeira 1941 -1942. Photograph donated by Mr J Chincotta.
Some numbers have been inserted to help in identifying names with the aid of key plan in the next page

Evacuees in Madeira

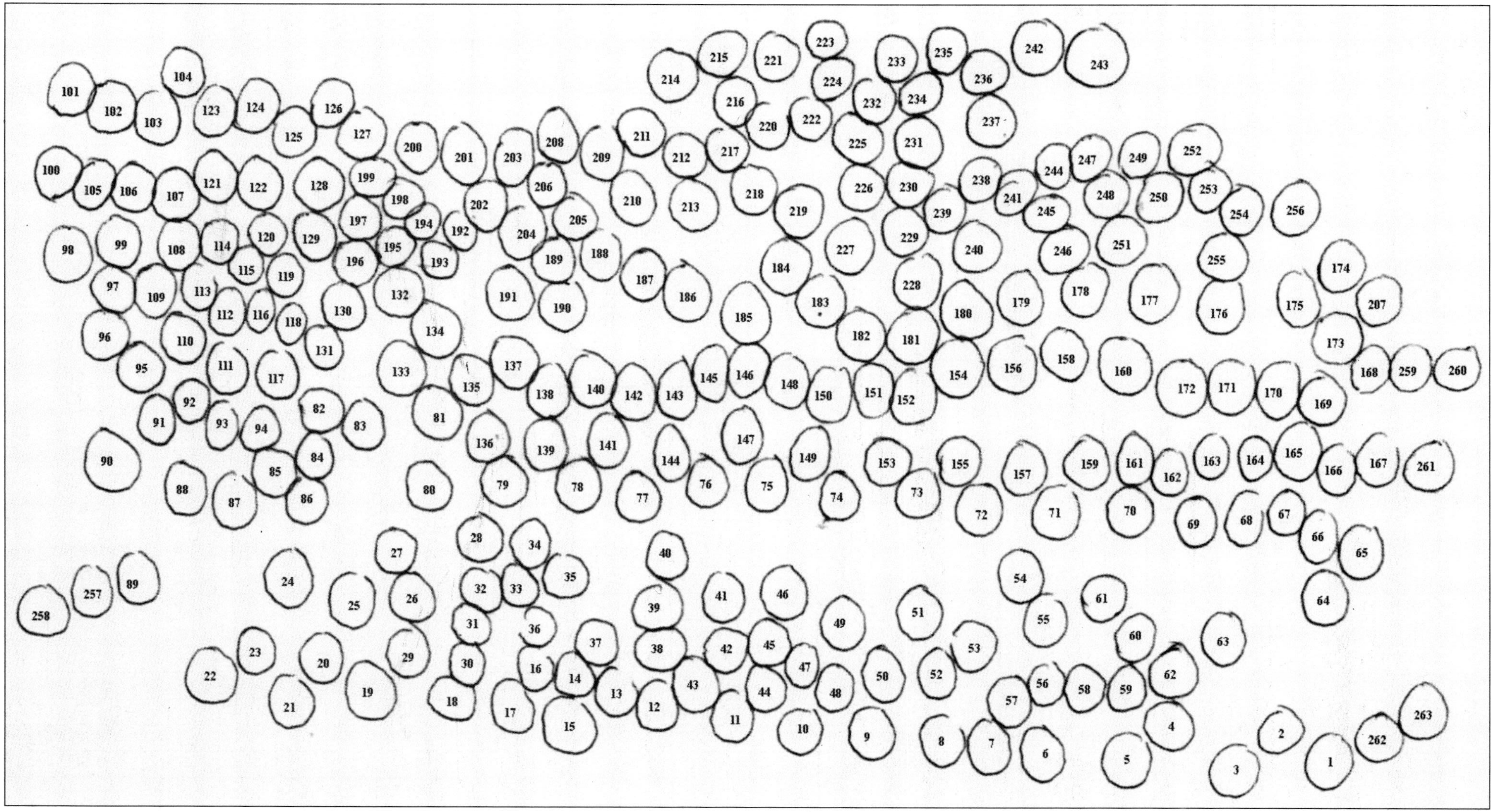

KEY TO HELP IDENTIFYING NAMES IN THE PHOTO SHOWN ON PAGE 54

"We Thank God and Englad.."

NAMES CORRESPONDING TO THE INSETS WITH NUMBERS ON PAGE 55.
T Signifies Teacher

1 Linares	31	61 Bugeja	91 Correa	121 Pons	151 Chiappe	181 Boulton	211 Carboni	241 Rodriguez
2 Peralta	32	62	92	122 Olivero	152 Codali	182 Morillo	212 Zayas	242 Vella
3 Correa	33 Garcia	63 Parody	93	123 Pitto	153 Azzopardi	183 Gracia	213 Cano	243 Alcantara
4 Barca	34	64 Balensi	94 Pereira	124 Yome	154 Canessa	184 Morello	214 Gracia	244
5 Moreno	35 Rodriguez	65 Chipulina T	95 Vella	125 Warne	155 Gilbert	185 Chincotta	215 Bottino	245
6 Diani	36	66 Maccari T	96 Moreno	126	156 Ballantine	186 Zammitt	216 Baker	246 Moreno
7 Peire	37 Ramirez	67 Cunha T	97 Bayardo	127 Bottino	157 Cavilla	187 Robba	217 Pisharello	247 Morillo
8 Morillo	38 Santos	68 Ross	98 Pisani	128 Viale	158 Brooks	188 Ferrary	218 Peralta	248 Noguera
9 Peire	39 Benyunes	69 Coelho T	99 Rodriguez	129 Nunez	159 Capurro	189 Attard	219 Pons	249 Canessa
10 Brooks	40 Raleigh	70 Romero T	100	130 Morillo	160 Diani	190 Capurro	220 Chichon	250
11 Wall	41	71 Canessa T	101 Goldwin	131 Baker T	161 Bugega	191 Casciaro	221 Perez	251 Holland
12 Restano	42 Santos	72 Carboni T	102 McEwen	132	162 Martin	192 Parody	222 Rodriguez	252 Coelho
13 Rodriguez	43 Serruya	73 Mr Andrews British Consul	103 Ferrary	133	163 Peire	193 Hathaway	223	253 Hoare
14	44 Santos?	74 Mr Power Headmaster	104 Goldwin	134	164	194	224 Garbarino	254 Coelho
15 Almeida ?	45 Eddings	75 Imossi T	105	135 Coelho	165 Balensi	195	225 Pereira	255 Miles
16	46 Portuguese national	76 Imossi T	106	136 Viale	166 Gilbert	196 Eddings	226 Bonfiglio	256 Warne
17 Viale	47 Benady	77 Warne T	107	137 Ferrary	167 O'Brien	197 Teuma	227	257 Formosa
18 Sacramento	48 Morello	78	108	138 Fabre	168 Alcantara	198 Yome	228 Robba	258 Morillo
19 Ramagge	49 Montegriffo	79 Alman T	109 McEwen	139 Laguea	169 Debono	199 Calamaro	229 Gaetto	259 Gracia
20	50 Viale	80 Richardson	110 Ruiz	140 Triay	170 Ferrary	200 Huart	230 Pisani	260 Picardo
21 Laguea	51 Ramagge	81 Teuma T	111 Bottino	141 Hume	171 Baglietto	201 Robba	231 Alcantara	261 Rodriguez
22 Morello	52 Yates	82	112 Hume	142 Ellul	172 Gracia?	202	232 Triay	262 Marfe
23 Laguea	53	83	113 Cruz	143 Pizzarello	173 Seruya	203 Calamaro	233	263 Sene
24 Morillo	54 Parody	84 Restano	114 Rodriguez	144 Danino	174 Olivero	204 Sene	234 Vinent	
25 Debono	55 Bensadon	85	115	145 Morillo	175 Montegriffo	205 Benady	235 Zayas	
26 Barca	56 Massias ? (Benzaquen)	86	116 Torres	146 Vinent	176 Miles	206 Chipolina	236 Canessa	
27 Huart	57 Pons	87	117 Eddings	147 Levi	177 Alcantara	207 not allocated	237 Peire	
28 Lavarello	58 Danino	88 Ramagge	118 Alcantara	148 Pizzarello	178 Silva	208 Gareze	238	
29 Catania	59	89 Codali	119 Picardo	149 Azzopardi	179 Canessa	209 Benyunes	239 Serruya	
30 Olivera	60 Noguera	90 Teuma	120	150 Neish	180 Sene	210 Sene	240 Baglietto	

Evacuees in Madeira

Other school activities consisted of organised outings to the various places of interest on the island. The photographs in this and the next page were taken during one of the school outings.

Above and on the top right hand corner photos taken during a school trip to Serra dos Santos on 26th June 1941. Photos Mr J Chincotta

Below are photographs of school children involved in outside school activities when they went on a trip to visit the Santo Do Serra. Photographs donated by Mr J Chincotta.

Photos taken during a school trip to Santo do Serra on 26 June 1941

As can be appreciated from some of the photographs many pupils were well above school age. However, rather than leaving these youngsters with very little to do it was preferable to keep them occupied by attending school.

Students at the steps of the school- in front of the school line is John Alcantara. Photo Mr L Pereira

Miss Carboni with students. In the photo are Berta Bayardo and Freddie Perez.. Photo Mrs Clark

One of the classrooms' students. Photo Mrs Clark

Students at the entrance of the school building to receive their certificates. Two of the students are Solomon Serruya and Emilio Peire. Photo Mr L Pereira

Students and teachers at the entrance to the school. PhotoMrs Clark

Senior students in the school patio. Photo Mrs Clark

Below are photographs of the teams which played for British School Football club.

The British School Football Club in Madeira. Photo donated by Mr M Robba
At the back L to R: Headmaster Mr N. Power Coll P.Gaetto M.Robba O.Robba Pitto M.Yome Rodriguez (Trainer)
Kneeling in front: A.Zayas E.Zayas Rodriguez (son of trainer) Pitto C.Huart

Another photograph of The British School Football Team. Photo donated by Mr L Pereira
At the back from L to R: F.Pitto J.Pearce A Perez C.Huart E.Peire J.Goldwin
Kneeling in front: C.Moreno P.Vella H.Ryan E.Campello A Nunez

On the second academic year since their opening, the schools were visited on the 26th November 1941 by the Civil Governor of Madeira, his wife, the Deputy Governor of Madeira, the British Consul and his wife as shown in the photographs.

Visitors, parents and families watching display by pupils.

The VIPs touring the school.

Pupils in front of the VIPs.

VIPs leaving the school premises.

Above the pupils giving a display in front of the VIPs.

Above another photo of the display by the children for the visitors.

All the photographs on this page were donated by Mr L Pereira.

The officials were taken round the schools to witness at first hand how the children were getting on with their schooling. Then they were later toured around the school to watch a display of physical education by boys and girls in the school playground. Photographs donated by Mr L Pereira.

According to official reports and the Madeira newspaper the Diario de Noticias the official guests were very pleased and impressed with the facilities being provided and with the standard of education afforded by the teaching staff.

According to an evacuee recollection about Christmas, he remembered that it was one of the best seasons in Madeira. Dances were held in the Casino which remained closed at other times owing to the fact there were no tourists as a result of the war situation. During Christmas the schools were decorated with the traditional Christmas trees. Below are two photographs taken during Christmas at school in Madeira. Photographs donated by Mr Pereira.

Above evacuees gathered for the Christmas party accompanied by officials.

The British Consul Mr Andrews, his wife and other officials visiting the school during Christmas.

The Sporting Of Madeira Football Team with Emilio Peire kneeling in the centre.

Another football team in Madeira with participants from Gibraltar are M.Robba, E.Ryan and F.Ptto.

The Sporting Club Da Madeira (Infantils) Team. In the team are Gibraltar Evacuees L.Olivero L.Pereira and C.Huart

Apart from the school football teams there were other football teams in which many Gibraltar evacuees took part, including the local football teams like the Sporting de Madeira.

Some of the natives of Madeira reciprocated by participating in a few of the evacuees' football teams. The photographs in this page show some of the football teams in Madeira.

As far as sports was concerned there was a miniature golf course and tennis court. At first these two sporting activities were new to most of the Gibraltar evacuees. It seems that after a lot of practice they soon took an active part in these sports. After a few sessions it was said that many of the evacuees became very skilled and competent in both tennis and miniature golf during their stay in Madeira. All the photographs on this page were donated by Mr L Pereira.

Being a subtropical climate region the sea around Madeira was relatively warm for almost all the year round. The months of December and January were the coolest. Except for these two months there was swimming practically throughout the whole year. As there were no real beaches in Madeira, most of the swimming had to be done at the lido. As can be seen from the photographs the lido comprised of an enclosure by the open sea.

A close view of the lido. Photo Mr Pereira

The Lido Photo Mr Pereira.

Residents at Lazareto on the cliff near the beach. At The Back A.Milan. Mid.Row M. Parody V.Martin F.Stagno M.Robba K.Bonfiflio. In Front M.Chincotta L.Parody K.Bonfiglio (Nee Robba). Photo Mrs Martin

The beach near the lido. Photo Mr Pereira

There was also the option of being able to swim from a pebble beach into the surrounding open sea. The evacuees living in the Lazareto being near the sea sometimes took the opportunity of bathing on a beach below the cliffs where there was always a lifeguard in case of any accidents.

Youngsters at the pebble beach near the lido. Photo Mr Pereira

During their stay in Madeira the evacuees organised many outings in the beautiful surroundings of Madeira as can be seen from the photographs displayed in this chapter. The photographs on this page where taken at the Quinta Blandis gardens. The evacuees in these photographs are in the majority, those who were residing at the Lazareto building where most of the Catalan Bay village evacuees were billeted. The photographs shown below were donated by Mrs Martin.

Gibraltar evacuees on a picnic at Quinta Blandis.
In the photograph are the following:
K.Bonfiglio (Mrs Martin) V.Pizzarello (Mrs Robba) C.Robba J.Revagliatte and Many Others from the Catalan Bay Village Living At the Lazaretto

Gibraltar evacuees at Quinta Blandis.
At The Back L to R: M.Robba J.Revagliatte F.Chincotta
Middle Row: L to R. M.Martin A.Revagliatte J.Revagliatte K.Bonfiglio and F.Martin
In Front L To R: K.Robba M.Martin M.Robba F.Stagno M.Chincotta K.Bonfiglio M.Parody A.Milan L.Parody

Evacuees in Madeira

Below pictures showing evacuees enjoying themselves at one of the verbenas organised in Madeira.

Evacuees at the verbena. Photo Mr L Pereira

Gibraltar Girls taking part in show at the verbena. Photo Mrs M Hook (nee Dalmedo)

Evacuees at an open air celebration. Photo Miss Sheryl Moya

Photo of a fancy dress competition held at the Savoy Hotel 1941. At the back L to R: Ena Macedo, Louis Pereira, Laura Macedo, Charles Olivero and Elena Campello. In Front: Lolo Olivero, Fabiola Macedo, Margot Pereira, Dolly Chichon and Albert Brooks. Photo Mr L Pereira

Lazareto building guitars' group
At the back L to R: J.Revagliatte E.MacarriC.Martins (Portuguese music teacher) J.StagnoA Revagliatte M.Robba
In front L to R: F.Chincotta D.Pizarello C.Robba
Sitting In Front V.Pisarello

Many evacuees, particularly youngsters, practised playing with stringed musical instruments as it was one of the most popular musical instruments in Madeira. After some basic lessons on guitar playing some of these youngsters eventually formed their own guitar playing groups like the one from Catalan Bay shown in the photographs. In addition to the guitarists group at the Lazareto there was also the local poet from Catalan Bay Albert Pizzarello who composed many poems. Below are two of the many poems which he dedicated to the Island of Madeira.

Guitar Group L to R: C.Robba M.Robba A.Revagliatte J.Revagliatte, F.Chincotta.

EVOCACIÓN

El sol se aleja y rútilos celajes
decoran el azul del firmamento,
mientras el mar, con suave movimiento,
orla la orilla con visos de encajes.

Ya las gaviotas, con caído vuelo,
graznando se dirigen a sus nidos.
Los áureos tonos desaparecidos,
las estrellas fulguran en el cielo.

La paz de que goza esta fértil tierra,
rodeada de un ambiente religioso,
arranca suspiros que mi alma encierra.

Recordando a mi querido Peñón,
y, al percibir el Ángelus, piadoso,
mueve mis labios férvida oración.

The above poem was published in the "O Jornal" Funchal, Madiera.

Evacuees dressed in typical Portuguese National Costumes. At the back L to R: M.Robba M.Robba J.Revagliatte V. Martin K.Robba C.Robba K.Bonfiglio A.Revagliatte. Kneeling F.Chincotta and J.Revagliatte

MI HOMENAJE A TI

Noble pinar de tierra lusitana,
crecido en verde, floreada alfombra,
con tu gentil saludo, de mañana,
me brindas la frescura de tu sombra.

Yo te admiro, gozando esta delicia,
con tu aspecto de verde quitasol.
Y mi ilusión alienta tu caricia,
cuando refulgen los rayos del sol.

Qué silencioso, al borde del camino,
te recreas en el grupo femenino
que, complaciente, acoges con respeto.

¡Ay! El día que de tí me haya ausentado,
cómo recordarás, emocionado,
la dulce poesía de mi secreto.

The above poem was composed at Lazareto in November 1942.

The photographs on this page were donated by Mr M Robba.

Many concerts and shows were held by the evacuees during their stay in Madeira. The photographs on this page were donated by Mrs M Lima (nee Eddings) and Mrs Hook (nee Dalmedo)

Below are photographs of girls taking part in a show at the Country Club. The proceeds from some of the events went towards the Benevolent Guild Fund.

Mrs Maruja Hook (nee Dalmedo) singing a Fado.

Below are photographs of concerts organised at the open air cinema.

One of the best-known participants in these charitable events was Mrs Maruja Hook (nee Dalmedo) who also used to sing Fados –typical Portuguese songs.

Photograph of Chapel at Funchal. Pictures above and below by Mr L Pereira

RECUERDO DEL SEGUNDO
ANIVERSARIO DE LA FESTIVIDAD DE
NTRA SRA DE LOS DOLORES
PATRONA DE LA CALETA DE GIBRALTAR,
Y DE LA SOLEMNÍSIMA MISA CANTADA
CELEBRADA EM SU HONOR EN SU CAPILLA DEL
LAZARETO DE FUNCHAL, MADEIRA,
EL DOMINGO 20 DE SEPTIEMBRE DE 1942
POR EL MUY REV PADRE
FRAY ARTUR ALVES PEREIRA O. F. M.
SUPERIOR DE LOS PADRES FRANCISCANOS
DE PENHA DE FRANÇA,
Y DE LA HORA SANTA Y LA PROCESIÓN DEL
SANTÍSIMO SACRAMENTO, CELEBRADA
POR EL INTERIOR DEL LAZARETO,
CON LA APROVACION DEL EXMO. SR.
D. ANTONIO MANUEL PEREIRA RIBEIRO
OBISPO DE FUNCHAL-MADEIRA,
A LAS 5,30 POR LA PAZ.
TODO A LA MAYOR GLORIA DE DIOS, Y DE LA
VIRGEM SANTÍSIMA,
NUESTRA SEÑORA Y MADRE.

HIMNO
A Nuestra Señora de los Dolores Patrona de la Caleta de Gibraltar
estrenado en el segundo aniversario de su festividad en su capilla del Lazareto de Funchal, Madeira.
El Domingo, 20 de Septiembre de 1942.

(2.ª EDICIÓN)

Como precio de amor y fé a la Virgen Santísima.
DE BENITO CASSAR SUAREZ.

1
En tus Dolores
Confían feliz,
Estos tus hijos
Reunidos aquí,
Y con entusiasmo
Y grande emoción,
Piden su retorno
Para su Peñón.
Coro
Virgen de Dolores
Patrona querida,
Por aquella Aldea
Dereis de mirár,
Librando a tus hijos
De qualquier peligro,
Sea de tierra,
Del aire, o del mar.

MONTIS INSIGNIA CALPE

4
Auxilio constante
Dios concedió
Aquellos que fueran
De Tu busca en pos.
De bienes y gracias
Colmados serán
Y la gloria eterna
Podrán alcanzár.
Coro
Tu Manto Señora
Siempre cubrirá,
Aquella montaña
De nuestra Ciudad.
Y aquellos hijos
Que anhelando están,
Celebrár tus Glorias
Los dias de la PAZ.

2
Van ya dos años
Mitiga el dolor,
De estár evacuados
De nuestro Peñón.
Por eso os pedimos
Con fé y devoción,
Aceptes la ofrenda
De nuestra oración.
Coro
Virgen Bendita
Oh Madre de Dios.
Guíanos al puerto
De nuestro Peñon.
Para en Tu Aldea
Poderte llevár,
Procesionalmente
[illegible]

3
Vos como Reina
Muy pronto podrás,
Llevarme a la Aldea
De mi Gibraltar,
Y a los evacuados
Que en Londrés están,
Asi los de Tanger,
Jamaica y Funchal.
Coro
Mater Dolorosa
Tened compasión
Del alma que llora
Esta separación,
Escucha amorosa
Nuestra petición
Y dadnos Piadosa,
Vuestra Bendición.

5
Oh Santa Maria
Aurora de PAZ,
De los hombres Madre
Al mundo salvád.
Veánte mis ojos
En aquel altár
Y te aclamen Reina
Todo Gibraltar.
Coro
Virgen de Dolores
A Inglaterra salvád.
Dadnos la Victoria
Y al mundo la Paz.
Salva y Bendice
A Tu Gibraltar
De los enemigos
De la Cristiandád.

6
Reina y Señora
Piedad y perdón
De esposas y madres
Llenas de dolor.
Se acabe esta guerra
Que es la destrucción
De seres queridos
Que claman a Vos
Coro
Virgen de Dolores
A Inglaterra salvad,
Dadnos la Victoria,
Y a los hombres Paz.
Haz que esta guerra
Se acabe en la tierra,
Y un dia leguemos
Tus Plantas a besár.

Above Copy of Ceremony Held On The 20th September 1940 at the Chapel in Lazareto to Commemorate the 2nd Anniversary of the Festivity of Patron Saint of the Catalan Bay Village the Hymn was first sung at this ceremony.

The Portuguese nationals and the Gibraltar evacuees who were predominantly Roman Catholics are seen participating fully in the many of religious activities held in Madeira.

Judging from the collection of personal photographs it seems that religious activities were very regular and no doubt must have played a very prominent role in life of the evacuees in Madeira. The next pages will consist of photographs related to these religious gatherings and activities in Madeira. Photographs shown below were donated by Mrs Martin.

Church Service at the Chapel in Funchal.

Church service at the Chapel in Lazareto.

Start of procession.

Gibraltar evacuees in a church procession in the vicinity of The Lazareto building in Madeira.
In The photo are Benito Cassar who looked after the chapel , Pepe Canessa and other Evacuees

A procession leaving the chapel at Lazareto
In the photo are Messrs B.Cassar, E.Macarri and M Robba among others.
Both photographs were donated by Mrs Martin

There were also the occasional religious pilgrimages to the Serra dos Santos like the one depicted on the photographs in this and the next pages.

The pilgrimage at Serra Dos Santo. Mr J Chincotta.

Above evacuees from the Lazareto buildings on a pilgrimage. Photo Mr F Chincotta.

Below evacuees and Madeira nationals up the mountain path. Photo Mrs Martin

Above evacuees gathered with priest at the Serra Dos Santos. Photo Mrs Clark

Photo above and below Mrs Martin

The Serra Dos Santos. Mrs Brittenden

Below are photographs taken during one of the pilgrimages at the chapel of the Serra Dos Santos.

Photo above and below Mrs Martin

Photo Mr N Chipulina. In the photo are Mr J Chipulina, other members of his family and Miss E Romero

From comments made by those who were evacuated to Madeira it seems that the health services provided for the evacuees was of a good standard. There were no cases of any evacuees requiring serious medical attention during their stay in Madeira. The change of environment did not seem to have any significant impact on the health of the evacuees except for some initial cases of mild digestive problems. There were also some minor outbreaks of skin irritation caused by the change in climatic conditions. After a few months the evacuees seem to have become used to the climatic changes. The evacuees at the Lazareto and Quinta das Cruzes buildings were provided with a hospital and infirmaries that were attended daily by a doctor and male nurse. Evacuees in category B were also provided with the service of another doctor. Mr Andrew Pereira managed a first aid service for the evacuees.

Below are copies of some the entries made by Mr Pereira in the first aid record book:

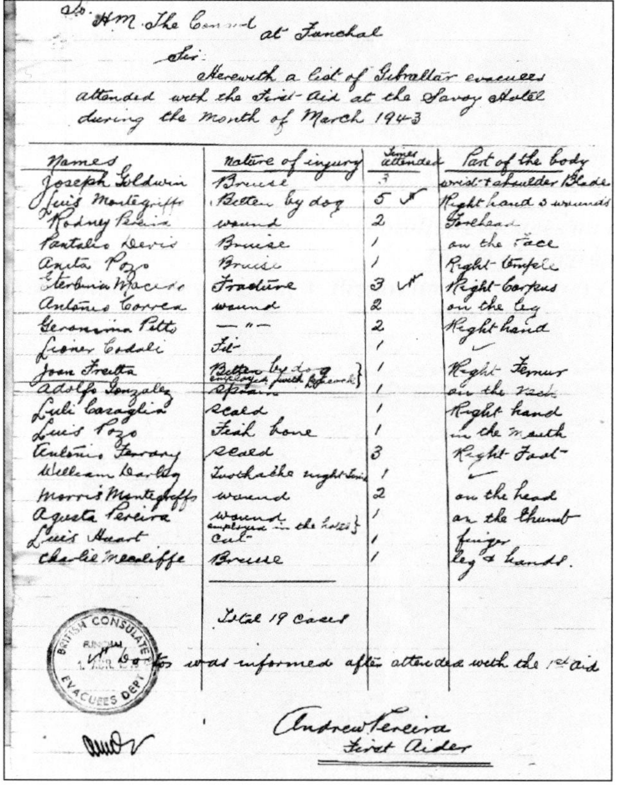

To H.M. The Consul at Funchal

Sir:

Herewith a list of Gibraltar evacuees attended with the first-aid at the Savoy Hotel during the month of March 1943

Names	Nature of injury	Times attended	Part of the body
Joseph Goldwin	Bruise	3	wrist & shoulder Blade
Luis Montegriffo	Bitten by dog	5 ✓	Right hand 3 wounds
Rodney Pereira	wound	2	Forehead
Pantaleo Devis	Bruise	1	on the Face
Anita Pozo	Bruise	1	Right temple
Eterbina Macedo	Fracture	3 ✓	Right Carpus
Antonio Correa	wound	2	on the leg
Geronima Pitto	— " —	2	Right hand
Lionel Codali	Fit	1	✓
Joan Fraetta	Bitten by dog employer's [illegible]	1	Right Femur
Adolfo Gonzalez	Sprain	1	on the neck
Lili Caraglia	Scald	1	Right hand
Luis Pozo	Fish bone	1	in the mouth
Antonio Ferrary	Scald	3	Right Foot
William Darby	Toothache night time	1	✓
Morris Montegriffo	wound	2	on the head
Augusta Pereira	wound employee in the hotel	1	on the thumb
Luis Hart	Cut	1	finger
Charlie Mccaliffe	Bruise	1	leg & hands.

Total 19 cases

✓ Doctor was informed after attended with the 1st aid

BRITISH CONSULATE FUNCHAL 1 ABR. 1943 EVACUEES DEPT

Andrew Pereira
First Aider

Occasionally, Mr Pereira had to attend also to allied servicemen who had to call at Madeira for medical attention. As can be seen from the notes and records kept during their stay in Madeira, the survivors were well looked after. All the copies of Mr Andrew Periera's records were copied by kind permission of his son Mr L Pereira.

Below is a copy of the first aid treatment given to survivors from the wrecked ship SS Moanda. As can bee seen from the notes at the end of their stay in Madeira, the survivors left perfectly cured.

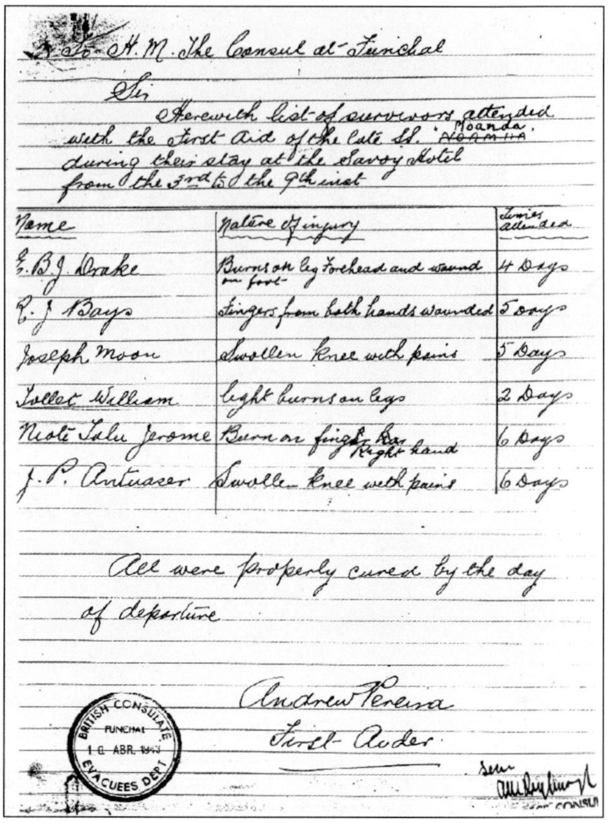

To H.M. The Consul at Funchal

Sir

Herewith list of survivors attended with the First Aid of the late SS. 'Moanda' during their stay at the Savoy Hotel from the 3rd to the 9th inst

Name	Nature of injury	Times attended
E.B.J. Drake	Burns on leg Forehead and wound on foot	4 Days
R. J. Bays	Fingers from both hands wounded	5 days
Joseph Moon	Swollen knee with pains	5 Days
Tollet William	light burns on legs	2 Days
Nioti Talu Jerome	Burn on finger Right hand	6 Days
J. P. Antuaser	Swollen knee with pains	6 Days

All were properly cured by the day of departure

BRITISH CONSULATE FUNCHAL 16 ABR. 1943 EVACUEES DEPT

Andrew Pereira
First Aider

Below is a copy of a letter of appreciation from the British Consul to Mr Pereira for his first aid services.

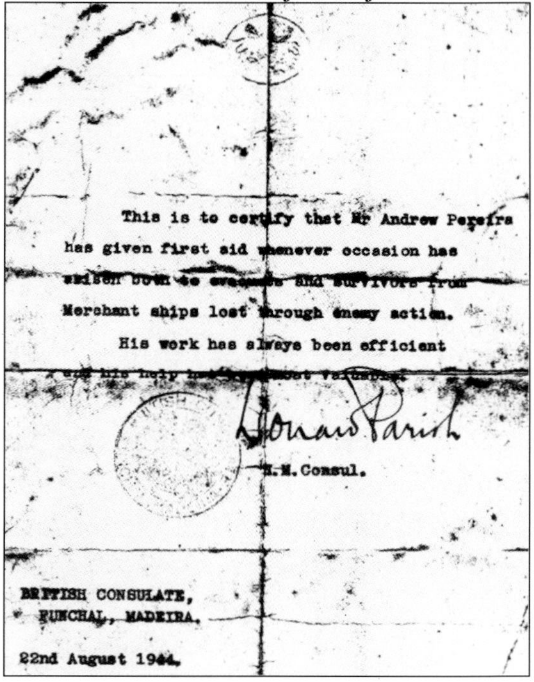

This is to certify that Mr Andrew Pereira has given first aid whenever occasion has arisen both to evacuees and survivors from Merchant ships lost through enemy action. His work has always been efficient and his help has been most valuable.

Donald Parish
H.M. Consul.

BRITISH CONSULATE,
FUNCHAL, MADEIRA.

22nd August 1944.

In Madeira there were Jewish evacuees who because of their religious traditions formed their own community in the island. This page depicts some photographs which show their place of worship, religious leaders and family reunions in Madeira. All the photographs on this page were donated by Mr M Belilo.

Mr Benaim Jewish Leader in Madeira.

Jewish representatives in Madeira

A party held in the Jewish Room.

The Synagogue above Mr Benaim's residence.

Members of a Jewish family outside their residence.

All the photographs on this page were donated by Mr M Belilo.

Jewish wedding.
On the extreme left is Mrs Rebeca Matana.

Guests at the wedding.

The wedding ceremony and reception.

Clarita's birthday party 15.10.1941.

Members of the Jewish community at the pier before embarking on the Indrapoera.
In the photo is Solomon Seruya.

Raquelita's birthday party 23.10.1941.

Although there were newspapers in Madeira which must have reported at length the war situation, the evacuees nevertheless seemed to have preferred to receive the war news from the BBC. This they did by listening to the wireless sets which in those days were considered a luxury item and therefore there were not many that could be found around.

Gibraltar evacuees in the lounge of the Savoy Hotel. Photo Mr L Pereira

At the Savoy Hotel there was a radio set on which the evacuees could tune to the BBC to find out how the war was getting on. With the aid of this radio, the evacuees designed a method which allowed them to keep track of how the war was developing and at the same time also keep a record of events. The method used consisted of a map of Europe on the wall at the lounge of the Savoy Hotel.

The men's club which was used a discussion forum. Photo Mr L Pereira

With marked drawing pins and strings, the Gibraltar evacuees plotted the position of armies on the different fronts in accordance with the latest news. This idea helped the evacuees to know at a glance how the war was developing on all fronts.

There was a club which was used by men where they had their reunion and where no doubt the war situation was one of the main topics of discussion.

An evacuee describing the map on the wall said that during the first year of the war those pins which indicated the position of the German forces were moving away from Germany in many directions throughout the rest of Europe. This was most noticeable from June 1941 onwards when Germany was set to invade Russia.

By the winter of 1941 most of these pins had been plotted eastwards parallel to the Russian borders from Leningrad down to Moscow and then Stalingrad. The rest of Europe was almost then occupied by Germany except for Switzerland in the centre and Spain and Portugal in the south of Europe.

This evacuees explained that as from the winter of 1943 the pins indicating the German armies started to move away from the Russian fronts and also in the south away from Italy. These changes were reflected by the movements of the marked pins on the wall map illustrating the trend of the war. Towards the end of 1943, it was also be seen on this map that the tide of the war had changed in favour of the Allies. By early 1944 the pins were convincingly moving in the direction from both the east and south pointing towards Germany. The evacuees were by then doubly happy about the war situation and optimistic of an early repatriation to Gibraltar. The whole idea was discontinued in May 1944 when the bulk of the evacuees were repatriated from Madeira.

Photo in recent years of the Savoy lounge where the evacuees kept in touch with the war developments by means of a wireless set during the evacuation. Photo Mrs R Field

City centre in Funchal during the evacuation.
Photo Mr Pereira

A recent photo of the city centre. Photo Mrs R Field

There were three main sources of grievances among the evacuees in Madeira. Despite the fact that the Island of Madeira is not that far from Gibraltar, relatives in Gibraltar were not allowed to visit the evacuees. Many representations were made to the Portuguese Government but it seems that it was not until about mid 1943 when relatives were allowed to visit the evacuees with a special visa.

Men arriving at Funchal to visit their families.
Photo Miss Sheryl Moya

There were also grievances expressed by the evacuees about the postal services to and from Madeira. The initial problem of mail between Madeira and Gibraltar stemmed from the fact that the British Government was insisting that as a war security measure that all mail from Madeira could only be sent either to UK or Portugal. In view of this policy the Portuguese authorities were not prepared to handle mail addressed to the Gibraltar evacuees. The whole matter took about a year for the problem to be resolved. This meant that for a whole year there was much anxiety among the evacuees of not knowing anything about the relatives in Gibraltar and vice versa. In order to by-pass this mail restriction some natives of Madeira agreed, for the sake of helping the evacuees, for letters to be addressed to their home until the problem was sorted out. There was a very high rate of unemployment in Madeira and this naturally, also had a negative impact on the standard of living of the natives of Madeira. Owing to the war situation leisure ships stopped calling at Madeira and as a result of this tourism fell dramatically having a very adverse effect on the economy of Madeira which was on the point of bankruptcy. I believe that it is fair to say that the economy of the island benefited substantially with the arrival of the evacuees who through their spending directly and indirectly helped to boost the economy of the island. The Madeira newspaper cutting shows in the introduction to this chapter shared this view.

Men arriving at Madeira to visit families.
Photo Miss Sheryl Moya.

Evacuees in Madeira

The total lack of employment was very distressing too for those young evacuees who had no personal income at all. Although they had plenty of leisure time with the island's almost perfect climate, they nevertheless saw that their youth years were being wasted. There were no prospects in terms of employment to be able to gain experience in any trade or career. In this respect many youngsters felt that their life was being frustrated due to the non-existence of employment opportunities. Some youngsters on reaching the appropriate age left Madeira to join the Gibraltar Defence Force (GDF) for a chance of a career opening and hopefully finding gainful employment. Shown in the photograph in the next column are Luis Pereira, Desmond Baker, Joseph Warne and Harry Chichon who like other teenagers decided to return to Gibraltar and join the GDF. They sailed to Lisbon and then travelled overland to Gibraltar. The other photographs show two groups of Gibraltar youths who like many had no prospects of finding employment during their stay in Madeira.

A group of youths at the Savoy Hotel Gardens In 1941.
Standing at the back L to R: James Rovegno, Charles Huart, Joseph Cerisola and Malik Robinson. Sitting in front Luis Huart, Joseph Goldwin, Anthony Ferrar, Albert Brooks and Luis Pereira.
Lying is Adolfo Gonzalez Photo Mr L Pereira

In the photo from L to R L.Pereira, Harry C hichon, Joseph Warne and Desmond Baker at Lisbon in their way to Gibraltar. Photo Mr L Pereira

Youths on a trip to the mountain. In the photograph is Berta Bayardo.
Photo Mrs M Clark

Soon after arriving in Madeira a benevolent guild was set up by Lady Liddell in order to help the needy evacuees and also the poor natives of Madeira with items of clothing and food. With the aim of raising funds for the guild, the evacuees held many charitable events. These events entailed the holding of concerts and theatrical shows.

Lady Liddell with the guild supporters. Photo Mr M Belilo

A verbena held in aid of the poor of Madeira. Photo Mr L Pereira

The Lady Liddell's Guild supporters in the garden. Photo Mr M Belilo

In addition to these events, every Gibraltar evacuee also contributed the sum of one escudo each a week to help the poor people of Madeira. There were many poor people in Madeira who were also helped by the benevolent guild.

Lady Liddell. Photo Mr M Belilo

The scope of this benevolent guild was later also extended to help with the sending of items of clothing for the fighting men and prisoners of war. A collection of many items of clothing were also sent to the victims of air raids in England.
Below is a cutting from the Gibraltar Chronicle dated 10th July 1941 describing the activities of Lady Liddell's Guild in Madeira.

LADY LIDDELL'S GUILD IN MADEIRA

A summary of the activities of Lady Liddell's Guild in Funchal for the three months ending May 31 shows that 194 oz. of wool, 55 dress lengths, 63 other garments and money grants to the value of Esc. 70.00 were given to the Gibraltar evacuees.

For men of H.M. Forces, including prisoners of war, 119 knitted comforts, 10 flannel vests, 24 handkerchiefs and 8 pairs of pyjamas were provided.

Garments (nearly all children's) sent to England for air-raid victims numbered 133, with a considerable quantity of used clothing. About 112 children's garments were also provided for the children of poor Portuguese in Madeira.

Through the columns of the *Diario de Noticias* Lady Liddell thanks all members of the guild for their continued support, and also all those who responded so generously to her appeal of April 22 for air-raid victims. The sum of Esc. 2,822.00 was received in response to this appeal as well as the used clothing mentioned above.

Children taking part in the matinee show of "La Rosa Del Azafran."

Show in aid of charity with children and adults taking part.

Concert held in aid of charity attended by the Governor of Madeira.

There were many plays organised in aid of charity as can be appreciated from the photographs displayed on this page. The main participants were the school children who despite the emphasis on the use of the English language, the children performed many plays and songs in Spanish.

In the above photo is Muriel Eddings (Mrs. Lima) and Fanny Ellul taking part in a play.

The plays where held at the main hall of the Savoy Hotel on Sunday 21 November 1943. The photograph at the top of the left hand column is from the matinee session of La Espigadora from the play of "La Rosa del Azafran." The funds raised were for the Gibraltar War Fund and local charities. The other two photographs below the one at the top of the left hand column were taken during another show held on Thursday 9th December 1943 and which was attended by the Governor of Madeira Don Gustavo Texeira Dias. This show was also in aid of the Gibraltar War Fund and local charity. Three of the girls in the picture shown at the bottom of the left hand column are Gladys, Tilly and Muriel Eddings. All the photographs on this page were donated by Mrs Lima (nee Eddings).

In Funchal the usual means of transport was a cart with sledges drawn by two oxen. The sledges had steel runners to slide on the roads constructed with cobblestones. To reduce the amount of friction, a man stood by the cart brushing the sledges with some sort of grease as the sledges moved over the cobblestones. These cobblestones were not placed uniformly and appeared to have been laid down in haphazard fashion. This made the road very uneven and in some places the stones had very sharp edges which made walking very painful for those not used to it. On the other hand it was interesting to see the natives walking barefoot with great ease over these stones without hurting themselves.

A cart for travelling up the hills. Photo Mrs Brittenden

The use of bicycle as mode of transport was also common. Mrs M Clark

Many women in Madeira were often seen carrying on their heads a basket fully laden with fruits, vegetables or flowers. They carried these loads, as in the picture shown below, with such great ease and perfect balance in order to stop the baskets from falling to the ground.

Typical scene in Madeira: A sledge cart drawn by oxen and woman carrying basket full of flowers on her head. Photo Mrs Brittenden

The cinemas in Madeira were mainly open air. Those evacuees who were not used to this, recall how strange it was to watch a film with the bare sky above. The films were usually very old and occasionally there were long breakdowns. Sometimes the breakdown went for so long that films were not shown completely. The American and British films were released in English with Portuguese sub-titles. There were occasions when the Gibraltar audience reacted to anything interesting said well before the Portuguese audience had a chance to the read the subtitles. This was more noticeable during a comedy film when there were occasional bursts of laughter by the Gibraltar evacuees well before the Portuguese audience could react to the jokes from reading the sub-titles.

During their stay, some evacuees recall seeing Portuguese men and women with their feet dyed in deep purple. This was as a result of having been working crushing grapes with their bare feet to squash out the juice to make the well-known Madeira Port wine. Workers were also seen bringing down the grapes from the farms on the mountains.

Above and below old photographs of grape vine workers. Mr J Chincotta

Wine workers.

During their stay in Madeira, the evacuees took the opportunity of visiting many places of interest on the island. Not far from Funchal was the fishing village of Camara dos Lobos with its colourful boats and houses. As is well known, this is where Sir Winston Churchill used to holiday. From the terrace of one of these houses he spent many hours painting and produced some of his famous pictures back in the 1950's.

The Camara Dos Lobos during the evacuation.

Near Funchal there was a sugar cane processing plant owned by a British company. Some evacuees explained that the sugar canes were carried on oxen-driven carts up a hill to the plant and that they used to grab hold of some of the canes to suck out the sweet juice. There were paths down the mountains called levadas. Rainwater came down these levadas and was collected in reservoirs, which supplied the people of Madeira with fresh water. All the photographs on this page, except the one at the top of the next column were donated by Mr.J Chincotta.

A more recent view of the Camara Dos Lobos.
Photo Mrs R Field

Above picture of the levadas during the evacuation.
Photo Mr J Chincotta

Photograph during the evacuation of the 16th Century Palace Fortress of Sao Lourenco.

One of the most famous historical buildings in Funchal is the Fortress and Palace of San Lourenco built during the time of the Spanish occupation of the island from 1580 to 1640. Below are some photographs of Funchal taken at the time of the evacuation and compared with recent ones. The pictures show different views of the cathedral in the centre of Funchal.

Picture of the Cathedral from the Bay of Funchal.

A Picture of the Cathedral from the City Centre.

The monument erected in honour of Joao Goncalves Zarco – Discoverer of Madeira.

All the photographs on this page, except the two shown in the next column, were donated by Mr L Pereira.

A recent picture of the Cathedral from the distance. Mrs R Field

Photo in recent years of the monument shown on the left hand column.
Mrs R Field

The above statue is near where the building of the Bank of Portugal now stands. During the evacuation the Golden Gate Hotel was near this statue.

On this page are recent photographs compared with the ones taken during the time of the evacuation in Funchal.

A recent picture of the Colegio Church. Mrs R Field

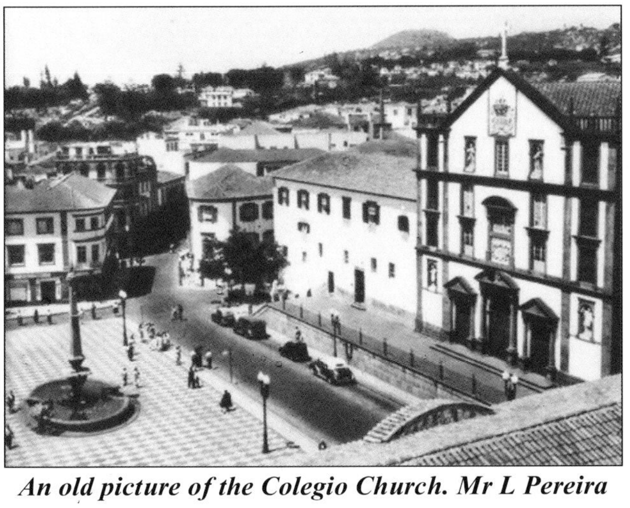

An old picture of the Colegio Church. Mr L Pereira

A recent view of the pier and harbour in Funchal. Mrs R Field

Old view of the Bay of Funchal. Mr J Chincotta

Modern sea front of the Bay of Funchal. Mrs R Field

View of the pier during the evacuation. Mr J Chincotta

The pier and harbour prior to World War Two. Mr J Chincotta

Since the evacuation many ex-evacuees have visited Madeira. Below is a cutting of a Madeira newspaper reporting one of such visits which served to recall the common past shared by both the Gibraltarian and Madeiran communities.

Recordar um passado comum

Gibraltinos visitam a Madeira

A Região Autónoma da Madeira está a ser visitada por um grupo de cento e dezassete gibraltinos, chegados a esta ilha no passado domingo num voo «charter» directo entre os aeroportos de Gibraltar e do Funchal, promovido pela «GB airways».

Recorde-se que, este foi o primeiro voo directo efectuado entre aquela colónia britânica e a Madeira, estando previstas mais duas operações do mesmo tipo para o próximo mês de Junho.

Nos últimos tempos, a Madeira tem sido frequentemente visitada por este povo que tem na região grandes laços de afinidade, já que foi precisamente na «Pérola do Atlântico» que encontraram refúgio quando eclodiu a II Guerra Mundial. Aqui viveram durante alguns anos, tendo alguns retornado ao país de origem e outros permanecido na

Quando regressou a Gibraltar, ficaram sepultadas no Cemitério de São Martinho a sua mãe e avó. Assim, além de guardar boas recordações do quotidiano madeirense, tinha igualmente deixado nesta ilha para sempre parentes de que também guarda «gratas memórias».

«Sentia muitas saudades da Madeira. Não queria morrer sem visitar esta ilha. Agora sim, isso poderá acontecer», disse Muriel Lima a este matutino.

Classifica esta viagem de «uma oportunidade fantástica» e demonstra-se surpreendida com o «grande desenvolvimento» da Região.

Sobre os custos da viagem à Madeira, considera-os «razoáveis» e revela mesmo que, «muitos gibraltinos aguardam os voos de Junho para passarem cá uns dias».

Regozija-se pelo facto de ter havido o primeiro voo directo entre as duas regiões, e considera que esta iniciativa «vai ao encontro dos desejos de muitos gibraltinos que ainda sonham em rever esta terra».

No que se refere a Gibraltar, disse-nos ser uma

titui um promontório rochoso situado a Sul da Península Ibérica, que fecha a baía de Algeciras a Leste.

Actual colónia britânica, é uma base aérea e naval de grande importância estratégica.

The boarding house at 155 Rua De Carreira where the Eddings Resided during the evacuation.

Among the many families who occasionally visit Madeira are the Eddings. Below is cutting of another Madeira newspaper which interviewed Mrs M.Lima (nee Eddings) during her visit to Madeira. Incidentally Mrs Lima speaks Portuguese.

O grupo de gibraltinos que se deslocaram em excursão à Região Autónoma da Madeira tem por objectivo visitar toda a ilha, como forma de reviver o seu passado neste arquipélago. Estão hospedados nas unidades hoteleiras desta cidade e têm já passeado pela costa Norte da ilha.

O «Diário de Notícias» conversou com a gibraltina **Muriel Lima, que passou nesta região a sua infância e grande parte da sua juventude.**

Juntamente com a família, Muriel Lima chegou à Madeira pela primeira vez em 1941, possuia então 10 anos de idade. Viveu cerca de seis anos na Rua da Carreira, n.º 155, tendo posteriormente regressado a Gibraltar, onde viria a constituir família e guardar na memória os «bons e tranquilos momentos passados no Golden Gate e no Teatro Municipal de Baltazar Dias».

parte dos géneros que consome, mas onde se vive bem. O clima é bom e há emprego para todos».

Segundo nos disse, «existe muitos portugueses a trabalhar em Gibraltar, sobretudo no sector terciário».

Acrescentou também que, a falta de espaço territorial para a construção de habitações é um dos maiores problemas que se colocam àquela colónia britânica, havendo já estudos para a construção de habitações na área marítima.

Relativamente a Espanha, diz «gostar muito do folclore e de passear por esse país ibérico, sobretudo agora que a fronteira foi aberta». Mas, afirma de forma peremptória que, «os gibraltinos nasceram debaixo da coroa britânica e não pretendem mudar de coroa. A nossa língua oficial é a inglesa e jamais a trocaremos pelo espanhola».

Em termos de localização geográfica, Gibraltar cons-

Muriel Lima, uma gibraltina que residiu na Madeira.

The photographs on this page, donated by Mrs Lima, where taken when she was on holiday in Madeira. They show her visiting her mother's resting place at the Santa Caterina cemetery and the place were she used to residę during the evacuation. Another frequent visitor to Madeira is Mr Luis Pereira who resided during the evacuation at Savoy Hotel.

Evacuees in Madeira

After the unveiling of the monument in memory of those evacuees who died in Jamaica, it was thought that a similar gesture should also be made for those evacuees who died in Madeira. A year later after many preparations all the necessary arrangements were in place for the unveiling ceremony at Funchal. The ceremony was held in April 2008 and was attended by the Mayor of Funchal Dr Miguel Felipe Machado de Albuquerque, the Mayor of Gibraltar Mr Clive Beltran. Mr Louis Pereira who thought of the idea of the monument and of arranging the trip for Gibraltarians was also present at the ceremony. The monument was built with limestone from the Rock and was erected next to a small chapel at Santa Caterina Cemetery. Because of the inclement weather, the ceremony invoking the presentation of the monument to the people of Madeira was held in the City Hall of Funchal.

Monument in memory of the Gibraltar evacuees who died in Madeira during the evacuation. Photo Wikipedia Free Encyclopaedia.

Following this ceremony contacts were maintained between the office of the Mayors of Gibraltar and Funchal with the object of establishing the twinning of the Cities of Funchal and Gibraltar.

These contacts culminated with the holding of official Twinning Ceremonies during May 2009. The first of the two ceremonies was held on Wednesday 6th May 2009 in Funchal Madeira. Gibraltar Mayor, Mr Solomon Levy, accompanied by his Personal Assistant, Mr Andrew Rowbottom, were present in Funchal for the historic signing Ceremony. They were hosted by the Mayor of Funchal, Dr Miguel Felipe Machado de Albuquerque, and guests of the President of the Madeira Government, Dr Alberto Joao Jardim. The second ceremony of the Twinning of Funchal and Gibraltar was held in Gibraltar in the Mayor's Parlour, City Hall on Tuesday 26th May 2009. Present at this ceremony were the guest of the President of the Madeira Government Dr Alberto Joao Jardim, the Governor of Gibraltar Sir Robert Fulton, the Mayor of Gibraltar Mr Solomon Levy, the Mayor of Funchal Dr Miguel Felipe Machado de Albuquerque and the Personal Assistant to the Mayor of Gibraltar, Mr Andrew Rowbottom.

In the photograph Guest of the President of the Madeira Government Dr Alberto Joao Jardim, Governor of Gibraltar Sir Robert Fulton, Mayor of Gibraltar Mr Solomon Levy, Mayor of Funchal Dr Miguel Felipe Machado de Albuquerque and Personal Assistant to the Mayor Gibraltar ,Mr Andrew Rowbottom at the Official Twinning Ceremony held at the Mayor's Parlour, City Hall on the 26th May 2009. Photo Johnny Bugeja – Gibraltar Chronicle.

CHAPTER EIGHT

EVACUEES IN THE UK

By September 1940 the bulk of the evacuees were already in London. They had arrived amidst sirens and air raids at the very height of the decisive historical Battle of Britain. By then London as well as many other British cities, were being heavily bombarded. Many ships were being sunk in the Atlantic Ocean, affecting seriously Britain's lifeline. Britain, as is well known, stood alone to repel the menace of the planned German invasion and with only a very small air force. The situation in Britain was a desperate one. Many evacuees with whom I talked about their recollections remember witnessing the "dog fights."

Gibraltar evacuees arriving in London. Holding left hand of the nurse is Laura Barea (Mrs Rovegno) and behind marked with a cross is her brother Adolfo. Photo Mr A Rovegno

This is how Salvador Lopez described his arrival in London. "Our journey to London was very exciting; I could not believe there were so many trees and greenery in the World. We could not control our emotions just looking out of the train window and seeing farm animals roaming free in beautiful fields. The train went through un-named stations. I was told it was because they did not want the German spies to know where they were. The houses well kept, appeared to have so much ground front and back, not like in Gibraltar with so many flats so close together, and no place to grow flowers except in pots, still we missed our Rock. After some hours in the train, I felt that it was slowing down and imagined that we were nearing our destination. We looked out of the window; the rolling hills were not longer there. The train slowed down to a very slow pace and then stopped very smoothly at a railway station full of military personnel getting on or off trains. We alighted from the train to board one of the buses waiting to take us away from the station. As soon as we stepped on the bus we went up to the top deck and rushed for the front seats before anyone else got there first. We never sat down; once or twice we went down to my mother to point out all the magnificent buildings and lovely places we were seeing for the first time. We noticed the excitement in her eyes, but we could also detect pain and worry obviously not knowing what was going to happen to us in this strange place. At last, the bus stopped outside this amazing building. Great shops on one side and a huge park on the other, we could not believe it when we were ushered inside. I thought it was the King's residence! It was called the Royal Palace Hotel in the centre of London."

My family in a Fulham studio shortly after arriving in London. Photo J.Gingell

The unfamiliar environment, the air raids, the climate and the separation of their loved ones made it very difficult for the evacuees to settle down in London. It was not until a year or so later, when the bombing eased, that many of the evacuees then began to do their best to adapt to the new situation. Even then there was still the anxiety being felt of not knowing how long the separation would last and what would be the outcome of the war itself. By then the Gibraltar evacuees began to the find means of getting on with their daily lives, as I will try to explain throughout the rest of this chapter about how the evacuees lived in London. Being called a refugee was something the Gibraltar evacuees resented very much, especially when said in an offensive tone.

In many instances, an explanation served to sort out things but not without the initial arguments. There were many refugees of different nationalities in London at the time and for the Londoners the Gibraltar evacuees were no exception because admittedly Spanish was spoken most of the time among the evacuees. However, in official circles, like in some of the debates in the House of Commons, the Gibraltar evacuees were also referred to as refugees.

When the evacuees arrived they were initially accommodated in the London Boroughs of Kensington, Barkingside, Bloomsbury, Westminster, Fulham and Wembley but owing to the subsequent bombing of some of the centres in these areas there were cases of evacuees having to be transferred to other centres in Wandsworth and Richmond where it was reckoned that the bombing was less intensive than in the centre of London.

This section about the London evacuation centres contains in alphabetical order all the information and illustrations that I have been able to obtain during my research of the places that were turned into evacuation centres. In the majority of the cases there are, to my knowledge, no original photographs available of the evacuation centres. For this reason I have had to rely on recent photographs of the existing buildings which at the time were used as centres. Most of these photographs were taken by my daughter Michelle during her numerous travels to the UK in connection with her regular treatment at the Royal Marsden Hospital. There were a few buildings that she was unable to take photographs of, as at the time, it was very inconvenient for her. Photographs of building like, for example, the Dean Hotel were obviously not available as it was completely destroyed by bombing. Where I have found it appropriate, I have also included a brief relevant history of the place where the evacuees were accommodated.

ANERLEY HOUSE

At Anerley House in Anerley Road, London SE 19 the officer in charge was Mr. F Fagan. There were only 23 evacuees accommodated. Apart from this, I have no other information or image of this centre.

BALMORAL

Balmoral at 37 Queen's Gate Gardens SW7 housed 172 evacuees. The officer in charge was Mr. A Mainwood but I could not find any information about who was the local delegate for this centre. At the top of the next column is the only image I have of what used to be Balmoral Hotel building taken in autumn 2006.

The entrance of what used to be the Balmoral Hotel. Photo my daughter Michelle

CAMPDEN HILL GATE

At the Campden Hill Gate hotel there were 305 evacuees. The officer in charge was Mr. C Thomson and the local representative was Mr. Dalli.

Building that used to be an evacuation center. Photo by my daughter Michelle.

Evacuees outside the British Empire Hotel.
In the photograph amongst the many evacuees are Mrs Violeta Golt (nee Lagares) Charles Sanz, Mrs Martinez mother of Sergio Martinez, Mr Agustin Huart and Major Joseph Patron

The British Empire and the Broadwalk Hotels, with nearly 300 evacuees, were at 28 and 11 De Vere Gardens respectively. The manager for both centres was Mr C Wright and the local representatives were Mr Bruzon for the British Empire Hotel and Mr Vella for the Broadwalk Hotel.

Evacuees outside the Broadwalk Hotel.
With the evacuees is Mr A.Huart and in front on the right hand side are Charles and John Tribello.

Runnymede House after the bombing on 21st September 1940. Photo Richmond Heritage Office

Gibraltar Evacuees at Richmond Park.
In the photograph are Aurelio Rodriguez, M.A.Rodriguez Richardson and their mother Mrs M Rodriguez who is kneeling on the extreme right. Photo Mrs Rodriguez Richardson

Courtlands evacuation centre consisted of luxury flats which at the time were selling at about £400. 438 evacuees were accommodated in this block of flats. From the information available, I know that many of the evacuees living in this centre were transferred following the bombing of the Dean Hotel in April 1941. The majority of these evacuees remained accommodated at Courtlands until they were finally repatriated in 1944. The block of flats occupied by the evacuees was called Runnyside House at Sheen Road. The officer in charge was Mr F Flagan and the local representative was Mr Correa.

At Courtlands as in many other centres, the evacuees had their own football team. With the vast recreational space available at Richmond Park, the evacuees were able to organise football matches and other recreational events. I think it is interesting to mention that according to the Richmond Heritage and Local History Office some of the flats were occupied by German nationals before the war broke out but obviously these left when the war with Germany became eminent.

Margot Barcio with her grandmother Mrs M Barcio at the entrance to Runnyside House in Sheen Road Courtlands. PhotoMrs M Gil

Miss Elena Gatt in the park near Courtlands. Photo Mrs E Mamo.

Evacuees gathered by Runnyside House, in Courtlands before leaving for Gibraltar.
Photo Mr M Infante

Some evacuees with officials at Richmond Park.
Back row ..?.. O.Smart H.Galia M.Rodriguez Mr Roberts (Manager)
Front row.G.Edwards A.Rodriguez M.A.Rodriguez Richardson Mrs Gaduzo George Gaduzo Goodman
Photo Mrs M.A. Rodriguez Richardson

Evacuees at the entrance to Courtlands in the photo is Elena Chini.
Photo Mr M Infante

Evacuees at a party in Richmond Park. Photo Mrs R Payas

The Barcio family at Courtlands: Francisco Barcio,
Mrs M.Barcio, Mrs Barcio, Margot Barcio and Alfred Barcio.
Photo Mrs M Gil

The Chini family at Richmond Park.
Catalina Chini, Antonia Chini, Elena Chini and Pepi Chini.
Photo Mrs E Mamo

Evacuees at Richmond.
In the photo are M.Oton, Goodman, M.Victory, A.Bonavia and Olivero.
Photo Mrs R Payas

Evacuees at a reunion at Runnyside House Courtlands.
Photo Mrs M.A.Rodriguez Richardson

Evacuees at Richmond Park. Photo Mr M Infante
In the photo left to right Julia Baldachino (Mrs Infante),
Mrs Julia Baldachino, Mrs Antonia Chini rest not known

Children at Courtlands Richmond.
In the photo are: E.Bagu, Tommy Neale,Arturo Pitto,A.Bagu,F.Bagu,J.Goodman,Tommy Power,Buttigieg,Salvador Pitaluga,Machado,R.Cassano,Betty Collins(Mrs Garcia)J.Bagu,Raggio,Macedo Sisters,L.Edwards,R.Rubbio,V.Rubbio,Ostengo Salvador MachadoHernandez and others
Photo Mr S Machado

Family evacuees in Richmond.
At the back L to R: Josefa Gatt, Elena Chini, Carmen Borge
In front L to R: Rosa Bossano and Violeta Gatt
Photo Mr M Infante

Girls at Richmond in the photo L to R: Rosa Olivero (Mrs Payas) M.Bacarisa, B.Collins, W.Collins, D.Collins.
Photo Mrs R Payas

As is well known the English philanthropist Dr Thomas Barnardo became the founder and director of the homes for destitute children. He was born in Dublin, Ireland, in 1845. His father was of Spanish origin and his mother English. After a period of preaching as an Evangelical Christian in the slums of Dublin he moved to London where he studied medicine to become a medical missionary. Whilst studying he soon discovered the plight of homeless children in London. Dr Barnardo delivered a speech about this problem at a Missionary Conference which was attended by Lord Shaftsbury who was so moved by what he heard that he offered Dr.Barnardo help to establish homes for these children. The banker, Robert Barclay also agreed to support the cause and in 1868, Dr.Barnardo had raised enough money to open his first home for destitute children. By 1878 he had established in London fifty orphanages, including his Village Home for Girls in Ilford. The Ilford Home for Girls became a complete community with seventy cottages accommodating over 1,000 children and with its own school, with its own laundry and a church.

By the time Dr Thomas Barnardo died on the 19th September, 1905, there were nearly 8,000 children in his residential homes, more than 4,000 were boarded out, and 18,000 had been sent to Canada and Australia. During the war Dr Barnardo's Homes in Barkingside accommodated 843 Gibraltar evacuees becoming the largest evacuation centre in London. In the next column is a cutting from the Ilford Recorder reporting the arrival of the first 400 Gibraltar evacuees on the 8th August 1940. The officer in charge of this evacuation centre was Mr R Summers and the local representative was Mr Abudarham.

The following is a brief summary from an evacuee at Dr Barnardo's Homes:

"In reality it was a lovely place, with cottages set among green fields and wooded areas. Each cottage accommodated various families as only one bedroom was allowed for each group. Food was served in a large hall which also served as a general meeting place. During air raids evacuees took refuge in small brick shelters that had been built in the gardens. I remember being told in school to crawl underneath the furniture when there was an air raid warning. After the all clear siren, my mother always had difficulty in dragging me out from under the wooden benches, as I was always very frightened.

We always, in any case, slept huddled together in the shelters, each grown-up holding us the young ones in their arms for warmth."

GIBRALTAR EVACUEES HAVE WAR HOME AT BARKINGSIDE 8/8/40 KPS

SPANISH COLONY AT GIRLS' VILLAGE HOMES

Ilford has a new community within its gates. Nearly 400 British subjects evacuated from Gibraltar arrived at Dr. Barnardo's Girls' Village Homes, Barkingside, last week-end. They will make this their war-time home.

(Ilford Recorder)

An Ilford Recorder reporter who paid the evacuees a visit wrote:

"Dog-tired after hours of travelling a party of evacuees from Gibraltar arrived at the Homes at 11.30 on Sunday night. Food and beds were ready for them and in a very short time they were settled in and ready to sleep.

The village is to be the evacuees' war-time home and after nearly a week they are now settling into a community which it is hoped will be a happy one for them during their enforced absence from their homes.

There are nearly 400 people, including many children staying there, and they are all British subjects though most of them speak Spanish. About 90 per cent of them can speak both tongues, but for those who do not speak English all the notices and sign posts erected for their guidance in the Village are both in Spanish and English.

A dinning room, hospital and recreation room are amongst the amenities which have been placed at their disposal in the Village as well as their own cottage home and even at this early stage these people, who are amazingly cheerful despite the natural sadness at having to leave behind their homes and their entire means of living but who are already looking to the future.

When I visited the Village which is now a copy of the Gibraltar colony, I found the friendliness of these vivacious folk almost overwhelming. Calling at one of the cottages to ask how the inhabitants were getting on I was conducted enthusiastically all over the homes by four charming women, two of whom only spoke Spanish.

Upstairs the beds were all neatly made, the living rooms were clean and tidy, and inside the kitchen an elderly gentleman spoke in grave appreciation of the stove on which he was placing some kettles for tea."

The Church at Dr Barnardo's. Photo Mr E Holt

Open air Mass at Dr Barnardo's Homes
Photo Mrs D Parody

Statue in memory of Dr Barnardo.
Photo Mr E Holt

Above a group of mostly elderly evacuees at Dr Barnardo's Homes.
Photo Mr E Pozo

Mrs M Brooks and Mrs V Santos
Photo Mr E Pozo

The Asquez family at Dr Barnardo's Homes. In the photo Mrs Emilia Asquez, with her children,Angela,Pepe and Laureano. Photo Mr J Asquez.

Children at Dr Barnardo's Homes.
In the photograph at the back L to R are Lilian Ramagge(nee Ellul) Cecilia Baldachino(nee Buzaglo) Joe Buzaglo
sitting in front from L to R Pepe L Moreno, Eric Ellul and John Ellul
Photo Mrs C Baldachino

In the photo are Doris Wahnon (nee De Las Heras) Mrs Victoria Wahnon,Leslie Wahnon and Mrs Annie Wahnon
Photo Mr L Wahnon

A children's party at Dr Barnardo's. Photo Mr V Gonzalez

Evacuees at Dr Barnardo's Homes. Photo Mrs C Baldachino
Back row L to R Mrs Herminia Buzaglo, ...?... Mrs Julie Ellul,..?... Mrs Alex Miles (nee Ellul). In front L to R: Cecilia Baldachino(nee Buzaglo),Joe Buzaglo and Mrs Carmen Motherhead (nee Ellul)

Leslie Wahnon by Dr Barnardo's Memorial in 1957.
Photo Mr L Wahnon

Leslie Wahnon by the door of his ex-Home in 1957.
Photo Mr L Wahnon

A.Brown,Mauro and other boys.
Photo Mrs M Brown

Leslie Wahnon outside his Home in 1942.
Photo Mr L Wahnon

Victor Gonzalez near his home.
Photo Mr V Gonzalez

Cecilia Baldachino(nee Buzaglo) and her brother Joe outside their residence at Dr Barnardo's Homes.
Photo Mrs C Baldachino

Albert Cruz and M.Juaquin.
Photo Mrs Cruz

Victor Gonzalez, J.Dyer and Luis Mauro
Photo Mr V Gonzalez

Visiting Dr Barnardo's homes Mrs Perera, her daughter Vicky and relative Francis Pitaluga

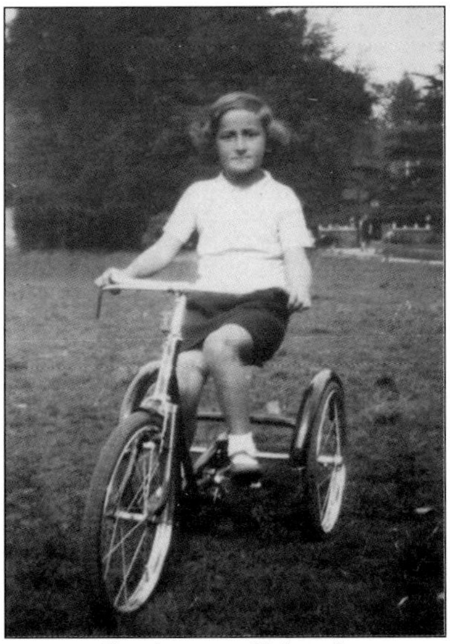

Sonia on a Tricycle
Photo Mr L Wahnon

Photo above and below Mrs V Soiza

Vicky Perera and Francis Pitaluga

Victor Gonzalez by fountain 1942

The photographs in this and in the previous page show the cottages which became the homes for evacuees at the Dr Barnardo's evacuation centre.

Leslie and Harold Wahnon with other children outside the Homes. Photo Mr L Wahnon

Cecilia Baldachino (nee Buzaglo) and her brother Joe playing in the snow at Dr Barnardo's. PhotoMrs C Baldachino

Mrs Gonzalez and another ex-evacuee visiting Dr Barnardo's Homes in 1992. PhotoMr V Gonzalez

Harold Wahnon with his tricycle Photo Mr L Wahnon

In the photo at the back left to right are Mrs Dorotea Wahnon, Mrs Victoria Wahnon…?...Mrs Annie Wahnon In front left to right Harold Wahnon, Leslie Wahnon, Sonia Wahnon (Mrs Pisani) Doris Wahnon. Photo Mr L Wahnon

Mrs Victoria Brown and her son Andrew. Photo Mrs M Brown

Mrs Wahnon with her sons Leslie and Harold to the dining room.

The Wahnons with relatives.

Mrs Wahnon with her sons and other children at the door of their Home.

Mrs Wahnon and niece Doris.

Mrs Wahnon and friends by the fountain.

Albert Cruz with his mother and grandmother (The above photo was donated by Mrs Cruz the rest of the photos were donated by Mr L Wahnon)

Mrs Wahnon and her sister in law.
PhotoMr L Wahnon

John Zayas,G.Formosa,A.Aguis(nee Sene) Margot Zayas(Mrs Byrne) Pepi Martinez
Photo Mr J Zayas

Harold and Leslie Wahnon with gas masks.
Photo Mr L Wahnon

Mr Wahnon with Mr Albert Martinez .
Photo Mr L Wahnon

Victor Gonzalez with his bicycle.
Photo Mr V Gonzalez

Victor Wahnon with toy horse.
Photo Mr L Wahnon

Mr Joseph Power with his son Richard.
Photo Mr R Power

Victor Gonzalez with his wife visiting
Dr Barnardo's in 1992.
Photo Mr V Gonzalez

Mrs Kitty Cruz with her grandchildren
Albert,Mirna and Louis.
Photo Mrs Cruz

Leslie and Harold Wahnon with grandfather
and cousin Noelia Gonzalez.
Photo Mr L Wahnon

John Martinez. Photo Mr C Martinez

Gladys Rolls and Andrew Brown.
Photo Mrs M Brown

GIBRALTAR BOY MISLEADS COURT

HAD INTERPRETER, BUT KNEW ENGLISH

AFTER an interpreter had been called in to help in the case of a boy Gibraltarian evacuee charged at Ilford Juvenile Court on Thursday with theft, it was revealed in a school report that he understood English perfectly.

Detective Cudmore said he went to Dr. Barnardo's Homes and said to the boy, "I am a police officer. I understand that you went to your employer's address and obtained from his wife the keys to the works and later on stole some cash from a desk in the office.' The boy replied, "I stole the cash, but not the cheque book."

Detective Cudmore said he asked the boy if he had any of the cash left. He said "No, I have been to Liverpool-street and spent it on food. I only had 7s.'

Detective Cudmore said the works were in Myrtle-road.

Mr. Ralph Summers, a warden, who acted as interpreter, said the boy admitted the theft of the seven shillings.

Mr. Summers explained that the evacuees who worked paid a small sum each week to the Ministry towards their upkeep. The amounts they were charged varied.

The Chairman, Alderman J. T. Sanders. "Would he be in fear of any penalty if he didn't pay his agreed contribution any week?"—No he had nothing to fear.

The Chairman: "If he had gone there without any wages he would have been treated the same?"—Oh, yes, he knows that.

Mr. Summers explained that there were 825 people in the centre, and of those there were only 216 who actually paid into the scheme. All the rest were maintained without any cost to them.

The Probation Officer said the boy's behaviour was such that efforts to help him had been baulked. He had not a relative or friend in this country who was in a position to take any responsibility for him at all. "He was adopted, as far as we can ascertain, and there is no one who can accept any legal responsibility," he added.

The Chairman: He comes to this country for security and protection, or is brought here for that purpose, and abuses the trust reposed in him by robbing his employer, and I think he understands what I say.

Speaking to the boy, the Chairman said "You have not acted fairly to us here. You have put us to a lot of trouble having everything interpreted to you in your native language. Here I have a report of your schoolmaster, in which he says 'He has been in this school for two years. He understands English perfectly, and can also speak English.' He also says, 'Whilst here he was a nuisance to everyone, and there is nothing good I can say about him. He can only behave himself well under discipline. Lying, deceitfulness and the use of bad language come easy to him. If he had one redeeming feature I should be only too glad to mention it, but he hasn't."

"This won't get you anywhere, neither in this country nor any other country," the Chairman told him. "You are under a big obligation to the people in this country for the safety of your skin and what is in your pocket. You will be fined 20s.; you understand that. You must take this as a warning; there will be prison next time."

On the left hand column a copy of the Ilford Recorder newspaper cutting about the boy who mislead the Courts.

Attached is a cutting from the newspaper 'The Ilford Recorder' about the case of a Gibraltar evacuee boy who was charged with theft and made the Ilford Juvenile Court believe that he could not understand English.

Evacuees at Dr Barnardo's Homes shortly after arriving Photo Mrs Hanglin

Gibraltar boy scouts with women's voluntary services

The Dr Barnardo's Homes prior to be converted in evacuee centres in 1939. The above photos were donated by the Ilford Local History Studies Office.

Above and below Mrs Mariola Summerfield (nee Benvenuto) with friends by the Duchess of Bedford Hotel in 1941. Photo Mrs M Summerfield

Mariola with friends. Photo Mrs M Summerfield

Mrs Summerfield(nee Benvenuto),Elsie Taylor,Victoria Chini, Conti,Olga Santos(Mrs Llanelo)Vicky Santos at At the Duchess of Bedford. Photo Mrs M Summerfield

Mrs Poggio visiting the Duchess of Bedford in the sixties. PhotoMrs Poggio

Mrs M Summerfield (nee Benvenuto) with friends by the Duchess of Bedford Hotel during the evacuation. Photo Mrs M Summerfield

On the left Mr John H Wilkie and Mrs Aurelia Wilkie with daughters Emily and Mari Photo Mrs Risso

At the Duchess of Bedford Hotel there were 417 evacuees. The officer in charge was Mr A Key and the local representative was Mr Oliver.

The Duchess of Bedford in Autumn 2006. The King's College be seen at the far end.
Photo by my daughter Michelle

Mrs Benvenuto in May 1941 with her children Mariola, Paul and Gustavo
near the dinning hut at the Duchess of Bedford. Photo Mrs M Summerfield

The Empress Hall was mainly used to accommodate temporarily about 700 evacuees. Within the precinct there were also many Jewish and Polish refugees. In September 1940, about a month after the arrival of the evacuees, a bomb exploded nearby causing damage which necessitated the transfer of the evacuees to other centres. The evacuees were at the time in a shelter nearby and fortunately no one was seriously hurt.

Above and below photographs of the Empress Hall in Lillie Road Fulham in 1935.

The evacuees had to sleep on the sits around the skating rink shown in the photograph. Photos the Fulham and Hammersmith Local History Studies Office

The Gibraltar evacuees at the Empire Pool Wembley.
Sitting in front are Salvador Mamo and Pepi Chini with Mrs C.Chini behind them.
Also in the group is Miss Herminia Cano later Mrs Mauricio and Salvador Orciel
Photo Mrs E Mamo

A postcard sent by an evacuee. Photo Mrs E Mamo

Children at the Empire Swimming Pool Gardens Wembley.
Photo Mr J Robeson, third from the left in the front row.

The Empire Pool, Empire Way, Wembley was designed by Sir Owen Williams and built in 1934 on the site of the British Empire Exhibition's Australian Palace. It was opened for the Commonwealth Games on the 27th July 1934. The pool was closed after the 1948 Olympic Games. The venue had been constructed to host swimming and ice skating competitions during the 1934 Empire Games. Over the years it hosted tennis, boxing, table tennis and cycle racing. In August 1940 it became the home of Gibraltarian evacuees until they were repatriated in July 1944. The officer in charge of this centre was Mr F Herbert and the local representative was Mr Attias. There were no major incidents and those evacuees who were designated to this evacuation centre stayed there throughout the whole period of the evacuation.

One of the most notable events held in this centre was a Gala Dance, which took place in July 1941 to raise money for a memorial fund in aid of the sunken battlecruiser **HMS Hood.** The dance was attended by many Gibraltar evacuees from different centres. The Mayor and Mayoress of Wembley and other well-known local persons were also in attendance at the dance. The Mayoress was presented with bouquet by an evacuee child who also placed the first coin in the box for the **HMS Hood** Fund.

Miss Herminia Cano with friend Miss Aida Attias.
Photo Mrs H Mauricio

Mrs Rocca with daughter Jeannette.
Photo Mrs J Randall

Salvador Mamo with tricycle at Wembley.
Photo Mrs E Mamo

Nurse with Jeannette Rocca.
Photo Mrs J Randall

Salvador Mamo holding the fort.
Photo Mrs E Mamo

Cousins Salvador Mamo and Pepi Chini.
Photo Mrs E Mamo

All the photos on this page were donated by Mrs J Randall

Mrs Rocca her daughter Jeannette. and Miss Mary Vella

Mr Pablo Vella her granddaughter Jeanette Rocca. and his daughter Mrs Rocca

Mrs Rocca, her baby Jeannette. Mrs Noguera and her son

Jeanette Rocca with the Wembley Building at the back.

Mrs Rocca with her daughter Jeanette.
Photo Mrs J Randall

Cousins Pepi Chini and Salvador Mamo.
Photo Mrs E Mamo

Roberto Ullger, Pepi Chini and Salvador Mamo.
Photo Mrs E Mamo

Aida Attias and Choly Stagnetto at the Empire Pool.
Photo Mrs H Mauricio

Mercy and Etty Povedano.
PhotoMrs Peto

Miss Mary Vella, Mrs Rosa Vella ,Mrs Jane Rocca and child Jeanette Rocca .
Photo Mrs J Randall

Evacuees in the UK

Children in the photo: A.Yeo,P.Hernandez,H.Requena P.Celecia J.Hernandez,G.Hernandez O.Requena J.Rocca A.Requena. Photo Mrs J Randall

Mrs Povedano with her daughters Noelia,Mercy,Lilian and Etty. Photo Mrs N Peto

Mrs Antonia Povedano with her daughter Lilian. Photo Mrs N Peto

Evacuees with the Wembley building in the background. Photo Mrs Randall

The Povedano family at Wembley. From L to R Noelia,Mercy, Mrs Antonia Povedano, Etty and baby Lilian. Photo Mrs N Peto

Mrs Rocca with her daughter Jeanette. The Wembley main building is in the background

The Grafton Hotel in Tottenham Court Road housed 342 evacuees. Despite being in the heart of London, this evacuation centre was very luckily spared from the intense bombing. There was in fact one incident when a bomb fell near the build putting off all the lightings. The officer in charge of this centre was Miss K. Richards and the local delegate was Miss Bebeagua.

The Grafton Hotel in 2004. Photo my daughter Michelle

The Grafton Hotel in the 20s. Photo Camden Historical Studies Office

The photographs on this page were donated by Mr J Guilliano. Mrs Guilliano with her son Joseph – one of the many families residing at the Grafton Hotel during the evacuation.

Mrs Guilliano with her son Joseph at the door to what used to be their room during the evacuation.

Mrs Guilliano and her son Joseph at the entrance to the Grafton Hotel.

Mrs Maria Guilliano at the roof of the Grafton Hotel.

Mrs Guilliano with her son Joseph near the Grafton Hotel.

Children at the Grafton Hotel. Photo Mr W Warwick
At the back L to R Risso Walter Warwick
Hubert Warwick Risso James Laguea
Sitting in Front:.....?..... .....?...... ......?.....

All the photographs on this page except the one below were donated by Mr Joseph Guilliano.

A children's party hosted by the Mayor of London and his wife at the Grafton Hotel in 1942. Joe and Leo Guilliano are in photo marked with crosses

Magician entertaining children at the Grafton Hotel in 1942.

A children's party hosted by the Mayor of London and his wife at the Grafton Hotel in 1942. In the forefront of the photo is Joe Guilliano holding a piece of cake.

Highlands Heath consisted of luxury flats, which were purposely built for private sale in 1936.

Below are some pages copied from the promotion brochure explaining the main features of the flats for sale. Publicity Material from the Wandsworth Heritage Office.

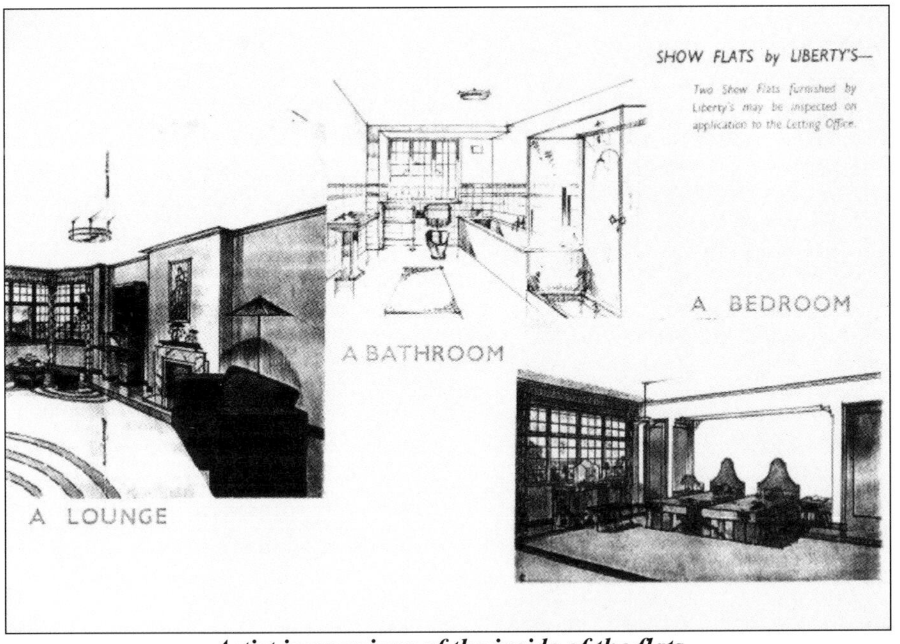

Artist impressions of the inside of the flats

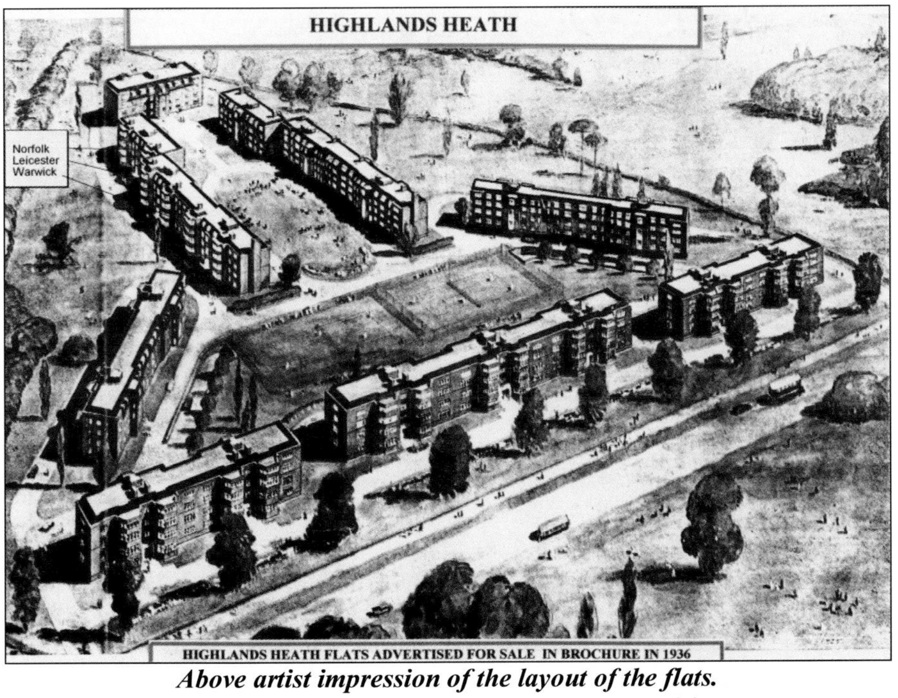

Above artist impression of the layout of the flats. The flats occupied by the evacuees are indicated with arrows

With the outbreak of World War Two, three blocks of flats included in this brochure were requisitioned by the British Government to accommodate 364 evacuees from Gibraltar. The officer in charge of this evacuation centre was Mr E Fround and the local representative was Mr Orfila.

Below is an extract of the information provided in the brochure.

The site is that of an old English House called "Highlands" on Putney Common, and every effort has been made in laying out the Estate to preserve the delightful gardens and the old mature timber. Miles of beautiful country, taking in Putney Heath, Wimbledon Common and Richmond Park, surround the Estate. The famous Roehampton, Coombe. Hill, Royal Wimbledon and Malden golf course are close at hand, and for those who ride, facilities are offered by several stables in the neighbourhood.
The brochure offer the chance to own a compact modern luxury flat – in the country and yet only 15/20 minutes by car or train from the West End and Theatre-land. That is what is actually made possible at "Highlands Heath," Putney."
The prices are from £145 for 1 Reception Room, 2 Bedrooms, Large Entrance Dining Hall, Kitchen, Bathroom with WC and additional separate WC.
And
2 Reception Rooms, 4 Bedrooms, Large Entrance Dining Hall, Kitchen, Bathroom with WC. Second Bathroom attached to best Bedroom, Cloak Room in Hall with lavatory basin and WC and additional separate WC. Maid's Bedroom with separate bath, lavatory and WC from £330.
Services in all the above flats include electric lifts, uniformed porters in attendance, constant hot water, central heating by means of radiators in all rooms and store room for tenants' boxes and luggage.

The blocks assigned to accommodate the evacuees were the **WARWICK, NORFOLK** and **LEICESTER.**
The rest of the blocks of flats were fenced off and all the facilities like the tennis courts etc were out of bounds for the Gibraltar evacuees. Incidentally, there was a shelter built underneath the tennis court and the roof of the shelter must have been so thin that anyone walking or playing on the tennis court could be heard in the shelter underneath. Some of the evacuees commented that in a direct hit no one would have stood a chance of getting out alive. There were plenty of open fields nearby where the youngsters could enjoy themselves playing. Nearby there was a pub called the Telegraph Inn where evacuees gathered occasionally to have refreshments especially after football matches.

Photo taken during the evacuation showing the blocks of flats. Photo Mrs E Azopardi

The blocks of flats were the evacuees were billeted. Photo taken in 2004.

Another recent view of the entrance to Highlands Heath in 2004.

The entrance to Highlands Heath in 2004

All the 2004 photographs on this page were taken by my daughter Michelle.

When I visited Whitelands College in February 2004 I took the opportunity of visiting with my daughter the blocks of flats, which were occupied by the Gibraltar evacuees during the war at Highlands Heath. The flats from what I gathered were still considered luxury flats. Upon enquiring about the prices, I found out that they were in the region of £200,000 in 2004. My daughter Michelle took the following pictures:

Norfolk House.

Warwick House.

Leicester House.

Francis Rocca playing with his sailing boat in a pond near Highlands Heath during the evacuation.
Please note presence of military vehicles in the distance.
Photo Mr F Rocca

Maricarmen Rebora in 1942.
at the entrance to her flat at Leicester House
Photo Mrs M Mamo

At the back Mrs Saldiva and Mrs M Rebora
In front L to R E.Ellul M.Saldiva A.Ellul M.Rebora and M.Linares
Photo Mrs M Mamo

Families at Highlands Heath.
Mrs Maruja Chichon (nee Cano) Lolo Cano Paul Cano Mrs Baldachino Mrs Carter Mrs Bautista Boys in front Baldachino and Joaquin Bautista. Photo Mr P Cano.

Maricarmen Rebora with grandmother Mrs Rebora in the fields at Putney Heath. Photo Mrs M Mamo

Another photo of Maricarmen at Highlands Heath.

THE HYDE PARK GATE HOTEL

At Hyde Park Gate Hotel at No.5 Hyde Park Gate there were 238 evacuees. The officer in charge was Mr J Thomas and the evacuees' representative was Mrs Shock from the Women's Voluntary Services.

THE IVANHOE HOTEL

At the Ivanhoe Hotel in Bloomsbury Street there were 478 evacuees. The officer in charge was Mr Frolic and the local representative was Mr Cavilla.

This evacuation centre had a very good football team as can be seen in the section about football in London. The photographs shown are of what is now the Marlborough Hotel but the building structure is the same of what used to be the Ivanhoe Hotel during the evacuation and up to the 70s.

The two photographs shown below of the Marlborough Hotel were taken by Mr D Parody.

KENSIGNTON PALACE MANSION

There were 448 evacuees accommodated at the Kensington Place Mansion in De Vere Gardens, Kensington. The evacuees used to call this centre the White Hotel presumably because it was all painted in white. The officer in charge was Captain E. Bateman. Towards the end of the evacuation it was hit by a flying bomb completely destroying part of the building and killing evacuee Mrs. Rosa Vella.

The Kensington Palace Mansion during the evacuation.
Photo Mrs M E Russo

Evacuees in a part near Kensington Palace Mansion.
Photo Mr J Aguilera

KENSIGNTON PALACE MANSION

The rear part of the building in 2006 of what was known during the evacuation as the Kensington Palace Mansion and was hit by a flying bomb. Photo Mr D Parody

All the following photos except the one at the bottom of the next column were donated by Mr James Aguilera.

In the above photo are Encarna Bosio and Maria Aguilera.

Pedro and Jaime Aguilera.

Above photo are Manolo Vella, James, Pedro and Laura Aguilera.

Joseph and Lawrence Mamo at the KPM. Photo Mrs P Mamo

At the King's College of House Hold and Social Sciences as it was known at the time of its release as an evacuation centre there were 329 evacuees accommodated. The officer in charge was Miss I Waugh and the local representative was Mr. Grech.

Evacuees in the main hall of the King's College – in the photo are Alfred Almeida and Victor Bossano.
Photo Mr V Bossano

Evacuees at the King's College.

The Entrance to the ex-King's College building in Campden Hill Gate.
The photos above and below were taken by my daughter Michelle

The ex-King's College building from the distance.

Two ex-evacuees - Mrs Bossano and her son Victor visiting the King's College in 1990.
Photo Mr V Bossano

At the Constance Hotel at 23 Lancaster Gate and at 55 Lancaster Gate there were 123 evacuees. The officer in charge for both centres was Mrs R Millar. The local representative for these centres was Mr Hanglin.

The Constance Hotel during the evacuation. Photo Westminster Local History Studies Office

Photo taken in 2005 of what used to be the Constance. Hotel. Photo by my daughter Michelle

The entrance of what used to be the Constance Hotel during the evacuation at 23 Lancaster Gate in 2006. Photo by my daughter Michelle

Bayswater Road leading to Lancaster Gate during the war. Photo Miss A Pardo

The surroundings to Lancaster Gate in 2005. Photo Mr M Pincho

All the photographs on this page were taken by my daughter Michelle.

At 90-92 Lancaster Gate there were 138 evacuees and the officer in charge was Mrs O. Henson. The local representative was Mr Hanglin.

Entrance to ex- 55 Lancaster Gate in 2006.

Entrance to the ex- 90-92 Lancaster Gate in 2006.

The ex- 55 Lancaster Gate building in 2006.

The ex- 90-92 Lancaster Gate building in 2006.

Manolo Pincho with his family visiting 100 Lancaster Gate building.

Manolo Pincho by the room where he used to live during evacuation.

Manolo Pincho recalling the many times that he used to cross this street during the evacuation.

Mrs Malenie Castle with her daughter Peggy and son Eddie at 100 Lancaster Gate.
Photo Mrs P Mamo (nee Castle)

All the photographs on this page, except the one shown above, were donated by Mr M Pincho.

Entrance to 100 Lancaster Gate.

At 100 Lancaster Gate there were 344 evacuees. The officer in charge was Mrs M V Steel and the local representative was Mr Mauricio.

At the entrance to the Royal Court Hotel.
At 105 Lancaster Gate in the photo are:
J.Noguera A.Rovegno L.Pardo A.Pardo and C.Asquez

Girls at the balcony of the Royal Court Hotel.
In the photo are Marina Linares, Concepcion Payas Angelina Palao and Kitty Casciaro

Girls at the Royal Court Hotel.
In the photo are L.Galliano L.Pardo A.Pardo and M.Casciaro

Arturo Pardo and family at the balcony of the Royal Court Hotel. The windows of 100 Lancaster Gate can be seen in the background

All the photographs on this page were donated by Miss Antonia Pardo. At the Royal Court Hotel at 105 Lancaster Gate there were 220 evacuees. The officer in charge was Major Bell and the local representative was Mr. Sampere.

Evacuees at the entrance to the Royal Court Hotel. In the photo are: Mariana Linares, Ena, Luis and Mario Sampere; Maribel Bellido; Paca Santos; Adelaida, Maria, Ricardo and Bienvenido Pereira Photo Mr L Linares

Evacuees at the Royal Court Hotel.
In the photo are: C.Correa, F.Pardo, A.Pardo, P and L Galliano, J.Williams, A.Pardo, A. Pardo, M.Pardo and L.Linares. Photo Miss A Pardo

Evacuees at the Royal Court Hotel.
Antonia Pardo with school friends
Photo Miss A Pardo

The ex- Royal Court Hotel building in 2005.
Photo Mr M Pincho

In the photo are Mrs Clemencia Sene her children Lilian and Cecil. Also in the photo are the Pardo sisters and Aida MacClaren. Photo Mrs L Baglietto

The Sene family:Mrs Clemencia Sene with her children Nobert, Cecil and Lilian. Photo Mrs L Baglietto

At the Linden Hall evacuation centre in 131/137 Cromwell Road there were 126 evacuees. The officer in charge was Miss O. Shore and the local representative was Father Azzopardi. The photographs on this page were taken by my daughter Michelle.

The entrance of what use to be the Linden Hall evacuation centre.

The ex – Linden Hall building currently known as the Kensington Rooms.

At Marlborough Court's evacuation centre in Pembroke Road, Kensington there were about 450 evacuees. The officer in charge was Mr A Lewington and the local representative was Mr Bellotti.

Part of the Marlborough Court building during the evacuation. Photo Mr Johnny Grech

The Infantes and related families at Marlborough Court. All from L to R at the back Mrs Mary Harrison (nee Infante) Juan Danino In the middle row Victor Infante Lourdes Infante (Mrs Cardona) Celestina Linares (later Mrs Danino) Maruja Linares, Marcelino Linares Sitting Mrs Oscaria Infante (nee Linares) Manuel Infante Mrs Eugenia Linares (neeInfante). Sitting on the floor is Mercy Infante (later Mrs Buhagiar) Photo Mr M Infante

Above youngsters at Marlborough Court in August1940. Above photos Mr Albert Moreno

A recent photograph of one of the entrances to Marlborough Court.
Photo Mrs Hernandez

Evacuees at a party held at Marlborough Court in 1942.
In the photo are bandmaster Juan Cruz, Aida Bugeya, Maruja Barabich, Elsie Sanchez, Manuel Infante, Pepe Moreno and other evacuees
Photo Mr J Sanchez

Evacuees at Marlborough Court. In the photo are Victor Infante, Albert Moreno and Victor Sciacaluga *Photo Mr J Sanchez*

A recent photograph of Marlborough Court building.
Photo by my daughter Michelle

Victor Infante.

Lourdes Infante (later Mrs Cardona).

Christmas party at Marlborough Court.
Photos above and below by Mr J Sanchez

Christmas party at Marlborough Court.
With the children is Miss Elsie Sanchez

Mrs Oscaria Infante (nee Linares) thinking about her sons Francis, Willaim and Manuel in Gibraltar.
All above photos Mr M Infante

THE MOSCOW MANSIONS

At the Moscow Mansions evacuation centre there were 213 evacuees. The officer in charge was Mr R MacQueen and the local representative was Miss D'Oyly from the Women's Voluntary Services in London. I have no images of this building.

NORTHWAY HOTEL

At the Northway Hotel in 70 Euston Square NW1 there were 91 evacuees. The officer in charge was Miss R Ross and the local delegate representing the evacuees was Miss Santos. I could find no images of this building.

THE NATIONAL HOTEL

At the National Hotel in Bedford Way evacuation centre there were 425 evacuees although according to my research there was at one time many more evacuees due to the transfer from the nearby bombed Raglan and Shelbourne Hotels in September 1940.

Mrs. Mary Borge with her children Rosa and Francis In a park near the National Hotel. Photo Mr F Borge

A pre-war postcard showing the entrance to the National Hotel. Postcard donated by Royal National Hotel

The National Hotel in the 60s. Photo Camden Local History Studies Office

Children from the National Hotel in a park nearby in the photo Miss Mary Mor (Mrs Martinez). Photo Mrs M Martinez

In Fitzjames Avenue, West Kensington there were two evacuation centres named North End House tower blocks A and B were there were 609 and 332 evacuees respectively. The officers in charge for A and B blocks were Mr. R.S.Asher and Mr N MacLeod and the local representatives were Mr Bruzon and Mr Benady respectively.

Above and below views of the North End House buildings in 1956. Photo donated by the Fulham and Hammersmith Local History Studies Office

Isaac Abensur gave the following account of his recollection when he arrived in England. "We were taken to London and placed in beautiful hotels, including some in the West End! Because of Jewish religion requirement, the Jewish community were gathered from different locations and sent to a residential building called the North End Block B. Here the Jewish community was provided with kosher meals and facilities for prayers. The manager was a charming, warm Scotsman, Mr N Macleod. They organised Scottish dancing for young girls. The Jewish teachers immediately organised religious classes and, of course, a managing committee was voted in. There were plenty of plays and concerts and not withstanding the constant bombings and the smog children enjoyed the benefits of a well ran community."

Ehat of Synagogue at North End House
Photo Mr M Belilo

Evacuees at the North End House block B taken in a studio at Hammersmith in 1942
At the back Cecil Holland and Abraham Beniso
In front Isaac L Attias, Isaac S Garson and Joseph Attias
Photo Mr A Beniso

Group of evacuees from North End House Block A. Photo Mr J Ferro
Back row L to R: 1. J.Ferrro 2..?....3...?...4...?...5 Sene 6...?....
Middle row L to R:1A.Camilleri 2 Vella 3Vella 4 C.Montero 5 O.Sene 6 Robles 7 J.Mamo 8 Smith? 9 E.Byrne 10.F.Origo 11.J.L.Olivero 12.?...13…?...14…?...
Front row l to R: 1..?...2…?...3 Alman 4 A.Olivero 5.Alman 6..?...7.LFerro 8.Sene 9...?...

Jewish children outside North End House Block B.
Back: Tito Gabay,Isaac Abensur,Batsheva Cohen,David Hassan,Clarita Massias,Abraham Massias,Simi Seruya.
Front: Yoita Bitton,DannyGabay,Sarah Hassan,Gladys Benady,George Benady,Sam Benady, Eddie Hatchwel,Benady,Simi Benady,Mark Benabu,James Nahon. Photo Mr M Belilo

A recent photograph of what used to be the Park Royal and Berkeley Hotels. Photo by my daughter Michelle

THE PARK ROYAL AND BAKERLEY HOTELS

At the Park Royal and the Berkeley Hotels in 25/31 Leinster Gardens in the Lancaster Gate area there were 179 evacuees. The officer in charge was Mr W W. Kealey and evacuee representative was Mr Segui.

Mrs Mary Mercedes Cartwright with her children at the Park Royal Hotel in Lancaster Gate. Photo Mrs Barbara Payne

SHAFTESBURY HOTEL

The Shaftesbury Hotel does not appear in the list of evacuation centres. However, Mr M Infante who gave me the photo at the top of the next column assured me that his family was billeted initially in this hotel before moving to the Marlborough Hotel evacuation centre. Another evacuee who also lived in this same evacuation centre was Mr Victor Gonzalez until his was moved to Dr Barnardo's Homes.

Shaftesbury Hotel in Shaftesbury. Avenue Photo Mr M Infante

The Gibraltar Chronicle cutting below refers to how the evacuees were settling after nearly a year in London.

NEW CENTRES FOR EVACUEES IN LONDON

Children's Health Benefits From Change of Climate

32, Sackville Street, Piccadilly,
London, W. 1.
20th April, 1941.

To The Editor, "Gibraltar Chronicle."

Dear Sir,—As you were kind enough to say that the notes I was able to give you while I was in Gibraltar would be appreciated, I am sending you some further notes about our people in London, which I trust will be found of interest.

Since the formation of the Inter-Departmental Committee, great progress has been made in obtaining new centres, which has enabled the numbers to be considerably reduced wherever these were excessive, and this has greatly added to the comfort of the evacuees.

Great advances have also been made in providing good shelters with bunks in all the centres, so that the evacuees do not have to go out to public shelters, as well as with the heating and the arrangements for schools.

In spite of the change to a much colder climate and in the food and habits of living, the incidence of sickness has been very low, and Dr. Durante tells me this compares very favouraby with the normal incidence in Gibraltar.

He also tells me that he has often watched the children playing football in the gardens and a fitter or happier-looking crowd of children could not be desired.

The fact that most of the younger members of the community are now employed and have other general interests to occupy them has made them more contented and happy.

As regards the children, apart from measles, which caused a good deal of sickness amongst them early in their stay in London, the incidence of children's ailments and infectious diseases has been noticeably low and they all look fit, healthy and happy, and I am of the opinion that the great majority have benefited by the change of climate.

Gibraltar Chronicle cutting dated May 1941.

The Royal Palace Hotel was constructed in the early 20th century and was considered one of the most luxurious hotels in London at the time. The photographs on this page show the building through the different periods of its history.

The Royal Palace Hotel about 1914.

The Royal Palace Hotel in the late 50s.Note part of the building destroyed during the bombing.

The demolition of the Royal Palace Hotel in the 60s.

At the Royal Palace Hotel in High Street Kensington there were over 613 evacuees being the largest of all the centres in the area of Kensington.

The officer in charge was Mr Metealfe and the local representative was Mr Murto. All the photographs on this page, except the one at the bottom right column were donated by the Kensington Gardens Hotel.

The finished Kensington Palace Hotel in 1965.

A recent photograph of the newly refurbished the now Kensington Gardens Hotel on the same site as the Royal Palace hotel.

Children at the entrance to the Royal Palace Hotel with their teacher. In the photo are Antonio Henrich, Jimmy and Johnny Edwards,Victor Spiteri,Johnny and Luis Fa. Photo Mrs Doris Gonzalez Edwards

Evacuees in the UK

Just a month after the arrival of the bulk of the evacuees in London, HM Queen Elizabeth, the Queen Mother paid a visit to the evacuees at the Royal Palace Hotel and the Kensington Palace Mansion. As can be appreciated from the photographs the evacuees gave the Queen a very cheerful welcome. She was presented with a bouquet by Margot Desoiza and later chatted with many of the evacuees who were eagerly awaiting her visit. When she left most of the evacuees were standing outside in the street near to their respective centres to greet and wave goodbye as the Queen left the area of Kensington.

In the photograph her HM Queen Elizabeth the Queen Mother talking with the Gibraltar evacuees during her visit to the Royal Palace Hotel on the 10 October 1940. Facing the Queen is Miss Hilda Viagas and near her are Mrs Dawes, Mrs Martin and Miss Cornelio.
Photo Gibraltar Heritage Trust

HM Queen holding the hand of child Adela Soiza (Mrs Hanglin).
Photo Mrs A Hanglin

The Queen's Secretary talking with Margot Desoiza.
Who handed the bouquet to HM Queen
Photo Mr Durrell

Above and below the Governor of Gibraltar Lt General Sir Noel Mason MacFarlane visiting children in a tea party. In the photo below accompanying the Governor is Father Azzopardi

The Governor Sir Noel Mason MacFarlane visiting the Royal Palace Hotel accompanied by Father Azzopardi

Children at a tea party.

The Governor of Gibraltar had been receiving letters of complaints about how the evacuees were being treated. In November 1943 he paid a visit to London and took the opportunity to see for himself how the evacuees fared at the various centres.

On this page are photographs taken when the Governor called at the Royal Palace Hotel evacuation centre. Commenting on his visit to London in his 1943/44 New Year's speech, the Governor said that the evacuees were ever so happy about the way they were being treated with many forms of entertainment provided during the Christmas period.
He continued by saying that despite the rationing, the food being provided was good and plentiful with the children having lots of fresh milk.

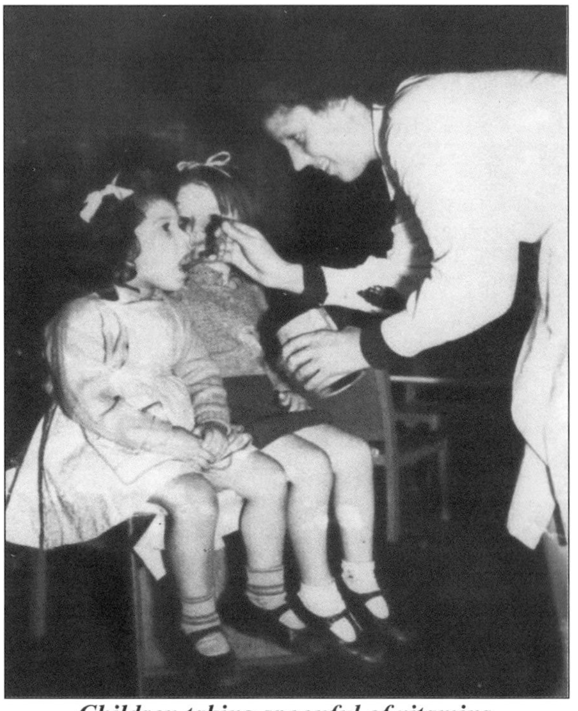

Children taking spoonful of vitamins.

All the photographs on this page, except the one below, were donated by Mr A Massetti.

Mrs Rosario Edwards with her children Jimmy and Johnny Edwards.
Photo Mrs Doris Gonzalez Edwards

On this page are photographs of some of the families at the Royal Palace Hotel.

Mrs Horrtencia Spiteri with her son Victor
Photos above and below by Mr V Spiteri

Henry and Victor Spiteri

Mrs Ana Maria Desoiza with children Tony and Margot at the Royal Palace Hotel   Photo Mrs V Desoiza

Richard and Joseph Evans.
Photo above and below Mr R Evans

Mrs Isabel Evans with her sons
Richard and Joseph

Adolfo,Isabel,Victor and Antonia Catania.
Photo Mrs L Holmes

"We Thank God and England.."

At St Katherine's College in White Hart Lane, Tottenham there were 300 evacuees. The officer in charge was Mr Brown and the local representative was Mr Becerra. The photographs on this page were donated by the Tottenham Local History Studies Office.

Aerial view of St Katherine's College.

A rear view of the west wing of St Katherine's College in 1931.

Students' study bedrooms were converted into families' bedrooms.

Mrs Josephine Alvarez with her children Humbert,Charles,Emilio,Francis and Arthur at St Katherine' s College. Photo Mr C Alvarez

At the St Katherine's College gardens Mrs Mansfield with daughter Silvia, Mrs Povedano with daughters Lilian, Noelia, Etty and Mercy. Tommy Mansfield is sitting in front.

At the St Katherine's College gardens Mrs Mansfield with her children Tommy and Silvia. Lilian Povedano standing on the right.

The Alvarez family at St Katherine,s College. Mrs Josephine Alvarez with her children Emilio,Francis,Arthur,Charles and Humbert. Photo Mr C Alvarez

The Students' common room was converted into living quarters Photo Tottenham Local History Studies Office.

Mrs Noelia Peto (Nee Povedano) At a studio in Tottenham.

All the photographs, except for the one at the bottom left hand corner were donated by Mrs N Peto.

THE RAGLAN AND SHELBOURNE HOTELS

The Shelbourne Hotel in Bedford Way in central London was converted into an evacuation centre the same as the Raglan and National Hotels also in Bedford Way but since they were destroyed by the bombing, fortunately with casualtie in October 1940, there seems to be no record of the number of evacuees or the centres' administrators.

My brothers and I on arrival at the Raglan Hotel.

The remains of the Shelbourne Hotel after the bombing. Photo Camden Local History Studies Office

ST.STEPHEN'S CLOSE

St.Stephen's Close evacuation centre in Avenue Road, St John's Wood there were 480 evacuees. The officer in charge was Major T.Sinclair and the local representative was Mr Bellotti.

Not very far from St.Stephen's Close is the famous Lord's Cricket Ground which was closed during the war although many services and school matches were played during the time of the war.

A few bombs of different types fell on the actual cricket ground, including a flying bomb. As far as I know St.Stephen's Close evacuation was not directly affected by the bombing.

Adolfo Bosio at the entrance to St Stephen's Close.

All the photographs related to St Stephen's Close were donated by Mr A Bosio.

Photo on the left , Adolfo Bosio with his wife (nee Freyone) and Adolfo's sister Olga visiting St Stephen's Close- Adolfo's wife former evacuation centre.

All the photographs on this page except for the one taken by my daughter Michelle were donated by Mrs V Desoiza.

Mrs Perera with her daughter Vicky and friend opposite the Thackeray Hotel.

The ex-Thackeray Hotel in 2006. Photo by my daughter Michelle

Vicky Perera and Charles Gonzalez at the entrance to the Thackeray Hotel.

Mrs Perera with her daughter Vicky at a park near the Thackeray Hotel.

At the Thackeray Hotel there were 279 evacuees. The officer in charge was Miss L Smith and the local representative Mr Soiza.

Livia Gill, Vicky Perera and Charles Gonzalez outside the entrance to the Thackeray Hotel. Please note that entrance decorations are the same during evacuation as in the photo taken in Jan.2006. Photo Mrs V Desoiza

A drawing of the Thackeray Hotel when constructed in 1914. Picture Camden Local History Studies Office

The entrance to what used to be the ex-Thackeray Hotel in Jan 2006. Photo by my daughter Michelle

An old postcard of the entrance to the Thackeray Hotel in the early twenties Picture Camden Local History Studies Office.

OTHER CENTRES

Other centres mentioned to me but which I have no images or information were the following:
The Russell Hotel, the Prince of Wales, Royal Patriotic School, and the Crystal Palace.

The three storeys Georgian Building in Chelsea named "Whitelands House." Photo Wandsworth Heritage Service

I think very few evacuees, if any, knew that the building at Putney, where they were living during the war, was owned by an institution with a very historical and educational significance. I, certainly, did not find out until I visited the College during the initial stage of my research. Because of the connection between Whitelands and the Gibraltar evacuees, I thought it would be of interest to the ex-evacuees that I should include in this documentary, although very briefly, the history of the Whitelands Training College. Whitelands is one of the oldest educational institutions in England. In 1811 the Church of England sought to meet the need for elementary education of the masses by setting up charity schools. Two years later it began to train teachers for these schools. The first of these training schools was in Baldwin's Gardens, Holborn and later in Smith Square, Westminster for the purpose of providing short practical teaching methods. The National Society of the Church of England founded two teachers' training colleges in January 1842 in Chelsea. One school was for men - St Mark's situated towards the Fulham end of King's Road and the other for women in a three-storied Georgian house at the junction with Walpole Street near Sloane Square, named "Whitelands House." By 1899 further buildings were erected above the school at Whitelands House to cater for its expansion. This included Whitelands' first own chapel since the school was founded in 1842. Throughout its early history the school had many famous benefactors including Baroness Burdett-Coutts, Charles Dickens and John Ruskin. It was John Ruskin who began the Whitelands College May Queen Festival in 1881, which was the origin of all children's May Day celebrations in England. By 1920 it was already becoming necessary to find a larger and new building.

After considering several places, it was decided to construct the new Whitelands Training College on a site called Melrose Gardens, by West Hill in East Putney. Sir Gilbert Scott the architect of the Liverpool Cathedral, the Battersea Power Station and many other famous building was commissioned to design the new buildings at Putney. Famous designers such as William Morris and Edward Bume-Jones contributed to the interior decoration of the building.

The Whitelands Training College built in 1931. Photo Wandsworth Heritage Service

The iron ornamented gates at the Whiteland House in Chelsea was brought to Putney where it was still when the photograph below was taken by my daughter in February 2004.

The iron ornament gates brought from Chelsea to Whitelands College in Putney. Photo taken by my daughter Michelle

By the time the new building was ready, Whitelands Training College had one hundred and ninety six students and seventeen lecturers. The new building at Putney was officially opened in June 1931 by Her Majesty Queen Mary. In 1939 there were already plans to celebrate the first centenary of the foundation of the College in 1941 but with the outbreak of war these plans had to be abandoned.

Students at the Whitelands College in Putney.
Wandsworth Heritage Service.

HM Queen Mary at the Whitelands Training College's opening ceremony in June 1931.
Wandsworth Heritage Service.

When the bombing started in 1940, the Whitelands' students like other students in London were evacuated. By early 1940, the College had been requisitioned by the British Government to house about five hundred Gibraltar evacuees who were to live there until it was bombed on Saturday 19th February 1944. On that Saturday, in the early hours of the morning the building was hit with incendiary bombs. The fire caused by these bombs spread very quickly and destroyed completely the entire roof and the whole of the top floor. Some serious attempts were made by the evacuees to put out the fire that became so intense that they were forced to abandon the building. The repairs to the roof and building started a few months after the bombing but because of the flying bombs its restoration works were disrupted causing much delay. As an interim measure, students were allowed to attend the College until gradually normal service was resumed after all the repairs were completed in 1948. Whitelands by then became a constituent College of the University of London's Institute of Education.

The post war years which brought a significant increase in the school age population in Britain meant a greater demand for more trained teachers. Despite the constraints placed by this on the College due to the shortage of rooms, it nevertheless continued to expand. By 1962 additional rooms to accommodate both teachers and students were built.

In 1975 Whitelands was made a founder member of Roehampton Institute becoming part of the University of Surrey.

A postcard of Whitelands College in the early fifties with the newly refurbished building and repaired roof.
Postcard by Mr H Zammitt

The last extension to the original plans, which consisted of accommodation space, was completed in 1998. Though the degrees issued by Whitelands were validated by the University of Surrey as from 1985, full university status was achieved in 2000, when the Roehampton Institute formally entered into federation with the University of Surrey and became known as the University of Surrey, Roehampton. In 2001 there were about 1,500 students who were attached to Whitelands College and 400 of these were resident on the campus. When I visited the College there were two students from Gibraltar: Guy Baglietto and David Banda. There was also a security officer from Gibraltar, Mr Joe Baglietto employed at the College.

At the start of the new academic year in August 2004 the students moved to another building called Parkstead House in the nearby town of Roehampton.

The building where the evacuees were housed in Putney was turned into residential flats after 74 years of its existence as a Training College. When I visited the College in February 2004 a road had already been built across what used to be until very recently the football pitch.

The Chapel in 1931.
Photo Wandsworth Heritage Service.

The Chapel in 2004. Photo Mr J Reading

A recently built road cutting across what used to be the Whitelands sports ground. Photo taken by my daughter Michelle.

I think it is also interesting to mention, that in the same place where the original Georgian Whitelands House was situated and demolished in 1932 another building was erected in 1937.

This building is also called Whitelands House and presently consists of flats and shops.

The larger building is Whitelands House built in 1937. Photos by my daughter Michelle

Like at West Hill and in Chelsea, the new building at Parkstead House also had a purposely built chapel in keeping with the Church of England tradition evident at Whitelands.

Entrance to Whitelands House at the end of King's Road. Photo by my daughter Michelle.

Since the evacuees left the building in that morning of February 1944 many since visited the building at West Hill. Although the present building still maintains most of its past architectural appearance, the historical link with the evacuees has now almost disappeared.

Like the rest of the other evacuation centres, Whitelands was administered by an evacuation committee which was responsible for the welfare of the evacuees. The managers at all the evacuation centres were appointed by the Ministry of Health. At Whitelands the manager was a Mr N S Davies and his deputy was a Mr Foley. There was also a representative from the Ministry of Health who was a Mr Frout. The Gibraltar members of the Whitelands evacuation committee were the following:
Mr A Lopez, Mrs Gaduzo, Mr R.Torrilla, Mr A Bosio, Mr Troice and Mr Bonilla.

The Whitelands College Evacuation Centre Committee.
L to R Mr A Lopez Mrs Gaduzo Mr Torrilla Mr Foley, Mr Davies (manager) Mr A Bosio Mr Troice and Mr Bonilla. Photo Mr J Morello

The main area of responsibility of the evacuation committee was to look after the welfare and safety of the evacuees in their respective centres. This task must have been, at times, quite arduous taking into account the circumstances which no doubt affected very adversely the life of the evacuees, viz, the bombing, the separation of families and those who became ill during the evacuation.
I remember Mr Antonio Lopez who was most of the time around the building walking with a stick making sure children behaved and did not destroy things. When there was an air raid warning, Mr Lopez also used to walk around the building to ensure that there were no visible lights during a period of blackout. There were quarterly meetings at alternative evacuation centres and the delegates from Whitelands at these meetings were Mr R Torrilla and a Mrs H J Lewin of the Women Voluntary Services. The distribution of mail for the evacuees was done from the main office situated on the left hand side of the entrance, shown in the picture above. When the mail arrived, Mr Davies used to call Miss Alicia Pitto who would help him with the distribution of personal mail.

The total area of Whitelands enclosure was about 12 acres which included many trees and open patches of grass. Within this area there were sporting and recreational facilities. The trees consisted mainly of chestnut, a few apple, cherry, pears, almond and oak trees. Around the perimeter of the building there were fences where plenty of mulberries and strawberries used to grow and which we used to pick when in season.

The mulberries in summer 2001.
Photo by my daughter Michelle

Behind the fences on the west side where there were many trees and there was an open field with some farming activities carried out by the then Royal Hospital for incurable diseases. On the east side there was a brick wall fence which together with the wooden fence on the west side enclosed the whole area. The exit and entrance to the whole precinct was via a gate at Sutherland Grove.

Antonia Gingell and Angeles Monteverde by the wall enclosing Whitelands College along Sutherland Grove Road. Photo Miss D Roman

Mr Antonio Lopez visiting the College in recent years. He was the grandson of Mr Antonio Lopez, Caretaker of Whiteland College during occupancy of Gibraltar evacuees. Photo Mr Salvador Lopez.

A view of the rear side of the main building in 2004
Photo by my daughter Michelle

The photograph above shows a view of the rear of the main building taken in winter 2004. From where the tree is, the ground sloped down gently for about 300 metres until it reached the very edge where the football ground was. The area covered by this slope from one end of the building to the other was quite large and was used by evacuees for various purposes. When snow fell, children used to roll and even attempt snow skiing on these slopes.

The entrance to the Whitelands Training College main building in 2004
Photo by my daughter Michelle

The sloping area was used for recreation and watching football matches played at Whitelands. The tennis court, which was beside the football ground, was used as an ice-skating ground whenever frozen puddles were formed within the tennis court. Sometimes during the winter period the evacuees used to fill the court with water in anticipation of freezing weather so as to be able to skate on the frozen puddles. The girls had their own basketball playing area. At the front of the building there was the main entrance as shown in the photograph. As you walked in, there were some steps, which led to the ground floor corridors and to the main hall.

On the left hand side before reaching the steps, was the administration office. When I visited the College the reception and administration offices were in the same place as they used to be during the time of the evacuation. Incidentally, the name of the architect of the building (Gilbert Scott) can be seen on the placard on my left hand side in the photograph of the main entrance. At this same entrance, during the evacuation, the firm Lyons made the deliveries of foodstuff. I remember seeing the lorry arriving on a few occasions unloading their goods. Opposite the main entrance was also the entrance to the Chapel, which we visited on that occasion in 2004. Readers may observe that the photograph of the Whitelands College evacuation committee was taken on the spot where I am standing.

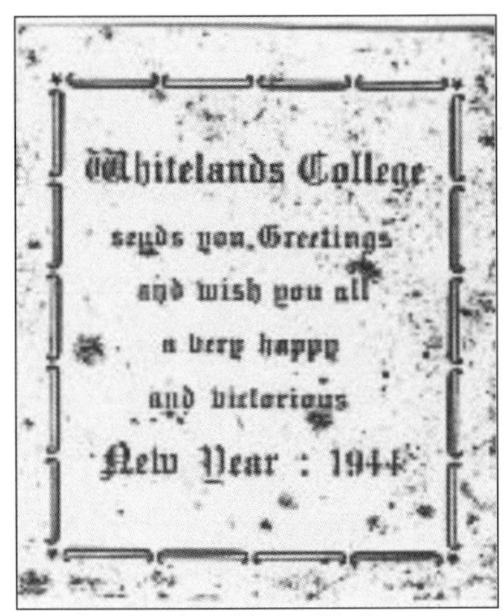

Souvenir of last Christmas at Whitelands
Photo Mr V Alecio

The hall was also large and was often used to hold meetings and for the displaying of notices of relevant interest to the evacuees. This hall was also used for photograph posing as can been in the collection of photographs about fancy dress competitions.

The main hall. To my left is the door to the dinning room and to my right the entrance to the theatre.

An aerial view of Whitelands showing the layout of the main building and surrounding campus. Photo Whitelands College Library

The photograph of the aerial view of Whitelands gives some rough idea of the size of the main building, the associated buildings, the campus and its football ground with its barely visible lines. In front of this building was the Whitelands Chapel. As can be seen from the photographs there were many apple and chestnut trees planted on the campus.

The chestnut tree where we often used to play.

The apple trees in the sloping campus.

All the photographs on this page, except the one of the aerial view of Whitelands College, were taken by my daughter Michelle.

As mentioned in the section about the history of Whitelands, by 1940 the British Government had already requisitioned Whitelands Training College to accommodate five hundred evacuees from Gibraltar. It was officially taken over by the Ministry of Works to turn it into an evacuation centre on the 6 March 1941. Immediately after this date there were already some evacuees at Whitelands as evidently shown from Maria Carmen Saltariche's birth certificate.

Families started to move gradually to Whitelands with the bulk of them coming from the National Hotel when this became overcrowded as a result of the transfer of evacuees from nearby Ragland and Rashbourne Hotels when they were bombed. (see Bombing Section).

According to the records, by late 1941 or early 1942 there were about 100 families living at Whitelands. One of the very latecomers to Whitelands was the Harper family.

The layout of the rooms with their common bathrooms and lavatories on each of the three floors was appropriate for the purpose that it had been designed for – a residential college for students.

Like in other evacuation centres, cooking in the rooms was strictly prohibited and evacuees had to avail themselves of the use of the dining room facilities. I remember that my aunt used to work in the kitchen and some times she was allowed to prepare typical local dishes. No doubt, my cousins, brothers and I must have got, the occasional extra helpings! Mrs Pitto also used to work in the kitchen. The dinning room was quite large and was very often used to hold dances and other entertaining functions.

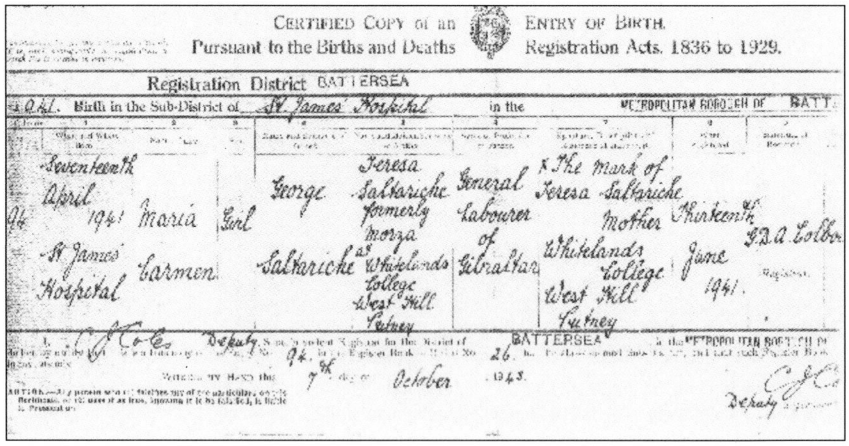

CERTIFIED COPY of an ENTRY OF BIRTH.
Pursuant to the Births and Deaths Registration Acts. 1836 to 1929.

Registration District BATTERSEA

1941. Birth in the Sub-District of St James' Hospital in the METROPOLITAN BOROUGH OF BATT[ERSEA]

94	Seventeenth April 1941 St James' Hospital	Maria Carmen	Girl	George Saltariche	Teresa Saltariche formerly Morza	General Labourer of Gibraltar	x The mark of Teresa Saltariche Mother Whitelands College West Hill Putney	Thirteenth June 1941	G.D.A. Colbo[...] Registrar

Whitelands College West Hill Putney

BATTERSEA METROPOLITAN BOROUGH

94 26

7th October 1948

Deputy

Copy of Maria Carmen Saltariche's Birth Certificate

Opposite the dinning hall there was a theatre but this and the library were kept closed during the whole occupancy of the evacuees.

The dinning room (Photo taken by my daughter Michelle)

There were rooms on the ground floor where there were mannequins dressed with garments appropriate for special occasions. I later found out in my research that these garments were used for the College's May Festival. And on the second floor there was the first aid room to treat minor injuries. On one occasion whilst playing near a tree, some children began to throw stones to bring down the "conkers" One of the stones went over the tree and unfortunately hit me on my head just above the forehead. I was taken to the first aid room covered in blood and was given a few stitches and a good bath afterwards. Despite the very long time, I still wear the marks of that injury.

May Festival Mannequin (Photo by Whitelands College)

Next door to the College was a hospital for patients who suffered from what was then classified as incurable diseases. The running of this hospital was then depended on charity and as a means of self-maintenance it had a working farm that included a pigsty. This farm can be seen from the aerial view of the hospital taken during the war years. There was a line of trees and a wooden fence (as indicated in the picture), which separated the College from the Royal Hospital.

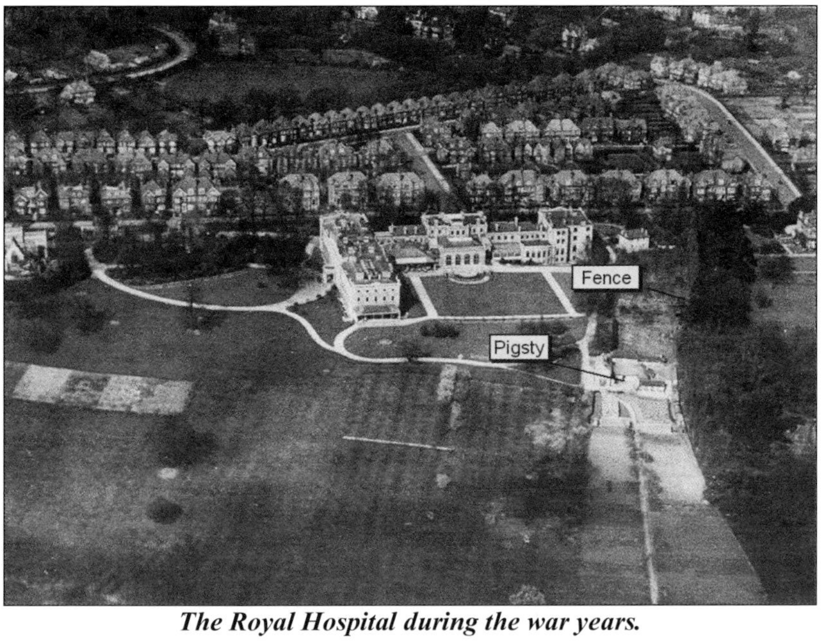

The Royal Hospital during the war years.

The farm keeper.

The photographs on this page were donated by The Royal Hospital for Neuro-disabilities.

Some of the evacuees were under the impression that it was a mental hospital. The scenario as seen from the College of patients moving about with difficulty or being carried on wheelchairs could have easily been misinterpreted as patients suffering from mental illnesses. Some children from the College jumped over the fence and ventured into the farm.

Those who had dared, told me of their experiences when they were repelled by the farm keeper with his air rifle. This rifle, which fired salt pellets, caused a lot of itching in the area of impact. "It didn't kill us, but the pellets were really itchy and the area of impact became very swollen and reddish, indeed," one of the then children explained to me.

Zoraida Hermida, who lived at the top floor, said that from her room window she was able to see the Royal Hospital and the farm. She said that sometimes, in the silence of the morning, she could hear the crying of the pigs when they were being slaughtered. "I could hear the terrible screaming noise made by the poor animals when they were taken to the slaughter house," explained, Zoraida.

I too from our bedroom window, one floor below Zoraida, could see the hospital working farm and much further afield. I remember spending many hours watching the mules and horses roaming around the field and also people working the farm. This hospital is now called The Royal Hospital for Neuro-disabilities. The hospital no longer has a farm but managed to retain some of the grounds, which are now used by the patients, and residents who are able to relax in the gardens. On my first visit to the College the students were actively involved in raising funds for the Royal Hospital for Neuro-disabilities.

The following are the names of the families that were accommodated and the names of the children who were born at the Whitelands Training College during the evacuation:

NAMES OF FAMILIES AT WHITELANDS DURING THE EVACUATION

ACOLINA	DAVIS	LOPEZ	PRESCOTT
ACRIS	DEBONO	MARTINEZ	RAMOGNIN
AGUILERA	DELLIPIANI	MASCARI	REYES
ALECIO	DUARTE	McKAY	RISSO
ALSINA	DYER	MENDEZ	RYMAN
AQUILINA	FALERO	MILAN	READING
BACARESE	FIGUERAS	MOLINARY	ROMAN
BALBAN	GADUZO	MONTADO	ROCCA
BALLOQUI	GALIA	MONTERO	RUIZ
BELLIDO	GARCIA	MONTOVIO	SACRAMENTO
BOSIO	GRACIA	MORELLO	SALTARICHE
BOSSINO	GERADA	MONTEVERDE	SANCHEZ
BROSCO	GIBSON	MORENO	SANPALO
BROTON	GINGELL	NACIMIENTO	SANTOS
BUTTIGIEG	GOMEZ	OLIVA	SANZ
CALAMARO	GONZALEZ	OLIVERO	SERRA
CAPURRO	GRIXTI	PAYAS	SHERIFF
CASSAR	HARPER	PELIZA	SIMONI
CAVILLA	HARRISON	PERERA	TORRILLA
CELECIA	HERMIDA	PILCHER	TRAVERSO
CHAPORRY	HOSKEN	PIPO	TRINIDAD
CHICHON	IGNACIO	PITTO	TROISE
CORTES	JIMENEZ	PODESTA	VASSALLO
COSTA	LEON	POGGIO	VIAGAS
CRUZ	LLAMBIAS	POWER	WINK
D'ALORTO	LOMBARD	PRATTS	ZAMMITT

BELOW IS THE LIST OF CHILDREN IN ORDER OF BIRTHS WHO WERE BORN DURING THE EVACUATION AND WHOSE PARENTS WERE LIVING AT WHITELANDS

NAME OF CHILD	DATE OF BIRTH	WHERE BORN	NAME OF PARENTS
SALTARICHE Maria Del Carmen	17 April 1941	St James Hospital Battersea	George and Teresa
BALBAN Maribel	28 September 1942	St Mary's Hospital Battersea	Alfredo and Juana
VASSALLO Horace	8 October 1942	St James Hospital Battersea	Carmelo and Gardenia
VASSALLO Louis	4 January 1944	St James Hospital Battersea	Carmelo and Gardenia
DUARTE Jeanette	6 January 1944	St James Hospital Battersea	Joseph and Encarnacion
LOPEZ Lydia	18 January 1944	St James Hospital Battersea	Joseph and Alice

Evacuees in the UK

Photograph taken in the Red Room. Photo Mr L Saltariche

Back row M.Sherriff Prescott H.Vassallo (child) M.Castro Troice Costa Payas (child) M.Payas (child) Ferris K.Ferris (child) Manuela Mascari V.Ferris (child)

Middle row Reyes Reyes (child) M.Balban (child) J.Balban M.Alecio (child) Canilla J.Canilla (child) ...?... S.Fiol (child) ...?... P.Moreno ...?... ...?... A.Saltariche L.Saltariche(child)

Front row: S.Balban ...?.... J.Prescott C.Prescott Saliva Saliva Fiol ......?.... L.Bellido

My son and I in the Red Room in 2004 where many of photos of the evacuees were taken.
It can be seen from the picture on the left that the tiles decorating the fire place are the same as they were sixty years before.

The Reading family on the steps near the School entrance
Photo Mr J Reading

John Reading with his sister Mercy during their visit to Whitelands in 2004
Photo Mr J Reading

There was also the occasional gathering of families at the Main Hall to collect the letters sent mainly by husbands in Gibraltar. During these occasions there were obviously moments of joy but also some of sadness among the families when they gathered in the hall. My mother used to get together with other evacuees in one of our rooms where she would write letters on behalf of some evacuees to families in Gibraltar. Among the Whitelands families there were a few additions as can be seen from the list of children born while the parents lived at Whitelands. There were also the unfortunate cases of those families who lost their loved ones whilst at Whitelands. The Readings as can be seen in the photograph above were in mourning when the photograph was taken, owing to the passing away of Mrs Reading's mother. Others who lost their loved ones during their stay at Whitelands were the Harrison's, the Alecio's, the Lopez's and a few others who I have not been able to get their names. They are all buried at the different cemeteries within the Borough of Wandsworth.

The above photograph was taken in a studio in April 1941 shortly after my family arrived at Whitelands Photo J.Gingell

Mrs Martinez with her daughter and son near to the entrance to Whitelands. Photo Mr J Martinez

Mrs Martinez with her son and daughter by the steps behind the main building. Photo Mr J Martinez

The Alecio brothers Victor and Hector in the C ollege Campus. Photo Mr H Alecio

The Whitelands building consisted of three floors; the ground, the first and the top floor. The evacuees were accommodated either on the first or top floor. This meant that there must have been an average of 250 evacuees on each of the first and the top floor. Some families were related to one another and had been together as from the start of the evacuation. Many helped each other and there was an atmosphere of companionship in case of difficulties. Shopping was mostly done in groups in order to make it easier to find goods, which were scarce. If any of the evacuees knew where to find these items they would tell other evacuees in the centres. There were also the bus routes to learn. Very few evacuees knew the routes and like everything some were quick to master the combination from one place to another. My Mother and another evacuee from Whitelands got lost in the smog on one occasion and thanks to a policeman who was nearby directed them to the nearest bus stop from where they were able to get to Whitelands.

The gate to entrance and exit of the Whitelands precinct leading to Sutherland Grove. Photo by my daughter Michelle

Whitelands, as described in previous pages offered a unique environment, which was ideal for recreational and sporting facilities. Families who came to visit the residents at Whitelands also enjoyed these facilities and when the weather permitted even family picnics were organised. I recall being with other children and parents in one of such picnics, which we enjoyed very much in a pleasant surrounding of many trees that grew within the campus.

The photographs shown on this page were taken on one of the many occasions when visitors came to Whitelands. Whenever there was a football match visitors and residents watched the matches from these slopes from where the football match could be viewed in its entirety. Photographs on this page were donated by Mrs R Martinez.

Rosa Cortes when she visited her Sister-in-law Mrs Victoria Cortes.

Salvador and Maricarmen Mifsud with their aunt Mrs Victoria Cortes when they visited Whitelands.

Rosa Cortes with the Harper sisters Aida and Kitty.

Maricarmen and Salvador Mifsud visiting their aunt Mrs V. Cortes.

The building that was named the York Hotel.
Photo by Mr D Parody

By the entrance to the York Hotel from L to R Laura Ferro, …?... Olga Ferro,…Ferro, Aida Ferro, Kitty Torrilla and Violeta Torrilla. Boy in front is Pepe Luis Ferro. Photo Mrs Monteverde (nee Ferro)

The back of the building in 2006. Photo Mr D Parody

At the York Hotel in Berner Street just off Oxford Street there were 310 evacuees. The officer in charge was Mr A Mildmaz and the local representative was Mr Baw. My family was transferred to this hotel about the beginning of April 1944. Just a few months afterwards a repatriation notice with reference No.511 was placed on the hotel's notice board at the reception and which included our family name. My mother was naturally full of joy in knowing that we were finally being taken back home. During our short stay at the York Hotel I recall that one afternoon, not long before we were due to leave for Gibraltar, there was, suddenly, a huge explosion. We were about to have our tea with some sandwiches. The windows were shattered, the cups and everything was thrown all over the room. I remember that there was a lot of dust which I suppose must have been brought about by what was to be a nearby bomb blast. In later years I got to know from my mother that this explosion was due to a flying bomb that had exploded in Goodge Street area killing an evacuee. According to official records the first flying bomb hit London on the 13th June 1944. Mr M Rodriguez in his book "I, Remember" makes mention about Miss Laura Sodi from the York Hotel who was killed by a flying bomb on the 19th June 1944. Perhaps some readers may have more information whether there was some connection about the explosion I am referring and Miss Laura Sodi's incident.

The greatest cause for concern among the evacuees in London was undoubtedly the bombing. Their relatives in Gibraltar were obviously equally worried about the fate of their loved ones in London. As soon as they arrived in the UK they were already witnessing the effects of the air raids. According to official sources, the first bombs were dropped in London on the 24th August 1940. By then there were already about 12,000 evacuees in London. From the start of the Battle of Britain on the 10th July and up to the month of September the Germans were attacking principally the airfields and radar stations to defeat Britain in the air in order to prepare for their planned invasion. Then as a means of demoralising the British public into submission, the Luftwaffe started bombing British cities. This change of tactics, as seen from a military point of view, gave the RAF a much needed breathing space to recuperate losses of aircraft and pilots in order to be able to defeat the Luftwaffe in the longer term, as indeed was the case.

Children leaving London. Photo The History Place

This bombing campaign of British cities known as the Blitz, continued until May 1941. For the first two months London was bombed continuously either during the day or night. As far as London was concerned the main area was the densely populated East End dockland and gas works. There was initially an intense attack that lasted 76 consecutive days and nights. Thousands of people were killed, injured or made homeless. The fires destroyed many areas of London. Residents sought shelter wherever they could find it - many fleeing to the underground stations that sheltered nearly 200,000 people during the night. The worst single incident occurred when 450 people were killed when a bomb destroyed a school being used as an air raid shelter.
Londoners were experiencing the same terror and destruction as other Europeans had suffered previously by the German well planned war tactics.

One of the first London bombing raids. Photo The History Place

During air raids people took shelter in warehouse basements and underground stations where they slept on makeshift beds amid primitive conditions with no privacy and poor sanitation facilities.

Londoners in the tube. Photo London Illustrated News

During this period of intensive bombing many Londoners, children in particular, were evacuated to remoter areas, which in some cases lasted for several years. In the case of those for whom evacuation was not a serious option, particularly the poor of London's East End districts, they put up with the bombing. There were occasions when some people did not emerge for weeks from the underground.

A Heinkel 111 bomber over Wapping and the Isle of Dogs in the East End of London on 7 September 1940. Wikipedia Free Encyclopeida.

Mrs Lourdes Galliano has contributed on many occasions with her own personal knowledge and experience on the subject of the evacuation, including, her own book "A Rocky Passage To Exile", which I highly recommend reading. As in many other occasions, Mrs Galliano has also very kindly offered to contribute in this documentary book with her own experience about the bombing in London as explained below:

"For no apparent reason, I have lately been recalling and reliving memories of "the Blitz"– which as evacuees from Gibraltar – we lived in London during World War II.

Seventy years is a long time - in fact it can amount to practically two generations – but to the people who lived that period – those experiences can still be clear and fresh in the mind.

We arrived in London in mid August 1940 little knowing what lay ahead.

On September 7th, a Saturday in the afternoon, the Germans had plans to destroy the City of London when over 300 bombers escorted by about 600 fighters took off and flew from France towards London – and achieved surprise.

The raid that took place was so intense that it started huge fires. The first wave targeted the docks, the arsenals and gas works which let the start of huge fires. The second wave went for central London where thousands of incendiaries bombs rained down on the selected targets and also on the rows of little houses where the workers and their families lived. In an hour and a half, London received one of its heaviest daylight raids of the war. By half past six the fires were just beginning to catch hold.

The blaze was so large and fierce that all other parts of London could see the red column of smoke filling the horizon. These fires would serve as beacons for the following waves of bombers. The bombs started falling all around us and we huddled together and prayed - not knowing that this was to become our daily life for the next four years.

When the siren gave its warning we picked up our gas mask, a blanket and pillows and some warm clothes and rushed downstairs to the lounge to take up our places for the night. My mother sat on an armchair, Rosary in hand, and we girls lay on our blankets on the floor. My father would put on his steel helmet and go upstairs to the roof to fire watch for incendiary bombs with the other men in the building. Soon came the drone of the Germans planes coming closer and closer - and someone always said " ahi vienen" " they are coming", and sure enough the bombs started to fall - each thump coming closer and closer – the next one? – no – not yet – then the explosions sounded in the other direction – they had missed us - thank God we had been spared! But no time to rejoice – the next wave of bombers was close behind – and so the pattern was repeated - "ahi vienen" – on the floor – pillows over your head – thump again and again – nearer – now overhead and passed – spared again – thanks be to God!

Windows broken children crying – the lights have gone- never mind – most of us had torches at the ready - then when they had passed we would relax and try to have a little sleep, till the " all clear" sounded, then we could sit up and talk and find out what had happened outside. T he street was full of rubble and broken glass and the firemen were putting out a fire up the street - and then amazingly a van would appear – it was manned by a group of elderly ladies and they stopped to distribute cups of hot tea and a little chat - it was a most wonderful sight.

And so dawn appeared – and the enemy disappeared – till the following night – when all would be repeated. For the "Blitz" it was here to stay."

Anti-aircraft guns in Hyde Park London. Wikipedia Free Encyclopeida.

I have been told of the many experiences lived by the evacuees when they first witnessed the devastation caused by the bombing. Whenever there was an air raid warning the windows had to be covered either with a black curtain or black paint, so that no light got out. The idea was obviously to make it difficult for the Germans bombers to find a target on which to drop their bombs at night. The actual air raids usually started with the sound of sirens, which made everyone run to their allocated shelters. This was followed by the frightening noise made by the aircraft engines, which was accompanied by the firing of anti-aircraft guns pounding incessantly. All these noises mingled simultaneously with the whistling sound made by the bombs before they hit the ground and exploded.

Manolo Pincho Lancaster Gate underground station on the spot where he spent many nights with his family during the air raids. Photo Mr M Pincho

The following is how some of the evacuees described the scene when coming out of the shelter or underground after an air raid:

Harry Fernandez said, "I could never go down to the shelter. I always got a very painful toothache, which made me stay half way down the stairs. It wasn't fear, as I was a member of the fire watching team and security – ensuring that the people pulled down their black outs etc."

Another evacuee said, "I can remember the all-prevailing smell of dust and powdered brickwork, the crunch of broken glass underfoot. Sometimes you could see a house sliced in half as though cut with a knife." Another said that he remembered seeing a bath hanging out of the window just held by the plumbing works. Many evacuees remembered how tired everyone looked, by the constant lack of sleep, and the worry of what was happening to your relatives either in other centres in London or back in Gibraltar. The stress, suffered particularly by women during the bombing must have been enormous. Many of them, like my mother, never really recovered from the trauma. Some evacuees also explained seeing mines hanging from buildings by parachutes. These mines generally arrived silently after the bombers had gone, usually when the fire and rescue workers had arrived. The blast from these devices was devastating, destroying hundreds of homes for hundreds of yards and maiming or killing anyone in the area.

The Germans dropped many parachute mines, which would hang, caught up in trees for days before exploding their massive charges. These were deliberately intended to inflict terror and kill civilians in large numbers. There were also thousands of incendiary bombs that would punch through slate roofs with a noise like pebbles. The chemicals and oils contained in these bombs would burn very fast and intensely to set roofs on fire in seconds.

A typical scene of London during an air raid. Photo The History Place

During a raid there would also be the continuous noise of fire engines racing from street to street and on many occasions unable to cope with the spread of fires. There were also the bells of the ambulances rushing to the affected areas, which, usually, were many in a single raid. In the mornings, after an air raid, it was very distressing to see all the damaged buildings and occasionally even the misfortune of witnessing the dead.

The evacuees, like the rest of the Londoners, were all in constant fear for their lives. The thought of being killed by the bombing was always constant in the minds of the evacuees. Some evacuees were trained as ARP wardens and also took charge of the auxiliary fire service in their respective centres.

A street scene on the outskirts of London after an air raid. Photo The History Place

Those appointed to the task of fire watching saw many building ablaze and also witnessed the anti-aircraft guns in actions with their deafening sounds. The Ministry of Home Affairs issued booklets giving advice and the procedures to be followed after an air raid with regard to destroyed or damaged homes, the food distribution, the taking care of the homeless and the tracing of missing friends or relatives. These booklets also gave advice on how to go about claiming compensation for any losses of items of furniture, clothes etc.

A street scene in central London like that experienced by Gibraltar evacuees. Photo The History Place

Although the most affected area of London was the East, because of the docks, other areas, like central London where most of the evacuees were initially accommodated also received a lot of punishment.

The climax of the raids on London came on the 10th of May 1941 when hundreds of bombers pounded the whole area causing the highest number of casualties. Among the well known buildings to be hit were the House of Commons, the Tower of London, the Law Courts, Westminster Abbey, Buckingham Palace, St. Paul's. and the Royal Mint. On that night almost 1,500 people died and 12,000 were injured. There was no gas, water or electricity for many days afterwards.

The of St Paul's Cathedral. during an air raid. Photo The History Place

Fire fighters struggling to put out fires in London. Photo The History Place

Parks were usually filled with anti aircraft guns and devices to prepare the barrage balloons that filled most of the London skies. By May 1941 Hitler called off the intensive raids in order to move his bombers east in preparation for Germany's invasion of Russia. Despite this, the Germans carried on bombing British cities although not on such a large scale as during the period of the Blitz.

In the next pages of this section on the bombing, I will refer to the bombing incidents that affected the different evacuation centres in a very approximate chronological order. On arrival many evacuees were taken to the Fulham Receiving Centre from where they were gradually taken to their designated evacuation centres in London.

A church in Fulham destroyed by the bombing. Photo the Fulham and Hammersmith Heritage.

A crater formed by a high explosive bomb by a nearby hospital in Fulham. Photo the Fulham and Hammersmith Heritage

In Fulham there was the Empress Hall in Lillie Road. From the information that I have been able to gather there were about 750 evacuees temporarily accommodated at the Empress Hall when they arrived in September 1940. According to some sources of information this was the first evacuation centre to be bombed. At the time of the bombing the evacuees were actually in the building's car park, which had been converted into a shelter. One evacuee recalls that there were fumes everywhere and someone cried that it was poisonous gas. The word soon spread around the shelter resulting in many of the evacuees becoming very hysterical. Fortunately the utter confusion that ensued did not last very long and everything soon returned to normal. After this incident the evacuees at this centre were soon found alternative accommodation. The skating rink, with its glass-constructed dome was obviously not in any way the ideal place to accommodate people during war torn London.

The ice skating rink building that was converted into an evacuation centre. Photo the Fulham and Hammersmith Heritage

The pictures of the Fulham area as can be seen show many of buildings, including hospitals, churches, schools and private dwellings destroyed by the bombing. Other London areas showed similar scenes.

A row of houses in Fulham completely destroyed. Photo the Fulham and Hammersmith Heritage

The next evacuation centre to be affected by the bombing was the Raglan Hotel in Bedford Way on the 15 October 1940. The Raglan was not completely destroyed but it was rendered unsafe and the evacuees were moved to the National Hotel by means of a passage, which communicated both hotels. The Raglan hotel was the evacuation centre where my family was initially billeted.

Gibraltar evacuees in the tube station.
In the photo is Albert Traverso with his mother. The other evacuees are Mrs Paterson, McGrail and Balloqui.
Photo Mr A Traverso

The picture of the Gibraltar evacuees in the tube was taken on 5 October 1940. It shows some Gibraltar evacuees in the Russell Square underground railway station only a few days before the nearby Raglan Hotel was severely damaged by the bombing.

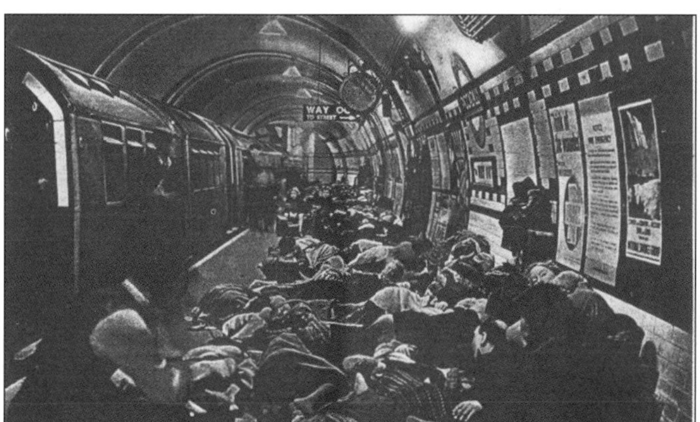

People sleeping in one of the underground stations.
Photo London Illustrated News

The other evacuation centre in Bedford Way, which was also affected, was the Shelbourne Hotel during the nights of 7/8 November 1940. In all the three hotels there were nearly 1,900 evacuees.

As a result of the transfer of so many evacuees to the National Hotel it became overcrowded and the authorities concerned had to transfer some of the evacuees to other centres. My family was transferred to Lancaster Gate where nearby there were many antiaircraft guns. My mother used to tell that the noise made by the firing of these guns was unbearable. We stayed there for a very short period and were then transferred to Whitelands College. The main criteria used for selecting the transferees were large families. Most of the families transferred were billeted either at Highlands Heath or at Whitelands College.

The composition of my family including my aunt and her three daughters was eight in all and suppose that that was the reason for our transfer to Whitelands.

The above photo shows the bombing site of the Raglan Hotel. Photo Camden Local History Office

The above photo shows the bombing site of the Shelbourne Hotel on 7/8 November 1940.
Photo Camden Local History Office

From the official archives in London, it is known that a high explosive bomb hit one of the blocks of flats on 21 September 1940. Some of these flats had, incidentally, been occupied by many German nationals who had obviously left Britain when the war with Germany was imminent. The damages caused to the blocks of flats, as can be appreciated from the photograph, were very extensive.

The flats at Courtlands destroyed by direct hit from a high explosive bomb on 21 September 1940 before the evacuees were moved there. Photo Richmond History Office

The photographs on this page of the antiaircraft guns and other devices were taken on the 10 October 1941 at Richmond Park on the Sheen Gate side. This was very near to where the Gibraltar evacuees were billeted. There is an anecdote, which I was told by one of the evacuees about an unexploded bomb that fell near Courtlands. It seems that on inspection by the bomb disposal experts it was found that the said bomb contained a lot of sawdust and sand. There was obviously a lot of speculation as to the reasons for the contents of this bomb. One of the many theories that tried to explain the mystery of these bombs was it was thought to be the work of some brave saboteurs working as forced labourers in the German ammunition factories.

A bus hit in the streets of London. Photo Mr S Lopez

I believe there were other similar cases of bombs that did not explode and which were thought to be the work of saboteurs. I do not know of any other bombing incident which affected the evacuees at Courtlands.

Antiaircraft gun site at Richmond Park.
Photo Richmond History Office

ATS Women handling a range finder.
Photo the Richmond History Office

Captain Margesson – Secretary of state for war visiting a gun site handled by ATS Women at Richmond Park.
Photo the Richmond History Office

Evacuees in the UK

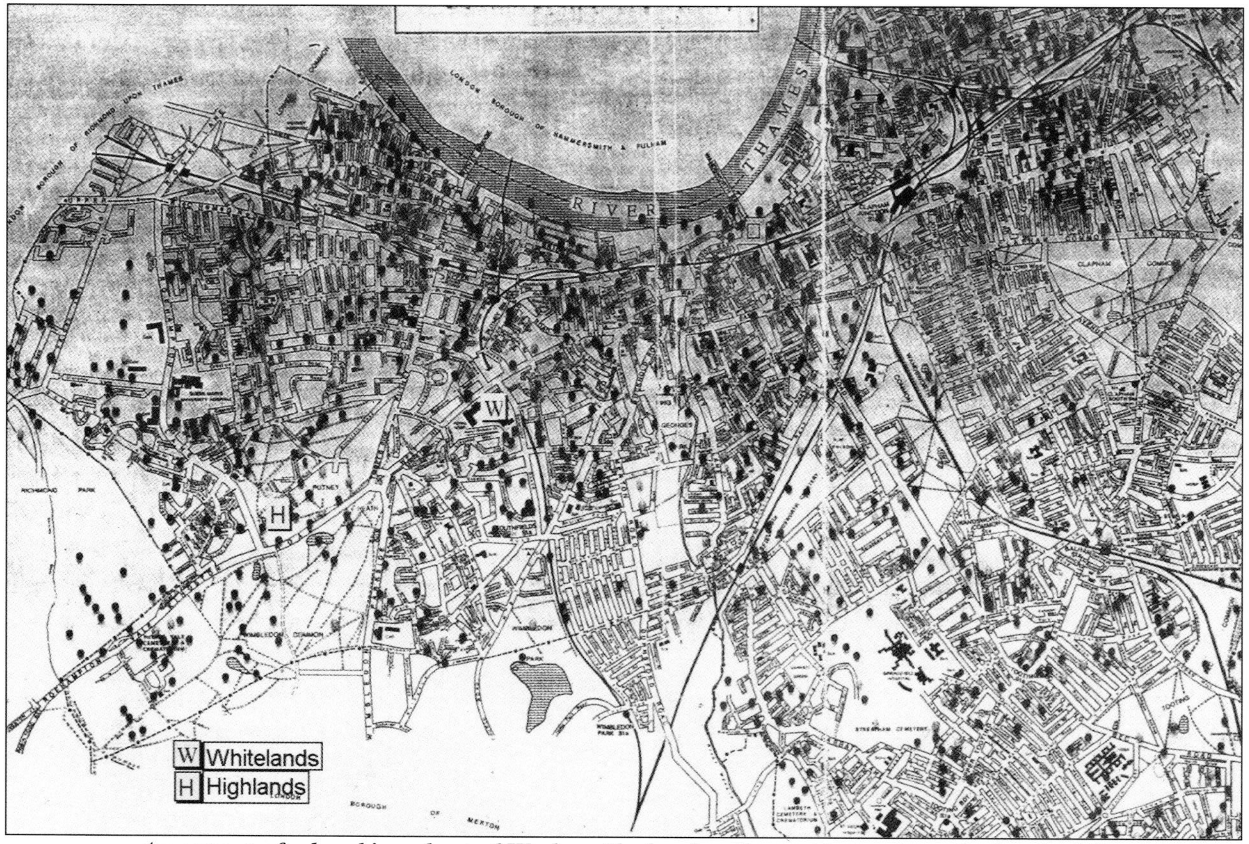

An extract of a bombing chart of Wndswotth showing the positions where the bombs fell
The positions of Whitelands and Highlands evacuation centres are indicated with a W and an H respectively.
Photo the Wandsworth Heritage Service)

The map at the top of this page shows the intensity of the bombing in the area of Wandsworth where it was calculated that during the World War Two 2,729 high explosive bombs and mines, 160 V1 bombs, 8V2 rockets and around 50,000 incendiary bombs were dropped. As a result 1,814 local civilians were killed during air raids and 8,868 were injured. Out of the 104,500 houses in the area, 6,672 were destroyed and 94,487 were damaged. In Wandsworth there were about 1,000 Gibraltar evacuees who arrived there from other centres as from April 1941 till 1944.

A public house after being hit by a high explosive bomb in November 194o. Photo the Wandsworth Heritage Service

A bus destroyed by high explosive bomb.
Photo History Place.

There was a bombing incident in which a few evacuees residing at the nearby Whitelands and Highlands evacuation centres had a miraculous escape. This incident occurred at the Black and White Milk Bar Restaurant and Dancing Hall in Putney on Sunday 7th November 1943. The bomb exploded at the corner of Putney Bridge Road and Putney High Street near the then Regal Cinema and the Putney Palace Cinema. People were leaving the two cinemas and queues were forming at the bus stop. Suddenly, a single plane swooped low, releasing a 500 kilogram bomb. According to investigations by explosive experts, this bomb had been fitted with a device designed to explode just above ground level. This technique seems to have been the major cause of the devastation.

On the evening of the incident like in many other occasions, there were a few Gibraltar evacuees in the dance hall. Among them were Gonzalo Aguilera, Aurelio Peliza, Willi Mendoza and a few others. They noticed that the bombing was getting very intense and in view of this, they decided to leave the place and return to their respective centres. Aurelio Peliza explained that a short while after they had left the dance hall, they heard a huge blast but they were not aware that it had come from the place they had left about fifteen minutes before. Salvador Lopez referring to this incident also explained that he and his friends had decided initially to go to the Black and White Milk Bar dance hall but on their way they changed their minds and went instead to visit friends at the Royal Palace Hotel evacuation centre. Both Salvador Lopez and Aurelio Peliza, who were working, at the nearby Melbray's Bakery, said that the next day on their way to work they got to know about the bombing incident and that rescue workers were still removing bodies from the rubble.

The corner of Putney Bridge Road and Putney High Street.
Photo the Wandsworth Heritage Service

There is a similar story of a family who also had miraculous escape. This family had come out of the cinema and had thought of going to the Milk Bar but in view of the anti-aircraft firing heard in the distance they decided instead to go home.

One of the family members had to get the bus from a station near the Milk Bar restaurant whilst the other members of this family had decided to go by trolley bus which was further away. In the meantime the anti-aicraft firing was intensifying with shrapnel falling near the bus queue with people having to take cover in the cinema foyer. This family member who was at the bus station walked over to another bus station where she stood a better chance of getting to her home earlier. As soon as she reached this other bus station there was whistling sound of a bomb followed by a huge explosion. There was smoke and flames that could be seen coming from where she had been standing before in the other queue. She walked back and found a very disturbing scene with bodies and injured people. Then she walked home very shocked. The other members of the family were already on the trolley bus when the bomb exploded and had thought that this other family member could have been on the bus queue. In the confusion that ensued they missed each other. When the one on the bus got home she thought the others would be there already but they were not. Thinking of the worst she went back to look for them. She had just reached the end of the road and found her family in a very distressed state. They fell into each others arms and wept. The other family members had also been looking through the dead and injured expecting to find her. It was not until the next morning that the whole family realised how much of a tragedy it had been, and how lucky they were since the crowded dance hall had taken a direct hit, and underneath was the Milk Bar. Over a hundred people had died that night many from the surrounding areas.

The bomb hit the Black and White Milk Bar at the corner of Putney Bridge Road, exploding on contact. The upper floor which was a dance hall was crowded with young people enjoying a Sunday night's entertainment. The dance floor collapsed onto the ground floor of the milk bar restaurant where there were about thirty customers. Miraculously, some received only cuts and bruises, while others were crushed by slabs of concrete. Rubble was strewn across the road and furniture store opposite had its stock reduced to matchwood. Flying glass also caused many injuries. The foyer of the Palace Cinema was used as first aid station before the injured were taken off to the neighbouring hospitals.
Then came the grim task of recovering the dead and injured from the heaped ruins. Some were lucky, escaping virtually unscathed, while others, who looked like they were unconscious, had been killed by the blast. The identification of the dead was difficult, especially in the case of women, who had become separated from their handbags containing their documents. It was weeks before some were reunited with relatives, as nobody knew to which hospital they had gone. A crane was brought to remove the large blocks of masonry and concrete. By the next day enough of the debris had been cleaned to allow the trolleybuses to pass. The final toll of casualties was 18 killed and 210 injured.

Above an extract from a report about the Black and White Milk Bar restaurant and dancing hall bombing incident. Cutting the Wandsworth Heritage Service)

The scene of destruction after the bombing. Photo the Wandsworth Heritage Service

Another interesting anecdote in connection with this bombing incident was that of Silvio Peliza and his band that had made arrangements to play at the Black and White Milk Bar dance hall on the night of the bombing. When they turned up to play they found that another band had been hired. Silvio was obviously very disappointed and felt very annoyed with the dance organiser.

After a lot of arguments and without getting much satisfaction by the way of an explanation, Silvio and his band gave up and left the place.

Relatives, friends and survivors being comforted by voluntary aid workers near the Regal Cinema. Photo the Wandsworth Heritage Service

The authorities concerned inspecting the damages. Photo the Wandsworth Heritage Service

This incident was according to official records, the worst war time incident in Wandsworth. What seems certain is that the Gibraltar evacuees had a very miraculous escape from this bombing incident.

There is a pub called The Telegraph Inn at Putney Heath, which is only a few meters from the entrance to the Highlands Heath flats. During the war evacuees who resided at Highlands Heath used to gather at this pub very often. It was a very convenient meeting place whenever there was a football match in the playing area near this pub. At the end of the match many players from the home, visiting teams and spectators gathered at the Telegraph Inn to chat about the football match and have a few drinks.

The Telegraph Inn in February 2004. Photo taken by my daughter Michelle

The Telegraph Inn during the evacuation. Photo the Wandsworth Heritage Service

According to the information supplied by the Wandsworth Museum there was an air raid in February 1944 when a high explosive bombs hit the area where the Telegraph Inn is situated. The explosion occurred at a time when there were many people in the bar. A Gibraltarian evacuee known as alias "Patente" used to work at the Telegraph Inn cleaning the place, collecting and washing the glasses etc. When the bomb exploded he was outside the building collecting the glasses from the tables. He was thrown in the air by the blast but fortunately escaped without a scratch. Many of those who were actually inside the building were service men that were perhaps enjoying a few days of leave. The majority were either killed or seriously injured by the explosion. The next major bombing incident affecting the Telegraph Inn building was caused by a flying bomb in August 1944. On this occasion the building sustained serious damage but according to the surveyors it was capable of undergoing repairs. Given this information it seems that the building was indeed repaired keeping its original structure and design as can be seen from the photograph of the Telegraph Inn in 2004.

Like in many places in London the flying bombs caused many deaths and completely destroyed many buildings. Near the Highlands Heath flats and the Telegraph Inn four flying bombs fell between 30 June and 21 August 1944.

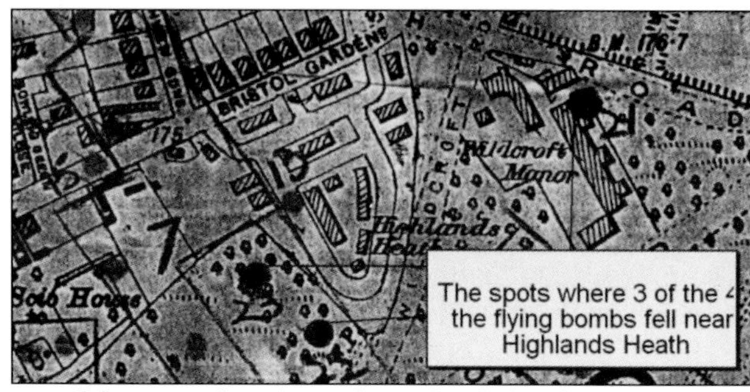

Diagram showing where the flying bombs fell. Photo the Wandsworth Heritage Service

By that time most of the evacuees accommodated at Highlands Heath had left. Luck, it seemed, was very often on the side of the Gibraltar evacuees. It has been said there was a general belief by many Londoners that the Gibraltar evacuees were blessed.

The dreaded flying bomb or doodlebug. Photo The History Place

As far as Whitelands was concerned, the official records reveal that there had been two minor bombing incidents prior to the arrival of the Gibraltar evacuees. These bombing incidents took place on the 9th October 1940 when the College suffered minor damages to its main buildings and more extensive damages to one of its houses named the Forest Lodge. The other bombing incidents occurred on the 15th November 1940 when much damage was inflicted on the Assembly Hall and roofs of the main building. A bomb also fell in one of the corners of the football ground in the campus. Since then there were no other bombing incidents within the area of Whitelands until February 1944. By then the Germany was fighting alone after Italy had surrendered in September 1943. The Russians were on the offensive and the Japanese expansion had been halted. In London the heavy aerial bombardment had receded considerably. Some of the men who stayed behind working on essential work in Gibraltar had already been allowed to take special leave to visit their relatives in London. There was, of course, an air of optimism but this seemed to be a little premature. During February and March 1944 the Luftwaffe attacked with so much strength that this spate of bombing became known as the "little blitz." or the "baby blitz" The air raid affecting Whitelands was reported by a Wandsworth newspaper as follows:

> "Putney received more attention than other areas. The raid took place in the early hours of Saturday 19th February 1944, which lasted for one and quarter hours. Among the bombs dropped were 100 incendiary containers, each holding 620 bombs. They fell over a wide area but fortunately they were of the non-explosive type. The contents of one container dropped along the length of Hazlewell Road and several houses were gutted by fire. Mayfield School and Whitelands College on West Hill were damaged and the District Line between East Putney and Southfields was closed because of an unexploded bomb in Sutherland Grove."

Wandsworth Heritage Services.

At Whitelands my mother never took us to the shelter, and therefore, we always sat in the corridor away from the windows whenever there was an air raid. She used to give two reasons for this. The first was that she believed that we stood a better chance by remaining in the main building than by going to the shelter. The shelter had been built underneath the tennis court and the actual layer of concrete must have been so thin that if one stood right underneath the tennis court, one could hear the sound of the tennis balls being hit with the racket or bouncing on the floor. Perhaps mindful of this, she used to say that in a case of direct hit the structure of the building offered better protection than the roof of the shelter. The other reason was that there was an elderly lady who lived with her daughter opposite our room who was most of the time on a wheelchair.

The corridor where we used to stay during the bombing. Photo taken by my daughter Michelle

My mother said that she felt sorry to leave this elderly lady alone with her daughter in the corridor when the rest went to the shelter. I think the name of this lady was Mrs Hortencia Barea related to the Pitto family. The night of the bombing we were all in the corridor. I distinctively remember when we got to know that the building had been hit. Then we started to leave the building and I noticed that the corridor was very badly lit and there was a lot of smoke. This was probably due to the electricity supply being cut off and the smoke must have come from the fire caused by the incendiary bombs.

The roof of the Whitelands College burning. Photo the Wandsworth Heritage Service

We were not very far from the fire escape doors and we soon were out of the building. My mother covered me with blankets and placed me near a tree well distant from the building. I also remember that from this spot I could see, behind the bare branches, the flames protruding from the roof and some of the windows. In the meantime I think my mother and my two older brothers went to salvage some of our belongings in the two rooms allocated to us.
It was in the early hours of the morning of Saturday 19 February 1944. The UK Met Office records showed that that morning it had been snowing slightly and the weather was freezing. After a very long while I remember that an army type lorry arrived and took us away. During my research I found out that my family was taken to a monastery at Lancaster Gate where we were given some hot drinks and then slept for the rest of the night. A few evacuees were offered to stay in some of the nearby houses along Sutherland Grove Road.

The spot from where I watched Whitelands roof burning. Photo by my daughter Michelle

Other evacuees were taken to other evacuation centres with the bulk transferred to a temporary centre in called the Camberwell Institute in Peckham Rye. See page 178 for details.
Other schools in the area near the Whitelands College were also hit within the same period. The St Mary's Church of England School in Felsham Road was hit the same night as the Whitelands College. The roof of this school was also destroyed.
Another famous school called the Mayfield School in Wandsworth was also hit during the same bombing period.

The Mayfield School in Wandsworth bombed on 25th February 1944. Photo the Wandworth Heritage Service

An elderly people's home was also hit very badly as can be gathered from a cutting shown below from the South Western Star newspaper dated Friday 25th February 1944.

AGED PEOPLE'S HOME HIT BY BOMB

Several people were killed at a home for the aged when part of the building in which they were sleeping were demolished by a bomb. Many of the survivors were later transferred to other institutions.

Newspaper cutting by the Wandsworth Heritage Service.

Between the nights of the 18th and 20th of February 1944, in addition to Whitelands bombing three other evacuation centres had been hit as follows:
A high explosive bomb hit the King's College at Campden Hill Road with residents having to be evacuated to neighbouring hostels. Although there were no casualties from the actual bombing it was reported that a Mr Joseph De Soiza had suffered a heart attack during the incident and died the next day at the hospital. Incendiary bombs also hit the Royal Stuart Hotel at Crowmwell Road, burning the roof of the hotel. The evacuees were transferred to the Moscow Mansion Buildings.
Incendiary bombs also hit the Constance Hotel at 23 Lancaster Gate. Residents there were moved to the evacuation centre at 100 Lancaster Gate. Fortunately, there were no casualties in any of these bombing incidents. I have gathered a few anecdotes related to the night of the bombing of Whitelands College from some of evacuees and which I have summarised in the next page.

Hector Alecio, although very young, he was already well aware that the evacuees were enjoying a comparatively quiet time in Whitelands after the initial heavy bombing suffered during the Blitz. He explained that on the night of the bombing of Whitelands, some evacuees got to know that the Germans were dropping lots of incendiary bombs to prepare the way for a spate of heavy bombing. That night Hector recalls that there were big fires all over London.

Yolanda Bacarese (now Mrs Tribello)
"My family were all in the shelter except my uncle Angel D'Alorto who was on fire watching duties. He had just gone to tell my aunts Aurelia D'Alorto and Francisca Pratts to rush to the shelter but before reaching the shelter we got to know that an incendiary bomb had hit the room where we lived. We later found that everything we had had been burnt, including my toys."

Arturo Harper
"That night many of the residents had gone early to the shelter. My father was like many other men on fire watching duties. He noticed from experience that there was going to be an air raid that night. He went to tell those who were still in their rooms to move quickly to the shelter. When they were about to go down to the shelter, the word got round very quickly that the building had been hit by a bomb. Those who were already in the shelter also got to know somehow of the bombing and wanted to get out of the shelter. Inevitably there were some clashes along the staircase between those who wanted to get in and those who wanted to get out of the shelter. There was for a while a great confusion which lasted until eventually everybody began to realise that they had to leave the building. By that time there was a lot of smoke in the corridors and many panicked and some even fainted."

Salvador Lopez gave a very vivid account of the night of the bombing. The following is as an extract of his recollections:
"That night we were extra vigilant, someone gave us to understand that he had seen what seemed to be small parachutes coming down with baskets attached. We looked in the direction that this person was pointing and noticed that these parachutes were released from a container when reaching a certain height and were then exploding all around the periphery of the building. Consequently, after a while there were fires all around us. Some of these fires managed to penetrate the building. All the firewatchers had stirrup pumps and buckets full of water. Everybody did a magnificent job in trying to put out the fires. As I was going to my flat, I heard a woman shouting that there was a fire on the stairs. I went with my stirrup pump and bucket and saw that a bomb had come through the window and the whole stair was full of black smoke. There was a horrific smell of acid. I placed a wet handkerchief covering my mouth and nose and tied it to the back of my neck. I aimed the hose in the direction of the fire and started pumping. I used half a bucket of water but the fire was just as fierce after several attempts with the pump. I managed to find a bucket and decided to get the water from a bathroom nearby and poured it on the fire. By that time almost everybody had left the building. One of the bombs had gone through the rafters and now the whole top floor was on fire. When I was coming down the stairs I heard lots of noises and got to know that my family were looking for me." Salvador also explained that when he left the building with his brothers he sat with the rest of the residents on the grass. At that moment and as a 14-year-old boy he said that he remembered feeling very proud of having helped to put out the fire. He, said, " I remember that they were all clutched to whatever possession they had managed to collect and watched how the rooms were burning little by little. Most of the women and children were grouped in the playing fields surrounding the building whilst the grown-ups salvaged personal effects and helped as best as they could. The fire brigade had been very busy that night and by the time they arrived at Whitelands the roof of the building was completely ablaze. All the evacuees who lived on the top floor had lost all their possessions."

Luis Saltariche who was then about 4 or 5 years old remembered how he was grabbed and then carried on the shoulder of a firewatcher who took him to the playground.

Zoriada Hermida, (now Mrs Santos) who was then about 11 recalled that they lived on the top floor. She explained that when they came out of the shelter all they possessed was what they were wearing. "My mother had a handbag where we kept our passports and some money – the rest of our belongings which were in our room were lost in the fire,"

Aurelio Bellido
Aurelio was on leave after serving in the dreaded Artic Convoys on **HMS Fulknore.** He had been celebrating his reunion with his family at Whitelands a few hours before the bombing. He had one too many and went straight to bed. Alfredo Balban who knew that Aurelio was still sleeping went into the room and carried Aurelio on his shoulder until he was safely out of the building.

Claudio Olivero
He was that night on shift work and did not get to know about the bombing until he arrived at Whitelands from work at about six in the morning. He said that when he arrived there was a lot of smoke coming from the building and although I told the fire brigade and the police that my family and I lived at Whitelands they would not let me pass.

Charlie Gibson
He was about 4 years and had spent the whole of that night crying from the time he left Whitelands until he reached the other centre. Charlie explained the reasons for this as follows: "My mother in the panic that ensued and to get out quickly from the burning building, accidentally pierced a safety in my chest's skin." Charlie was obviously in a terrible pain and was crying all the way until his mother found out that it was the safety pin that made him cry all the time.

John Reading
He was about 4 years old and recollects that when they went back the next day to pick up their belongings he was very saddened to see the state of his toys. "I had a toy horse, which was made of some sort of cardboard material. When we entered our room, the toy horse was floating and disintegrated in the water that been poured by the fire fighters to extinguish the fire"

Adolfo Bosio
"We returned to Whitelands the day after the bombing to look for our things and found that everything was burnt. On top of a burnt chest of drawers there were a few coins stuck together." The coins because of the intense heat had been fused together on the point of melting as can be seen in the picture. The three coins consisted of a 2s. 6d, a 2s and 6d coin. They are still kept by Adolfo as a memento of that terrible night at Whitelands College.

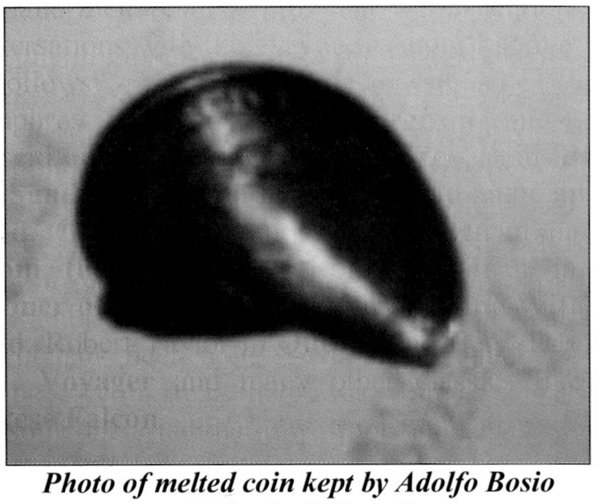

Photo of melted coin kept by Adolfo Bosio
Photo by J.Gingell

Pepi Davis. (Now Mrs Bula)
"Before the air raid started, I had been to The Plaza cinema at the end of Sutherland Grove and remember that I had been to see the film **Now, Voyager** starring Bette Davis and one of my favourite actors of the time – Paul Henreid"
Many of those who remember explained that on the night of the bombing some of the evacuees were taken to private houses in the periphery of Whitelands. They said that they were given tea and biscuits. Below are some of the houses along Sutherlands Grove where most probably some evacuees spent the night when Whitelands was bombed.

The houses in Sutherland Grove Road.
Photo by my daughter Michelle

The Whitelands centre, from the information I have been able to gather, was perhaps the only centre where the evacuees had attempted to put out the fire caused by incendiary bombs but naturally without succeeding and luckily without any casualties.
On the same night of the Whitelands' bombing there were other buildings similarly bombed, regrettably with casualties, as can be seen from an extract of a Wandsworth newspaper copied below:

THREE FIREWATCHERS LOSE THEIR LIVES

Commercial premises which were struck by incendiaries caught fire and three firewatchers, Messrs. Holloway, Greenaway, and Aird, were trapped and lost their lives.
In another area a bomb damaged a branch bank, a church, and other premises. Several people were injured by flying glass.

FAMILY UNDER DEBRIS

For some hours after the raid rescue workers were still digging for members of a family named Smith who were believed to be trapped under the debris of a large house converted to flats, which [illegible]

THE WEDDING PROCEEDED

A Roman Catholic church suffered from blast. A wedding which had been arranged to take place was held, despite the damage. Two other churches were damaged. A nun at a convent in the neighbourhood said "Although there was a lot of dam

Wandsworth newspaper cutting from the Wandsworth Heritage Services

Some years later when we talked at home about the evacuation etc, my mother used to tell me that when she came out of the building she noticed that in every direction that she looked there were buildings on fire. She used to say that it seemed as if the whole of London was burning that night.

The map showing the position of the bombs dropped at Whitelands.
Photo the Wandsworth Heritage Service

Arthur Harper explained that on his returned to Whiteland to collect some of the belongings left behind, he noticed that on the ground near the main building there were two bombs. The bombs were embedded and slightly covered by grass and leaves. The bombs were small in size and of incendiary type similar to the ones shown in the diagram below:

Incendiary bombs similar to the ones seen by Arthur Harper.
Photo Museum of London

The Wandsworth newspaper the South Western Star of the 25th February 1944 reporting on the air raids included the following about the bombing of Whitelands:

ROOF OF REFUGEE BUILDING BURNT

The roof of a building in which 500 refugees from Gibraltar were billeted was set on fire by incendiaries. None of the refugees were injured. Next day they returned to salvage their possessions. Damage was done mainly to the roof.
Delayed action bombs were dropped on several places. A Mr Sheridan said, "Even the bombs that didn't explode seemed to shake the ground like an earthquake."
A school from which the children had been evacuated was hit by incendiaries. The caretaker Mr Davenport, his wife and their two daughters were in their shelter at the time. Mrs Davenport told a reporter "We could not get out at first because of burning incendiaries at the front, but we managed to get out at the back."

Copy from a Wandsworth newspaper reporting the bombing of Whitelands College. Cutting the Wandsworth Heritage Service

Below is an extract from a letter sent by the Whitelands College Seceretary Miss L S James when she was reporting the bombing incident to the Whiteland's Central Board of Finance.

"Dear Mr Sawden,

I am sorry I have to report that the College has once again been unlucky and was hit by incendiary bombs on Friday. The roof and the top storey of the central block of the building have been severely damaged by fire. The two wings are intact except for two small holes in the roof of the East wing. The Chapel is all right. I am glad to say that the refugees were evacuated from the building at once and that there were no casualties. "

Many of the residents at Whitelands were moved temporarily to a building, which in later years was referred to by many evacuees as simply Peckham. The manager of Whitelands College, Mr Davies, accompanied the evacuees to this place in Peckham Rye. I suppose that the reason for this was that he must have remained responsible, through the Ministry of Health, for the evacuees assigned to him as the officer in charge. The building belonged to the Camberwell Institution and it was in Gordon /Consort Road. Prior to the war it was known as the Board of Guardians' Workhouse. It was a very dilapidated building and it had been used for some time as a home for destitute people and was then officially known as the Camberwell Institution.

The building at Peckham were evacuees were accommodated after Whitelands' bombing. Photo Southwark Local History Studies Office

I recall that we all slept in a large room with two rows of beds one on each side of the room with a passage in the middle: just like hospital wards in the old days. The beds were placed very close to each other. There was a partition between this room and another room where there were two similar rows of beds.

Above what the rooms looked liked.
Photo Southwark Local History Studies Office.

I believe one room was for women, and children up to the age of twelve and the other room for men and boys from 13 upwards.

The rooms were lit with very small gas lamps fitted on the wall above the beds. I remember that out of curiosity I touched the lit gauze in the lamp. The gauze was so fragile, that it disintegrated completely the minute I touched it. After speaking to someone who still remembered this building in Peckham he assured me that the main reasons why we left Peckham was because of the intense bombing and firing at enemy aircraft. I remember too that my mother used to tell me that the bombing in this area was so intense that representations were made to the Ministry of Health to take us somewhere else. There were other evacuees who believe that the reason why the area received so much bombardment was because there were military installations right underneath the building. One evacuee assured me that he had seen tanks and guns underneath the building. From this transit centre at Peckham Rye families were sent to different evacuation centres in London. According to well-documented reports that I received from contacts related with my research in the UK, Camberwell and Peckham Rye were one of the most heavily bombed areas of London. 90% of the houses in the area were damaged, 1,000 people were killed and over 5,000 were seriously injured.

The place was built in 1878 as a workhouse by the Camberwell Board of Guardian for inmates to perform manual work such as chopping wood by men while women were employed doing laundry. In 1933 it was taken over by the London County Council as a reception centre for homeless men. It was closed in 1986 and the building demolished in 1996.

Judging from the sequence of my family movements since the bombing at Whitelands, I reckon that we must have been living at this building in Peckham Rye for about a couple of weeks or so. We left Peckham Rye and were then transferred to the York Hotel, at Berner Street just off Oxford Street.

Shortly after arriving in London there was a bombing incident at the Royal Palace Hotel causing injuries to Mrs Lara and her daughter. Mrs Lara suffered severe injuries to her breast and a piece of shrapnel hit Mrs Lara's daughter on her right leg which was also severely burned by the acids contained in these types of bombs. Mrs Bugeja still wears these acid scars on her right leg. Both Mrs Lara and her daughter were conveyed to St.Mary Abbott's Hospital where Mrs Lara's mother had already been admitted because of some ailments in her legs. Whilst in hospital Mrs Lara was also very concerned about the fate of her other three children: Joe, Jimmy and Mati of whom she had not heard since the bombing incident. After some enquiries by the hospital staff, Mrs Lara was told that her children were well and safe. But this was not the end of the Lara's bombing ordeal. St Mary Abbott's Hospital was also bombed shortly after on Saturday 14th September 1940 resulting in the first Gibraltar evacuee casualty. As a result of this bombing the Laras were transferred to another hospital in Staines.

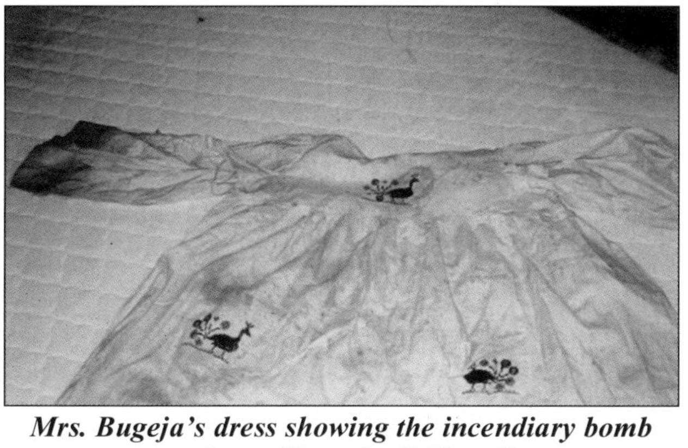

Mrs. Bugeja's dress showing the incendiary bomb stains. Photo by J.Gingell

There was another incident when Alec Grech, who was two years old, was taken with indigestion disorder to St Mary Abbott's Hospital in Kensington. Whilst there a flying bomb hit the hospital on the 17th June 1944 killing many people, including patients, but luckily, Alec was apparently the only child who survived in the children's ward. Alec's family was residing at the King's College when they heard the explosion.

Evacuees went to tell Alec's father that the hospital had been hit by a flying bomb and that only one child had survived. Mr.Grech without telling his wife rushed to hospital to find what happened. Alec's father took his friend with him because he did not dare to find whether it was his son who had survived the explosion. The surviving boy suffered head and face injuries which made it very difficult to identify. Mr. Grech was obviously very much relieved when at last his friend emerged from the damaged hospital to tell him that his son was alive.

Harry Fernandez, Alec's brother-in-law remembers witnessing a horrible scene when he saw many people killed near a tobacconist shop by the De Vere Gardens. This incident was caused accidentally by a shell fired from one of the A.A. guns in Hyde Park. Among the dead was a lady who Harry recognized as only an hour before she had been to Harrods where Harry was working and spent about £80 – a lot of money during the war. "When I saw her next she was lying on the street in a pool of blood," said Harry.

Near to the evacuation centres in Kensington High Street was the Lady of Victories Church which was run by nuns during the war. In one of the early air raids on the 13th September 1940 this church was badly hit by a high explosive bomb. As can be seen from the photograph it was very extensively damaged. In the photograph there are Gibraltar evacuees looking at the damages. The evacuees are on the left Mrs Magdalena Schembri, in the centre Miss Flori Schembri (now Mrs Ballard) and on the far right is Miss Violet Yeo (now Mrs Morello).

The Lady of Victories Church after the bombing on the 13th September 1940. Photo Mr P Cano

A German bomber crashed between the King's College and the Duchess of Bedford evacuation centres. Mrs.Mariola Summerfield(nee Benvenuto), then a sixteen year-old evacuee at the Duchess of Bedford evacuation centre explained briefly what had happened. "When the bomber crashed we were in the shelter and many of us heard a sudden thud. After the all clear was sounded, we came out of the shelter and immediately we saw this massive aircraft lying on the road between the buildings of the Duchess of Bedford and the King's College. It was still smoldering but apparently there had been no explosion or fire. We were not allowed to get near and all those people residing along the road were told to stay well away from the aircraft. Some of the older evacuees commented that it seemed that the aircraft had dropped whatever bombs it was carrying before crashing because otherwise there would have been some explosions. It was also noticed that one of the aircraft propellers had apparently come off its shaft, presumably on impact, and had gone hurling through a window on the first floor of the Duchess of Bedford centre. In its path, the propeller had passed over a cot where moments before going to the shelter a baby had been sleeping. The wrecked aircraft was cleared very quickly by the fire fighters and the salvage squad."

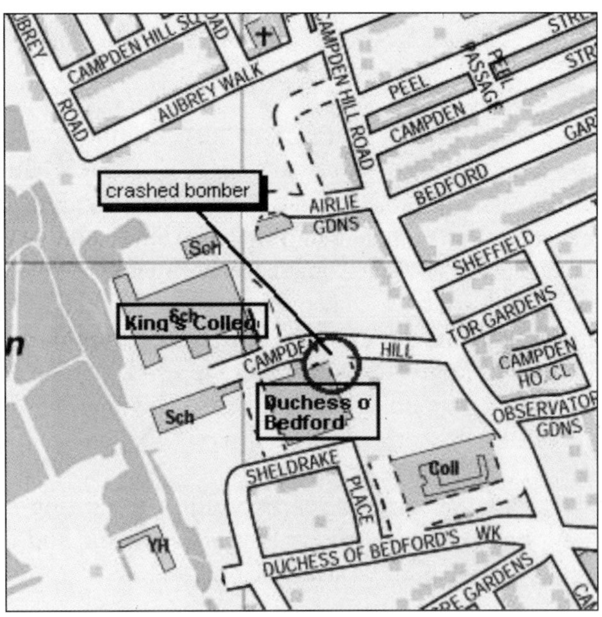

Sketch showing where the German bomber crashed. Sketch created by J.Gingell

I was told by another evacuee that the incident was reported in one of the leading newspapers in London showing a picture of the aircraft with evacuees standing outdoors during the night. It was also reported that the German crew had been apprehended.

Mrs Mariola Summerfield still keeps a German pilot's cap badge which she found at the site of the crash. Many evacuee children collected pieces of shrapnel which they exchanged. Others like Victor Infante of Marlborough Court found part of a bomb component which he brought with him and still keeps it as a souvenir.

Above a bomb component found and retained as a souvenir by Victor Infante. Photo by Mr V Infante

At the same time that the German bomber crashed, some clusters of bombs also fell near the area of the Duchess of Bedford and the Kings College. Before that night's bombing, Silvio Peliza and his band had been playing at the Royal Palace Hotel. Normally, when they finished playing they used to carry their instruments to the next arranged dance venue which on that occasion was to be the Duchess of Bedford. But that night they were tired and they decided to leave the instruments at the Royal Palace Hotel until the next day. The place at the Duchess of Bedford where Silvio had intended to leave the instruments for the next night's performance was very badly damaged by one of the bombs that hit the Duchess of Bedford.

Many Gibraltar evacuees were engaged as air raid wardens in their respective centres. Below is a copy of the certificate appointing Mr. Manuel Infante as an Air Raid Warden at Marlborough Court.

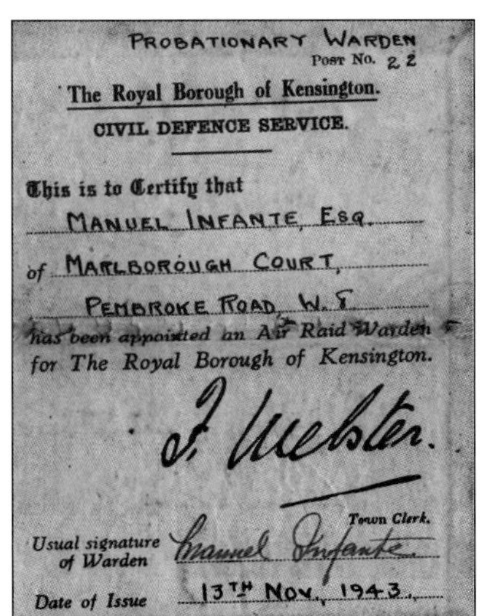

PROBATIONARY WARDEN
Post No. 22

The Royal Borough of Kensington.

CIVIL DEFENCE SERVICE.

This is to Certify that MANUEL INFANTE, ESQ. of MARLBOROUGH COURT, PEMBROKE ROAD, W. 8 has been appointed an Air Raid Warden for The Royal Borough of Kensington.

J. Webster
Town Clerk.

Usual signature of Warden: Manuel Infante

Date of Issue: 13TH NOV., 1943.

Mr. Infante's Warden Certificate.

Within weeks of the arrival of the evacuees in the UK and a week after the start of the Blitz saw the first Gibraltar casualty on the 14th September 1940. Fourteen months old Mario Massetti from the Royal Palace Hotel was at the time at St Mary Abbott's Hospital in Kensington with his brother Angel, who escaped with only minor injuries. In the hospital, were also at the time, three members of the Lara family (see page on bombing in Kensington). The next fatal casualty was that of Mr Henry Balestrino at the Dean Hotel on the 18th April 1941. He was a firewatcher and apparently he came out of the shelter to check that everything was all right when suddenly there was an explosion, which killed him instantly. The evacuees had to leave the shelter with some difficulty because part of the pavement had been lifted by the blast and was blocking the exit of the shelter. After a lot of effort by the fire fighters etc to clear the rubble the residents of the Dean Hotel managed to get out. Once out, they noticed that the Dean Hotel had been completely destroyed and also learned about the death of Mr Balestrino who only moments before had been with them in the shelter.

The evacuees were taken away from the scene of the disaster to other places. Mrs Chini and daughter Elena, as always, locked the doors of their rooms before going to the shelter and carried the keys with them. Mrs Chini, in the confusion, inadvertently kept the keys to her room in her pocket. The family of Miss Elena Chini who later married Mr Manuel Infante still keeps the keys to their rooms at the Dean Hotel as an evacuation memorabilia and most probably the only key left of the Dean Hotel.

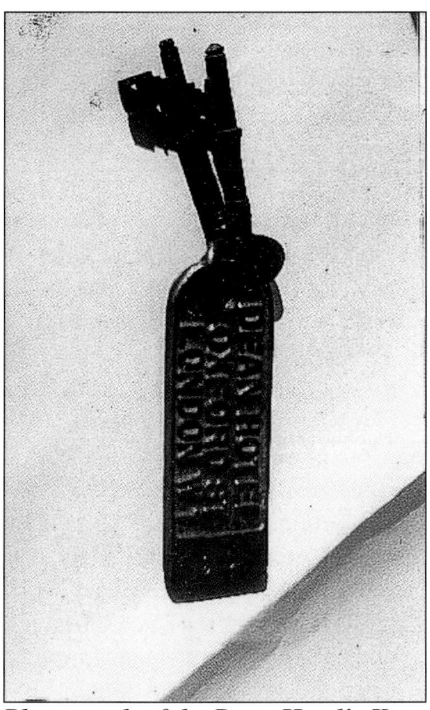

Photograph of the Dean Hotel's Keys. Photo by Mr M Infante

The Harewood and the British Empire Hotels were also hit on that same day but all the casualties reported were injuries of a minor nature, although the buildings were extensively damaged. The next fatal victim as a result of high explosive bombs was Miss Gardenia Morello, an evacuee from Lancaster Gate. It occurred during a day raid when Miss Morello took shelter in a nearby building and was killed by the bomb blast.

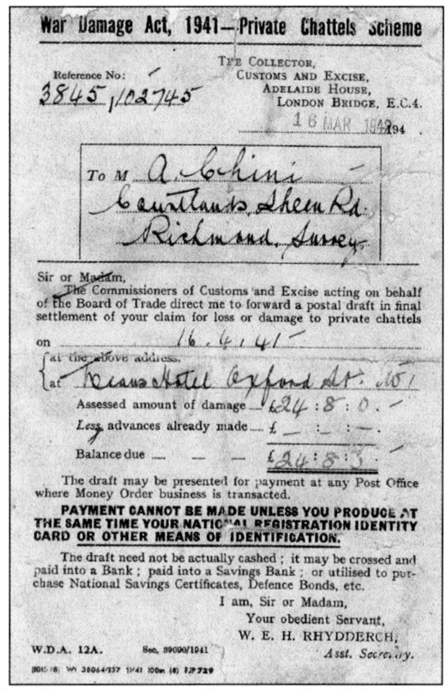

War Damage Act, 1941—Private Chattels Scheme

Reference No: 3845/102745

The Collector,
Customs and Excise,
Adelaide House,
London Bridge, E.C.4.
16 MAR 1942 194

To M A. Chini
Courtlands, Sheen Rd.
Richmond, Surrey

Sir or Madam,
The Commissioners of Customs and Excise acting on behalf of the Board of Trade direct me to forward a postal draft in final settlement of your claim for loss or damage to private chattels on 16.4.41
~~at the above address.~~
at Dean Hotel Oxford St. W1

Assessed amount of damage £24 : 8 : 0.
Less advances already made £ — : — : —.
Balance due £24 : 8 : 0.

The draft may be presented for payment at any Post Office where Money Order business is transacted.

PAYMENT CANNOT BE MADE UNLESS YOU PRODUCE AT THE SAME TIME YOUR NATIONAL REGISTRATION IDENTITY CARD OR OTHER MEANS OF IDENTIFICATION.

The draft need not be actually cashed; it may be crossed and paid into a Bank; paid into a Savings Bank; or utilised to purchase National Savings Certificates, Defence Bonds, etc.

I am, Sir or Madam,
Your obedient Servant,
W. E. H. RHYDDERCH,
Asst. Secretary.

W.D.A. 12A. Sec. 39090/1941

Receipt for compensation received by Mrs Chini for damages to her belongings in the Dean Hotel bombing. Copy Mr M Infante

There were no more fatal casualties until the onset of the flying bombs, which started from the 13th June 1944 causing the deaths of six evacuees. By then the evacuees were only a few weeks from being repatriated. The flying bomb victims in chronological order were: Mr Francisco Pereira from Linden Hall on the 17th June 1944, Miss Laura Sodi from the York Hotel in Goodge Street on 19th June 1944. On the 30th June 1944 Mrs Joaquina Ryan and her son Andrew were killed at the Australiasian Hospital in Dr Barnardo's Homes.

The following are newspaper cuttings reporting the flying bomb incident at Dr Barnardo's home and the killing of the Gibraltar evacuees.

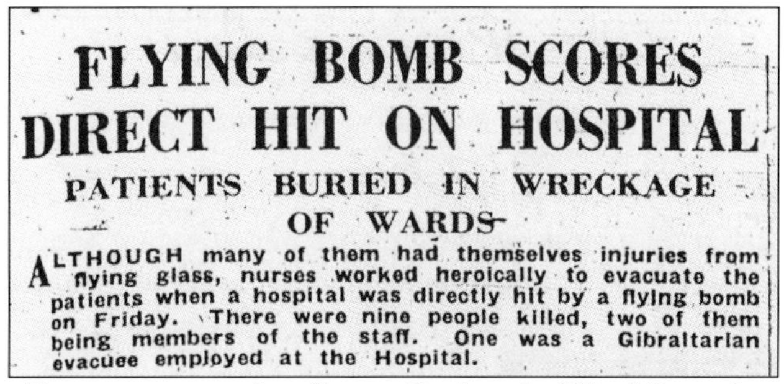

FLYING BOMB SCORES DIRECT HIT ON HOSPITAL

PATIENTS BURIED IN WRECKAGE OF WARDS

ALTHOUGH many of them had themselves injuries from flying glass, nurses worked heroically to evacuate the patients when a hospital was directly hit by a flying bomb on Friday. There were nine people killed, two of them being members of the staff. One was a Gibraltarian evacuee employed at the Hospital.

Newspaper story heading. Cutting the Ilford Recorder

The bomb crashed between two of the single-story wards, almost completely destroying both. All the other wards were damaged. One of the nurses had a miraculous escape. She was standing outside a ward next to one of those destroyed, when she heard the bomb coming and stepped behind the blast wall at the entrance to the ward. There was a deafening roar and a cloud of dust went up. One of the patients not far from the nurse was killed.

Almost at once rescuers were busy among the heaps of shattered wood and brickwork which were all that remained of the wards.

The nursing staff evacuated the patients from the wards, and put them on the lawn outside the hospital where they were given cups of tea while they waited for the ambulances which were to take them to other hospitals. The patients, who included men and women appeared to be quite composed.

When the patients had been attended to, the nursing staff were busy getting out the beds, and other articles from the hospital.

Close to the Hospital is a Day Nursery where war-working mothers leave their children.

This building had its windows blown out and suffered other damage, but the children and staff were all in the brick surface shelter a few yards away. The children had been taken to the shelter. On this occasion such members of the staff who remained in the Nursery went to the shelter when they heard the bomb approaching.

A number of houses in which Gibraltarians evacuees are quartered were damaged and so were other houses in neighbouring roads. A fire station also lost its windows.

The Matron of the hospital said afterwards, "We were flooded with help of all kinds from people of whom I could keep no record, and I should like to express to them our very great gratitude. The work of the Civil Defence and ambulance services was beyond all

Newspaper coverage of flying bomb incident.
Cutting the Ilford Recorder

In connection with this bombing incident at Dr Barnardo's, it is interesting to mention that Henry Massetti was at the same hospital with a sprained ankle on a bed beside Andrew Ryan who was lying on a mattress on the floor because there were no more beds available.

RYAN, Andrew, age 22. Son of William Ryan, of 4 Cumberland Road, Gibraltar, and of Joaquina Ryan. 30 June 1944, at Australasian Hospital, Barkingside.

RYAN, Joaquina, age 50. Wife of William Ryan, of 4 Cumberland Road, Gibraltar. 30 June 1944, at Australasian Hospital, Barkingside

Extract from the list of casualties showing the names of Mrs Ryan and son Andrew. Cutting the Ilford Recorder

Henry's mother decided to take her son out of the hospital because she felt very apprehensive about the bombing and Andrew Ryan took over Henry's bed a few hours before the blast.

The front wing of the Australasian Hospital at Dr Barnardo's Homes. Photo Mr E Holt

Another evacuee, Victor Gonzalez, gave his account of moments before the flying bomb hit the hospital. He said: "We were in the school play ground when the teacher came rushing and told all the children to run to the shelter. A while later we heard a tremendous explosion. The floor of the shelter seemed to have lifted and there was a lot of dust everywhere. When eventually we came out of the shelter we got to know that the hospital at Dr Barnardo's had been hit and that there were casualties. I also remember seeing an ambulance which had its doors wide open and could see the corpses covered with sheets and which impressed me for the rest of my life."

The other two flying bomb casualties were that of Mrs Rosa Vella and Mrs Dolores Garcia from Kensington Palace Mansion on the 18th July 1944 when they were preparing their luggage to be transferred to Northern Ireland.

Altogether, three evacuees died from conventional bombing and in just one month six evacuees fell victims of the flying bombs. Taking into account that there were over 12,000 evacuees in London there is a consensus of opinion that the evacuees had been extremely lucky.

As mentioned in the section about the bombing, the Gibraltar evacuees arrived in London at the very height of the Battle of Britain. Wartime London, from where the great majority of the British children had been evacuated to other safer places, was not the ideal place to attend school. The bombing naturally, placed major obstacles when trying to make the necessary arrangements for the Gibraltar children to attend school. Mothers were understandably apprehensive to send their children to distant schools. Consequently, arrangements were made as far as possible, for children to attend school within their respective centres or as near as possible but not more than a couple of miles away. Added to this was the fact that the Gibraltar children took sometime to get used to living in London.

Children in a school near the Thackeray Hotel. In the photo are Francis Borge, Charles Gonzalez and Vicky Perera. Photo Mrs Desoiza

The majority of the Gibraltar children had had their schooling disrupted by the war, due to the time spent in French Morocco, the sea journeys before arriving in the UK and the natural difficulty to adapt to normal school routine in London. All in all, it took nearly a year for the majority of the children to be able to start attending school on a regular basis. The other obstacle was the appointment of the necessary teaching staff for nearly 3,000 children of school age ranging from 5 to 16 years old. There were very few teachers available in London, as the majority of them had been enlisted. Many of the teachers were women plus a few men who had to be recruited from among some of the evacuees who had no qualifications and not much teaching experience either. There were also some English teachers who initially had some difficulties in communicating with many of children, particularly those in the primary age group, who were not very fluent with their English. Arrangements were made to deal with these difficulties by grouping the Gibraltar children in all their respective evacuation centres. Some buildings like the Victoria and Albert Museum had some of the rooms converted in classrooms.

There were some cases of children of different ages in the same classroom and some who did not attend school at all during their time in London. As an anecdote, Sergio Martinez said that the cost of the bus journey to the Victoria and Albert Museum School was 1 ½ pence (0.6p) and that there was a Gibraltarian, Mr Benady, who had been employed as a bus collector since before the war. Because he was Gibraltarian some of the children tried to take advantage to travel free to school. By concentrating many of the children within a centre it had its drawback in the sense that it affected their chance of practising English as the children tended to speak with each other in the vernacular. The curriculum consisted mostly of elementary subjects like reading, writing and arithmetic.

Below are cuttings from the Ilford Recorder commenting about the Gibraltar school children at Dr Barnardo's Home.

YOUNG BRITISH SUBJECTS ARE LEARNING ENGLISH HERE

IN a hall in the grounds of Dr. Barnardo's Girls' Village Homes at Barkingside, a young Ilford schoolmaster and his assistants are teaching 300 young British subjects to speak English, and he is finding it an intriguing experience and, in return, is acquiring some phrases of Spanish.

The young scholars of this schoolmaster – Mr. Emmett – come from Gibraltar. Early last summer they and their mothers, together with some elderly men, were evacuated from "The Rock," as it is affectionately known among this little colony of some 800. Some of them went to French Morocco at first, but when the French collapsed they were sent back to Gibraltar and then embarked for Britain. Many of them had a long and very arduous sea journey before they reached Barkingside in the care of Mr. Victor Ramagge, who before the war owned a flourishing stationer's business on the Rock, and is now a voluntary worker in charge of a large family. He is Assistant Commandant at Barkingside.

KEEN TO LEARN

Mr. Emmett told me that he found the children very anxious to attend school, and many were sorry that they could go only for half of each day, for the boys attend one session and the girls the other. He had found them very keen on painting and drawing and exceedingly quick to learn. Some of the elder children had learned English in Gibraltar, but the younger ones had to be taught, and were just learning.

What he had noticed above all else was the extreme pride the children took in the fact that they were British subjects. They constantly referred to that.

Mr. Ramagge spoke with deep appreciation of the work that had been done for his "family" by the women of the W.V.S. The W.V.S. prepared the Village for the guests from Gibraltar, and were there ready and waiting when they arrived, some of them at 3.0 in the morning. Since then they had done a great many things, among the chief being to supply clothing, which is particularly necessary in the cold weather for people who have known no cold weather.

Mr. Ramagge desired to thank them all for what they had done.

But the healthy, smiling faces of the children were probably the best thanks that could have been given to the W.V.S. workers.

Cutting from Ilford Recorder.

Governor of Gibraltar Lt General Sir Noel Mason MacFarlane visiting the nursery at the Royal Palace Hotel.
In the photograph is also Father Azzopardi and Miss Olga Massetti
Photo Mr A Massetti

School children at St Katherine's College evacuation centre
with teacher Miss Laura Freyone.
Back row L to R: M.Moreno L.Alvarez Maribel Vinet ,M.Povedano (Mrs Cruz), T.Dalmedo I.Becerra.
Front row L to R: L.Baglietto M.Romero Violeta Thornton (Mrs Zammitt) ,L.Pons, M.Baldorino
Photo Mrs N Peto(nee Povedano)

For the younger children there were nurseries which were run by the WVS. The children were sent to schools which were the nearest to the evacuation centres.

A Nursery at the Royal Palace Hotel. In the photo are Frank and Adela Soiza (Mrs Hanglin) Taking care of the children sitting in the left hand corner is Miss Olga Massetti. Photo Mr E Vallejo

Children at a Nursery in Holland Park. In the photo are Sonia Lopez, Emily Wilkie, Elsie Reyes, Rosy Baldachino, Angeles Baldachino and Conchi Clark Photo Mrs Risso

Children from the York Hotel attended initially the St Patrick School in Soho which was destroyed during an air raid, fortunately it happened when it was closed. In view of this, they had to be taught at the York Hotel by Gibraltarian teacher Miss Anita Bezzina.

Photo Mr J Soiza

In the above photos taken on the roof of the St Patrick School is Gibraltar teacher Miss Anita Bezzina. Among the children are: Antonio Rocca, Antonio Lavagna, Rafael Galdez, Joseph Soiza, Luis Chipolina, Juan Serra, Marilu Catania, Milagro Requena (Mrs Bugeja), Alex Santos, Adameberry and Pepe Requena.
Photo Mr A Lavagna

About 200 boys and girls of all ages attended school at the converted classrooms in theVictoria and Albert Museum. Below are two groups of boys.

Photo Mr A Traverso

Photo Mr A Traverso

Below two groups of school girls who attended the adapted classrooms at the Victoria and Albert Museum.

Photo Mr A Traverso

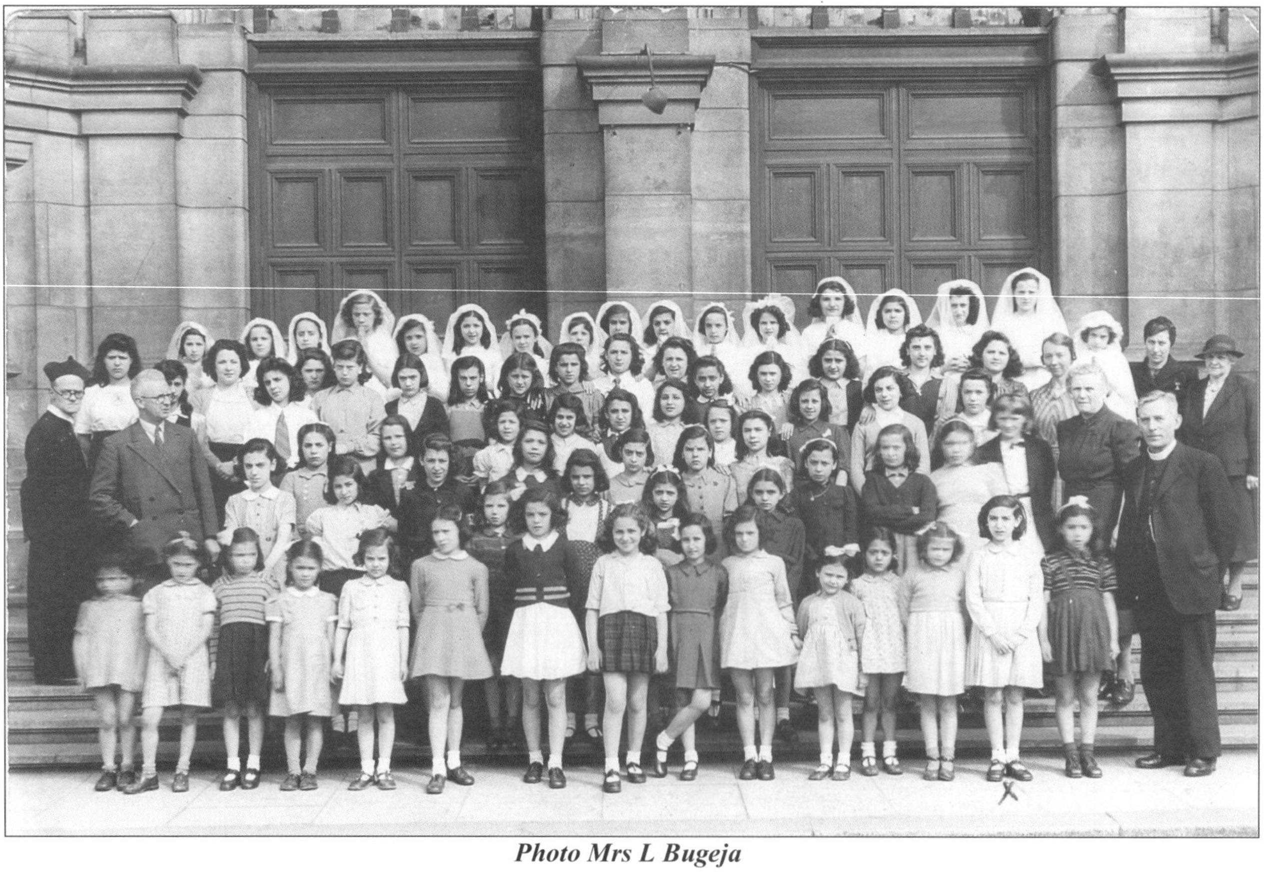

Photo Mrs L Bugeja

All the photographs on this page were donated by Mr M Belilo. The photographs are of the Jewish children residing at the North End House.

A School Play.

In the school canteen.

School children in a brides and fairies play.

Children at the Empire Pool Wembley School with teacher Miss Mary Vella.
In the photo are Salvador Mamo, Alex Requena,Jeannette Rocca,(Mrs Randalll) Tommy Finlayson,Laura Dellipiani(Mrs Gabay),Angela Camisuli,Anthony Dellipiani, Arthur Wall,Ruiz brothers and Joe Robson.
Photo Mrs E Mamo

The Opening of the Calpe Institute at 28 Lancaster Gate in June 1943.
In the photo are Major Patron, Archbishop Amigo, Mr Gaggero and Mr A Huart. Photo Mr L Massetti

By 1942 provisions were made for the selection of the more academically advanced evacuees to attend secondary level education by means of attainments reached in various subjects. About 80 students obtained scholarships to places in secondary schools. In 1943 a building was obtained in Lancaster Gate, named the Calpe Institute to serve as a culture centre and also provided the more senior evacuees pupils with the facility to further their studies.

Evacuees in the UK

A Gibraltar teacher with school children in Kensington Gardens.
In the photo are brothers Joseph and Horacio Franco
Photo Mr P Franco

School children living at the Royal Court Hotel at 105 Lancaster Gate.
In the photo Antonia Pardo among other school friends
Photo Miss A Pardo

Infant school children in Hyde Park. Photo Mr A Traverso

EDUCATION FACILITIES FOR EVACUEES

Schools For Gibraltar Children In U.K., Jamaica & Madeira

We have received through official channels the following account of the educational facilities provided for Gibraltar evacuated children in the United Kingdom, Madeira and Jamaica.

UNITED KINGDOM

In November, 1940, the Minister of Health established a committee to organise a systematic arrangement for the education of the evacuee children, some 2,880 boys and girls between the ages of five and 16.

The provision of accommodation and staff took some time and buildings such as the Victoria and Albert Museum have had to be adapted to school purposes. Actually, school facilities are provided within two miles of each evacuation centre.

As almost all the children are Roman Catholics, the co-operation of Roman Catholic authorities has been sought and, although accommodation has been provided only in one Roman Catholic school, in the other schools the L.C.C. have selected Roman Catholic teachers for the work. Nineteen lay teachers among the evacuees have been employed.

As many of the L.C.C. teachers are not acquainted with Spanish, they are experiencing some difficulties, particularly with the lower stages. The teachers, however, speak well of the brightness and general intelligence of the children. It has also been difficult to ensure both enrolment and regular attendance, but the attention of parents has been drawn to their legal liability and possible penalties. Parents who cannot provide the necessary school clothes, raincoats or footwear are helped to procure them.

Pupils between the ages of 12 and 16 who have qualified by their attainments are being admitted to approved secondary, central or junior technical schools. Some 80 pupils are already receiving post-primary instruction.

The L.C.C. has opened 24 classes for the teaching of English, commercial subjects, music and other subjects for adolescents who wish to continue their studies. Some women evacuees are attending a secretarial training school under priva management.

Community and welfare work has bee entrusted to the Women's Voluntary Se vices Association, who in turn have en listed the aid of the Boy Scouts, Gi Guides and Red Cross Victoria League.

Organised educational work includ classes for French, dress-making and phy sical training. Entertainment activiti include football, billiards, musical an dramatic societies, debating clubs, fencin and boxing and children's dances.

The Gibraltar Government and the S cretary of State attach great importanc not only to progress in the English lan guage, but also to the acquisition of Eng lish atmosphere and traditions.

Above is a cutting from Gibraltar Chronicle dated 5th July 1941 reporting on the educational facilities provided to Gibraltar evacuee children in the UK, Madeira and Jamaica.

The evacuees at Whitelands had the advantage of having the school and nursery facilities within the College building. The campus also offered many recreational and sporting amenities for the school children. These arrangements gave parents the comfort of knowing that their children were within easy reach in case of an air raid.

The arched doors were the entrances to the school and nursery at Whitelands. Photo by my daughter Michelle

Pupils like in some other centres had to be placed in age groups from five to twelve years of age. The nursery was for children between three and four plus. Children of the same age groups from Highlands Heath which was only about 15 minutes walking distance, also attended school at Whitelands or a school at the nearby village of Roehampton.
Those who recollected schooling at Whiteland said that subjects taught were very basic and apparently the classrooms lacked many normal facilities. Although I was just over three years old I remember being in the nursery and then attended my first ever schooling at Whitelands. We used to memorise the alphabet by singing it like in the old days of schooling. I also remember enjoying myself very much when we used to play with plasticine, coloured chalks or crayons. Apart from these few glimpses, I do not remember much more about my schooling days at Whitelands. As there were no facilities at Whitelands to cater for children above the age of twelve, children in that age group had to attend other Schools in London. One of the schools mentioned to me was the Henry Thornton Secondary School in Clapham Common. Others, depending on their academic standards, were selected to attend the Pitman's College at Brook Green, Hammersmith. This was a commercial type of school where students studied office procedures like typing, filing and shorthand. The Headmaster at the Whitelands School was Mr McCarthy and the teachers were Mrs Ryan, Mr Pedler, Mr Jackson, Miss McNamara, Miss O'Connor and also two local teachers, Mr John Hermida and Miss Amanda Alecio. Mr Hermida also helped some evacuees at Whitelands when there was a need for formal letter writing. On some occasions, when there was a need for translation, he also accompanied some mothers to places like hospitals.

Michelle at the steps leading to the school. Photo taken by J.Gingell

Mr John Hermida. Photo Mrs Z Santos(nee Hermida)

Miss Amanda Alecio. Photo Mr Alecio

Photograph of the school boys in the Red Room at Whitelands College.
5th Row:L.Harper J Lopez A.Reading A.Bosio V.Balban F.Acolina A.Zammitt A.Lopez (caretaker)P.Harrison J.Gerada Chappori C.Mascari
4th Row:F.Brosco H.Payas T.Power J.Balban G.Gaduzo J.Capurro L.Pilcher Viagas T.Hosken E.Brosco M.Cruz
3rd Row:R. Capurro J.Olivero A.Pitto J.Acolina L.Bellido S.Costa A.Gingell G.Saltariche T.Zammitt S.Hermida R.Capurro
2nd Row: Perera Galea Galea ...?..... H.Chichon J.Mascari J.Harrison Reyes F.Balban ....?... ...?... C.Montado J.Reading
Front Row:Torrilla Fiol Brosco Morello Perera C.Gomez Perera Perera Santos. Photo Mr T Power

"We Thank God and England.."

Photograph of school children in the Red Room at the Whitelands College. Photo Mrs Mato(nee Harrison)
5th Row: L.Gomez ...?.. Z.Hermida I. Capurro J.Hosken E.Gerada A.Mascari M.Acolina V.Pilcher M.Mascari
4th Row:Figueras l. Payas ...?.. S. Zammitt O.Montado M.Harrison A.Olivero A.Saltariche P. Grixti M.Prescott M.Reading
3rd Row:Broton,J, L.Celecia M.Gingell N.Harrison M.Cruz V.Olivero E.Rayman ...?... A.Saltariche Brosco K.Ferris(child)
2nd Row:L.Montado J.Viagas T.Alecio E.Gerada M.Bosio Y.Bacarese M Saltariche M.Montado V.Ferris M.Garcia
Front Row: J.Saltariche Reyes M.Alecio ....?..... L.Prescott J.Gingell

Gibraltar evacuees attending a school in Bloomsbury in 1941. In the photo are Chipolina, Luis Wood, Michel Lombard, Llanelo and John Victor. Photo Mr J Victor

Children in a private school in Hampstead Heath. In the photo at the back row third from the left is Plinio Oliva the only Gibraltar pupil in this school Photo Mr P Oliva

In early 1944 when plans for the repatriation were already well in advance, schooling in London suffered still more disruptions which was worsened due to a spate of intensive bombing followed by the onset of the flying bombs which forced the evacuees to leave London in anticipation of the intended plans.

In the case of those who were caught in the first years of schooling in London in a way benefited from the point of view that they were able to acquire from the very outset more fluency in English.

This seemed to be more so in the case, of those children who were evacuated to Northern Ireland where they continued to attend schools where they had to speak only in English. Many of the children who had spent a few years in Northern Ireland were noticed, in many cases, to be more fluent with their English than the average children who came back much earlier to Gibraltar.

The assessment from official sources about the provision of educational facilities for the evacuees, given the existing world conflict, was reckoned to be reasonably satisfactory although in some cases the practical contents were deficient. A few families who had left the evacuation scheme sent their children to privately arranged schools as the one in Hampstead Heath.

Some of those who were of school age during the evacuation expressed the view that their schooling was severely disrupted in London and that it affected their opportunities for employment when they reached their adolescence. Other evacuees who were caught in their last few years of schooling believe that the standard of the subjects taught was such that it would not have been of much use for those who were already advanced in their studies. For the teenagers there was also the attraction of finding well remunerated work as there was much demand for unskilled work and this led to some of these evacuees leaving school much earlier than normally expected. Some evacuees were able to work and carry with their academic studies on a day release basis like John Victor who in 1942 was able to work for a Ford main dealer and also attend a technical school for theoretical and academic studies.

After the Blitz, the evacuees were able to begin to settle down and look for sporting activities like the formation of football teams in many evacuation centres. Among these teams there were many Gibraltar evacuees who were keen football players. They demonstrated their skills and gave very good performances at the different matches played throughout the period of the evacuation. By early 1941 the London Gibraltarian Football Association was founded under the sponsorship of the Ministry of Health and presided by Mr Farrow.

Photograph taken on the occasion of the formation of the Gibraltar Football Association. In the photograph with Major Patron are A.Galia J.Milan J.Sanchez A.MacMahon Earle F.Barcio Avellano J.Ochello J.Candeas H.McIntosh and others. Photo Mr J Ochello

The Gibraltar Football Association's committee was composed of some Gibraltar evacuees and chaired by a Mr Sleight. A cup competition between the different centres was held with a view of choosing teams to play either in the senior or junior division. The senior division was for older boys and some men and the junior for boys in their early teens. Matches were usually played on Saturdays. Most of the centres played at nearby parks like those evacuees living at Courtlands who played at Richmond Park. There was another suitable playing area at Highlands Heath near a cricket club at the top of Putney Hill. Whitelands, as can be seen from a photograph in this section, had an adequate football ground.

In the pages that follow there are photographs of a number of teams from the various centres. Judging from the different reports it seems that the evacuees at Ivanhoe, Highlands Heath, Duchess of Bedford, Whitelands, Dr Barnardos, Lancaster Gate and Courtlands had very good teams. There were a few mentions in the press about the Gibraltar evacuees football teams like, for example, the Ilford Recorder dated 2 October 1941, which I have copied in the next column.

"Gibraltar Evacuees Are Keen Footballers"

The boys of Gibraltar who, as evacuees from their homeland, are living at Dr Barnardo's Homes, Barkingside, are keen sportsmen. Mr Gilkes, mainspring behind adult football here now, has been interesting himself in them. Unfortunately, he was unable to fit their football team into the Ilford War League, but he is trying to find games for them. I saw some of them playing on the Barkingside Recreation Ground on Saturday, with coasts as goalposts. It struck me that they have some players of real promise among them. There was some exceedingly good ball control, a feature of most continental football, those who know the game there tell me, it would be interesting to see these lads in real action, and I am hoping it can be contrived. Mr Gilkes, who is also a table-tennis fan, says he took along some good exponents of that game to try out the Gibraltar talent recently, and found it very good. They have also some billiards players, and are now anxious to get a table for use. Has anyone got a billiard table to spare? "

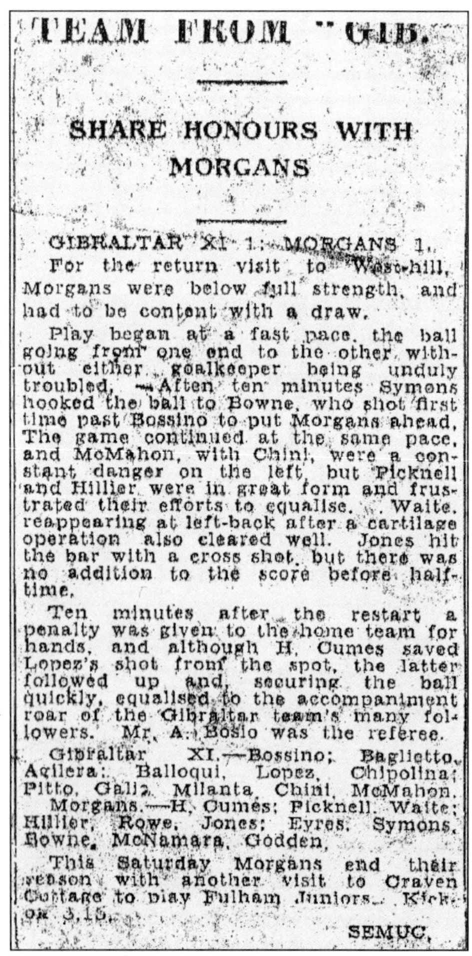

TEAM FROM "GIB."

SHARE HONOURS WITH MORGANS

GIBRALTAR XI 1: MORGANS 1.

For the return visit to West-hill, Morgans were below full strength, and had to be content with a draw.

Play began at a fast pace, the ball going from one end to the other without either goalkeeper being unduly troubled. After ten minutes Symons hooked the ball to Bowne, who shot first time past Bossino to put Morgans ahead. The game continued at the same pace, and McMahon, with Chini, were a constant danger on the left, but Picknell and Hillier were in great form and frustrated their efforts to equalise. Waite, reappearing at left-back after a cartilage operation also cleared well. Jones hit the bar with a cross shot, but there was no addition to the score before half-time.

Ten minutes after the restart a penalty was given to the home team for hands, and although H. Cumes saved Lopez's shot from the spot, the latter followed up and, securing the ball quickly, equalised to the accompaniment roar of the Gibraltar team's many followers. Mr. A. Bosio was the referee.

Gibraltar XI.—Bossino; Baglietto, Agilera; Balloqui, Lopez, Chipolina; Pitto, Galia, Milanta, Chini, McMahon.

Morgans.—H. Cumes; Picknell, Waite; Hillier, Rowe, Jones; Eyres, Symons, Bowne, McNamara, Godden.

This Saturday Morgans end their season with another visit to Craven Cottage to play Fulham Juniors. Kick-off 3.15.

SEMUC.

A report from a sports magazine about a game played at Whitelands. Cutting Mr J Harrison

As can be seen from the copies of football league tables and fixtures shown on this page practically every evacuation centre had its own football team. Many of these teams had also their own trainers, referees and linesmen.

By October 1941 football was already becoming a regular feature in providing leisure, sports and entertainment for the evacuees in London. Some of the most important matches were played at Wormwood Scrubs in Shepherds Bush where there were many pitches. In the north of London there were other pitches used by the evacuees to play football. Many evacuees attended these matches as spectators and also as supporters of their respective teams. I remember that at Whitelands many evacuees gathered at the top of a slope surrounding the pitch from were they watched the matches being played, which was at a lower ground level. I also remember that on many occasions when there was a football match, Alfredo Balban, who for many years used to play in the Gibraltar Sea Scouts Band,entertained the spectators with his bagpipe which he played by going round the pitch until the match started.

By October 1941 teams in both the senior and junior league divisions were in their starting positions in accordance with the standard of play. Some teams were by then being rated as favourites like Ivanhoe in the senior league and Lancaster Gate in the junior league table. Highlands Heath and Courtlands reached the finals in the junior league. The match was played on Saturday 9th May 1942 at the Queen's Park Rangers football ground in Loftus Road, Shepherds Bush with kick- of at 2.45pm. The admission fee was sixpence and children three pence. All the proceeds from this match went to the Spitfire Fund.

The Courtlands team players were C.Bacilisco, A.Savignon, M.Gatt, W.Sanchez, J.Serra, E.Cerisola, P.Garcia, G.Danino, C.Rodriguez, V.Figueras and J.Perez.

Their combination was blue shirts with white sleeves and white shorts.

The Highlands Heath team players were M.Azopardi, J.Dalli, L.Raggio, M.Apap, P.Cano, J.Reyes, T.Long, A.Rodriguez, M.Rodriguez, P.Cardona and V.Long. Their combination was red and black-stripped shirts and black shorts that had been manufactured using blackout curtains cloth

THE LONDON GIBRALTAR FOOTBALL ASSOCIATION LEAGUE TABLES AS ON OCTOBER 1942

SENIOR LEAGUE

TEAM	PLAYED	W	D	L	F	A	POINTS
LANCASTER GATE	4	4	-	-	22	0	8
COURTLANDS	4	4	-	-	14	5	8
WHITELA\NDS	4	3	-	1	12	14	6
DR BARNARDO'S	4	3	-	1	6	4	6
ROYAL PALACE HOTEL	4	3	-	1	5	4	6
WEMBLEY POOL	4	2	1	1	15	10	5
ROYAL STUART	4	2	1	1	1	9	5
MARLBOROUGH COURT	4	2	-	2	11	12	4
NORTHE END HOUSE	3	2	-	1	10	3	4
ST STEPHEN'S CLOSE	2	1	-	1	6	1	2
DUCHESS OF BEDFORD	4	1	-	3	9	15	2
KING'S COLELGE	4	0	1	3	1	8	1
HIGHLANDS HEATH	2	0	1	1	3	4	1
BRITISH EMPIRE	3	0	-	3	2	11	0
KENSINGTON P.M.	4	0	-	4	1	20	0
INVANHOE	4	0	-	4	3	1	0

JUNIOR LEAGUE

TEAM	PLAYED	W	D	L	F	A	POINTS
IVANHOE	4	4	-	-	44	12	8
DUCHESS OF BEDFORD	4	3	-	1	12	5	6
DR BARNARDO'S	3	3	-	-	18	1	6
COURTLANDS	3	2	1	-	9	6	5
KENSINGTON P.M.	3	2	1	-	16	15	5
ROYAL PALACE HOTEL	4	2	1	1	20	22	5
THACKERAY	5	2	1	2	20	40	5
WHITELANDS	4	2	-	2	15	10	4
LANCASTER GATE	3	2	-	1	21	5	4
WEMBLEY POOL	4	2	-	2	26	14	4
NORTH END HOUSE	4	1	-	3	1	18	2
YORK HOTEL	4	1	-	3	2	30	2
NATIONAL HOTEL	3	1	-	2	3	19	2
PARK ROYAL	4	1	-	3	16	30	2
ST.KATHERINES	4	0	-	4	7	3	0
ST STEPHEN'S CLOSE	4	0	-	4	0	0	0

At the match there were many evacuees from most of the evacuation centres. The Highlands Heath team won the match by four goals to nil. Tony Rodriguez scored the first goal, and Tommy Long scored two goals. Just before the match ended Victor Long scored the fourth goal. Manolo Rodriguez (captain) missed a penalty. The Higlands Heath team, which was not considered a favourite to win the final match, could not believe that they had won the junior cup. The referee was A.A.Victory and the linesmen were M.Balloqui and E.Baglietto. After the game there was a short display by the sea cadets and then afterwards everybody took their places again to watch the senior league final between Dr Barnardo's and the Ivanhoe team. Dr Barnardo's team consisted of the following players:
M.Lavagna, J.Cruz, H.McIntosh, M.Aguis, E.Power, A.Abudarham, J.Victory, J.Perez, M.Mena, F.Baglietto and A de La Paz.

Their combination was white shirts with red chevrons and white shorts.
The Ivanhoe team players were:
E.Medina, A.Cavilla, L De Soiza, E.Sanchez, J.Candeas, A.Rocca, Bacarisa, J.Sanchez, C.Lima, S.Martinez and H.Cocklan. The referee was W.H.Metcalfe and the linesmen were A.Bosio and J.Sevilla.
The match started at 4.30 pm and about ten minutes later Hector Cockland scored the first goal. Then Sebastian Martinez scored the second goal for Ivanhoe. Before half time Dr Barnardo's drew with two goals by Frank Baglietto. In the second half Ivanhoe won the match with two more goals by Charles Lima and Hector Cocklan. At the end of the match, the captains of both the Ivanhoe and Highlands Heath teams, Juan Candeas and Manolo Rodriguez respectively led their players to the rostrum to receive the winners' cups and medals from the President of the Association. This ceremony was followed by the presentation of medals to the players of the runner-ups teams.

HIGHLANDS TEAM - JUNIOR CUP WINNERS IN MAY 1942
Back row: Mr Gracia (trainer) Mario Apap John Dalli Paul Cano Michael Azopardi Juan Reyes Hector Hermida. Front row: Tommy Long Tony Rodriguez Manolo Rodriguez (Captain) Pedro Cardona Victor Long (Photo Mr P Cano)

THE TEAM FROM COURTLANDS AT THE QPR'S FOOTBALL GROUND
Back row E.Baglietto (linesman) P.Garcia C.Rodriguez G.Danino H.Balestrino V.Figuera Perez A.A.Victory (referee). Middle row: E.Cerisola P.Serra V.Sanchez. Front row L.Gatt C.Basilisco A.Savignon (Photo Mr C Basilisco)

According to those who still remember both matches and the impression gathered from the general public, the matches were played in a sporting manner with good football and much excitement. The matches also provided many enjoyable afternoons for the evacuees.

The Ivanhoe Team – Winners of the Senior Cup in May 1942.
Photograph taken at the QPR Football Ground.
Standing L To R A.Candeas A.Cavilla E.Medina L.De Soiza,M. Costa.
Sitting In Middle: E.Sanchez J.Candeas A.Rocca.
Kneeling In Front: C.Bacarisa J.Sanchez C.Lima S.Martinez H.Cocklan. Child is son of Spanish Refugee Named Caballero. Photo Mr J Candeas

Dr Barnardo's Football Team.
Back row left to right: J.De La Paz J.Victory M.Agius M.Mena M.Lavagna J.Abudarham H.McIntosh E.Power J.Gatt
Kneeling in front: J.Cruz A.De La Paz F.Baglietto J.Perez. Photo Mrs De La Paz

According to a report in the London Evening Standard in May 1942 there were many Gibraltar evacuees footballers.

After this season there seem to have been some disruption in the line up of the different teams. The main reason for this was that many of the players in the junior teams had attained the age of 16 plus and were therefore promoted to the senior division teams. Strangely enough, I was told that senior players from other centres filled the gaps left by those who had been promoted in order to raise the standard of the teams concerned. It seems that some of the players recruited in this manner were not of the expected standard and others failed to turn up for training due to personal reasons.
As a result of this, some teams found it difficult to compete and the final arrangements for the finals of the 1942/43 season had to be abandoned.
Notwithstanding this, some of the teams continued playing between the different evacuation centres and against London teams. As can be seen from the photographs in the next pages the teams continued playing friendly matches. Many of these matches were played at the Whitelands College football ground.

The Ivanhoe football team in their club at the Ivanhoe Hotel.
At the back ….?.... ….?.... …..?....
Middle Row standing:….?... J.Sanchez S.Martinez C.Lima …?... H.Cocklan …?...
Sitting: A.Candeas …?... …..?... J.Candeas ….?... L.DeSoiza ….?...
Sitting on the floor: A.Rocca E.Medina A.Cavilla
Photo Mr C Cumbo

The QPR football ground at Loftus Road just after the war.
PhotoQPR Football Club

I think football was one of the most popular of all the activities at Whitelands. I believe this was due to the fact that it was perhaps the only evacuation centre, which had its own proper football ground. There is an anecdote about the football ground which although it may not sound important I nevertheless believe I should mention it.

The Whitelands Football Ground.
Photo by my daughter Michelle

In November 1940, before the Gibraltar evacuees were accommodated at Whitelands, a high explosive bomb exploded in one of the actual corners of the football ground making a very deep crater. Apparently this crater was never filled up properly and throughout the whole period of the evacuation matches were played despite an acute dent on the ground. The actual corner with the dent was on my right hand side in the picture above.

There is another anecdote about the goal posts and the flag poles which to me sounded somewhat hilarious. At first, I thought this anecdote only applied to Whitelands. However, I later found out that all the centres carried the same routine. It seems that each centre had its own set of goal posts and corner flagpoles, which the teams used to take with them wherever they played. At the end of each game, these were removed and stored at their respective centres. The reason for this was that apparently there was a great shortage of firewood and if the wooden posts were left behind they would run the risk of soon being turned into firewood.

In charge of the football ground at Whitelands was Mr Arturo Pitto who made sure that the pitch was properly marked with the appropriate lines etc before the start of a game. Mr Adolfo Bosio, who was a member of the evacuation committee, was usually involved with the refereeing of matches.

On the next column there is a typical football notice which appeared in the Sunbury Sports Notices. A dance with music by the Gibraltarian Dance Band is also announced in the same notice. In the next column there is a copy of a report by Mr R.Torrilla, which appeared in the Sunbury weekly sports magazine about a game at the Whitelands football ground between the Morgans F.C. and the Whitelands Football Team. The report was titled: **"Fine Game at Whitelands"**

Sunbury Football Club Notices

EASTER ATTRACTIONS
IN AID OF THE ROYAL AIR FORCE BENEVOLENT FUND

EASTER SATURDAY, APRIL 24th –

SUNBURY v. DUCHESS OF BEDFORD F.C.
For Cup presented by R. Avellano, Esq.
At Benwell Meadow Kick-off 3 p.m.

DANCE — AT THE REMEMBRANCE HALL
MUSIC BY THE GIBRALTARIAN DANCE BAND
7.30 p.m. till 11.30 p.m.

EASTER SUNDAY, APRIL [illegible] –

DUCHESS OF BEDFORD F.C. v. INVANHOE F.C.
Both Gibraltarian Teams Kick-off 3 p.m.

EASTER MONDAY, APRIL 26th –

SUNBURY v. OLD TIMERS
Annual match for the "Brown" Challenge Cup

A Copy of the Sunbury Football Club Notices.
Cutting Mr J Harrison

The best game seen this season at Whitelands was played on Sunday when Morgans F.C. were visitors. Against these formidable opponents Whitelands put up a remarkably good show.

The game started with great enthusiasm. Gallia was promising and nearly scored the first goal for Whitelands. A corner was given against Morgans, but Picknell intervened and the ball was passed to McNamara who on several occasions tried shots but without success although he showed grand ability. Balloqui was out of play for a few minutes owing to injury, but resumed play after attention by the trainer (Mr J. Duarte). Morgans were playing a little bit rough. Their first goal, scored by C. Howard, was clearly offside, but the referee was uncertain and obviously nervous during the game. Whitelands were playing fast football Sanchez scored the first goal for Whitelands, but was a bit slack, P. Troice was the outstanding player on the field. Arnold was a difficult man to pass but Fhirman was the best player in Morgans team. Another clear penalty against Morgans was ignored by the referee and the match was suspended for a few minutes but resumed with a protest from Whitelands President and Secretary (Mr. J. Oliva and Mr. A. Bosio). Lopez was a bit uncertain but gave a great exhibition. The first half ended Whitelands 1, Morgans 1.

The second half started with some hard tackling by Morgans, the referee still showing favouritism for them. McMahon scored for Whitelands with a tremendous shot from the penalty area. He was playing excellently and P. Brosco and Gallia were also good.

Coughman scored the second goal for Morgan and Simons the third, and it was in that exciting quarter of an hour that Gallia scored the third goal for Whitelands, the game thus finishing a draw 3—3.

Morgans—T. Cumes; F. Arnold, A. Meldrum; D. Reeson, E. Picknell, W. Bovington; T. Coughman, McNamara, G. Simons, C. Howard, S. Fhirman.

Whitelands—J. Bossino; E. Baglietto, J. Ochello, A. Reyes, A. Lopez, M. Balloqui; Sanchez, P. Brosco, P. Troice, A. Gallia, McMahon.

RALPH. TORRILLA.

Copy of Report by Mr R.Torrilla.
Cutting Mr J Morello

The Whitelands College football team.
At the Back: J.Duarte (trainer) Lombard A.Reyes Llambias (goalkeeper) M.Balloqui V.Aguilera J.Pitto P.Galia
In Front: G.Aguilera E.Garcia A.Lopez A.Galia M.Pitto
Child J.Duarte Child Alex Lopez Both photos Mr A Reyes

The Duchess of Bedford football team at Whitelands.
At the back: Antonio Dalmedo George Yates Antonio Moreno Ernest.Baglietto Gustavo Chipolina N.Victory Antonio Olivero
In front: Carlos Borge Chiara Juan Milanta Chini Albert McMahon

Teams Receive Bouquets from Girls from Respective Centres.
Left to Right: Antonio Lopez (Whitelands) Alicia Pitto (Whitelands) Lourdes Bau (Duchess of Bedford) Ernest Baglietto (Duchess of Bedford). Note the people watching the game.
Photos Mr A Reyes

Presentation of Trophies at the Whitelands College Football Ground.
....?... A.Pitto L.Bau Avellano A.Candeas Lombard? M.Lima

Back row: Albert Reading Victor Figueras
Middle row: Plinio Harrison, Victor Balban, John aViagas ,Adolfo Bosio, F.Brosco A.Pipo
Front row: Joe Canepa, Tito Figueras, George Gaduzo, John Olivero, Lionel Bellido
Photo by Mr A Harrison

Back row L to R: Pepe Peliza, Chappory, J.Brosco, Jose Harrison, F.Brosco, Plinio Harrison.
Front row: Manolo Cruz, Johnny Martinez, Joe Canepa, Tito Figueras, Charles Traverso .   Photo Mr E Brosco

With a football ground within the Whitelands College campus, the boys had access to play there almost every day. As soon as the evacuees moved to Whitelands in April 1941 they began to organise football matches. The school boys like the older boys had their own football team combination of shirts and shorts. Their colours were white shirts, white shorts and white socks with red stripes.

In the photograph at the top of the left hand column the Whitelands Boys' Football Team can be seen in full gear at the actual football ground. The photograph at the bottom of the left hand column was taken by the main Whitelands College building.

The girls also had their own basketball team but I have not been able to find a photograph to display.

There was a lot of open space around the building for children to play other games without the need to go outside the enclosure. This gave mothers peace of mind in knowing that their children were safe and in case of an air raid they were very near the building's shelter.

The Ivanhoe football team at Whitelands.
C.Lima E.Power....?...... J.Candeas S.Martinez ...?.... ...?... ….?....
J.Sanchez Chini E.Medina Neale. Photos Mr J Candeas

The Duchess of Bedford team at Whitelands.
Standing L to R C.Harrison Garcia J.Ochello J.Sanchez M.Balloqui
J.Candeas..?... S.Martinez A.Lopez Earle A.Bosio
Kneeling L to R Silva H.Neale A.Moreno,L. De Soiza A.Galia A.McMahon

Because Whitelands had its own football ground, many teams from the different evacuation centres came to play there. The most regular visitors were the Ivanhoe and the Duchess of Bedford teams. It is interesting to note that some players in the Ivanhoe team also played for the Duchess of Bedford team. Likewise there are players in the photograph who normally played for the Whitelands College team but also played for the Duchess of Bedford team. In the Ivanhoe team is Eladio Power who normally played for the Dr Barnardo's Team. Likewise, M.Balloqui and A.Lopez who normally played for the Whitelands team and are also in the photograph with the players from the Duchess of Bedford team.

The reason for showing the photograph of the houses at Sutherland Grove Road is to highlight the fact that these were the same houses which are shown in the photograph of the Ivanhoe team at the Whitelands football ground. As mentioned in the chapter about the bombing, these houses were the ones where the Gibraltar evacuees were taken during the night of the bombing of the Whitelands College on the 19th February 1944.

Above a photo taken in 2004 of the same houses shown below during the evacuation. Photo taken by my daughter Michelle

The Ivanhoe Football Team at Whitelands.
J.Ochello M.Balloqui J.Candeas A.Moreno A.Lopez J.Sanchez
S.Martinez L.De Soiza H.Neale A.Galia A.McMahon Photo by Mr J Candeas

The photograph below shows one of the many occasions when teams from different evacuation centres went to play at the Whitelands College football ground. The team is that of the Duchess of Bedford but there are also some players from the Whitelands College team in the photograph.

The full contingent of the Ivanhoe football team at Whitelands.

Standing L to R Garcia ...?... G.Duarte...?... ...?...L.De Soiza M.Balloqui A.Lopez S.Martinez...?.... J.Sanchez Joyce A.McMahon Earle Baglietto? A.Dalmedo Chipolina A.Pitto....?... Ghio A.Lopez. Kneeling L to R: A.Bosio C.Harrison Avellano A.Galia A. Moreno J.Candeas J.Ochello H.Neale Silva Felice E.Medina

Photo by Mr J Candeas

The photographs shown below were taken by the Highlands Heath flats in Putney Heath when the team won the Junior League Cup in May 1942. The goalkeeper, Michael Azopardi is holding the cup.

Left to right: J.Reyes H. Hermida T.Long T.Rodriguez J.Dalli M.Azopardi P.Cano M.Rodriguez P.Cardona V.Long M.Apap Gracia (Trainer) Photo Mr M Rodriguez

At the back: Tommy Long Mr Gracia (trainer) Highlands Heath Manager
Third row: Mr Macedo Tony Rodriguez Pedro Cardona Manolo Rodriguez Hector Hermida
Second row: Mario Apap Paul Cano Juan Reyes. In front: John Dalli Michael Azopardi Lili Raggio
Photo Mr P Cano

Below are photographs of the Wembley and the Duchess of Bedford evacuation centres' teams. Note the badge on the shirts of the Wembley team is GE, which stands for Gibraltar Evacuees.

The Empire Pool Wembley evacuation team.
Back row L to R: T.Finlayson M.Silva J.Garcia F.Fortunato A.Ruiz I.Attias R.Attias C.Silva A.Victory
Sitting in front L to R: W.Bado J.Castro M.Rodriguez I.Duo. Photo Mr J Garcia

The Duchess of Bedford football team.
Back row L to R: Avellano ?Mrs & Mr Key (Manager Duchess of Bedford)....?... E.Baglietto J.Ochello J.Milanta Earle Ruiz Parody Santos....?....
Front row L to R: Joyce McCarthy Chiara Chini Moreno Bear Beiso. Photo Mr J Ochello

Despite the fact that the official football arrangements were not working as well as anticipated some teams nevertheless carried on arranging their own competitions. This is demonstrated by the fact that the Lancaster Gate centre formed the Calpe Football Club and won the minor football league for the 1943-1944 Season.

The Lancaster Gate Senior Football Team 1942.
Standing L to R: J.Gomez G.Gonzalez E.Victory M.Glynn H.Trinidad L.Massetti Kneeling in front L to R: M.Gonzalez H.Alman F.George J.Mauricio J.Bossino J.Porro...
Photo by Mr L Massetti

The Lancaster Gate Team. Photo Mr F Ramirez

In the photograph above are two well-known local football players of the 50s – the brothers Pepe and Jaime Ramirez. The team coach was Mr Rolf Torrilla standing on the left of the back row.

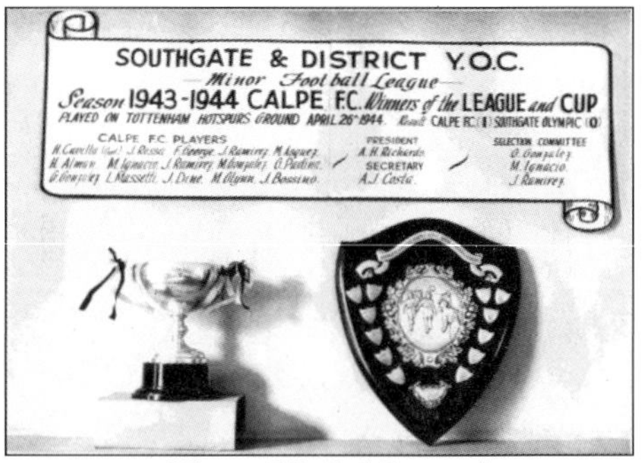

Photo Mr L Massetti

Above the cup and shield won by the Calpe Football Club formed by evacuees at Lancaster Gate. The club president was A.H.Richards and the secretary A.J.Costa.

The match took place at the Tottenham Hotspurs ground at White Hart Lane on the 26 April 1944. The result was:
Calpe F.C.-1 Southgate Olympic –0
The players for this match were the following:
H.Cavilla (capt) J.Ressa F.George J.Ramirez M.Asquez H.Alman M.Ignacio J.Ramirez M.Gonzalez G.Padina G.Gonzalez L.Massetti J.Dine M.Glynn J.Bossino

The team selection committee was composed of the following members: G.Gonzalez M.Ignacio and J.Ramirez

Judging from the above, it seems that the evacuees continued playing football until shortly before they were being repatriated. By the time this match was played more than 2,300 evacuees had already been repatriated to Gibraltar.

The North End House football team.   Mr Photo Mr M Belilo

Courtlands football team at Richmond Park
Back row l to r: A.Figueras P.Garcia G.Danino C.Rodriguez V.Figueras Perez Serra (trainer)
Middle row l to r: E.Cerisola P.Serra V.Sanchez
Front row l to r: L.Gatt C.Basilisco A.Savignon
Photo Mr C Basilisco

When the war broke out in September 1939, the British Government immediately imposed a ban on assembly of crowds and as a result the Football League competition was brought to an end. However, soon afterwards permission was given for football clubs to play friendly matches but the number of people that could be gathered to watch these matches was limited to 8,000. This was later increased to 15,000. The London clubs played friendly matches which the evacuees were able watch on Saturdays.

The old Arsenal football stadium at The Valley. Photo Wikipedia Free Encyclopedia

Within these friendly matches, evacuees had the great opportunity of being able to watch teams like the Chelsea, Arsenal, Fulham, Tottenham Hotspurs and other well known London football teams from many of the other London football clubs.

Luftus Road Stadium just after the war ended. Photo QPR Football Club

Although many of the players were enlisted, some were allowed to play for their own clubs or other clubs as guests. Some of the famous players seen were Stanley Matthews, Wilf Mannion, Raich Carter and many players of international repute.

The Fulham F C Stadium at Craven Cottage. Photo Wikipedia Free Encyclopedia

The Chelsea Football ground at Stamford Bridge just before the war. Photo Chelsea Football Club

White Hart Lane Stadium.

There was a contingent of refugees who were mainly from the Basque country. They had a club near Lancaster Gate called El Hogar Español and one of the key players in this Spanish team was Emilio Aldecoa who on one occasion played at the Whitelands football ground. He arrived in England as a Spanish Civil War refugee in 1937. Emilio Aldecoa Gomez began his football career with Wolverhampton Wanderers in 1943 becoming the leading scorer. In 1945 he moved to Coventry City. In 1947 he returned to Spain joining Atletico Bilbao. He made one appearance for the Spanish national team, as a substitute in a 2-1 win against the Republic of Ireland in May 1948 at the Montjuiic Stadium, Barcelona.

As from 1949 until 1954 he played for Real Valladolid, Barcelona, Sporting de Gijon and Girona FC where he subsequently became manager. From 1966 to 1967 he managed the CD Condal and the Real Valladolid football clubs. He became assistant manager of Birmingham City between 1960 and 1962.

Emilio Aldecoa.
Photo www.euskomedia.org

Some of the men who were allowed to visit their families in London under the special leave arrangements were well known local football players like Alfredo Duarte (El Chino) and Miguelito Goodman. During their visit they formed a combined team with players of other centres and played at the Whitelands College football ground. I was told that the shirts that they were wearing in the picture with diagonal stripes were that of the Prince of Wales F.C.team in Gibraltar. The shirts were brought by one of the players who visited his family in London.
One of the most popular players during the evacuation was Joaquin Sanchez. He told me that he had played on some occasions for the QPR club and I understand from many who remembered him that he always gave a good performance. Joaquin Sanchez, in a conversation with me mentioned an anecdote when he was playing at the Whitelands football ground. He explained that Gonzalo Aguilera, from the Whitelands team, tried to take the ball from Joaquin, when he (Joaquin) was about to pass the ball to one of his team-mates. Gonzalo was hit accidentally by Joaquin and suffered a compound fracture in his leg. Joaquin carried on explaining that it was a clean pass but it was one of those accidents that happen so often in football.

A combined team with some visitors from Gibraltar.
Back Row: J.Gonzalez S.Duarte M.Balloqui A.Duarte M.Goodman A.Lopez A.Pitto H.Aguilera
Front Row: A.Reyes J.Bossino J.Ochello A.Galia.
Photo Mr A Reyes

Joaquin Sanchez and Joe Gingell posing after having a chat about football in London

Some of the players who played for the evacuation teams continued playing football when they returned to Gibraltar. The main football clubs were then Gibraltar United, Prince of Wales, Britannia and Europa. I remember watching many good games by these teams in the early fifties and also when they combined against visiting teams like Atletico Madrid. On one of those occasions, I remember getting an autograph from Larbi Ben Barek, when he came to Gibraltar with Atletico de Madrid.

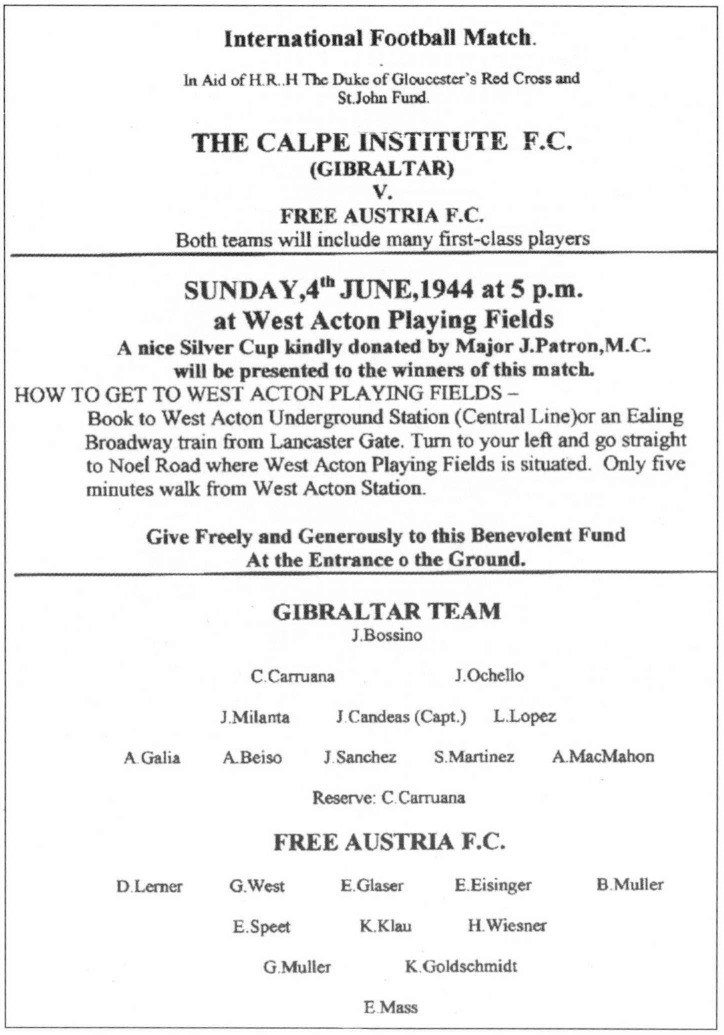
International Football Match.

In Aid of H.R..H The Duke of Gloucester's Red Cross and St.John Fund.

THE CALPE INSTITUTE F.C.
(GIBRALTAR)
V.
FREE AUSTRIA F.C.
Both teams will include many first-class players

SUNDAY,4th JUNE,1944 at 5 p.m.
at West Acton Playing Fields
A nice Silver Cup kindly donated by Major J.Patron,M.C. will be presented to the winners of this match.

HOW TO GET TO WEST ACTON PLAYING FIELDS –
Book to West Acton Underground Station (Central Line)or an Ealing Broadway train from Lancaster Gate. Turn to your left and go straight to Noel Road where West Acton Playing Fields is situated. Only five minutes walk from West Acton Station.

Give Freely and Generously to this Benevolent Fund At the Entrance o the Ground.

GIBRALTAR TEAM
J.Bossino
C.Carruana J.Ochello
J.Milanta J.Candeas (Capt.) L.Lopez
A.Galia A.Beiso J.Sanchez S.Martinez A.MacMahon
Reserve: C.Carruana

FREE AUSTRIA F.C.
D.Lerner G.West E.Glaser E.Eisinger B.Muller
E.Speet K.Klau H.Wiesner
G.Muller K.Goldschmidt
E.Mass

Copy of the notice about the international games. Poster by Mr J Candeas

One of the last matches to be played by the evacuees was that made up of a selection from the different evacuation centres and known as the Gibraltar Team. This team played against teams of refugees of different nationalities in London. The Gibraltar team played on Sunday the 4th June 1944- a few days before the onset of the flying bombs.
The Gibraltar team consisted of J.Bossino as goalkeeper, J.Ochello, C.Caruana, J.Milanta, and J.Candeas as captain, L.Lopez, A.Galia, A.Beiso J.Sanchez S.Martinez and A.MacMahon and they played against a team called the Free Austria F.C.
There were teams from Spain and Britain. The games were played at West Acton Playing Fields in aid of the Red Cross and St. John Fund.

Below a photo of a combined Gibraltar team. In the picture are: Llambias, A.Galia, A.Pitto, A.Reyes, A Lopez, Pitto, Lombard, G.Aguilera, M.Balloqui and a few others. Photo Mr A Reyes

The other sports practised were boxing for boys and netball for girls. In the photograph below are the girls from Dr Barnardo's Homes receiving the winning trophy from Mrs MacFarlane, the wife of the Governor of Gibraltar who had been visiting the evacuees in London in May 1943. As can be seen from the Ilford Recorder cutting the ceremony was recorded by the BBC. Cuttings were provided by the Ilford Recorder.

'GIB' CHILDREN WIN CUP

GOVERNOR'S WIFE AT BARKINGSIDE

The wife of the Governor of Gibraltar, Mrs. Mason MacFarlane, visited Gibraltar refugees at the Barkingside Village Homes on Saturday and presented a cup to the girls' netball team after they had beaten a team of evacuees from Kensington Palace.

The ceremony took place after a tea had been provided and the B.B.C. recorded the ceremony for broadcasting to Gibraltar.

Olga Cornelio, captain of the team, received the cup and each member of the team had a medal.

They had been trained by Mrs. Watson and Mrs. Allen, of the Ilford W.V.S.

The team was Olga Cornelio, Julio Cruz, Maribel Cornelio, Violet Mauro, Maribel Garcia, Olimpia Danino, and Muriel Cartwright.

At Dr Barnardo's Home a Sports Day event for Gibraltar evacuees took place and the results were reported in the Ilford Recorder in September 1943.

'GIB' EVACUEES SPORTS DAY

At the Barkingside Village Homes, on Saturday, Gibraltarian cyclists could be seen racing under a horizontal wire strung with rings. If they were successful in passing a stick through one of the rings, they tugged and unravelled a gay streamer of red, white and blue.

This was an event in the "Sports Day" of the Gibraltarian evacuees—the culmination of the little fun-fair they had had on Thursday, Friday and Saturday of last week, and on the same three days the week before. A special prize went to the girl, Victoria Vinales, who made the best attempt in the one mile flat race. Alderman A. W. Green attended, with Mrs. Green, who presented the prizes. The results were:—

40 yds. flat race (children 7—10).—1, O. Orfila; 2, J. Baglietto.

80 yds. flat race (10—14).—M. Martinez. (14—20).—1, B. Ryan; 2, J. Orfila. Special to first girl, O. Alvarez. (Over 20 yrs.).—F. Baglietto.

25 yds. egg and spoon (girls 7—10).—M. Borge.

40 yds. egg and spoon (girls 10—14).—D. Tacon.

25 yds. wheel-barrow (boys 10—14).—A. Gareze and partner.

One mile flat race (open 16 and up).—J. Orfila.

40 yds. skipping race (girls up to 14).—F. Rocca.

60 yds. blindfold race.—C. Alvarez and A. Gareze.

40 yds. slow bicycle race (open).—B. Ryan.

Long jump (boys under 14).—M. Martinez.

Long jump (over 14).—J. Martinez.

100 yds. walking race (open).—J. Orfila.

Bicycle ribbon race (open).—1, A. Delapaz; 2, J. Victory.

When war was declared in September 1939, all the cinemas in London and other British cities were closed for safety reasons but were back in business within a week because it was realised that the nation needed entertainment to keep up its spirits. Cinema going was seen as particularly vital when the war was not going as well. In this sense the news was heavily controlled by the Ministry of Information. Its main purpose was to keep the nation's morale up by giving out the message that Britain was winning the battle. During the Battle of Britain it was said that the figures that were given out for the enemy planes were inflated.

At home people listened to the radio. Mostly to comedy broadcasts designed to keep up morale. As from the beginning of 1942, entertainment went back to normality after the worst part of the war was over. It is generally believed that this morale boosting propaganda had a significant importance on people's attitude towards the war.

Sometimes the cinemas were referred as 'picture houses' and were considered safe places to be during a bombing raid. Very often people went to see morale-boosting films with a war theme. There was also then the novelty of Hollywood movies in colour. People also relied on the cinema to keep them informed about what was happening in the war. Pathe or Movietone were in charge with the releasing of the latest war news on the big screen. As far as the Gibraltar evacuees were concerned cinema going was also one of the main sources of leisure and entertainment for evacuees in London. During that time the cinema industry was going through an epoch, which has been described as the "Golden Age" of cinema entertainment. The cinemas, also known as the 'dreams palaces', offered the public an escape from the realities of everyday life. In London the cinemas and mainly those of the West End received all the latest films, which the evacuees were in a way privileged to enjoy. Those were the days of classic movies that even more than sixty years later are still shown on some TV channels. Some of the most popular film stars and their related films that were mentioned in conversations with the evacuees whom I spoke with are follows:

Humphrey Bogart, Ingrid Bergman and Paul Henreid in **Casablanca,** Tyrone Power in **Blood and Sand,** Errol Flynn in **Robin Hood** and **Captain Blood**, Gary Cooper and Ingrid Bergman in **For Whom the Bell Tolls**, Ronald Colman in the **Prisoner of Zenda,** Clark Gable in **Gone With the Wind**, Robert Taylor in **Queens** and Betty Davis in **Now, Voyager** and many other classics like the **Maltese Falcon.**

Like with many other means of getting on with life in London, people also attended cinemas despite the bombing. Going by what I been told by some of the evacuees, there were occasions that even when an air raid was announced on the cinema screen very few, if any, left the cinema. The film, which could be said to have had the greatest impact on the evacuees, was **Blood and Sand** shown during the summer of 1942 throughout many of the cinemas. When this film was shown at the Plaza Cinema near the Southfield Underground Station it attracted a very large audience from both the nearby Whitelands and Highlands Heath evacuation centres in Wandsworth. Some of the evacuees who still recall this film explained that during the show there were many evacuees who shouted "ole" appropriately timed with the execution of the 'lidia' performed by Tyrone Power.

After the shows there were also many who tried their best by pretending to be bullfighters. Those who dared demonstrate their understanding of bullfighting, the aficionados, did so by holding their jackets or other garments with one hand and pretended to execute the passing of the bull. Passers-by who did not know what the whole thing was about, must have obviously watched their gestures with great perplexity. One of the most popular film stars of the time was perhaps Errol Flynn who performed in most of the adventures/action films.

Errol Flynn who starred in many adventure films. Photo Wikipedia Free Encyclopedia

The war seemed to give the British film industry a boost which helped the image of Britain at war. Among the best known films in this category were **In Which We Serve , Went the Day Well? The Day Will Dawn.** There were films which, while set in wartime, were very much about the people affected by war rather than battles. They told the story of the resistance movement in occupicd France Norway and Holland. They were also intended to boost up the will of the people to continue the struggle and at the same to convince them of the German brutality in occupied countries. The British cinema industry was largely controlled by the Ministry of Information which was responsible for the publicity and propaganda aimed for the national cause. The Ministry of Information advised producers on subject matter and helped with the actual making of films which served to convey thoughts on supporting the national cause. Another objective was also the need to inculcate on the people a sense responsibility in not giving away information which could be harmful to the national security. In pursuance of this policy posters were sponsored by the Ministry of Information could be seen at the cinema foyers beside the actual film posters throughout the whole country. Generally, before the main show began, that is, the film itself, there was the news about the war giving an update account of the war situation. When evacuees arrived in 1940 the news shown on the cinemas were very damaging to the morale but by the autumn of 1943 the news became to be more optimistic and hopeful for a victorious end. The prices of tickets were about 1s.6d (7.5p) for adults and 9d (3.75p) for children. My collection of the information about cinemas refers mainly to some of those in the SW London area where there were many cinemas. The most frequently attended are mentioned in my narrative about cinema entertainment.

The Regal Cinema in 1937.
Photo the Wandsworth Herritage

The Odeon Cinema where the Regal Cinema used to be.
Photo taken in 2004 by Mr J Collado.

The Regal Cinema was in Putney High Street near the corner with Putney Bridge Road and Felsham Road. It belonged to the ABC circuit of cinemas. As can be seen from the recent photograph of Putney High Street the cinema there is now called the Odeon. Near to this cinema were the Putney Hippodrome in Felsham Road and The Putney Palace as part of the Gaumont circuit of cinemas. There were many films seen by the evacuees in these cinemas. One of the evacuees recalls watching the film the Sea Hawk starring Errol Flynn or the Tarzan films by Johnny Weissmuller and his wife Jane played by Maureen O'Sullivan. The Putney Hippodrome in Felsham Road was attended by many evacuees in the Wandsworth area. Some of the most famous film stars enlisted to encourage others to enlist. One of these films stars was Clark Gable who attained the rank of captain taking part by flying in actual combat missions over Germany. When the war was still on Clark Gable starred in a film Combat America based on his own war experience.

The Wandsworth Palace in the early 20th Century.
Photo Wandsworth Heritage Service

The Wandsworth Palace in the 50s.
Photo Wandsworth Heritage Service

A photograph in recent years of what used to be the Wandsworth Palace during the evacuation.
Photo Mr J Collado

When opened in 1906 the Putney Hippodrome was the only purpose built music hall in the area and was called the Putney Empire Palace of Varieties. Many famous artists appeared there. The appearance of the film industry defeated it and it became a cinema in 1924 until 1961 when television defeated cinema. The Plaza was the nearest cinema to the Whitelands and Highlands Heath evacuation centres.

The Putney Hippodrome in the 50s.
Photo Wandsworth Heritage Service

One of the most classic films during the war, Blood and Sand, was shown in this cinema and I was told that it was packed with Gibraltar evacuees from both centres. There were also films shown for the younger viewers. Some of these films which were shown during the war years have since become classics. When enquiring for my research I was told those lived near the building that when this cinema closed it became an arcade for gaming machines and then more recently a bingo hall.

The building where the Plaza Cinema used to be.
Photo taken by my daughter Michelle

The Wandsworth Palace was also one of the most popular cinemas in Wandsworth for those evacuees who lived at Highlands and Whitelands College. This cinema as well as the Putney Palace Cinema in Putney High Street was part of the Gaumont circuit of cinemas in the area.

A photo in recent years of the Grand in Clapham Junction.
Photo Mr J Collado

The Empire Cinema
in Leicester Square before the war.
Photo Wikipedia Free Encyclopedia

Recent picture of the Empire Cinema in Leicester Square.
Picture Wikipedia Free Encyclopedia

During the 40s many love stories were screened in London. Among these were "Gone With the Wind" and "Rebecca."
In St. John's Hill , Clapham Junction there was the Imperial Cinema a name which was retained until 1973 when it was taken over by a new proprietor Mr Fred Clarke who named it the Ruby Cinema closing in 1981 as one of the last surviving cinemas of its kind in Battersea. The Ruby Cinema closed on 22nd August 1981 with the film starring Harrison Ford in "Raiders of the Lost Ark". It was demolished in December 1982, and a branch of Barclay's Bank now stands on the site.

The Globe Cinema.
Picture Wandsworth Heritage Service

Photo of Clapham Junction in 2004 showing where the Imperial Cinema used to be. Photo Mr J Collado

The Imperial Cinema in Clapham Junction in the very early 20thCentury. Photos above and below Wandworth Heritage Service.

The entrance to the ex-Imperial Cinema in 1981.

At St John's Hill, Clapham Junction and not very far from the Imperial Cinema there were two more cinemas. They were the Grand now a musical community centre and the Granada Cinema at the very end of the road. When my family was transferred to the York Hotel, which must have been about end of March, or beginning of April 1944, we were in an area where there were the most luxurious cinemas in London. Certainly much better than those we went to when we were living at Whitelands. I remember on one occasion seeing a few films in a cinema which was near the York Hotel in Oxford Street. In one of these cinemas, which to me looked quite big, I remember seeing for the first time a coloured film. The film was Ali Baba and the Forty Thieves. I think the film stars were John Hall and Maria Montez. I am not sure whether, the then famous Sabu, starred in this film or in another which was very similar called The Arabian Nights. I also remember seeing in one of the cinemas in the same area what I think was my first ever science fiction film. I believe it was called the Iron Man which was about a robot or something similar. There were also the well known Cinemas like the Empire and the London Hippodrome in Leicester Square. Throughout the war there were many posters displayed at the cinema foyers and which were intended to boost morale or recruit people into employment and also in the armed forces.

Picture Wikipedia Free Encyclopedia

The Granada at Clapham Junction during the war.
Photo Wandsworth Heritage Service)

The Granada in the 50s.
Photo Wandsworth Heritage Service)

A recent photo of what used to be the Granada Cinema.
Photo Mr J Collado

Whilst living at the York Hotel, I remember going also to some of the games shops where my brothers and I played a few times. I believe these gaming shops were around Leicester Square or Piccadilly Circus. What I do remember is giving a few tries to one of those machines, which you try to grab things with a mechanical hand inside a glass cubicle. On one occasion I also remember going to the Madame Tussaud's Museum. As I went down one of the stairs in the museum, I recall seeing a replica of Hitler with his typical brown shirt and the arm band with the swastika. We also went to Hyde Park where there were lots of barrage balloons, and if I remember rightly, I think I saw some anti aircraft guns as well in the park.

Cinema frequented by evacuees at Peckham Rye. Photo Southwark Local History Studies Office.

John Victor pointing to the Royal Hotel National where he was accommodated during the evacuation. Photo Mr J Victor

John Victor who was lodged at the National Hotel during the whole duration of the evacuation explained that on many occasions he used to go to watch movies at the many of the cinemas situated in central London.

I think I should end this chapter about cinema entertainment in London with a very interesting anecdote about a resident at Whitelands who took part in a film with none other than the then very famous star James Mason.

Andres Harrison, then in his early teens, was resident at Whitelands. Whilst in central London he was approached by some film producers from the famous Twentieth Century Fox and offered him role in a film. Andres was very excited and was obviously very interested in the idea. Andres, there and then, accepted the offer of becoming an instant film star.

The actual film makers were British Lion Ltd and hired Andres for a casting where he played the role of an Arab bell boy. The scene in which Andres took part was a railway station in Algeria. The actual filming was naturally made in a London studio with a lot of artefacts simulating a railway station.

Andres explained that he recalled that he was all the time in the studio where all the noises, effects etc associated to a railway station were produced.

Andres said, "It seemed so real that it felt as if I were in an actual railway station. I could hear the hissing and clanking of a train when it is approaching and stopping by a railway platform. However, despite the fact that after seeing the film several times, to see myself, I have never managed to do so."

Andres said he was paid 5 guineas, which in those days was equivalent to about one month's salary. The film company also paid for the taxi to take him back to the Whitelands College.

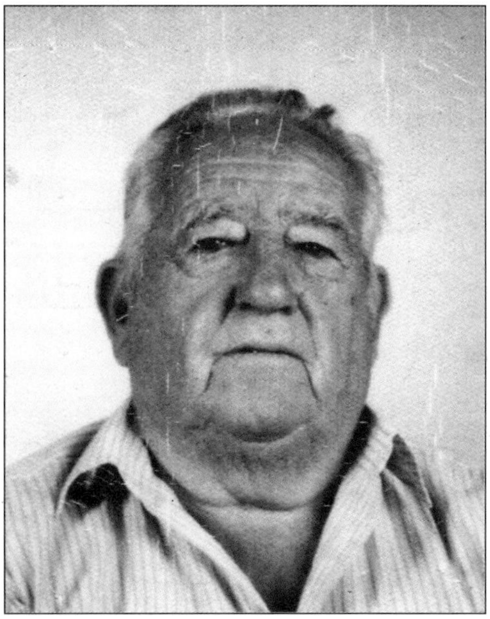

Andres Harrison.

From what I have been told, the style of music during the war revolved around the big bands that were very popular in those days. Many of the singers of that era entertained crowds with their unique brand of music. The style of music at the time of World War Two also reflected the difficulties that Britain was going through while still maintaining a positive attitude about a victorious future. Many of the singers managed to become famous in the history of music. Even now some are still regarded as initiators of a particular style of music during the war years. Although there were many people dying in the war the musical performers continued to help people to take their mind off of the bad news. They not only continued to make fun music, but many of them also took their talents to the troops to keep them entertained and boost their morale. The songs were also intended to help the public overcome the stress of the war and relax when the occasion permitted. One of the most popular singers during the Second World War was undoubtedly DameVera Lynn who used to sing many morale boasting songs. Her repertoire was quite extensive and the songs which are recalled by the majority of the evacuees are the White Cliffs of Dover, There'll Always be an England, We'll Meet Again and many others. The 40s were also the years with fast, frantic, mainly American style of dance music, like boogie-woogie or jitterbug with dances being held everywhere.

Vera Lynn. Photo Mr Mark Dowd of Topfoto.co.uk

The other popular singers of the war years that came to minds of those I talked with were Anne Shelton, the romantic music from the famous Geraldo and his orchestra. I think Anne Shelton's most favourite songs amongst the evacuees were, "Kiss me my love", "Begin the Beguine" and "Lay down Your Arms"

Anne Shelton. Photo Mrs Kelly Richards – Photo WWW Anne Shelton Co UK

There was also the legendary Andrew Sisters who also became one of the most popular singers during the Second World War and some years after. Among the best known songs of the time by the Andrew Sisters were: Round the Apple Tree, Don't Fence Me In, Pistol Packin' Mama and for the evacuees I think it was their version of Amapola.

Despite the dangers posed by the bombing, the Gibraltar evacuees also did their best to organise different types of entertainments in almost every centre. Once the bombing eased the evacuees were able the hold concerts, dances, plays and other forms of entertainment more frequently. Bands were formed and played at different evacuation centres. Among the many songs of the time there were also typical songs relating to Gibraltar like the very popular "Llevame donde Naci." One of the slogans created by the Gibraltar entertainers was "We cannot take you home but we can make you feel at home"

The "Harry And His Victory Rascals" band at Whitelands College.
***Standing Left to Right:** George Holzen (a Belgian pilot) Salvador Sciacaluga, Pepe Roman, Harry Fernandez Manuel Gonzalez Sitting with drums Alfredo Balban. Photo Mr Golt*

Harry Fernandez who led The Harry and His Victory Rascals' Band played in 219 dances between 18 October 1940 and 11 June 1944. At Whitelands, alone, he played 159 times. From a very detailed record kept by Harry Fernandez of his band activities, I found out that the fees charged to the centre for each session was £4.10.0d and the entrance fee to a Fancy Dress Ball was 1s.6d. In nearly four years the band made a total of £921.8s. 2 1/4d. Harry's records of his band activities included a copy of a contract to play at Linden Hall. The contract as can be seen was signed by the officer in charge of the Linden Hall, Miss Olga Shore and the band leader Harry Fernandez. Below the copy of the contract is the actual advert announcing the Fancy Dress Ball which took place on Sunday 14 November 1943. The dance, I understand, was well attended by many evacuees who were more in the mood for dancing due to the fact that the war situation was looking more promising for a return to Gibraltar, as implied by the lyric of the music played at the dance.

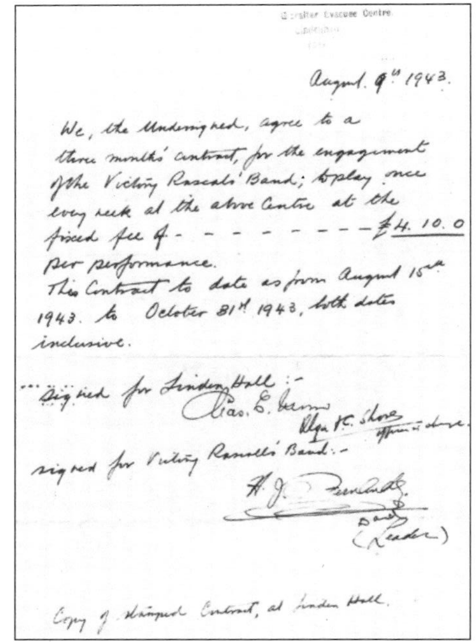

August. 9th 1943.

We, the Undersigned, agree to a three months' contract, for the engagement of the Victory Rascals' Band; to play once every week at the above Centre at the fixed fee of - - - - - - - - £4.10.0 per performance.
This Contract to date as from August 15th 1943. to October 31st 1943, both dates inclusive.

Signed for Linden Hall :-
Olga E. Shore

signed for Victory Rascals' Band:-
H. J. Fernandez
Band Leader

Copy of Original Contract, at Linden Hall.

Above copy of original contract. Copy Mr H. Fernandez

Copy of advert placed in the different centres announcing Fancy Dress Ball at Linden Hall. Copy Mr H.Fernandez

The Gibraltar Victory Band led by Juan Cruz was, as can be seen from the photographs below, also had a very large string orchestra. The photographs were taken on an occasion when they played at Dr Barnardo's Home for a charitable cause. The photographs on this page were donated by Mr E Cruz.

The Juan Cruz's Gibraltar Victory String Orchestra playing at Dr Barnardo's Homes.
At the back: J.Ochello Vicotory Olivero A. Bugeja J.Cruz ...?... ..?... Olivero .....?...
Front row: Barea ..?.. ....?..... T.Cruz ...?... ....?.. J.Osborne W.Feetham G.Yeats.

The Juan Cruz Band playing at Dr Barnardo's Homes.
From L to R: Juan Cruz W.Feetham, G.Yeats, Olivero, Barea.

The photographs below shows the Juan Cruz's Gibraltar Victory Band when at Marlborough Court evacuation centre in Pembroke Road where the band originated.

The Juan Cruz's Gibraltar Victory Band.
Back Row L to R Alex Osborne Alfred Bugeja jnr Joseph Bugeja Snr
Front Row L to R Mr J.Cruz Harry Payas Juan Dalli Johnny Osborne
Emilio Gomez Ernest (Tito) Cruz. Both photos by Mr E Cruz

Sitting in front are Mr Juan Cruz …..?.... ….?...... .Mr Alfred Bugeja.

Below are photographs of the Gibraltar Victory Band conducted by Juan Cruz when performing at Dr Barnardo's home in Barkingside.

The Juan Cruz's Gibraltar Victory Orchestra.
From L to R: Tito Cruz Olivero Victory ...?... ...?... ...?... Juan Cruz Photo by Mr E Cruz

Silvio Peliza and his Band back in Gibraltar. Photo by Mr S.Peliza

Another band which was very successful was the Rock Jokers which initially consisted entirely of accordions. It was started by Silvio Peliza at 92 Lancaster Gate, known as the White Hotel. The manager of this hotel gave them a room for rehearsing. The band also played at various evacuation centres becoming very popular. The name of the band was later changed to The London Rhythm Kings when they changed to a dance band with a mixture of instruments. From then on they acquired more popularity and played not only at the evacuation centres but also at many London venues like the White City Hall. Silvio explained that at this place they played on the stage which was in the centre of a huge hall and the dancers, hundreds of them, danced around the stage. "It was a huge success", said Silvio.

Below is a copy an admission ticket to a Grand Dance in aid of the Gibraltar London Scouts group to the music of The Rock Jokers Orchestra.

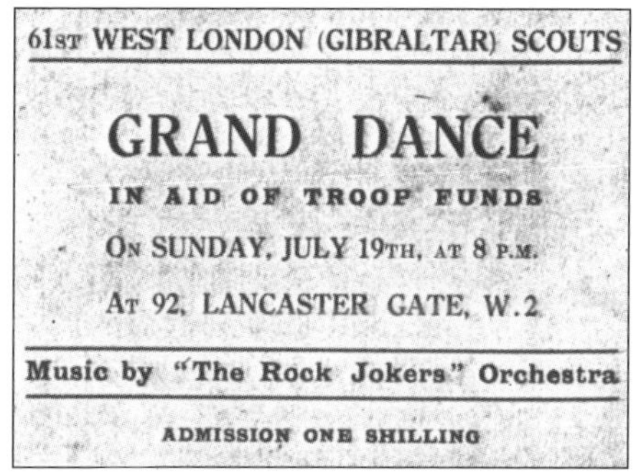

61ST WEST LONDON (GIBRALTAR) SCOUTS

GRAND DANCE

IN AID OF TROOP FUNDS

ON SUNDAY, JULY 19TH, AT 8 P.M.

AT 92, LANCASTER GATE, W.2

Music by "The Rock Jokers" Orchestra

ADMISSION ONE SHILLING

The band also played on many occasions at the Hogar Espanol, the residence of the Spanish refugees in London at Lancaster Gate. In January 1944 the band was requested by the president of the El Hogar Español to perform at the BBC studio with the aim of accompanying a Spanish refugees' singing group with his music. The band was paid by the BBC two and half guineas for their performance. Silvio and his band even played to collect funds in aid of the Russian Army led by Marshal Timoshenko and fighting in Stalingrad. Among the many places where the London Rhythm Kings performed was at The Calpe Institute New Year's tea party in 1944. Below is a copy of the institute's thank you letter.

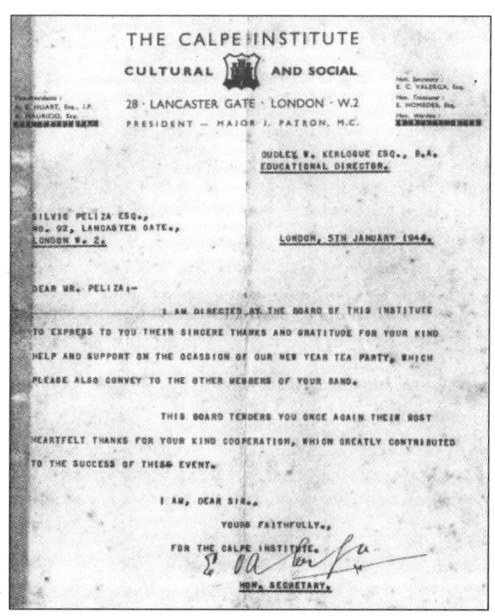

THE CALPE INSTITUTE

CULTURAL AND SOCIAL

28 · LANCASTER GATE · LONDON · W.2

PRESIDENT — MAJOR J. PATRON, M.C.

Hon. Secretary: E. C. VALERGA, Esq.

Hon. Treasurer: E. HOMEDES, Esq.

DUDLEY W. KERLOGUE ESQ., B.A.
EDUCATIONAL DIRECTOR.

SILVIO PELIZA ESQ.,
NO. 92, LANCASTER GATE.,
LONDON W. 2.

LONDON, 5TH JANUARY 1944.

DEAR MR. PELIZA:-

I AM DIRECTED BY THE BOARD OF THIS INSTITUTE TO EXPRESS TO YOU THEIR SINCERE THANKS AND GRATITUDE FOR YOUR KIND HELP AND SUPPORT ON THE OCASSION OF OUR NEW YEAR TEA PARTY, WHICH PLEASE ALSO CONVEY TO THE OTHER MEMBERS OF YOUR BAND.

THIS BOARD TENDERS YOU ONCE AGAIN THEIR MOST HEARTFELT THANKS FOR YOUR KIND COOPERATION, WHICH GREATLY CONTRIBUTED TO THE SUCCESS OF THIS EVENT.

I AM, DEAR SIR.,
YOURS FAITHFULLY.,
FOR THE CALPE INSTITUTE.
HON. SECRETARY.

The North End House Band led by Pepe Luis Gomez also played at many centres including at Whitelands College where the photograph shown below was taken. Mrs Dolly Caruana also performed at the piano with the North End House Band.

North End House Band.
Mesod Serruya (Drums) Joseph Bossano (Piano)Pepe Luis Gomez (trumpet) Albert Vinales (violin) J.Victory (banjo) J.Cornelio (alto saxo) A.Sciacaluga (soprano saxo). Photo Mr P L Gomez

Another well known band was that formed by Gibraltarian evacuee James Chipolina. Before the evacuation James, who had a passion for music, performed on many occasions at the Theatre Royal. When evacuated to London he worked his way up in the world of music and became a vocalist with the famous Edmundo Ross Band. Due to professional reasons he had his named changed to Santiago Lopez. Soon after leaving Edmundo Ross Band, Santiago formed his own band which concentrated on Latin American music.

Santiago Lopez and his wife Ursula during one of their performances. Photo Mr F Rocca

During the war he entertained the troops under the auspices of the Entertainers National Services Association. His band also played at the BBC, at the Queensbury All Services Casino and the Royal Albert Hall along with internationally known orchestras like Victor Sylvester, Geraldo, Edmundo Ross, and others like Roberto Inglez. During this time Santiago was also given very wide publicity by the British press for which he became very popular. Santiago was also very keen on horses, specialising in Arab Horses. During a visit of King Hussein of Jordan to the Astor Club in London he met Santiago. From then on he became much acquainted with the King Hussein of Jordan who named Santiago a Master of the King's Horses. The evacuation provided Mr Chipolina the great opportunity of becoming famous in what he loved doing. There were much smaller bands like the one formed by a group of girls in addition to the main band at North End House shown in the photo below.

In the photo are Carolina Bishop, Flordeliz Caballero. Photo Mr J Ballester.

Evacuees in the dance hall at the Royal Palace Hotel. Photo Mr A Massetti

Among the evacuees there was also a variety group called the Tariks led by Louis Vincent. Productions of local concerts were also staged in many centres. Another well known evacuee who used to play and also teach the piano was Mrs Maria Isabel Soiza (nee Salvado). She resided initially at the Thackaray Hotel and later moved to the York Hotel.

The Tarik Band led by Luis Vincent when entertaining evacuees. at the North End House. Photo Mrs A Lara

At the Whitelands College like in many other centres the dining room was used to hold dances almost every weekend. I remember on one occasion when a grand dance was held in the dining room. I think it was the last Christmas we spent at Whitelands. The dining hall was fully decorated with "cadenetas." I distinctly remember also seeing a replica of an aeroplane constructed with foil paper. It was hanging from the ceiling looking very impressive.

This decorative aeroplane had been constructed by Angel D' Alorto, an avid manufacturer of toys during the evacuation.

Years later, after the war, Mr D'Alorto used to own a toy shop in Gibraltar.

There were no resident bands at Whitelands but I remember that Alfredo Balban entertained the evacuees by playing his bag pipe within the College precinct. Alfredo used to walk round the gardens or the corridors and was followed by children who had a great time. When there was a special football match he also played at the start of the match. While Alfredo played his bag pipe he was accompanied with a display of Scottish dances by the lovely dancers Lourdes and Mini Bosio who also resided at Whitelands. There were other forms of musical entertainment like listening to music from wireless sets and playing records on hand-wound gramophones. The wireless set had been issued by the authorities concerned to every centre. In some centres, where practicable, pianos were also provided for musical entertainment.

At Whitelands the radio and gramophone were kept in a large room where there was a table set aside with chairs to listen to the radio, play records and organise parties, indoor games and bingo sessions as a way of providing other forms of entertainment. Children were not allowed to go into this room whenever there was a function going on but they would nevertheless, listen to the music from the outside of the room.

There were also many evacuees who took part in variety shows, concerts and plays at different evacuation centres as can be seen from the photographs shown in the next few pages. Below are photographs taken at Highlands Heath on the occasion of a variety show organised by Mr G.Linares.

Photograph of a Variety Show by Evacuees at Highlands Heath.

Standing on back in the centre of the picture is G.Linares
Standing L to R: McCarthy W.Mendoza M.Macedo N.Trinidad Mi.Azopardi L.Netto P.Cano T.Cano V.Chipolina Borda Ma.Azopardi A.Peliza F.Cano C.Baldachino A.Garro B.Bensusan A.Peliza.
Sitting left to right F.Rocca ...?... L.McCarthy A.Cano A.Duo V.Netto Linares. Bensusan Z.Patterson P.Cardona. Photo Mr J Lima

Photograph of a variety show by evacuees at Highlands Heath.
Back row standing left to right B.Bensusan A.Peliza Mi.Azopardi T.Cano A.Garro C.Baldachino C.Cano M.Macedo McCarthy Ma.Azopardi A.Peliza P.Cano L.Netto W.Mendoza N.Trinidad
Slightly in the middle standing with right hands up : V.Netto Z.Patterson A.Cano
Kneeling : C.Trinidad L.McCarthy E.Bensusan D.Duo
Sitting on the ground N.Linares F.Rocca. Photo Mrs L Olivero(nee Netto)

Almost the same group as above.
Back row left to right: P.Cano A.Peliza Mi.Azopardi L.Netto McCarthy C.Baldachino F.Cano Ma.Azopardi A.Garrro N.Trinidad G.Mendoza G.Linares. Sitting in front from left to right: M.Macedo A.Cano T.Cano L.Trinidad D. Duo E.Bensusan N.Linares .Duo A. Peliza Z.Patterson V.Netto B.Bensusan
Photo Mrs E Azopardi

The children also took part in many plays as can be seen from the photograph in this and the next page. The photographs below were taken during a Christmas play in Highlands Heath.

In the photograph marked with a cross is Francis Rocca.

Amongst the children in the photo are Francis Rocca and George Azopardi.
Photos Mr F Rocca

Above from L to R: …?...,J.Nahon,S.Seruya,…?.. ,D.Gabay,G.Benady…?....,…?....

Above at the back from L to R: …?...,C.Massias,…?...,O.Hatchwel,…?...,D.Hassan,B.Israel,…?...,
Sitting C.Bensadon A. Massias

Above from L to R:…?...,…?...,…/…,B.Israel,O.Hatchwel,..?.., B.Cohen,…?...,C.Bensadon,...?...,G.Benady,Benady.
The photographs above were taken during school plays
organised by the Gibraltar Jewish evacuees at North End House.
Photos Mr M Belilo.

Above and below children taking part at a Christmas Play at the Royal Palace Hotel.
Photos above and below Mrs LBugeja

Above children in an open air Peter Pan play at Dr Barnardo's Homes.
Above photo Mr L Wahnon

Evacuees in the UK

A children's play at Northern House. Mrs A Lara

Celebrating Christmas at Dr Barnardo's Home. Photo by Mr J Zayas.
Below cutting from the Ilford newspaper the Recorder reporting
On the entertainment of Gibraltar children at Dr Barnardo's.

GIB. CHILDREN SEE PANTO.

The child evacuees from Gibralter, who are staying at Dr. Barnardo's Homes, Barkingside, were entertained by the W.V.S. at that Centre, to a talkie cinema show, kindly given by Mr. Pritchard of Ilford, on January 6th. During the evening a party was held, the following artistes helping, Mrs. Phyllis Baker, with her accordian, Madame Morgan, songs at the piano, Dorrie Gilbert, comedian, and Mazeda, a charming girl who thrilled everyone with her delightful singing and dancing.

On Thursday and Friday, January 7th and 8th, 150 children enjoyed themselves at a matinee of "Cinderella" at the Ilford Hippodrome. The W.V.S. ladies in charge, Mrs. Allen, Mrs. Peel, and Mrs. Carter thank all who helped to give the children such a happy time.

On the left cutting from the Ilford Recorder referring to the Panto show.

Children at Dr Barnardo's watching a puppet show. Amongst the children are Hubert Corby and his sister Doris (Mrs Parody).
Photo Mrs D Parody

Children show at Dr Barnardo's Home
In the photo are :R.Sherriff, D.Corby (Mrs Parody),H.Corby, H.Osborne,D.Wahnon,King, E.Power, J.Asquez. Photo Mr J Asquez

Below are the details of the participant in a Cinderalla play organised by Silvio Peliza and his band staged at 92 Lancaster Gate on Wednesday 3rd March 1943 at 6.30 pm.

1ST PART	2nd PART
Selection by Silvio Peliza and his Band **"CINDERELLA"** **Prince Charming**....... Pat Tait **Cinderella...**............ Lourdes Linares **Lady Julia**.............. Mary Lou Pallas **Ugly Sisters**..............Angela Reading Elizabeth Casia **Cook**....................... Alicia Fenwick **Matilda...**............ .Ida Padina **King**...................... Alicia Fenwick **Queen...**................. Mary Louisa Fenwick **Fairy Godmother** Angela Nogueras **Bobo** Matilde Schembri Announcers, Heralds, Courtiers, Mice Bats, Fairies, Servants Acacia Pereira, Lilian Sene, Ida McLaren, Carmen Serra, Alicia Asquez, Laura Gomez, Ida Asquez, Margot Serra, Viola Linares, And Ernestina Victory.	**Top Hat Dance**.............Elena Rodriguez **Russian Dance**. Mary Lou Serra JosephineBanda Claudia Ignacio **Spanish Dance And Song** ... Regina Knapp **Three Little Sisters** ...Ida Padina ...Lilian Sene .... Acacia Pereira **Polka.** **......**Claudia Ignacio Mary Lou Serra Mr W. Perera and his harmonic **Dance**.................. Ruby Caetano **Song**..................... Aurelia Borge **ClownDance**......... Matilda Schembri **Selection By Band** **God Save The King**

Similar entertainments involving plays, variety shows and many fancy dress competitions were also held at different evacuation centres as can be appreciated from the photographs in this section about entertainment.

At Whitelands two plays were organised and staged by Mr Ralf Torrilla. These were "El Macareno" and "La Cueva del Albaizin" He also produced a sketch entitled "Hay Lyons Hoy Mr Lyons. According to him (Mr.Torrilla), his favourite poem was "A Mi Pequeña Patria" written in 1943. It was first recited for the evacuees at Whitelands College and then, by popular demand, at many other evacuation centres in London.

"A Mi Pequeña Patria"

Inspiración sana y pura
Yo busco cada mañana
De la luz de la razón
No creáis que sea la ambición
De retener a mi tierra
Que la añoro con pasión
Lo medito y lo pienso
Lo justifico y lo acato
Aunque comprendo mil veces
Que estoy lejos de hallarlo
Solución inesperada es lo único que espero
Para el día de mañana
Ya todo abra terminado
El calvario de mi alma,
La pesadilla constante
Que me atormenta mi alma,
Será ilusión vespertina
De nuestra patria querida
Que aunque pequeña es tan grande
Que a las grandes las eclipsa.

Yo no soy ilusionista
Solo redacto mi mente
Como idea definida
Y nada tiene valor
Ni nada complace o sirve
Si no amas como yo
La tierra donde naciste!

Poem donated by Mrs Sonia Golt (nee Torrilla)

Evacuees in the UK

One of the most well known functions during the evacuation was that organised by the BBC and staged at the King's College on the 3rd May 1942. It was reported in the Gibraltar Chronicle on 29th July 1942. The recordings were used in the first edition of the series ***Gibraltar in London*** on the 15 September 1942. It was then broadcast to Gibraltar at monthly intervals until the summer of 1944 when the evacuees left London.

GIBRALTAR EVACUEES FROM ALL OVER LONDON BROADCAST TO–"THE ROCK"

These pictures, taken in a B.B.C. studio, show talented Gibraltar evacuees in London giving their own broadcast concert to Gibraltar.

They came from various centres all over London, where they are now living, to give an enthusiastic and entertaining performance.

Above, six-years-old Laura Diaz, is photographed singing "Mi Jaca," in which she was accompanied at the piano by Mrs. D. Caruana.

On the right (top) is a scene from the Spanish operetta, "La Rosa del Azafran", being sung by (left to right) Miss Orensia Ghio, Miss Elena Cruz, Miss Angeles Usifredo, Miss Noelia Mosquera, Miss Araceli Lopez, Mr. Louis Gomila, Miss Luisa Lopez, Miss Carmen Ghio, Miss Maruja Lopez and Mrs. L. Gonzalez. They were accompanied at the piano by Mrs. Frances Calamaro.

Above pictures from a show held at the King's College by the BBC on the 3rd May 1942.
Mr Manuel Infant is sitting in front.

Another function arranged by the BBC was held at Marlborough Court evacuation centre and which is depicted in the photograph shown below.

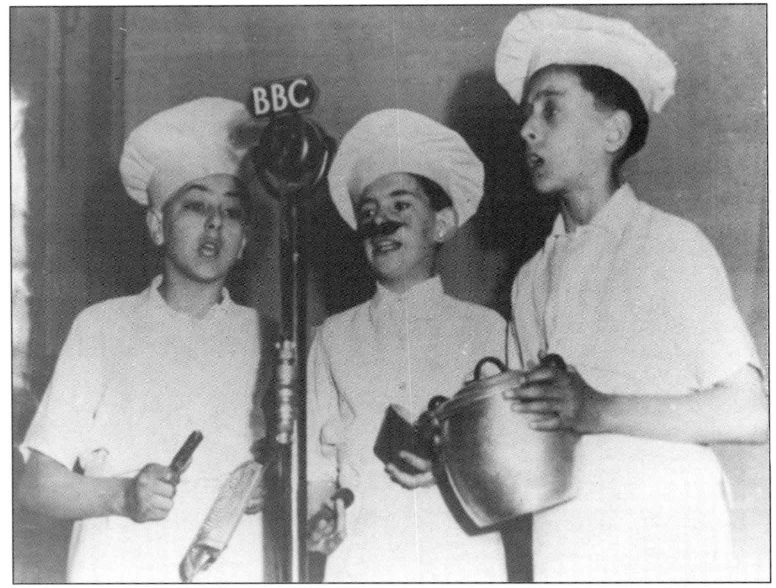

Taking part in a show arranged by the BBC at Marlborough Court evacuation centre.
In the photo from L to R Marcelino Linares, Victor Sciacaluga and Victor Infante.
Photo by Mr V Sciacaluga

Many of the evacuation centres organised fancy dress competitions as can been seen from the photographs which I have been able to obtain during my research and have displayed in the following pages. The variety and quality of the different dresses produced for these events are really first class taking into account the shortage of materials.

Left to right A.Acolina G.Olivero L.Aguilera M.Harrison G.Mendez L.Harrison.
Photo the Harrison family

Back row left to right: M.Costa E.Leon P.Davis
Front row Left to right E.Acolina J.Martinez (Winner) C.Montado M.Harrison. Photo Mr J Martinez

Back row left to right ...?... E.Leon ....?...F.Acolina (winner as Charlot) M.Acolina A.Saltariche E.Acolina
Front row left to right V.Pilcher L.Pilcher A.Montado A.Olivero L.Montado M.Reading G.Gaduzo.
Photo Mr L Saltariche

Back row from left to right : R.Gingell M.Davis (Winner as Maria Antoniette) L.Power
Front row left to right: A.Celecia M. Martinez Trinidad O.Harrison C.Harrison A.Acolina.
Photo the Harrison Family

"We Thank God and England.."

At Whitelands College the fancy dress competitions were mainly organised by Mr Ralf Torrilla who also organised many plays, concert and recitals.

Back row R.Gingell J.Gingell S.Balban Ferris F.Balban Fiol Acolina G.Olivero M.Saltariche
Third row ...?... ...?.... V.Olivero...?.... ...?...J.Canilla...?...C.Mendez...?... ...?... ....?...
Second row W.Nacimiento Nacimiento ...?... ...?....J.Viagas ...?.. ...?... ..?... ...?..... ...?...L.Montado(winner as nurse)
Front row Barea M.Payas ...?... W.Gomez H.Hosken ...?... A.Lopez C.Gibson ...?.... ...?.... Photo by Mr C Gibson

Back row C.Montado L.Bellido J.Balban G.Saltariche C.Montado J.Oliver Brosco J.Harrison J.Martinez G.Costa
Third row M.Prescott Figueras Zammitt Payas H.Payas Gerada O.Broton,J.Broton, J.Lopez M.Capurro M.Balban
Second row C.Hosken M.Olivero L.Bosio L.Montado E.Gerada Martinez M.Costa ....?.....
First row J.Cavilla G.Peliza J.Peliza Y Bacarese A.Celecia L.Power R.Capurro J.McKay Trinidad M.Davis.
Photo Mr M Balban

George Gaduzo.
PhotoNeilston Local History Office

Joe Gingell

Mrs Wahnon with her sons Leslie and Harold taking part in a fancy dress competition.

Leslie Wahnon taking part in a variety concert at Dr Barnardo's.

L.Wahnon in a school play of " Peter Pan" at the Mossford School.

Leslie Wahnon and cousin Dorothy Wahnon in a variety concert.

All the photographs on this page were donated by Mr L Wahnon.

Victor Spiteri at the Royal Palace Hotel in fancy dress competition.   Photo Mr V Spiteri

Children at Dr Bernardo's Home in an open air play of Peter Pan.   Photo Mr L Wahnon

Joseph and Richard Evans taking part in a fancy dress competition at the Kensington Palace Mansion. Photo Evans brothers

This gaily-dressed group of Gibraltar children caused considerable interest recently, when they appeared in the High-road in Spanish costume. They are living at Dr. Barnardo's Homes.

The above photo was taken from a cutting of the Ilford Recorder.
At the back second from the right is Leslie Wahnon. Photo by Ilford Recorder

Fancy dress competition held at Dr Barnardo's Home.
In the photo standing in front on the extreme right is Joe Ballantine
and on the extreme left in air force uniform Harold Wahnon. Photo by Mr L Wahnon

Elena Bagna(Mrs Alman) at a fancy dress. competition at the 100 Lancaster

Rosy and Kiko Borge winners of a fancy. dress competition at the National Hotel

Elena Bagna(Mrs Alman) at 100 Lancaster Gate.

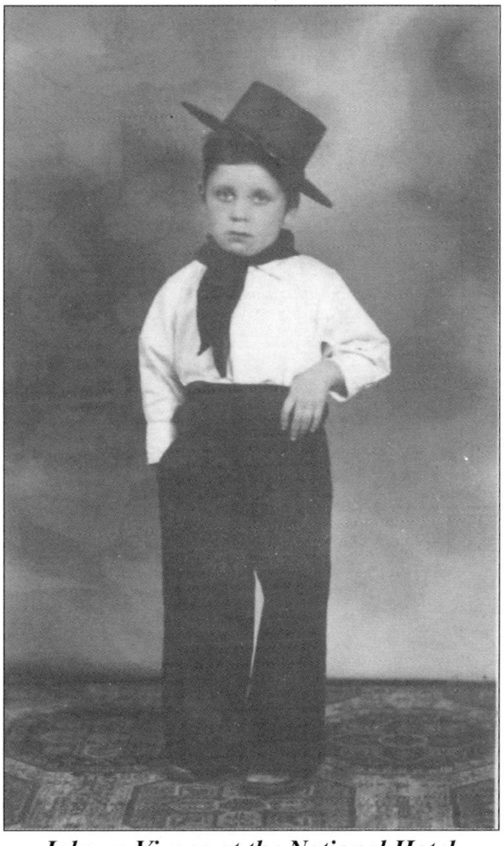

Johnny Viagas at the National Hotel.

Aida Perez and Mariola Benvenuto(Mrs Summerfield) at the Duchess of Bedford. Photo Mrs M Summerfield

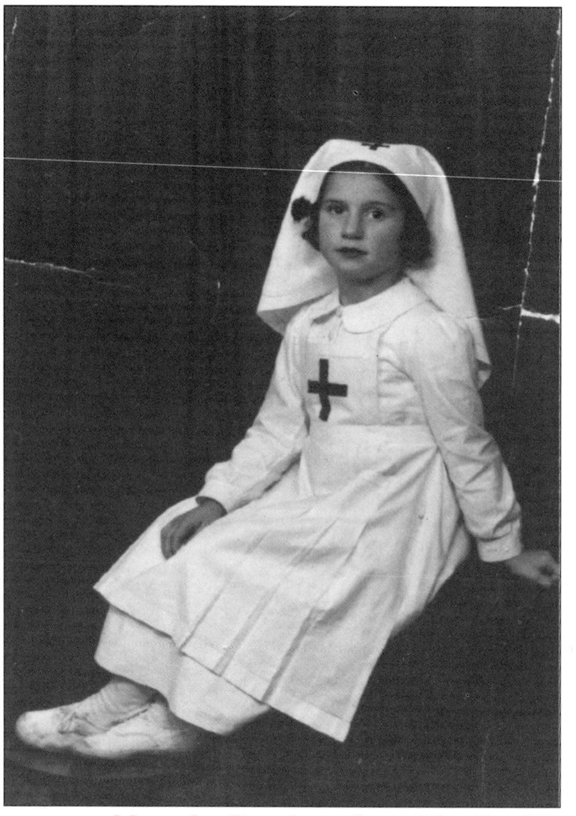

Mercedes Povedano (later Mrs Cruz) at St Katherine's College. PhotoMrs M Cruz

Lygia Bugeja at the Royal Palace Hotel. Photo Mrs L Bugeja

Albert Cruz at Fulham. Photo Mrs M Cruz

Mariola Benvenuto (Mrs Summerfield)
at the Duchess of Bedford fancy dress competition.
PhotoMrs M Summerfield

Girls taking part in a dressing competition
at Marlborough Court.
In the photo are Lourdes Infante standing in the middle at the back and Mercy Infante sitting on the left hand
Photo Mr M Infante

Francis Rocca and ...?.... at Highlands Heath.
Photo Mr F Rocca

Leslie and Harold Wahnon
At Dr Barnardo's.
Photo Mr L Wahnon

In addition to the leisure activities and the many forms of entertainment organised by the evacuees, the Ministry of Health in conjunction with the Gibraltar Evacuation Committee representatives also arranged outings and tours around London for different age groups of evacuees. The photographs in this section were taken during some of these tours. The tours included visits to the different places of historical interest.

Children from different centres for a day outing at Hampstead Heath.
In the photo taking care of the children is Mr L.Mañetto. Among the children is Eligio Vinet.
Photo Mr C Rodriguez

Evacuees at Richmond Park. Photo Mr M Infante

The photograph below shows the children boarding the bus to take them on a tour around places of interest. Note the evacuees carrying the boxes containing the gas masks. The historical places were Hampton Court, Windsor Castle, The Tower and London Bridge, St Paul's Cathedral and many other places. There were also large gatherings of evacuees at the different parks in London like Richmond.

Evacuees on a bus trip. Photo Mrs P Mamo(nee Castle)

One of the many places of interest included also a visit by school children to the London Zoo of which a photograph is shown below:

A visit by school children to the London Zoo. Photo Mr J Zayas

The photograph below shows evacuees from different centres in London taking part in games during an outing to Hampstead Heath.

Gibraltar evacuees playing games at Hampstead Heath during an outing. Photo Mr C Rodriguez

Gibraltar Evacuees posing for a photograph at Richmond in the Summer of 1942
In the photo are Rosa Payas (nee Olivero), Rosario Galliano, M.Savignon,A.Savignon, J.Bagu, M.Finlayson, Miss C Hernandez,Salvador Machado Hernandez,Juani Bagu,Guillermo Hernandez, Aida Raggio,Minerva Danino(Mrs Ramirez),Juanito Goodman,Rodolfo Torrilla Photo Mrs R Payas

Below are photographs taken at one of the evacuees' outings at Richmond Park. During one of these visits the evacuees were taken to see Windsor Castle.

Photos Mr M Infante

Evacuee children in a London park.
Sitting at the extreme end is Miss Olga Massetti. Photo Mr A Massetti

The above close up photograph was taken during an outing at Hampstead Heath.
In the forefront of the photograph is Eligio Vinet and the extreme right is Paco Jurado both from the Royal Stuart Hotel
Photo Mr M Infante

Below are pictures taken during the boat sightseeing trips along the River Thames. Photos donated by Mr C Rodriguez.

The photographs below show evacuee children in London when they were taken on a boat tour in the River Thames to watch the London scenery. Photos Mr C Rodriguez

Gibraltar evacuee children on a river boat trip in London.

Evacuees on a sight seeing trip along the River Thames.

Below pictures of trips along the River Thames with a recent photograph of the Tower London seeing by the evacuees across the river on their boat trip.

Evacuees on the river trip. In approximately the centre of the boat is Mr and Mrs Norton. Photo Mrs Gill (nee Norton)

Evacuees gathered after an outing at a park near Northern End House. With them are Louis Vinent and his band- The Tariks. Photo Mrs Lara

A close up picture of evacuees on the river boat.   Photo Mr C Rodriguez

*Children on a river trip to see places of interest.   Among those in the photograph are the following: J.Mamo,C.Montegriffo,A.Olivero,Vella,L.Ferro,J.Ferro,L.Estella,Sene,V.Zammut,M.L.Zammut,C.Montero,M.Pizzaro, J.Olivero,(Vinales),LMontegriffo(Pilcher),P.Olivero (Brooks) and Asquez\
Photo Mrs P Mamo(nee Castle)*

Evacuees in the UK

Left to Right A. Roman E., Sanchez and Adolfo Barboro from Ivanhoe Hotel.
Photo Mr J Sanchez

Johnny Mascarenhas and his sister Nora with other children.
Photo Mr J Mascarenhas

Carlos, Olga and Isabel Montero.
Photo Mr C Montero

Mrs K Amores, Aurelia Wilkie Emily Wilkie Maria Dolores Wilkie.
Photo Mrs Risso

"We Thank God and England.."

In this page are photographs of evacuees enjoying an outing to Hyde Park.

Mrs Benvenuto at Hyde Park with her sons Paul and Gustavo.
Photo Mrs M Summerfield

Children in Hyde Park. One of the carers, second from the right is Miss Olga Massetti.   Photo Mr A Massetti

From L to R Magi Pardo, Pastori Cavilla, Paul Cano, Maruja Chichon and Hemmi.
Photo Miss A Pardo

Evacuee children playing in Hyde Park during one of the outings. Photo Mrs L Bugeja

When the evacuees became more accustomed to London, they ventured to visit families in the different evacuations centres. They also visited places like Trafalgar Square, which seemed to be one of the most favourite places to have photographs taken.

A Group of Gibraltar evacuees at Trafalgar Square during one of the many organised trips around London. In the photo is Miss A.Pardo. Photo Miss A Pardo

Mr Anthony and Mrs Victoria Catania with their daughter Antonia. Photo Lavina Holmes

Antonio Dalmedo with his recently married wife Carolina at Trafalgar Square . Photo Mr Dalmedo

Anna Pozo Maidi Walker Mary Hermida Boys Alfred and Emilio Hermida. Photo Mr E Pozo

Mr and Mrs Norton with their son Johnny in 1943. PhotoMr.Gill (nee Norton)

L to R: Regina Lima..?... Margarita Marchavello, Celia Bossano. Photo Mr V Bossano

Mrs Victoria Benvenuto by the Round Pond At Hyde Park. Photo Mrs M Summerfield

At the back L to R: Mrs Regina Lima amd Mrs Celia Bossano Kneeling L to R: Andres Bossano and Victor Bossano. Photo Mr V Bossano

Adolfo Barboro and his wife Maruja (nee Candeas) on honeymoon. Photo Mrs Barboro

Above and below the Macedo family.

Mrs Mascarenhas with her children Johnny and Nora and other children. Photo Mr J Mascarenhas

At the back L to R: Mrs Maria Macedo, Mrs Ana Macedo with Maruchi Macedo and Miss Rosa Macedo. In front Anne Macedo and Hector Macedo. Photos Mrs M Martinez

This page shows a collection of postcards of places of interest visited by the evacuees during some of their tours sponsored by the British Council.

Big Ben as seeing during the war.
Photo The History Place

Gibraltar evacuees posing in photo studio after a sightseeing tour in London.
In the photo Maribel Dalmedo(nee Butterham), Ofelia Cano,(nee Carreras).
Photo Mr M Chichon

Evacuees on the Putney Bridge.
Mrs Ana Hernandez (nee Jimenez) with other evacuees
Photo Mrs Brittenden

Evacuees in the area of Putney
In the photo are Mrs Ana Hernandez (nee Jimenez), Mrs M Poggio and another evacuee Photo Mrs Brittenden

The Victor family at a studio in Oxford Street in 1942
At the back Mary and Jane.
In front Hortensia, Mrs Maria Victor and John.
Photo Mr J Victor

Scouting and the Girl Guides movements were soon started in almost every evacuation centre. There were for the younger children the Brownie Packs in many centres too. The picture below shows the Boy Scouts at the Royal Palace Hotel where there were so many that they had their own Company.

Boys Scouts at the Royal Palace Hotel.
In the photo are Paul and Joseph Lara
Photo Mrs L Bugeja

As at the Royal Palace Hotel, the Girl Guides at the National Hotel were so many that they had their own company too.

Girl Guides at a park near the National Hotel.
At the back L to R: Sonia Duarte, Olga DeVeras, Sonia Almeda, Mary Mor, Dorothy Brown ….?....
Sitting in front L to R: Viola Abudarham Betsy Brown …..?......
PhotoMrs M Martinez

Below is an extract from the Gibraltar Chronicle published in May 1941 referring to the formation of Scouts, Girl Guides and Brownies activities in London.

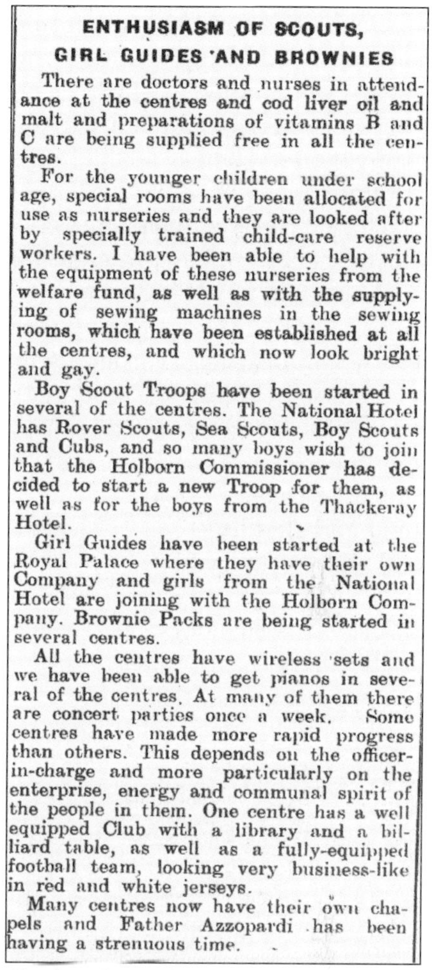

ENTHUSIASM OF SCOUTS, GIRL GUIDES AND BROWNIES

There are doctors and nurses in attendance at the centres and cod liver oil and malt and preparations of vitamins B and C are being supplied free in all the centres.

For the younger children under school age, special rooms have been allocated for use as nurseries and they are looked after by specially trained child-care reserve workers. I have been able to help with the equipment of these nurseries from the welfare fund, as well as with the supplying of sewing machines in the sewing rooms, which have been established at all the centres, and which now look bright and gay.

Boy Scout Troops have been started in several of the centres. The National Hotel has Rover Scouts, Sea Scouts, Boy Scouts and Cubs, and so many boys wish to join that the Holborn Commissioner has decided to start a new Troop for them, as well as for the boys from the Thackeray Hotel.

Girl Guides have been started at the Royal Palace where they have their own Company and girls from the National Hotel are joining with the Holborn Company. Brownie Packs are being started in several centres.

All the centres have wireless sets and we have been able to get pianos in several of the centres. At many of them there are concert parties once a week. Some centres have made more rapid progress than others. This depends on the officer-in-charge and more particularly on the enterprise, energy and communal spirit of the people in them. One centre has a well equipped Club with a library and a billiard table, as well as a fully-equipped football team, looking very business-like in red and white jerseys.

Many centres now have their own chapels and Father Azzopardi has been having a strenuous time.

Cutting from the Gibraltar Chronicle

Gibraltar evacuee Scouts in Holborn.
Photo Mr F Curtis

Due to the fact that most young men were in the Services there was a great demand for labourers both male and female. At first there were many impediments for evacuees to find work. However, soon after the evacuees had settled down, the rules restricting the employment for evacuees were more relaxed. For those evacuees who wanted to work there were many jobs available in the then London labour market. Many of the factories changed their production line to meet the war effort requirements of the Government.

Within Wandsworth and nearby there were Gibraltarian evacuees from Whitelands and Highlands working in some of these factories and shops. The following are the names some of the nearby firms:

Crown and Bedding
near Wandsworth Prison
Pre-war: bedding items.
Wartime: canvas, bags, parachutes, beds etc.

Starkie Gardner at Southfields
Peacetime: Escalators for shops and undergrounds.
War Time: Equipment for minesweeping and aircraft petrol tanks etc.

Morgan Crucible at Battersea near Bridge Road
Engineering and manufacture of carbon brushes for motors, generators etc

Tate and Lyle at Wandsworth
Sugar refining

Prices at York Road Wandsworth
Candle making.

Two of the Alecio brothers were employed in the repair of sewing machines and production line belts. Also making spare parts for items such as, parachutes, fuel tanks, radiators and so on. Another of the Alecio brothers was employed in a bakery near Putney Bridge called Melbrays. This firm produced meat pies, jam tarts and other confectioneries. Hector Alecio explained to me that he remembered when his brother, who was only fifteen, came back from work. He usually arrived late in the evenings, always with burns in his arms and hands due to the hot jam tarts. Hector also explained that his brothers' earnings never reached £3 per week and out of that they paid National Insurance and had some money deducted to cover their upkeep at Whitelands. Also working in Melbrays bakery were Salvador and Antonio Lopez from Whitelands College and Paul Cano and Manolo Rodriguez from Highlands Heath. In this same firm, there were also about twenty Gibraltar female evacuees employed. Salvador told me "I still carry burn marks on my arms from the trays that we had to remove from the hot ovens. When needed, we had to unload bags of flour and stack them in the store. Salvador said, "Considering that we were between 14 and 15 years of age I think we were doing a very tough job."

Antonio Reyes from Whitelands worked in a nearby branch of the famous Gordon Gins Distilleries. Antonio later moved to a mattresses making shop where he was employed in filling up the mattress. There he met his future wife Maruja Olivero who used to saw up the mattresses.

Kitchen helpers at the Broadwalk Hotel,De Vere Gardens.
In the photo are Mrs Maria Josefa Caballero, Mrs Catalina Lombard (nee Walker), Mrs Lucy Santos. Photo Joseph Ballester

Kitchen helpers at Lancaster Gate.
Back row Mrs B Sene..?...Mrs Victory MrsL.Ignacio Mrs Figuera. Middle row Mrs L Danino Mrs M Serra Mrs R.Danino Mrs E.Noble. In front Mrs Olivero Mrs A Rocca. Photo Mrs Rodriguez

There were also opportunities offered by the Government for young people to take up short-term trade training courses. Manolo Rodriguez, Victor Bossano, Ernest Asquez and William Mondoza from Highlands Heath each took up these courses in mechanical engineering at a training centre in Hounslow West. Manolo Rodriguez worked for some time in this trade before returning to Gibraltar. Harry Fernandez, from Marlborough Court found a job at Harrods where he worked until he left London in 1944. He said that even up to very recent years he was given special treatment when ever he visited Harrods. The photos below were donated by Mr M Infante.

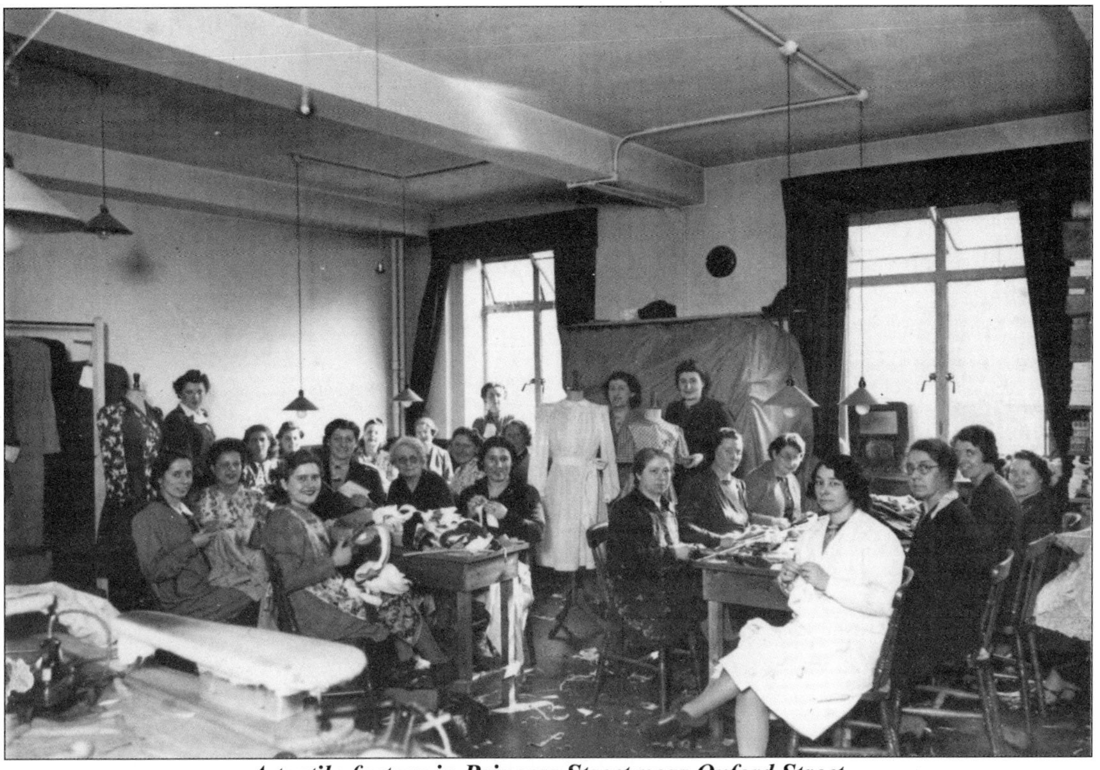

A textile factory in Princess Street near Oxford Street.
In the photograph are Miss Elena Chini and Violeta Gatt from the Dean Hotel

The same clothing factory as above where evacuees who were accommodated at the Dean Hotel used to work.
In the photograph are Miss Chini and her cousins Miss Gatt and Carmela Baglietto.

There were many job vacancies in demolition work where good wages were paid but it entailed very dangerous work. A few evacuees took up this work but soon gave it up. For women there were apparently other jobs available mainly in the textile industry. Many evacuees at the Dean Hotel and the York Hotel used to work in clothing American factory called the Style Dresses at Princess Street near Oxford Street.

Evacuees at the Style Dress Factory. In the photo are Miss Luisa Ferro, Miss Dellipiani and Josefa Martinez from the York Hotel. Photos Mr M Infante

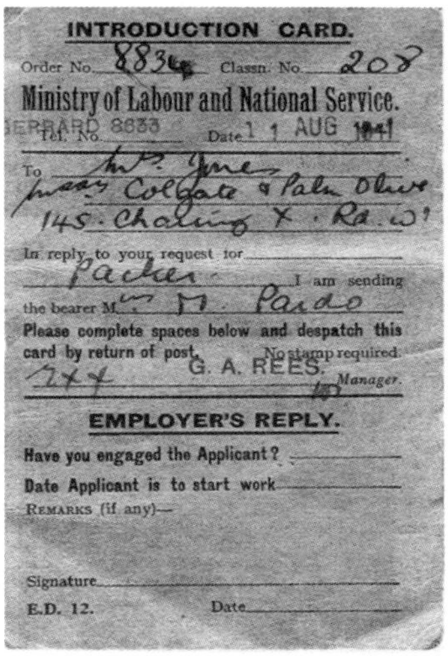

INTRODUCTION CARD.

Order No. 8834 Classn. No. 208

Ministry of Labour and National Service.

Tel. No. GERRARD 8833 Date 11 AUG 1941

To Mr. Jones, Colgate & Palm Olive, 145. Charing X. Rd. W1

In reply to your request for Packer I am sending the bearer Miss M. Pardo

Please complete spaces below and despatch this card by return of post. No stamp required.

G. A. REES. Manager.

EMPLOYER'S REPLY.

Have you engaged the Applicant?

Date Applicant is to start work

Remarks (if any)—

Signature

E.D. 12. Date

Copy of an introduction for employment card by Miss A Pardo

Evacuees from Lancaster Gate working in an Army procurement factory. In the photograph are Miss E.Pardo (Mrs Moreton) Miss I Pardo (Mrs Santos) Miss L Porro Miss J Silva. Photo Mrs I Santos

Above Miss M Pardo's introduction card when she went for an interview to be employed with Colgate and Palmolive Ltd in Charing Cross.

Below is an example of an insurance contribution card. Copy Mr Infante

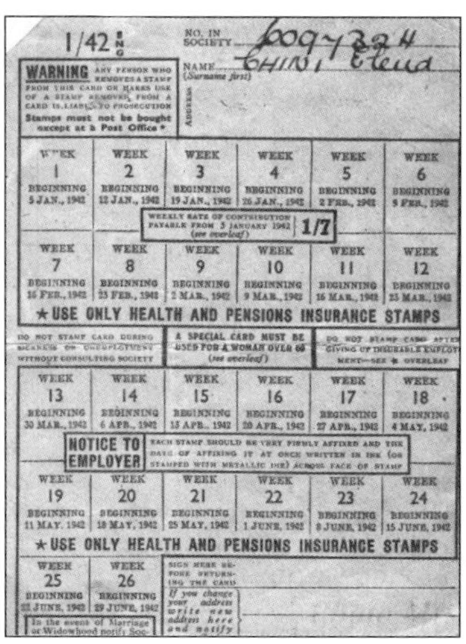

1/42

NO. IN SOCIETY 6009-7324

NAME (Surname first) CHINI, Elena

WARNING ANY PERSON WHO REMOVES A STAMP FROM THIS CARD OR MAKES USE OF A STAMP REMOVED FROM A CARD IS LIABLE TO PROSECUTION. Stamps must not be bought except at a Post Office*

WEEK 1 BEGINNING 5 JAN., 1942	WEEK 2 BEGINNING 12 JAN., 1942	WEEK 3 BEGINNING 19 JAN., 1942	WEEK 4 BEGINNING 26 JAN., 1942	WEEK 5 BEGINNING 2 FEB., 1942	WEEK 6 BEGINNING 9 FEB., 1942
WEEK 7 BEGINNING 16 FEB., 1942	WEEK 8 BEGINNING 23 FEB., 1942	WEEK 9 BEGINNING 2 MAR., 1942	WEEK 10 BEGINNING 9 MAR., 1942	WEEK 11 BEGINNING 16 MAR., 1942	WEEK 12 BEGINNING 23 MAR., 1942
WEEK 13 BEGINNING 30 MAR., 1942	WEEK 14 BEGINNING 6 APR., 1942	WEEK 15 BEGINNING 13 APR., 1942	WEEK 16 BEGINNING 20 APR., 1942	WEEK 17 BEGINNING 27 APR., 1942	WEEK 18 BEGINNING 4 MAY, 1942
WEEK 19 BEGINNING 11 MAY, 1942	WEEK 20 BEGINNING 18 MAY, 1942	WEEK 21 BEGINNING 25 MAY, 1942	WEEK 22 BEGINNING 1 JUNE, 1942	WEEK 23 BEGINNING 8 JUNE, 1942	WEEK 24 BEGINNING 15 JUNE, 1942
WEEK 25 BEGINNING 22 JUNE, 1942	WEEK 26 BEGINNING 29 JUNE, 1942				

WEEKLY RATE OF CONTRIBUTION PAYABLE FROM 5 JANUARY 1942 (see overleaf) 1/7

★USE ONLY HEALTH AND PENSIONS INSURANCE STAMPS

A SPECIAL CARD MUST BE USED FOR A WOMAN OVER 60 (see overleaf)

NOTICE TO EMPLOYER

★USE ONLY HEALTH AND PENSIONS INSURANCE STAMPS

If you change your address write new address here and notify

HM Queen Elizabeth talking to Miss Lourdes Montegriffo (Mrs Pilcher) from North End House working in a tent factory. Photo IWM.

Photo taken in London on the 15 July 1943 of work mates in the Ticty. Snack Factory in the photo are Margari, Obdulia, Melle and Luisa. Photo Mrs Rodriguez

For women in addition to the jobs available mainly in the textile there were also others more directly oriented to the war industry. By 1942 there were many Gibraltar evacuees employed in many different type of work. J. Lyons & Co. in Cadby Hall employed many evacuees. Nearby this firm there was a post office where some Gibraltar evacuees were employed. Evacuees had to conform to labour employment requirements in term of insurance and tax.

In 1942 at Ford's main dealer told John Victor that he was a very promising apprentice and arranged with a technical institute in London in association with London City Council for him to attend classes on a day-release basis to study basic engineering.

Miss Carmen Rodriguez (Mrs Torres) receives National Savings Certificate at the Eric Hart Ltd annual factory party from Alderman G.C.Brooks, Chairman of the St Marylbone Local Saving Committee. In the photo are Mr and Mrs Hart, principals of the blouse and dress manufacturing firm in Oxford Street. Also in the photo is Mrs Maria Adela Finlayson Photo Mr M Infante.

John Victor in 1941. Photo Mr J Victor

Evacuees working in Kensington. At the back left hand corner is Miss Lourdes Sheriff (Mrs Barker) next is Nydia Gomez and at the right hand corner is Miss Victoria Parody (Mrs Berry). Photo Mrs Cavill

Telegraph Messengers in London. In the photo is Sidney Walker. Photo Miss A Pardo

Many evacuees were also involved in charitable and voluntary work as depicted by the photographs on this page

Lady Mountbatten during the opening of the exhibition held on the 17th September 1943 organised by the BBC. The exhibition entailed some handwork done by some evacuees for prisoners of war. Mrs. Ana Hernandez is first on the left of the photo. Photo Mrs Brittenden

Lt General Sir Noel Mason MacFarlane. with kitchen helpers at Royal Palace Hotel . Photo Mr A Massetti

Gibraltar evacuees in the British Red Cross. Photo Mrs Summerfield

In April 1942 it was reported by The Times that the Duchess of Gloucester visited an Exhibition and Sale of Work of Evacuees from Gibraltar, at Gloucester House, Park Lane. In August 1943 a sale of work done by Gibraltar evacuees had been held in London where nearly £600 had been raised for the Red Cross and St. John fund for prisoners of war. The photos below show Gibraltar evacuees engaged on voluntary work.

Evacuees helping the British Red Cross. Photo Mrs M Summerfield

Gibraltar evacuees in the Women Voluntary Services In the photo is Mrs Victoria Freyone Langtry. Photo Mrs Bosio (Nee Langtry)

The Plessey's underground factory at Ilford. Photo Mrs Santos

From my own research I believe that the accommodation provided to the evacuees was adequate given the circumstances. However, I came across a report from a leading UK newspaper making reference to complaints about accommodation and that apparently nothing had been done to ameliorate the matter despite repeated requests made through the Ministry of Health. The reporter of this article quoted as examples of overcrowding the following:

"In one small room there were a mother, five children, and an elderly male relative. There were inadequate washing conditions and no running water. In another were a married couple and five daughters, aged from 10 to 24. These evacuees were promised another room a year ago at another room but nothing has happened. Another room had to house a mother, four sons (some grown-up), and an elderly man and woman. These are a few cases, and worse cases of overcrowding are alleged both by the evacuees and people interested in their welfare. The atmosphere of the rooms is drab and depressing, and there is an entire absence of amenities which might help to relieve the gloom of exile."

Food in London was to my understanding was definitely the subject of many quarrels and complaints between the evacuees and the managers of some of the evacuation centres. Many of those who were evacuated to the UK were of the view, that given the war situation, no one could say that they were left without food at any time. However, there were those who said that in their view the chief causes of complaint was about the English cooking which was not of style and liking preferred by the evacuees. In some centres, to overcome this problem, it had been suggested that instead, the evacuees should be allowed to cook their own food.

BACALAO PROVES TO BE A POPULAR DISH

Food, naturally, continues a difficult problem, due to the difficulties of obtaining the classes of food the people are accustomed to, and a Food Advisory Committee has been formed which has done a good deal of very useful work, the members of which are Mrs. Casaglia, Mrs. Bado, Mrs. Durante, Miss Perez, as well as Mr. Benhayon.

In the last few days they have tried out such dishes as bacalao, almondigas and rosto, which have proved very popular. The bacalao was especially successful, and the staff at one of the centres, who, never having seen it before and disliking the smell, had to be coaxed into trying it, all finished by having a second helping.

An attempt at olla de coles was not so successful, but these efforts to vary the diet and to give them, as far as possible, the type of food to which they are accustomed, are very much appreciated.

It seems that in some centres this suggestion was put practice and evacuees helped with the cooking of the food as was the case at one of the centres at Lancaster Gate shown in the photograph below:

There was also the problem that many evacuees had to find food, occasionally, from other sources, including the black market.

One of the most common recipes which have been mentioned in many conversations about food in the UK was that of the typical bone with bacon used as the main ingredient or a whole chicken. Both were regarded as luxurious dishes. I remember that my mother on one occasion even went to the extreme of giving us " churros" – fritters, but I have no idea how she went about to get the ingredients and utensils to frying them..

There was also the, almost constant, controversy about the evacuees wishing to cook their meals in their allocated rooms for the sake of making it more appetizing. One of the most notorious cases related to the issue of food was that of a complaint by the residents of Marlborough Court in Pembroke Road, Kensington. The matter became so complex that those engaged in the dispute with the managers of this evacuation centre were involved court proceedings. The issue first sparked off in the public domain when a lawyer representing the evacuees, Dr H Newcome Wright wrote a letter about the treatment of the evacuees in The Times newspaper. In the letter Dr Newcome Wright was very critical of the way the evacuees were being treated by the Ministry of Health, which was responsible of the welfare of the Gibraltar evacuees. He mentioned in his letter, as a case in point, that a family, including several small children, had to spend the night out after expulsion for not complying with the dinning room rules. The matter reached Parliamentary level with Mr Brown, Minister for Health having to answer questions about these issues from Members of Parliament. Some evacuees were of the view that sometimes food was being wasted at the centres when many seamen were loosing their lives to ensure provisions.

This page contains newspaper cuttings with reference to the Gibraltar evacuees in London. Below is a copy of a London magazine on an exclusive about the Gibraltar evacuees.

GIBRALTAR IN BLOOMSBURY

NOTES FROM THE COUNCIL MEETING

THE Ministry of Health has confessed itself unable to carry out its own avowed policy of child evacuation, since it has decided that the Gibraltar children in Holborn and other parts of central London must stay where they are and risk the bombs.

These children have been brought 1,200 miles from their homes presumably partly for their own safety, and have been dumped in some of the worst blitzed areas in London.

Westminster City Council approached Holborn Borough Council in August pointing out that no attempt appeared to have been made by the Ministry to evacuate the Gibraltar children to a safe reception area.

It was suggested that the two Councils should together make strong representations to the Ministry to remove the children to a safer place. Holborn agreed and the protest was sent.

The reply said that the Minister was well aware of the risk to which the children were exposed and he wished to send them to the country in the same way as other London children. The Minister pointed out, however, that owing to the "family group" mode of life of the Gibraltar Community, it had been found impossible to billet them on householders in the country as had been done with English children.

The Ministry therefore arranged to accommodate families in self-contained colonies and as the evacuation areas were already full, London was the only place where sufficiently large premises could be found to contain them.

Shelters had been built at the centres and they are being filled with bunks, said the letter.

Everything is being done to lessen the dangers to which the children may be exposed, the Ministry added.

And so the matter rests.

Children who were forced to leave their sunny Mediterranean homes are now put up in commandeered London hotels while Ministers warn us that this winter's air raids may be even heavier than last.

HOLBORN OUTLOOK

Page 2—This Month's Heroes.
Page 4—Sad Short Story.
Page 5—Fighting Fire Bomb Fritz.
Page 6—Let the People Read.
Page 8—Cookery Class.

The Monthly Magazine for Holborn Tenants — November 1941 — Price 2d

MOH & GIB KIDS

These children need a better playground than the street.

THE Ministry of Health has confessed itself unable to carry out its own avowed policy of child evacuation, since it has decided that the Gibraltar children in Holborn and other parts of central London must stay where they are and risk the bombs.

"Bloomin' foreigners" has too often been said in our tube shelters when the Gibraltar mothers and children have taken refuge there. We sometimes forget that they have been compulsorily evacuated from their sunny homes to one of the most blitzed areas of London.

Of the 18,000 Gibraltese in London, many are billeted in three Holborn hotels. They have their food, prepared from Spanish recipes, brought direct from Lyons, Cadby Hall, yet life is unfamiliar to them. They are having to try and adapt themselves to a completely foreign mode of living in our anything but warm and sunny climate. They have no homes to be interested in, none of their accustomed social life and only a minute amount of pocket money.

Many of the women have succeeded in getting sewing jobs and some of the older boys have joined London demolition squads. The children have made the streets their playground and are a menace to the traffic and to themselves for Holborn's green open spaces and unused squares are closed to them.

Is it right that these refugees should be brought to the very centre of blitzed London? Could they not be taken to some of England's vast empty country houses where they could live cheaply and safely? They are British citizens and deserve to be treated equally with English evacuees.

Meals on Wheels

Holborn is to benefit by the generosity of the American Book Trade which has presented two mobile canteens to Britain. One of these has been earmarked for use in this Borough. It will be operated by the Church Army.

The boy in the forefront in Boy Scouts uniform is believed to be Francisco Gaiviso. Cuttings by Mr F Curtis

Other well known newspapers like the Daily Express and The Times contained regular articles on how the evacuees were customizing to life in London with regard to food, shopping, children education, entertainment etc.

Back in Gibraltar there were also very regular articles which appeared in the local newspapers referring to the Gibraltar evacuees. As a result of this incident, many letters, articles and even reports of debates in the House of Parliament were published in the UK newspapers. The following is a summary of one of these letters "…people in England were aware that all the civilians in Gibraltar not employed on defence were compulsorily evacuated in 1940, when it was thought that a siege of Gibraltar was imminent. …..that what the British public was not aware was that these loyal subjects from Gibraltar, of all classes, most of whom who had lost their means of livelihood and were penniless, had been crowded by the Ministry of Health, who had undertaken the responsibility for them, into single rooms and that in many cases unmarried adults of both sexes had been living and sleeping in the same room." The author of this letter stated that he had information of many such cases where up to nine adults, male and female; five had been sleeping and living in the same room, in some cases, for nearly three years. Referring to the dinning arrangements he said that the last meal of the day at the centres was at 5.30 p.m., and the evacuees were not allowed to take this meal up to their rooms. Those who were working and came in late, sometimes 8 or 9 at night, had to take their chance of having food kept for them, and a cup of tea kept warm from tea-time. The meal, he carried on saying, had to be paid there and then whether the evacuees took it or not. He also stated that all requests by the evacuees to have their own ration books and to cater for themselves were refused. That any complaints or attempts to bring pressure upon the Ministry were countered by eviction, and that the evacuees had neither furniture nor the means to pay the present price of furnished rooms so the threat they were faced with was a most serious one. The matter received so much publicity that it reached Parliamentary level with the Minister of Health being asked about the living conditions of the Gibraltar evacuees in London.

During the middle of 1943, the Gibraltar authorities approved a scheme that allowed the men who stayed behind to visit their families in London. Judging from reliable sources it seems that about 300 men took advantage of this scheme to travel to UK on special leave. I remember that my uncle John paid us a short visit to Whitelands. He brought with him a tin, which to me looked like one of those old Oxo tins. We all sat around the kitchen table whilst we watched my uncle opening the box.

In the photo above my cousin Rose Gingell with photo of her father- my uncle. Photo Mrs Roman

In the box, as far as I can remember, there were a few chorizos, some cloves of garlic and few packets of saffron. These ingredients were obviously not available in London at the time and I suppose that my aunt who used to work in the kitchen at Whitelands must have put in good use all these ingredients to prepare a typical local dish.
My father, who like many was working in the Dockyard on essential repairs to the Royal Navy ships, was unable to visit us.
Not long after the war, many like my father were awarded, the civilian defence medal in recognition for their service to the Royal Navy during the war years. By the end of 1943 there were already plans to repatriate the evacuees and therefore by the early part of 1944 the first evacuee started to arrive.

The scheme for visiting families was abolished which meant that I had to wait yet another year to see my father. When we were evacuated I was 2 years old and the only means I had to remember my father until we met again was a greeting card that my father sent to us at Whitelands for Christmas 1941. It was kept on what was like a chest of drawers placed adjacent to the window. I still cherish this Christmas greetings from my father.

The Christmas card, which my father sent for Christmas 1941. Postcard by J.Gingell

From what I understand priority was being given to those families who had been separated during the war and who could be claimed by anyone who had stayed behind in Gibraltar. These criteria placed my family for an early repatriation. But the bombing of Whitelands in February disrupted things a bit as we had to be transferred to another evacuation centre, namely the York Hotel. The Normandy landing in June caused the postponement of the second party from the UK until end of July 1944 and hence prolonged the chance of seeing my father for another few months.

Christmas greeting card sent to Mr Manuel Infante by his son Manuel who was in the Police Force in Gibraltar Photo Mr M Infante

During the four years that the evacuees resided in London many died of natural causes. I have been given to understand that the majority of evacuees who died in the area of Kensington were buried at the Gunnersbury Cemetery in Kensington. Shortly after arriving in London 22 months old boy Jose Barcio died on the 22nd September 1940 and is buried in this cemetery.

Mrs Francisca Barcio with her son Jose.
Photos above and below by Mrs Diaz

Resting place of Jose Barcio
At the Gunnersbury Cemetery

Gunnersbury Cemetery at Gunnersbury Avenue
Kensington London W3.

Other places where many Gibraltar evacuees were buried were at the, Earlsfield, Magdalane Road, Garrett Lane and at Putney Vale cemeteries in Wandsworth where relatives of the Alecios, Harrisons, Readings and Lopez who died while residing at Whitelands and or at Highlands Heath.

The resting place of Mrs Magdalena Harrsion
at Earlsfield Cemetery, Wandsworth
(Photo by Mrs N Attias (nee Harrison)

It has been estimated that about 200 evacuees died in the UK from natural death and the bombing.

Putney Vale Cemetery, Wandsworth. Photo Mr Paul Huppert

During my research I was able to get in touch with Mrs Dinorah Markel daughter of Mrs Juaquina Ryan who was very anxious to find out where her mother and brother were buried. We exchanged information to find the relevant cemetery and possible records. After a few months it was confirmed that Mrs Juaquina Ryan and her son Andrew were buried at the St Patrick's Roman Catholic cemetery on the 8th July 1944. Mrs Juaquina Ryan and her son Andrew were killed by a flying bomb at Dr Barnardo's Hospital on the 30th June 1944. See pages 181 and 182.

The St Patrick's Roman Catholic Cemetery at Leytonstone,Essex.
Photo Mr Geoff Gillon

There were some families who had relatives or acquaintances outside London and moved to live with them as was the case of the Ellul's, Facio's, Gonzalez's, Stagno's and Cavilla's who managed to leave their respective evacuation centres in London to live in the mining village of Cowie in Scotland. All the photographs on this page, except the one below, were donated by Mrs L Ramagge.

In the photos above at the back L to R Lilian Ellul (Mrs Ramagge)Fr Bracelin's niece, Mercedes Facio(Mrs Ramirez, Mariluz Facio (Mrs Murphy) In front L to R Eric Ellul, Charles Facio and John Ellul. Photo Mr C Facio

Other families like the Tricos moved to Wales whilst the Povedanos moved to Kent but they (the Povedanos) soon went back to London because the bombing in Kent was as bad as in London. Those who left the scheme were responsible for finding their own private accommodation and for their maintenance. Those who left the evacuation scheme forfeited any privileges or rights associated with the Evacuation Scheme. However, evacuees who left the scheme were always able to return to the Evacuation Scheme if they wished to do so.

At St Margaret's School in Cowie. At the back L to R: Carmen Stagno, Francis Stagno In front L to R: Mercedes Facio (Mrs Ramirez), Mariluz Facio (Mrs Murphy) Janet Gonzalez and Lillian Ellul (Mrs Ramagge)

According to the Gibraltar Government archives there were evacuees living outside the evacuation in other cities of England, Wales and Scotland.

In the photo above from L to R: E.Ellul,J.Ellul,Lilian Ellul, C. Stagno, F. Stagno

In the photo above from L to R J.Ellul,C.Cavilla, C.Facio and Tito Gonzalez.

In the photo above Lilian, Eric and John Ellul.

ALPHABETICAL LIST OF EVACUATION CENTRES IN THE LONDON

NAME OF CENTRE	ADDRESS OF CENTRE	NO OF EVACUEES	0FFICER IN CHARGE
ANERLEY HOUSE	ANERLEY ROAD ANERLEY	23	MR F FAGAN
BALMORAL	37 QUEEN'S GATE GARDENS SW7	172	MR A MAINWOOD
BRITISH EMPIRE HOTEL	28 DE VERE GARDENS W8	154	MR C WRIGHT
BROADWALK HOTEL	11 DE VERE GARDENS W8	145	" " "
31/60 CAMPDEN HILL GATE	31/60 CAMPDEN HILL GATE W8	305	MR C THOMSON
CONSTANCE HOTEL AND 55 LANCASTER GATE	23 LANCASTER GATE W2	123	MRS R MILLAR
COURTLANDS	SHEEN ROAD RICHMOND, SURREY	438	MR A FLANN
DEAN HOTEL	DEAN STREET W1	?	?
DR BARNARDO'S HOMES	BARKINGSIDE ESSEX	843	MR R SUMMERS
DUCHESS OF BEDFORD	CAMPDEN HILL GATE W8	417	MR A KEY
EMPRESS HALL	LILIE ROAD FULHAM	750	LONDON COUNTY COUNCIL
GRAFTON HOTEL	TOTTENHAM COURT ROAD W1	342	MISS K RICHARDS
HIGHLANDS HEATH	BRISTOL GARDENS PUTNEY HEATH SW15 WANDSWORTH	364	MR E FROUND
HYDE PARK GATE HOTEL	5 HYDE PARK GATE W8	238	MR J THOMAS
IVANHOE HOTEL	BLOOMSBURY STREET WC1	478	MR F FROLIC
KENSINGTON PALACE MANSION (NORTH BLOCK)	DE VERE GARDENS KENSINGTON W8	448	CAPT.H BATEMAN FOX
KINGS COLLEGE OF HOUSE HOLD AND SOCIAL SCIENCE	CAMPDEN HILL ROAD W8	329	MISS I WAUGH
3/4 LANCASTER GATE 105/7 LANCASTER GATE	LANCASTER GATE	220	MAJOR J BELL
90/92 LANCASTER GATE	LANCASTER GATE W2	138	MRS O HENSON
100 LANCASTER GATE	LANCASTER GATE W2	344	MRS M V STEEL
LINDEN HALL	131/137 CROMWELL ROAD SW7	126	MISS O F G SHORE
MARLBOROUGH COURT	PEMBROKE ROAD KENSINGTON W8	452	MR A LEWINGTON
MOSCOW MANSION	224 CROMWELL ROAD W5	213	MR R MACQUEEN
NATIONAL HOTEL	BEDFORD WAY WC2	426	MR H HESFORD
NORTH END HOUSE TOWER BLOCK A	FITZJAMES AVENUE WEST KENSINGTON W14	609	MR R S ASHER
NORTH END HOUSE STAR BLOCK B	Do	332	MR N MACLEOD
NORTHWAY HOTEL	70 EUSTON SQUARE NW1	91	MISS R ROSS
PARK ROYAL HOTEL AND BERKELEY HOTELS		179	MR W.W.KEALEY
RAGLAN HOTEL	BEDFORD WAY WC1	400	MR ALEXANDER
ROYAL PALACE HOTEL	HIGH STREET KENSINGTON W8	613	MR W .H. METCALFE
ROYAL STUART HOTEL	161/169 CROMWELL ROAD SW5	213	MRS M OXLEY
SHELBOURNE HOTEL	BEDFORD WAY WC1	350	MR FROLIC
ST KATHERINE'S COLLEGE	WHITE HART LANE TOTTENHAM N17	300	MR BROWN
ST STEPHEN'S CLOSE	AVENUE ROAD ST JOHNS'S WOOD NW	480	MAJOR T E SINCLAIR
THACKERAY HOTEL	57 GREAT RUSSEL SQUARE WC1	279	MSS L SMITH
WEMBLEY POOL	WEMBLEY MIDDLESEX	427	MR F HERBERT
WHITELANDS TRAINING COLLEGE	WEST HILL PUTNEY SW17	475	MR H DAVIES
YORK HOTEL	BERNERS STREET W1 OFF OXFORD ST.	310	MR A MILDMAZ

CHAPTER NINE

EVACUEES IN JAMAICA

As mentioned in Chapter Six the first group of those evacuated to Jamaica arrived on the **SS Neuralia** on 25 October 1944. As soon as the **SS Neuralia** berthed, the officials who had been appointed to be in charge with the managing the camps went on board to greet the Gibraltar evacuees.

SO, THIS IS JAMAICA!

CENTRE: A Gibraltar Senora and her little girlie make a charming picture framed by the porthole as they smiled with Jamaicans on the wharf on their arrival yesterday. LEFT: a scene of the disembarkation showing some of the evacuees coming down the gangway. RIGHT: piling luggage into one of the omnibuses in which the evacuees were speeded away to Camp Gibraltar Mona.

Headings of a Jamaica newspaper cutting reporting the arrival of the evacuees on the 25th October 1940.

1,100 EVACUEES NOW AT GIBRALTAR CAMP

First Batch Ended Long Voyage Yesterday

1,100 EVACUEES NOW AT GIBRALTAR CAMP

First Batch Ended Long Voyage Yesterday

Jamaica yesterday became a haven of safety to 1,100 civilian evacuees from Gibraltar, key to the Mediterranean, the British fortress that has withstood frontier sieges for six centuries or more.

Four thousand miles away came these evacuees from the famous British stronghold of the Mediterranean. They experienced sixteen days of excellent weather in the dash from the war zone to sunny Jamaica. Hundreds of Jamaicans lined the waterfront. Thousands lined the streets through which the buses took the arrivals to the Mona camp and warmly welcomed them, in a typical Jamaica manner.

History was made in the island as the ship steamed in with its human cargo, for it was the first close up this island has yet received of the devastating European war. Pathetic scenes were witnessed as these haven seekers from Gibraltar, mostly women and children, had their first greedy glimpses of the country, which they will make their home till Hitler is forever crushed.

Aged men and women—one Senora having just celebrated her 90th birthday peeped out of port holes to see the people, who will be their friends for—who knows when? Tears trickled down aged faces and young ones too. Many of these people have left behind their sons, their husbands, their fathers, their uncles, their brothers and their sweethearts to defend Gibraltar, who they may never see again.

"We know that Gibraltar will never fall into enemy hands," one woman sobbed, "but we know that for some of us, too, there will never be a reunion with some of our loved ones."

SEVERING OF TIES

For many of these people it means their tearing away from their life-long home, it means the abandoning of their homes and possessions, their business and everything that they hold dear.

"Rule Britannia," sang the diving boys as they collected pennies thrown at them from the decks of the ship. The evacuees with their Moorish, Spanish and English background and 100 per cent pro-British political outlook, smiled and even joined in the famous patriotic song.

"We prefer to die before we give over one inch of Gibraltar to the Germans," one businessman declared. "That is the spirit of the Gibraltarian. We are all definitely anti-Nazi."

Of the 1,104 arrivals, 185 are males, 673 are females and 246 children, under 12 years of age. A large proportion of the male arrivals are aged men and comparatively young fellows still in their teens. The youngest arrival is a two day old baby, who was born in Caribbean waters. The safe arrival of these people from Gibraltar's 15,000 civilian population, revealed as splendid an organisation as can be desired in these difficult war days.

Mr. B. D. Austin Cathie, retired Registrar of the Supreme Court of Gibraltar, was in charge of the evacuees on sea. There also accompanied them Dr. J. E. Murray, a Colonial Medical Officer and three Sisters.

Inspector Cano, of the Gibraltar Constabulary, Sergt. Richardson and several special constables also accompanied the evacuees. The Inspector and Sergeant and their families will take up residence at Mona, but the constables will return to the Mediterranean.

MET THE SHIP

Down at Port Royal to meet the ship were Mr. E. A. Rae, Manager of the Camp; the Very Rev. Fr. Feeney, Father Superior of the Roman Catholic Church and member of the Camp Gibraltar Committee; Mr. J. B. L. Taylor, Drs. Gideon and Johnson and Landing Waiters of the Customs Department.

At the pier to welcome the arrivals and among those first to board the ship, alongside the Royal Mail Line pier, were the Hon. Major Simms, Mr. J. L. Worlledge, Capt. H. de B. Tupper, Inspector Langdon, Mr. C. W. Varney and the Naval, Police and Customs officials.

"What is our Camp like," was the first question the evacuees asked "Gleaner" representatives when they boarded the ship. They were happy to learn that there will be modern conveniences to which they are accustomed.

Of course, the majority of the young people speak English and even some of the older ones. English, they explained, was compulsorily taught to-day in Gibraltar schools. French and Spanish, they said were also taught. They spoke Spanish, because Spain was so close to them and because of the twenty thousand Spaniards that came over from the border every day to work as domestics and dock-yard hands.

Messrs. Worlledge and Taylor and others supervised for several hours the getting off of the evacuees to their buses. Members of the Transport Authority assisted in the direction of 15 buses that plied to and back from Mona. There were eight stretcher cases and they were taken to the Camp by the ambulance, the Kingston Fire Brigade co-operating also in taking off the arrivals.

PROTECTION EXCELLENT

The evacuees tell gripping stories of Gibraltar and its preparedness for the conflict. The 5½-mile long by 3½-mile wide fortress, some 1,400 feet above sea level, they say, is able to repulse any modern attack. Air raid shelters are all built in the rock, British civil engineers having drilled and blasted ten tunnels at strategic points.

With the country being free from debt and the people having fairly good credit balances in the banks the wartime protection is excellent, deep bomb-proof shelters at the terrific price of some £100,000 giving complete protection to 15,000, even if enemy planes plastered Gibraltar with one and a half ton bombs.

"Our morale and courage are peak high", and ex-Inspector of Civil Police stated. "We are firm in our conviction that Hitler and his aide, Mussolini, will meet their end in this war. It is the general opinion of the people in

(Continued on Page 19)

Among the officials was The Very Reverend Father Thomas Feeney, who was going to play a very prominent role in the running of the Gibraltar camp. When the evacuees disembarked they assembled on the quayside where there were already 35-seater buses waiting to take the evacuees to Camp One. The Jamaican Boy Scouts helped the evacuees with the loading of the luggage on the buses. Along the road to the camp there were also many Jamaicans who had turned out to greet the evacuees with cheers as they were driven along the road in the direction of the campsite. Volunteer priests and nuns helped to guide the evacuees to their quarters from the main gate on the road to August Town. When the evacuees entered their respective quarters they found that their beds were already made for them by courtesy of Catholic schoolgirls anxious to make the evacuees welcome.

The newspaper cutting below is a continuation of the main heading "1,100 Evacuees Now at Gibraltar Camp" shown in the previous column.

1,100 Evacuees

(Continued from Page 1)

the Mediterranean. that the Italians will play Germany a trick, as they had done in the last war."

Miss Mary Deely, with an English background, and a school teacher, who did A.R.P. work, spoke of the special defence work the men of Gibraltar are doing to-day. She is of the opinion that Spain will never fight with the Axis as the country was too poor. Of the 18,000,000 Spanish people, she said that 17,000,000 are pro-British. "Spain will starve if she ever went to war," she stated.

HAD DIFFICULT JOB

Thanks to Jamaica for her warm welcome were expressed by Mr. Austin Cathie, officer in charge of the evacuees on their long voyage to Jamaica.

Mr. Cathie, who has just retired as Registrar of the Supreme Court of Gibraltar, undertook the task of managing the voyage to Jamaica, and all the evacuees testify to the excellent manner in which he did that job. He will leave Jamaica shortly for England.

"We must thank the people of Jamaica for their very warm welcome," he said, "and I have just cabled to the Governor of Gibraltar telling of our safe arrival and of the fine welcome we have received."

Upon arrival, Mr. Cathie rushed off to Camp Gibraltar, Mona, where he helped the local management supervise the arrival of the evacuees by bus from the pier and helped see to their comfort.

Mr. E. A. Rae, Camp Manager; Very Rev. Father Thomas Feeney, S.J., and the able social service company of priests and nuns, saw to the quartering and feeding of the evacuees as they arrived in bus loads and had everything going efficiently by sunset.

The newspaper cuttings shown on this page are articles published by the Jamaican newspaper The Gleaner when reporting the view being expressed by the Gibraltar evacuees after a few days in the camp.

EVACUEES BUOYED BY CONFIDENCE IN BRITAIN

Majority in Good Spirits as They Express Expectation Of Early Victory and Re-union With Relatives and Friends.

As one speaks with the evacuees who landed here on Friday afternoon, one is impressed with their deep-seated loyalty to and love of Britain, their faith in her might and their sincere belief that the war will soon end in an overwhelming victory for our arms. It might have been this belief that so buoyed them up; for the majority displayed the best spirits both at the wharf and when seen later at their

One young bride—she had been married only a few months when she had to leave Gibraltar and her husband—chatting to the reporter over a cup of coffee, a favourite Spanish drink, voiced the hope that soon she would see her husband. She was the Senora Carmen Vaggliotto, a charming brunette of the typical Spanish type.

Sitting beside her was the Senorita Baldacchino who, with a deep blush, told how she had left her fiance behind. "You must be very sad?" she was asked. "No," came the quick reply. "You see, soon the war will be over and I will go to see him again and then we will be married."

Another senorita, Miss Celia Gomez, could not quite see why they had been made to leave. "Gibraltar is so strong and so are the British. The other day, a large number of planes came and attacked us, but it was surprising how little damage they did, considering their numbers. The place is strong, and we have very good shelters".

PROUD OF BEING BRITISH

All emphasized that they were British and told the reporter: "Long live Britain. Yes, we are English subjects just as you are. We love her."

Three sisters, the youngest well over 50, were among the evaçuees. They were accompanied by their brother, who was over the half-century mark himself.

"We used to be dressmakers before the war", they told the reporter, "and used to be able to make our living well enough. We were happy. Now, we are here; but we hope to be back one day."

When they were assured that the country was a fine one, and that they would like it, they smiled their hope in which their brother Baldomero, who did not say much, joined. They gave their names: Concha, Rosalia, Ofelia and Baldo mero Hemmimi.

NOT ALL SPANISH

Not all of the refugees were Spanish in origin or birth. There was one elderly Scot with his wife, a very amiable couple, who spoke longingly of old Scotland. Mr. Proctor came originally from "gode olde Lockerbie" in Dumfries; but had spent 37 years on The Rock where he met his wife.

They were a very interesting couple and spoke with an accent which was an intriguing mixture of the rich Highland brogue and Spanish.

"I served in the regular army until 1912." Mr. Proctor told the reporter "when I left for Gibraltar, where I had, in the meanwhile, married. On the outbreak of the war, I joined up, was wounded twice, for which I received three medals" the medals were displayed on Mr. Proctor's breast. "After the Armistice, I left England for Gibraltar and served with the Government. Up to the outbreak of war, I was Office Keeper in the King's Yard."

Mr. and Mrs. Proctor have left their son and daughter behind, in Europe. Their son is with the British Mediterranean fleet, and their daughter is married and lives in England with her husband and four children.

HUMOROUS PAIR

A very humorous pair too, and truly Scot. The proverbial humour of their race has certainly stood them in good stead; for they must have found it difficult to pull up their old roots, as it were, at such a late stage—Mr. Proctor is 60 and Mrs. Proctor is 54.

Mrs. Proctor was not quite sure she would like the place, but qualified the statement with the observation that to each his own home seemed best.

This son of the clans, despite his 60 years, had offered his services to Britain.

They described how they had been bombed before they left. "French planes came over", said Mr. Proctor, "and, among other places, laid waste the King's Yard. They were French planes but we are sure that they were flown by German pilots."

INTERESTING GROUP

One of the most interesting groups was the Lucia family, consisting of Mrs. Lucia, soft-spoken, fair-haired, and still attractive matron of 49, her daughter Maruja Lucia, her little baby boy, a sister and nephew. They had left the rest of the family in Gibraltar. The Lucia's could not speak any English, having, as they explained, attended only the Spanish school on The Rock.

Mrs. Lucia was sad almost to the point of tears. In her picturesque language she told how she had had to leave behind her husband and her son, both of whom are working for the government.

Asked whether she liked it here, she replied: "I love Gibraltar very much, as naturally it is my home; but here looks a pretty place with kind people and I would not be so anxious to return if only my husband had been able to accompany me here.

FIANCE LEFT BEHIND

Her daughter, Maruja, a lively and charming brown-haired girl of 18, had her gaiety tinged with a spot of sadness for she too had left some one very dear behind.

"We would have been married by now, had the war not broken out", she told the reporter. "But I do not mind, I expect to see him soon; for soon Britain will win, and we will meet again."

It was from Mrs. Lucia one gathered something about the living condition on the rock. She said her husband worked for about 50/- weekly and her son earned an additional 30/-. But the cost of living was less than here, for they could rent a house of four or five apartments for 45/- per month, and food was not such a big item on their budget.

The first impressions gathered by the evacuees on their arrival in Jamaica were that of a strange land of extreme climatic conditions and with a very dense and a great variety of flora. There were many tropical fruits like, for example, the mangos never sampled by the evacuees before. There were many types of insects all over the place that the evacuees had never seen before either. I believe one of the most fearful of these insects was the scorpion which was considered very poisonous. These insects could be found anywhere, even under the pillow or in a shoe. During their stay in Jamaica there were the occasional earth tremors and hurricanes which are very characteristic of that part of the world. There was also the occasional down pour of very heavy rain followed suddenly by a clear blue sky. The majority of the Gibraltar evacuees had, obviously, not witnessed any of these things before.

On one occasion the grass, trees and the whole flora turned suddenly from its natural colour of green to a very pale yellow. The explanation given for this sudden change in colour was that the dust from a volcano that had erupted in Mexico had been blown by the wind and had settled in the area of Jamaica.

The cuttings shown on this page are from the Jamaican newspaper The Gleaner giving a detailed report about the second group of evacuees who arrived on the **SS Thysville**.

As explained in the report they were met by the camp commandant, the manager and the Rev.Father Feeney. The new group of evacuees were also assisted in the disembarkation by some of the evacuees which had arrived a few weeks before.

MORE EVACUEES ARRIVE — here they are— some of the nearly 400 evacuees who arrived from Gibraltar on Friday for the duration of the war. The youngest is but a month old and the oldest about 80. Nearly three fourths of the arrivals are women. The small male population suffered a loss by the death of one man while the ship was just a couple of days out from Gibraltar. Mr. J. Macneil Hunter, Glasgow-born Gibraltarian, who was in charge of the evacuees at sea, and to whom the Gleaner is grateful for these pictures, is seen at the extreme left corner (below) having a peaceful smoke.

Nearly 400 More Evacuees Here

Arrivals Yesterday From Gibraltar Confident Britain Will Win War. Had Uneventful Trip

400 Evacuees Here Yesterday

A SECOND AND SMALLER detachment of evacuees arrived from Gibraltar yesterday to join the Camp at Mona property. The four hundred newcomers landed at No. 1 Railway Pier and appeared on the whole cheerful after their long and hazardous voyage.

Among them are a few cripples who were conveyed to ambulances while the others, mostly very old or very young persons travelled by bus to the Camp—the youngest arrival is a year-old child.

Immediately after the vessel docked it was boarded by Capt. H. de B. Tupper, Harbour Master; Mr. J. L. Worlledge, Commandant in charge of the Gibraltar Camp at Mona; Mr. E. A. Rae, Manager of the Camp; Very Rev. Fr. Feeney, Supericr in charge of Jamaica Catholic Missions; officials of the Naval Intelligence and H. M. Custom who welcomed the Evacuees to Jamaica.,

All of them smiled cheerfully as they stepped from the ship's gangway to the pier to board the 12 buses which took them to their future abode. Only one very old Sencra shed tears as she was carried on a stretcher to an ambulance. A curios crowd gathered before the entrance to the pier in Harbour St. and locked on as bus-load after bus-load roared past conveying the evacuees to Mona.

Mona's Evacuee Camp population took a near 400 climb yesterday, with the arrival of 302 more evacuees from Gibraltar, Britain's impregnable Mediterranean fortress. Of the arrivals, nearly three fourths are women. The youngest arrival is a one-month old baby: the oldest about 80 years. Death boarded the ship some two days out from Gibraltar and claimed 45-year-old Julio Peralta, dockyard worker, with a heart attack, the body being buried at sea in the presence of his sorrowing relatives.

Unlike the other ship, which brought more than a thousand evacuees to Jamaica, less than three weeks ago, there was no birth on board.

Thirty-four Spaniards, who had fled from the Franco government and had been living in Gibraltar for some time are among the new arrivals.

"A beautiful trip", all the passengers affirmed. "It could not be better." There were only about 12 stretcher cases and these were all taken by ambulance to the Camp's hospital at Mona.

Cinema shows and concert and dancing parties featured the entertainment on the hazardous 16-day journey. "The Captain and officers lent themselves very genially to the comfort of all," declared Mr. J. Mac neill Hunter, Glasgow born Gibraltarian, who was in charge of the evacuees on board. "There is nothing but the highest praise for the treatment that has been rendered to the evacuees on board. We are deeply gratified."

SMILE IN SORROW

With smiles, many of the new arrivals covered sad thoughts and fearful hearts as they got off the big ship and boarded omnibuses at No. 1 pier for their six-mile drive to the place that will be their home for who knows when- "But we are not a bit down-hearted,' in true Gibraltarian fashion, one aged man declared. "We know that the Mother Country will smash Hitler and his degrading aide. And who knows? Some of us are looking forward to returning home by next summer when everything is all over."

An end of the conflict before the summer of 1941 is the opinion of many evacuees. So confident are they as to the ultimate end.

A sprinkling of prominent Gibraltarians featured the passenger list. Among these are Mr. Hunter and his Gibraltar wife, a leading business woman; Mr. John M. Porral, a Barrister at Law, who had been called to the Bar at Inner Temple for nearly half a century—since 1892; Mr. Richard Barratt, Secretary of Gibraltar's 19-year-old British Legion; Mr. John B. Arias, former Chancellor of the Spanish Consulate in Gibraltar; Mr. Jose Saldena, retired Inspector of Dock Yard Police and Mr. Salvador Lara, of Barclays Bank staff, who are accompanied by their families.

Mr. Hunter, who acted as officer in charge of the evacuees at sea is no stranger to Jamaica. He was here during the last war, spending about a fortnight, while on his way from Australia. As a cricketer—although he is now 67—he takes a great interest in the grand old game. He had met George Headley and our other cricketers in Australia some nine years ago. He is the oldest playing member of the Gibraltar C.C.

EVENTFUL VOYAGE

Giving up his position as A.R.P. Warden to come over with his wife, Mr. Hunter spoke quite enthusiastically about the crossing. "We have had no eventualities to talk about, as the trip had been very enjoyable," he said. He explained that the Spaniards, who had accompanied them over were Spanish refugees, who were unable to return to Spain after the Civil war and were taken care of by the people of Gibraltar.

"The people are all for the allies," he said, when discussing the war. "The feeling is, that there will be a decisive victory and that Spain, although forced by Germany, will probably hold out and keep out of the war; at least she will not go on the axis side."

Through the effort of Mr. Richard Barratt, Secretary of the British Legion in Gibraltar a Poppy Day collection was taken on board the ship and the sum of £14. 12s. 1½ netted, which will be handed over by him to the Colonial Secretary of Gibraltar.

Very few civilians are left now in Gibraltar, according to Mr. Barratt. As a matter of fact, there are none left to be evacuated as those en tho rock are those who are actually working with the Government, doing military work or connected to the City Council. There were practically no women left with the exception of a few, who were doing special work. All the other civilian evacuees are now in England, Madeira and other places.

When this second group of evacuees arrived there were also many Jamaican boys, with the rest of the waiting crowd at quayside.

These boys as in the case of the first group of evacuees also dived for coins that were thrown from small boats alongside the arriving ships. These evacuees were also met later at the entrance to the camp by the previous group of evacuees. Both groups became very emotional as they kissed and hugged each other.

When the order was given that civilians from Gibraltar were going to be evacuated to Jamaica an old sugar plantation site known as the Mona Estate was identified as an ideal place to construct the Gibraltar Camp and to be located at the foot of Long Mountain near the Hope River as can be seen in the map shown below:

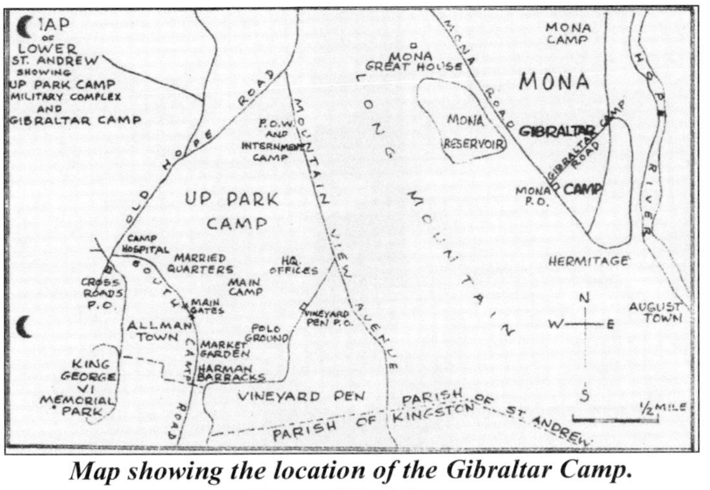

Map showing the location of the Gibraltar Camp. Picture Mr A Lara

It was initially intended for the camp to have capacity to accommodate 4,000 evacuees and then it was decided to build an additional camp to accommodate altogether up to 9,000 persons. The site was 7 miles by road from Kingston. The construction site was also near to the services which were need for the essential maintenance of a small township.

Aerial view of the Gibraltar Camps by the Long Mountains. Photo Jamaican Newspaper The Gleaner

A closer view of the huts. Photo Miss S Moya

As will be explained in this chapter, only one camp was occupied by the Gibraltar evacuees. The site for the construction of the two camps covered an area of 252 acres of which 85 acres were allocated for Camp One, 114 acres for Camp Two and 53 acres for the camp hospital. Because of the urgency, a simple barracks design had been chosen for the overall construction. At the entrance to the camp were the main administrative offices, the main stores, the police station and barracks. Close to these buildings were the motor transport garage, carpenters' shop, the cooks' quarters and chauffeurs. There was another building called the Matron's quarters where the medical staff used to reside. There were three large halls and each of these halls had a stage erected. They had been purposely designed to provide cinema, dances, concerts and any other form of entertainment for the evacuees. There was also a firewood store. The almost all-wooden buildings were purposely constructed to meet all the basic needs of the evacuees. The camp had been built near Kingston's main supply services with the idea of providing essential services like water and electricity. The main telephone service was also near the camp.

Metal tank installed to supply Gibraltar Camp residents

The Gibraltar camp fresh water supply tank with capacity to hold 130,000 gallons of water. Photo Mr A Lara.

The first administrative task was to establish a camp committee for the running of the camp. The members of the committee appointed to administer the camp were the Commandant, the Manager and two Roman Catholic Priests. The responsibility for the administration of the camp in terms of security and discipline was initially given to Major Henry Simms but soon afterwards it was handed to Mr Worlledge who became Camp Commandant. Ex-major Mr E. Rae became his deputy.

Mr Worlledge
Camp Commandant
Photos above and below the Catholic Opinio Magazine.

E. A. RAE,
Manager of Camp Gibraltar

A special police force recruited entirely from Gibraltar evacuees with the necessary experience were also employed to assist with matters of discipline. The Reverend Father Thomas Feeney, father superior of the Roman Catholic Church and his brother Father William Feeney were members of the Camp Committee. When the evacuees arrived there were many Jamaicans who were allowed to sell their wares and it was possible to buy chickens and other country produce.

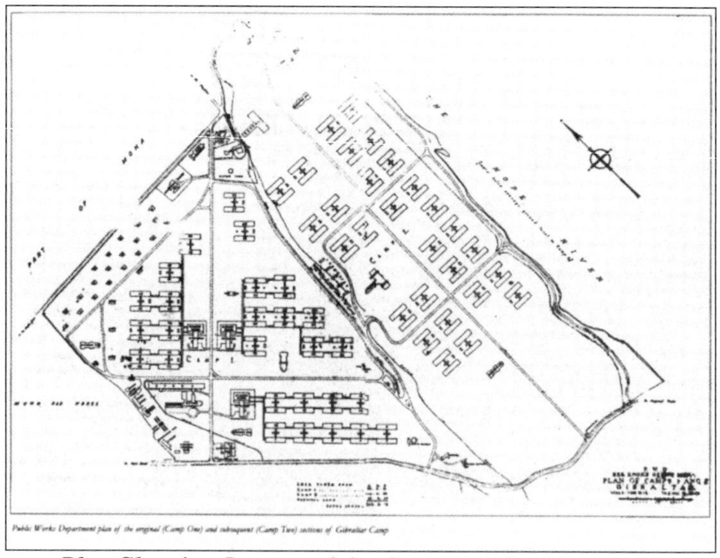

Plan Showing Layout of the Camps. Plan Mr A Lara

Road to the Camp. Photo Mr A Lara

But this arrangement did not last very long as they were no longer allowed to enter the Gibraltar Camp. To buy anything extra, which could not be found in the camp store, the evacuees had to go shopping to a market at Papine, which was a town about a mile away from the Camp. The bus terminus to go to Kingston was also at Papine.

Evacuees shopping at Papine. Photo Mrs Wood

One of the three large recreational halls in the camp.
Photo Mr Zammitt

Inside the Administration Office.
Catholic Opinion Newspaper.

Camp limitation notice.
Photo Mrs Wood

A Recent Photograph of one of the remaining buildings of what used to be the Gibraltar Camp. Photo Mr A Lara

Alma Cantillo at the information office within the Camp.
Photo Mr A Lara

There was a post office and the first things the evacuees did on arrival were to send cables and letters to tell their families in Gibraltar about their safe arrival in Jamaica. The Camp rules made it a prerequisite for every evacuee to reside in the camp. The entrance and exit from the Gibraltar Camp was very restricted and only the evacuees and those who were duly authorised were allowed inside the camp. The evacuees were issued with passes which they had to show on leaving and entering the camp.

As part of the arrangements for the evacuation to Jamaica, the Governor and the Catholic Bishop of Gibraltar had requested the then Governor of Jamaica Sir Arthur Richards to ask the local Catholic Church to become involved in the welfare of the Gibraltar evacuees. In line with this policy, the Roman Catholic priests and nuns were placed in charge of the educational, religious and social aspects of the camp. Father William Feeney became the Roman Catholic Chaplain at the Gibraltar Camp.

The Entrance to the Camp. The Administrative Block is on the right of the photograph. Photo Mr C Moore

It seems that one of the initial problems encountered by the evacuees was the question of the allocation of accommodation in accordance with family composition. Although this was seemingly sorted out after some intervention, this problem cropped up again at a later stage in the camp.

The Priests' Quarters. Photo Mr C Moore

The Matron's bungalow in the Camp. Photo Mr C Moore

Two Franciscans, two Sisters of Mercy, two Dominicans and two Native Sisters moved into the Nunnery which was the only two-storey building on the site near the Camp. Food and lodging was the main task that had to be handled by the camp committee. Each unit, which was in a form of a bungalow, could accommodate up to six evacuees.

Sisters and Nuns by the entrance to the Nunnery. Photo Mr E Enriles

The rules for the administration of the camp were well displayed as can be seen of the copies reproduced below:

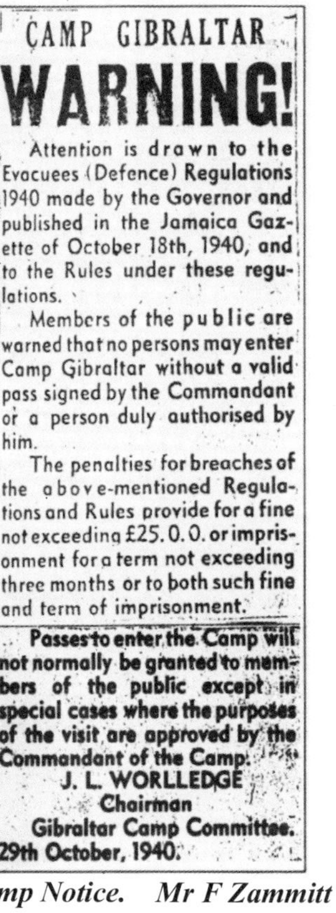

CAMP GIBRALTAR

WARNING!

Attention is drawn to the Evacuees (Defence) Regulations 1940 made by the Governor and published in the Jamaica Gazette of October 18th, 1940, and to the Rules under these regulations.

Members of the public are warned that no persons may enter Camp Gibraltar without a valid pass signed by the Commandant or a person duly authorised by him.

The penalties for breaches of the above-mentioned Regulations and Rules provide for a fine not exceeding £25. 0. 0. or imprisonment for a term not exceeding three months or to both such fine and term of imprisonment.

Passes to enter the Camp will not normally be granted to members of the public except in special cases where the purposes of the visit are approved by the Commandant of the Camp.

J. L. WORLLEDGE
Chairman
Gibraltar Camp Committee.
29th October, 1940.

Camp Notice. Mr F Zammitt

Any evacuee found contravening the above rules was liable to a fine of £25 or 7 days imprisonment at the camp prison. There were a few incidents involving some evacuees and outsiders breaking the camp rules which resulted in penalties being imposed.

Evacuees in Jamaica

There were 31 large housing units or bungalows and each of these could accommodate up to 60 evacuees. These units measured 150 feet long and 25 wide with a 7-foot-wide veranda on each of the long sides. Each unit was subdivided into two rooms twinned to one another by walkways with a sanitary annexe measuring 50 feet by about 14 feet shared between two living quarters. There were also 20 smaller units designed to accommodate smaller family groups. One of the bungalows had been reserved for the elderly and invalid evacuees.

Mrs L Romero with other evacuees utside the hut. Photo Miss S Moya

Entrance to the hut. Photo Mr E Enriles

A persisting complaint about the living accommodation at the camp was the lack of privacy. The dividing "walls" between huts were made of bare plywood that did not reach the ceiling. Therefore any conversation or other noises were easily overheard.

Boys outside one of the wooden units showing the verandas. Photo Mr Zammitt

Members of the Enriles family sitting outside the hut. Photo Mr E Enriles

There was ample space between one hut and the other. The photographs on this page give some indications of what the huts looked like and how the evacuees lived in the camp. Every room opened out on to the veranda and by sharing this veranda families could be allocated their respective rooms in line with the size of the family.

Mrs Mercedes Palma with huts in the background. Photo Mrs McNiece

Evacuees M.Cano,O.Carreras and V.Carreras. Photo Mr E Enriles

The rooms in these units contained basic furniture needs like beds, tables and chairs. A wire fence enclosed the whole area.

View of a couple of huts. Photo Miss S Moya

Evacuees outside kitchen. Photo Mr F Mosquera

The health care of the evacuees was seen to, initially, at a small hospital until a larger one was completed. The larger one had capacity for up to 100 beds with all the main facilities to look after the health care of the evacuees. This consisted of a maternity ward, an operating theatre, a dental clinic and an outpatient's cares facilities. There were quarters for the hospital staff and sanitary inspectors. The small hospital at Camp No.1 was converted into a maternity ward with six beds after the hospital at Camp No.2 was ready for use.

Some of the Gibraltar nurses receiving tuition in nursing. Photo Mrs A Perez (nee Cano)

Shortly after arriving in Jamaica there were some cases of contagious diseases related to scabies and inflammation of the eyes among the children. There was also a report of an outbreak of head lice. All these three cases affecting the health of the evacuees were dealt with very efficiently with the help of the nursing nuns. According to some of the evacuees who were very young at the time, most of the children had their tonsils removed as a precautionary measure against infections.

The Gibraltar Camp Medical Staff in October 1944. Photo Mrs A Perez (nee Cano)

In view of the many insects in the island many evacuees suffered the occasional insect bites which required the attention of the health services in the camp. Some of Gibraltar evacuees were recruited as nurses and received training to assist in the hospital camp. Some of these recruits were able to obtain qualifications which qualified them as equivalent to enrolled nurse.

The dental and sanitary clinics. Photo Mr C Moore

HYGIENE INSPECTION OF CAMP GIBRALTAR STAFF

Employees at Camp Gibraltar were required last week to submit to inspection of their person by the chief nurse of the Sanitary Department acting on orders effective from Monday, 21st. instant. The new regulation is interpreted as an additional effort to improve health conditions at the Camp.

Employees' heads and legs were examined, it is understood, and the majority of the staff have submitted to the inspection in a spirit of loyal co-operation. A very few persons have. however, chosen to regard the recent hygiene order as being personally humiliating to them and one individual is said to have left the employment of the Camp as a result of his refusal to be examined. Periodic inspection will continue as long as the authorities consider it necessary.

Sir Frank Stockdale, Comptroller of the Welfare and Development Fund, and the Labour Adviser attached to his staff, Mr. F. A. Norman, will visit the Camp on Wednesday of this week.

A few more male evacuees arrived this week and have taken up residence at the Camp.

Press cuttings about the health and hygiene at the Gibraltar Camp. Mr F Zammitt

Throughout the stay of the evacuees in the camp it seems that their health and hygiene were in good hands judging from the different newspaper cuttings. As can be seen from the photograph below there were many nurses employed to look after the 1,500 evacuees in the camp.

Gibraltar nurses at Gibraltar Camp Hospital.
At the back L to R: E.McKintosh, E.Nyberb (Swedish) P.Edwards A.Baker(Mrs Johnson)M.Orfila,(Mrs Soleci)E.Manser,P.Zammitt(Mrs Baker)In front R.Ballester,E.Sacramento,E.Celecia.
Photo Mrs A Perez (nee Cano)

Children's ward nurses in the Camp Hospital.
Photo Mrs A Perez (nee Cano)

Gibraltar nurses in the Camp. Photo Mrs A Perez (nee Cano)

PUBLIC HEALTH WORK AT GIBRALTAR CAMP

Dr. I. J. Cruchley, Medical Officer of Health, Kingston, has been seconded for special duty at Mona —to direct measures under the Public Health Law at Gibraltar Camp.

The M.O.H. has already entered upon the duties he has been detailed to carry out at the township for evacuees who arrived last Friday. Dr. Watson, Assistant M.O.H., has been transferred from St. Andrew to Kingston to act in the highest capacity, while Dr. Lightbourne is in charge of Public Health work in St. Andrew.

A cutting from the Jamaica Times related to health matters in the Gibraltar Camp.

EVACUEES PRAISE HOSPITAL TREATMENT

The conscientious, efficient and hard work being done by the Doctor, the matron and the staff of the Gibraltar Camp Hospital among the evacuees has been attested to by many of the patients.

Among these are two ladies who were so pleased with the kindness they had received and the patience with which they were attended that they begged that the public know of their gratitude. They are Mrs. Manser and Mrs. Carrol who were recently dismissed from the hospital after a severe bout of illness.

Press story from the Jamaica Times praising the hospital treatment

In accordance with above story published in a Jamaican newspaper it seems at least some evacuees regarded the medical services as good. However, in early 1941 rumours were reaching Gibraltar that the standard of health and sanitation being provided at the Gibraltar Camp was not of the standard that it was expected. A press communiqué was issued from the camp as shown below denying such allegations.

Press Communique

GIBRALTAR EVACUEES IN JAMAICA.

His Excellency the Acting Governor is in receipt of a telegram from the Officer Administering the Government of Jamaica indicating that it has been reported to him that false rumours are being spread in Gibraltar concerning the sanitation and health at the Evacuees Camp there.

The telegram categorically states that there is no truth whatsoever in the rumours and that the health and sanitation conditions are of the best. Any information regarding the source of these lying and mischievous rumours would be gladly received by the Honourable Colonial Secretary.

21-1-41.

Extract from a newspaper in Gibraltar.

Press Communiqué denying charges.
Mr F Zammitt

The educational needs of nearly 330 children of school age were catered for as from the beginning of 1941.

School Children with Teacher C.Gomez in Jamaica.
Photo Mr F Zammitt

Teachers and senior evacuee pupils in Jamaica.
At the back: Violeta Martinez F.Villa Adelaida Banda Mariluz Peralta, Pauline Romero, Alice Peralta, Berta Gomez, Sara Hatchwell
Sitting in front are the teachers with Head teacher Sister Xavier sitting in the centre of the picture. Photo Mr A Traverso

School children. Photo Miss S Moya

The school was fully equipped with the usual standard tables, blackboards, text books and all the necessary stationery items required for the teaching of all elementary subjects including music. The school catered for children up to the age of 14.

Below cutting from The Gleaner commenting on the opening of school facilities for evacuees.

Steps Being Taken For Education Of Evacuee Children

Steps are being taken by the Gibraltar Camp authorities to provide for and in some cases complete the education of the evacuee children of school age of which there are at present 331 between the ages of 4 and 15. Of that number 66 are between 4 and 7 and must be taught in infant schools.

The authorities have no wish that these unfortunate victims of the war should grow up illiterate and so are at present building class rooms for them. It is understood that four of the older boys who have either passed or are preparing for the Junior and Senior Cambridge examinations will be sent to St. George's College to complete their studies. The older girls will in due course complete their education either at the Alpha Academy or at Alvernia.

As a part of this educational scheme, it is the purpose of the committee of management to bring out to Jamaica a sufficient number of Christian Brothers who taught these children in Gibraltar. The Christian Brothers fill the same role in education in Gibraltar as the Jesuit Priests do here. They are very popular with the Gibraltareans and their names seem to be always on the lips of the refugees.

A representative of the Christian Brothers now in New York, Bro. Patrick Ryan who taught in Gibraltar 31 years ago, will probably visit the island in the very near future for negotiations in this matter.

FOR THE GIRLS

In the meanwhile sufficient teachers are available both among the evacuees, some of whom have taught in Gibraltar, and among the local Sisters, who will in any case take care of the education of the girls. It is only with regard to the education of the big boys that the authorities are not so fortunately placed and it is here that the Christian Brothers must come in.

The Very Rev. Fr. Feeney, Father Superior at Winchester Park, and a member of the committee of management, who is in charge of these educational matters told the "Gleaner" on Saturday that preparations were also under way for the selection and development of a representative football team which when ready might serve as a new source of competition to the local Private Secondary Schools and the Manning Cup teams.

With regard to the class rooms at Gibraltar itself, two ordinary long houses, partitioned into class rooms will admirably serve the purpose and will also fit in with the whole general principle of economy which is being followed.

“ We Thank God and England..”

The school curriculum was in line with the Gibraltar system of education. Those children who were beyond secondary school age and wished to achieve a higher level of academic education were given the opportunity to attend the Secondary Schools in Jamaica. As in the case of the school children in Madeira, the British Government also gave much emphasis to the need of encouraging more fluency in the English language. The policy was to bring education in line with British culture and traditions so that when the Gibraltar children left Jamaica they were academically prepared as British Citizens.

Teachers Mrs. Tucker and Miss V.Azzopardi outside the classroom. Among the children are R.Enriles sitting beside Mrs Tucher and Violeta Gomez (Mrs. Ballestero) marked with a cross. Photo Mr E Enriles

Teachers Mrs Tucker, A.Celecia, Sister Jones and Mrs Lola Romero outside the classroom.Among the school boys are E.Enriles,V.Yeo, M.Cooper,J.Remolines and among the girls are the Flower sisters,Devincenzi,Collado,Azzopardi and Silva. Photo Mr E Enriles

At the back L to R Palmero, Str.Jean, Str Xavier, P.Zammitt, C.Gomez, O.Buttigieg, A.Celecia and V.Azzopardi. In from L to R Str Filomena, Bead, Emmanuelle, F.Tucker, L.Romero Fr W Feeney. Photo Mr F Zammitt

Because of the many babies born shortly after the arrival of the evacuees, provision was also made at the camp for a school nursery. This also meant that eventually there was a need for extra infant classrooms. The school had a large playground where the boys played football and the girls basketball. Physical education was also included in the curriculum. The teaching staff consisted of a head teacher and five Sisters of various Orders. There were nine Gibraltar lay teachers who were selected from amongst the evacuees and a Jamaican teacher.

The Catholic Opinion published an article about the opening of the Camp Gibraltar School. As can be seen from the cuttings they give detailed accounts of the arrangements made to open the school, the appointment of teachers and facilities provided.

FR. LEO T. BUTLER, S.J.
Supervisor of Catholic Schools

HON. B. H. EASTER,
Director of Education

OPENING OF SCHOOL. — The Camp Gibraltar School was opened on the 20th of last month, with a registered attendance of two hundred and thirty children. SISTER XAVIER is in charge of Sixth Standard; SR. EMMANUEL and MRS. GARCIA control the Fifth; SR. BEDE looks after the Fourth; MISS GOMEZ is occupied with Third; MISS BROWN and MISS ZAMMIT take care of the Second; SR. DIVINE HEART, MRS. ROMERO and MISS CELECIA are in charge of the First; and SR. BERCHMAN, MRS. TUCKER and MISS PALMERO teach in the Kindergarten class.

The class rooms are large and airy. Blackboards have been put in their places: and benches and desks are in every class. The compound includes four buildings, united by covered runways. The fourth structure is devoted to Domestic Science, and at present sewing is done there. The buildings adjoin the Church, and are set back from the road some sixty or seventy yards, leaving a splendid stretch of green-covered field, dotted with trees, for a playground. Gravel-walks are being built, in order to prevent wet feet.

On the 27th of last month LADY RICHARDS, accompanied by MRS. PENNANT, paid the school a visit. On arrival the party was met by the Acting Commandant, MR. J. L. WORLLEDGE, VERY REV. FR. THOS. FEENEY, S.J. and REV. FR. LEO BUTLER, S.J. LADY RICHARDS and party went to each class, offered a word of encouragement to the children, and expressed delight at the work done in the short space of one week after the opening.

With the opening of school, the 8 o'clock Mass has become the Children's Mass. FRS. W. FEENEY and THOS. HENNESSEY are kept busy with children's confessions on Saturday afternoons, and the number of children at Holy Communion on Sundays is increasing weekly. The children's choir sing at the 8 o'clock Mass, and the young

Very Rev. Fr. Superior
T. J. FEENEY, S.J.
In Charge of Religion, Education and Recreation at Mona

Primary school children. Photo Mrs Bossino

School children. In photo are Enrique Mauro Maria Mauro and Jose Molinari. Photo Alfred Balban

Below cutting from the Gibraltar Chronicle of May 1941 referring to opening of school in Jamaica.

JAMAICA

A "Gibraltar Camp School" was start on the 16th January, 1941. Three hu were transformed into schoolrooms whi provide ample accommodation. The classrooms are spacious, well-lighted a ventilated and have been generously equi ped. For the Infant department the r quisite kindergarten has been provided.

The staff consists of one Head teach and 14 assistant teachers, composed five Sisters from the Convents of King ston, nine selected Gibraltar evacuees a one Jamaican.

The course of study is the same as i Gibraltar schools. Several boys and gir who wish to continue their schooling b yond the age of 14 years have been ad mitted to the public secondary schools the island.

By April last, 114 boys and 120 gir had been enrolled. The number is i creasing weekly.

The camp contains a recreational h with ping-pong tables and sets, gam sets, dominoes, cards and an electric gr mophone with amplifier and records. Ba concerts and cinematograph entertai ments are provided regularly. There i also a well-supplied reading room.

There were three dining rooms, which had been allocated to cater for different groups of evacuees according to age and family composition. There were three daily sitting arrangements in each of the dining halls. These consisted of breakfast, lunch and supper. This meant that a great deal of the time was spent by the evacuees near and around the dining halls. The quality and quantity of food served in the camp was reasonable but it was not cooked in a way which was as appetising or as palatable as the evacuees would have liked. This in itself was the cause some problems, among the evacuees who occasionally complained about the food.

Adult evacuees in the dining room. In the forefront is Mr Lara.   Photo Mr J Parody

Evacuees during breakfast. In the photo is Mrs L Romero. Photo Mrs P Wood

Gibraltar evacuees employed with the kitchen staff.   Wikipedia Free Encyclopedia

The idea of cooking food to the liking of the evacuees was slightly sorted out when some of the evacuees offered to help with the menu and the distribution of food.

Above two missionary Sisters and a group of evacuee girls about to serve their fellow Gibraltarians. Photo Mr F Zammitt

Again the idea of serving food at the table did not remedy entirely the whole problem, as by the time the evacuees sat on the table the food was normally cold. One of the caterers, Peter McCaulay, from the Canadian Regiment at Jamaica introduced a system similar to a self-service canteen. With this system the evacuees could collect their own food directly from the kitchen on a tray and take it to their respective table. Like in a self-service canteen the food was ready for collection within a specified time.

Evacuee children in the dinning room. Photo Mr C Moore

Below a detailed account of the new system of serving food in the camp dinning room as published in a Jamaican Times in November 1940.

NEW SYSTEM FOR FEEDING EVACUEES

Presence at Gibraltar Camp of members of the military over the week-end gave rise to certain speculations and rumours some of which were to say the least fantastic. To get the truth of the matter, the Gleaner approached the Commandant and is now able to allay all fears.

Recently, the authorities at Gibraltar had to turn to the sergeant chefs of the military to show them how to serve meals as quickly as possible to the thousand-odd evacuees lodged there. The old system of feeding them showed leaks and inconveniences and in compliance with the request of the Gibraltar Commandant, the C.O. at Up Park Camp despatched two of the quarter-master sergeants to show how the military cook and dine.

Last week, Col. Kaye, the C.O., at the personal invitation of Mr. Worrledge, visited Gibraltar to see how his men were progressing. The C.O. was accompanied by Lt. Davies and a quarter-master sergeant. The visitors inspected the ranges and saw the meals served and were pleased at what they had seen.

The new system of serving meals is called the cafeteria system. Formerly the evacuees were made to sit at long tables, when two from each table would bring in in large vessels the soup and the meat, etc. These two would then share the meals for everybody at their particular table. This system soon proved to be imperfect; and involved a long wait during which the soup would get cold. Often enough, too, those deputed to do the sharing were not able to hold the scales evenly nor cater successfully to the special tastes of the diners.

NEW SYSTEM

The military sergeants changed all that. No longer are the people requested to sit at table and wait for the food to be brought to them. Instead they themselves queue up before the kitchens, and one by one, they pass the vessels with the food steaming hot. Each evacuee asks for and receives the quality and the amount of food he or she desires; the vessels remain hot to the end. Now evacuees do not have to rush in to get their places at tables. They begin to dine at 12 and the meal hour continues for one hour. So they may come in at their convenience at any time during that hour.

There are three dining rooms, designated A, B and C. Each caters to a different set of evacuee. One caters to the mothers with children under 5, one to mothers and children under 15 and the other to the people of other ages.

Evacuees were not allowed to compete for employment in the Jamaica labour market but in order to avoid idleness as much as possible, opportunities for employment were given to the evacuees within the camp. Eventually about 400 evacuees were employed in the Camp.

Evacuees employed as kitchen helpers. Photo Mr F Mosquera

The jobs in which the Gibraltar evacuees were mainly engaged were those in the bakery and laundry services which had been run, initially, by the Jamaicans. Some Gibraltarians were also employed to help in the kitchen. Others were allowed to perform in trades like in the carpentry and butcher shops. Although many of the evacuees engaged in these trades had no previous experience many of them eventually gained the necessary skills and reached a reasonable level of competence in their respective trades.

Young evacuees acquiring skills in carpentry shop. Photo Mr C Rebora

There were also opportunities to be employed as police constable and in the fire brigade within the camp as can be seen from the pictures shown in this page.

Evacuees employed as fire fighters. Wikipedia Free Encyclopedia

Gibraltar evacuees employed in the Gibraltar Camp Police Force. Wikipedia Free Encyclopedia

The seamstresses at work. Wikipedia Free Encyclopedia

The Canteen in Jamaica run by evacuees. Photo Mr E Triay

A wider view of the canteen. Photo Mr A J Santos

Evacuees employed in the Camp Office.
In the photo are Miss O Carreras and Miss A Sita.
Wikipedia Free Encyclopedia

Within the camp there was also a store where items of shoes, clothing, sweets, stationery and many others goods could be obtained on sale. The management of the canteen in the camp was given to Gibraltar evacuee Mrs Dalmedo with the help of six paid assistants. There was a policy to involve the evacuees as much as possible in the running of the Gibraltar Camp. To comply with this policy, the older boys helped to unload and store goods in the kitchen and the dining rooms. Some of the senior girls were also engaged with helping in the kitchens with various jobs. These activities went a long way in helping with the food distribution including some modifications at a later stage.

The delivery of mail in camp was carried out by Gibraltar evacuee Mr Ernest Lara seen in the picture below.

Mr Lara – The Camp Postman.
Photo Mr A Lara

Gibraltar girls helping in the camp.
The Catholic Opinion

Those evacuees who could not be found a job were paid unemployment benefit at the rate of about 2s.6d (12.5p) a week.

Given that the majority of the evacuees were Roman Catholics, religious activities played a very significant part in the life of these evacuees in Jamaica.

The Above Postcard from Jamaica Shows the Holy Trinity Roman Catholic Cathedral in Kingston. Photo Mr C Moore

* *The Roman Catholic Church was built in 1810 by a Spanish merchant. It was destroyed in the earthquake of 1907. It was rebuilt and it is Kingston's largest church and the mother church of the Catholic community. The Cathedral's large rose windows, massive reinforced concrete walls reaching up 26m to its striking copper dome make it one of Kingston's most attractive buildings.*

Father Thomas Feeney in addition to his appointment as a member of the management committee of the Gibraltar Camp was also the Father Superior of the Roman Catholic Church in Jamaica. He and his brother William with the assistance other priests, sisters and nuns were naturally very much involved in religious activities as can be appreciated from the photographs in this chapter. The church building within the camp was quite large with capacity to accommodate about 500 worshippers. There were facilities for a choir with the provision of an organ. Daily church services were held. There was a convent for the nuns and a hostel for the resident priests. In the photographs on the following pages the Gibraltar children can be seen celebrating the Holy Communions and Confirmations. Throughout the year all the religious feasts were observed and celebrated. In the photographs shown in this chapter, the Gibraltar children can also be seen taking part in the Corpus Christi procession held in the Gibraltar Camp.

Inside the Camp Church. Photo Mrs P Wood

Occasionally the evacuees were taken to the main Roman Catholic Church in Kingston shown at the top of the page.

CHOIR FROM CAMP GIBRALTAR SING IN R.C. CATHEDRAL

A party of 38 voices drawn from the Chapel choir at Camp Gibraltar, Mona, honoured Gaudete Sunday with a musical programme at the evening service in Holy Trinity Cathedral on Sunday night last. Miss Valverde, one of the evacuees, officiated at the organ for the major portion of the programme, Mr. Arthur Chevolleau, organist of the Cathedral taking the Tantum Ergo at Benediction and playing Viviani's "Silver Trumpets" as the recessional.

The congregation were very pleased with the high standard of the programme by the evacuees, and at the close of the service introductions were made. Two youngsters of the choir acquitted themselves admirably in solo parts in two of the items. The order of service was as follows: two hymns, followed by the sermon by Fr. Thomas O'Lalor S.J., another hymn the O Salutaris, the Tantum Ergo, another hymn, and the recessional. Miss Valverde made a very good impression in her contributions on the organ, and the hope was expressed that further opportunity would be afforded her in this capacity.

The Holy Trinity Cathedral choir and instrumentalists will repeat at the Camp Gibraltar Chapel, on Christmas morning at 9 o'clock the Mercadante's Mass in B flat to be rendered by them in Holy Trinity Cathedral Xmas Midnight Mass.

Above and below cuttings from Jamaican Times Newspaper.

There was also a small chapel for evacuees who were members of Anglican denomination. This chapel was also provided with an organ.

CAMP GIBRALTAR

The Anglican Community had a New Year's Party at the camp on Friday, 3rd January. Friends and relations were invited and in all there were about 60. Owing to the generosity of a few friends in Kingston and St. Andrew and some hard work on the part of some of the ladies, especially Miss E. Manser and Mrs. Griffin, the company enjoyed a sumptuous repast during the course of the evening. They were very pleased to welcome the Acting Commandant, and the Deputy Commandant and Mrs. Rae. There were games and fun for old and young and time passed only too quickly. At the end of the evening Miss Deeley entertained the company with songs and Mrs. Rae kindly distributed prizes to the winners of the various games. Thanks are due to the Camp authorities for allowing the use of various crockery and cutlery and of the Recreation Hall.

Most of the children born in Jamaica were baptised in the Gibraltar Camp Church. Equally children at their appropriate age received their first Holy Communion and were confirmed in the Camp Church, which had been built specifically for the religious requirements of evacuees.

Nuns with evacuee children in the Camp.
Photo Mrs V Ballestero

The above photographs show girls, nuns and Girl Guides taking part in the Corpus Christi Procession.
Photo Mrs V Ballestero

Girls about to take part in their First Holy Communion.
Photo Mr E Enriles

Photo Mr E. Enriles.

Photo Mr E Triay.

CORPUS CHRISTI PROCESSION

THE CORPUS CHRISTI PROCESSION at Gibraltar Camp, last Sunday morning, was an impressive spectacle. Over 1,000 persons took part. This picture shows a nun with some of the little schoolgirls—hijas de Maria—during the procession.

Photo Catholic Opinion.

A USA dirigible over the Church. Photo Mrs P Wood

Gibraltar Youths and Adults in a Religious Grouping in Jamaica Sitting in front are Mr Carreras, Mr Macia, Mr N.Mosquera and Father William Feeney. Standing at the back with the auxiliary force cadets is John Parody. Photo Mr J Parody

Gibraltar young evacuees with nuns at a religious gathering. Photo Mr Triay

Gibraltar evacuees in a procession. Photo Miss S Moya

CONFIRMATION AT GIBRALTAR CAMP

Sixty candidates were presented for confirmation at Camp Gibraltar yesterday afternoon, His Lordship Bishop Emmet officiating, assisted by Rev. Frs. Gladstone Wilson, William Feeney and T. J. Hennessey. His Lordship also preached the sermon.

Previous to the confirmation service, a procession of scouts, rovers and guides was held with Fr. Wilson as Master of Ceremonies.

Afterwards, the Bishop visited the Hospital and blessed the sick, as well as the new surgery building.

At 7.30 in the evening the Bishop officiated at the Sodality Reception in the Camp Church when 125 candidates were received.

HOLY WEEK — The first Holy Week at Camp Gibraltar has come and gone. Early in the week our Church was a place of great activity. The good Sisters aided by many Sodalists prepared the repository, rehearsed the girls for the Holy Thursday procession and practised for the two High Masses which were sung on Holy Thursday and Easter Sunday.

The repository was erected at the gospel side of the Sanctuary and was covered with beautiful, flowing folds of white silk. The contributions from the Evacuees for flowers and candles were many and generous. On Holy Thursday, after the High Mass, twenty white-robed little girls strewed flowers before Our Blessed Lord as He proceeded to the altar of repose. During the day, school children and adults kept vigil before the Blessed Sacrament.

On Friday morning the Mass of the Presanctified was celebrated after the return of the procession from the altar of repose. In the afternoon the Three Hours service was conducted in Spanish. FR. WILLIAM FEENEY preached and PETER CARRERAS did the reading. MR. MOSQUERA's choir provided apt and excellent music.

Saturday morning the Paschal Candle was blessed after which a low Mass was said. The High Mass on Easter Sunday was sung by REV. FATHER HENNESSEY, S.J. The Sodality Choir rendered the Missa de Angelis.

The newly organized altar-boys society, the two fine choirs and the graciousness of the youngsters who marched in the procession were important factors in our quite devotional Holy Week.

SODALITY ACTIVITIES.—Under the zealous direction of FR. THO. HENNESSEY, and the perseverance of SISTERS BEDE and FRANCIS, the Young Ladies' Sodality continues to thrive. The consultors are: CELIA GOMEZ, JOSEPHINE ZAMMITT, PEPITA ZAMMITT, VICTORIA AZZOPARDI, MERCEDES CANO, OPHELIA CARRERAS, EMELIA MCINTOSH, LOURDES MCGILLVARY, MAGDELENA ORFILA, EULALIA MARTINEZ, CATHERINE OLIVERO, DORIS SHERIFF, ANGELES COCHRANE, VICTORIA MCKAY and IRMA.

The first General Communion of the Sodality took place on the 9th of March, and brought out over one hundred young ladies to the communion rail.

Two socials were held during the month. The first was of an impromptu nature, when FR. HENNESSEY spoke on "Rome", whilst the second consisted of a musical programme, interspersed with dancing.

On the 25th of last month, the feast of the Annunciation, the first meeting of the married Ladies' Sodality took place. After the recitation of the Rosary, the REV. FR. WM. FEENEY, in a short address, told the Sodalists that he felt sure that the devotion to our Blessed Mother, which is outstanding in the Iberian Peninsula, would flourish here. He pleaded for fidelity to the Sodality, observing that faithfulness would have the triple effect of increasing personal holiness, drawing down blessings on their families, and bringing the assurance of Our Lady's protection on their husbands and sons who were in Gibraltar.

A beautiful companion statue to that of the Sacred Heart has been set up on the Epistle side of the Sanctuary. It is the gift of generous benefactors, to whom the church authorities are deeply grateful. As is clear, the statue has helped to intensify devotion of the two Sodalities to Our Blessed Mother, and is certainly an extra adornment to the church.

CANDLE STANDS.—In order to allow the carrying on of the laudable practice of burning candles before the Sacred Heart and Blessed Virgin's statue, two metal candle holders have been constructed.

Above cuttings from the Catholic Opinion describing some of the religious activities in the Gibraltar Camp.

Evacuee Girls taking part in Holy Thursday. Photo Mrs V Ballestero

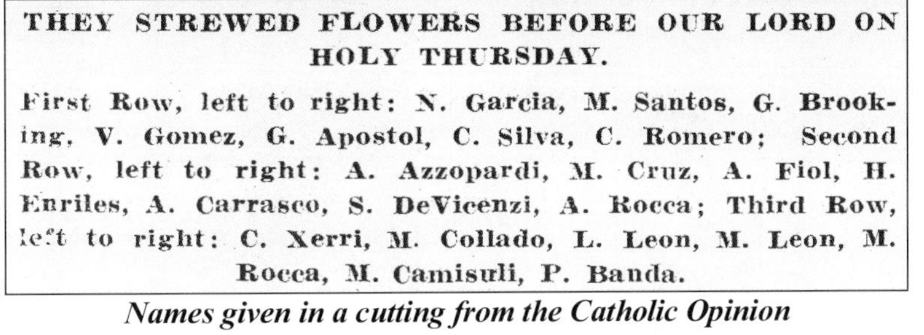

THEY STREWED FLOWERS BEFORE OUR LORD ON HOLY THURSDAY.

First Row, left to right: N. Garcia, M. Santos, G. Brooking, V. Gomez, G. Apostol, C. Silva, C. Romero; Second Row, left to right: A. Azzopardi, M. Cruz, A. Fiol, H. Enriles, A. Carrasco, S. DeVicenzi, A. Rocca; Third Row, left to right: C. Xerri, M. Collado, L. Leon, M. Leon, M. Rocca, M. Camisuli, P. Banda.

Names given in a cutting from the Catholic Opinion

Gibraltar evacuees taking part in religious activities. Photo Mr F Zammitt

All the photos on this page were donated by Mr F Zammitt.

Holy Communion at the Camp.

Above Church service at the Camp.

In the photo L to R: L.Orcese, L.Gomez, P.Zammitt, Fr Buckley, P.Romero, L.Carreras ..?..

Corpus Christi Procession.

As can be demonstrated from the photographs in this page there were many religious activities in which the evacuees participated fully in the camp. All the photographs on this page were donated by Mr Frank Zammitt.

The idea of forming a football team with players recruited from among the Gibraltar evacuees was very early in the minds of the administrators. This came about after the administrators watched the style of football being practised by the evacuees when playing casually in the camp.

The following story; the first about football in the camp, appeared the Jamaican Times on Friday 27th December 1940 .

EVACUEE FOOTBALL.

We are reliably informed that there are times when the Very Rev. Fr. W. Feeney, S.J., Father Superior of the Roman Catholic Mission, and a member of the managing committee of Camp Gibraltar, cannot look Mr. J. L. Worlledge, Auditor General and Acting Camp Commandant, in the eye.

The position is this. The Very Rev. Father decided from early after the arrival of the evacuees from Gibraltar to show them how football is played. He therefore, went to the trouble of getting a team of tots up at the camp; but they were badly beaten by the Gibraltar eans. Profiting from experience, he brought a second and bigger team; but they too were defeated. Much disillusioned, the Father Superior still had up more teams; but on Saturday last, his latest team met with a four-nil defeat. This team consisted of big, hefty fellows, sporting the famous light blue of the Dragons.

Frankly, these evacuees play a very fair brand of football. They use the short passing tactics—so reminiscent of the old 'Christians'—with effect, have fine ball control and should give our Manning teams considerable trouble.

We suggest that the J.F.A. come to the aid of the Rev. Fr. Superior and arrange a match, say, first of all against the Alpha Boys, the Aguilar Cup champions, and then ask either St. George's or K.C. to finish the lesson—if they can!

The Gibraltar football team in the Camp. Photo by Mr F Zammitt

After a few trial matches a team was finally selected from the players who had shown from the very beginning a keen interest in football. By the beginning of 1941, that is, a few months after the arrival of the Gibraltar evacuees, formal football matches were already being played

The Gibraltar team practising in the Camp. Photo Mr F Zammitt

Many fine games were observed and the Gibraltar team managed to beat some of the local teams. A team was finally selected to play against some of the Jamaican football teams on an informal competitive basis.

Space was not an impediment as there was ample terrain available to have a sizeable football pitch. As soon as possible a football ground was marked within what had been earmarked to become Camp No.2.

On Friday 29 August it was officially announced through the Jamaica Daily Express that the opening of the Camp Gibraltar football ground would take place the following day Saturday 30th August 1941 at 4.30 pm.

Below extract from the Jamaica Daily Express announcing the opening of the football ground

Football At Gibraltar Camp

Official opening of the Camp Gibraltar Football Ground will take place at 4.30 p.m. on Saturday of this week. There will be an opening match between the Camp Gibraltar team captained by Ignasius Zannit and a team from the Fleet Air Arm.

There will also be a flag raising ceremony when the flag will be raised by Commander Hawkins and Mr. E. A. Rae, Camp Commandant. The public will be admitted to the ground for a subscription of 6d. per person.

The ground is situated at Camp No. 2, and the South-end gate will be the one in use. A large gathering is expected to witness the match and ceremony.

The Gibraltar Football Team. 6th from the left is Frank Valverde. Photo Miss Sheryl Moya

The inauguration ceremony of the new football ground was initiated with a friendly match that was played between the RN Fleet Air Arm and Gibraltar Camp football team.

OPENING OF PLAYING FIELD AT CAMP GIBRALTAR

Commander Hawkins, of the Fleet Air Arm, hoisting the Union Jack at the Gibraltar Camp sports ground opening ceremony on Saturday afternoon last. Others in the picture, taken outside the pavilion, are acting Commandant E. A. Rae, acting Deputy Commandant G. P. Brown, the Father Superior, Mr. Herbert Macdonald, Mr. H. N. Walker, and Mr. F. O. Romney.

TEAMS WHICH TOOK PART IN MATCH AT CAMP GIBRALTAR

Members of the Gibraltar Camp Football team (bottom) who defeated the Fleet Air Arm (top) in a friendly soccer tussle on the new Camp sports ground on Saturday afternoon. For some time there has been displayed a healthy rivalry between the two teams. Just a week or more ago the Camp team had defeated them three nil. The winners have to their credit a string of successes since their organisation as a club. At the official opening match on Saturday Commander Hawkins of the Fleet Air Arm hoisted the Club's Union Jack and acting Commandant Rae kicked off.

Playground Opened At Camp Gibraltar

Home Team Win Football Match Marking Occasion

Most of Gibraltar Camp's 1,600 evacuee population and their guests and friends took part on Saturday afternoon in the opening of the Camp's four-acre sports ground.

Commander Hawkins, of the Fleet Air Arm, officially opened the beautiful and spacious ground on the southern end of the Camp by hoisting the Union Jack in front of the pavilion, while the big crowd cheered, clapped wildly and sang. The Commander was assisted by Mr. E. A. Rae, acting Commandant.

COLOURFUL CEREMONY

Quite colourful was the ceremony of the opening of the ground. After tea in the Directors' room, acting Commandant Rae and Mrs. Rae being host and hostess to 20 or more, the Alpha Industrial School Band, under Mr. Neilson, led a parade of Gibraltar Girl Guides under Sister Emanuel and Boy Scouts under Scoutmaster A. Gomez and Assistant Scoutmaster Joseph Dalnado.

In front of the pavilion the procession was formed while the two football teams took up positions nearby.

At the Flag Pole, where the principal ceremony took place, there were Commander Hawkins, the Very Rev. Fr. Francis Feeney, Mr. Rae, Mr. G. P. Brown, (acting Deputy Commandant), the Rev. Fr. Hennessy, (Games Master of the Camp), Mr. Herbert Macdonald, President of the J. F. A., and others.

Mr. Rae then kicked off for the opening match in which there was witnessed a keen struggle between the two teams among whom a keen rivalry has been existing for some time. Just a week ago the Gibraltarians had defeated them 3—1 in a well fought game.

Captain I. Zammit led the victorious Camp team on Saturday, while Mr. T. Cullen was the skipper of the Fleet Air Arm side. A Fleet Air Arm officer refereed.

Both sides played a dashing game, but displayed very little co-operation. Gibraltar's two goals were scored one each in the first and second halves.

At the conclusion of the match the visitors were given rousing cheers for their plucky fight.

Bishop Emmet headed the large crowd of visitors who witnessed the game from the lines. Others seen included Dr. and Mrs. Cyril Gideon, the Rev. Frs. Wm. Feeney, Dooley, Donohue, Cruchley, Welch and Ochs, Mr. Cyril Walker, and Captain Jones.

The Gibraltar team was captained by I.Zammitt and the Fleet Air Arm team by Mr T.Cullen. The match ended in a two-nil victory for the Gibraltar Team. The cuttings on this page are from the Jamaica Times newspaper referring to the opening of the football ground.

At the start of the football season the Gibraltar Team was entered into the Junior League. According to the attached newspaper cuttings the Gibraltar Camp had a very good team and beat a few teams in Jamaica.

Military And Camp Gibralta[r] Teams To Take Part In J.F.A. Competitions

Camp Gibraltar have entered fo[r] the Junior League, and Commandant Ernest Rae seems to expect bi[g] things from them. During last season they played many friendly matches, and so must have moulded themselves into a team by now. Outstanding among their players are said to be two dumb brothers. We look forward to their debut.

"LINESMAN"

GIBRALTAR FOOTBALL TEAM

On Sunday last I saw the evacuee team play the Local Forces. The latter won, with the score 2 goals to nil. The evacuees had the chance to score at least 5 goals. In fact they did everything except score.

What was wrong with the team? I felt that they could be faster on the ball, that they might be too slow for teams like Kingston and St. George's and the Printers.

While their backs individually were good, their understanding was not good. Zammitt, the captain, at left back was dependable; but he and his mate had apparently no concerted plan of action with the result that there was not enough covering done.

Xiberes at outside right and Zammitt at inside are good, particularly Zammit.

I saw Arias their renowned centre-forward. He did not impress. He looked more than a trifle slow and a bit lacking in control. Neither is he blessed with zeal for arduous work: likes the ball to be sent to him where he can just kick to the uprights. He does seem, however, to know where the uprights are, and possibly, when he gets more acclimatized he might if very well fed score goals: for in fairness to him, I may say that he may not yet have gotten off his sea-legs.

This fact I noted, however, which is important: every individual member of the team shaped like a footballer and could answer most of the questions on kicking and passing set them. But their speed and understanding........umph!

THE JAMAICA TIMES,

KEEP COOL, GIBRALTAR

I am one of those who have been much impressed with the clever game played by our visitors at Mona, but I would like to give them a friendly word of advice—don't get rattled when you are bowled over by a hefty but perfectly fair charge. The players on the team are all on the light side, and naturally they fare second best in an encounter. As against that, they are much faster than most of our players, and if they make use of this asset, the question of lack of weight would hardly ever arise.

Many visitors came to the Gibraltar Camp to watch the football matches. It seems that outsiders were only allowed to go into the Gibraltar Camp when there was an away football team playing.

Frank Valverde one of the key players in the Gibraltar Team. Photo Mrs Valverde

The Gibraltar team was, as can be seen from the Jamaica Times newspaper cutting shown below, entered in the Senior Football League.

GIBRALTAREANS ENTER SENIOR FOOTBALL LEAGUE

"I tell you, sir, I do not say we will win, but we are going to give a good account of ourselves in your Senior League competition. You saw us in action recently?"

"No, but I saw you last year against teams which would be moderately good in what we call our Manning Competition out here; and I was impressed. I was of the opinion, however, that while you would be very considerable in the Junior League, you would not be able to hold our senior men."

"That was last year, sir; we are a very changed team now. In addition, we have recently been considerably strengthened by one of the best footballers Gibraltar has produced, Arias, who will play at centre forward. Oh, we have a strong combination, don't you fear."

The speaker and I were in the Recreation Hall at Camp Gibraltar He was not drinking. he does not drink—I mean 'hot and rebellious liqueurs'. Neither do I. He was shortish but of stocky build with a prominent nose an a humorous twinkle in his honest English eyes. He had spent over three decades in Gibraltar; knew the Latin temperament inside out and not unlikely had imbibed some of it. He is the manager of the Evacuee team which will play Senior Cup Football this season.

Around us stood ten likeable lads, on the short side, but of respectable build, of the type that would be at their best, if the world agreed to adopt the garb of Tarzan; for one does not realise the presence of muscles until one is surprised by them when the owners don shorts. You see, I have seen these boys in action: they are the Evacuee team.

The manager is a Mr. Barrett. He chats eloquently and profoundly of the game and, during his long stay on 'The Rock', identified himself with it always. He and a committee of four rule the team. The captain is Senor Zammitt.

IMPRESSIVE CONFIDENCE

Manager and team gathered around me. They were not boastful; but they were confident. Mr. Barrett oozes confidence and the lads assimilate it. They told me their hopes: they are very keen.

I felt impressed. Would they humble the pride of Island football! They did not say they would; but they would not say they couldn't. I was impressed. You see they were not drinking. We parted over bottles of Coca-Cola for which they paid.

They have great faith in this new man Arias. From their reports, he is a sort of genius. Mr. Barrett and his committee (he introduced me to two of the members, Mr. A. B. Hassan and Sr. M. Navas) have great faith in every member of the team. The team seem to have great faith in Mr. Barrett and the committee. Mr. Barrett says that every man on the side can acquit himself well in any position on the field. There is versatility for you!

Besides, it is not true that they use only the shortpassing tactics. "We can readily change to the tactics which seem best advisable to beat our opponents." And they have beaten a lot of opponents since preparation for the season began. Played 34 matches, won 24, drawn 7 and lost 4. Scored 106 goals as against 42 netted by their foes. Good going that, say I.

I said good-bye and felt that whatever happened, whether they won or not, these boys should be the attraction of the season and one of the most colourful teams we have had for quite a while.

Above and below newspaper coverage about the entry of the Gibraltar team in the senior football team.

Football Results

In a very close, fast, and attractive Senior League Football Match played at Mona, yesterday afternoon the Gibraltarians defeated the Y.M.C.A., one of last year's most powerful teams, by one goal to nil. The teams fought a goalless first half, the only goal scored coming late in the second half.

St. George's Old Boys, the Senior League champions, defeated Jamaica Constabulary by two goals to nil, in their first meeting of the football season yesterday afternoon. in the presence of a good-sized crowd at New Asylum.

In the Senior League, the Gibraltar team was required to play a higher quality football as explained in the Jamaica Times newspaper cutting shown below:

The ten clubs including Gibraltar which entered the senior league.

TEN CLUBS IN THIS SEASON'S SENIOR LEAGUE

Railway, Police, Camp Gibraltar And Military Additional Entries

NEW ENTRIES.

The four new Senior League clubs are: Railway, Kingston Police, Camp Gibraltar and the Military. In the case of Railway however, it is only a matter of returning to their own, which fact was more than expected after the request of this privilege was turned down last season and following their impressive performance.

"Camp Gibraltar will provide the colour of the coming football season", said one competent authority to me. At first we were made to believe that they had applied for the Junior League, but the evacuees are confident and they would have regarded it an insult to have been regraded to the lower league.

That they are enthusiastic goes without saying, and in friendly matches, played not only last season, but praticuarly recently preparatory to their entry into Jamaica's highest class of football, they have been building up something of an invincible record. Only late last week the Melboune Senior League team were held 3—3 on their new ground at Camp Gibraltar.

And something of that new ground. It is already voted probably the best football field in Jamaica. "It is a billiard table", says the same authority. If that is so, it is a natural incentive to good football, and I shall take the earliest opportunity of not only seeing this football mecca, but seeeing the Gibraltar team in action. Will they supply the colour to the expected struggle among St. George's Old Boys, the champions; Y. M. C. A., and a possible resurrected Kingston?

The evacuees are said to be adepts at the short passing, which the Sherwood Foresters used with such telling effect against our club teams and Jamaica combination up to three seasons ago. Also they can shift to the long passing game to suit the exigencies, but like most of the latin teams to have visited Jamaica do not shoot as promptly as they should after good outfield work puts them in an advantageous position. However, it is said that their centre-forward will be a revelation to local football.

"LINESMAN."

One of the many matches played in the Senior League outside the Gibraltar Camp was in the Spanish Town football ground on the 4th November 1941 as reported in the Jamaica Times newspaper cutting shown below:

GIBRALTAR F.C. TEAM TO PLAY AT SPA. TOWN TOMORROW AFTERNOON

The Gibraltar football team are due to make their appearance in St. Catherine to-morrow afternoon, when they play the Government School Old Boys, one of St. Catherine's oldest football teams, in a match arranged on behalf of the Cayman Fishing Disaster Fund.

Play takes place at the Old Constabulary Barracks, Spanish Town, widely known grounds of the Government School Old Boys, and is due to commence at 4.15 o'clock.

Above coaching the Gibraltar team

THE GIBRALTAR TEAM

The "Rock Scorpions" of the Gibraltar team are liable to sting our local Tigers, Dragons etc., before the season is through, and their entry will add very greatly to the interest of the season, for they are a fast, colourful and plucky side; and, on their own ground, probably as good as any team in the competition—though they do not control the ball, or themselves, quite so well on the fast, dry grounds in the city area. They tackle with great vigour and pluck; and, as they have their fair share of the Latin temperament, have already struck quite a few sparks both against St. George's and the Y's—a matter they want to be rather careful of, since it doesn't take much to get a rough game going with most Jamaica sides.

The Jamaica Times newspaper cutting reporting on the Gibraltar team on 17th October 1941.

The Gibraltar team also lost some of the games in the senior league as reported in the various sports columns of Jamaica Times newspapers copied below:

OLD BOYS BEAT GIBRALTAR 2-0

St. George's Old Boys defeated the Gibraltar side two goals to nil in a Senior League match full of incidents at Winchester Park yesterday, Arthur Mackenzie scoring both goals.

St. George's scored in the first five minutes, Mackenzie driving in a long low shot which went through the goalie's legs. After this the Gibraltareans, very fast on the ball, and passing neatly, pressed hard, and there was a lot of rough play, the referee not keeping the match well in hand.

Gibraltar got a penalty but the centre forward booted it over the top.

Going downhill in the second half St. George's had somewhat the better of play and should have had a penalty, the left back handling the ball badly, but the referee took no notice of it.

Just before time, Mackenzie scored again with a grand shot, a left hook which clean beat the goalie.

For St. George's, Delgado in goal, Peter and Mackenzie were outstanding; for Gibraltar, the right back, centre forward and left wing.

G. St. C. S.

JAMAICA DAILY EXPRESS

WEMBLEY STILL SHOW FORM

By Beating Gibraltar Camp 1-0.

Wembley have certainly proven themselves the surprise packet of the current season.

Yesterday afternoon they gained another step in their aspirations for Senior Cup honours this season by nosing out Gibraltar Camp by one goal to nil scored by Peterkin.

Again this was a match, in which it is almost impossible to explain how many more goals were not actually scored, as the many opportunities were in abundance, but the shots essayed were either ill-directed or else weak in the extreme. Eventually Peterkin scored the only goal of the match to give his side victory. The Gibraltar Camp forward line was always in the picture, but their finishing was practically non-existent.

On some occasions there were naturally criticisms about the style of football played by the Gibraltar teams as can be gathered from the football reports shown below:

POOR FOOTBALL FEATURES OPENING MATCHES

I almost said 'Ichabod' or did I say it? Now I come to think of it, I should have, after seeing the opening match of the Senior Cup Football season on Wednesday.

I was at Sabina Park where the "Tigers" defeated the evacuees by two goals to nil. The victors were not the old tigers we used to know. Wednesday's editions were the domesticated type, if there is such a thing as a domesticated tiger.

You got the impression that more than half the team—really not the whole—could use only **one** foot and that through some prank of mischievous Fate, they had been put in positions on the field in which they had to use the other foot. Result—a lot of men kicking and, oh yes, hustling quite a lot; and there was the ball; but just a couple of footballers and just a little football. Ichabod!

THE EVACUEES AGAIN

Can't some one tell our friends from Gibraltar that the five forwards cannot play effectively in a dead straight line and that when all rush up to the goal keeping that line religiously and geometrically straight, they give a lot of work to their half line, who, instead of being a mixture of defence and offence, must now play the one role of defenders. Also that when this line is so advanced, little chance will there be to cash in on the mistakes of the enemy custodian or the other opposing defenders.

Will some one also get it into the heads of the Gibraltar backs that it is disastrous for both backs to advance also in this straight line parallel to touch against the attack of the opposing side; for in the case of a break through there is no one to cover up or shield the custodian!

I could almost cry when I saw them use that formation at Sabina Park. I nearly reached for my kerchief and it is hoping I am that they won't do it again. Right now I am **not** feeling well; I am not feeling well at all.

The Gibraltareans in addition to being slow had a strange forward line: they all swarmed up the field in a beautifully straight line, leaving all the work to the halves: and the two backs again showed that they have not fully discovered the art of covering each other.

Some nice tactical movements initiated by their half line in the second deserved to bear fruit. On one occasion, the left half took the ball down field but when all his men were positioned and he could have passed advantageously, he still held on and was robbed. On other occasions, forwards received nice passes but were too slow in getting going.

A very poor display of football.

The Camp doctor and his wife amongst other VIPs watching a football match. Photo Mr F Zammitt

A few months after entering the Football Senior League the Gibraltar teams were apparently not allowed to compete in further football matches. This was due to some trouble related to the alleged misconduct of some of the evacuees during the initial games against some of the Jamaican teams. In this page are some of the stories published in the Jamaica Times newspaper related to the football match incident which prevented the Gibraltar team from continuing to participate in future football competitions.

THE MONA INCIDENT

An outrage unprecedented in the history of football in Jamaica occurred at Mona last Saturday, when Paul Chevannes, the referee of the match between Gibraltar and the Kingston Club, was assaulted by a member of the Gibraltar team, who disagreed with a penalty award against his team. For a player to strike another in the heat of the game has happened before, fortunately on occasions few and far between, but for a referee to be attacked and made the subject of a brawl is definitely the limit. The Jamaica Football Association acted promptly in the matter and held an emergency meeting on Tuesday afternoon, and four of the Gibraltar team were suspended for varying periods, the maximum being two years.

At the same time, the Council accepted the wihtdrawal of the Gibraltar team from the Senior Competition, and they can consider themselves lucky that the Council allowed this, as expulsion would have meant that they could not have played no more football whatever. As it is, they can still play friendly games, but of course the suspended players cannot take part.

It is regrettable that such a thing should have happened in their first year of football out here, but they only have themselves to blame.

The above reported incident took place in November 1941. No doubt this must have been a big blow to some of those Gibraltar players who were keen sporting footballers.

The Gibraltar Team in Jamaica. Photo Miss S Moya

Evacuees in Jamaica

The girls had their own netball team which was also very active in the sports ground available at the Gibraltar camp. Other sporting activities in the camp consisted of boxing and cricket for boys and basket ball for girls.

The girl basket ball team. Photo Mr E Enriles

FAIR GIBRALTAREANS TACKLE LOCAL NETBALL TEAM

The fame of the evacuees' football team has been circulating in municipal circles: so many teams have they whipped. Now the girls have begun to show what they can do with netball and on Wednesday last they journeyed down to Alpha and there engaged the girls of the elementary schools whom they defeated.

Above and below cuttings from the Jamaica Times.

Within the range of indoor games there were table tennis, draughts, dominoes, darts, cards playing and, of course, the popular tablita. In the camp there was a room with an electric gramophone with an amplifier and a collection of records.

FAIR EVACUEES AT PLAY AGAINST ALPHA.

(ABOVE.)—On Wednesday last week, netballers from the Evacuee Camp at Gibraltar, journeyed to the Alpha Convent and engaged the girls of the Elementary School. The evacuees won.

Some of the Gibraltar Netball Team Supporters

At the back from L to R: J.Agius, A.Remolines, V.Victor, E.Enriles, M.Peralta, P.Leon.

Sitting in front L to R.: Britto, A.Sherrif. D.Enriles,C.Enriles,J.Alvarez, C.Enriles,I.Enriles.

Photo by Mr E Enriles

With the idea of having the young evacuees fully occupied it was decided to set up and organise the Girl Guides and Boy Scouts movements within the camp. The idea attracted much interest among the young evacuees and by April 1941 the first Girl Guide Troop was formed. Then by June 1941 the Boy Scouts troop was also started.

Girl Guides parading to investiture ceremony.
Photo Mr F Zammitt

GIRL GUIDE COMPANY ADDS TO CITY LIFE OF GIBRALTAR CAMP

MRS. KELLY LAWSON, Island Guide Commissioner investing the Camp Gibraltar guide company. In the picture also is Sister Emanuel who organised the Company.

Photo Mr E Triay. Cuttings are from the Catholic Opinion

As can be seen from the photographs the Girl Guides took a very active part in the Guides movements during their stay in Jamaica.

On this page the Girl Guides are shown taking part in the investiture ceremony which took place at the Gibraltar Camp on Sunday 25th May 1941.

THE Gibraltese, though far from the comfort and atmosphere of home, by their very determinedness "to make the best of it" here display the grand British spirit, of carrying on under any and all conditions.

With each succeeding day the thousands of Gibraltar evacuees are settling down to normal life in Jamaica almost as though their lives had never been disturbed by the turmoil of war.

Latest innovation to the Camp, which is rapidly transforming itself into an autonomous city, is the first Girl Guide Company. The Company was organized and trained by Sister Marie Emanuel (a Jamaican, and former Kathleen Clough) who works alongside the religious authorities in the camp, and Miss Eileen O' Flanagan.

The troupe, consisting of twenty-one Guides, five Rangers and six guiders was enrolled on the 4th of April by Mrs. C. M. Kelly Lawson, Island Guide Commissioner, and presented so disciplined an appearance as to earn the compliment of the Commissioner.

VIPs watching the investiture ceremony.
Photo by Mr F Zammitt

Girl Guides displaying colours after the ceremony. Photo by Mr F Zammitt

In this page there are more pictures related to the Girl Guides activities in the Gibraltar Camp.

From L to R Troop Leaders A.Banda,A.Peralta,F.Villa,P.Romero and V.Martinez

Above and below guides and nuns by the camping site.

Guides in Kingston with the nuns.

Girl Guides attending mass in the Camp.

Above Girl Guides saluting the flag.

…?.... C.Gomez, Sister …?....   O.Buttigieg…….?...
…?....P.Zammitt, Mrs Griffin….?......
Photo Miss S Moya

As can be gathered from the pictures the Gibraltar Girl Guides in Jamaica were kept very busy by attending many parades and other associated activities. All the photographs on this page except the one above were donated by Mr Frank Zammitt.

In this page there are more photographs depicting the Girl Guides activities in the Gibraltar Camp.

Girl Guides.
From L to R: Celecia, ..?.. C.Gomez, Mrs Griffin,...?...

In the photo L to R are Girl Guides.
A.Peralta,F.Villa and P.Romero

All the photographs on this page were donated by Mr Frank Zammitt.

The same as the Girl Guides the Boy and Sea Scouts were formerly invested at the Gibraltar Camp in a ceremony, which took place on Saturday 23rd July 1941. In this page are photographs of the investiture ceremony. All the photographs on this page were donated by Mr Frank Zammitt.

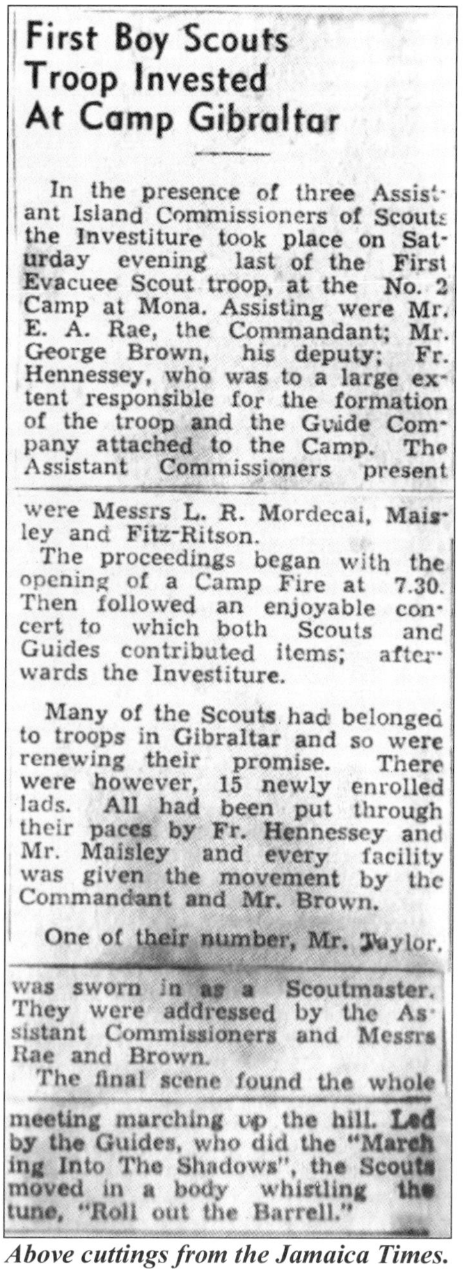

First Boy Scouts Troop Invested At Camp Gibraltar

In the presence of three Assistant Island Commissioners of Scouts the Investiture took place on Saturday evening last of the First Evacuee Scout troop, at the No. 2 Camp at Mona. Assisting were Mr. E. A. Rae, the Commandant; Mr. George Brown, his deputy; Fr. Hennessey, who was to a large extent responsible for the formation of the troop and the Guide Company attached to the Camp. The Assistant Commissioners present were Messrs L. R. Mordecai, Maisley and Fitz-Ritson.

The proceedings began with the opening of a Camp Fire at 7.30. Then followed an enjoyable concert to which both Scouts and Guides contributed items; afterwards the Investiture.

Many of the Scouts had belonged to troops in Gibraltar and so were renewing their promise. There were however, 15 newly enrolled lads. All had been put through their paces by Fr. Hennessey and Mr. Maisley and every facility was given the movement by the Commandant and Mr. Brown.

One of their number, Mr. Taylor, was sworn in as a Scoutmaster. They were addressed by the Assistant Commissioners and Messrs Rae and Brown.

The final scene found the whole meeting marching up the hill. Led by the Guides, who did the "Marching Into The Shadows", the Scouts moved in a body whistling the tune, "Roll out the Barrell."

Above cuttings from the Jamaica Times.

A group of Boy Scouts at ease.

Below more pictures of the Gibraltar Boy Scouts investiture ceremony from Jamaica Times newspaper cuttings.

Commandant's Wife Presents Camp Scout Troop With Colours

In a colourful little ceremony at Camp Gibraltar yesterday afternoon. Mrs. E. A. Rae, wife of the Acting Commandant, handed the Gibraltarean Scout Troop their new flag, which is the gift of the now famous Evacuee artist, Mr. Benunes and Mrs. Benunes. Mr. and Mrs. Benunes did an invaluable bit of work and the gift was highly appreciated. Hundreds of evacuees turned out to witness the ceremony. Mr. Leslie R. Mordecai, and Mr. Maisley, Scout Commissioners took part, while several visitors, the Acting Commandant Mr. E. A. Roe, and his Deputy, Mr. Brown looked on. Fr. Hennessey, who has worked hard on the troop, Mr. Rae, Mr. Mordecai and Mr. Maisley addressed the scouts. The company of Camp Girl Guides and several visiting scouts were in attendance.

AS GIBRALTAR SCOUT TROOP RECEIVE COLOURS

SCOUT COMMISSIONER LESLIE R. MORDECAI and Assistant Scout Commissioner Maisley, attended Camp Gibraltar, on Sunday last to assist in a pleasant ceremony—the presentation of colours to the Evacuees Scout Troop. The flag was presented by Mr. and Mrs. Benunes, an evacuee family. Mr. Benunes is a noted and brilliant artist and the flag was made by him, assisted by his wife. Mrs. Rae, the wife of Acting Commadant E. A. Rae, handed the colours to the Company, while Messrs. Mordecai and Maisley spoke to the boys complimenting them upon their smart appearance and giving them useful advice.

Below Boy and Sea Scouts outside their headquarters.
Photo Mr F Zammitt

Investiture Of Rover Scouts At Gibraltar Camp

(Contributed)

On Saturday January 24, fourteen of our visitors at Gibraltar Camp were invested as Rover Scouts. This Rover Crew, under its leader Rover Scout Hugh Padina, has not long been formed but has already shown a great interest in Rovering.

The Investiture itself was performed by Rover Scout Leader Padina, assisted by his second, Rover Francis Sardena, under the direction of Mr. Hugh Mazely, Honorary secretary of the Jamaica Boy Scouts Association.

Mr. D. T. M. Girvan, Deputy Camp Chief, representing the Island Commissioner (on leave) and the Acting Island Commissioner, spoke on behalf of the Boy Scouts Association and welcomed the newly invested Rovers to the ranks of scouting. Messrs Frank Muirhead and Gerald Hall acted as sponsors to the Rover Squires as they undertook their greater duties as Rover Scouts. Mr. Donald Fitz-Ritson, Assistant Island Commissioner, was present also.

Rovers from the Molynes Crew were in attendance together with representatives of the Guiders and Rangers from the Gibraltar Camp Companies.

After the ceremony, the Camp Commandant, Mr. E. A. Rae, welcomed the new rovers in the name of the Camp. The Rt. Rev. Thomas A. Emmet, Roman Catholic Bishop in Jamaica, addressed the newly invested Rovers and gave them his blessing.

A combined church parade of Rovers, scouts and guides was present at Mass on Sunday morning. This was followed by an Investiture Breakfast for the Rovers which the Camp Commandant and Mrs. Rae attended in company with the Rev. Wm. Feeney to the Sacred Heart Church at Camp Gibraltar.

Above cutting from the Jamaica Times.

Girl Guides involved in cooking.
Photos Miss S Moya

As explained in previous pages, within the Gibraltar Camp there were three halls, purposely built for the recreational and entertaining needs of the evacuees. The halls were used to show films twice a week. Dances and plays were also held in the halls.

Above are Lourdes Barrett (Nee McGillivray) and Nemesio. Mosquera. Photo Mr F Mosquera

Girls taking part in Portuguese Dance "El Fado." Standing at the back L to R S.Axisa, R.Richardson, P.Romero Kneeling L to R: M.Trinidad, A.Arias, A.Celecia L.Copello H.Yeo Photo Mr F Zammitt

Girls in taking part in "Manton Granadino." At the back L to R B.Gomez, R.Richardson, V.Martinez, A.Arias, L.Copello, S.Axisa, A.Banda, M.L.Trinidad. Kneeling H.Yeo and P.Romero. Photo Mrs A Banda

There were some Gibraltar evacuees who became very popular within the camp by demonstrating their talents when taking part in shows and other functions which went a long way to entertaining the evacuees who were thousand of miles away from home.

Below is well known local comedian Nemesio Mosquera with other participants in a comedy show. Photo Mr F Mosquera

Below is a copy of the notice placed in one of the newspapers advertising the show mounted by the Gibraltar evacuees in the camp theatre.

TO NIGHT!!

You Have A Definite Date At The

WARD THEATRE AT 8.30,

To See "Gibraltar Comes To Town"

GRANDIOSO!! MAGNIFICO!!

MUY PRECIOSO!!

FOR THE WAR FUND.

SEATS 3/-, 2/6 and 1/-.

Space donated by "ISSA'S" of King St.

The Show Notice. Mr F Zammitt

Nemesio Mosquera with Other Participants in Comedy. Photo Mr F Mosquera

The cuttings on this page are from the Jamaica Times reports about the variety concerts performed by Camp Gibraltar Calpe Society.

Gibraltar Comes to Town!

Gibraltar Evacuees Concert at Ward Theatre.

on 2nd. December 1941.

FOR WAR FUNDS

·Box Plan now open at Cocking's. 21 Church Street.
Space generously donated by — UNITED FRUIT CO..

The Play "La Estudiantina" With Maruja Chipolina, Nemesio Mosquera, H.Rodriguez, J. Britto, J.McGillivray and J.Barea. Photo Mr F Mosquera.

"GIBRALTAR COMES TO COME"

"Ooh—I want to woo!" or how they make love in Gibraltar. A scene from a really different show at the Ward Theatre on Tuesday December 2, in aid of War Funds, which will be presented by the evacuees at the Camp.

"GIBRALTAR COMES TO TOWN."—(Above.)—A scene from Gipsy Feast at "White Horse Inn"—at the variety concert presented in the Ward Theatre on Tuesday night by the Gibraltar Camp Evacuee "Calpe Society," in aid of the War Fund. The attendance was very small, but the performers turned in a rollicking good show, and won rounds of applause.

Variety Concert By Camp Gibraltar "Calpe Society"

Gibraltar Camp Evacuees "Calpe Society" came to town in right regular style on Tuesday night last—presenting a Variety concert in the Ward Theatre in aid of the War Fund. The attendance was very small, hence the able manner in which the performers delivered the goods was the more commendable.

Among those present to contribute their moral and financial support to the worthy cause were the Hon. F. L. Brown, Acting Colonial Secretary, and Mrs. Brown, His Lordship Bishop Emmet, S.J., D.D, Mr. F. E. Lyons, J.P., Commandante E. A. Rae and Mrs. Rae.

The Jamaica Military Band under Captain Jones rendered a number of items, and accompanied the tap dancing numbers, whilst piano accompanists were Mrs. G. Valverde, Miss C. Valverde, and Miss Hazel Lawson—the latter accompanying Mr. Danino who gave a violin solo and had to respond to an encore.

Hit number of the evening—because of the mirth and gay abandon in which the players entered into the proceedings, was the Gipsy Feast at "White Horse Inn'—stars being Miss Jane Jiminez, Miss I Axisa, Mr. N. Mosquera, and Miss L. McGillivary. The latter and Mr N. Mosquera had the house laughing throughout their number "El Pato & La Pata"—the duck and the drake make love—the drake gets too friendly, so the duck leaves in a hurry; also in "Los Claveles", a comic duet.

Little Miss B. Benatar pleased with her "Top Hat" number, and "Down Argentina Way".

Smart and snappy was "Molinos de Viento" in which the Cadets enjoyed reading love letters, save and except the bosum, who was dubious and suspicious of his.

Mr. N. Mosquera, director and stage manager must be compli- [illegible] the get-up and pre- [illegible] the programme.

A variety concert entitled "Gibraltar Camp comes to Town" was presented in the Ward Theatre last night by the Gibraltar Camp Evacuees Calpe Society in aid of the war fund. The attendance was small but the performers neverthe less gave of their best. Among those present were the Hon. F. L. Brown, acting Colonial Secretary, and Mrs. Brown, and His Lordship Bishop Emmet, S.J., D.D.

This page shows some of the photographs taken at the different plays held at the camp. Musical entertainment was provided by the Jamaican Military Band which performed twice weekly at the Camp. All the photographs and cuttings on this page were donated by Mr Frank Zammitt.

A Mexican Show.

A zarzuela in the camp theatre.

Participants in one of the many variety shows.

A School Children Play.

Bright Concert At Camp Gibraltar

Camp Gibraltar evacuees held a very successful concert in their theatre on Monday evening last. A very appreciative audience consisting both of Jamaicans and Gibraltareans left quite satisfied with the entertainment.

Among the non-evacuees present were Hon. B. H. Easter, C.B.E., Director of Education; His Lordship Bishop Emmett of the Jamaica Vicariate; Mr. and Mrs. P. E. N. Mortimer, Mother Jones of the Immaculate Conception Convent, Constant Spring; and Mr. and Mrs. E. A. Rae, Acting Commandant and his wife, also the Deputy Commandant, Mr. C. P. Brown, and Mrs. Brown.

A play in English: "The Night Watchman" was one of the most attractive features of the programme. This play depicted how the spirit of goodwill came to a little village at Christmas time.

Attractive too were the Nativity Tableau; and the "Santa Claus" workshop in which the children of the camp took part and acquitted themselves splendidly. In addition, there were singing and dancing.

At the conclusion of the programme, the Hon. B. H. Easter congratulated the artistes on their fine performance and wished them a Merry Christmas and a Happy New Year.

Musical entertainment was provided by the Jamaican Military Band which performed twice weekly at the Camp. All the photographs and cuttings on this page were donated by Mr Frank Zammitt.

Some evacuees put forward their own personal ideas as a means of creating amusements and attractions with the aim of making life more enjoyable in the camp. One of the many entertaining activities was the holding of fancy dress competitions.

Gibraltar girls in Mexican dresses.
At the back L to R: A.Banda,..?.., N.Bear, Yeo, P.Zammitt
Sitting: ..?.. L.Marquez, M.Dalmedo.

In Gibraltar national costumes.
At the back L to R: ..?..,...?..., A.Alman, Valverde, S.Axisa,..?... In front: Rebora, Chipolina, L.Beiso.

In Hungarian national dress.
L to R: P.Zammitt and L.Gomez.
Photo Mr F Zammitt

A mixture of national costumes.
At the back L to R: Beiso, Pisimbo, F.Villa, ...?.. ,..?....
In front:..?.. ,...?...,...?....,...?......

In Hawaiian Dresses. Photo Mr E Triay
At the back L to R: A.Peralta, P.Marquez, O.Carreras,...?....,...?......
In front:..?.., M.Peralta,..?..., Celecia

Miss P Marquez taking part in the "El Pericon" Argentina dance.

All the photographs on this page were donated by Mr F Zammitt.

In addition to the concerts, fancy dress competitions and plays there were other forms of entertainment as depicted on this page.

Mr Ernesto Lara who took it upon himself to build A replica of the World War Two battleship HMS Nelson. Photo Mr A Lara

It Was Fun Aboard H.M.S. Nelson For These Girls

Pretty girls donned officers' uni forms to parade on a Float which represented H.M.S. Nelson, at Camp Gibraltar's Fair on Saturday.

H.M.S. Nelson Now At Camp Gibraltar

The model of H.M.S. Nelson donated by Hardware and Lumber Ltd. to the West Indian Publishing Company's Cigarette Fund which was won by Master David Smith, son of Inspector and Mrs. Clive Smith of Clarendon has been donated by Master Smith to Gibraltar Camp, where it has been gratefully received and will be a source of great pleasure to the residents there, no doubt serving to remind them of happier times when this great battleship was often to be seen on her visits to the real Gibraltar. The "Nelson" "sailed" up to the Camp on Thursday morning last.

The newspaper cuttings are from various newspapers in Jamaica reporting the Scottish Regiment entertaining the evacuees in the Gibraltar Camp.

Members of the Scottish Regiment at Camp Gibraltar

The skirl of the Scottish Bagpipes filled the air at Camp Gibraltar, as these gallant boys swung into march and into tune with their bagpipes.

Films were also shown in the camp as can be seen from the following notices.

There will be a moving picture show at Camp Gibraltar tonight, commencing at 7:30 o'clock, when, in addition to shorts and news reel the feature film "Captain Moonlight" will be shown.

The Jamaica band playing at the Gibraltar Camp during the Empire Day celebrations. Photo Miss S Moya

To do away with the monotony at the camp, music was broadcast via a system of speakers, which were also used to make any announcements concerning the evacuees.

A choir was formed in the Gibraltar Camp to entertain the evacuees and on the occasion described in the press cutting headed "Camp Gibraltar Artists Entertain at Mulry Hall." The purposely built hall at the camp was used twice weekly to show films. The press cutting shown below refers to a film shown about life in the Gibraltar Camp.

Press cutting from the Daily Gleaner about Gibraltar Camp artists.

CAMP GIBRALTAR ARTISTS ENTERTAIN AT MULRY HALL

In appreciation of the hospitality and kindnesses shown them since their arrival in Jamaica, and in support of a very worthy and deserving cause, the St. Vincent de Paul Society, a concert party from Camp Gibraltar, presented a highly entertaining concert in the Mulry Hall on Thursday night to a capacity house.

With few exceptions, the entire programme was presented in Spanish but every item on the somewhat lengthy but excellently arranged programme, was executed with marked ability and well received by the audience.

His Lordship Bishop Emmet attended. and in the large company of Jesuit Priests present were: the Very Rev. Fr. Thomas Feeney, S.J., Father Superior; Rev. Fr. John Williams, Rev. Fr. County, Rev. Fr. Gladstone Wilson, Rev. Fr. Balleau, Rev. Fr. Dooly, Rev. Fr. Krim, Rev. Fr. Fox, Rev. Fr. Coakley and the Rev. Fr. Heefernon. Sisters from the various Convents were also present.

Following a short introductory speech by the Father Superior, the Rev. Fr. John Williams, who is attached to Camp Gibraltar, took the chair, introducing each item to the audience.

The programme was opened with the chorus........"Land of Hope and Glory".... impressively sung by a party of twelve young women, and this opening number received the treemndous applause of the audience it so well deserved. Of the other numbers two which stood out prominently were the song of Master Julio Torres and Schubert's Serenade' beautifully rendered by Miss Blanche Rosetti, excellently accompanied by Miss Doris Sheriff, accompanist of the evening.

Julio Torres.

Below cutting from the Jamaica Times about cinema entertainment at the Gibraltar Camp.

SCENE FROM "THE GATE AT GIBRALTAR"

A scene from the film of the evacuees at Camp Gibraltar, which was directed and produced by Duncan Keith Corinaldi and had its premiere at the Carib Theatre last night. Here are two clerks attending to the orders of fellow evacuees who are made to feel as much at home as possible.

Film Of Life At Camp Gibraltar At Carib Theatre, Is Well Produced

Easily one of the best photographed motion pictures ever made in recent years in Jamaica is Duncan Keith Corinaldi's "The Gate at Gibraltar", the film of the life of the evacuees at Mona, which had its premiere at the Carib Theatre last night.

For aptness and skill of commentary, for clearness and beauty of scenes, especially the panoramic shows and the closing scene, for realism and dignity of setting, the film marks a new "high" in local bid for notice in the cinema world.

The theme is a simple one, without devious plots; but so great is the coherence that the interest is sustained throughout. Besides, the strongly prophetic note contained appeals to the lover of democracy and England. One will marvel at the miracle of efficient planning which is Camp Gibraltar. Those who have never been within its portals will see it turned inside out. The film has succeeded in conveying to the audience the vast amount of work already done and the vast amount of work which the daily running of the camp entails.

As a director Mr. Corinaldi shows talent. There are many scenes of the highest excellence. He caught the subtle changes in the moods of the evacuees—their despondency when they landed; their resilience of spirit, as the "blues" gave way to cheerfulness and hope, thawing before the sun of kindness and care which the authorities turned on them. The closing scene, however, where Fr Feeney, the brother of the Father Superior and Camp Chaplain, is shown saying mass, with the evacuees' faces showing devout and exalted, was given a dignity and vividness which a Hollywood director might have been proud of.

The evacuees themselves proved very facile and photographed well. The shots of the Blue Mountains and its foothills in panorama show the startling grandeur of Jamaica's scenery.

An outstanding contribution to the film is the commentary done by Dudley G. MacMillan, noted advertising expert. Apt and graphic in almost every single cut, his commentary will grip the audience with its eloquence and carry them along.

Appropriately, too, as the film winds up to the finale, the solemnity of the church setting will be found to be matched and enhanced by the language, and the audience can not but leave touched to the core.

Apart from the variety shows, concerts, cinemas and musical entertainment there were also other leisure activities like planting flowers, knitting sessions, trips, picnics etc as can appreciated from the photographs on this page. All the photographs on this page were donated by Mr Frank Zammitt.

A trip to the mountain.
Among the evacuees are Mrs L Romero, Tucker, P.Edwards, A.Baker, C Gomez, P Zammitt, Marquez and C.Baker

Leisure gardening: L.Gomez, C.Gomez, P.Zammitt, M.Orcese and L.Orcese

Knitting Classes.
Among those in the photo are E.Hill, V.Azopardi, L.Orcese, P.Baker

Among those at the picnic are V.Carreras, P.Romero, A.Peralta, M.Peralta, A.Banda

A party

The Pub.

Planting flowers .

With the weather being very warm throughout most of the year there were many evacuees who very often either went to the beach or to the swimming pool in Kingston. On this page are pictures of evacuees enjoying a day at the swimming pool in Kingston and Springfield.

Above and below view of the swimming pool. Photos by Mr A Lara

Postcard showing swimming pool by Mr C Moore

Gibraltar evacuees at the beach. Photo Miss S Moya

Nuns and evacuees at the swimming pool. At the back L to R: A.Baker, H.Dalmedo, M.Trinidad,…?...,..?..., Mrs Griffin Sister Emmanuel and other sisters are on the forefront. Photo Mr F Zammitt

At the swimming pool in Springfield. On the left hand is C.Gomez with other evacuees. Photos above and below Mrs A Banda.

At the swimming pool in Springfield. At the back from L to R: Mrs Griffin, A.Baker, P.Breeze..?..H.Dalmedo, P.Edwards, Sitting on the middle steps: L to R: P.Zammitt and C.Gomez In the pool L to R: B.Casciaro, A.Azzopardi, M.Trinidad, A.Banda, A.Peralta, H.Yeo.

Evacuees in Jamaica

On this page are the pictures taken of the evacuees when they went to the beach for a swimming and sunbathing.

Evacuees at the beach. Photo Mr A Lara.

Mrs Violeta Victor (nee Mor) at the beach. Photo Mr E Triay

Members of the Lara family at the beach. Photo Mr A Lara..

Teachers Mrs L Romero, P.Zammitt, C.Gomez, O.Buttigieg, Tucker, V.Azzopardi A.Peralta and M.Trinidad with school childrenJ.Dalmedo, P.Romero, A.Banda, J.Enriles, J.Banda.Azzopardi, M.Collado. A.Agius, E.Enriles and M.Camisuli. Photo Mr E Enriles.

EVACUEES ENJOY TRIP TO COUNTRY

Gibraltar Evacuees had their first glimpse of rural Jamaica when, on Sunday last, a party of 39 headed by Sr. John Bonnici, visited Dunn's River Falls in St. Ann. The party consisted of 9 men, 4 boys, 10 elderly ladies and 16 senoritas.

The party were delighted with the trip. They expressed surprise at the beautiful countryside, the nice views, the roads and the hospitality of the country people who waved to them as the bus went along.

Their leader is an interesting person. Of a large family of some 40 people who had been evacuated, he and one other member had come to Jamaica. His wife and daughters and grand-child with other relatives, near and distant, had been evacuated to England.

A marine engineer, he actually volunteered his services as second engineer on the ship that brought his batch here. He served in the mercantile marine during the last war and hopes to be able yet to serve "my king and country".

It is expected that more of these trips will be arranged. The evacuees subscribe to the entire cost of the trip, even to the food taken along.

Above cutting Jamaica Times.

EVACUEES VISIT HOPE GARDENS

A party of evacuees from Gibraltar Camp visited Hope Botanical Gardens on Monday, and another party went yesterday afternoon. There were 48 in yesterday's group and over 50 in Monday's. Both groups were attended by Roman Catholic priests and some of the sisters at the Camp.

The Very Rev. Fr. Feeney, S.J., Father Superior at Winchester Park, and a member of the Managing Committee of Gibraltar Camp, and his brother Fr. William H Feeney, S.J., camp chaplain, were in charge yesterday. The parties consisted for the most part of young ladies who had been working hard in the camp, assisting with the serving of meals and other domestic duties. The outing was in the nature of a reward, and a rest. The girls were accompanied by little boys and girls of more tender age.

The visitors evidently admired the garden, although, according to some, it did not surpass their own Alamada Gardens at home. They displayed a great deal of interest in the orchids as well as the birds living in cages nearby. After having their fill of sight-seeing, the party romped around and sang, and one of the fathers took both snaps and movies of the youngsters as they played.

The party then sat down to a repast of dixie doodles, arranged games, the winners of which were given more dixie doodles, and after about three hours spent in this enjoyable way, the party returned home.

Above cutting Daily Gleaner

Recreational outings were organised by the camp administrators. There were the occasional trips to places of interest in Kingston and much further away like Springfield, near the mountains on the northwest area of Jamaica. These outings proved very exciting and enjoyable for the evacuees. The pictures on this page and in the next show the evacuees enjoying themselves on one of those occasions when they visited Kingston to see places of interest like the Hope Botanical Gardens. There were also shopping sprees to the street market in Papine. Here fruits and vegetables were very fresh and cheap. Some evacuees even recall getting some fruits like bananas and mangoes free.

Evacuees on a shopping spree. Photo Mr E Triay

A postcard of the Hope Botanical Gardens from Mr C Moore

The Jamaican Military Band entertaining the evacuees. Photo Mr E Triay

The photographs below show some evacuees when they went to one of the outings in Jamaica.
All the photos on this page Mr E Triay

In the photo above are M.Peralta, I.Enriles and A.Peralta and V.Victor (nee Mor)

In the photo above are G.Robles, A.Villa, V.Martinez, M.Fiol, V.Victor(nee Mor) and the Agius sisters.

During the first Christmas in Jamaica one of the main trees in the camp was decorated to resemble the traditional Christmas Tree – including the lights. On the first Christmas Eve celebrated in Jamaica the evacuees gathered round the tree to wish each other the season greetings. They tried their best to be as cheerful and merry as possible but at the back of their minds there was the constant memory of their relatives in Gibraltar and also those, who in some cases, had been evacuated either to London or Madeira.

The Christmas decorated tree. Photo Mrs Valverde

The nuns and the Camp Manager went round the camp giving Christmas presents to every evacuee. Given the deep feeling of nostalgia that existed among most of the evacuees, owing to the war situation, Christmas celebrations was said to have gone much better than expected. Frank Valverde constructed a model of the Rock of Gibraltar with many details, including the lightings. It was placed near the Crib giving a special attraction. At the moment that the lights of the model were switched on, nearly every evacuee present at the Christmas party started to sing “Mi Gran Peñon” with many letting off their emotions as they sung. The flag which had been designed and manufactured by a Gibraltar evacuee was raised in the middle of the camp. Christmas parties for the children and the adults were also organised as can be seen from the photographs displayed.

Evacuee Artist's Work

The camp at Gibraltar is to fly the Gibraltar flag as well as the Union Jack. The above design was made by a young artist among the refugees who had done similar work for the government of Gibraltar before he landed here.

Bright Concert At Camp Gibraltar

Camp Gibraltar evacuees held a very successful concert in their theatre on Monday evening last. A very appreciative audience consisting both of Jamaicans and Gibraltareans left quite satisfied with the entertainment.

Among the non-evacuees present were Hon. B. H. Easter, C.B.E., Director of Education; His Lordship Bishop Emmett of the Jamaica Vicariate; Mr. and Mrs. P. E. N. Mortimer, Mother Jones of the Immaculate Conception Convent, Constant Spring; and Mr. and Mrs. E. A. Rae, Acting Commandant and his wife, also the Deputy Commandant, Mr. C. P. Brown, and Mrs. Brown.

A play in English: "The Night Watchman" was one of the most attractive features of the programme. This play depicted how the spirit of goodwill came to a little village at Christmas time.

Attractive too were the Nativity Tableau; and the "Santa Claus" workshop in which the children of the camp took part and acquitted themselves splendidly. In addition, there were singing and dancing.

At the conclusion of the programme, the Hon. B. H. Easter congratulated the artistes on their fine performance and wished them a Merry Christmas and a Happy New Year.

Cuttings from the Daily Gleaner and the Catholic Opinion newspapers.

Gibraltar Evacuees Look Forward To First Xmas Here

The evacuees at Camp Gibraltar are looking forward to their first Christmas away from home and it is an open secret that the whole population of 1,500 will be visited by Father Christmas. The authorities already have secured Christmas presents which are all parcelled up and ready for Christmas Eve when at 8 o'clock in the evening, distribution will take place.

The Evacuees will spend Christmas day in camp. As most of them are Roman Catholics they will, with their own choir, celebrate Midnight Mass at Gibraltar. The camp chaplain, the Rev. Fr. Feeney will be the celebrant.

At 9 o'clock on Christmas morning, the Holy Trinity Cathedral Choir at full strength, with Mr. Chevolleau at the organ and Mr. Jackie Lewis, will assist in a service at the Camp.

Later, the evacuees will have dinner in dining rooms specially decorated for the occasion. The afternoon will be given over to sports and games. At night, certain trees will be illuminated so as to add to the attractiveness of the camp. This Mr. MacDuff of the Jamaica Public Service Co. has kindly offered to do free.

There is little chance that there will be a lack of money among the evacuees at this time. Many of them have been receiving monies quite regularly from their folk in Gibraltar. It will be remembered that the able-bodied men were left behind in occupations of one kind or another. These men send money regularly to their relatives among whom are wives, mothers and sisters.

Besides, there are several pensioners who are entitled to pay from the Imperial Government.

AIR OF CONTENTMENT.

The Gleaner also learnt from authentic sources that at the local Gibraltar as many as 291 Gibraltareans are employed and receive pay weekly. Some are employed to do clerical work, some are mechanics, carpenters, plumbers; girls work in the canteens; there are orderlies, a dentist assistant; special district constables of which there are 15. They are paid on a lower scale than the Jamaicans having regard to the fact that they receive their board and lodging free.

There is a general air of contentment and happiness about the camp. The best of relations seem to exist between the officials and their charges. Without hesitation individuals approach the camp Commandant Mr. J. L. Worlledge or the deputy Mr. E. A. Rae and make their requests or ask information and each is made to feel at home.

On Saturday the camp team consisting wholly of evacuees played a strong team from St. George's past and present boys. A very big crowd of evacuees turned out to watch the struggle. They were very enthusiastic; they sang or shouted cries in Spanish to egg their men on. These men for the greater part of play were all over the local team and at the end of play the score was 4-nil to Gibraltar.

The Gleaner understands that the Very Rev. Father Superior has been fetching all kinds of team against the refugees and he is now with his back against the wall as every one of his offerings has been humiliated.

Comments by the Jamaica Times newspaper.

This page contains newspaper cuttings referring to how the evacuees spent the first Christmas in Jamaica.

The Christmas Party for children in the camp in the forefront to the right is Violeta Gomez (Now Mrs. Guerrero). Photo Mr C Moore

Children at a Christmas Party in the Camp. Photo Mr A Balban

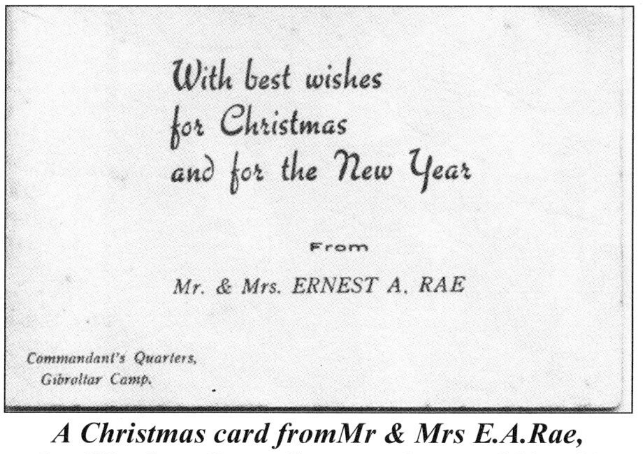

With best wishes
for Christmas
and for the New Year

From

Mr. & Mrs. ERNEST A. RAE

Commandant's Quarters,
Gibraltar Camp.

A Christmas card fromMr & Mrs E.A.Rae, the Gibraltar Camp Commandant and his wife.

Below cuttings from the Jamaica Times reporting how the evacuees spent their first Christmas in Camp Gibraltar.

Christmas At Camp Gibraltar

Christmas at Camp Gibraltar was observed with gaiety, ceremony and song. From 8 o'clock on Tuesday evening until night again covered the camp on Wednes day the unfortunate victims of totalitarian aggression received Christmas cheer and showed themselves as happy as could be expected under the circumstances. Outstanding among the events were the distribution of presents, the visit of the full choir of the Holy Trinity Cathe dral on Wednesday morning, and the hoisting of the Gibraltar flag, also on Christmas morning.

On Christmas eve at 8 o'clock, as previously arranged, presents were distributed in the huts to every evacuee. The presents, which had been neatly parcelled were brought down from the Nuns' quart ers. On each was written the name of the recipient; it was handed out by the sisters themselves.

The Acting Commandant, Mr. J. L. Worlledge, together with the Deputy Commandant, Mr. E. A. Rae, and the Father Superior, the Very Rev. Fr. T. J. Feeney, S.J., visited nearly all the houses during the distribution and were obviously most gratified at the pleasure each evacuee showed on receiving his or her present.

HUMOROUS INCIDENT

According to rumour, a touch of humour obtruded itself, and was appreciated by all parties concerned. Unwittingly, the packers had put in one of the parcels a tube of toothpaste among other articles. The recipient, after examining some of the other articles, took up the tube, glanced at it, for moment looked puzzled and then with a broad smile displayed his toothless gums to the amusement of everyone including himself.

In the meanwhile, the big tree in the camp was lighted and looked perfectly marvellous with its five different coloured lights, and a big diamond-shaped star perched on top.

After the distribution was over, the evacuees got ready and later attended midnight mass.

There was little sleep in the camp for the remainder of the night.

At 9.30 on Christmas morning, the full Cathedral choir arrived and celebrated the Mercadante's mass, which was sung at the opening of the Roman Catholic Cathedral some 30 years ago.

HOISTING OF FLAG

Shortly afterward, there took place amidst tears and sighs the hoisting of the Gibraltar flag—a red and white creation with a castle neatly worked in the centre in gold and with a golden key suspended from the castle, indicating, presumably, that Gibraltar is the key to the Mediterranean. This flag is to be seen at the eastern end of the Administrative buildings.

As the hundreds of evacuees looked on while two members of the Jamaica Constabulary sent up their flag, they sang "God Save the King", led by the Roman Catholic Cathedral choir. After the "King", the evacuees then sang the Gibraltar anthem in which a little boy led off and was then accompanied by the hundreds of voices of his fellow countrymen.

Then the Cathedral choir and the entire gathering went to the Camp Hospital where they sang carols for the amusement and edification of the sick. Followed a tour of Camps 1 and 2 by the visiting choir.

The rest of the day was given over to games and at night there was a concert which the evacuees themselves had arranged.

EVACUEES MARK EMPIRE DAY AT CAMP GIBRALTAR

On Empire Day, the loyal inhabitants of Gibraltar's colony in Jamaica celebrated with a pleasant, simple but impressive little ceremony at Mona, in which children of the school and guides belonging to the Camp company played the leading role. Acting Commandant Rae, too, was given an important part: not only did he deliver an address explaining the significance of Empire Day, but he planted a tree, "The Glory of the Forest" in memory of the occasion.

A well got up programme, consisting of songs and recitations was rendered by individuals and groups of students and guides. With the exception of the singing of the Gibraltarean 'National' anthem, the whole programme was rendered in English. Voices of boys and girls rose clear and sweet on the morning air; and their efforts were made even more attractive by the traces of accents that obtruded themselves frequently.

Acting Commandant Rae talked briefly on the importance of Empire Day. Empire Day, he explained, was the birthday of the late Queen Victoria, during whose reign the British Empire had grown to most of its present wide extent. Her parents had well named her Victoria which meant victory; for thanks to the foresight and courage of the queen, the British peoples had successfully fought for freedom, personal liberty of the individual as well as for the extension of the empire.

The Queen-Empress had always adopted a liberal attitude to the colonies and both Gibraltar and Jamaica had reasons to be grateful to her. Gibraltareans had benefited by the declaration which made the 'Rock' a free port. During her reign, the abolition of slavery in Jamaica became a fiat accompli.

FREEDOM THE KEYNOTE

One great keynote of her reign, therefore, was freedom. In celebrating her birthday, it was necessary to think of her fairmindedness. How logical, therefore, it was that all true Britishers should continue the fight for the retention of the freedom which she worked so hard to afford us.

In these troublous times, when dictators ran amuck in Europe, threatening the world with loss of liberty, it behoved everyone to stand firm and remember the traditions of freedom which the great Queen-Empress helped to maintain.

At the conclusion of the Acting Commandant's speech, the Union Jack was dipped by a smart colour party, coached in their duties by the sisters attached to the Camp.

Assisting in the planting of the tree was Mr. Joseph Hill, a Gibraltarean, who is a veteran of two wars, the Boer war and the World War No. 1. A pensioner, he was sent here with his fellow evacuees as he had passed the age for active service.

Among those present at the function were Mr. E. A. Rae, the Deputy Mr. Brown, Fr. William Feeney, chaplain of the Camp, and the sisters in charge of the school and the hospital.

The Jamaica Times newspaper cuttings on this page, as can been seen, gave much coverage about how the evacuees celebrated Empire Day at the Gibraltar Camp. The celebration was reported as simple but impressive with the children playing the leading roles.

ON MONDAY LAST, Empire Day was 'kept' up at Camp Gibraltar. School children, girl guides from the Camp troop, priests and nuns attached to the Camp attended and listened to a patriotic address delivered by the Acting Commandant Mr. Ernest Rae. In the picture, Mr. Rae is seen planting a tree "The Glory of the Forest" in memory of the occasion. Assisting him is Mr. Joseph Hill, a retired veteran of two wars, and standing is Mr. Brown, Mr. Rae's deputy. Fr. William Feeney, S.J., Camp chaplain is at the extreme left.

Above evacuee Mr Joseph Hill veteran of two wars planting a tree at the Gibraltar Camp.

GIBRALTAR EVACUEES CELEBRATE EMPIRE DAY

(Below.) In a pleasant but impressive ceremony, Evacuees kept up Empire Day on Monday last at Mona. A section of the group of school children and Guides who rendered an enjoyable programme of patriotic songs and recitations. The Acting Commandant Mr. E. A. Rae addressed the assembly and then planted a tree, "The Glory of the Forest" in memory of the occasion.

Above Gibraltar evacuees celebrating Empire Day on the 1st June 1941.

Table set for the Empire Day morning party. Photo Mrs P Wood

During the evacuees' stay in Jamaica, the Governor Sir Arthur Richards and his wife visited the Gibraltar Camp several times. Attached are newspaper cuttings from the Daily Gleaner and the Jamaica Times mentioning the different occasions on which the camp was visited by the Governor and/or his wife.

Governor's First Visit To Evacuees, Camp On Monday

Paying an unexpected visit to Camp Gibraltar at Mona on Monday afternoon at five o'clock, His Excellency Sir Arthur Richards received a hearty welcome from the Evacuees, which was significant of their loyalty to the British throne and all that it stands for.

As His Excellency entered the camp, the Jamaica Military Band for the first time that day, playunder Lieutenant Jones, which had been playing on the grounds ed God Save The King, while the Evacuees stood to attention.

His Excellency was conducted to the chief dining room, and meanwhile being loudly cheered, he inspected the kitchen staff, and saw arrangements for dining.

Speaking through a microphone to the Evacuees gathered around Kitchen A, His Excellency told them that we in Jamaica were trying to do everything that would make them happy and enjoy the convenience of their home at the Gibraltar Camp. Loud applause followed this speech, and under a cheer leader, three cheers were given His Excellency, and expressions of gratitude were made by the gathering concerning what Jamaica was doing for them.

Thanking the Evacuees for their co-operation, which consisted of voluntary service in the kicthen and at table by about 120 Evacuees, His Excellency then passed to Room No. 2, where a similar procedure followed. This dining-room is for mothers and children under five.

Next to be inspected, were the stores and canteen, and the arrangement of these was described as excellent, by the Governor.

His Excellency was then introduced to the various workers at the canteen and kitchen, and proceeded to inspect the Administrative offices. He also made suggestions in regard to the enlargement of the offices for the heads of staff.

His Excellency surveyed the second camp from the nearby hilltop. Returning to the Administration Offices and before leaving for King's House at a quarter after six, His Excellency expressed his appreciation, and tendered his congratulation to the members of the committee.

The Jamaica Military Band will play at Gibraltar Camp every Monday and Friday, from 4 to 5 p.m.

AT CAMP GIBRALTAR FUNCTION

LADY RICHARDS received a warm welcome on Saturday, when she attended the Garden Party at Gibraltar Camp in aid of war funds. Her Ladyship, who presented the prizes for the various competitions, is seen inspecting the Gibraltar Boy Scouts. Accompanying her are Mr. P. E. N. Mortimer, Manager of Barclay's Bank; Mr. E. A. Rae, Commandant of the Camp; and Mrs. Dalmedo.

Above details of first visit to the camp by Sir Arthur Richards on Saturday 2nd November 1940.

Lady Richards Pay Visit To Evacuees Camp

ON 2-HOUR INSPECTION TOUR, SHE SEES EVERY ASPECT OF LIFE IN COMMUNITY.

Lady Richards, wife of His Excellency the Governor, paid her first visit to Camp Gibraltar yesterday, accompanied by Lady Furness, and made a two-hour tour in which she inspected every aspect of the life of this novel community, bringing comfort and smiles to these victims of aggression.

In turn she was entertained by them, a troupe of 20 children putting on a surprisingly fine show which consisted for the most part of choral selections beautifully rendered, the little artistes being accompanied by one of thei· number. It is likely that this troupe will be heard over the local radio shortly.

Arriving at 10.30 in the forenoon, Lady Richards was welcomed by the Acting Commandant, Mr J. L. Worlledge and Mrs. Worlledge, the Very Rev. Fr. Thomas Feeney, S.J., a member of the committee of management; Mr E. A. Rae, manager of the camp; Mrs F. E. V. Smith and Sisters Xavier and Bede.

The party immediately proceeded to the administration offices through everyone of which Lady Richards was shown. Then they motored to the long house or store-room, the Alladin's cave of supplies, containing furniture, linens, groceries, together with banana and fish rooms. When Lady Richards entered the linen room, mosquito nets were being furnished as a protection for the babies' cribs; as many as 35 children under the age of 5 came with this first contingent of evacuees.

Across the road to the northward lies the canteen now completely organised and almost completely stocked. Lady Richards was introduced to the heads of departments and various members of the staff. She was told that eventually it was hoped to staff as many Camp positions as possible with evacuees.

EVACUEES AT WORK.

Leaving the canteen, Lady Richards went to see the first reception room to be completed (and which will be opened for the first time this week as a temporary place of worship for members of the Anglican and Jewish faiths) and also saw many of the evacuees engaged in washing of clothes, conveniences for which have been provided as the evacuees prefer to do their own washing.

Followed a visit to two of the three-roomed cottages occupied temporarily by 8 Roman Catholic sisters who are assisting in the social services and the hospital work of the camp. It was at this point that Lady Richards was entertained by the troupe. She was also presented with a fine bouquet of flowers.

Lady Richards next did the Hospital. Some 18 dispensary cases had been treated that morning and Lady Richards moved from bed to bed giving a few words of consolation, and lingering long enough at each bedside to make the sufferers all happy and grateful for the visit.

Then came what perhaps was the *piece de resistance* of the entire trip—a trip to the 3 dining rooms. Here Lady Richards was cheered to the echo; for the house "was in session". She waited until the entire service of meals (the actual serving) had been completed which was done in the remarkably short time of 10 minutes, so efficient has been the arrangements for the service.

In each house a different group is catered for. In C, are served all the mothers with children under 5; in B mothers and children under 14 and in A all other adults. This arrangement helps greatly in overcoming difficulties such as those of diet.

HER EXCELLENCY LADY RICHARDS
Who Visited School at Camp Gibraltar

The first visit to the camp by Lady Richards on Thursday 7th November 1940.

In order to encourage youth activities for the older boys an auxiliary force was formed to assist with the miscellaneous running of the camp. They were very often called upon to help with numerous tasks in order to take an interest in the smooth running of the Gibraltar Camp.

Gibraltar evacuees Youth Auxiliary Force. Photo Mr J Parody

Gibraltar evacuees Youth Auxiliary Force on parade. Photo Mr F Zammitt

YAF Cadet Ernest Lara.
Photo Mr A Lara.

There were many opportunities within the confinements of the camp, for the evacuees to be able to pose for photographs. In this and in the next page are some of the photographs taken of evacuees in groups and alone.

Photo Mr E Triay.

Sitting on the right of Mrs P Zammitt is her nephew Michael Zammitt. Photo Mr M Zammitt

Photo Mr E Triay.

Mrs Violeta Victor (Nee Mor) . Photo Mr E Triay

Photo Mr E Triay.

Mrs Mercedes Palma. Photo Mrs M McNiece.

Large groups of evacuees who had become acquainted with each other because of the proximity of their living huts gathered together to have photographs taken as shown below.

Evacuees near the medical centre. Photo Mrs V Ballestero

A group of evacuees outside one of the camp huts.
At the back from L to R: V.Martinez, V.Carrera, F.Villa, C.Gomez, R.Richardson, A.Torres, M.Peralta, H.Yeo, B.Gomez, A.Peralta, M.Valverde. In front L to R: B.Casciaro, R.Carreras,….?......, A.Banda, A.Azzopardi and P.Romero. Photo Mr F Zammitt.

Evacuees in Jamaica

In this page are photographs of groups of families taken at the camp.

Mr Lara with evacuee girl. Photo Mr A Lara

Mrs Violeta Victor (Nee Mor) with her niece.
Photo Mr E Triay

Mr Mosquera, family and other relatives.
Photo above and below Mr F Mosquera

Tea time outside the hut. Photo Mrs P Romero

The Lara family with other evacuees and Jamaicans.
Photo Mr A Lara

Mr Mosquera with wife and son.

The photographs on this page were donated by Miss Sheryl Moya.

Attached are some of the children's photographs which I have been able to collect during my research.

Manolo Santos with playing horse.

Violeta Gomez and cousin Francis Mosquera playing with bicycle. Photo Mr F Mosquera

The Torres and Romero families.
Above photo and the one at the bottom right hand corner by Mrs P Wood

Manolo Santos watering plants in the garden by his hut.

Manolo Santos with cousins.

Mrs Lola Romero with her children Pepe, Pauline and Carmenia.

Many Gibraltar children were born in Jamaica. According to a report in the Jamaica newspaper, 'The Gleaner', about 100 Gibraltar evacuee children were born in Jamaica. The photographs shown in this page were taken in 1993. They show the remains of what was the maternity wing during the time of the evacuation.
Mrs Lilian Gomez (nee Borastero) was one of the many children born in Jamaica. When she went on holiday to Jamaica in 1993 she made a point of visiting the place were she was born and also Father William Feeney who baptised her.

Mrs Gomez, Fr. W. Feeney and Manolo Gomez.

In the photograph above Mrs Gomez is being accompanied by Father William Feeney outside the chapel where she had been baptised in 1940.

In the photograph above is Mrs Lilian Gomez (Nee Borastero) with Father William Feeney.

At the top of the right hand column is another photograph of what used to be the maternity wing during the evacuation.

A photo of part of what used to be the maternity wing.

A photograph of what used to be the maternity ward.

The photographs on this page were provided by Mr and Mrs Gomez.

In Jamaica there were marriages between evacuees and also a few between evacuees and Jamaicans. The first marriage between evacuees was held at the Gibraltar camp on the 21st July 1941. The couples were Alfonso Manito and Miss Aurelia Fernandez. Another marriage reported by the Jamaican newspaper 'The Catholic Opinion' was that of Mr Alfred Mansfield to Miss Domingo Busutil.

FIRST COUPLE WED AT CAMP GIBRALTAR

"ROCK" ROMANCE RIPENS ON JAMAICA'S SOIL.

Local Gibraltareans flocked by the hundreds yesterday morning to the Roman Catholic Church in their camp to witness the first wedding ceremony to be solemnised between members of their group since they landed in the island many many months ago.

The happy couples were the Sr. Alfonso Manito and Senorita Aurelia Fernandez. Fr. William Feeney, Camp chaplain, assisted by Fr. Hennessey, S.J., officiated.

The Deputy Commandant Mr. C. Brown, gave away the bride.

Assisting in the ceremony were Miss Mary Deely and Mr. Julio Torres, the latter known as the Gibraltar 'Bobby Breen.' Miss Deely rendered Gounod's "Ave Maria." Mr. Torres sang "Salve Virgo Pura."

Senora Manito was quite chic in

MR. & MRS. ALFONSO MANITO

tailored black and white ensemble, while her bridesmaid, Mrs. V. Fernandez was similarly dressed. Groomsman was Mr. V. Fernandez, a brother of the bride.

The couple left for Mandeville to spend their honeymoon in a car to take them thither which had been placed at their disposal by a member of the Commandant's staff. Last week-end, Mr. Manito who is on the clerical staff of the Commandant's office, was given a purse by his co-workers.

Mr. Manito told a 'Gleaner' reporter that he knew his wife before they left Gibraltar for this island but that romance had actually ripened here. He has no relatives in Camp Gibraltar. Neither are the bride's parents here.

Romance On "The Rock" Culminates In Jamaica

Wedding At Gibraltar Camp Yesterday

Axis submarine warfare failed to stop Mr. Alfred Mansfield, a native of Gibraltar at present attached to the Gibraltar Camp Fire Brigade as a driver, from culminating his three years engagement to Miss Domingo Busutil.

Mr. Mansfield should have been evacuated to England, but took the risk of crossing the Atlantic on a tanker to Curacao where he took another tanker to Jamaica, in order to keep his appointment and to be near his mother.

The wedding which took place in the Sacred Heart Roman Catho-

MR. & MRS. ALFRED MANSFIELD

lic chapel at Gibraltar Camp yesterday morning was largely attended, with Fathers Feeney, Buckley and Butler officiating.

The bride was charmingly attired in a picturesque gown cut on princess lines, the billowy skirt making a formal train reminiscent of the Victorian age. Her head-dress was a short veil of tulle falling from a coronet of orange blossoms. She carried a bouquet of asters and asparagus ferns.

The bride was attended by her mother-in-law, Mrs. Mansfield, with little Miss Angeles Duo as trainbearer. Mr. Manuel Busutil was bestman. During the ceremony Mrs. Garcia sung "Ave Maria."

After the ceremony, the reception was held in "Hut" 51 after which the couple left for South Camp Road Hotel, and thence to Mandeville for their honeymoon.

The Commandant made everything as convenient as possible for the couple.

Among those present were: Mr. and Mrs. Manuel Busutil, father and mother of the bride, Mrs. Elizabeth Mansfield, Mother of the groom, Mr. E. A. Rae, Commandant, Mr. G. P. Brown, Deputy-Commandant, Mr. and Mrs. C. H. Harris, Mr. Fabian Lopez, Mr. A. L. Manito and Mr. A. L. Hatchwell.

Taking home the typical bridal cakes in Jamaica. Photo Mrs P Wood

On Monday 28th October 1940, only two day after the arrival of the evacuees in Jamaica, the Daily Gleaner reported the death of the first evacuees as shown below.

Gibraltar Evacuee, Age About 76. Dies

One of the 1,100 evacuees who arrived here on Friday from Gibraltar died on Saturday night. His name was John Parodie, age about 76 years.

The old man suffered from a bad heart, and was said to be unwell before embarking ship for Jamaica. Probably the long voyage across and other circumstances hastened his end.

Funeral service was conducted yesterday afternoon by the Rev. Fr. Francis J. Osborne S.J., pastor of St. Ann's Church and interment took place in the Catholic section of the May Pen Cemetery.

The next two deaths occurred on Saturday 23rd November 1940 and on 24th January 1941 as reported by the Jamaica Times in the cuttings shown below:

EVACUEE DIES

Mariah Risso, an evacuee at Camp Gibraltar, died at the Kingston Public Hospital on Saturday and was buried yesterday.

She was about 40 years of age and had not been, it is said, in the best of health. She was admitted to the Hospital on Friday. A post mortem examination was performed.

EVACUEE DIES

Catalina Berto, 74-year-old evacuee of Camp Gibraltar, died on Wednesday night at the Camp. Her body was taken to the public morgue and the interment took place yesterday afternoon at the Roman Catholic cemetery. She had not been enjoying the best of health and was in the Camp hospital.

The funeral was attended by a number of evacuees.

There was a sudden death of a relatively young evacuee on Wednesday 5th February 1941 as reported by the cutting of the Daily Gleaner shown below.

Police Probing Death Of Gibraltar Evacuee

The "Gleaner" understands that the St. Andrew Police are investigating the death of one of the evacuees at Camp Gibraltar. She was Mrs. Adelina Fiol who died under somewhat peculiar circumstances on Sunday last.

The death of this comparatively young woman—she was only 37 years of age—made it seem necessary to have an autopsy performed. When this was done on Monday, the decision reached was that an investigation was necessary. The viscera was sent to the Island Chemist and the Police began active work on the case.

The woman was ill for a few days prior to her death and had been treated at the Camp hospital; but despite the most careful attention she passed away.

Mrs. Fiol leaves two children, aged 9 and 7, who arrived in the island with her.

Unfortunately there were many other cases of evacuees who died of natural causes. In 2007 an obelisk was erected near to what used to be the Gibraltar camp in memory of all the evacuees who died in Jamaica. The idea was initiated and seen through its completion by Mr Anthony Lara whose grandmother died in Jamaica.

Below are the names of evacuees who died in Jamaica as inscribed at the bottom of the obelisk.

Above and below view of the obelisk. Photo Mr A Lara

Obelisk . Photo Mr A Lara

Evacuees in Jamaica

In Jamaica there were three modes of transport: the buses, the tram cars or the horse drawn carriages. The photographs on this page depict the three methods of transport used by the evacuees to travel in Jamaica.

The horse drawn carriage called "La Guaga" by the Gibraltar evacuees.
Photo Mr F Zammitt

Gibraltar evacuee teachers on a tram car.
In the photo are Mmes C.Gomez, Josephine Zammitt, Tucker, V. Azzopardi and Lola Romero.
Photo Mr F Zammitt.

The Gibraltar Camp Bus. Photo Miss Sheryl Moya

Evacuees waiting for the bus at the camp bus top. Photo by Mrs V Ballestero

Above another example of the different forms of transport in Jamaica.
Photo Mr F Żammitt

In the camp the washing was carried out in a communal laundry as can been seen from the photographs taken during a laundry session. Water for the washing was supplied from what used to be, an old aqueduct which was used at one time to irrigate the sugar plantations in that part of the camp.

The huge washing tubs in the camp.

Evacuees in camp laundry. Photo Mrs V Ballestro

Hanging the washing at the laundry. Photo Mr F Zammitt

As explained at the beginning of this chapter, the first thing the evacuees did when the reached Jamaica was to inform their relatives in Gibraltar of their safe arrival. This was done by means of telegraphic cables, normal letters or postcards. However, according to other sources of information the postal room in the camp began to operate from November onwards but the Camp Post Office was not officially opened until 1st April 1941. All letters sent or received had to go through the censorship system that operated everywhere during the war. One evacuee who mentioned in a letter to her husband that she had seen an American dirigible (see photo on page 295) over the camp had it crossed out by the censorship. Below are examples of letters sent and received at the Camp giving an indication of how dispersed families were during the war.

Below are envelopes of a letter sent by Rosa Perera, living in Hut 48 Camp Gibraltar to Air Coporal R.Perera serving at RAF Station Takoradi in West Africa.

Below is copy of a letter sent to Mrs Mary Del Rio Gibraltar Camp Hut 41 by Leopoldo Del Rio Aptdo.aereo Cali (Valle) Republica de Colombia.

Below the copy of the letter sent by Mrs Olga Asaisa Gibraltar Camp Hut 15 to Mrs Agustina Axisa No.57 Great Russell Street (Thackeray Hotel) London WC1

Postcard from New York dated 26 May 1943 sent to Ernest Rodriguez, Gibraltar Camp Hut 24.

Below copy of envelope of letter sent to R T.Baker Wilson's Ramp, Gibraltar.

Copies of addressed envelopes were donated by Mr C Moore.

Articles of clothing pour into Winchester Park which has become a major depot of supplies for the stricken areas. Dresses, Suits, Shoes and gaily coloured women's hats are heaped into this pile waiting to be ru hed to the impoverished. But larger supplies are still needed. This particular allotment, comprising more than a thousand pieces of clothing was contributed by the evacuees at Camp Gibraltar, and was consigned to Morant Bay and adjoining territory. Mr. Frank Tucker, Captain Josephine Zammitt, Lieutenant Celia Gomez and Pauline Romero, all from the Camp, are shown in the above picture.

Above newspaper clippings from the Jamaica Times referring the Gibraltar evacuees when they collected articles of clothing to help the impoverished natives. In the photograph are Gibraltar evacuees Misses Celia Gomez, Josephine Zammitt and Pauline Romero.

Gibraltar Girl Guides and Boy Scouts helping with the collection of debris from the hurricane. PhotoMrs Wood

The Governor of Jamaica visiting the stricken areas. Cutting the Jamaica Times newspaper.

A couple of months before the Gibraltar evacuees were due to leave a very strong hurricane hit Jamaica on Sunday 3rd September 1944 causing many damages. The Gibraltar evacuees as can be seen from the cuttings of the 'The Catholic Opinion' shown below helped in many ways to assist the needy Jamaicans in the stricken areas.

GIBRALTAR CAMP AND RELIEF WORK

The evacuees of Gibraltar Camp, on realizing the destruction caused by the hurricane, spontaneously offered to help the poor victims. On Saturday, August the twenty-sixth, it was announced in the kitchens at noon that the girl guides would visit the huts, soliciting help. Half a dozen groups were organized, and they started out on their mission of mercy. The response on the part of the people was most generous. They were well received everywhere.

On Sunday evening, they reported at the priests' house to Fr. Butler and Fr. Buckley, counted the money, and realized that they had picked up seventeen pounds, five shillings and two pence. The three sodalities—Married Ladies, Children of Mary and the Men—each volunteered to give a pound from their funds, and thus the handsome sum of twenty pounds, five shillings and two pence was realized. The pieces of clothing collected by the guides amounted to one thousand and sixty. To these, Mr. Dent added nineteen: making a total of one thousand and seventy-nine articles of clothing. On Tuesday morning, August the twenty-ninth, Captain Josephine Zammitt, Lieutenant Celia Gomez, and Pauline Romero, of the group that collected the most money, accompanied Father Buckley to Winchester Park, where Mr. E. A. Rae permitted the contributions to be turned over to Father Superior, to be distributed to the poor by the Saint Vincent de Paul Society.

May God bless the evacuees of Gibraltar Camp! May He continue to bless them; and may He lead them safely, in the near future, to their beloved homes that nestle so sweetly beneath the Rock of Gibraltar.

FR. BUCKLEY

ST. VINCENT DE PAUL SOCIETY STORM RELIEF FUND

Winchester Park	£40	0	0
Particular Council St. Vincent de Paul Society	20	0	0
Members St. Vincent de Paul Society, Holy Trinity Conference	5	0	0
Evacuees, Gibraltar Camp	20	5	2
Wherry Wharf (Stephanie and Michael Isaacs)	5	5	0
Total:	£90	10	2

Other contributions of money and/or clothing will be very welcome and may be forwarded to Very Rev. Thomas J. Feeney, S.J., Winchester Park, Kingston, for the St. Vincent de Paul Society.

The postponement of a further batch of evacuees from UK meant that the Gibraltar Camp Two remained unused for almost a year after which it was thought to be put in use as a military barracks for Jamaican troops. Having these troops living very near the Gibraltar Camp was seen as cause for concern to the Roman Catholic Church in view of the many young female evacuees who were living so near. Representations were soon made to both the Governors of Jamaica and Gibraltar. Both Governors concurred with the view that it would be too risky to have coloured troops next door to so many young girls. In view of the opposition expressed at official level the idea was cancelled altogether. In a note explaining the cost of the camp to the Treasury, a Colonial Office official said:

"The camp was constructed at very great speed under strong pressure from this end to use the utmost expedition, and that may well have increased the cost. In the circumstances, it is little short of lamentable that we should only have been able so far to arrange for some 1,500 evacuees to occupy the camp. It may be that the proposal to send some of the evacuees from this country to the West Indies will be revived. We can only hope that by these or other means the vacant accommodation will, sooner or later, be turned to practical advantage."

Early in 1941 it was thought to use Camp Two to accommodate refugees of different nationalities but the Gibraltar Camp Committee was opposed to such an idea on the grounds that it was going to be very detrimental for the morale of the evacuees. Despite this, Camp Two was used for the accommodation of internees. A passage of about 200 yards wide was constructed in order to separate the two camps. In addition to these internees by December 1941, the British Government, the Polish Government in exile and the American Jewish Joint Distribution Committee agreed to send Polish Jewish to Jamaica.

Jewish refugees arriving at Jamaica from Lisbon on the Serpa Pinto. Cutting from Jamaica Times

The first group of 152 refugees arrived on the Portuguese ship the **Serpa Pinto** in January 1942. Their maintenance was paid for by the Jewish Joint Distribution Committee. Over the next few years, small groups of Jewish refugees continued to be brought from Spain and Portugal.

Victims Of Hitler, Here, In Need Of Help

Within the last two months a number of refugees from Europe arrived in Gibraltar Camp. They are all of Polish origin and the majority of the Jewish faith.

Before the war, they lived in various countries, and some of them were prosperous merchants and in professions in Berlin, Paris and Brussels.

Driven from their homes by Hitler and his hordes and deprived of their possessions they fled to Lisbon, where they remained until recently. The Portuguese Government having ordered them to depart a charitable organisation in America, established to succour the victims of religious persecution, arranged with the Imperial Government to house these refugees in Jamaica, cost of which is being defrayed by the organisation.

Unfortunately, most of these refugees arrived quite penniless and without adequate clothing for the tropics, and through the good services of the Rev. H. P. Silverman and other Kingston gentlemen, a small sum of money has been subscribed towards relieving the immediate wants of these poor people.

It is possible, however, that further funds may be required later on, and the Gleaner is informed that it is certain that the charitable public of Jamaica will not fail to help these sad victims of the most bestial brutality in the world's history.

Above Jamaica Times cuttings referring to the arrival of refugees at Camp Two.

Polish Refugees Here

THE EDITOR, Sir:—Referring to an article published in the "Daily Gleaner" headed **"Victims of Hitler Here in Need of Help"** we beg you to publish the following.

We have been very surprised to see that it had been found necessary to make an appeal on public charity on our favour without asking us for agreement or advice on this behalf. Although being in a somewhat difficult situation we do not wish by any means that such public appeals for us should be made.

Regarding the mentioned good services of Rev. H. P. Silverman, they consisted in a gift of £10—which we refused to accept. We wish nevertheless to express our gratitude to Mr. S. Cohen and M. Mathalon, for their organising of a helpful action for those being most in need of our group. Unfortunately their efforts were in vain.

We are, etc.,
Committee of the Polish Group
per (Dr.) N. BIDERMAN, M. GRUN, A. P. RINGER, S. ROSENBAUM.
Gibraltar, June 6.

POLES HERE MARK INDEPENDENCE DAY

Ceremony Of Celebration Held In Camp At Mona.

Jamaica's Polish community, in a brief but touching ceremony, celebrated their National Day of Independence in the No. 2 Camp, Mona, yesterday afternoon. In their strange but soft and attractive language, they sang fervently their National Anthem and prayed for their dead, for Britain's King and the Polish Prime Minister and for victory.

Witnessing and assisting in the observation were the Very Rev. Thomas Feeney, S.J., Fr. Butler, S.J., the Acting Commandant of the Camp, Mr. E. A. Rae and Mrs. Rae; the Deputy Commandant, Mr. C. Philpotts Brown and Mrs Brown.

In true Polish tradition, the small community, consisting of under 200 souls, reasserted their belief in the rightness of their cause and the inevitableness of a United Nations' victory.

As can be seen from the newspaper cuttings there was a very large contingent of Polish refugees who celebrated Poland's Independence Day in Camp Two. There were 34 Jewish Gibraltarians who had been allocated a bungalow exclusively for their use. They also had their own purposely built Synagogue. Rabbi Silverman looked after the religious affairs like kosher food and other matters affecting the Jewish evacuees.

The newspaper cuttings from The Jamaica Times and The Daily Gleaner refer to an address given by Rabbi Silverman about Jews in Gibraltar. One of the Jewish girls Tany Conquy was 14 when she arrived with her family.

"I remember my first sight of Jamaica," she said.

"It was beautiful. We ate in huge dining halls, and there were separate kitchens for kosher."

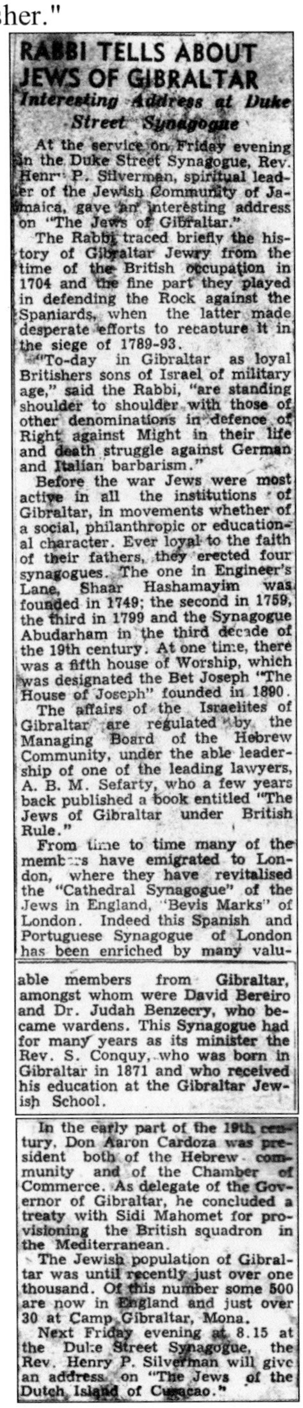

RABBI TELLS ABOUT JEWS OF GIBRALTAR

Interesting Address at Duke Street Synagogue

At the service on Friday evening in the Duke Street Synagogue, Rev. Henry P. Silverman, spiritual leader of the Jewish Community of Jamaica, gave an interesting address on "The Jews of Gibraltar."

The Rabbi traced briefly the history of Gibraltar Jewry from the time of the British occupation in 1704 and the fine part they played in defending the Rock against the Spaniards, when the latter made desperate efforts to recapture it in the siege of 1789-93.

"To-day in Gibraltar as loyal Britishers sons of Israel of military age," said the Rabbi, "are standing shoulder to shoulder with those of other denominations in defence of Right against Might in their life and death struggle against German and Italian barbarism."

Before the war Jews were most active in all the institutions of Gibraltar, in movements whether of a social, philanthropic or educational character. Ever loyal to the faith of their fathers, they erected four synagogues. The one in Engineer's Lane, Shaar Hashamayim was founded in 1749; the second in 1759, the third in 1799 and the Synagogue Abudarham in the third decade of the 19th century. At one time, there was a fifth house of Worship, which was designated the Bet Joseph "The House of Joseph" founded in 1890.

The affairs of the Israelites of Gibraltar are regulated by the Managing Board of the Hebrew Community, under the able leadership of one of the leading lawyers, A. B. M. Sefarty, who a few years back published a book entitled "The Jews of Gibraltar under British Rule."

From time to time many of the members have emigrated to London, where they have revitalised the "Cathedral Synagogue" of the Jews in England, "Bevis Marks" of London. Indeed this Spanish and Portuguese Synagogue of London has been enriched by many valuable members from Gibraltar, amongst whom were David Bereiro and Dr. Judah Benzecry, who became wardens. This Synagogue had for many years as its minister the Rev. S. Conquy, who was born in Gibraltar in 1871 and who received his education at the Gibraltar Jewish School.

In the early part of the 19th century, Don Aaron Cardoza was president both of the Hebrew community and of the Chamber of Commerce. As delegate of the Governor of Gibraltar, he concluded a treaty with Sidi Mahomet for provisioning the British squadron in the Mediterranean.

The Jewish population of Gibraltar was until recently just over one thousand. Of this number some 500 are now in England and just over 30 at Camp Gibraltar, Mona.

Next Friday evening at 8.15 at the Duke Street Synagogue, the Rev. Henry P. Silverman will give an address on "The Jews of the Dutch Island of Curacao."

There were other Jews of different nationalities, but mainly Polish, who had come to Jamaica as refugees from the menace of the Nazis. They had been settled in what became known as Camp Two. There were, according to some reports 1,400 Jewish refugees in this camp. Apparently for some unknown reason they did not mix with the Gibraltar evacuees.

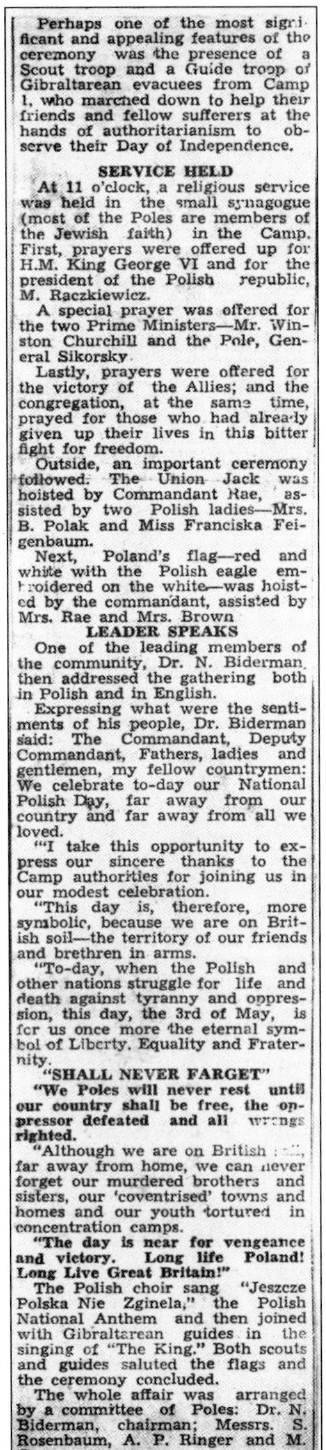

Perhaps one of the most significant and appealing features of the ceremony was the presence of a Scout troop and a Guide troop of Gibraltarean evacuees from Camp 1, who marched down to help their friends and fellow sufferers at the hands of authoritarianism to observe their Day of Independence.

SERVICE HELD

At 11 o'clock, a religious service was held in the small synagogue (most of the Poles are members of the Jewish faith) in the Camp. First, prayers were offered up for H.M. King George VI and for the president of the Polish republic, M. Raczkiewicz.

A special prayer was offered for the two Prime Ministers—Mr. Winston Churchill and the Pole, General Sikorsky.

Lastly, prayers were offered for the victory of the Allies; and the congregation, at the same time, prayed for those who had already given up their lives in this bitter fight for freedom.

Outside, an important ceremony followed. The Union Jack was hoisted by Commandant Rae, assisted by two Polish ladies—Mrs. B. Polak and Miss Franciska Feigenbaum.

Next, Poland's flag—red and white with the Polish eagle embroidered on the white—was hoisted by the commandant, assisted by Mrs. Rae and Mrs. Brown

LEADER SPEAKS

One of the leading members of the community, Dr. N. Biderman, then addressed the gathering both in Polish and in English.

Expressing what were the sentiments of his people, Dr. Biderman said: The Commandant, Deputy Commandant, Fathers, ladies and gentlemen, my fellow countrymen: We celebrate to-day our National Polish Day, far away from our country and far away from all we loved.

"'I take this opportunity to express our sincere thanks to the Camp authorities for joining us in our modest celebration.

"This day is, therefore, more symbolic, because we are on British soil—the territory of our friends and brethren in arms.

"To-day, when the Polish and other nations struggle for life and death against tyranny and oppression, this day, the 3rd of May, is for us once more the eternal symbol of Liberty, Equality and Fraternity.

"SHALL NEVER FARGET"

"We Poles will never rest until our country shall be free, the oppressor defeated and all wrongs righted.

"Although we are on British soil, far away from home, we can never forget our murdered brothers and sisters, our 'coventrised' towns and homes and our youth tortured in concentration camps.

"The day is near for vengeance and victory. Long life Poland! Long Live Great Britain!"

The Polish choir sang "Jeszcze Polska Nie Zginela," the Polish National Anthem and then joined with Gibraltarean guides in the singing of "The King." Both scouts and guides saluted the flags and the ceremony concluded.

The whole affair was arranged by a committee of Poles: Dr. N. Biderman, chairman; Messrs. S. Rosenbaum, A. P. Ringer and M. Grun.

In late 1943 the male internees previously housed at Up Park Camp where prisoners of war were held were sent to Camp Two. The addressed envelopes were donated by Mr C Moore.

Below are examples of letters sent from camp two to families of internees in the United States of America.

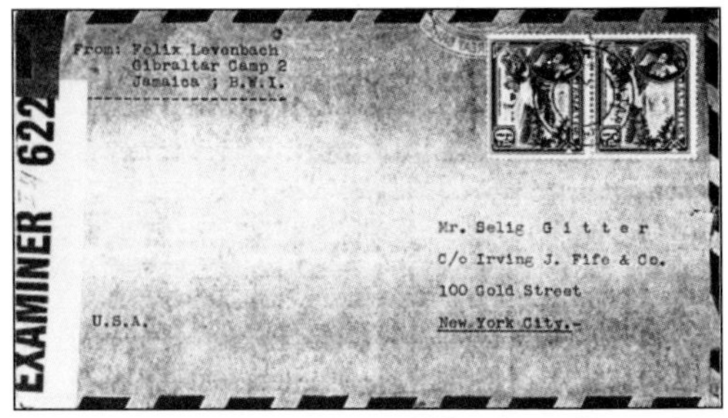

Letter from Internee at Gibraltar Camp 2 to Family in New York.

Above Letter from Prisoner to Family in New York.

Another letter from an internee at Gibraltar Camp Two to family in New York.

The women and children in Hanover Street Camp also started to arrive at the Gibraltar Camp No.2. These internees which numbered about 60 consisted mainly of Italian and German families. They were living in British West Africa when the war broke out and were shipped to Jamaica.

The internees were housed in eight barracks. There was also a dining hall, school and staff quarters and even a sports field and each month movies were shown.

Plays and concerts were staged occasionally and the children were taken on field trips. Generally speaking the evacuees seemed to have settled well although occasionally there were bound to be some problems linked to the administration of the camp, particularly, matters regarding the breach of camp rules. The Jamaican newspaper 'The Gleaner' published an article accusing the Camp Commandant of behaving in a dictatorial manner in the handling of the camp owing to its reporter not being allowed to enter the camp because he had forgotten to bring his pass.

No pack, however, would be complete without its joker, so we now have our own "little" Ernest Rae of "Gibraltar", complete with sports model concentration camp, scuttle helmet, and off-with-his-head manners.

The other day the Gleaner had something rather important to ask the Gibraltar Commandant, so important that we actually sent up our News Editor, Mr. G. V. Barton, supported by a staff reporter, to look after the job. Now "Father B's" job in news editing the Gleaner is one of those whole time jobs where you work overtime in your spare time, so about the only time he ever goes out on an assignment is on a really bloody murder, ("B" loves to dip his pen in gore) or chasing an elusive U. S. President round the harbour and environs. So it can readily be imagined that we really wanted to find out something.

In due course this Press Delegation arrives at the frowning portals of Camp Gibraltar, and sends in to request can it see the Deputy Commandant. The answer, conveyed by an orderly, from the Deputy Commandant in the best Berchtesgaden style that "The Deputy Commandant did not want to see the Gleaner"—and that of course was that!

These things undoubtedly have their funny side, equally undoubtedly they have their serious side —and free British subjects are getting thoroughly disgusted with the dictatorial attitude taken up to-day by so many of our officials, particularly when one remembers that the life blood of the Empire is now being spent in fighting this very attitude.

* * *

Copy of article published by the Daily Gleaner.

A few days later, an anonymous letter appeared in the same newspaper denying the accusations. Following this letter, there was an official denial in the by The Gleaner newspaper.

Another newspaper 'the Spotlight' reported that the accusations were unfounded after a reporter found for himself how well the evacuees were treated when he visited the camp.

Camp Gibraltar—Evacuee's Complaint As To Conditions

THE EDITOR, Sir:—I read in yesterday's issue of your paper that your News Editor was recently refused entry to Gibraltar Camp by order of our local dictator. Of course, he was refused entry through the "gloomy portals" (by the way we always refer to the prison gates as "gloomy portals").

His visit might have coincided with a mealtime. He would then have seen the bad catering and indifferent cooking to which we are treated and the unpleasant conditions under which it is served to us. The founder of the Camp has unfortunately sailed for his home at Gibraltar, satisfied that he has left us in safe and happy conditions until the war, which has deprived us of our homes and livelihood, is over. It is the greatest wish of all of us that he could see how the people he has entrusted us to have developed into dictators, small in their way but definitely to be felt. Whole families in the Camp who have been sufficiently lucky to catch the dictator's aproval are employed at 10/- and 15/- a week, each member, in spite of the fact that the head of the family is drawing a government pension. For the unlucky (or untactful) ones amongst whom there are many capable professional and reliable workers, they must eat their hearts out for work, and a little wage to supplement the poor food and the little money they have managed to bring with them. What is to happen when their small savings are exhausted no one can foretell. But all this is of no interest to our own particular dictators. I can give you the name of an ex-serviceman, a member of the British Legion, who has received no pension since he came to the Camp, and has not yet obtained the necessary interview with the Camp authorities. He is still trying to break through the bodyguard.

I quite realize that owing to the war there is intense suffering throughout the world, but that does not excuse unpleasant conditions that could be avoided. We all like Jamaica and we deeply appreciate the great kindness and sympathy we are receiving from outside the Camp, but we do feel that having been brought here under military exigencies, thereby depriving us of homes and means of livelihood, we should be treated as responsible human beings, and not mere nuisances to provide a living for a few petty officials. I am enclosing my full name and address, but not for publication. If my name is published, the writing of this letter might be termed insubordination, and dire punishment for that, as you would see in the printed rules if you were permitted to see them, is deprivation of food which, bad as it is, would be unpleasant for me as I am one of the unfortunates in the Camp who at present "have no visible means of support."

I must apologise for bothering you with such a long letter, but several of us have been threshing round lately trying to find a responsible and independent person outside the Camp who might take up our cause and it seems as if you, Mr. Editor, might be that person.

I am, etc.,

"ONE OF THE EVACUEES."

Camp Gibraltar,
January 18, 1941.

However, further accusations, about the handling of the Gibraltar Camp came also from a Jamaican councillor who publicly criticised the management of the camp by the Jamaican authorities.

Amidst these criticisms, some Gibraltarians who had visited their families in the Camp commented very favourably of how the evacuees were being looked after. However, another Jamaica newspaper printed an official denial of the accusations about the treatment of evacuees.

CAMP GIBRALTAR

Official Denial Of Evacuee's Charges

With reference to a letter which appeared in the "Gleaner" of Tuesday, January 21, signed "One of the Evacuees," a Government spokesman issued denial of the charges contained therein, as follows:

He denied that the camp was referred to by the evacuees as "the gloomy portals." Everything compatible with discipline was done to make the evacuees feel at home. Their liberty was not curtailed; they often left the camp at 8 o'clock in the morning and could remain out as late as 10 p.m.

There was no attempt at dictatorship; the most pleasant relations existed between the authorities and the evacuees and neither the commandant or the deputy commandant was inaccessible.

Over 400 of the evacuees were employed in different tasks in the camp, and their weekly paybill amounted to £229 1s. 9d. There was no discrimination when these people were being employed.

An ex-serviceman had been appointed as chief of the Special Police which consisted wholly of Gibraltareans. He was a most efficient man with 28 years service in the Gibraltar Police.

The delay in the paying over of pensions to some of the pensioners from Gibraltar was not the fault of the local authorities and steps had been taken to adjust matters with the Gibraltar Government.

Yet again another Jamaican newspaper came out in defence of the authorities responsible for the Gibraltar evacuees. At that juncture the whole matter seem to have acquired a political flavour in Jamaica's internal politics.
About a year later after the letter in the previous column was published, an incident took place when some evacuees insisted in the taking of meals outside the dining room. As a result a few evacuees were arrested and one was fined and others reprimanded. The incident came to the knowledge of families in Gibraltar by means of a leaflet, notes and letters which made mention of this and various other complaints.

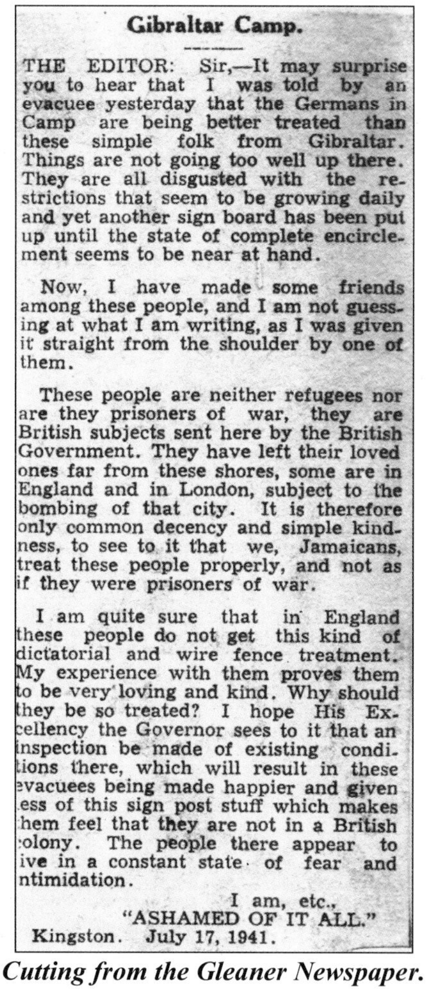

Gibraltar Camp.

THE EDITOR: Sir,—It may surprise you to hear that I was told by an evacuee yesterday that the Germans in Camp are being better treated than these simple folk from Gibraltar. Things are not going too well up there. They are all disgusted with the restrictions that seem to be growing daily and yet another sign board has been put up until the state of complete encirclement seems to be near at hand.

Now, I have made some friends among these people, and I am not guessing at what I am writing, as I was given it straight from the shoulder by one of them.

These people are neither refugees nor are they prisoners of war, they are British subjects sent here by the British Government. They have left their loved ones far from these shores, some are in England and in London, subject to the bombing of that city. It is therefore only common decency and simple kindness, to see to it that we, Jamaicans, treat these people properly, and not as if they were prisoners of war.

I am quite sure that in England hese people do not get this kind of ictatorial and wire fence treatment. My experience with them proves them o be very loving and kind. Why should hey be so treated? I hope His Excellency the Governor sees to it that an inspection be made of existing conditions there, which will result in these evacuees being made happier and given ess of this sign post stuff which makes hem feel that they are not in a British olony. The people there appear to ive in a constant state of fear and ntimidation.

I am, etc.,
"ASHAMED OF IT ALL."
Kingston. July 17, 1941.

Cutting from the Gleaner Newspaper.

The Colonial Secretary in Gibraltar wrote to Jamaica requesting information on the allegations circulating in Gibraltar about the evacuees in Jamaica. Upon investigation, again most of, if not all, the allegations cited in the letters and pamphlets were rejected in total. One evacuee with whom I talked with about the food etc in the camp said that on one occasion they were given pies filled with sardines for about four days in a row. He said that the evacuees expressed their annoyance by throwing the plates with the sardine pies all over the dining room.

Below is a road sign which serves as an historical reminder, of what was once the Gibraltar Camp.

A clear reminder of the Gibraltar Camp.
Photo Mr A Lara

After four years, almost exactly to the day, came the turn of the repatriation of the evacuees in Jamaica. How did the evacuees fare during these four years in the Gibraltar Camp? There are varying versions of how the Gibraltar evacuees lived in Jamaica. From what I have researched it seems that those in charge of the evacuees did their best to look after their well being in the prevailing circumstances. The majority of the evacuees were very appreciative that everything possible was, all the time, being done on their behalf. However, the evacuee's minds and hearts were, naturally, all the time with their loved ones who remained behind in Gibraltar or were evacuated to other places. Their stay in distant lands, no matter how well they were, was no substitute for their homes in Gibraltar. When the time for departure came, many Gibraltarian women went to the Papine market to say goodbye to those with whom they had had much contact with. The Gibraltar evacuees were received with many hugs from the Jamaicans who were sad to see the evacuees go. Very recently during my research, I came across a web page referring to the Gibraltar Camp. The following is an extract from this web site referring to an interview with someone who remembered the Gibraltar evacuees.
"Chances are that not many Jamaicans know much about Gibraltar Camp or Gibraltar, but Peter McCaulay believes the Gibraltarians remember Jamaica. Towards the end of our interview, McCaulay recounted how a few years ago when he and his wife, Dawn, visited Gibraltar, they wound up with a taxi driver who, on hearing where they were from, excitedly told them that his grandparents had come to Jamaica during World War II and that Jamaica held a special place in their hearts."

CHAPTER TEN

GIBRALTAR DURING THE WAR

When Britain declared war on Germany in September 1939, the people of Gibraltar had already witnessed very recently the horrors of the Spanish Civil War affecting many families in Gibraltar with close relatives in Spain. Some Gibraltarian families who had been residing in Spain decided for their own safety to come over to live in Gibraltar. Also some Spanish nationals who had taken refuge in Gibraltar during the Spanish Civil war were still living in Gibraltar for fear of reprisals.

Above is a photo of the shelter at Line Wall Road built during World War Two. Photo by J.Gingell

Gibraltarian men were by then enlisting in the newly formed Gibraltar Defence Force and other Services like the police. Guns and searchlights were being installed in strategic positions around Gibraltar. Also about a dozen air raid shelters were constructed around Gibraltar.

Members of the Gibraltar Defence Force at the Europa Point Anti-Aircraft defences during WW2. Photo Mr Ferrary

An RAF search and rescue squadron and a naval task force known as Force H were ordered to be stationed at Gibraltar at the very initial stages of the war. Places which were considered military strategic areas in Gibraltar became out of bounds for civilians.

An immediate curfew was imposed and some blackout exercises were carried out. During the war Gibraltar underwent many physical changes commensurate with a war situation. There were many places fenced with barbed wire, iron pikes and concrete fortifications mounted on strategic positions in the event of an attack. In a short period of time Gibraltar was transformed into a fully-fledged military fortress. The most significant changes from a military point of view were that of the Victoria Gardens with its racecourse converted into an airstrip.

Guns at the top of the Rock. Photo Mark Bruzon

Guns at the Detached Mole. Photo Mr Ferrary

Below is a copy of a Government notice referring to a blackout notice.

GOVERNMENT NOTICE No. 72.

With reference to Government Notice No. 54 dated the 11th of April, 1940, it is hereby notified for general information that Tests in connection with the Gibraltar "Black-out" system will be carried out on Sunday night, 19th May, 1940.

2. In their own interests and that of the safety of Gibraltar, the public are earnestly requested to obey the following instructions in every detail:—

(a) From 9.45 p.m. to 10.15 p.m., as many lights as possible should be exposed. Householders should have their shutters open and allow the lights in rooms to shine out.

(b) From 10.15 p.m. to 11.00 p.m. there will be a complete black-out. The signal to begin blacking-out will be the firing of one gun from Devil's Gap Battery. The Public are particularly asked NOT to begin blacking-out before this signal.

3. Should the Exercise have to be cancelled owing to bad weather the Public will be informed at 6 p.m., the 19th of May, through Radio Distribution, and by announcements from the Police loud-speaker van.

Colonial Secretary's Office,
Gibraltar, 16th May, 1940.
(M.P. No. 80/38 (2)).

By Command,
ALEXR. E. BEATTIE,
Colonial Secretary.

The other major physical change was the excavation of miles of tunnels to prepare Gibraltar in case of a prolonged siege. Among the many facilities made available in these tunnels were included a hospital, quarters, fuel storage tanks, a fresh water supply system, a communication centre and two generating power stations. These changes proved in many instances Gibraltar's value as a fortress during the war in the protection of convoys sailing into the Mediterranean Sea and became vital for the invasion of North Africa. From the beginning of July 1940 and until 1943 Gibraltar suffered the occasional aerial bombardments from both the Vichy French aircraft based in French Morocco and the Italian aircraft based in Sardinia. The worst of all the bombings carried out by the Vichy Air Force occurred from 24th to the 25th September 1940 in reprisal for the British attempted occupation of Dakar on the 23rd September 1940.

GIBRALTAR RAIDED BY OVER 100 PLANES

Several Enemy Aircraft Shot Down

Fortress B.H.Q. has issued the following communique relating to yesterday afternoon's raid:

"A further air raid on Gibraltar by large numbers of French aircraft was made to-day.

The Air Raid Warning was given at 14.33 hrs. and was shortly followed by heavy anti-aircraft barrage fire and the dropping of the first load of bombs.

Continuous waves of bombers dropped their bombs, most from a great height, until 16.50 hrs.

It is estimated that over 100 aircraft dropped some 300 bombs of varying sizes.

A large proportion of bombs dropped in the sea and on the barren parts of the Rock, but many fell on buildings, roads, and old defences.

Considerable damage was again done to private property and Government offices, but there was very little damage to Military works and personnel.

One small ship was hit and subsequently sank in the harbour.

There were a number of casualties, including some fatal ones.

The Fortress A.-A. fire was most effective and the Gunners stood up to the heavy bombing magnificently.

Several enemy aircraft were shot down; three for certain, and two more, possibly."

Above and below cuttings from the Gibraltar Chronicle reporting the details of the air raid.

CEREMONY OF THE KEYS FOLLOWS AIR RAID

"After an afternoon of intense air bombardment Gibraltar's high morale remains entirely unaffected and the traditional Ceremony of the Keys was carried out in the presence of His Excellency the Governor with full ceremonial."

The bombing stopped the day after the British withdrew from Dakar but Gibraltar had already suffered heavy damages. Despite the bombing the ceremony of the keys went ahead as reported in the Gibraltar Chronicle. It was estimated that about 500 bombs were dropped with most of them falling in the sea; some of the bombs that fell in Gibraltar killed six civilians and damaged many buildings.

A photo of the damage caused by the bombs in September 1940. Photo Mrs L Galliano

The civilians killed were Mrs Mercedes Crisp,(56) Miss Josefina Crisp,(23) Master Francis Crisp (15)and Mr Francisco Crisp (59) living at Naval Hospital Road and also Mrs Leopordina Borda (21) who lived near Scud Hill. The names of the casualties were obtained with the kind help of Mr Alfred Ryan, Superintendent of the Gibraltar Cemeteries.

One of the Vichy aircraft, theMartin-MarylandF167, which bombed Gibraltar. Photo Wikipedia Free Encyclopedia

Italian and Vichy French aircraft continued to attack Gibraltar but with very little success. The bombs usually fell in the sea since most of the time the aircraft could not approach the Rock as they were soon repelled by the anti aircraft batteries.

The Rock searchlights in action during an air raid. Photo Wikipedia Free Encyclopedia

Between September and October 1940, there were strong reasons to believe that Germany was planning to capture Gibraltar with Spain's assistance. Franco in those early days of war was praising both Germany and Italy and was even decorated with the Italian Order of Annuziata. It was also known that there were frequent meetings between foreign ministers Ribbentrop of Germany and Serano Suñer of Spain. Credence to this information was given when Hitler and Franco held their historic meeting at Hendaye on the 23rd October 1940.

A French bomb hitting the North Front area. Photo Mr G Cano

The intended plan to capture Gibraltar which is said to have been discussed at this meeting became historically known as "Operation Felix."

Hitler and Franco meeting in Hendaye. Photo Mr Franz Penskofer and Mr Martin Nuza.

During the summer and autumn of 1940 the Germans carried out detailed reconnaissance missions from the Spanish hinterland to study the Rock's defences in order to plan their intended attack on Gibraltar. The plan was said to entail rapid entry through Spain (with or without permission). With Gibraltar captured, the Strait would be closed to the Allies forcing shipping to steam all the way around the Cape of Good Hope to enter the Mediterranean Sea via the Suez Canal.
The actual military operation to seize the Rock was to start in January 1941 with an initial very heavy bombardment by planes leaving from France but landing afterwards at Spanish air bases. This was to be followed by a sea and land invasion of troops.
In the event of a successful capture, contingency plans called Operation Tracer were drawn up by the military authorities in Gibraltar for a few men to hide themselves inside the Rock. Two small openings were made on the face of the Rock so that these men could secretly watch the enemy activities. One opening faced the east and the other the west. The idea was for them to report all enemy movements and operations to London with the aid of secret transmitters. They would have enough supplies to last for one year but were not to come out of this hiding place unless Germany was defeated within a year. The plan was tried very extensively from the point of view of all the necessary requirements, such as, equipment, food, exercises, clothing and the psychological effects on the men. However, as the war developed the plan was never required to be put into practice.
Little seems to be known generally of a secret plan prepared by the Spanish military command to capture Gibraltar in the summer of 1940. Franco awaited the expected German victory in the Battle of Britain to give his blessing to this plan which never materialized. The plan called Operation C entailed a lot of logistic planning including the evacuation of the civilian population because it was intended to use mustard gas.
On the 3rd November 1940 the destroyer **HMS Greyhound** was deployed to intercept the Italian submarine the Michele Bianchi that was operating in the Strait of Gibraltar.

HMS Greyhound. Photo Old Ship Gallery

Depth charges were launched and after a while the submarine was seen making for the port of Tangier (then in control of Spain) when **HMS Greyhound** was attempting to ram the submarine, as it could not fire because it was already in what was considered to be Tangier's jurisdictional waters.
In November 1940 two Spanish Savoia 17 type aircraft which had been spotted shadowing British ships were mistakenly shot down by British fighters not very far from the Balearic Islands. The incident was settled diplomatically.

During the early part of 1941 Vichy French aircraft carried out various attempts to bomb Gibraltar. The aircraft were soon repelled by the anti-craft guns emplaced in many of the strategic areas in different parts of the Rock. During these bombing raids some of the bombs fell in the sea or on the beaches of La Linea. On the 12th July 1941 bombs from an Italian aircraft hit a house at the corner where Calle Lopez de Ayalla and Calle Duque de Tetuan meet. Six people were killed and another eleven were wounded. Other bombs dropped by this aircraft fell on La Linea's western beach but did not explode. A few days later two Italian aircraft attempted to bomb Gibraltar but were caught by the searchlights and fired upon. One of these aircraft dropped the bombs on the western side of La Linea. Two bombs exploded at a Polo pitch and an unexploded bomb fell in the River Chacon. One of the aircraft was hit and crashed in Los Barrios. Photos of the bombing shown below were donated by Sñr Luis Javier Traverso from La Linea Historical Archives.

Above and below the scene of destruction caused by the Italian bombs

Known as the "Floating Trojan Horse of Gibraltar", the Italians devised a craft called the human torpedo or chariot and was launched from submarines specially designed to carry these special torpedoes.

800 px -Piaggio – the type of aircraft that dropped the bombs in La Linea. Photo Regia Marina

The Italian submarine Scire was the one which carried out most of these attacks in Gibraltar.

The Italian submarine Scire carrying the "chariots." Photo Regia Marina

Once launched, the torpedoes were guided by the frogmen in the direction of the desired target. On the 24th September 1940 the Scire left La Spezia carrying three manned torpedoes to carry out similar attacks but the intended targets had left Gibraltar before Scire arrived at the scene. In October 1940 the Sciré again headed for Gibraltar carrying three manned torpedoes and eight crewmen. The manned torpedoes entered the harbour, but were abandoned and later they were washed ashore at the Espigon Bay without being able to damage any of the ships in the harbour. Then in November 1940 another attempt was made but the operation failed completely when they were only about 30 metres from the target that was to be the battleship **HMS Barham.**

HMS Barham. Photo Old Ship Gallery

On the 25th May 1941 the Scire arrived in the Bay of Gibraltar carrying three manned torpedoes secretly loading them in Spain with six crewmen. They found no warships in Gibraltar because by then they had left as part of the Royal Navy's deployment in the search for the German battleship Bismark.

A photo of a human torpedo. Photo Regia Marina

On the 21st September 1941 there was another attack but the operation was discovered and many of the craft destroyed. However, others were able to penetrate the Gibraltar defences and managed to sink two tankers, the Denbydale, the Fiona Shell and the armoured British merchant ship Durham. The Warmer Castle was also sunk. Later in the war the Italians instead of using the submarine Scire, resorted to a less risky method by swimming from Puente Mayorga were they had managed through contacts in Spain to hire a house called Villa Carmela which became a secret operational base to carryout attacks on Gibraltar.

The Villa Carmela. PhotoRegia Marina

On the night of the 13th-14th July 1942 the Italians swam towards Gibraltar carrying limpet mines to be attached to the hull of the ships in harbour. On that night the ships Meta, Shuma, Snipe and the Baron Douglas were sunk. On the night of 15th September 1942 the Italian swimmers managed to defy the increased British vigilance in the bay and sank the ship Raven's Point.

When Italy declared war Britain on the 10th June 1940 she attempted to scuttle ships in the Gibraltar Bay. One of the ships involved was the Olterra which was immobilised near the shores of Algeciras.

Undetected by the British, the Olterra had a special underwater compartment constructed from where the chariots could be launched to proceed directly across the bay to Gibraltar. The first attack from the Olterra was carried out in December 1942 but failed. On the 17th December 1942 six Italian frogmen on three torpedoes left the Olterra to attack the British warships **HMS Nelson, HMS Formidable**, and **HMS Furious**. A British patrol boat killed the torpedo's crew with a depth charge. Their bodies were recovered and buried at Gibraltar with full military honours. A British patrol boat detected another torpedo, which was pursued and shot at, capturing its two crewmen. The remaining manned torpedo returned to the Olterra.

The Italian ship Olterra anchored at Algeciras. Photo Regia Marina

No further attacks were made until 7th May 1943 when three manned torpedoes left the Olterra in bad weather but managed to reach their targeted ships. As a result, the merchant ships Pat Harrison, the Marhsud and the Camerata were sunk. The last of this type of action by the Italians took place on the 3rd August 1943 sinking the US ship Harrison Gray Otis, the Norwegian tanker Thorshovdi and the British merchant ship Stanbridge.

The damaged Norwegian tanker Thorshovdi. Photo Siri Lawson.www.warsailors.com

On the 2nd October 1943 a larger Italian frogman-carrier left Italy with plans to attack Gibraltar. The boat was 33 feet long and carried four frogmen. The surrender of Italian forces to the Allies cancelled the whole operation. At the same time that the Italians were engaged with their maritime actions they also carried out some aerial bombardment on the 24th September, the 20th October, the 8th and 14th November 1942 but most of the bombs dropped fell, either in the sea or in La Linea.

During the war many aircraft patrolled the areas around Gibraltar. One of the best known aircraft was the Catalina. It was a Catalina which spotted the **Bismark** in the Atlantic and which led to the subsequent chase by naval units in the Atlantic. Included in the chase from Gibraltar was **HMS Ark Royal**, which contributed to the sinking of the **Bismark** on the 27th May 1941 by damaging her steering gear with torpedoes, launched from her Swordfish aircraft.

Spitfires and Hurricanes being assembled at North Front. Photo Mark Bruzon

A very well known event that took place near Gibraltar was that of the sinking of **HMS Ark Royal**. On the 12th November 1941 while returning from her task of delivering aircraft to Malta, a torpedo from a German U-boat hit the aircraft carrier **HMS Ark Royal**. Many attempts were made to save her from sinking with a rescue operation from Gibraltar. She began to list badly and then sunk the next day when she was only 25 miles from Gibraltar.

HMS Ark Royal sinking off Malaga in November 1941. Photo Royal Naval Museum

That same year on the 7th December 1941 came the terrible news from far away in the Pacific Ocean about the surprise attack on Pearl Harbour by the Japanese Imperial Navy. The USA had gathered a substantial number of her ships at Pearl Harbour as part of her Pacific Fleet. Many of these ships were either sunk or severely damaged and over 2,300 personnel were killed.

The battleship USS Arizona sinking in Pearl Harbour. Photo The History Place

The next day as part of a general Pacific campaign, the Japanese launched an assault on Hong Kong forcing its surrender on Christmas Day. Soon after came the fall of Singapore which Churchill considered one of the most humiliating British defeats of all time. The same day that the USA declared war on Japan, Germany also declared war on the USA in the hope that Japan would help Germany by attacking the Soviet Union. Japan did not oblige Hitler who made the fatal mistake of allowing the USA to enter the war in Europe. By July 1942 Churchill had already placed Gibraltar under the command of General Eisenhower and of Operation Torch. His operational headquarters were within a chamber constructed inside the Rock

Sir Winston Churchill in Gibraltar with Governor Sir Noel Mason MacFarlane. Photo Wikipedia Free Encyclopedia.

The Victoria Gardens at North Front were converted into a military aerodrome with rocks excavated from tunnels inside the Rock. All the photographs on this page were donated by Mr Mark Bruzon.

Guns within the Dockyard.

About 100,000 troops had also converged on Gibraltar to take part in the North African landing. In November 1942 when the operation was finally launched about 400 aircraft, which had been assembled at the North Front, flew across the strait to land on captured airfields in North Africa. British and Americans troops landed at Algiers, Oran, and Casablanca meeting very little resistance and quickly driving inland. On the 15th November 1942 the French in Africa joined the Allies.
Operation Torch was the first necessary step to prepare for the invasion which Churchill came to call "the soft underbelly of Europe" which entailed Italy's removal from the war and the subsequent invasion of southern France. In less than a year since the launching of Operation Torch Italy surrendered on the 23rd September 1943 and a few weeks later declared war on Germany.

Aircraft ready to take off for the North Africa landing.

EISENHOWER SETS PRECEDENT AT GIBRALTAR

Was First Foreigner in British History to Take Command of Rock

By WES GALLAGHER

Allied Headquarters, North Africa, Dec. 5 (Delayed) (AP).—Lt.-Gen. Dwight D. Eisenhower commanded the British fortress of Gibraltar during the first days of the North African operations, thus being the first foreigner in two centuries to control that rock of British Empire.

Security reasons restricted the announcement until today. (Censorship further delayed publication of the despatch even after it was written.)

In the world's safest air raid shelter under 1,400 feet of solid rock in offices carved from limestone, the Allied staff worked 24 hours a day under the United States commander.

"Never in my wildest dreams in my West Point days did I ever think that I—an American general—would ever command the British fortress of Gibraltar," Eisenhower declared one day at a press conference at his office in the Rock.

Gibraltar was under his command only because he was Allied Commander-in-Chief and Gen. Mason MacFarlane, who actually is in charge, was temporarily under his orders.

Above a cutting from an unknown newspaper when General Eisenhower took command of Gibraltar

By then French Morocco was already on the side of the Allies. The Russians continued to make advances on the Eastern Front. The Battle of the Atlantic was effectively over and in the Pacific the US forces were overcoming the Japanese in their occupied areas. Also plans were already being prepared for the Normandy landing in June 1944.

Guns at the top of the Rock.

Franco had declared in March 1943 that he wanted an agreement with the Allies to defend Western Civilisation. In November 1943 he returned to a policy of neutrality from his previous one of non-belligerency. Within this context Franco was quoted as saying that he had never been allied to the Axis powers. When Hitler got to know about this, he was quoted as saying that Franco's nerve had no limits. By then the war, as far as Gibraltar was concerned, in terms of hostilities, was practically over.

Naval units at Gibraltar making preparations for Operation Torch. Photo onboard of HMS Bermuda from Mr L Burrill – webmaster@hmsgangestoterror.org

Describing the Allies achievements up to then, Sir Winston Churchill in one of his many famous war speeches said, "This is not the end. It is not even the beginning of the end. But it is, perhaps, the end of the beginning."

Plaque by the American War Memorial Steps in memory of Opèration Torch. Photo by J.Gingell

Another event that occurred during the war was when General Sikorsky was killed in an aircraft, which crashed after a few moments of taking off from the newly constructed military runway.

On the 4th July 1943 a converted Liberator bomber from RAF Transport Command took off from Gibraltar for England. The aircraft climbed normally from the runway, levelled off to gather speed but then suddenly lost height and crashed into the sea on the eastern side of the Rock.

General Sikorski and 15 others were killed. The sole survivor was the Czech-born pilot, who was rescued by an RAF launch. The bodies of 5 passengers and crew, including Sikorski's daughter, were never found.

General Wladyslaw Sikorski with General Gort inspecting Gibraltar defences. Photo Wikipedia Free Encyclopedia

At the time of mentioning this incident in my book, the cause of the death of General Sikorski was being investigated by the Polish authorities and concluded that the death was caused by the injuries from the plane crash. Some documents about this incident are still kept secret at the Public Records Office in the UK.

Monument and plaque to commemorate the 60th Anniversary of the death of General Sikorski At bottom of the slate there is an inscription that reads:
NON OMNIS MORIAR –*Not all of me shall die*
Photo by J Gingell

There are some researchers that believe that General Sikorski's death was not an accident but an act of sabotage for his accusations about Stalin's alleged killing of Polish Officers. Speaking with a Pole about this incident, he maintained that Sikorski was an obstacle in the good relations that the Allies wanted to keep with Russia in order to defeat the Germans.

During the war there were acts of sabotage carried out by agents recruited by the German intelligence service. Two of the agents captured were Luis Lopez Córdon Cuenca and José Martin Munoz.

Cuenca was charged with "acting with intent to assist the enemy, and with having in his possession a bomb intended to cause an explosion in the dockyard." In his trial Cuenca said that he did not know that the package he delivered to a house in Gibraltar contained a German-made bomb. He was convicted on 31 August 1943 and was sentenced to death.

Munoz, a worker from La Linea, was accused of having caused a suspicious fire in the Gibraltar dockyard on 30 June 1943. He was also charged with having hidden a bomb in the coal-hole of a local café. He was sentenced to death for having acted with "intent to assist the enemy by an act designed to impede naval operations or to endanger life."

Both men were hanged in Gibraltar on 11 January 1944.

The other saboteur was Gibraltar born Jose Estelle Key. During his arrest he was found carrying information, which he was intending to transmit to the Germans. Key was taken to the UK and charged under the Treachery Act. He was executed at Wandsworth Prison on 7 July 1942.

In an article about espionage a British journalist commented that it was possible to pass secret information to Berlin about Gibraltar by walking in ten minutes across to the frontier. The same reported carried on saying that the fact that there were about 6,000 Spaniards entering and leaving the fortress made the task for the security forces very difficult. And that the reason why there had been only a few cases of sabotage was owing to their successful policy of taking preventive measures. It is a well known fact that there were many German spies watching movement of ships, troops and aircraft from across the surrounding towns on the Spanish hinterland. Admiral Canaris, Chief of the German Military Intelligence visited Spain frequently and has been mentioned in researches on the subject to have been seen in the vicinity of Los Barrios for possible contacts with British agents seeking an agreement to end the war.

The Gibraltar – Spanish Frontier during the war. Photo Mr M Bruzon

During the Second World War Gibraltar became conspicuous for the absence of children, women and elderly people. The civilian population, consisting mainly of men, who remained behind to work on essential services in Gibraltar totalled about 4,000. There were at the time an average of about 30,000 troops stationed in Gibraltar. Below a group of men who worked in essential services for the military authorities and the police force. Many Gibraltarians also served in the war. A very detailed account of their services in the war can be found in Mr Eric Canessa's book "They Went To War."

Men working for the essential services. left to right: Ernest Gilbert, Alfredo Ferro, Peter Ferro, Alberto Victory, and Victor Ferro and Antonio Ferro. Photo Mr Gilbert

Thousands of Spaniards came daily to work but left before the curfew time. Gibraltar was not as heavily attacked as had been expected although there were contingency plans for a mass evacuation of troops and civilians working in the fortress. Most of the time there was very little to do after work with the streets remaining almost empty just before the start of the curfew time at eleven at night.

The main sources of entertainment during the day and at weekends were football, hockey and other sports or indoor games. The ground stands were usually full up when there was a special match being played.

The Gibraltar United Team- winners of the 1943-44 League. Photo Gibraltar Football Association

Visiting ships also played football matches at the naval football grounds. Below is a photograph of **HMS Hood's** football team when they played against another Royal Navy ship's team.

HMS Hood football team at the naval ground. Photo HMS Hood Association.

A few musical bands used to perform in dances held in the Assembly Rooms, hotels and clubs. Along Main Street there were about 4 or 5 saloon bars/cafes. Some of the names of these places that come to mind are the Trocadero, the Royal, the Suizo and the Universal where Spanish dancers performed. There were the forces cinemas like the Naval Trust, the Garrison Cinema at the Ince's Hall and the Globe. The local cinemas were the Rialto and the Theatre Royal where many Spanish-speaking films were shown. The entrance fee was about 6 old pennies (2 ½ p). Shops were replenished all the time with basic food supplies. Fruits, vegetables and groceries were available all the time. Other items found were those, which were considered luxurious at the time like the nylon stockings, watches, radios, ballpoint pens, cosmetics etc.

Spanish dancers at the Royal Hotel Bar. Photo Mr J Chiara

Outside Gibraltar was the special annual attraction of La Linea's fair ground. Below are some Gibraltarian men who stayed working for essential services having time off to enjoy at the La Linea fair.

In the photo Messrs J Sacramento, Davis. Photo Mr H Sacramento

Below a Gibraltar Chronicle advert on cosmetics available from boutiques in Gibraltar.

In October 1943 the Secretary of State for the Colonies visited Gibraltar and made various announcements in connection with Gibraltar's post war plans as described in the copies of the cutting from the Gibraltar Chronicle shown on this page.

GIBRALTAR WELL ADVANCED WITH POST-WAR PLANS: COL. STANLEY

By Gibraltar Chronicle Staff Reporter

AFTER an extensive tour, during which he has urged colonial governments to prepare now for reconstruction after the war, the Secretary of State for the Colonies, Colonel the Right Honourable Oliver Stanley, P.C., M.C., M.P., arrived at Gibraltar to find its plans for post-war development "well up in the list" among colonies whose schemes have already been drawn up.

During his visit to Gibraltar he has studied with officials of the Colonial Government some of the Colony's most pressing needs, including housing, which he regards as the major problem of the moment.

"YOUR WORK A SOVEREIGN CONTRIBUTION"

Fortress Stronger Today Than In All Its History

BROADCASTING to the people of Gibraltar over Radio Distribution last night, Colonel Stanley declared: "Whatever the dangers of the past, today we can face the future with confidence. Thanks to the skill of your commanders and the unremitting labour and devotion of all the services the fortress of Gibraltar stands stronger today than in all its long history.

"It is true that, owing to the fortunes of war, Gibraltar's role has not hitherto been spectacular. But it has nevertheless been vital. Many times during the past four years the men who so skilfully direct our strategy have had reason to be grateful to and for Gibraltar.

"It has been a great pleasure to spend even a few hours in this historic place — a place which is not only one of Great Britain's most loyal and ancient colonies but also one of its greatest fortresses.

"You have had to suffer in common with us in Great Britain the privations inseparable from war. But in the evacuation of your women and children and of all the men not required for the Colony's war effort you have borne a special burden.

The Leave Scheme

"The evacuation was a vital necessity but His Majesty's Government, which was forced to take that hard decision, appreciates to the full the sacrifices it has entailed.

"We are doing and will do all we can for the comfort of those evacuees in England. But England today is not a very comfortable place; England, too, is something of a fortress now, and you must be patient in the face of our many difficult problems. Those in Jamaica and in Madeira are faced with special difficulties, which it will be my constant endeavour to overcome.

"I was very glad recently to introduce the leave scheme and I am pleased to hear that it is working successfully.

"To those who have stayed behind I should like to express the gratitude of His Majesty's Government. Whether you are a worker in the Dockyard or the War Department, for the City Council or the Colonial Government, your work, done under conditions of exceptional difficulty and discomfort, has been a sovereign contribution to the war effort of the Colony."

These were among points emphasised by Colonel Stanley at a Press conference at The Convent yesterday, when discussing aspects of post-war development in Gibraltar.

Pointing out the present difficulties of obtaining labour and supplies due to diversions to meet wartime needs, he declared that as soon as the existing demands on these services eased up it should be possible to make great advances.

MAJOR PROBLEMS

"It is quite clear," said Colonel Stanley, "that your two major problems in Gibraltar are education and housing — and I am not sure that I would not put housing first.

"One of the most important factors in education is the standard of housing conditions, and that is a question which I have been particularly discussing with the officials of the Colonial Government here."

Emphasising that the aftermath of the war would probably prevent the immediate solution of war-time problems, Colonel Stanley warned:

"We must not expect that on the day Germany is defeated and peace is declared all these problems are going to become easy. The difficulties now existing will continue and may in some cases be accentuated for a time.

PUT THINGS RIGHT

"Our problems cannot be solved in a day, but plans can be laid now and as conditions improve we can build up. We must not, however, raise people's hopes and then cause them disappointment."

Asked how Gibraltarians at present evacuated in London and employed in war industries at home were going to be re-absorbed into employment in Gibraltar after the war, Colonel Stanley said:

"Many of them should come back with a very useful industrial education. I think they will return with a greatly widened outlook and even if existing conditions were intolerable before the war they could be much more intolerable afterwards. We intend to put that right as soon as we possibly can and to start the process as soon as the opportunity occurs."

He added that it was intended to put more local people into the Colonial administration — but that again depended on the educational facilities available to give them the necessary opportunity.

INTEREST AROUSED

"Although our Colonial administration has much to its credit, a great deal has been left undone," he said. "My great hope is that the interest which has been awakened among the people of Great Britain in the Colonies will increase.

"I am sure we shall be able to help you after the war with many of your problems, although I think you will agree that His Majesty's Government, like other people, is liable to help those who help themselves."

Resident-General of French Morocco Visits the Rock

His Excellency the Resident-General of French Morocco, M. Puaux, paid an official visit to His Excellency the Governor and Commander-in-Chief, Gibraltar, yesterday.

HE was accompanied by Col. Vitrolles, of the French Air Force, Colonel Duval, his secretary, Mr. Stonehewer-Bird, British Consul-General at Rabat, and members of his personal staff.

On arrival by air at North Front, M. Puaux was received by the Governor, who was accompanied by Vice-Admiral Sir Harold Burrough, Flag Officer Commanding Gibraltar, Air Commodore Simpson, the Colonial Secretary (the Hon. Miles Clifford), Maj.-Gen. F. G. Hyland, Deputy Fortress Commander, and members of the French military and naval mission.

TOUR OF ROCK

Mr. Puaux inspected a guard of honour provided by the Herts. Regiment, and was the guest of the Governor at a luncheon at The Convent.

During the course of his visit he was conducted round some of the main tunnels and points of interest in the fortress and later toured round the Rock in a motor launch.

He left with his entourage by air for Rabat last night.

French Morocco General visits Gibraltar.

At that time many Gibraltarian workers were already able to visit their relatives in London and Madeira by taking special leave arranged for that purpose. During the repatriation the AACR played a very prominent role in speeding the process.

Italian Tanker Surrenders, Comes To Gib.

BY CHRONICLE STAFF REPORTER

THE 5,000-ton Italian tanker Olterra, which was anchored in Gibraltar Bay when Italy entered the war in 1940, has surrendered to the British naval authorities at Gibraltar under the terms of the Allied armistice agreement with Italy under which Italian ships at sea or in neutral ports were required to make for British bases.

The tanker, which was loaded with oil, was scuttled and beached in Spanish waters. Later, she was salvaged and towed into Algeciras.

She had been unable to escape for three and a half years for fear of seizure by the British. On surrender she was taken in tow by tugs and brought into Gibraltar harbour.

ONE OF SIX

All the members of her crew except the chief engineer had left the vessel since its enforced "internment" and had returned to Italy.

The chief engineer, who remained in Algeciras, accompanied the ship to Gibraltar.

The Olterra was one of six Italian ships anchored in the roadstead on June 10, 1940, when Mussolini declared war on Great Britain.

The above cutting from the Gibraltar Chronicle reported the surrender of the Italian Tanker Olterra that had served as an operational base for Italian frogmen during the war. Its surrender was in line with the armistice arrangements made with Italy that required that all ships in neutral ports had to be handed to the nearest British bases. Also interesting at the time was the visit of the official from French Morocco in support of good relations with Britain.

The Governor Sir Noel Mason MacFarlane through the Forces radio summed up the war situation in his new year speech in December 1943 as reported in the Gibraltar Chronicle cutting shown below.

GIBRALTAR'S SHARE IN THE MEDITERRANEAN VICTORIES AND THE DEFEAT OF THE U-BOATS

NEW YEAR'S DAY MESSAGE BROADCAST BY HIS EXCELLENCY THE GOVERNOR AND C.-IN-C.:

ANOTHER year of war behind us . . . and here we are again for the fifth time on the wartime threshold of another year. New Year's Day is in many ways a good time for taking stock. And stock-taking on this New Year's Day is a very much more congenial and encouraging task than it has been on its four wartime predecessors.

Repatriation of the evacuees as soon as conditions permit

I think that we can safely say that 1943 has fulfilled, and even possibly more than fulfilled, the most optimistic hopes that we were justified in entertaining a year ago. Just think for a moment of the situation that I've just summarised for you — and then of the results which the last year has brought.

In the Mediterranean theatre we have, at great cost to our enemies, cleared them completely from the African continent. We have taken Sicily, Sardinia and Corsica. We have secured the downfall of Mussolini and his fascist government and have granted their successors first an armistice and later the status of co-belligerents.

We have in our hands, or co-operating with us, practically all the powerful Italian Fleet. Our Armies have liberated southern Italy; we have made our first bridgehead into the continent of Europe; and we are not far from being within striking distance of Rome itself.

In Russia our stout allies have gone from strength to strength and have surged forward irresistably. As Gaspadin Kalinin said only yesterday, they have already liberated more than two-thirds of the vast territories overrun by the German hordes. Every German counter-stroke has been ultimately held and thrown back. Today with General Winter beside them, the Russian armies would appear to have worked their way forward into strategic positions of the greatest importance.

Germany: A Lesson

In the air war, quite apart from the colossal contribution made by the Allied air forces in the vast combined operations which we have so successfully undertaken, they have devastatingly carried the war into the enemy's vitals.

For once, and at long last, the German people are being made to learn something of what war means in one's own country. Many is the number of their factories, industrial plants, shipyards and ports which have been completely wrecked or terribly knocked about. Many of their principal cities and towns have been largely laid waste.

And as the ring round Germany's so-called European Fortress gradually narrows — already the targets of Southern Germany and the oilfields of Rumania are within effective range of our Italian airfields — this bombing will increase and grow inexorably in intensity. The Luftwaffe has had its days. The German people are on the eve of a dark night.

IN the Atlantic the combined efforts and indefatigable endurance of the Royal Navy and the Allied navies, of the Royal Air Force, of Coastal Command and of the Allied air forces have at last succeeded in dominating conclusively the U-boat threat which at one time assumed the proportions of a menace which bade fair to become critical. The good work of 1942, which culminated in the launching of the North African operation with literally negligible losses from U-boat action, has been continued and consolidated in 1943.

It was vital that a solution to the U-boat problem should be found. It has been found. The United Kingdom — and don't forget Gibraltar too — are being fed and supplied largely from overseas. The menace of the U-boat can never be completely eliminated but thanks to the Merchant Navy and to the ascendancy gained by our sailors and our airmen, and to the work of the allied shipyards, we have safely rounded a corner which has taken a lot of turning. We can now strike against the enemy within reason pretty well wherever we choose.

But with all these successes behind us and with the forces and resources of the Allies gathering strength everywhere for the critical fighting of the year that is starting, perhaps the most encouraging augury of final — and let us hope relatively speedy — victory lies in the extent to which the collaboration and coordination of effort of the United Nations have increased and been consolidated during the past twelve month.

Prospects Brighter Now

The leaders and the principal executives of the major partners of the United Nations have met in conference and we can rest assured that the individual resources at their disposal should now be employed in accordance with collective plans designed to achieve the speediest possible defeat of our common enemy.

May our great leader, the Prime Minister, who has played so great a part since we had our backs to the wall in 1940, make a swift recovery from his recent illness and be rapidly and fully restored to strength to lead us to final victory.

Gibraltar's Share

How do all these mighty happenings affect us here in Gibraltar? What are and what will be their results and repercussions upon us? It must be obvious to everyone that there is a definite limit to what it is possible to say. But within that limit there are one or two things that I'd like to mention.

Firstly, there is Gibraltar's share in at least two of our major successes of the past year — the victories in the Mediterranean and the defeat of the U-boats.

In the first we have played a bigger part both directly and indirectly than is immediately apparent to the average inhabitant of the Rock. But it has been a big part and a very important part and it has been continually and very fully appreciated by all concerned. As success followed upon success the tide of amphibious war receded from Gibraltar. But the fact that the Rock stood, as you and your immediate predecessors have made it, did a very great deal towards not only making our initial descent upon North Africa possible but assisting very materially its subsequent magnificent exploitation.

In the U-boat war the part played by light forces of the Royal Navy and by the R.A.F. Units of Coastal Command based on Gibraltar has been indefatigable and memorable. The garrison of the Rock is proud of being charged with the protection here of the sister Services. It has warmly welcomed the recent promotion of

of war we are in a position to take advantage of this strength.

That does not mean that we can for one moment relax our vigilance or that our responsibility for the security and the guarding of our charge is in the slightest degree diminished. But it does mean that the volume of work to be done simultaneously has diminished and it does mean that a proportion of our garrison who fill static roles need not necessarily be up to the athletic standards demanded by modern operations in the open field.

There are many of you on the Rock who are highly trained, young and fit soldiers. You want to have a chance of getting away and playing your part in the big events which this year will clearly bring. Some of your comrades have already left and I hope that many more of you will get their chance. We can fill your place with trained men who may be a bit older than you and no longer able to do the 100 yards in level time but whose value if it comes to a static scrap will be equal to yours — and that is saying a lot. Our training camp in North Africa has done much towards making up for restricted training facilities here.

No Relaxation

There is still much to do here and there is still the all-important task of guarding our domain. There will be many who will not be able to get away to fight in the open; there is a limit for obvious reasons. And those who stay will find that there is still much to be done and that there can be no sort of relaxation in vigilance and in training. These are matters in which only the highest standards can be expected or permitted in war time.

But prospects are less indefinite and a bit less gloomy than they used to be. Length of service on the Rock has gradually been reduced to not very much more than two years, and two years is the figure to which I hope to be able to work in the not-far-distant future. As far as amenities and recreation are concerned we are all doing our best and on the whole I don't think we've been too badly off during the past year.

I have great hopes that the establishment which the Y.M.C.A. are shortly going to open on the Alameda will be a great boon to the whole community and go far to fill a hitherto more or less unfilled gap in our social amenities.

BEFORE I come to an end I want to say a few words to my Gibraltarian listeners. I have just returned from a short visit to London and spent a considerable part of my time going round with my wife, who knows most of them intimately now, a number of the centres in which our evacuees are accommodated. I also discussed the question of the possibility and practicability of at least making a start in the fairly near future with repatriation.

I took Bishop Fitzgerald with me and we both spent many hours visiting all your relatives and friends in many of the centres

CHAPTER ELEVEN

THE FIRST REPATRIATES -1944

By late autumn the military authorities considered that Gibraltar was no longer vulnerable to enemy attacks and therefore saw no reasons for not allowing the repatriation of the civilian population. About that time the Governor visited London with the aim of having detailed discussions with the British Government on the policy to follow for the return of the evacuees. The main problem affecting their return was the very acute shortage of accommodation in Gibraltar. Some of existing buildings, which were going to be used to accommodate the repatriates, required extensive refurbishment. Essential domestic utilities like cooking appliances, lighting and running water had still to be installed in many buildings before being allocated as dwellings. The other equally important requirements that needed to be put in placed before the return of the evacuees were normal schooling facilities and medical services. On the other hand, the British Government was, for various reasons, pressing at the same time for the urgent return of Gibraltar evacuees. London, in particular, had also an acute shortage of accommodation which from the British Government point of view was one of the reasons for the urgent return of the evacuees.

A Resettlement Board was set up to deal with all matters affecting the repatriation. The first meeting of this body was held in early December 1943. The Secretary of the Board was Mr Derek Alexander Lucas. The two main tasks of the Board were to draw up a list of evacuees in the three different locations and to establish the priority rules for the repatriation of about 16,000 evacuees.

The Governor in his 1943-44 New Year's message said that his intention was to start the process of repatriation as soon as possible but without making any commitment as to any specific date. He also mentioned that the decision of setting out the priorities was going to be left to the local repatriation committee but that the first priority would be given to those evacuees who had near relatives or dependants that remained in Gibraltar during the war. In the next column is an extract of Governor's Speech in relation to the repatriation.

Repatriation As Soon As Conditions Permit

The Governor's Message—From Page Two

Nothing in this world is perfect. War must inevitably produce hardships and abnormal situations. It is asking much of a community to separate the major portion of it from the remainder; to separate families from their men for three and a half years; and to settle these families in conditions of housing, food and life generally very different from those to which they have been accustomed.

Cordial Relations

I am satisfied that this is very fully realised by most of those responsible for our evacuated families in London. Quite frankly, in most of the centres I found a very happy family spirit, and the relations between your families and those in charge of the administration of the centres were in most cases delightfully cordial and friendly. In one or two cases where I found definite overcrowding the families concerned had been offered more spacious accommodation, but they refused to move to another centre as they were very happy where they were and did not want to leave the staff of the centre they were in.

On the food side much has been done to provide items normally not procurable in England, and the rations are good and plentiful. The children, especially, are extremely well looked after and get plenty of milk. In most centres they have very cheerful nurseries. Plenty of entertainment was being provided over the Christmas season, and in many cases the children were rehearsing shows of their own.

THE Calpe Institute for boys — in which, as in many activities, Major Patron has given much assistance—is a great success and a very nice place. Many of those in the centres have found occupations — many of them in war work. I spoke with a fair number and all seemed well satisfied with their work and conditions. I talked individually and collectively with many of your relatives and friends — far too many to remember them individually or to bring you messages from them.

I spoke in Spanish to many of the older ones who in contrast to the younger generation have not made much progress in English. I found them all remarkably cheerful, they had practically no grouses except minor ones, were on the best of terms with those in charge of the centres and had only one main and oft-repeated question: "When can we get back to Gibraltar?"

As I've already told you, that was one of the main objects of my visit. It is my firm intention to commence repatriation as soon as the progress of the war and the shipping situation permits. In this I had the wholehearted support of all the ministries involved, with whom I discussed the situation.

Provisional Dates

We got down to fixing provisionally a good deal of detail. Priorities will be left to our local repatriation committee here. First priorities will be the near relatives and dependents of all of you who have born the heat and burden of the day out here for the past three and a half years. Jamaica will get highest possible priority in the earlier categories.

We fixed provisional numbers and dates. We discussed rebuilding and new building problems here. In fact we went a long way towards setting the ball rolling. But in wartime there are always unforeseen factors. And I am not going to make any definite promises until final decisions have been taken at home and the word go has been given I don't want to give you cause for disappointment and I don't intend to do so.

But I can give you this one assurance. That all the ministries concerned in London are now determined to commence repatriation just as soon as the many factors involved make it possible for the War Cabinet to give a definite decision. We are a very great deal nearer the realisation of our hopes than we were a year ago. For my part, I and the local Government are going right ahead and flat-out to ensure that all possible preliminary work and arrangements are completed so that when we get the word we can go right ahead. As I told you, I am promising absolutely nothing. But I hope and pray personally that it won't be long . . .

In wishing you all, individually, happiness and the best of good fortune in the New Year, I wish also that your hopes may come true.

As from early 1944 the administrative authorities and those who remained behind had most of its attention on the repatriation of the evacuees. In addition to the priorities given to the different group of evacuees there was also the question of deciding at which rate the evacuees were going to be allowed to return. This last aspect of the repatriation, as will be seen, was going to prove the most difficult task ahead.

As from the very outset the British Government was insisting that the evacuees should return to Gibraltar at a rate which the Government of Gibraltar was unable to cope with. In early March an official notice as shown below was placed in every evacuation centre in London. As can be seen from this notice, arrangements were being made to repatriate evacuees as soon as possible upon the availability of ships and that it would take some time to complete the whole repatriation.

Below copy of notice issued to all evacuation centres in London.

It is nearly four years since a large proportion of civil population was evacuated from Gibraltar. This evacuation was rendered necessary solely in the interest of the prosecution of the war, and it has always been the intention that evacuees should be repatriated as soon as the war situation permitted. Arrangements are now being made for a limited number of evacuees to return to Gibraltar. At present these arrangements apply only to the evacuees in the United Kingdom. They will be extended in due course to those in Madeira and Jamaica also.

It must be clearly stated that no promises can be given regarding the repatriation arrangements. Progress will depend upon the availability of ships for the journey and to the extend to which accommodation can be released and made ready in Gibraltar. It will probably be a considerable time before all the evacuees can return. But a beginning is in sight. The selection of individuals and families for repatriation is in the hands of a Committee in Gibraltar. Those selected for the first party will be notified immediately.

Following this official notice, an article appeared in the Gibraltar Chronicle on the 11th March 1944 described as a "Decision behind the Agreement." Below is an extract from this article.

FAMILY REUNION BEFORE REBUILDING

Gib. Plan Speeded Up

Gib. Plan Speeded Up

By Chronicle Staff Reporter

SUBJECT TO THE OVERRIDING CONSIDERATION OF SHIPPING, UPON WHICH THE WHOLE SCHEME DEPENDS, DETAILED PLANS HAVE NOW BEEN COMPLETED FOR THE REUNION IN GIBRALTAR OF ALL FAMILIES SEPARATED FOR MORE THAN THREE YEARS BY COMPULSORY WAR-MEASURE EVACUATION.

IN the hands of Ministerial departments in Whitehall today is a complete list of priorities, on the basis of which this great family reunion move will be carried out.

This list has been compiled by the Resettlement Board in Gibraltar after an exhaustive analysis of the recent civilian repatriation census.

All arrangements which it is possible to make from now on for the return of wives, children and dependants from all evacuation centres—London, Jamaica and Madeira—will involve a strict application of the priorities which the list lays down.

Behind the official announcement yesterday that initial steps have been taken for the first party of evacuated Gibraltar civilians to return lies a decision which affects the whole policy of planning Gibraltar's future:

Board's Big Task

The return of families has precedence over all schemes of reconstruction, even to the extent of risking inconvenience owing to lack of adequate accommodation.

The priorities affect principally the wives, children and other dependants of married men who have remained in the colony on essential work throughout the war, and the near relatives — mothers, fathers, sisters, brothers — of unmarried men similarly placed.

Extract from the Gibraltar Chronicle announcing the arrangements for repatriation.

A day after this article appeared in the Gibraltar Chronicle, a statement was issued by the Colonial office in Gibraltar warning the evacuees of the inadequate living conditions in Gibraltar by pointing out that it was more overcrowded, shabbier and uncomfortable than ever. That those who wished to return early would have to put up with very adverse accommodation facilities. That although the Gibraltar Government did not wish to delay their return unnecessarily, it would have to postpone the repatriation for years in order to remedy living conditions in Gibraltar. The statement also stressed that essential commodities like food, clothing furniture and other household goods were very scarce and expensive. That there were no educational facilities and that it would take some time before they could be provided at a satisfactory standard. The statement ended that the warning was not issued to discourage evacuees from returning but to make them fully aware of what to expect if they decided to be repatriated and advised them to have patience until conditions could be improved. Names of families selected for repatriation were placed in their respective evacuation centres in the UK. Below is, as an example, the copy of the notice placed at the York Hotel.

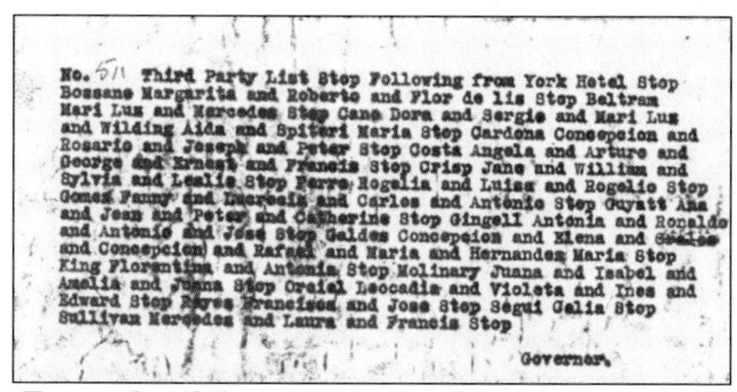

No. 511 Third Party List Stop Following from York Hotel Stop Bossano Margarita and Roberto and Flor de lis Stop Beltran Mari Luz and Mercedes Stop Cano Dora and Sergio and Mari Luz and Wilding Aida and Spiteri Maria Stop Cardona Concepcion and Rosario and Joseph and Peter Stop Costa Angela and Arturo and George and Ernest and Francis Stop Crisp Jane and William and Sylvia and Leslie Stop Ferro Rogelia and Luisa and Rogelio Stop Gomez Fanny and Lucrecia and Carlos and Antonio Stop Guyatt Ana and Jean and Peter and Catherine Stop Gingell Antonia and Ronaldo and Antonio and Jose Stop Galdes Concepcion and Elena and [illegible] and Concepcion and Rafael and Maria and Hernandez Maria Stop King Florentina and Antonia Stop Molinary Juana and Isabel and Amelia and Juana Stop Orciel Leocadia and Violeta and Ines and Edward Stop Reyes Francisca and Jose Stop Segui Celia Stop Sullivan Mercedes and Laura and Francis Stop

Governor.

Example of the repatriation lists that appeared in the evacuation centres in London. Source Gibraltar Government Archives.

During the initial stages of the repatriation arrangements, London was again being heavily bombarded, giving credence to the British Government's view that the evacuees should leave London soonest. By that time the approximate number of evacuees to be repatriated from the different destinations was as shown below.

UK	12,000	Madeira	2,000
Jamaica	1,500	Tangier	700
Spain	100		

Approximate total to be repatriated : 16,300.

As explained at the end of the previous page when the repatriation of the first party was being planned, London was again under a series of sustained bombing attacks. Many evacuation centres were affected in a spate of bombing which became known as the "baby blitz." During that period Whitelands College, Kings College, Hyde Park Gate Hotel, the Constance Hotel and the Royal Stuart Hotel evacuation centres were damaged by the bombing but fortunately there were no casualties or serious injuries. However, all the evacuees living in these centres which totalled more than 1,100 had to be found alternative accommodation when there was already a severe shortage of useable buildings. In order to deal with this difficult situation many evacuees were being transferred by mid March 1944 to transit camps in Chorley in Lancashire or Neilston and Bridge of Weir, in Renfrewshire, Scotland for their safety and to await their earliest repatriation opportunity. Although ships were still urgently needed for the war, some troopships were becoming available and the opportunity was taken to make full use of convoys on the way to Gibraltar to repatriate the evacuees from UK. According to the Secretary of the Evacuation Reunion Association in the UK one of their members, Miss Maisie Prest, who helped with the evacuation of British children had also volunteered to help organise the welfare of Gibraltar children and adults, who as she put it, was hard to believe that they had spent four years of the war in London before being transferred to Scotland.

Miss Maisie Prest

The first party of repatriates from UK totalled 1,367. They spent about a few weeks at Neilston and then were taken to Greenock to sail on the **Duchess of Richmond** and the **Antenor** with 1,170 and 197 repatriates respectively.

The SS Duchess of Richmond as it was about to berth. Photo Mr J Morello

One evacuee remembers that the journey took about 5 days and a Royal Navy destroyer escorted them all the way to Gibraltar with fine weather throughout the whole journey. The ships arrived on the night of the 5th April 1944 and dropped anchors in the Bay of Gibraltar.

The SS Antenor. Photo Old Ship Gallery

In the morning of the following day which was Maundy Thursday the 6th April 1944 the ships berthed near to where the three-legged crane used to be in the dockyard. Then the evacuees were allowed to disembark and taken by army lorries to their respective dwelling places.

Evacuees on board the Duchess of Richmond. In the forefront are Mrs Canepa and her son Joe (ex-commissioner of police). Photo Mrs M Summerfield

As expected there was a lot of jubilation in town when the ships arrived in port with the first contingent of evacuees. The families of those evacuated were naturally waiting to welcome their arrival.

The following is a reproduced cutting from the Gibraltar Chronicle of Thursday 6th April 1944.

The employers had granted the relatives special leave for the special occasion. The evacuees had made the journey under the supervision of Miss Edge of the Ministry of Health assisted by Mr and Mrs Jackson of the same department. The ship's captain told the Chronicle that the evacuees had collected £12 to purchase books for the ship's company as a memento and token of their gratitude.

The photograph above shows Miss Elena Chini talking with a Gibraltar Chronicle reporter. Photo Mr M Infante

The first evacuee to disembark from the **Duchess of Richmond** was Miss Elena Chini. Behind her came her mother Mrs Antonia Chini.

Below is an extract from the interview given by a reporter from the Gibraltar Chronicle to Miss Elena Chini - the first evacuee to disembark. "We are very happy to be home. We thank God and England for our safe return." Miss Chini said that she had been working on war production at an English factory in London.
Mrs Margarita Barcio aged 64, who was the third repatriated to leave the ship said. "How glad I am to be back in my Rock again." She too was from the Courtlands Evacuation Centre in Richmond.

The children, whose age ranged from two years to eight, were soon scrambling ashore and before long the parties had been taken to dispersal points and quickly whisked away to their homes by excited relatives and friends.
All the repatriates agreed that it had been a splendid trip. One of the ship's crew expressed the feelings of the remainder when he said: "I wish we were always on the Evacuee Run."

Below a cutting from the Richmond and Twickenham Times of Saturday 22nd April 1944.

AT HOME AGAIN.

Gibraltarians Welcomed at "The Rock."

Mrs. Woodley, of 14, Manor-road, has kindly sent us the following extract from a letter written by her son, L.A.C. K. E. Woodley, who is with the R.A.F. at Gibraltar, telling of the return home of Gibraltarians who were evacuated to this country five years ago. Some of them had lived at Courtlands, Richmond. The letter, written on Good Friday, stated:

The first batch of evacuees to return found wet weather, but rather warmer than England. Spirits amongst the Gibraltarian menfolk ran very high—they have done for some time past; but the actual arrival ——! The number although not very large is noticeable in town, for it is very strange to see youngsters, and stranger still to see English style of clothes, after the persistent black of the Spanish. When they came from the dockyard to the City Hall everywhere around that neighbourhood was full of waving arms, handkerchiefs, tears, laughter, surprised looks on the faces of five-year-olds on "seeing" Gib. (home!) for the first time. The parents were speaking "Spanish," but the kids still talk English, so we can understand (?) them.

Transport was provided for the repatriates by the military authorities who quickly conveyed the families to the four allocated transit centres and other dispersal points.
The Governor was thanked by the AACR publicly through a letter in the Gibraltar Chronicle for having arranged the repatriation of the Gibraltar evacuees.

Below is another extract from the Gibraltar Chronicle

FIRST TIME ON THE ROCK

"Babies born in England who had not seen the Rock before were among the most interesting of the home coming party. To them Gibraltar was as strange as England had been to the evacuees in 1940.
The first official who arrived to greet the travellers was the Colonial Secretary, Mr. Miles Clifford, who addressed them over the ships' loud-speakers. His Excellency the Governor and Commander-in-Chief, Lieut. General Sir Ralph Eastwood arrived as the evacuees began to disembark and went aboard one of the ships."

Photo above shows some of the evacuees arriving on the tender from the SS Antenor. Photo Mrs C Cavill.

Below Mrs Vella and her daughter Loli disembarking. Photo Mr J Asquez

Chronicle Staff Reporter

VARIED in all other respects, reactions of the first 1,400 evacuees on returning to Gibraltar after their three-and-a-half-year stay in England are unanimously similar on one point—appreciation of the preparations made to receive them.

Yesterday I toured the four special transit centres—Hotel Cecil, Gaviño's, Loretto Convent North and St. Mary's Senior School—and found satisfaction among those who have had to occupy temporary homes which, although perhaps not ideal, are at least clean and comfortable.

Most successful are the dining arrangements at the Cecil, where 1,650 meals are being served daily, with no time wasted between sittings and—up to now—no complaints received.

★

LOCAL business firms are cooperating with the authorities and an exceptionally high standard of catering has been achieved.

Presented free of charge on Thursday were 60 dozen tins of beer and 100 bottles of cordials by Messrs. Saccone and Speed, in addition to refreshments also supplied by Messrs. Baglietto and Company. Completing the day's gifts were 600 lbs. of fish and 100 lbs. of prawns from Mr. Abelardo Escobar.

Lunch yesterday comprised four courses—including the best butter—and equalled that obtainable in the best of Gibraltar's hotels.

Rapidly gaining great popularity with the returned evacuees is the Cecil's restaurant superintendent, S.Q.M.S. Frank Pooley of the R.A.S.C. (EFI). Tireless in his efforts, Pooley has succeeded where failure would have been easy.

HIS Excellency the Governor, Lieut.-General Sir Ralph Eastwood, chats with the returned families on the quayside.

HOW do people find Gibralta after nearly four years' ab sence? It would appear tha there are two distinct schools o thought on this subject.

First there are the ideas—ver definite—of the older generation Thankful to be home, they stil find Gibraltar the best place in th world, although England's kind ness is something they will al ways remember.

The citizens of tomorrow, how ever, seem to have doubts. Cer tainly they are glad to be back but the exigency of war has show them wonders which the Gibralta of today has little to rival.

London was a city of glamou and excitement which does no slip so easily away from the mind of youth as from those of thei elders. Frankly many young Gil raltarians would like—some day—to return to the heart of the En pire of which they are a sma but important part.

ONE significant benefit derive by youth from its stay i England has been a fluency in th English language. Take, for ir stance, little eight-year-old Pete Aguilera, with whom I chatte yesterday.

Peter started school in England and soon was speaking English so well that even his own family were occasionally puzzled. On such occasions, however, Peter would obligingly switch back into Spanish.

During our talk Peter told me what he thought of England — "all right but not so good as here" — while at the same time backchatting over his shoulder to his father in Spanish.

Pleasant changes for all concerned are the absence of blackout and Gibraltar's climate. There has been rain since their arrival but, as they point out, "this is nothing compared to winter in London with its frost and fog."

Above ,among the first group of repatriates awaiting transport to their place of abode , are Tony Perera and his sister Silvia

A helping hand – a smile - reunion

Above and on the left typical scenes as the first of the Gibraltar's evacuated families came home – a helping hand from the transport that took them from the ships to the dispersal points; a smile from one of the young generation, glad to be home.

Family reunion

Below: Raining, but the weather could not check the smiles of the evacuees as they landed.

The photo above and below show the first repatriates who arrived on the SS Antenor landing at North Mole.

Above photo Mrs C Cavill

In this are some clippings from the Gibraltar Chronicle showing the arrival of the first repatriates.

Clipping from the Gibraltar Chronicle showing one of the many children born in Britain arrive in Gibraltar for first time.

JOURNEY'S END—a group of evacuees alight at a dispersal point to meet their menfolk.

In the photo Angeles and Hector Gomez re-united near their place of abode in Irish Town after 4 years of separation. Photo Mr J.Victory-Gomez.

Evacuees taken to their places of abode by settlement personnel PC Joseph Danino and Mr Oscar Chichon. Photo Royal Gibraltar Police. Below cutting from Gibraltar Chronicle.

Gibraltar Is A Town Of Smiles Today: Big Welcome For Evacuees

THERE HAVE NOT BEEN SO MANY HAPPY FACES IN GIBRALTAR FOR AS LONG AS ONE CAN REMEMBER AS THERE WERE TODAY WHEN THE FIRST 1,400 EVACUEES RETURNED TO THEIR HOMES AFTER 3½ YEARS' ABSENCE IN ENGLAND.

IT was Gibraltar's Good Thursday—and the biggest "Easter Egg" anyone could wish to have. If the town was not bedecked with flags, it was certainly wreathed in happy and contented smiles.

Fathers, husbands and other relatives of families evacuated since 1940 gathered at the allotted points in the town early this morning to welcome these first arrivals.

Meeting of the Alvarez family after four long years.

By about the beginning of May 1944 the authorities in London had already plans well in hand for the repatriation of the second group of about 500 evacuees mainly because of the shortage of accommodation in London from where there were already reports of many cases of people squatting. Coinciding with the repatriation of this group of evacuees from London was the preparations by the Allies for the invasion of Normandy which was obviously bound to clash with the repatriation process. In the meantime these evacuees were being taken to the transit centres in Scotland and the north of England as can be seen from the Ilford Recorder cuttings.

Evacuee children lying flowers at Dr Barnardo's Tomb. In the photo are left to right Hubert Corby, Victor Schembri and Doris Corby (Mrs Parody.) Photo Mrs D Parody

Below a cutting from the Ilford Recorder showing the evacuees leaving Dr Barnardo's

ILFORD SAYS GOOD-BYE TO GIBRALTARIANS

Before departing for their own country, after nearly four years here, a group of Gibraltarians in Dr. Barnardo's Village Homes, Barkingside, laid flowers at the foot of the memorial of Dr. Barnardo, for, as was said by one of them, "Looking after us and guiding us while the enemy was striking hard."

In the Village Homes on Friday, the Mayor of Ilford, Alderman Russell Daniels, Councillor A. W. Green, and members of the House Committee said farewell to 80 Gibraltarians who were departing.

Standing under chestnut trees, on the edge of their football pitch while the sun was streaming down, the Gibraltarians cheered the speakers as complimentary remarks were made of how they had been moved from one danger area to another in the first days of the war, and how they had lived in Ilford, and made the best of it.

Councillor Green said, "On behalf of the borough we would like to say goodbye before you go back to Gibraltar. I am very pleased to see you have laid flowers at the memorial of Dr. Barnardo. It was many years ago that I knew Dr. Barnardo, and I can honestly say there was never a finer man. He started these homes with practically no money at all, and worked till they grew into something more than a place for children without parents.

"You are British. You have simply come from one part of the Empire to another, and we have done our best to treat you the same way as our own people. We have tried to educate your kiddies as our own, and have given them the same opportunities regarding secondary schools and elementary schools. They have had an excellent teacher, Mr. Emmett (loud cheers), who undoubtedly has done his best for you."

The Mayor said "For the Gibraltarian children in years to come, their stay in Dr. Barnardo's home will bring back pleasant memories that will be passed on to their children. We have done our best for you in the Homes, and on behalf of the borough we wish you a speedy safe return home."

Members of the house committee made speeches wishing their fellow people a safe journey, and hoping to be with them in Gibraltar very soon.

Mr. F. W. Emmett, the shoolmaster, who appeared to be enormously popular, was asked to say a few words. He said, "I would like to say that I and other teachers, have done our best for the kiddies. It was 12 years ago that I went to Gibraltar, never dreaming in years to come I would be teaching you in Ilford. In the near future I will come to Gibraltar and look some of you up."

Councillor Green reported on their departure at the Ilford Education Committee on Monday, and referred to the spontaneous gesture of the children in placing flowers on the tomb of Dr. Barnardo.

The Mayor described the scene, and Alderman Braithwaite spoke of his visits to the Homes.

Councillor G. F. Tyler said he would like to pay a tribute to Mr. Emmett and his staff, who had done wonders under difficulties. "They will go back with a greater opinion than ever they had of this country," he said.

The next cutting on the left from the Ilford Recorder of the 18th May 1944 refer to the Gibraltar evacuees when they were leaving Dr Barnardo's Homes on their transfer to Neilston.

In a broadcast on the 25th May 1944, came the bombshell, when the Governor referred to the effect of a recent ban on travelling from the United Kingdom and the disappointment felt by everyone concerned. The Governor said it was the start of a decisive period of the war, and it was therefore necessary to suffer restrictions and also disappointments. He made particular mention of the evacuated families in Jamaica, who, he said, were uppermost in the thoughts of the Government but that their return at the moment depended on shipping. The reason for the priority given to those in Jamaica was because owing to distance they had been unable to be visited by relatives in Gibraltar within the Special Leave Scheme. Before the broadcast the Governor told reporters that the people of Gibraltar could hope to have a bigger say in the management of their own affairs in the future and that plans for the advancement of social welfare, education, and labour conditions were under consideration by the Colonial Office. He also said that he thought that the people of Gibraltar would have to undertake greater responsibilities and that they might be expected to play a permanent part in the defence of the Rock.

“We Thank God and England..”

As mentioned in the previous page, because of the travelling restrictions from the United Kingdom and the lack of shipping from Jamaica, the Governor had suggested to the Colonial Office in the UK to allow instead for the return of about 1,000 evacuees from Madeira. This suggestion to repatriate the bulk of the evacuees in Madeira was also made in order to cushion the effects of the disappointment felt in Gibraltar about the delay in repatriating evacuees in the UK. Local poet Alberto Pizzarello composed a poem for this occasion and which I have reproduced below:

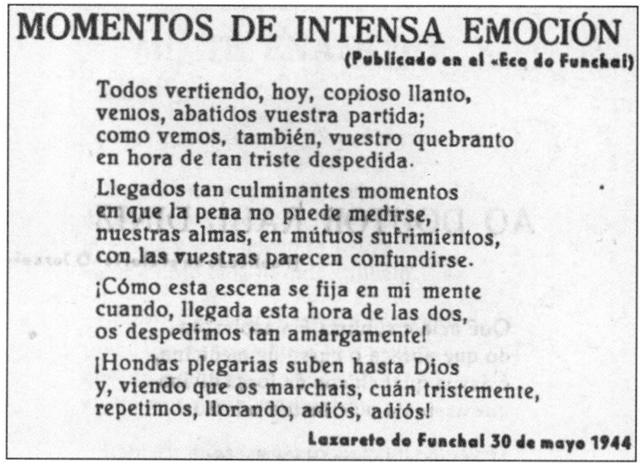

MOMENTOS DE INTENSA EMOCIÓN

(Publicado en el «Eco do Funchal)

Todos vertiendo, hoy, copioso llanto,
vemos, abatidos vuestra partida;
como vemos, también, vuestro quebranto
en hora de tan triste despedida.

Llegados tan culminantes momentos
en que la pena no puede medirse,
nuestras almas, en mútuos sufrimientos,
con las vuestras parecen confundirse.

¡Cómo esta escena se fija en mi mente
cuando, llegada esta hora de las dos,
os despedimos tan amargamente!

¡Hondas plegarias suben hasta Dios
y, viendo que os marchais, cuán tristemente,
repetimos, llorando, adiós, adiós!

Lazareto do Funchal 30 de mayo 1944

Copy of poem by Mrs Martin.

Members of the Jewish community in Funchal waiting to board the SS Indrapoera. Photo Mr M Belilo

Group of evacuees preparing to depart. Photo Mr L Pereira

Above the SS Indrapoera and two escort destroyers getting reading to leave Funchal. Photo Mr J Chincotta

The first party of evacuees from Madeira totalling 977 arrived at Gibraltar on board the Dutch ship **SS Indrapoera** on the 31st May 1944.

The SS Indrapoera. Photo Old Ship Gallery

The Destroyer HMS Vanoc. Old Ship Gallery

By that time a good number of evacuees in Madeira were also making their own private arrangements either to move to Spain or to Tangier. On the same day that the evacuees arrived from Madeira, it was announced that all Gibraltarian males between the ages of 18 and 22, including returned evacuees not engaged in war work, would be called up for six months' military service as A.A. gunners in the Gibraltar Defence Force embodied since the outbreak of war. The destroyer **HMS Vanoc** shown in the photograph above and other destroyers escorted the **SS Indrapoera** to Gibraltar. In the next column are the photographs of evacuees arriving at Gibraltar onboard the **SS Indrapoera**. With the arrival of this first group there still remained about 700 evacuees in Madeira. As soon as the families of those remaining in Madeira were able to provide adequate accommodation in Gibraltar arrangements were made to repatriate them. Many of these evacuees as will be explained in the next pages took four long years to return to Gibraltar. During this time, some of them made their trip first to Lisbon and then arrived in Gibraltar by travelling overland.

Evacuees Arriving At Gibraltar on the Indrapoera In the photo are W.Pissani J.Chiappe and sister, .Julie Canepa (nee Dobinson), John and Arthur Chincotta, Amelia McClaren (nee Parody), Jane Farrugia, Charo Llufrio (nee Vinent), the Macedo sisters, Mrs Chincotta, Maruja and Vitoty Cassaglia. Photo Mr J Chincotta

In front are the Caetano family Isabel, Maria and Isobelita Caetano also in the photo is Angela Jane Clancy. Photo Mrs Dalmedo (nee Caetano)

The photographs and the Gibraltar Chronicle cuttings on this page show the first contingent of evacuees to arrive from Madeira on the 31st May 1944.

Above evacuees onboard the Indrapoera getting ready to disembark. In the photo are Vivienne Llufrio, John Rosales and Victor Balloqui. Photo Miss S Moya

An elderly evacuee disembarking

MORE EVACUEES COME HOME

BACK from Madeira after four years' evacuation, about 1,000 Gibraltarians were welcomed by His Excellency the Governor and Lady Eastwood when they disembarked yesterday.

Pictures, story—Page 3

The photograph above shows the Governor of Gibraltar, Sir Ralph Eastwood and his wife meeting some of the evacuees as they disembarked from the SS Indrapoera.

JUST a few of the 1,000 who returned, waiting for transport after disembarking from the repatriation ship. Everyone was glad to be home, but full of appreciation of the treatment accorded them in Madeira.

Evacuees returning from Madeira.

4 YEARS IS A LONG TIME: AND THEN THE

Boy who came home got 'lost'

Chronicle Staff Reporter

THIRTEEN - YEAR - OLD Felix Ernest Pizzarello came home after four years in Madeira—and got 'lost.'

Most of the 1,000 Gibraltarians who came back yesterday had disembarked. It was a smooth, uneventful disembarkation. It began ahead of schedule. And it was going well.

Then Mrs. Pizzarello stood on the quayside, looked around, and said: "Where is my son?"

Mysterious . . .

TRANSPORT was waiting to take Mrs. Pizzarello to Scud Hill. Her disembarkation card was numbered 9, and there at No. 9 transport stand was the Scud Hill party. But Felix Pizzarello was missing.

His card had also been marked 9. But mysteriously, in the short time that it took to get from the ship to the waiting trucks, it had got altered to 14.

Someone had decided that the only destination Master Pizzarello could have was Catalan Bay. And the Catalan Bay transport left No. 14 stand.

Mr. E. Pizzarello, Registrar of Gibraltar Supreme Court, was waiting patiently at Scud Hill for the arrival of his family. Four years is a long time.

No, not here

THE position on the quayside was explained. His Excellency the Governor heard of the affair. gave instructions: "Send a car at once to Catalan Bay and have the boy brought back."

At Catalan Bay the truck from stand No. 14 had safely transported its passengers. Families clambered down to be welcomed by their menfolk.

Still on the lorry was Felix Pizzarello. No, they said, he doesn't belong to Catalan Bay. Forty other Pizzarellos might. But not Felix.

At Scud Hill Mr. Pizzarello was waiting.

Driver decides

OFFICIALS were despatched. Everything would be put right. The disembarkation must go on. Transport could not be delayed.

So Mrs. Pizzarello boarded the lorry at No. 9 stand, left the welfare of her lost son to those who were hot on the scent, and set off to meet her husband.

At Scud Hill she was welcomed by Mr. Pizzarello, who had been waiting four years. And by Master Felix Pizzarello who had been waiting four minutes. In either case, it seemed a long time.

Waiving regulation schedules, the driver of the truck had decided that if Felix Pizzarello, back from Madeira, belonged to Scud Hill and not to Catalan Bay, then to Scud Hill he should go.

So the boy who got lost got there first. "*Someone*," he said, "altered my card."

Well treated

YESTERDAY'S party was the second to return to Gibraltar since the resettlement scheme began earlier this year. Of the colony's 15,000 evacuees about 2,400 are now home.

About 500 remain in Madeira, where—say those who landed yesterday—the treatment they have been accorded during the past four years has been exceptionally satisfactory.

On the left hand column is a cutting from the Gibraltar Chronicle of Thursday 1 June 1944 reporting the missing of thirteen-year-old boy Felix Pizzaerello who was sent by mistake to Catalan Bay when he arrived with his parents from Madeira. When the boy's parents reported him missing instructions were given by the Governor to bring the boy back from Catalan Bay where the boy had been taken by mistake.

As can be seen from the schedule shown below, some of the evacuees took a very long time to be repatriated. The main reason for this, as in the case of those who were in Northern Ireland, was the serious lack of accommodation, which prevented them from returning sooner to Gibraltar.

SHIP	DATE OF ARRIVAL	NUMBER OF EVACUESS
INDRAPOERA #	**31 MAY 1944**	**977**
LIMA *	**SEPTEMBER 1944**	**36**
LIMA *	**OCTOBER 1944**	**76**
LIMA *	**NOVEMBER 1944**	**21**
CABO DE HORNOS *	**APRIL 1945**	**134**
CARVALHO ARAUJO *	**MAY 1945**	**99**
BATORY #	**JUNE 1945**	**193**
LIMA *	**MARCH 1946**	**31**
LIMA *	**MAY 1948**	**32**

= Sailed directly to Gibraltar
* = Sailed to Lisbon then made it overland to Gibraltar

The Portuguese ship SS Lima. Photo Old Ship Gallery

The Portuguese ship **SS Lima** which made the usual run between Funchal and Lisbon was used at times to repatriate five separate groups of Gibraltar evacuees. From Lisbon these groups of evacuees had to travel overland via Spain to get to Gibraltar.

The **Cabo de Hornos** was a Spanish ship which was on her way back from her normal route from South America and called at Funchal on the 1st April 1945. Whilst there, 134 evacuees were embarked and then taken to Lisbon and hence travelled overland to Gibraltar.

The Spanish Liner Cabo De Hornos. Photo Old Ship Gallery

The Portuguese ship the SS Carvalho Araujo. Photo Old Ship Gallery

The sixths group of evacuees travelled on the **Carvalho Araujo** which was a Portuguese ship that made the run between Madeira and Lisbon. On the 11th May 1945 she called at Funchal on her regular schedule and took to Lisbon 99 evacuees who then returned overland to Gibraltar.

After a year there were still over 250 evacuees awaiting repatriation from Madeira. These evacuees returned in the following chronological order:

The Polish liner **Batory** which had brought back evacuees from the United Kingdom was then requisitioned to call at Funchal to repatriate 193 evacuees from Madeira on the 24th June 1945. After the return of these evacuees just over 60 evacuees remained in Madeira.

As there were only 10 pupils and two teachers, the British School for Gibraltar Children closed shortly after in July 1945. About half of these evacuees returned in March 1946 and the other half, that is, about 30 evacuees had to wait a further two years until May 1948. Both groups sailed from Funchal to Lisbon on the **SS Lima.**
Regrettably like everywhere there were evacuees who died and are buried in Funchal.

Below is a photograph of the Jewish Cemetery.

Jewish Cemetery at Funchal where some evacuees are buried as detailed below: Samuel M Benady (1940) Donna Hassan Bentata (1942) Abraham Benzecry (1943) David Cohen (1941) Esther Benaim Hassan (1942) Estrella Labos (1943) Modehay Labos (1942) Baruj Tobelemn (1942). Photo Mr M Belilo

The Christian cemetery at Santa Caterina is also shown in the photograph below. I have been informed that this cemetery has been modified since the time of the evacuation.

The photograph above shows Mrs Lima visiting her mother's resting place during one of her holidays in Madeira. Photo Mrs Lima.

When the first group of evacuees were repatriated from London there still about 10,000 left to repatriate. During the time that the second group of evacuees were being moved from London, there was increasing fear in Gibraltar that the Allied plan to invade Europe was bound to bring reprisals from Germany on South East England, especially in London. Feeling very concerned that these reprisals could cause many casualties among the Gibraltar evacuees, representatives from the Association for the Advancement of Civil Rights (AACR) were urging the Governor to remove the Gibraltar evacuees from London as soon as possible. When preparations were put in place for a gradual repatriation, the fears expressed in Gibraltar were realised as London was being attacked with flying bombs. Those evacuees who were destined to be repatriated continued to be moved either to Chorley in Lancashire or Neilston and Bridge of Weir in Scotland. My family was at the York Hotel when we received the news that we were going to be repatriated to Gibraltar. The order came a week or so after having witnessed the blasting effects of flying bomb which fell in Goodge Street. I think it was about the end of June 1944 when we left London from Euston Station. I remember when we were waiting for the train the air raid siren was sounded and we took shelter in the nearby underground. After, what seemed to me like an endless journey, we arrived at Euxton near Chorley during day time. We alighted from the train and walked across a field to the huts where we were going to be housed. The place consisted of rows of some sort of bungalows on the outskirts of the town not very far from the railway lines. During my research, I learned that the camp near Chorley was also very near a large munitions factory called the Royal Ordnance Factory in the village of Euxton.

The factory workers, I was told, used to mingle with the Gibraltar evacuees. They were mainly women who wore wooden shoes, similar to the Dutch clogs and their hands were usually stained with some sort of yellowish powder. I also found out that this yellowish stain was because of some chemicals normally used to make gunpowder and that the wooden shoes were worn to avoid the risk of any sparks through friction. I think we stayed there for just a few weeks but some of the evacuees like my mother managed to travel to Preston for shopping goods that could not be obtained in the village.

The huts in the transit camp at Chorley during 1940s
Photo : Francis Frith Collection and Chorley History Library.

In Gibraltar the families at that time were very concerned about the menace posed by the flying bombs. In view of this the AACR decided to hold a public demonstration in early July 1944.

2,000 take part in Gibraltar's demonstration

Chronicle Staff Reporter

TWO THOUSAND PEOPLE including women and children, took part last evening in a public demonstration designed to draw the attention of the authorities to the desire of the colony for the return of evacuated families without further delay.

Assembling in Market Place, they marched quietly through Main-street, where shops were closed and all business had temporarily halted, passed Government House and into Alameda where they dispersed in orderly fashion.

Banners carried at the head of the procession had such inscriptions as: "Bring our Dear ones before it is too Late"; "Jamaica is Hell"; "Ban must not Apply to our Evacuees"; "Free Women and Children from the Bombs."

The demonstration, held under the auspices of the Association for the Advancement of Civil Rights—whose President and Committee headed the march—passed off without any incidents, all orders from the Association's delegates being strictly obeyed.

Above report by the Gibraltar Chronicle on the public demonstration held by the AACR on the 4th July 1944.

About mid July 1944 we left Chorley by train bound for Glasgow. We arrived at Glasgow and soon after we were taken by bus to Greenock. Before boarding the ship we were given something to eat. I remember I had a plate of porridge with salt instead of sugar, as we normally have it. I must have been very hungry because I remember eating it all. From this place, which looked to me like a huge hangar, we proceeded to embark on the **Stirling Castle.**
Those evacuees who were sent either to Neilston or Bridge of Weir told me that they managed, on a few occasions, to travel to the nearby city of Glasgow. Since it was mid summer they also enjoyed viewing the beautiful scenery offered by the Scottish countryside. At Bridge of Weir the evacuees saw some prisoners of war near a farm and there was also a Polish camp in a place called the Johnstone Castle. The old and recent photographs of Bridge of Weir were donated by Mr Walter McAllister.

Old photograph of Bridge of Weir.

A postcard of Bridge Of Weir sent by an evacuee.
Postcard by Miss A Pardo

Some of the very young evacuees remember playing by the River Weir where they used to catch toads or slide down the bank slopes on top of corrugated iron sheets. Other youngsters also remember going in a farm near the camp to get some fresh vegetables.

A view of the huts in the camp.

The transit camp from the distance.

A recent view of the remaining buildings.

The church near the camp.

The transit camp at Neilston was very similar to that at Bridge of Weir. There was a wire fence surrounding the transit camp and some evacuees believe that this camp had been used before for prisoners of war. The huts had bunk beds and a few chairs. According to other evacuees whom I spoke with the evacuees were served communal food, which was not very much of the liking of most of the evacuees. In the mornings they usually had some porridge. The camp was near a railway station and nearby was an Oxo branch office and shop as shown in the photograph below.

Gibraltar Evacuees With The Staff of the Oxo Office near the Transit Camp at Neilston. At the back in the centre is Mrs Anna Hughes of the Oxo Office. The three boys at the back are left to right Jimmy Rosado, Louis Lombard and Willie Chamberland. The two boys in front are Francis Cotterill and Francis Apap. Photos above and belelow Mr William Chamberland

In the above photo from L to R.Willie Chamberland,Francis Apap,Jimmy Rosado,Louis Lombard,Galliano ,Francis Cotterill

There where were also many refugees of different nationalities, but mainly Norwegians, living in similar camps near the Gibraltar evacuee transit camp at Neilston. Some of the local people living near the camps were under the impression that the Gibraltar evacuees were from Malta.
During their short stay the evacuees made many friends from the surrounding neighbourhood as can be seen from the two photographs on this page.

According to the information given to me from my inquiries from the Scottish National Archives, the camps sites were removed between the late forties and early fifties. Mrs Noelia Peto visited Neilston in the late 50s when she took the photo below showing the remains of the camp site.

Mrs Peto (nee Povedano) by the remains of the once transit camps at Neilston in 1959. Photo Mrs N Peto

Leslie and Harold Wahnon with acquaintances in Neilston. Photo Mr L Wahnon

The Village of Neilston. Photo Mr M Infante

After the public demonstration held in Gibraltar on the 4th July 1944, the Colonial Office in the UK was insisting on the increasing agreed quota of repatriates to avoid casualties among the evacuees. By then four evacuees had already been killed by the flying bombs.

The Normandy Invasion 6th June 1944.
Photo US Army Center of Military History

The AACR also inquired from the Colonial Secretary that in view of the fact that British women and children were being evacuated from London what arrangements were being made to remove the Gibraltar evacuees whose early repatriation had been postponed. A few days later a couple of stories appeared in the Gibraltar Chronicle about the British women and children who were leaving London for safer places in England. One of the stories (shown in the next column) was published beside an official statement announcing the removal of all Gibraltar evacuees from London. The same day that this statement was made in the Gibraltar Chronicle two more Gibraltar evacuees were killed by flying bombs when they were preparing their luggage to be transferred to Northern Ireland. See Page 182.

Official statement

Following is the text of an official statement issued from the Colonial Secretariat:

"Arrangements have been made to move from the London area all evacuees remaining in evacuation centres."

Above copy of official statement.

Those evacuees who were not categorised for immediate repatriation to Gibraltar were being diverted to Liverpool from were they were sent directly to Northern Ireland. In early August 1944 it was announced that after the arrival of the first two contingents from the UK and the one from Madeira, the next in the priority list were the evacuees in Jamaica.

GIB. EVACUEES GOING TO NORTH IRELAND

THE Government of Northern Ireland have undertaken to accommodate nearly 8,000 evacuees from Gibraltar pending their repatriation, cabled Reuters correspondent in Belfast last night.

The evacuees, who arrived in London in August, 1940, will now be accommodated in camps in Northern Ireland. Belfast expects the first arrivals very shortly.

Below the story about Londoners Escaping from the flying bombs together with the heading about evacuees leaving for Northern Ireland.

The total number of women and children who have left London to escape the threat of the flying bombs is now more than 171,000.

Going smoothly

Reports from the Midlands and the North indicate that the billeting of the evacuees has, generally speaking, proceeded smoothly. Thus about 2,500 were billeted voluntarily at Kettering while compulsory powers were used to billet a further 250.

The Mayor of Blackpool said that about 1,600 children were found accommodation on the day they arrived in the town and 650 mothers and children were billeted the following day, with the exception of 13 mothers and their families who were billeted within 48 hours.

Huddersfield has taken 2,000 Londoners voluntarily and similar reports have come from many other centres.

Room with view

Nearly 1,000 dissatisfied evacuees have returned to their homes—not all of them with genuine grievances. For example, a party of 30 arrived at Lytham St. Annes in Lancashire and demanded to be billeted together and on the sea front. Because this was impossible they declined separate billets and returned to London.

In some instances, however, mothers have been billeted in what to Londoners must be regarded as very isolated spots.

The President of the Mineworkers Federation, Mr. W. Lawther, said yesterday: "The miners organisation will place all their welfare facilities at the disposal of mothers and children who have been evacuated from London."

In the Metropolitan area army patrols have mounted guard over the blasted shop of a jeweller where it was feared that priceless gems were being trodden underfoot in the debris.

Born in raid

Children were being shepherded from one school when the windows were blown out of their frames by an exploding flying bomb, but nobody was hurt.

Following the explosion of another bomb a woman was trapped in wreckage for over seven hours before being rescued alive. In another part of London a doctor was lowered three times into a bomb cavity to assist an aged woman, her son and daughter-in-law who had a baby aged 10 weeks.

At Dagenham a baby was born in an Anderson shelter while flying bombs were falling. Both mother and child are well.

The Stirling Castle carrying American troops as part of A United States military convoy in preparation for the D-Day Landing. Photos NARA

The Stirling Castle disembarking US Troops at Liverpool. Photo US Army Center of Military History

The **Stirling Castle** was due to sail on the 18th July 1944, the same day of the official announcement in the Gibraltar Chronicle that the all the evacuees were going to be removed from London. However, it turned out that **Stirling Castle** was unable to sail until the 26 July 1944. According to an official version the reason for the delay was due to mechanical trouble in the device, which converted seawater into fresh water. Others, when I talked to them about it, speculated that the reason for the delay was that it was waiting for clearance from the military authorities owing to possible enemy submarine activities on the scheduled route. There are others who believe that the reason was really that the **Stirling Castle** had to wait for the escorts to arrive but had been delayed due to unforeseen reasons. When it sailed it was carrying 3,161 repatriates making it the largest contingent of evacuees to be repatriated in a single trip. Both the **Stirling Castle** and her sister ship the **Athlone Castle** were built in 1936 with a tonnage of 25,550 grt.

In 1940 both ships were requisitioned for troopship duties and were capable of carrying 6,000 persons each in a single journey. In 1941 the **Stirling Castle** was kept on a 7-day standby, as part of a 12,000 strong force, in case it became necessary to occupy the Azores and/or the Canary Islands in case Gibraltar was captured. Towards the end of 1943 it started carrying troops from the United States to the United Kingdom as part of Operation Bolero in readiness for the D-Day landings. Shortly after this mission, the **Stirling Castle** was tasked to sail to Greenock from where she was to collect the second contingent of evacuees to be repatriated to Gibraltar from the United Kingdom. Her war services ended in 1945 having steamed over 500,000 miles and carried a total of 128,000 troops.

There is an anecdote which I found very humorous and which I feel I should narrate. After a long wait the **Stirling Castle** was finally slipping its moorings and moving very slowly from its berth. At that moment, someone noticed that there was a cat in the water struggling to stay afloat between the **Stirling Castle** and another ship in the harbour. Naturally, the cat had very soon caught the attention of most of the passengers on both ships. After a little while, someone in the tugboat, assisting the ships to move away from their berths, though of lowering a thick rope from one of the cranes. The cat, desperately trying to get out of the water, immediately grabbed the rope. Very carefully and with precise timing the cat was hoisted. There was then a tremendous applause from all the passengers, as the cat was brought to safety on the tug's deck.

After leaving the Princes Pier at Greenock, the **Stirling Castle** sailed through the River Clyde, and I recall that the ship moved very slowly as it negotiated along the narrow passages of the river and saw people along its bank.

The Princess Pier, Greenock.
Photo McLean Museum

The weather was fine with good visibility and we could see the distant highlands, which are characteristic of the Scottish regions. As soon as the **Stirling Castle** left the Firth of Clyde and entered the Irish Sea, war ships were waiting to escort her to Gibraltar. According to the Ministry of Defence sources, three war ships escorted the **Stirling Castle.** The warships were the **HMS Argonout,** a cruiser and two destroyers, **HMS Wakeful** and **Wager.** They escorted the **Stirling Castle** throughout the journey until it reached the proximity of the Strait of Gibraltar.
One evacuee remembers that during the journey there was an episode concerning a submarine. Apparently, this submarine popped suddenly out of the water creating a lot of panic among the passengers who were naturally very concerned not knowing whether it was friendly or foe. But very soon the passengers were put at ease when it was announced that it was a friendly submarine. The ship had no armament other than a few anti-aircraft guns, which were useless to repel any enemy submarines. There were the occasional exercises onboard to prepare for any eventuality that required the abandoning of the ship. This drill entailed the wearing of life saving jackets, the testing of its gadgets and also the orderly assembling on the upper deck to await instructions from the officers and crew. There were a few of these training sessions but fortunately the real need for this drill never materialised. The few guns that were mounted were also fired occasionally in exercises during the journey. Those who remember said that although the guns known as Pomp-Pomp guns were not very big, they nevertheless made a lot of noise since they were all firing at very short intervals simulating a real air attack.

A 'Pomp – Pomp" anti-aircraft gun.
Photo Wikipedia Free Encyclopedia

The cruiser HMS Argonout. Old Ship Gallery

The Destroyer HMS Wager. Old Ship Gallery

The destroyer HMS Wakeful. Old Ship Gallery

The **Stirling Castle** arrived on Tuesday 1 August 1944. As she was approaching the Bay of Gibraltar an RAF Sunderland, amphibious aircraft, flew a few times at low altitude near the **Stirling Castle**.

An RAF Sunderland amphibious aircraft.
Photo Wikipedia Free Encyclopedia.

She entered the Admiralty Harbour and berthed alongside the three-legged crane on that same morning with the repatriates remaining in the ship overnight.
I was then six years old and I remember it was very hot that night and many of the passengers remained for most of the night on the upper deck. Many of us, the children, stayed playing until very late on the upper deck.

Evacuees on the decks of the Stirling Castle.
Cutting from the Gibraltar Chronicle.

In the morning having been checked for identity and other requirements by the regulating authorities, the evacuees were finally allowed to disembark in the morning of Wednesday the 2nd August 1944. They were greeted by families and friends who had been eagerly waiting since very early in the morning for the repatriates to leave the ship.

Below the Gibraltar Chronicle mentioning the two evacuees who were born on the journey from Greenock to Gibraltar.

— THEY WERE BORN ON VOYAGE

HOME this morning: 3,161 Gibraltar evacuees, the eldest a lady of 89, the youngest—a boy eight days old and a girl five days old, hardly evacuees—both born on the voyage.

Stirling Lima was born on July 24, Hortensia Arsina on July 27. Captain of the repatriation ship presented a miniature silver cup to Stirling and a silver spoon to Hortensia on behalf of the ship.

Party is the third contingent of evacuees to disembark, the second from the United Kingdom since April 6. The journey, Miss Margaret Smailes, Ministry of Health official in personal charge of the party, told a Chronicle representative, was uneventful and "everyone endured it well."

Today's repatriation brings the total number of evacuees now home to 5,575—4,575 from the United Kingdom, about 1,000 from Madeira.

Still to be repatriated are 7,000 in the United Kingdom—6,800 now in Northern Ireland and 200 in London; 1,400 in Jamaica; 500 in Madeira; about 750 in Spain and Tangier.

Roughly 3,500 of the civilian population have remained in Gibraltar engaged in essential war work throughout the war.

Picture of the arrival by Official Photographer.

GIBRALTAR CHRONICLE
First Published 1801
2 Library Gardens. Tel.: A. 589/597.

WEDNESDAY, AUGUST 2, 1944.

RETRIBUTION

BY THEIR REPLY to Gen. Eisenhower's pledge to bring to swift justice those who commit atrocities against the resistance movement in France the Germans characteristically show their determination to continue what is by all laws nothing short of murder. Villages burn—and no German excuses or explanations can serve to cover the deliberate intent with which these acts are perpetrated.

We have already had the general pledge of the United Nations that those responsible shall be taken back to the scene of their crimes and there judged in accordance with the laws of the countries they have victimised. We have had a number of specific pledges, such as that to bring to justice those who murdered the 50 officers in Stalag Luft 3.

Gen. Eisenhower, however, was mainly concerned to save from murder those who are his own soldiers, for the French Army of the Interior is an integral part of the Allied Forces of which he is Supreme Commander. His pledge is made necessary by the savage order issued by Field-Marshal von Rundstedt on June 6, which threatened with summary execution all French people assisting the Allies in any way.

It is a disgraceful order, which reveals the fear of the oppressor for the oppressed. It has had terrible consequences, such as the massacre of Oradour; and no apologist can pretend, as some tried to do about the murder of the air forces officers, that a merciless Gestapo and not the German Army was responsible.

Above is a cutting from the Gibraltar Chronicle referring to comments by General Eisenhower about crimes being committed by the Germans.

In front to the right is Mrs Rodriguez (nee Rocca). Photo Mrs Rodriguez

Group on the left: Mrs Antonia Povedano with her daughters Noelia, Mercy, Etty and Lilian. PhotoMrs N Peto

In the photo are Mrs Clemencia Sene, Mrs Martinez (Mrs Sene's mother) Lilian Sene (Mrs Baglietto) Cecil and Nobert Sene Photo Mrs L Baglietto

In the photo are MariaSantos (Brooks), Antonia Santos, Joseph Santos (Pepin), Margot Santos (Pizarro) and Mrs Hortencia Spiteri. Photo Mr J Lima

Passengers disembarking from the Stirling Castle.
In the foreground Miss Lourdes Reading (later Mrs McGrail).
Photo Mrs McGrail

After disembarking, the passengers were taken to their respective place of abode in army lorries. My family were temporarily accommodated at the Cecil Hotel in Main Street. I remember that when we had settled down, my father had ordered special lunch for us at the Grand Hotel (where Barclays is now), near to the Cecil Hotel. The dining table was dressed with a bowl of grapes and a sugar melon already sliced. This immediately captured my attention; I had never seen these fruits before! I remember that very near the Cecil Hotel there was the Majestic Store where I think the Star of India is presently. I used to go there when my mother wanted anything from the grocers. See the prices of fruits and vegetables then in the next column.

Evacuees being taken to their place of residence.
Photo the Bula family.

By that time, in view of the fact that about 6,000 evacuees had already returned, the Colonial Office had announced that improved educational facilities had been planned by a committee in Gibraltar in preparation for the return of the children from England, Jamaica, and Madeira. One of the main recommendations made by this committee, and which had been accepted by the Secretary of State for the Colonies, was the immediate appointment of a director of education.

The new appointed director was to be Dr. W. H. Howes Ph.D., Principal of the Norwich City College and Arts School, who would be leaving for Gibraltar as soon as possible.
His first duty on arrival was going to be to advise on emergency arrangements for the schooling of children who had already returned.

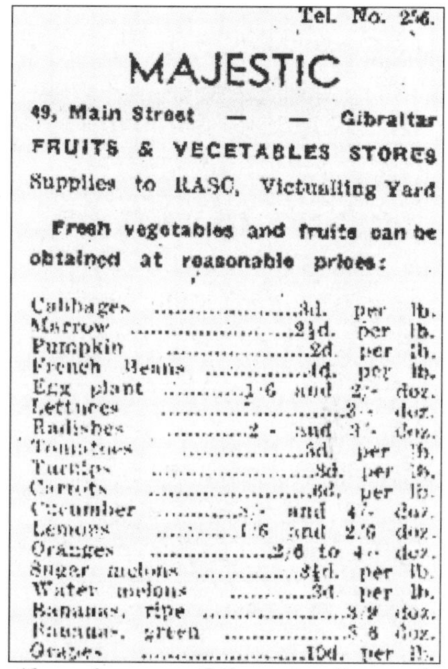

Tel. No. 256.

MAJESTIC

49, Main Street — — Gibraltar

FRUITS & VEGETABLES STORES

Supplies to RASC, Victualling Yard

Fresh vegetables and fruits can be obtained at reasonable prices:

Cabbages ....3d. per lb.
Marrow ....2½d. per lb.
Pumpkin ....2d. per lb.
French Beans ....4d. per lb.
Egg plant ....1/6 and 2/- doz.
Lettuces ....3/- doz.
Radishes ....2/- and 3/- doz.
Tomatoes ....5d. per lb.
Turnips ....3d. per lb.
Carrots ....6d. per lb.
Cucumber ....3/- and 4/- doz.
Lemons ....1/6 and 2/6 doz.
Oranges ....2/6 to 4/- doz.
Sugar melons ....3½d. per lb.
Water melons ....3d. per lb.
Bananas, ripe ....3/9 doz.
Bananas, green ....3/6 doz.
Grapes ....10d. per lb.

Above is copy of the price list at the Majestic Stores published in the Gibraltar Chronicle on the 2nd August 1944:

After the arrival of the first two groups of evacuees from the UK and the one from Madeira a smaller group of evacuees which had been transferred to one of the camps of Northern Ireland were also being repatriated. On the 25th August 1944 it was announced that 550 evacuees were on their first stage of their journey to Gibraltar. The majority of them had been living in evacuation camps in Co. Antrim since their transfer from London nearly a month before. This group of evacuees was to be the first contingent to be repatriated from Northern Ireland – a protracted process that would last until 1951.

On the 28th August 1944 a story titled "Sweet Home for Evacuees" which I have copied below appeared in a Northern Ireland newspaper reporting on the departure of the first group of 488 evacuees from Northern Ireland.

These evacuees and the other two groups that followed had been transferred temporarily from London to Northern Ireland. The first of this group of evacuees embarked on the troopship the **Highland Brigade** reaching Gibraltar on the 2nd September 1944.

SWEET HOME FOR EVACUEES.

DEPARTURE TO GIB.

FIRST BATCH LEAVE.

The first batch of the evacuees for Gibraltar, who have been resident in Northern Ireland for some weeks past, left Belfast to-day on the first stage of their journey home.

There were 400 in the party, mostly women and children, and they joined 200 others who were already on board the ship.

It is understood that repatriation will be carried out at frequent intervals until the whole of the 6,000 odd evacuees have been sent home.

To-day's batch came from camps in Co. Antrim and they were carried in N.I.R.T.B. buses from the camps to the docks, where they were met by Mr. A. P. FitzGerald, of the Ministry of Health and Local Government, and bidden God-speed on behalf of his department.

Miss Whitehorn, of the British Council, who has been here making contacts with the Northern Ireland Ministry of Education in connection with plans for the continued education of the children while in Ulster, also saw the emigrants off.

THE ROCK OF THEIR DREAMS.

Practically everyone in the party was laden with parcels and everybody was smiling in anticipation of what lay at the end of the sea voyage.

The oldest man in the party, Diego Mena, who stated he was 74, and looked hale and hearty, said he wanted home. He liked Ulster all right and the people were all right and were kind to him, but he wanted back to the Rock, where his home was.

Mena's attitude was typical of all the other evacuees. They had all enjoyed their stay, but there was a nostalgic atmosphere that could be sensed almost in the people's eyes.

A little family party consisted of an elderly woman, Mrs. Lourdes, of Town Range, Gibraltar, her daughter-in-law, Mrs. Ellen Santos, of the same address, her two children and her brother Francis Santos.

Their faces beamed as they spoke of home in a mixture of broken English and Spanish. They were leaving behind other relatives who, they hope, will be included in the next batch.

HUSBAND NAVAL POLICEMAN.

Mrs. Santos' husband is a British naval policeman, and she hoped when she got home to find him safe. She has not seen him for four long years, and she could be pardoned for saying that Ulster was not her home and that she was counting the hours to see her own house again.

Mrs. Lourdes proudly showed an antique gold signet ring she was wearing—a collector's piece. In place of the signet was a miniature photograph of a young man in uniform.

"MY SON," SHE PROUDLY SAID.

"That is my son," she said, and as she passionately kissed the photograph tears came into eyes that showed that she had looked on much sorrow.

As the buses arrived the staff checked the papers of the evacuees expeditiously, and they were soon on board.

Above the newspaper cuttings about first evacuees to leave the camps. Copy Mr V Gonzalez

Above evacuees ready to embark after leaving the camps.
Photo Mr V Gonzalez

The Troopship Highland Brigade. Photo Old Ship Gallery

Repatriates onboard the Highland Brigade.
At the extreme right are Mr. M Infante and family from Marlborough Court and then Camp No1 in Northern Ireland.
Photo Mr M Infante

By mid September 1944 the bombing of London with the flying bombs and the V2 rockets had ceased and the priority for returning to Gibraltar shifted to the evacuees in Jamaica. However, before then, two more contingents of evacuees arrived from Northern Ireland. The second contingent of just about 40 evacuees from Northern Ireland and about 400 from UK embarked on the troopship **Almanzora** reaching Gibraltar on the 5th October 1944.

The troopship Almanzora. Old Ship Gallery

The last group of evacuees to leave the UK with some from Northern Ireland made it on board the troopship **Elizabethville** which arrived in Gibraltar on 25th October 1944 with a total of 150 evacuees.

The troopship Elisabethville. Photo Old Ship Gallery

After these two groups of evacuees from Northern Ireland it was stated that no more evacuees could be repatriated until Gibraltar was ready to cope with the increase in the civilian population. On the other hand the British Government was insisting on a speedy repatriation of all the evacuees. The then Governor, Sir Ralf Eastwood, kept stressing from the very beginning, that the rate of repatriation depended very much on the availability of adequate accommodation. A Times correspondent commenting on this subject said that housing was probably Gibraltar's biggest post-war problem and that the official housing figures for a population of 20,000 people in 1938 showed that 17,000 lived in 608 tenements; 2,500 in 390 houses of three rooms; 300 in 63 two- roomed houses, and 100 in 35 one-room dwellings.

The lack of accommodation was made worse by the fact that the 2,000 to 3,000 Gibraltarians who were living in Spain before the evacuation had now to be found accommodation in Gibraltar. In addition to this problem, there were some buildings that had been demolished or bombed during the war. Also those who had been living in serious overcrowded conditions before the war expected to be brought back to more decent standard of accommodation. Faced with these tasks, the Gibraltar authorities wanted to slow down the repatriation process by the acceptance of all concerned on an agreed quota in line with the availability of accommodation in Gibraltar. The Government of Gibraltar's basic argument was that there was no point in repatriating evacuees when there was no place to accommodate them or adequate facilities available. On the other hand the British Government view was that evacuees should not be prevented from being repatriated just because of lack of accommodation and if that was the case then temporary housing had to be provided.

In the picture L to R are Julio Ryan …?. . Mosquera….?…Antonio Lopez. Photo Mr A Ryan

The evacuees in the above picture are holding a placard which reads as follows:

God Bless Gibraltar
We Do Not Want To See
You Any More
Living In These Huts Is A Crime
We Are Not Prisoners Of War

The evacuees in Jamaica were repatriated on the 10th October 1944. The ship tasked for this purpose was the **Duchess of Richmond** which had repatriated the first party of evacuees from the United Kingdom on the 6th April 1944. Apart from a few evacuees who had to stay behind for personal reasons, all the evacuees, totalling about 1,500, were repatriated in one single trip on the 10th October 1944. The ship after leaving Jamaica proceeded to the island of Bermuda where the evacuees stopped for three days. During their short stay in Bermuda, an evacuee recalled that one of the days was a Sunday and a priest from Bermuda celebrated mass on board the **SS Duchess of Richmond.** She then steamed across the Atlantic in a convoy with American troopships escorted by two British destroyers. Before arriving at Gibraltar it stopped at Casablanca where it stayed for only a few hours to disembark several Spanish refugee passengers. It then sailed to Gibraltar where it arrived on 26th October 1944.

Above copy from the Gibraltar Chronicle showing evacuees arriving on the Duchess of Richmond on the 26th October 1944.

Evacuees disembarking from the Duchess of Richmond on the 26th October 1944. Photo Mrs Wahnon

The Fernandez family together again after 4 long years. Photo Fernandez family

On the return of the evacuees from Jamaica, the Governor of Gibraltar sent a letter thanking the Jamaican people – noting that the Gibraltarians remembered that Jamaica gave them sanctuary and made them welcome.

HOME—1,500 evacuees from Jamaica. And these pictures of their homecoming tell their own story. Farthest-travelled of all Gibraltarians forced by war to leave their homes, first on the Government's priority list but delayed in their return by overriding demands on shipping, they disembarked yesterday after an uneventful journey.

The Garrison Band was there to play for them as they landed, and His Excellency the Governor and Lady Eastwood were among the first to welcome them. Rear-Admiral H. R. Marrack, Brigadier C. S. Vale, the Hon. Colonial Secretary, Mr. G. Miles Clifford, and members of the Resettlement Board—all of whose "priority" evacuees have now returned—were on the landing pier.

Within two hours disembarkation had been completed, and all members of the homecoming party with relatives in Gibraltar had been reunited with them. As on previous occasions, a detachment of St. John Ambulance Brigade gave valuable assistance to the sick, aged and children, while a military party handled the luggage.

The commander of the ship said that Gibraltarian V.A.D. members aboard ship from Jamaica had performed excellent work during the voyage.

—Pictures by Official Photographer.

Above, copy from the Gibraltar Chronicle.

ONE scene typical of many in Gibraltar yesterday, when the last of the "majority" evacuees— 1,500 of them—arrived home from Jamaica. Neighbours turn out to wecome Elena and Margot Borge as they arrive at their Lynch Lane home.

Above and below copies from the Gibraltar Chronicle.

And another . . . Many willing hands hasten to aid an evacuee as she "disembarks" a second time—this time from transport which carried the homecomers to their dispersal points.

With the arrival of the 1,500 evacuees from Jamaica on the 26th October 1944, the balance still to be repatriated was approximately another 8,000 made up of about 500 in Madeira, 500 in Spain and Tangier, 7,000 in Northern Ireland with about 200 still in mainland Britain. By the end of 1944 the British national press was already giving coverage about the evacuees in Northern Ireland. The following is a summary from the comments made by one of the reporters.

Officials had informed the evacuees that the question of repatriation was entirely one for the authorities at Gibraltar, and that war-time conditions, including shortage of housing, were chiefly responsible for delaying their return. That while everything possible was being done to make life comfortable, the conditions left much to be desired and were unsuitable for people accustomed to a Mediterranean climate. The evacuees had complained to this reporter about the bitterly cold winter, of their small allowances, the primitive sanitary arrangements, and lack of essential amenities. The essential services were run by the evacuees, and cooks, cleaners, and labourers who received local rates of pay. That all the evacuees were supplied with food and received, in addition, a weekly allowance amounting to 5s. for those over 15, 8s. 6d. for married couple, and 2s. 6d. for each child. Most of the, evacuees were said to be not too badly clothed, but all were finding that their present living conditions were very severe on clothing, especially shoes. The W.V.S., who had a representative at each camp, assisted the mostly in need with gifts of clothes and footwear, but the supplies were said to be far from adequate. The children attended their own camp school, and those of suitable age received free education in secondary and technical schools in Belfast and other towns. There was an unattractive, although well equipped, sick-bay, and a doctor who attended daily. Health at the camp was good and there had been few cases of sickness. Cooking was done in a communal kitchen, and each person received rations similar to those available to residents in Northern Ireland. Each Nissen hut was divided into two small compartments and furnished with a table, one or two rough wooden chairs, and beds according to the number of occupants. There were no carpets or boards to cover the damp concrete floors. A stove and oil lamp supplied heat and light. The camp toilet, which consisted of about 20 cold water taps pouring into long wooden troughs, was unheated and totally unsuitable for the women. When reporters arrived there was no electricity supply in the camp, although electric light was going to be shortly installed in the dining-rooms, kitchens, and recreation rooms of all the camps but not in the living quarters, where it was needed most. The next Chapter "Evacuees in Northern Ireland." will explain in much more detail how the evacuees lived in the camps.

CHAPTER TWELVE

EVACUEES IN NORTHERN IRELAND

The Monarch of Bermuda arriving at Belfast from Liverpool with many evacuees who had left London.

By August 1944 over 4,500 evacuees had been repatriated from the UK to Gibraltar (about 1,400 on the 6th April and about 3,100 on the 2nd August), most of the remaining evacuees totaling nearly 7,000, who also left London between 18th and 24th July were transferred to the camps of Northern Ireland. About 200 evacuees consisting of those who were hospitalized and their families were still living in London.

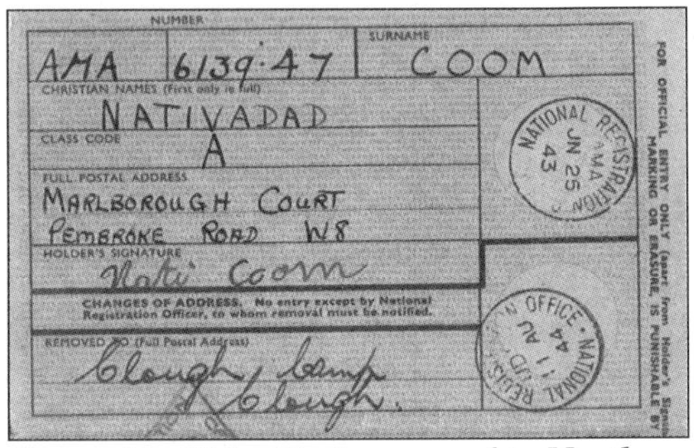

NUMBER AMA 6139·47
SURNAME COOM
CHRISTIAN NAMES (First only in full) NATIVADAD
CLASS CODE A
FULL POSTAL ADDRESS MARLBOROUGH COURT PEMBROKE ROAD W8
HOLDER'S SIGNATURE Nati Coom
CHANGES OF ADDRESS. No entry except by National Registration Officer, to whom removal must be notified.
REMOVED TO (Full Postal Address) Clough Camp Clough.
FOR OFFICIAL ENTRY ONLY (apart from Holder's Signature) MARKING OR ERASURE IS PUNISHABLE BY
NATIONAL REGISTRATION JN 25 43
NATIONAL REGISTRATION OFFICE 1 AU 44

Example of identity to proceed to Northern Ireland. Copy Mr C Coom

Evacuees disembarking at Belfast.

View of huts on arrival.

Evacuees arriving at the camps in Ballymena.

Office for the distribution of coupons.

All the photographs on this page were donated by the Gibraltar Museum.

The evacuees transferred to Northern Ireland followed a different route to those being repatriated to Gibraltar. They travelled from London through Rugby arriving at Liverpool non-stop.

At Liverpool they stayed for a couple of days during which time all the administrative procedures related to their identification and eventual accommodation were carried out. From then on they were embarked on the ships to take them to Belfast. On reaching Belfast they were treated to milk and biscuits before they were put on the buses that were waiting to take them to their respective camps. Once in the camps they had something to eat and then each family group was given the keys to their respective huts in the camp. The photographs on this page were donated by the Gibraltar Museum.

The administration office at Ballymena where the keys to the huts were handed to family groups.

It was summer and the evacuees were delighted to be in the splendour of the beautiful countryside as opposed to the rigour of life in London. They were obviously feeling gladly relieved from the dangers of the recent spate of the flying bombs. Many newspapers picked up the news about the arrival of Gibraltar evacuees like, for example, the Northern Whig and Belfast Post which carried an article about the arrival of 3,600 Gibraltarians in Ulster.

The Gibraltar evacuees with Mr William Grant, Minister of Health.

SPANISH ACCENTS IN CO. DOWN

LOYAL PEOPLE FROM GIBRALTAR

IDLENESS PROBLEM

The soft Spanish accent coming from a very ardent Briton can be heard in the highways and byways of County Down to-day.

A "News-Letter" reporter yesterday visited several of the camps occupied by civilians from Gibraltar, and found it a novel experience to listen to the "whoa" of the County Down farm hand on one side of the road and fluent Spanish, accompanied by much gesticulation, on the other.

These people from Gibraltar are as British as the Union Jacks which fly over their camps. Call them Spanish and they will soon let you know that, though the great majority speak naturally in that tongue and have Spanish names, it practically amounts to an insult.

One old lady, a grandmother, indicated the attitude of them all, when she was asked if she would not have preferred to stay in Spain when the "Rock" had to be cleared of civilians. She replied in broken English: "Well, we might, but we could not tell what side Franco would take at that time."

The Ministry of Health have done a fine job in helping these people to settle down in a strange land. There are problems, of course, and those who can speak English will tell you that the chief one, strange as it may seem, is idleness. The problem is not so acute with the women, for they have children to look after and huts to keep clean. The men, however, are a different proposition. Most of them, and the younger people, were working in the South of England before they were shipped to Ulster. They were all in good jobs—typists earning £5 a week, and even a cloakroom attendant, who made as much as £15 every week.

OUT OF RANGE

Consequently many of them did not take very kindly to being transported to an area where they can earn little or nothing. They are, however, very thankful to be out of the range of the flying bomb, and the children are already putting on weight from the healthy life they are leading, plus a generous supply of milk.

Mr. William Grant, Minister of Health, inspected the camps yesterday and talked with the committees which the men have set up. He explained that employment could not be found as easily in the heart of the countryside as it was in London, and that Ulster had some thousands of her own workless. The question, however, was engaging the attention of the authorities, as was, too, that of the education of the children.

The evacuees all speak highly of the kindness which they have received from local residents—but one thought dominates the minds of them all: "How soon will we get home?"

There are few restrictions at the camps. They can come and go practically at will. They must be on time for meals; but if they are away overnight visiting another camp they are expected to inform the Group Warden. Rations are on exactly the same scale as for the ordinary citizen.

Above newspaper cuttings reporting the arrival of evacuees in Northern Ireland. Copy Mr V Gonzalez

The camps in Northern Ireland were originally constructed as an emergency for the civilian population when Belfast was subjected to heavy bombardment but they were never intended for long-term use. Then early in January 1942 when America had already been a month into the Second World War, the camps were put in full use to accommodate US troops who were stationed in Northern Ireland. By 1944 it was estimated that there were about one hundred thousand American troops in Ulster.

American troops in one of the camps.
Photo US Army Center of Military History

When the US troops were transferred to Southern England in preparation for the Normandy Landing, the camps fell into disuse but they were very soon prepared to accommodate the 7,000 Gibraltar evacuees transferred from London. The camps were located within the surroundings of the countryside with its picturesque farms and houses.

A typical Nissen hut. Photo Mrs Beniso

The huts, called Nissen, after their inventor, were built with corrugated iron sheeting and cement floor. They measured about 36 feet long by about 16 feet wide and divided in half. Each half accommodated an average of four to six persons. The furniture in the huts consisted from four to six bunk beds to each half.

There was also a table, a cupboard, a chest of drawers and a wardrobe. In the middle of the room there was a stove. The huts, although fitted with stoves to heat them up, were not the ideal place to live, particularly during the severe winter weather associated with Northern Ireland. There were communal toilets with little or no privacy and no protection from the inclement weather, especially for the elderly. Some evacuees explained that during a period of heavy snowing they had to creep through the windows to get out of the huts and then remove the snow with shovels from the door so that the rest of the family could get out of the hut. It was well established that the evacuees did not have suitable clothing for the winter

The stove used to warm up the huts.
Photo Mr V Gonzalez

a

Mr. Grant, Minister for Health, with other UK Officials looking at the allocation of camps in Northern Ireland.
Photos above and below were donated by the Gibraltar Museum

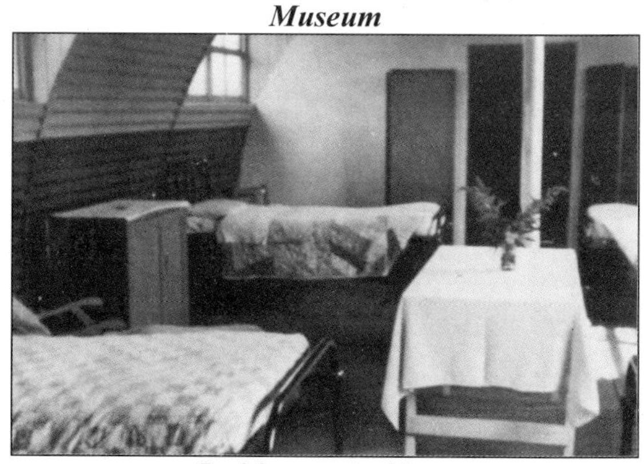

Inside a typical hut.

Camp 17 at Carryduff was the largest of all the camps. It had been converted into an evacuees' camp at the very last moment in addition to the original 16 camps to accommodate a larger than estimated number of evacuees. Below are photographs and notes about the camp at Carryduff near Belfast.

An aerial view of Camp No.17 Carryduff.
Photo Mrs M Lopez

NISSEN HUTS & EVACUEE OCCUPANTS

1a:	JUAN ORFILA (Mgr Orfila's father) with two sons & one daughter
b:	ERNESTO MORELLO (uncertain whether with family or alone)
2a:	JULIO ABUDARHAM and family (three sons & one daughter)
b:	(i) CELECIA - (ii) MARIO SILVA (School Teacher) and family
3a:	GEORGE WHITE and family
b:	CALAMARO and family (one daughter)
4a:	FRANKIE BAGLIETTO and family (nicknamed 'Horrores')
b:	(i) CORNELIO - (ii) ALBERTO FERNANDEZ and family
5a:	SALVADOR MACLAREN and family
b:	JUAN MILAN and ROBLES families
6a:	LIONEL RAGGIO and wife
b:	ANTONIO GARCIA and family
7a:	MRS FOSTER (nicknamed 'La Reina Mora')
b:	JOE JURADO and family
8a:	DICKIE DYER (Boxer) and family
b:	(i) VICTOR IGNACIO and family - (ii) JIMMY DURANTE and family
9a:	LEO GUILLIANO and family (two sons & two daughters, the youngest being born in the Camp)
b:	PACO GUILLIANO (Leo's brother) and wife Helena
10a:	(i) MESODA BENGGIO - (ii) MOMMY ACRIS with wife and daughter (iii) LUISA GUILLIANO and son PEPE (Leo's mother and brother)
b:	(i) ALEJANDRO WHITE and family - (ii) EDUARDO PALMIER & family

NOTE: (i), (ii) & (iii) denote sequence of residence

Details of evacuees living at Carryduff.

Evacuees inside their hut.
Photos above and below were donated by the Gibraltar Museum

The majority of the camps were totally removed from the main towns giving a sense of isolation, particularly in the winter months. There were reports of rats roaming in the fields that found their way in the camps. Despite the cold and damp weather, the general state of health among the evacuees was good and there were only a few cases requiring special medical attention, which were not attributed to the environment. The layout of the camps was generally speaking like in the diagram below: Diagrams created by Mr J Guilliano.

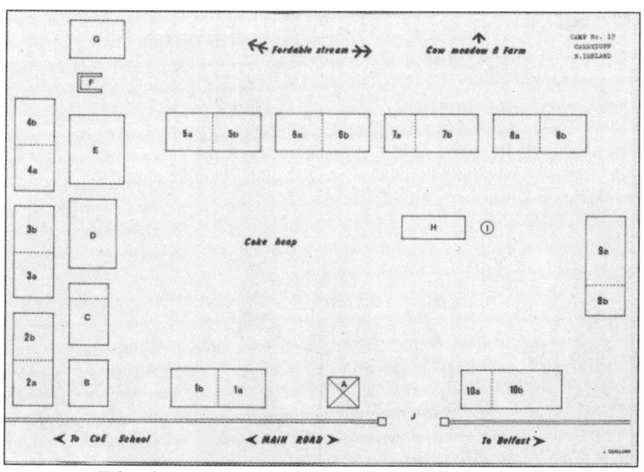

The layout of camp no.17 at Carryduff.

Layout of huts in a camp at Ballymena.

Carryduff was the only camp that had a supply of electricity.

The Camp Committee at Camp No.3 – Crossgar
L to R: A.Sciacaluga, L.Randall Bro. Murphy J.Forbe, Cerisola, Aonso. Photo above by Mr A Sciacaluga. The rest of the photographs were donated by the Gibraltar Museum

Mr. Walker Assistant Secretary, Mr. Fitzgerald, Principal Officer and other officials of the Ministry of Health and Local Government meet the committees of Girls' and Men's Club in Dunnaird Camp.

The registration office at Ballymena.

Each camp had their own representatives and there was also an overall committee to deal with matters affecting all the evacuees in Northern Ireland.

One of the committee where Mr L Bruzon represented the evacuees.

Below are the names with the corresponding numbers of the 17 camps in Northern Ireland.

COUNTY DOWN
1 Clough
2 Cargagh
3 Crossgar
BELFAST
4 Saintfield
17 Carryduff
COUNTY ANTRIM
5 Tawnybrack
6. Moorfields
7. Castlegore
8. Dunnaird
9. Drummock
10. Aghacully
11. Breckagh Bridge
12. Corby Bridge
COUNTY LONDONDERRY
13. Ballyarnett
14. Molennan
15. Warbleshinney
16. Tagherian

In the camps there were huts allocated for the use of minor health services particular for children as shown in the photographs on this page.

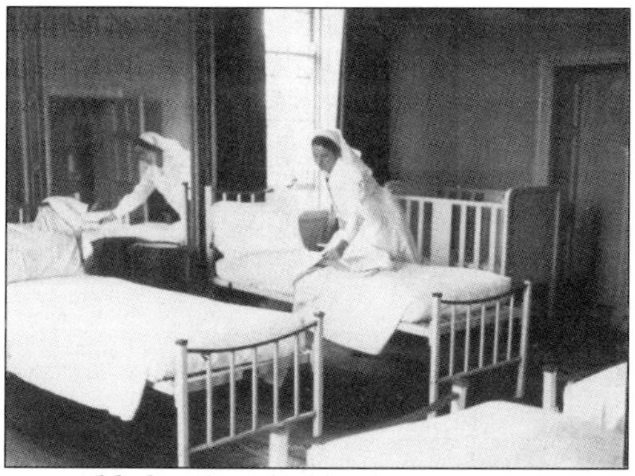

Above and below hospital in the town of Ballymena.

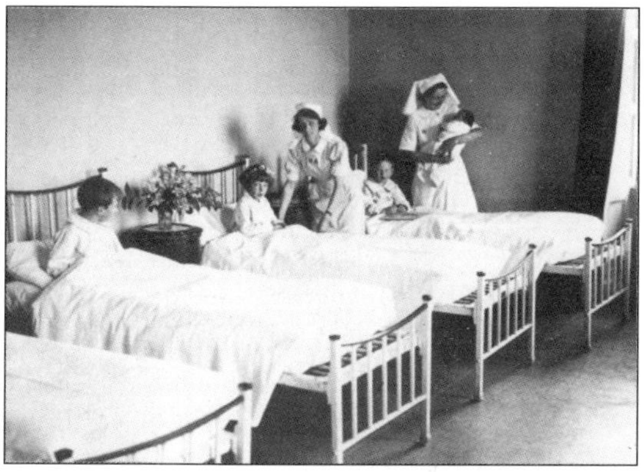

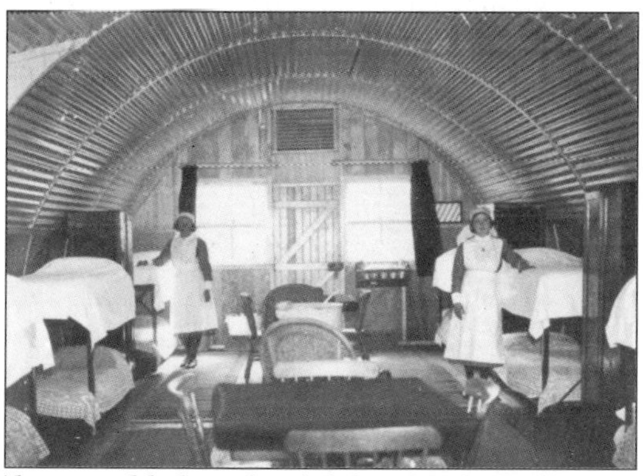

Above and below the sick bay hut in Ballymena.

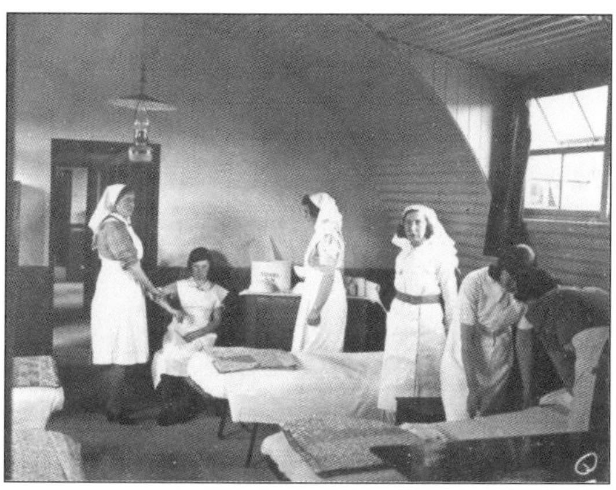

Cases of ill health requiring more specialised attention were taken either to the nearest town hospital or to Belfast. All the photographs on this page were donated by the Gibraltar Museum.

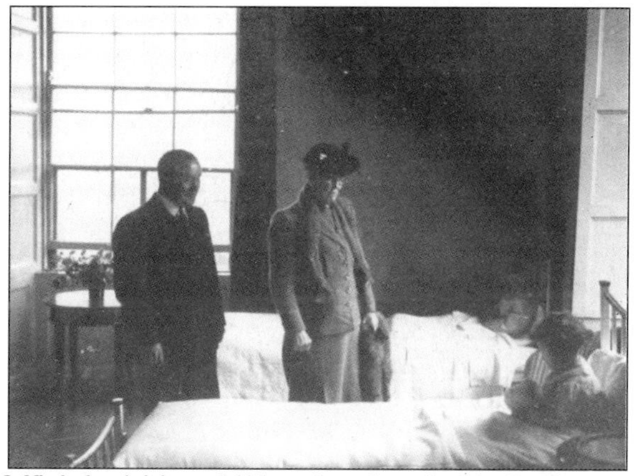

Officials visiting children in a hospital in Ballymena.

Above and below a nurse looking after children in a hospital in Ballymena.

The arrangements for the provision of food were often a source of discontent in the camps because of either the cooking or the food itself, which was often not to liking of the evacuees. In this page there are photographs taken in the dining rooms in the camps of Ballymena.

The photos below show the children in the dining room.

However, with regard to the food prepared and supplied from the camp kitchens where there were evacuees involved there seemed to be no real complaints about either the quality or the quantity of food.

Being in a farming environment there were plenty of fresh products like meat and poultry. Fresh milk was available every day all the time.

Evacuee exchanging view with official about food

Below vacuees in a dining room in one of the camps in Ballymena.

Lorry delivering food provisions to the camps in Ballymena.

All the photographs on this page were donated by the Gibraltar Museum.

One of the first administrative priorities were the arrangements for the children to attend school since most of them had missed a lot of formal schooling due to the lack of continuity experienced during the last months in London. As I understand, all camps had facilities for children to attend primary schools. Like in London and elsewhere during the evacuation, many of the teachers in the camps were laypersons. For the secondary aged children there was the opportunity of attending public schools in Belfast.

Singing lessons in the classroom.

A classroom in one of the Ballymena camps.

Playtime at school in Ballymena.

These children were selected by sitting a test by which they were assessed in order to allow them to be placed in the appropriate classes in accordance to their attained level of academic standard. There were also nursery facilities in some of the camps.

The old school near camp no.2 (Cargah). Photos above and below Mrs E Alman

Mrs Elena Alman (nee Bagna) visiting what used to be her school at Cargagh.

Elena photographed above visiting what used to be her school in Camp No.2 in Cargagh. She remembered that her teachers were Misses O'Driscol and Killroy who lived not very far from the camps.

Teacher with children in a Ballymena Camp.

All photographs except those by Mrs E Alman were donated by the Gibraltar Museum.

"We Thank God and England.."

The photographs on this page show groups of nursery and school children and youths.

Nursery children in Camp No.10 (Aghacully)
With the children are Miss I.McGreech and Miss Lourdes Padiña.
Photo Mr V Gonzalez

A nursery in Ballymena. Photo Gibraltar Museum

Children outside a school hut in Northern Ireland.
In the photo is Betty Collins (Mrs Garcia). Photo Mrs Garcia

Schoolchildren at Camp No.10 Aghacully. Photo Mr F Bocarisa
In the photo is local lay teacher Mr. Alecio also among the children is Francis Bocarisa

In the photo are Mrs Ana Bagna,Mrs Carmen Wall andMrs Olga Alman.
Photo by Mrs E Alman

The lack of employment opportunities in Northern Ireland had a very negative effect in the attitude of many of the evacuees who at times manifested symptoms of boredom and a feeling of neglect by the authorities concerned. At one stage the evacuees were provided with some financial assistance of about 8s.6d a week for a period of six months, which was considered inadequate for the subsistence of a married couple. Some evacuees found gainful employment on a rotational basis in the camp kitchens as shown in the photographs. The money that some evacuees had managed to save as a result of working in London was being spent in buying goods, which were not generally available in the camps or with their ration books.

Kitchen workers in Camp No.15 (Warbleshinney)
In the photo are Mrs Walker, Mañetto ,Bossano, and Parody
Photos above by Mrs Lane (nee Mañetto) and below by Mrs Ferro.

Kitchen workers in Camp No.10 (Aghacully)
At the back from L to R are: Messrs Trico, Nunez, Morrison (camp manager) at the very end Mr Azzopardi. Sitting at the table from L to R are Mrs Ratcliffe, Mrs Ferro (nee Galbarino) Mrs Nunez and Buckley.

Above an below attending the kitchen ovens and hot plates.
Photos Gibraltar Museum

Kitchen workers in Camp No.10 (Aghacully)
Among the back row L to R are Mr Buckley, Mrs Nunez, Mr Trico Mrs M.Simone Among the middle row L to R is: Mr Morrison (camp manager), Mrs M.Azzopardi, and Mr Bossano. Among those sitting in front L to R: Mrs Ferro (nee Galbarino) Mrs Nunez and Mrs Buckley. Mrs. F Piris is also in the photo. Photo Mrs Ferro

In the photo are Mr. A.Garcia, Mrs. Raggio, M.Rubio,…?..,…?.... Mrs R.Olivero, Padina,..?... Kneeling : M.Raggio…?... R.Olivero (Mrs Payas). Photo Mrs Payas

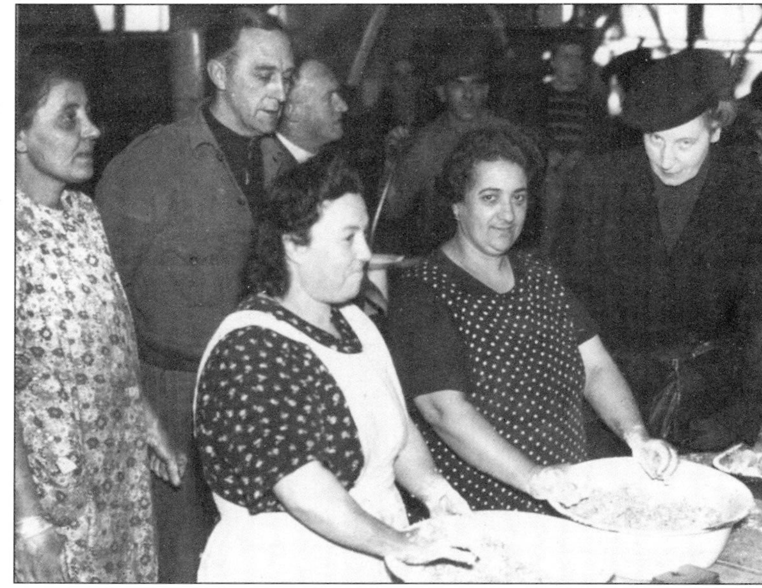

Above and below kitchen workers in Ballymena. Photos above and below Gibraltar Museum

The photographs shown in this page are of the kitchen workers in the camps of Ballymena. All the photographs on this page were donated by the Gibraltar Museum.

Administrative and kitchen staff.

Making a start in the kitchen.

Getting the dinning room ready.

Loads of loaves of bread in the kitchen.

It is interesting to know that in the camps where the evacuees were gainfully employed there were no signs of quarrels between the evacuees and the wardens. There were also some evacuees who were unofficially employed in the collection of potatoes in order to earn a bit of extra money. I believe that the going rate at the time was two old pennies per full bucket. They worked practically the whole day picking potatoes. The daily income was about 10 shillings (50p), which in those days was considered good extra money.

Carpentry work.

Children collecting potatoes. Gibraltar.

Above and below evacuees employed in the collection of potatoes. In the photo is John Mascarenhas. Photos by Mr J Mascarenhas

Potatoes collectors.

Textile factory in the camp at Ballymena. Photo Gibraltar Museum

Some of the evacuees who had skilled trades were able to find work outside the camps even though there were restrictions that did not allow the Gibraltar evacuees to compete for jobs in Northern Ireland. Among those who found work as plumbers were Alberto Fernandez, Salvador McClaren and Leo Guilliano. They were employed by Harland & Wolfe in Belfast in the refit of the liner "Reina Del Pacifico." When the refit was completed the ship sailed across to the Clyde for speed trials, which were completed satisfactorily, though slight overheating was observed in one of the engines.

The liner Reina del Pacifico. Photo Old Ship Gallery

On Friday 12th September 1947 during the return voyage to Belfast, while speed was being increased, all four engines exploded without warning. In an instant the engine room was almost completely destroyed. When rescuers entered the engine room they found fires breaking out and bodies everywhere in an atmosphere of thick smoke. The sad result was that twenty-eight workers had died, either instantly or from their injuries and a further twenty-three were hurt. The Reina Del Pacifico drifted for a couple of days until tugs arrived to tow her back to the Belfast dockyard. Leo Guilliano was the only Gibraltarian worker on board during the trials. Ten minutes before lunch, Leo decided to go aloft to wash his hands and was lucky enough to escape the brunt of the engine room explosion and able to return alive and unscathed, albeit rather grimy with soot and grease.

Gibraltar workers on the Reina Del Pacifico From L to R: Alberto Fernandez, Leo Guilliano and Salvador McLaren. Photo Mr J Guilliano.

Like in every location where the evacuees were taken, and in Northern Ireland too, they tried as much as possible to settle and make the most of their stay with the difference that in their case they were liable to be repatriated in individual groups at any given moment and thus disrupting any entertainment plans and arrangements. They organized plays, groups, concerts, arts and crafts exhibitions and there was even an information bulletin called The Camp Courier.

Gibraltar Evacuees in Show in a Nissen hut in Camp No 10 Northern Ireland Left to Right Antonia Galia (Mrs Calamaro) Zoraida Hermida (Mrs Santos) Lourdes MontegriffoChica Bensadon Aida Sanchez Lourdes Padina (Mrs Baglietto) Cornelio. Photo Mr J Guilliano

THE GIRBRALTAR VICTORY BAND IN NORTHERN IRELAND During a concert held at Camp No. 1(Clough) in 1945. At the Piano Harry Fernandez Ernest Cruz (accordion) Jacinto Ventura (guitar) Juan Cruz (conductor) Walter Feetham (mandolin) Thomas Estella (mandolin) Juan Ochello (banjo) Lionel Victory (drums). Photo Mr E Cruz

Below are the names of the participants who took part with the Victory Band in the concert held at Clough in 1945.

Ladies Chorus

Mrs J.Bado, Mrs V. Bado, Misses R.Lavagna, J.Lavagna, A.Lavagna, A.Ochello, V.Alvarez, T.Alvarez, M.Grech H.Peire, M.Macedo, E.Sanchez, L.McEwan

Men's Chorus

Messrs.S.J.Sciacaluga, M.Sciacaluga, J.Bado, S.Holliday, A.Beiso, A.Garcia, J.Moreno, B.Martinez, C.Harrison, J.Martinez, M.Axisa, J.Peira, J.Kinder, L.Kinder, V.Sciacaluga, O.Victory

Children's Play

Girls – O.Ocana, L.Chichon, L.Ochello L.Burke
Boys - A.Ocana O.Victory A.Chichon, H.Ullger, J.Cruz, J.McEwan, J.Worley, A.Worley G.Worley

Scenographer – Mr J.Cruz

Make –up – Mr J.Saccone.

Wardrobe – Mr B.Martinez
Costumes – Mr.V.Calderon

Prompters – Messrs A.Almeida and J.Moreno

Carpenters and Decorators – J.Cruz, M.Axisa, C.Harrison, S.Holliday, A.Estella, B. Martinez, J.Sene A.Beiso.

In the next pages there are photographs of the different plays and concerts organised by the evacuees and many of the participants.

“We Thank God and England..”

In the photo are :Pepe De La Cruz, Pepe Martinez, Joe Formosa, Johnny Martinez, Lionel Santos .

In the photo are :Victor Gonzalez, Joe Formosa, Pepe De La Cruz, Johnny Martinez, Muriel Cartwright.

In the photoa are :Pepe Martinez, Amanda Martinez, Victor Gonzalez, Joe Formosa, Alminda Tonna, Hilda Tonna, John Martinez, Captain Bateman Fox, Muriel Cartwright,Mrs. Bateman Fox, Johnny Martinez, Pepe De La Cruz.

In the photo are :Amanda Martinez, Pepe De La Cruz, Johnny Martinez, Joe Formosa, Flocy Cartwright, Victor Gonzalez, Alminda Tonna, Muriel Cartwright
All the photos in this page Mr Clive Martinez.

Evacuees in Northern Ireland

The photo below shows the evacuees who took part in a concert held at Camp No.10 - Aghacully.

Evacuees taking part in a show at Camp 10.Aghacully
In the photos are Mr A Garcia and his son Tony.
Sitting in front in the middle is Laura Diaz (Mrs Pizzarello).
Photos above and below Mr A Garcia

The photo below shows the evacuees who took part in the Grand Concert held at the Clough – Gibraltar Evacuee Camp No.1. Photo Mr H Fernandez

Participants of a variety show held at the social club in Camp No.17 Carryduff. Photo Mr J Guilliano

Entertainment group in Northern Ireland.
Among those in the photo are: Angeles Olivares(Mrs McKay) Flordeliz Ignacio, Obdulia Pipo,Olga Ramos,Mercedes Ruiz, Lourdes Randall, Margot Mesilio, Emily Olivares(Mrs Latter) Mercedes Ignacio, Mariluz Olivares,Lourdes Olivero,Alicia Galia, Anne Parody, Johnny Ramos,Juan Ramos, Alberto Sciacaluga,Pipo,Chipolina, Manolo Celecia.Br.Murphy.
Photo Mrs Latter

A Band Formed By Evacuees At Camp No 2 Cargagh, Cough Country Antrim. Photo Mr V Gonzalez
Back row J.Felices,Perera,A.De La Paz,H.Mackintosh
Front row: P.Gomez,A.Martinez, J.Noguera,A.Agius, J.Dyer,F.Ferro Photo Mr V Gonzalez

Participants of a variety show held at camp No.3 Crossgar.
L to R: Momo Ignacio Ignacio A.Sciacaluga Ignacio Victor Ignacio. Photo Mr A Sciacaluga.

Below participants of a show held in one of the camps in Northern Ireland. Photos Mr V Gonzalez

Back: L. Santos, A. Martinez, L. Cartwright, Tonna, ...?, Jones, H. Cartwright, Alvarez, Jones, Navas, C. Mena, Sanchez, Baglietto, ...?, B. Mena.
Standing: J.Martinez, V. Gonzalez, J. Formosa, J. Fa, Prescot, ...?, L. Hitchcock, J. Ellul, Baglietto, T. Martinez, A. Ferro, J. De La Cruz.
Sitting: M. Dalmedo, B.Rice, J. Catania, Jones, J. Martinez, (Capt Fox & Wife), Perera, J. Noguera, Victory, Rice, Powel, J. Fa, Dalmedo, Dalmedo, ...?, Tonna, Olivero, Rammage, ...?, Formosa, Navas, Alvarez, Catania.

Below: J. De La Cruz, A. Martinez, J. Martinez, Ellul, J. Formosa, Jones, J. Fa, F.Cartwright, J. Catania, ...?, Prescot, Tonna, V. Gonzalez, Alvarez, A. Ferro, M. Cartwright, L. Hitchcock.

Photograph of the quartet Luisa Fernanda.
In the photograph from left to right are Salvador Sciacaluga,
Elena Nacimiento(Mrs Bado) Salvador Holiday and Juan Bado. Above photo Mr V Sciacaluga

Above and below a Gibraltar football team in Northern Ireland.
Among the players are F.Asquez, M.Asquez, and V.Balban
The coach is M.Asquez Snr.

Outside the football Club.
In the photo are M.Asquez, V.Balban, and Alfredo Balban

Although there are not many photographs available of the football teams in Northern Ireland, it was nevertheless a popular sport among the evacuees. A story published in 1985 by a Northern Ireland newspaper mentioned as one of the highlights of the Gibraltar team known as 'The Rock' when they reached a final in 1945 against BB United. Also as in other destinations, evacuees did their best to demonstrate their passion for football. Boxing in those days was also a very popular sport among the evacuees. Attached to this page are photographs of the football team with its club in one of the camps. In the Ballymena camps there was also a boxing club. All the photographs on this page were donated by Mrs Asquez.

Manolo Asquez.

....?... .J. Castro M.Asquez.

Boxing enthusiasts at Ballymena.

Evacuees in Northern Ireland

As well as football and boxing there were other amateur sports, like cycling and indoor games in Camps in Northern Ireland. In this page are some of the photographs taken at the indoor games and cycling sessions.

Breckagh Bridge Club Table Tennis winners.
From L to R; L. Quelcuti, A. Dalmedo, L.Debono (captain), E.Piris, J.Contreras, E.Garcia.
Photo Mr V Gonzalez

Darts Champions at Carryduff Social Club.
Among the players is F.Baglietto. Photo Mr J Guilliano

Manolo Asquez, Victor Balban, Freddie Asquez? ……
Photos above and below Mrs Asquez

Freddie Asquez ,Victor Balban and .?...

As a means of entertainment, there were also evacuees involved with hobbies to make the best of their spare time. In December 1946 a grand exhibition of arts and crafts was held at the Ballymena Town Hall. The articles on view in the various classes were classified as of a high standard and aroused considerable interest among the many who visited the exhibition. It also gave visitors an opportunity to appreciate the abilities of many of the young people in the Camps. The Mayor of Ballymena, Councillor Patrick Murphy, formally opened the exhibition. Mr. Newe, Senior Camps Inspector presided at the opening ceremony and welcomed the Mayor. Mr.Newe then expressed thanks on behalf of the Ministry of Health and Local Government to Mr McClelland, Principal of the Ballymena Technical School. The Mayor said that the exhibition contained a very interesting and attractive display of work. And that it was obvious that a good deal of time and energy had been put into the arrangements for the exhibition for which the people of Gibraltar could well be proud of the result.

Above and below Mr R. Torrilla showing his exhibit, a replica of a Nissen hut to the Camp Officials. Photo Gibraltar Museum

Photo Mr Torrilla.

Below are the lists of prizewinners published by the Camp Courier. Copies provided by Mr V Gonzalez.

The Prizewinners were:—

WOODWORK.

Class 1.—Any article in Woodwork. Best original Design.
1st. Victor Gonsalez, Camp No. 2, Cargagh.
2nd. E. Poggio, Camp No. 4, Saintfield.
3rd. A. Ballester, Camp No. 9, Drummuck.

Class 1.—Any toy, suitable for children, 6-10 years of age.
1st. E. Poggio, Camp No. 4, Saintfield.
2nd. Victor Balban, Camp No. 4, Saintfield.
3rd. A. Alecio, Camp No. 11, Breckagh Bridge.

Class 3.—Any article for use in the home.
1st Victor Gonsalez, Camp No. 2, Cargagh.
2nd. A. Ballester, Camp No. 9, Drummuck.
3rd. Louis Jurado, Camp No. 17, Carryduff.

THE CAMP COURIER.

Class 4.—Any toy suitable for children, 10-14 years of age.
1st. Tony Raggio, Camp No. 17, Carryduff.
2nd Francis Martinez, Camp No. 10, Aghacully.
3rd. A. Rubio, Camp No. 8, Dunnaird.

Class 5.—Any article in woodwork. Confined to members of a Camp Club.
1st. Charles Raggio, Camp No. 17, Carryduff.
2nd. Victor Gonsalez, Camp No. 2, Cargagh.
3rd. F. Asquez, Camp No. 4, Saintfield.

SOFT TOYS.

Class 6.—Doll made from rags, etc.
1st. V. Poggio, Camp 4, Saintfield.
2nd Violetta Victory, Camp 4, Saintfield.
3rd. L. Castro, Camp 4, Saintfield.

Class 7.—Animal made from rags, etc.
3rd. Mrs. L. Griss, Camp No. 8, Dunnaird.

Class 8.—Animal made from rags. Confined to members of a Girls' Club.
3rd. Ida Netta, Camp No. 10, Aghacully.

WOOL-WORK.

Class 9.—Dressing Jacket. Hand-knitted.
1st. Pilar Danino, Camp No. 17, Carryduff.
2nd. Mary Poggio, Camp No. 4, Saintfield.

Class 12.—Pair of Gloves.
1st Pilar Danino, Camp No. 17, Carryduff.
2nd. Mrs. Mauro, Camp No. 5, Tawneybrack.
3rd. Miss A. Cornelio, Camp No. 5, Tawneybrack.

DRESS-MAKING.

Class 15.—Dress, Coat or Skirt for child under 14 years.
1st Mrs. Acris, Camp No. 17, Carryduff.
2nd. Mrs. Ana Calamaro, Camp No. 17, Carryduff.

Class 16.—Any Article for an Adult. Made from an old garment.
1st. M. Saltariche, Camp No. 4, Saintfield.

Class 19.—Work-bag or Tea-cosy. Made from Felt.
1st. M. Earle, Camp No. 4, Saintfield.

Class 20.—Fancy Rug. Made from sacks or other material. Natural or dyed colours.
1st. F. Bautista, Camp No. 10, Aghacully.

Class 22.—Flowers, wax on natural stems.
1st. J. Collado, Comp No. 10, Aghacully.

Class 23.—Paper Flowers.
1st. Mrs. Earle, Camp No. 4, Saintfield.
2nd Mr. McCarthy, Camp No. 4, Saintfield.
3rd, Mary Poggio, Camp No. 4, Saintfield.

Class 24.—Shopping bag, string.
1st. Mr. Edward Piris, Camp No. 11, Breckagh Bridge.
2nd. Mrs. Mauro, Camp No. 5, Tawneybrack.
3rd. Mrs. Resso, Camp No. 5, Tawneybrack.

Class 25.—Raffia Work.
1st. J. N. Walker, Camp No. 4, Saintfield.

Class 26.—Tea Cloth or table centre—string.
1st. Mrs. Martinez, Camp No. 5, Tawneybrack.
2nd. Edward Piris, Camp No. 11, Breckagh Bridge.
3rd. Angeles Morello, Camp No. 17, Carryduff.

Class 27.—Model Ship.
1st. J. Poggio, Camp No. 4, Saintfield.
2nd. Chas Morello, Camp No. 17, Carryduff.
3rd. J. McCarthy, Camp No. 4, Saintfield.

Class 28.—Model, any Article.
1st. Manuel Durante, Camp No. 17, Carryduff.
2nd. J. Lima, Camp No. 9, Drummuck.

Class 29.—Any fancy article (Small).
1st Mrs. Elena Guilliano, Camp No. 17, Carryduff.
2nd. Mrs. M. Serra, Camp No 8, Dunnaird.
3rd. Edward Piris, Camp No. 11, Breckagh Bridge.

CHILDREN'S CLASSES.

Class 30.—Hand-writing. English. Confined to Camp Schools. Not less than 25, and not more than 50 words.
1st George Gaskin, Camp No 5, Tawneybrack.
2nd. John Garcia, Camp No. 11, Breckagh Bridge.
3rd. Carlos Saltariche, Camp No. 9, Drummuck.

Class 31.—Sketch from Nature, or Still Life. In pencil.
1st. Ana Lane, Camp No. 10, Aghacully.
2nd. C. Saltariche, Camp No. 9, Drummuck.
3rd. Manuel Muscatt, Camp No. 11, Breckagh Bridge.

Class 32.—Sketch from Nature or Still Life, in water colours.
1st. Isabel Caballero, Camp No. 10, Aghacully.
2nd. Carlos Saltariche, Camp No. 9, Drummuck.
3rd. L. Macedo, Camp No. 8, Dunnaird.

Class 33.—Home-made stuffed toys.
1st. Rose Attard, Camp No. 11, Breckagh Bridge.
2nd. Manola Cefai, Camp No. 11, Breckagh Bridge.
3rd. Rose Duarte, Camp No. 11, Breckagh Bridge.

Class 34.—Composition. My Ambition. Not more than 250 words.
1st. Gilbert Carmen, Camp No. 10, Aghacully.
2nd. Araceli Candeas, Camp No. 5, Tawneybrack.
3rd. Violet Victory, Camp No. 4, Saintfield.

(Continued at foot of next page).

Class 35.—Best named collection of Leaves.
1st. Manola Cefai, Camp No. 11, Breckagh Bridge.
2nd. Josephine Duarte, Camp No. 11, Breckagh Bridge.
3rd. Joseph M. Reyes, Camp No. 11, Breckagh Bridge.

Class 36.—Toy made from fir cones, acorns and twigs.
1st. Pupils of Class 2, No. 1 Camp, Clough.
2nd. Josephine Durante, Camp No. 11, Breckagh Bridge.

Class 37.—Best Model of an Ulster Farmyard.
1st. Pupils of Class 4 and 5, Camp 8, Dunnaird.
2nd. Pupils of Class 2, Clough, Camp No. 1, Co. Down.

The evacuees, who in the majority, were Roman Catholics observed and celebrated most of their religious festivities. The differences that exist between Catholic and Protestant people of Northern Ireland inevitably cropped up every now and then. But these differences were never extended to include Gibraltar evacuees who had no difficulty in associating with Northern Ireland people of either denomination. Many evacuees were baptised, received their first Holy Communion, celebrated their Confirmation and were also united in holy matrimony in Northern Ireland.
This page shows the Corpus Christi Procession with the traditional group of children taking part in the processions.

Above and below evacuees taking parting the Corpus Christi Procession. Photos above and below Mr M Infante

Gibraltar evacuees taking part in a procession in Northern Ireland.

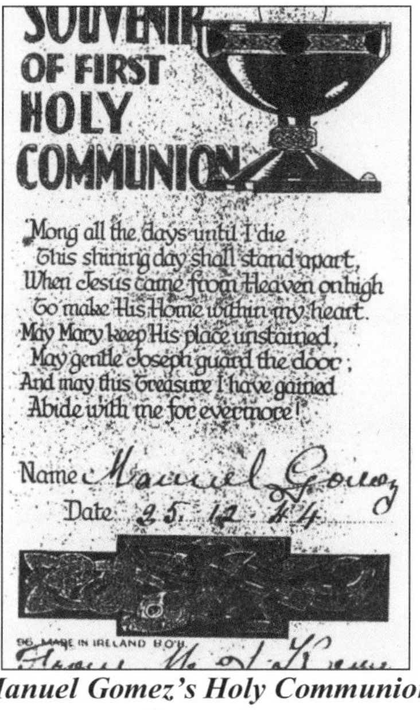

SOUVENIR OF FIRST HOLY COMMUNION

Mong all the days until I die
This shining day shall stand apart,
When Jesus came from Heaven on high
To make His Home within my heart.
May Mary keep His place unstained,
May gentle Joseph guard the door;
And may this treasure I have gained
Abide with me for evermore!

Name Manuel Gomez

Date 25. 12. 44.

MADE IN IRELAND

Manuel Gomez's Holy Communion Souvenir.

The Immaculate Church of Mary at Drumbo where Maria Luisa Guilliano was baptised. Photo Mrs M Lopez

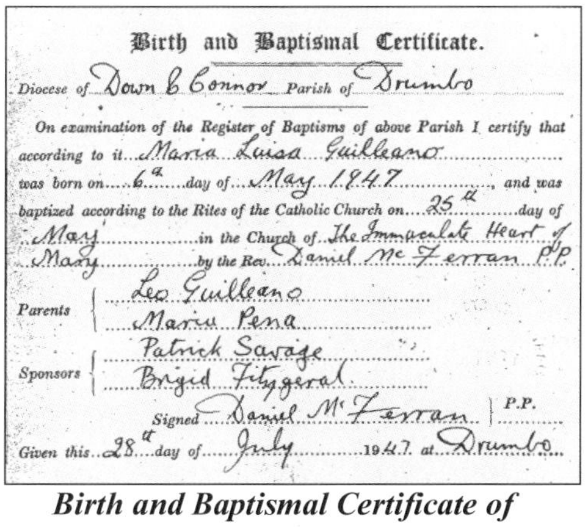

Birth and Baptismal Certificate.

Diocese of Down & Connor Parish of Drumbo

On examination of the Register of Baptisms of above Parish I certify that according to it Maria Luisa Guilleano was born on 6th day of May 1947, and was baptized according to the Rites of the Catholic Church on 25th day of May in the Church of The Immaculate Heart of Mary by the Rev. Daniel McFerran P.P.

Parents: Leo Guilleano; Mariu Pena

Sponsors: Patrick Savage; Brigid Fitzgeral

Signed Daniel McFerran P.P.

Given this 28th day of July 1947 at Drumbo

Birth and Baptismal Certificate of Maria Luisa Guilliano.

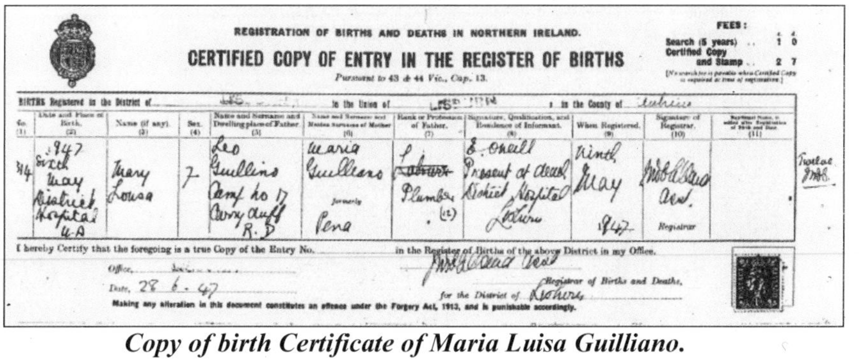

REGISTRATION OF BIRTHS AND DEATHS IN NORTHERN IRELAND.

CERTIFIED COPY OF ENTRY IN THE REGISTER OF BIRTHS

Pursuant to 43 & 44 Vic., Cap. 13.

FEES: Search (5 years) 1 0; Certified Copy and Stamp 2 7

No. (1)	Date and Place of Birth (2)	Name (if any) (3)	Sex (4)	Name and Surname and Dwelling place of Father (5)	Name and Surname and Maiden Surname of Mother (6)	Rank or Profession of Father (7)	Signature, Qualification, and Residence of Informant (8)	When Registered (9)	Signature of Registrar (10)	(11)
44	1947 Sixth May District Hospital	Mary Louisa	F	Leo Guillino Camp No 17	Maria Guilleano formerly Pena	Plumber	E. Oneill Present at death District Hospital	Ninth May 1947	Registrar	

I hereby Certify that the foregoing is a true Copy of the Entry No. in the Register of Births of the above District in my Office.

Date, 28 6. 47

Registrar of Births and Deaths, for the District of

Making any alteration in this document constitutes an offence under the Forgery Act, 1913, and is punishable accordingly.

Copy of birth Certificate of Maria Luisa Guilliano.

I think the Gibraltarian Jews were all accommodated at Camp No.4 Saintfield in County Down. This page contains photographs of Jewish families in Northern Ireland. All the photographs except the one below were donated by Mrs Beniso.

Gibraltar evacuees at Camp No.4 Saintfield.
At the back L to R: Joseph Gabay Rev.Benzibra, Harry Porter, Alfonso Moss, Mesoda Benady, David Cohen, Abensur and George Azopardi. In front L to R.Tommy, George Nahon (young woman) Benady, Monolo Segui, Jose Castro, Hatchwell and G.Azopardi Granddaughter – Maricarmen Netto. Photo Mr A Moss

Evacuees at Camp No.4 Saintfield where many Gibraltar Jews were accommodated.

Mrs. Beniso (nee Cohen) round about Camp No. 4 Saintfield.

Above and belowMrs R Beniso and friends with Lord and Lady Moore in their Manor next door to Camp No.4.

Above and below Rachel Cohen (Mrs. Beniso) with her friend.

Evacuees in Northern Ireland

Families obviously kept together during the evacuation. In this and in the next page there are photographs of families in Northern Ireland.

Mr George Saltariche with wife Teresa and daughter Ana in Camp No.14. (Molennan).
Photos above and below Mr L Saltariche

The Saltariche children in the snow in Camp No.14.
At the back L to R: Asuncion, George and Ana
In front are: Luis, Mary and Juan

Mr Moses Abecasis and his wife Herminia with children Manolo and Mercy Baglietto and Gentila Abecasis. Photo Mrs M Brown

Manolo Gomez with his family at Camp No.5 (Tawneybrack).
Photo Mr M Gomez

Johnny Sanchez at Camp No.1 (Clough). Photo Mr J Sanchez

Josephine Poggio in Camp No.13 (Ballyarnett). Photo Mrs Poggio

Mary Saltariche with friend.
Photo Mr L Saltariche

Alex Grech around the camp.
Photo Mr A Grech

This page contains photographs of different groups of families in Northern Ireland.

Evacuees at Camp No.11 (Breckagh Bridge).
In the photo are Charlie Hayward, L.Prescott, Porter and M.Gracia. Photo Mrs Balban

The Pratts family. Photo Mr Pratts

The Macedo Family.
In the photo Mrs Ana Macedo, Mrs Encarnacion Macedo, Rosa, Anne, Hector and Maruchi Macedo. Photo Mrs M Martinez

The Mañetto family at Camp No.15 (Warbleshinney)
In the photo are Mrs Candelaria Mañetto her son Luis and daughters Aurelia and Anne. Photo Mrs L Lane

Johnny Viagas.

Anita Rocca.

The Power family.
At the back Mr Joseph Power with son Clive and wife Mabel. In front Eddie, Daisy, Gladys and Richard Power. Photo Mr R Power.

The Torres family.
L to R: Mrs Maribel Torres, Irene Torres (girl standing on chair)
Gladys Torres, Peseda Torres (Mrs Robba)
Mercedes Torres (Mrs Gonzalez) Mr Miguel Torres.
Photo Mr V Gonzalez

The Macedo Family in Camp No.9
(Drummock).
In the photo Mrs Ana Macedo, Anne, Hector,
Rosa, Maruchi and Mrs Encarnacion Macedo.
Photo Mrs M Martinez

The Celecia Family at Camp 15 (Warbleshinney).
From L to R: Aida Celecia (Mrs Bautista), Margot Mahoney,
Olga Celecia, (Mrs Sanchez), Lauri Celecia (Mrs Savignon),
Regina Davies, Antonia Celecia (slightly at the back) and Rafael
Celecia Photos above and below MrJ Bautista

Luis,Aurelia and Anne Mañetto.
Photo Mrs L Lane (nee Mañetto)

The Bautista family in Camp No.14 (Molennan) in 1946.
Left to Right: John Bautista, Mrs Herminia Bautista,
Mr Henry Bautista and Joe Bautisa

The Rocca Family. Photo Mr A Rocca

The photographs in this page are of the Gulliano's family who were in Camp No.17 (Carryduff).

Mr Leo Guilliano with sons Leo and Joseph.

Mrs Elena with husband Paco Guilliano, nephews Leo, Joseph and niece Magnolia.

All the photographs on this page were donated by Mr J Guilliano.

Mrs Guilliano with their children Leo, Magnolia and Joseph.

Leo and Joseph Guilliano with other children.

Joseph, Magnolia and Leo Guilliano.

Antonio and Carolina Dalmedo with their Son Joseph Luis Dalmedo in Ballymena. Photo Mr Dalmedo

Francis Rocca with his uncle Alex Chipolina. Photo Mr F Rocca

The Chipolina family.

Mr Freddie Parody with his wife Anna and children Anthony and Alex in Camp No.11 (Brechagh Bridge). Photos above and below Mr F Parody

Victor Gonzalez with fiancé Mercedes Torres. Photo Mr V Gonzalez

Anthony and Alex Parody in Camp No.11 (Breckagh Bridge)

The photographs on this page are of the Sene and other families who were in Camp No. 11 (Breckagh Bridge) – Aughafatten.

In the photo Mrs Isabel Sene with daughters Lourdes and Laura. the child is Lilian Lima.

In the photo Mrs Sene with daughter Laura and son Victor. the child in front is Lilian Lima.

In the photo at the back from left to right: Laura Sene, J.Ferrary and I.Garcia. In front from L to R Bruzon, Garcia ..?.. , Bruzon, M.Bruzon.

Miss Angela Sene (Mrs Lara).

Mr and Mrs Sene with their daughter Maribel.

All the photographs on this page were donated by Mrs A Lara.

Evacuees in Northern Ireland

In above photo taken in Dec. 1945 are Rogelio Borge, Humberto Garcia, Pepe Lombard, Andres Savignon, Pepe Serra, George Epsworth and Jaime Savignon. Photo Mr A Savignon

Evacuees at Camp No.1 (Clough). Photo Mr J Sanchez

Evacuees in the snow in the photo are Anne and Hector Macedo. Photo Mrs Martinez

Evacuee children. In the photo is Victor Risso and Peter Grima. Photo Mrs Risso

Gibraltar evacuees visiting the Town Hall at Ballymena.
In the photo are Pepe Luis Gomez,HenryViñales and Juan Rodriguez.
Photo Mr H Viñales

Evacuees at Camp No. 8 (Dunnaird).
Among those at the back are Borge, Hernandez, Lombard, Bagu and Cassano. Amongst those in front are Pitto and Attias. Photo Gibraltar Museum

Evacuees from different camps. In the photo among the evacuees is A.Sciacaluga.
Photo Mr A Sciacaluga

Photo of group of evacuees taken on 24.8.1946
and sent to Alberto Santos. Photo Mr A Santos

Evacuees in Northern Ireland

Evacuees at Camp No.16 (Tagherian).
Amongst the children marked with an x is Mariola Aldorino.
Photos above and below Mrs Reading(nee Aldorino)

Evacuees in Camp No.5 (Tawnybrack).
In the photo are Miguel, Aida and Eduardo Cornelio and Manolo Gomez.
Photo Mr M Gomez

Evacuees in Camp No 16. (Tagherian).
Amongst the children is Mariola Aldorino

Evacuees at Tawnybrack CampNo.5 in Ballymena.
The nurse with children is Miss Olga Massetti. Photo Mr A Massetti

At the back from L To R Andrea Ferro,Daisy Power, Maribel Torres,Elena Bagna,Gladys Power , Rosario Gomez. In front are L To R Marcelino Mena, Richard Power and Manolo Valarino. Photo Mrs H Alman

Evacuee children. On the extreme right is Sonia King (Mrs Jezzard). Photos above and below Mr D Jezzard

Group of evacuees with Monolo and Freddie Asquez. PhotoMrs Asquez

Evacuee children at the back second from the left is Sonia King (Mrs Jezzard).

Evacuees in the snow. In the photo are Miss Montado and Mrs Grima. Photo Mrs M Martinez

Among are Manolo and Freddie Asquez. Photo Mrs Asquez

The selections of photographs on this page were taken in the camps of Ballymena. All the photographs on this page, except the two shown below, were donated by the Gibraltar Museum.

In the photo from left to right are Mrs M Hernandez, Mr R Hernandez and Mrs M Fernandez. The children are Josephine and Mari Carmen Hernandez. Photo Mrs M Hernandez

Conchi,(later Mrs Ramirez),Charles(later Bishop of Gibraltar) and Joe Caruana. Photo Mr J Caruana

On the left hand side of the picture above are Freddie and Manuel Asquez.

The photographs on this page were taken in the camps of Ballymena. All the photographs on this page except the one below were donated by the Gibraltar Museum.

Evacuees at Camp No.10 Aghacully. Photo Mr S Chipolina

Mr William Grant – Minister of Health with evacuee children.

Evacuees in Camp No.10 (Aghacully) In the photo are Carlos Saltariche, Antonio Saltariche, Antonio and Francisco Martinez, C. De Santos, Collado and Nicolas Risso. Photo Mr L Saltariche

Evacuees in camp No.14 (Molennan) .In the photo is Carlos Saltariche. Photo Mr L Saltariche

Wilfred Francis with his aunt Elvira Sheriff (nee Francis) in one of the camps in Ballymena. Photo Mr W Francis

Mrs Isabel and Mr Manolo Asquez. Photos above and below Mrs Asquez

Evacuee in the farm near Camp No.14 (Molennan). In the photo is Mary Saltariche. Photo Mr L Saltariche

Freddie Asquez.

Some evacuees celebrated as much as four Christmases in the camps. Below are cuttings from the camp magazine titled the Camp Courier reporting about the activities in the camps during Christmas 1946. - the third Christmas in Northern Ireland and the sixth away from Gibraltar. Copies of Camp Courier by Mr V Gonzalez.

Clough.

Highlight of the Christmas festivities in Clough was the Children's Party in the Recreation Hall, when Father Christmas came loaded with sweets, chocolates and toys, to the joy of the little ones. There was a gay atmosphere at this attractive Christmas Day party, the arrangements for which were in the capable hands of a Committee representative of the Camp residents. They left no stone unturned to make the children happy.

"Sticky Apples" contributed by the Camp Staff were an extra treat which the kiddies enjoyed. The festivities concluded with a most enjoyable dance.

Saintfield.

The Feast of Christmas was opened with Midnight Mass in the Camp on Christmas Eve, which attracted a large congregation, and was celebrated by Rev. J. Barrett, B.A., Camp Chaplain. Particularly impressive and devotional was the rendering of the sacred hymns by the Camp Choir.

The children had a Christmas Tree and a gay party all to themselves, with gifts of chocolates, apples and—yes—bananas, followed by high tea. A little bird tells us they did enjoy themselves.

The Men's Club had its big "do" on Boxing Day—a real "banquete" which everyone thoroughly enjoyed and to which all did full justice. The "feast" was followed by a very attractive dance, songs, etc.

The Girls' Club had a most enjoyable evening, with more good things to mark the festive season. The singing was specially attractive.

Everyone in the Camp worked hard to make this Christmas a memorable one, and while it would be wrong to single out individuals for special praise, everyone felt that Mr. Matos, president of the Men's Club, worked a major miracle in perfecting the arrangements. Others who helped in a special way were Mr. Walker, Mr. Alfonso Moss and Victor Balban. The Girls' Club arrangements were under the capable supervision of Mrs. Earle, the Misses Lina Castro and Aida Abensur and their band of hard-working young ladies who did most of the behind-the-scenes jobs. Music was supplied by Messrs. Sanders, McCarthy, Aldorino and Balban (Gibraltarian Piper).

Carryduff.

On Christmas Eve members of the Men's Club were the guests of the Roosevelt Street Youth Centre, where they were treated right royally and with true Ulster hospitality. The Centre's relations with the Camp Club are of the friendliest, and the

Below message from the Rt Hon.William Grant, J.P., M.P., Minister of Health and Local Government.

On the occasion of the issue of this special edition of the "Camp, Courier", I take the opportunity of 'Wishing all the Gibraltarian evacuees in Northern Ireland the Compliments of the Season: This will be your third, Christmas here, and I am sure you are all looking forward to the day when you will return to-your homeland. Over four thousand of your compatriots have returned home since you came to Northern Ireland, and I understand that a further party of two hundred or more, mainly elderly people is due to sail shortly.

Unfortunately, it may be some time before the last repatriation party leaves, but I can assure you that until that happy time arrives my Ministry will do all in its power to make the stay of those who remain, as comfortable and pleasant as the circumstances will allow.

I wish all of you, and especially the children, a very Happy Christmas, and I. hope that your dearest wish, that is, to return to Gibraltar will, come true in. the not too distant future

Cutting about Christmas in the camps continued from previous column.

Gibraltarian community in Carryduff wish to thank the Roosevelt Street boys and girls for their many kindnesses.

A special dance on Christmas night attracted a large crowd, and was most enjoyable. On Boxing Day the kiddies in the Camp were entertained by the Club to a truly delightful party, and a specially handsome Christmas Tree. It is a safe bet that the children will not soon forget this event, and the Club deserves warm congratulations upon the excellence of its arrangements.

On New Year's Eve some fifty boys and girls from Roosevelt Street were the guests of the Camp Club, where they were entertained to supper, and afterwards to a well organised and most attractive dance. Certainly the visitors enjoyed themselves and spoke warmly of the hospitality and kindness of their Gibraltarian friends.

Tawneybrack.

The Men's Club presented a gay scene on the occasion of the Children's Party on Christmas Day. It was most attractively decorated and it was evident that the Club members spared no pains to make the occasion one which the children would appreciate. And appreciate it they did! Their delight with the arrangements and the excellent tea provided was evident.

The Girls' Club members looked after the tea arrangements, and the general organisation was perfect.

Mr. Candeas addressed the children as did Mr. A. McCormick, Camp Warden, who, while wishing everyone a "Merry Christmas" on behalf of himself and the Staff, expressed the warm wish that they would celebrate the Feast next year in sunny Gibraltar.

Dunmaird.

Miss McKee, C.C.R., provided a special treat for the Nursery children. The nursery was delightfully decorated, and from an attractive Christmas Tree each child received a small present. Following tea, the children entertained the grown-ups to a charming concert.

Another special treat for the tiny tots was provided by the Camp Staff.

Specially memorable was the Children's Party organised by the Men's Club. Following tea, each children received a gift, these being distributed by the Warden, Mr. J. Davidson; Miss Patton, Asst. Warden, and Mr. S. McDonald, Catering Manager, on behalf of the Club. The three officials mentioned, in turn got a very pleasant surprise

Below another Christmas massage From Mr J.N.Walker, Chairman, Central Clubs Committee.

"I am glad to have this opportunity to send warm greetings to the young men and women of the Camp Clubs and all my fellow Gibraltarians in Northern Ireland and back home in Gibraltar.

Christmas is very much the Festival of the Family, when we forget our troubles and anxieties and think only of those family associations which are so very dear to all peoples everywhere, but so especially dear to us. As young and old gather within the family circle—a magic circle of love, faith and courage—there will be thoughts of home and of pleasant things, of the joy that will be ours when again we hear the Christmas Carols echo from the blue skies which keep watch upon our dear Rock.

That the time of waiting may not be long is the dearest prayer of all of us in the Camps.

But, while we wait, let us fit ourselves to grasp with a full heart and a generous courage those opportunities which must, inevitably, come our way when our exile is ended and we come home again. To-morrow is for the young people of Gibraltar, and I know they will be worthy of it.

May God bring you, each of you, every happiness in the coming year."

Despite the fact that the sea temperature surrounding the beaches of Northern Ireland are not particularly appetising for swimming, the evacuees who were used to more warm sea temperatures nevertheless managed to go to the nearby beaches. Whether they actually went for a swim is something I do not have any evidence except the photos in this page.

Above and below female youngsters and children at the beach near Ballymena. Photos Mrs E Alman

Although Mrs Elena Alman had no photographs from the time of the evacuation she had the above photographs taken went she visited the Tyrella Beach, near Newcastle in County Down the same beach she used to go to during the evacuation. Photo by Mrs E Alman

Another photo of Elena at Tyrella Beach with her husband Adolfo. Photo by Mrs E Alman

Children going for a ride in a farm cart in Ballymena. Photo Gibraltar Museum

Youngsters gathered for a reception given to the Rt.Rev.Monsignor Flanagan at Carryduff Camp. Photo by Mr V Gonzalez

During their stay in Northern Ireland many marriages and births took place. The marriages were: Mr Michael Joseph Torres to Miss Maria Delcarmen Rodriguez at the All Saints' Church in Ballymena. Miss Angela Sene to Mr Ernest Lara in the nearby chapel at Aughafatten.

Mr. Michael Joseph Torres and Miss Delcarman Rodriquez (centre) leaving All Saints' Church, Ballymena, after their wedding in 1945.

The newly wed couples with Father Dominic McHugh who officiated at the ceremony and Mrs Lara's parents Rogelio and Isabel Sene. The photos above and below were donated by Mrs Angela Lara.

Families and friends greeting the newly wed couples.

Other weddings celebrated during 1945 were that of Mr Frank Bau to Miss Maureen Shields at Broughshane. Also married from the same camp was Miss Carmen Peñalver to Hugh Hunter McKay at the Presbyterian Church. As to births the ones I know from my research were Mrs Sonia Golt (Nee Torrilla), Mrs Lourdes Lane (nee Mañetto), and Mrs Lopez (Nee Guilliano)Miss Sonia Peñalver, Mr Albert Poggio, Mrs Priscilla Sacramento and many others. The subject of the evacuation has, occasionally, been given press coverage in Northern Ireland and which over the years has renewed close links with Gibraltar. It would be practically impossible, in terms of space, to refer to every single newspaper that I have acquired during my research. A Northern Ireland newspaper story in the 50s quoted below drew comparison between the Gibraltar evacuees and the Hungarian refugees who arrived at Ulster seeking political asylum during the uprising in 1956. The Cuttings were donated by Mr V Gonzalez.

MENTION of the arrival in Ulster of Hungarian refugees reminds me of the time when we were hosts to the people of Gibraltar, who came here when "evacuated" from London at the time when the "doodle-bugs" were doing so much damage, and who spent years here in sixteen camps situated in Counties Antrim, Down and Derry.

I was appointed to the staff of one of these camps when it was being built to accommodate expected refugees from the parts of France then being overrun by the Nazis. We lived "rough" in those early days, our sleeping-place being Nissen-type huts heated by coke stoves, with two-tier iron beds, washing facilities being provided by tin basins, hot water coming (when at all) from the central kitchen where the cooks worked under primitive conditions to supply food for us all.

There was a large building, one of the first constructed on the site, which was literally crammed to the roof and doors with everything from bedding, basins, tables, chairs, cutlery, delph, hatchets, saws, buckets, soap, candles, coal buckets and shovels to field-kitchen boilers, pots, pans, and garden tools. One of the first jobs we tackled was the arrangement of this higgledy-piggledy chaos into some semblance of order and accessibility. Then we had to transport by hand and assemble in each of the 120 Nissen huts everything necessary for the expected occupants, who were expected to number about 1,000. (In fact at one time we had 1,200 in our particular camp.)

When we came next day to record their names we were in for another surprise. There were O'Reillys and O'Kanes, O'Briens and Murphys among the Yeos and Gonsalez, and there were Patricks and Bernards and Dannys among the Miguels and Vincenzos of the Christian names. The greatest surprise was when one of them addressed me in Irish, and he seemed more than surprised when my fluency fell far short of his! It seems that most of them had been educated at the schools of the Irish Christian Brothers, and some of the Brothers had taught them the Gaelic tongue.

An Artistic People

THEY were a very artistic people, and the women had what a Braid woman called "great hands"—a fact which I as storekeeper became painfully aware when I found the small children walking about in beautifully-fashioned siren suits which had been made from some of the dark blankets I had issued when colder weather came.

In the musical field they were very accomplished, both as instrumentalists and singers, and during their stay they gave many most enjoyable concerts, and when the first Christmas came they made many lovely toys for their children.

Some of them were gifted painters, and I have before me, as I write, a beautiful painting in oils of Gibraltar, the work of a certain Senor Mannia, who he presented to me before I left the camp.

Well, they are back on their beloved Rock long ago, but they left an enduring memory behind of a very likeable people, and I wonder if any or many of them recall the years they spent among us. And do they still wear the "snood," a form of headgear which they made fashionable for some time in Ulster?

In recent years groups, who in the main were those who were evacuated to Northern Ireland have visited the sites of the camps in Northern Ireland. In October 2005 one of these groups visited the camps accompanied by the Bishop of Gibraltar Monsignor C.Caruana and Father C.Azzopardi to take a replica of the statue of the Lady Of Europe to Northern Ireland. See Chapter 16.

Mr. and Mrs. Alman with Mayor of Ballymena Councillor Tommy Nicholl. Photos above and below by Mr and Mrs Alman

Victor Gonzalez recollecting his young days in camps. Photo by V Gonzalez

Manolo Gomez visiting the camp site where he and his family were accommodated at Camp 5 Tawnybrack in Kells. Photo by Mr M Gomez

Mrs. Elena Alman (nee Bagna) by the same wall as in the photo below. Photo by Mrs E Alman

In the photo L to R Carlota Navas, Mabel Power and Daisy Pike. Photo by Mr R Power

The resting places of some of the evacuees was also visited. Photo by Mr M Gomez

The remains of what used to be the Laundry at Camp No.13 (Ballyarnett)

“We Thank God and England..”

The photographs on this page were taken during the October 2005 visit to the camps in Northern Ireland.

Bishop C.Caruana, Father Azzopardi and Mr Archie Patterson. Photo by Mr M Gomez

Visiting the camp sites in Northern Ireland from Left to Right Johnny Grech, Johnny Sanchez, Victor Gonzalez and Clive Coom. Photo by Mr C Coom

What used to be the laundry at Camp No.1 (Clough). Photo by Mr C Coom

Group of ex-evacuees who visited the camps in October 2005. Photo by Mr M Gomez

One of the many families who visited the Northern Ireland camps in recent years was the Guillianos.

Above Mrs Maria Luisa Lopez (nee Guilliano born in Northern Ireland) visiting the remains of what used to be the dinning room at Camp No.17 Carryduff.

Mrs Maria Guilliano visiting the resting place of her brother-in-law, Mr Joseph Guilliano

Above and below Mrs Maria Guilliano with her daughter and son-in- law visiting the remains of one of the huts in what used to be Camp 17 Carryduff.

Mrs Guilliano visiting the resting place of Parish Priest Daniel McFerran who baptised her Northern Ireland born daughter Maria Luisa seen in the photograph accompanied by her husband Mr Lopez who was also evacuated to Northern Ireland.

All the photographs on this page were donated Mrs M Lopez.

Return from the Rock

Mrs Angela Lara, who along with her late husband Ernest was a Gibraltarian evacuee at Breckagh Bridge Camp outside Broughshane back in 1945, was back in Ballymena last week for the first time since leaving some sixty-two years ago. Mrs Lara, who was guest of Ballymena Mayor Ald James Alexander , also met Canon Dominic McHugh who was the Chaplain to the camps, married her and her late husband in All Saints Church in 1945. Also included are Mrs Lara's daughters Elizabeth and Eileen and Breda Watterson, who runs the All Saints parish website. BT23-112JC

A Gibraltarian woman, who was evacuated to Ballymena from 'The Rock' during World War II, has made her first visit back to the borough in 62 years.

Mrs Angela Lara, 81, was accompanied last week on her emotional trip down memory lane by two of her five children, Eileen and Elizabeth, who had been planning their mother's return to Ballymena for almost two years with the help of All Saints parishioner, Breda Waterson.

"One of the daughters was doing some research on churches in Ballymena and came across our website," said Breda.

"We started sending e-mails to each other and that started me off on my own research and I found the priest who married Angela all those years ago," she explained.

Mrs Lara and her late husband, Ernest, lived at the Breckagh Bridge Camp, outside Broughshane, during their evacuation and were married in 1945 at St Patrick's church, The Braid, by Canon Dominic McHugh, who was chaplain to the camps.

Their wedding was the first Gib wedding to take place in the borough and the occasion was marked by wife of the Lord-Lieutenant of County Antrim, Lady O'Neill, who sent the bride a bouquet of flowers on the morning of the ceremony.

Memories of the nuptials came flooding back to Mrs Lara last Tuesday when, thanks to Breda, she met the man who performed the ceremony all those decades ago, Canon McHugh, at a civic reception in her honour hosted by Ballymena Borough Council.

Breda, who co-ordinates the All Saints Church website, took the visitors under her wing during their three-day visit and treated them to a tour of Ballymena, the evacuee camp sites, the North Coast and Giant's Causeway and, with the help of the Local Studies archives at Ballymena library, sourced a group photograph taken on Mrs Lara's wedding day.

She also took them to visit the site of the Braid Chapel where the ceremony took place.

"It was a very busy three days and Angela did have a fantastic time although she was sad her husband, Ernest, wasn't with her," said Breda.

"She remembered quite a lot about Ballymena such as the Town Hall and the bank at Broadway.

"It was her first footstep back here since she went home to Gibraltar and although she's now 81 she did say she'd love to come back," said Breda.

"Her daughters also plan to bring their families over some time," she added.

In the interim, Breda will be incorporating a special feature on the Lara family's historic and rather emotional visit into the All Saints website shortly and also has a feature on the wider subject of Ballymena's Gib. camps in the pipeline.

Anyone keen to find out more can log on to www.ballymenaparish.org

The most recent visit to the camps was arranged by the Lara family through their contacts in Ballymena. The cutting shown above reproduced by the Gibraltar Chronicle explains in detail the main reasons for the Lara's family visit to Northern Ireland.

Mrs Lara with her daughters Elizabeth and Eileen at the site of what used to be Camp No.11. Photo Mrs Lara.

As explained in the cutting shown at the top of this page, the Lara family were taken to see the remains of the camp were Mrs Lara was accommodated during the evacuation. The above photograph shows the plaque that was placed in 1998 to mark the 50 anniversary of the closure of the camps in July 1948.

Mrs Lara and her daughters were also the guests of the Ballymena Mayor Ald James Alexander who presented Mrs Angela Lara with a memento souvenir on behalf of the Ballymena Borough Council.

Photo of souvenir presented to Mrs Angela Lara. Photo J.Gingell

In 2006 in conjunction with the twinning between the Cities of Ballymena and Gibraltar a delegation headed by the Mayor of Gibraltar visited the town of Ballymena and the camp sites in Northern Ireland. The idea of establishing the twinning of both towns was in recognition of the memories that still exist in the hearts and minds of the people of Gibraltar and Ballymena.

Mayors Clive Beltran and Tom Nicholl.

Visiting the remains of buildings.

The remains of what used one of the camps in Ballymena.

Delegation visiting the cemetery where many Gibraltarian evacuees were buried.

In order to have a rough idea of what the camp environs looked like, I have included photographs taken during the twinning tour to show some of the remains of the camps in Northern Ireland. All the photographs on this page were donated by Mr L Bonavia.

The Gibraltar delegation visiting the All Saints Chapel at Ballymena. The statue on the left hand corner is of Our Lady of Europe taken during the visit in 2005.

Above picture shows the remains of one of the stoves used to warm up the huts during the evacuation.

Camp No.10 Aghacully, Augafatten, County Antrim.

Camp No.8 Dunaird, Broughshane, County Antrim.

Above the remains of the building that was the camp kitchen during the evacuation in Northern Ireland.

Camp No.11 Breckagh Bridge, Aughafatten, County Antrim.

The Gibraltar delegation's visit was reciprocated by a delegation from Ballymena led by Alderman James Alexander, Mayor of Ballymena, including the three former Mayors and other leading officials on Saturday 9th September 2006. A group of Ballymena Borough residents with local connections also took part in the programme of events. Both the Mayors of Ballymena and Gibraltar exchanged speeches and then proceeded to the signing of a Memorandum of Understanding based on the historical links between the two communities. The signing ceremony which was attended by many guests, including some ex-evacuees, was held outside the City Hall on Tuesday 12th September 2006.

Above Alderman James Alexander Mayor of Ballymena and Gibraltar's Mayor Clive Beltran signing and exchanging copies of a Memorandum of Understanding.

CHAPTER THIRTEEN

REPATRIATION OF EVACUEES IN NORTHERN IRELAND AND REMAINING IN THE UK

The protracted repatriation process from Northern Ireland was to last from about the end of 1944 until late 1951. I must say that I found this part of my research the most controversial of all. It seems that the main source of grievance affecting the majority of the evacuees was the understandable continued desire to be repatriated to Gibraltar. From the very outset the matter became a constant source of dispute between the British Government, the Gibraltar authorities and those seeking the speedy return. Throughout all this time many meetings and demonstrations were held to bring pressure upon the pertinent authorities to repatriate the evacuees. The authorities concerned were in turn saying all along that the process was going to be necessarily long due to the shortage of housing, the inadequate facilities available in Gibraltar for schooling, medical and hygiene. Added to this was the phasing out of part of a very large military garrison of about 30,000 to make room for the repatriated civilian population. The grievances affecting the evacuees in Northern Ireland ranged from the lack of employment, the non-entitlement to social benefits, and the extreme cold weather without proper heating facilities and the uncertainty of not knowing exactly when they could return to Gibraltar. Throughout the whole period there were conflicting views emanating from those in the camps, the officials, and those who were demanding their return on the grounds of living conditions in the camps. On the one hand the officials usually reported the conditions of the evacuees as fairly adequate given the circumstances of the war, which forced the authorities concerned to take the evacuees to Northern Ireland. However, the views of those making the complaints usually described the conditions at the camp as appalling, although there were also some who sounded very grateful, for the way they were being treated. I have attempted to include as much information as possible of some of the main highlights in connection with the Northern Ireland repatriation controversy.

By late 1944 the pertinent authorities were already being urged to expedite the repatriation of the remaining evacuees in Northern Ireland. The Governor reported that he was receiving letters and telegrams from the evacuees urging him to authorise their immediate repatriation. The AACR was also complaining to the then Colonial Secretary Mr Miles Clifford about the suffering of the evacuees in Northern Ireland.

The issue became more tense when Mr Clifford replied that the evacuees were happy to put up with the camps' conditions when they escaped from the flying bombs and they could not expect to be moved again back to England at their convenience. The Governor was also stressing at the time that no promises had been made of an early return.

"Appalling conditions" alleged in Ireland

A.A.C.R. URGE RETURN OF GIB. EVACUEES

A six-point resolution calling on the Government of Gibraltar and the authorities in the United Kingdom to carry out the immediate repatriation of all evacuees, and suggesting measures to overcome accommodation difficulties at present impeding the measure, was unanimously approved by members of the Association for the Advancement of Civil Rights who packed the Theatre Royal last night.

PRESIDENT of the Association, Mr. Albert Risso, declared that this was not the time to judge responsibility for the non-return of evacuees still in Northern Ireland. It was the time to get together to endorse the points of the resolution with a view to affecting their prompt repatriation.

The resolution described the meeting as being "fully conscious of the hardships which the Gibraltar evacuees in Northern Ireland are undergoing by being compelled to live under the most appalling conditions," and suggested the following action to remove obstacles to their return:

"Board changes"

1 Immediate derequisitioning of property still in the hands of the military authorities.

2 Handing over to the Colonial Government of all military married quarters and other property.

3 Closest cooperation by all Government Departments concerned in the building —with top priority in every way — of temporary dwellings.

4 Free exercise by the Resettlement Board of all properties vested in it under the Defence Regulations, and allocation of all available accommodation by the Board.

5 Reconstitution of the Resettlement Board to include more members of the Association for the Advancement of Civil Rights as soon as possible.

The fact that the majority of evacuees in Northern Ireland had been deprived of their luggage, which had been mistakenly sent to Gibraltar, made it still more imperative to carry out the most immediate repatriation, the resolution added.

It was decided that a public demonstration should accompany the deputation handing the resolution to His Excellency the Governor.

Report on the meeting held on the 6th December 1944.

On the 6th December 1944 a meeting was convened by the AACR at the Theatre Royal where it was demanded from both the Government of Gibraltar and the authorities in the United Kingdom to carry out the immediate repatriation of all remaining evacuees in Northern Ireland.

The first official visit to ascertain conditions in the camps took place at the end of January 1945 when it was already reported that the evacuees would not be happy until they returned to Gibraltar.

Coinciding with the AACR meeting a deputation composed of representatives from the camps travelled to London to meet officials at the Colonial Office where they made specific complaints about the dictatorial treatment the evacuees were receiving from some wardens in the camps. The Ministry of Health on investigating the complaints came up with totally different explanation to that given by the local representatives. Further investigations were carried out by officials to find out what were the conditions in the camps and to report their findings. From their investigations it emerged that the evacuees were found to be somewhat confused by hearing different accounts from a variety of official and unofficial sources. Lack of work was mentioned as an issue of great concern and that to make up for financial hardships they were using up the savings made in London. In this respect it was recommended that the evacuees had to be gainfully occupied if they were to stay much longer in the camps and if that was not possible, then they had to be told without any ambiguity when they were going to repatriated. It was also mentioned in their findings that although the people of Northern Ireland were very friendly, the evacuees could not help feeling like displaced people, abandoned and in isolation. The reports concluded that, in any case, the evacuees would never feel happy until they were returned to Gibraltar or were told conclusively that their waiting would not be long.

The Cap Tourane. Photo Old Ship Gallery

Groups of evacuees who had been categorised as first priority but were left pending on the availability of ships to be repatriated were arriving despite the difficulties explained. The first of this group consisting of 170 evacuees arrived on the 15th January 1945 on board the **Cap Tourane.**

A second group of 285 of evacuees arrived on board the Troopship **Carthage** on the 23 April 1945.

The Carthage. Photo Old Ship Gallery

At that stage the possibility of taking the evacuees to Tangier, French Morocco, and Spain, or even back to England, was being considered but the suggestions were completely discarded as impracticable. Throughout the early part of 1945 priority was being given to families who could be claimed by relatives and friends and who could provide accommodation in Gibraltar.

By the time these groups of evacuees arrived, it was certain that the war in Europe was coming to a definite end. On the 1st May 1945 Germany announced that Hitler and his wife Eva had committed suicide. Meanwhile millions of German soldiers were surrendering and it was logical to think that the war with Germany was practically over.

As can be seen from the story that appeared in the Gibraltar Chronicle copied below Admiral Doenitz had by then ordered his submarines to abstain from any act of war.

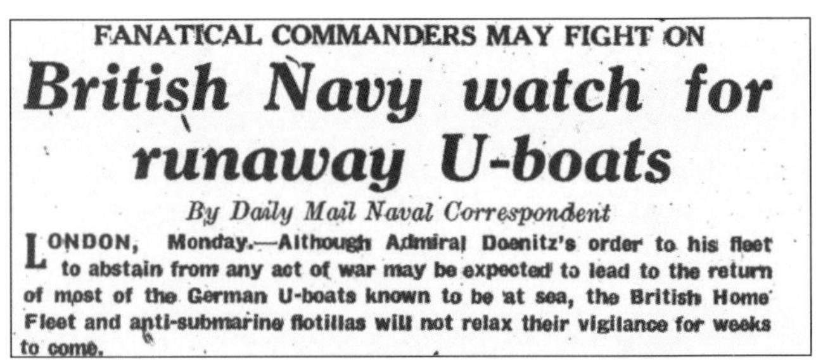

FANATICAL COMMANDERS MAY FIGHT ON

British Navy watch for runaway U-boats

By Daily Mail Naval Correspondent

LONDON, Monday.—Although Admiral Doenitz's order to his fleet to abstain from any act of war may be expected to lead to the return of most of the German U-boats known to be at sea, the British Home Fleet and anti-submarine flotillas will not relax their vigilance for weeks to come.

Whilst awaiting the announcement of the formal surrender of all German forces, the allied countries were preparing to celebrate VE Day. In Gibraltar the details of the celebration were published in the Gibraltar Chronicle as shown in the cuttings on the next page.

When it was announced that the war was going to end within the next day or so, the Gibraltar Chronicle carried an article explaining the events which were going to be held to celebrate the end of the war and Victory in Europe – VE day. The Theatre at the Ince's Hall was showing a film by Metro-Goldwin-Mayor titled **AIR RAID WARDENS** which seemed to be very appropriately shown for the occasion. The film was comedy by the then very famous comedians Stan Laurel and Oliver Hardy.

VE SALUTE

Thanksgiving: victory march and funfair

GIBRALTAR'S fortress guns are waiting to fire their victory salute. A 21-round salvo from the "heavies," timed to herald peace in Europe within a few minutes of the Prime Minister's broadcast announcement of the end of hostilities, will be followed the same evening by a general barrage and a firework display from Detached Mole.

Subject to any last-minute alterations necessitated by the time at which Mr. Churchill's broadcast is made, Gibraltar's VE-Day celebrations have been completed almost down to the last detail.

They include a broadcast by the Governor and Commander-in-Chief on VE-Day itself, a public holiday, special church services, a victory parade in which service and civilian defence organisations will take part, and a funfair in Alameda Gardens open to all members of the Forces and local residents.

A VE-Day football match is also being arranged by the Joint Services Football Committee.

Governor's speech

The following communique outlining proposed peace celebrations was issued by the Colonial Government yesterday:

1 The day on which the announcement of the termination of hostilities in Europe will be made is referred to in this Notice as VE-Day.

2 The announcement of the cessation of hostilities in Europe will be made by the Prime Minister by wireless broadcast. Shortly after the Prime Minister's announcement a message from His Excellency the Governor and Commander-in-Chief to the people of Gibraltar will be broadcast by Radio Gibraltar and Radio Distribution. Advance notice of this broadcast will be given.

Church services

3 Arrangements have been made for churches of all denominations in the Colony to be open for prayer and thanksgiving after the Prime Minister's announcement on VE-Day. If the Prime Minister's announcement is made after 6 p.m. on VE-Day the churches will be open during the day following VE-Day at 9.30 a.m. Official services of thanksgiving will not be held on VE-Day but on a day to be announced in due course as a day of thanksgiving. On the day of thanksgiving official services will be held.

4 H.M. the King will broadcast at 9 p.m. double British summer time on VE-Day.

5 The day following VE-Day will be declared as a public holiday unless VE-Day falls on a Saturday, in which case the Monday following will be a public holiday.

Joint parade

6 A victory parade in which members of the fighting and civilian services will take part will be held on the Saturday following VE-Day unless VE-Day fails on a Thursday or Friday in which case the parade will be held on the next Saturday but one after VE-Day. H.E. the Governor and Commander-in-Chief will take the salute at Casemates Square. A further announcement with regard to the arrangements for the victory parade will be made later.

7 A salute of guns will be fired upon the announcement of victory.

8 Special entertainments will be provided in the Alameda Gar- at 6 p.m. on VE-Day unless the announcement of the cessation of hostilities is made after midday in which case the entertainments will be held at 6 p.m. on the following day.

Above and in the next cutting explaining the events taking place to celebrate VE Day.

The Gibraltar Defence Force marching towards the Alemeda Parade for the VE –Day celebration. Photo Mr Ferrary.

On the 7th May 1945 it was officially announced that Germany had surrendered unconditionally. The next day the formal documents of surrender were signed and thus the war in Europe was finally over.

Below is the wording of the instrument of surrender. Copy The History Place

ACT OF MILITARY SURRENDER

1. We the undersigned, acting by authority of the German High Command, hereby surrender unconditionally to the Supreme Commander, Allied Expeditionary Forces and simultaneously to the Soviet High Command all forces on land, sea and in the air who are at this date under German control.

2. The German High Command will at once issue orders to all German military, naval and air authorities and to all forces under German control to cease active operations at --2301-- hours Central European time on -- 8 May-- and to remain in the positions occupied at that time. No ship, vessel, or aircraft is to be scuttled, or any damage done to their hull, machinery or equipment.

3. The German High Command will at once issue to the appropriate commander, and ensure the carrying out of any further orders issued by the Supreme Commander, Allied Expeditionary Force and by the Soviet High Command.

4. This act of military surrender is without prejudice to, and will be superseded by any general instrument of surrender imposed by, or on behalf of the United Nations and applicable to GERMANY and the German armed forces as a whole.

5. In the event of the German High Command or any of the forces under their control failing to act in accordance with this Act of Surrender, the Supreme Commander, Allied Expeditionary Force and the Soviet High Command will take such punitive or other action as they deem appropriate.

Signed at RHEIMS at 0241 on the 7th day of May, 1945.
France

On behalf of the German High Command.

JODL

IN THE PRESENCE OF

On behalf of the Supreme Commander, Allied Expeditionary Force, W. B. SMITH
On behalf of the Soviet High Command, SOUSLOPAROV

F SEVEZ, Major General, French Army
(Witness)

The Signing of the Instrument of Surrender. Photo The History Place

A German captured submarine being towed into the Gibraltar harbour. Photo Mrs Desoiza

Celebrating VE Day in London. PhotoThe History Place

Gibraltar like the rest of the Allied countries was set to celebrate the end of the war in Europe – VE Day. By then nearly 9,000 evacuees had already been repatriated with many of them still living in transit centres scattered around Gibraltar.

Mr Churchill, Mr Atlee and Mr Bevan at VE Day in London. Photo The History Place

We were living at the Cecil Hotel and I remember watching from the entrance to the hotel many people gathered along Main Street.

Main Street in 1945 by the junction to Tuckey's Lane. Photo reproduced from the Gibraltar Chronicle.

Among the crowd in Main Street there was a group of people dragging a dummy of Hitler with his special mustard coloured uniform and the usual red armband with a swastika. I remember seeing some people dragging this dummy along Main Street whilst others were having a go at sticking a wooden sword in it.

Main Street decorated to celebrate VE Day Photo reproduced from Gibraltar Chronicle.

Gib. celebrates

OPEN-AIR DANCING AT FUNFAIR

Prominent Gibraltar citizens have donated about £700 towards today's victory celebrations on the Rock.

At Alameda, chief centre of celebration, where the long-planned funfair will be in full swing, 100,000 cigarettes, 8,000 pints of beer, 10,000 sandwiches, 3,000 bottles of lemonade and about 5,000 cups of tea will be distributed free of charge.

SPECIAL illuminations have been erected at the fair, which has a wide variety of sideshows. A space has also been left open for dancing.

During the night the garrison military band will play near the Eliott monument from six o'clock till midnight: The King's speech will be broadcast through loudspeakers.

'Coronation' flags

Union Jacks which quickly appeared in Gibraltar streets yesterday afternoon as news spread that the war in Europe was over had been held in stock in the town since as far back as Coronation Day. Most of them were made in Germany.

Reason for German flags was easy to discover. Officials of the Gibraltar War Fund who sold them to the public had been faced with a peculiar decision. Practically the only flags in the town were 92 dozen of these German-made Union Jacks. It was a question of German Union Jacks — or a restricted display of thanksgiving.

An official of Gibraltar War Fund told the *Chronicle* yesterday: "The only flags obtainable were those held in stock since before the war. They were bought in England for the Coronation."

Below celebrating VE day at the Alameda Grand Parade.

Photo Mrs Desoiza.

Despite the many difficulties mentioned in the previous pages, evacuees were being repatriated, albeit, in small groups. About 280 repatriates arrived on the troopship **Highland Monarch**.

The Highland Monarch. Photo Old Ship Gallery

The next month saw the arrival of 778 evacuees from Northern Ireland on board the Polish liner **Batory** on the 22nd June 1945

The Batory. Photo Old Ship Gallery

Another report was submitted to the authorities in connection with the evacuees in Northern Ireland. The report's basic findings were that the evacuees had to be removed from the camps as soon as possible and returned to a Mediterranean country or transferred back to mainland Britain. Other recommendations specifically mentioned in the findings were the urgent need to improve housing conditions in Gibraltar. The suggestion was once again made of a campsite in Tangier as an alternative to already rejected suggestions of a campsite in Spain. By that time the Ministry of Health was informing the Colonial Secretary in Gibraltar that the conditions in the camps had improved significantly in the last few months. Simultaneously, the evacuees in Northern Ireland were being informed that the general conditions of living with respect to accommodation, schooling and health care were not very good in Gibraltar. This seemed to have influenced the thinking of many evacuees who were feeling reluctant to return to Gibraltar for fear of living in worse conditions than in the camps.

Dr.Kauntz, an official from the UK, visited Gibraltar in July 1945 to assess and report on the health services available in Gibraltar. In his report he stated that the health authorities, owing to the serious overcrowding in Gibraltar, were unable to cope with the workload and he strongly recommended that unless certain of the recommendations were put in place no more evacuees should be repatriated.

The Bergensfjord. Photo Old Ship Gallery

During July 40 evacuees arrived on the Norwegian ship **Bergensfjord** on the 23rd July and 423 on the troop ship **Ascania** on the 26th July 1945.

The Ascania. Photo Old Ship Gallery

On the 31st July 1945 the Gibraltar Chronicle announced the construction of flats for a thousand families.

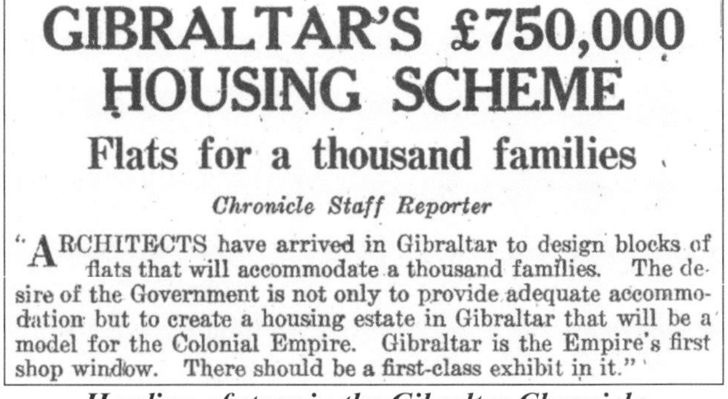

GIBRALTAR'S £750,000 HOUSING SCHEME

Flats for a thousand families

Chronicle Staff Reporter

"ARCHITECTS have arrived in Gibraltar to design blocks of flats that will accommodate a thousand families. The desire of the Government is not only to provide adequate accommodation but to create a housing estate in Gibraltar that will be a model for the Colonial Empire. Gibraltar is the Empire's first shop window. There should be a first-class exhibit in it."

Heading of story in the Gibraltar Chronicle about the construction of flats.

GIBRALTAR'S NEW HOMI

ARCHITECTS' drawing of one of the 60-flat blocks to be erected between Kingsway and Governor's Meadow under the Government housing scheme. The picture shows how use is made of the rising ground so that every flat has an unobstructed view. The drawing and full plans and perspectives of the are on view to the 4 p.m. and 8 p.m. to Friday of next Calpe Institute.

Handing the Press an announcement by the Secretary of State for the Colonies on local repatriation and housing, yesterday the Colonial Secretary (Mr. R. C. S. Stanley), used those words to describe what may be called the Government's "middle term" scheme—that part of the permanent programme that will have to be completed before all Gibraltarians can be repatriated.

Seventeen blocks of five or six-storey flats—eleven of which will be erected on sites already chosen in Kingsway, Governor's Meadow, and Sandpits areas, and two on "Old Man's Garden," south of the Rock Hotel—are being so designed as to preserve the present natural amenities and to provide a "practical opportunity for good living."

They will cost three-quarters-of-a-million pounds, but will be subsidised so that rents will be within the means of "tenants with small incomes."

The architects, Mr. Robert Atkinson, F.R.I.B.A. and Mr. A. F. B. Anderson, F.R.I.B.A., have already made their preliminary survey.

Saturation point

Referring to immediate repatriation prospects, Mr. Stanley said that we had almost reached saturation point. Not only dwellings but medical and educational services had to be provided as the people returned.

"The world-wide shortage of nursing sisters is acute. It is the duty of patriotic Gibraltar women to take advantage of the recently advertised scheme for the enrolment of assistant nurses" he said.

Explaining that overcrowding is causing considerable anxiety to the health authorities, Mr. Stanley added that a proportion of the temporary houses now being erected will have to be allocated to its relief.

A substantial part of these temporary dwellings will be available in October. The principal items in this programme are houses in Glacis road, conversion of Hargraves Barracks and the use of Nissen huts whenever possible.

The Nissen huts on the Alameda however, will be used to accommodate extra labour needed to carry out the permanent scheme.

From the official statement it is clear that some 2,000 people may have to wait some time for new permanent buildings before they can return to Gibraltar.

Asked if they would be sent to Tangier, Mr. Stanley said that he had "no information to give."

10,950 back

The following is the text of the official announcement received by the Gibraltar Government from the Secretary of State which is being published simultaneously in England and Northern Ireland:

The Secretary of State for the Colonies has had under consideration a preliminary report from Sir Findlater Stewart, G.C.B., G.C.I.E., C.S.I., who was appointed earlier in the year to investigate the question of the resettlement of evacuated Gibraltarians whom it has not yet been possible to repatriate.

The report shows that the measures taken by the Government of

The new temporary accommodation consisting of houses already under construction or shortly to be built mentioned in the press report refer to the bungalows at Glacis Road. These houses were due for completion between October and November 1945. As to the Nissen huts, these were those which had been built by the Army in 1942, mainly to accommodate troops for the North African landing. After the war they were refurbished to accommodate families who had repatriated but were still living, in transit centres like the Cecil Hotel, the Little Sisters of the Poor and a few others. Most of these families were moved from the transit centres to the Nissen huts during autumn 1946.

Gibraltar to utilise existing housing accommodation have already permitted the return of a substantial proportion of the evacuated population (10,950 up to June 30, 1945, including those repatriated before Sir Findlater Stewart began his enquiry) and these measures coupled with the provision of new temporary housing will enable further repatriation to be carried out during the next twelve months.

It was estimated on June 30 that it would be possible for about one thousand more Gibraltarians to return and reside with friends and relatives possessing accommodation certified by the local health authorities to be sufficient for the purpose.

Serious overcrowding

New temporary accommodation consisting of houses already under construction or shortly to be built, of military barracks and other buildings that are being converted into flats, and of Nissen huts, which it is proposed to erect on sites suitable only for buildings of a very temporary character, will together accommodate about 1,600 more persons.

It is hoped that a substantial part of this new temporary accommodation will begin to become available about the end of October (a few flats have already been completed and occupied).

It will not however, be possible to allocate all this new temporary accommodation for the reception of Gibraltarians from overseas because, as a first measure, it is essential to relieve a number of cases of serious overcrowding in small tenements, which are causing anxious concern to the medical authorities.

Steps must also be taken to re-accommodate some of the occupants of transit centres who are living under conditions that, if prolonged, would constitute a potential danger to health.

Over 2,000 left

When these cases of overcrowding have been relieved the Government of Gibraltar will utilise new temporary accommodation as it becomes available in order to release occupied premises claimed under the provisions of Gibraltar Government Notice No. 213 of 1944 by owners or tenants who cannot return to Gibraltar until the present occupants of the premises claimed by them have been accommodated elsewhere.

It is estimated that after the return of all those who have been authorised to live with friends or relatives in Gibraltar as well as those for whom the provision of new temporary housing will make accommodation available, there will remain —apart from Gibraltarians who have taken up or expect to take up residence in England under private arrangements—over 2,000 Gibraltarians to be repatriated, of whom nearly all are at present in Northern Ireland.

It will not be possible for those remaining Gibraltarians to return to Gibraltar until permanent buildings, to be erected by the Government of Gibraltar, are ready for their reception.

Two-year scheme

Proposals for the construction of blocks of flats to provide accommodation for one thousand families have received the Secretary of State's approval and a firm of architects has already been engaged.

It is hoped that this scheme will be completed in about two years from the date of commencement of building and that the preparation of designs and plans and the engagement of contractors can be hastened so as to enable building to begin very early in 1946.

The scheme, will be subsidised by the Government of Gibraltar in order that rents may be within the means of tenants with small incomes. Further details of this scheme will be announced by the Government of Gibraltar as early as possible.

The question of the arrangements to be made for those Gibraltarians who cannot be received in Gibraltar until permanent building accommodation is provided is receiving the urgent consideration of the Secretary of State.

Despite the reference made with regard to the completion date of the new housing scheme in the above article, the blocks of flats were not actually completed until about 1950, that is, four years later!

The Alameda Estate buildings completed in 1950 showing some Nissen huts on the right of the picture. Photo Mr E Vallejo

The Glacis Road estate in the late fifties. Photo Mr E Vallejo

The Nissen Huts at what is now the Laguna Estate. The actual Laguna can be see in foreground. Photo Mr E Vallejo

Although the war had ended in Europe the war in the Far East and principally in the Pacific was far from over. Japan by then was almost finished but they were still fighting to the bitter end. The few aircraft they had left were used as the ultimate weapon – the Kamikaze. These were, as is well known, suicide missions designed to inflict heavy damages to the Allied warships in the Pacific. The photographs on this page were donated by The History Place website.

A Kamikaze plane heading for the USS Missouri.

The Americans in their effort to finish the war and avoid the killings of thousands of their fighting forces also resorted to their newly invented ultimate weapon of mass destruction – the atomic bomb. Whether the dropping of these bombs was necessary to end the war and avoid further killings is an issue that continues to be debated since.

Atomic bomb dropped on Nagasaki.

The use of the atomic bombs on the cities of Hiroshima and Nagasaki compelled Japan to surrender.

US President Mr Harry Truman announcing the surrender of Japan.

The Japanese signing their surrender on the battleship USS Missouri.

Celebrating end of World War Two in New York.

As a result of Dr Kauntz's assessment on the medical facilities available in Gibraltar, the Governor informed London that the next group of evacuees should not be repatriated until more hospital staff were recruited and temporary accommodation was made available. He also requested London that Dr Kauntz's recommendations with reference to the medical and accommodation matters were implemented as soon as possible so as not to delay any further the repatriation arrangements.

In September 1945 the AACR held another meeting to denounce the way the authorities were handling the plight of the evacuees in Northern Ireland.

Below is an extract from a report on the meeting held on the 16th September 1945 urging the return of the evacuees in Northern Ireland.

"Disgusting conditions"

Mr. Risso announced that a committee had been appointed by the association consisting of Messrs. E. Salvado, A. Morillo, C. McGrail and himself, to deal with matters relating to the deputation that will leave Gibraltar early next month to interview the Secretary of State for the Colonies.

It had been decided, he said, that the deputation should first visit the Northern Ireland evacuees before seeing the Secretary of State.

Mr. Louis Bruzon, who recently arrived in Gibraltar from the U.K., told the meeting that he had lived for some time in Northern Ireland and had found the conditions in which the Gibraltar evacuees were living disgusting. It was intolerable that they should remain there another winter.

Referring to Mr. Risso's remarks about Major Patron, Mr. Bruzon said that Major Patron's attitude while acting as Commissioner to the evacuees in England had been most unsatisfactory.

He had always supported the official view against the general interests of the evacuees and had on many occasions obstructed the work of his (Mr. Bruzon's) executive committee.

Two more years

To show the "lack of any sense of urgency on the part of the authorities in handling repatriation", Mr. Bruzon referred to the appointment of Sir Findlater Stewart, who after seven months, he said, had submitted a preliminary report on his visit to Northern Ireland and Gibraltar, in the face of which the authorities now suggested that it would be necessary for more than 2,000 Gibraltarians to be compelled to live in exile for a further period of two years" (shouts of No, No!).

"This should not be tolerated and should be regarded by the whole community as an insult," declared Mr. Bruzon, who said he was convinced that there was sufficient accommodation to receive all those still in exile.

At this meeting it was also announced that a delegation was travelling to the UK to meet with the Secretary of State for the Colonies to deal with the policy of not allowing further repatriation until Gibraltar's schooling, medical and accommodation facilities were adequate.

The Secretary of State's reply to the Governor's request was not helpful and the affected evacuees in the camps began to complain when they came to know that those who required medical attention were not being allowed to be repatriated.

Below copy of telegram sent by evacuee Francisco Jurado saying that he is happy to leave Camp No.13 (Ballyarnett) in Londonderry on the 28th August 1945.

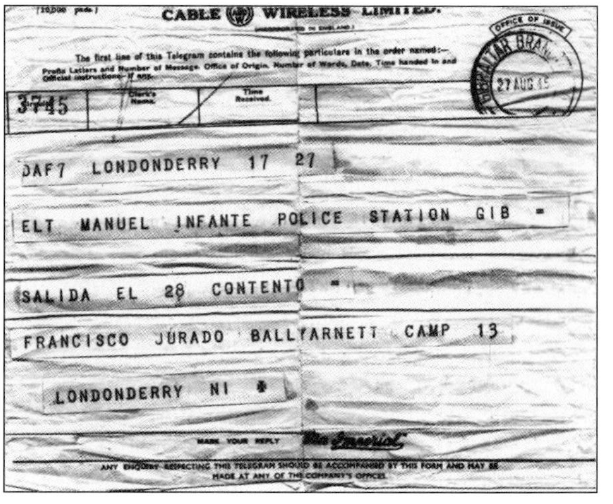

CABLE & WIRELESS LIMITED.

3745

DAF7 LONDONDERRY 17 27

ELT MANUEL INFANTE POLICE STATION GIB =

SALIDA EL 28 CONTENTO =

FRANCISCO JURADO BALLYARNETT CAMP 13

LONDONDERRY NI +

In September 236 evacuees returned from Northern Ireland on the troop ship **Eastern Prince.**

The Troopship Eastern Prince. Photo Old Ship Gallery

The reaction to the Secretary of State for the Colonies' statement was followed by another public meeting held on the 14th October 1945 to protest at was considered an insult to the people of Gibraltar to have to wait another two years before the evacuees could return from exile.

The speakers at the meeting informed the public that they considered it an injustice in not allowing the evacuees in question to be repatriated on the grounds of inadequate health care in Gibraltar and that the two-year waiting period announced by the Secretary of State for the Colonies for the return of evacuees in camps was not going to be tolerated. At the end of the meeting the AACR urged the Gibraltar Government that evacuees should not be stopped from returning to Gibraltar if their departure had been approved by the Resettlement Board or they had acquired the rights to return. The Governor informed London that his request for medical assistance had been misunderstood and that evacuees should not be deprived from being repatriated because of their medical conditions. Also that the ones already held back for medical reasons should be allowed to proceed regardless. A Government notice setting out the conditions for repatriation on health grounds was promulgated in the Gibraltar Chronicle on the 16th October 1945.

GOVERNMENT NOTICE No. 171.

It is notified for general information that in view of reports by the Medical authorities regarding the serious and increasing danger to public health caused by the conditions of overcrowding in Gibraltar and the lack of medical facilities due to the inability to obtain the additional nursing staff that must be secured before further hospital accommodation can be provided, it has been necessary to postpone the repatriation of any further parties of Gibraltarians until the nursing staff position has improved. Every effort has been and is being made by the Government and by the Secretary of State for the Colonies to obtain additional nursing staff.

2. This temporary postponement will not apply to the next party of about 450 persons who are expected to arrive in Gibraltar shortly from Northern Ireland, but persons likely to need hospitalisation will not be included in this party.

By Command,

R. C. S. Stanley,
Colonial Secretary.

Colonial Secretariat,
Gibraltar, 15th October, 1945.
(M.P. No. 0029/178).

Mr Stanley, the Gibraltar Colonial Secretary held a press meeting to defend the Gibraltar Government's policy in not allowing further repatriates until Gibraltar was ready in terms of accommodation and medical facilities to accept them. The Councillors of the newly reconstituted City Council of Gibraltar were very critical of the military authorities for not helping by releasing buildings to alleviate the shortage of housing in Gibraltar. On the 24th October 1945 the Secretary of State for the Colonies stated in the House of Commons that it was impossible to repatriate the 3,000 evacuees in Northern Ireland until the additional accommodation became available in Gibraltar.

A.A.C.R. ATTACK COLONIAL GOVERNMEN'

No power given to public opinion

GIBRALTAR'S PROBLEMS

THE system of government in Gibraltar was strongly criticised at a meeting of the Association for the Advancement of Civil Rights held at the Theatre Royal yesterday.

Mr. S. P. Triay, outlining the aims of the A.A.C.R. deputation to the United Kingdom—which is to seek an interview with the Secretary of State for the Colonies—said there were many acute problems to be solved in Gibraltar. Prominent among them were rents, wages, repatriation and the cost of living.

Some of their problems were old, some of them arose out of the war, and some were possibly caused by misunderstanding or failure to interpret and give effect to public opinion.

Main grievance

The system of government in Gibraltar, said Mr. Triay gave no power whatever to public opinion, which could be followed or ignored at the discretion of the Governor, or sometimes the Colonial Secretary.

"Even dictators admit that it is not possible to govern for long without or against public opinion. Gibraltar is no exception and our main grievance is that public opinion has no constitutional means of converting itself into law.

"This situation" went on Mr. Triay, "makes it more necessary than ever that the dictatorial powers of the Governor and the Colonial Secretary should be exercised in patient and elaborate cooperation with the people of Gibraltar, by which I necessarily mean the majority of the people of Gibraltar.

No cooperation

"No one will deny that we have reached a stage when cooperation between the Governor and the Colonial Secretary, on the one hand, and the majority of the people of Gibraltar is non-existent. It is idle to discuss who is to blame—maybe the people are to blame—but we can't change the people, and as cooperation is an urgent necessity we must ask for the change of the Governor and the Colonial Secretary."

Adding that it might be argued that the picture he had drawn of the absolute powers of the Governor and the Colonial Secretary was exaggerated because of the existence of the Executive Council Mr. Triay declared:

"We feel that, if the Governor really wants to make sure that the Executive Council conveys to him the true feelings of public opinion, so long as the present system of government remains it should at least be elected by the people, either totally or in a majority."

Deputation of four

Mr. Albert Risso (president of the A.A.C.R.) announced that the the committee had nominated Messrs. S. P. Triay, E. J. Alvarez, J. T. Ellicott and himself to form the deputation. These nominations were approved by a unanimous vote of the meeting.

Mr. Risso said that up to now the sum of £215 12s. 10d. had been collected towards the expenses of the deputation. He pointed out that this was not enough and appealed for further subscriptions.

Mr. Triay said that he had already contacted Mr. D. N. Pritt, M.P., who was willing to accompany the delegation to the Secretary of State, for the Colonies and it was hoped that other M.P.s would help the deputation in its task.

Petition to Governor

Mr. Louis Bruzon told the meeting that he would continue his demands for the speedy return to Gibraltar of the 3,500 Gibraltarian evacuees who had been away for over five years and who were deprived of their right of residence.

On the day the deputation left Gibraltar for the United Kingdom, he said, a petition containing thousands of signatures, urging the prompt repatriation of these evacuees, was to be presented to the Governor.

Above report on a public meeting held in 14 October 1945.

The nominated AACR delegates as reported on the previous page left Gibraltar in early November for London after a memorandum had been handed to the Governor criticizing him and the Colonial Secretary. The last group of over 500 evacuees to be repatriated in 1945 arrived on the 22nd November on the converted troopship **Cilicia.**

.

The converted troopship Cilicia.
Photo Old Ship Gallery

Meanwhile the Colonial Government kept stressing that there was not much prospect of many of the evacuees being returned before the first housing project had been completed in October 1946 which meant another year at least. It was also being stressed that it would take another two years for permanent accommodation to become available for the returning evacuees. When the evacuees learnt about this, they held demonstrations in the camps demanding their repatriation.

Gibraltar evacuees staging a demonstration in Northern Ireland. Among the evacuees in the picture above are Andrew Ferrary, Isabel Schembri, Pepi Ferrary and Micheelle Schembri. Photo Mr V Gonzalez

Since the British Government was unable to supply nurses, to alleviate the nursing problem, four nurses were recruited and sent for training to the UK in November 1945.

On the right a Gibraltar Chronicle article about nurses undergoing training in the UK.

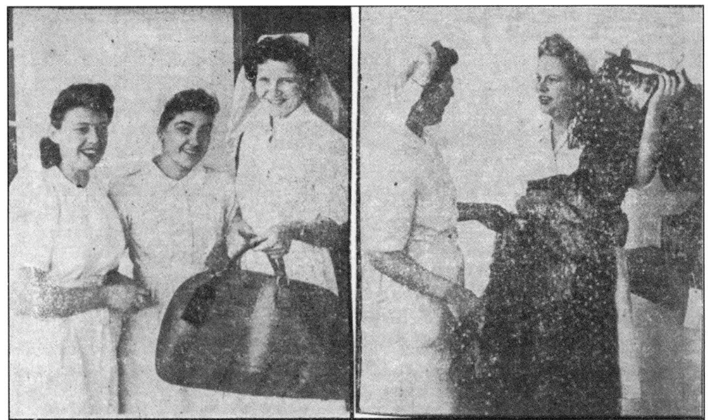

FIVE nurses at Gibraltar's Colonial Hospital are busy packing their belongings. In a few days' time they will be off to England — to train at Croydon Hospital for the status of State registered nurses under the new colonial medical re-organisation scheme. During the evacuation they were able to further their training in Jamaica, have since served six months at the Colonial Hospital, hope after their return from England to become nursing sisters. Yesterday the Matron, Miss Jane Reilly, gave a tea-party in their honour at the hospital.

Left: Miss Esther Manser and Miss Emilia McIntosh are packing their off-duty dresses—in anticipation of relaxation from the hard work that lies ahead. Right: Miss Mary Orfila, Miss Acacia Baker, Miss Pauline Edwards.—*Army Photo Unit.*

Gibraltar's need of nurses

GIBRALTAR'S King George V Hospital could be opened in a few days if nursing staff were available.

This opinion was expressed yesterday by Dr. R. A. W. Procter, Senior Medical Officer, who emphasised the seriousness of the position caused by the shortage of nursing staffs in Gibraltar.

In an effort to expedite the recruitment of nursing sisters from either Great Britain or Eire Dr. Procter is flying to England shortly.

No children's ward

He told a *Chronicle* representative that following recent repatriation the women's section of the Colonial Hospital was congested. There were at present 33 chest cases and seven mental cases at the hospital, which had no children's ward. The position would be greatly improved, he said, when the Government was able to open the King George V Hospital and a part of the Mental Hospital.

Yesterday three new nursing sisters arrived on board the S.S. "Celicia" but this is not enough in view of the fact that the staff of State registered nurses is considerably below strength and that it has proved impossible so far to obtain the necessary complement of locally recruited assistant nurses, of whom 19 are required either at the Colonial or at King George hospitals.

Training in U.K.

Dr. Procter referred to the "further training" scheme for nurses, under which Gibraltar girls wishing to become State registered nurses can be sent to England and thus be given a chance to make nursing a worth-while career.

He said that girls who were interested in this scheme should get into touch with Miss J. Reilly, the Matron at the Colonial Hospital, who would give them fuller particulars.

The local assistant nurses already working in the hospital were giving excellent service and had enabled many difficulties to be overcome. "But," added Dr. Procter, "until King George V Hospital is opened the medical position will remain precarious and no further repatriation of evacuees from Northern Ireland can be recommended." **H.H.W.**

The AACR delegates who had paid a visit to London and the camps returned to Gibraltar in early December 1945. The outcome of their visit was reported by the Gibraltar Chronicle shown in the cuttings below:

WORKMEN'S COMPENSATION ON THE WAY FOR GIBRALTAR

INSTRUCTIONS given by the Secretary of State for the Colonies (Mr. George Hall) for the introduction of workmen's compensation legislation in Gibraltar were mentioned by Mr. S. P. Triay at a meeting held by the Association for the Advancement of Civil Rights in John Mackintosh Square yesterday.

Mr. Triay and Mr. Albert Risso (President of the A.A.C.R.) were reporting on their visit, with two other members of the association, to England to lay before Mr. Hall a list of grievances concerning the government of Gibraltar.

Loud applause greeted Mr. Triay's statement on workmen's compensation, legislation for which, he said, was to be introduced shortly. The deputation had been sympathetically received by Mr. Hall, who had listened to them attentively for over an hour. He had promised to consider the points of their memorandum and give a written reply in due course.

A barren rock

During their visit to England, said Mr. Triay, they had been made painfully aware that very little was known by the public about conditions in the Crown Colonies, so far as the man in street was concerned, Gibraltar was a barren rock somewhere in the Mediterranean.

Because of the supposedly magic phrase that "Gibraltar is a Fortress", he went on, the people of Gibraltar up to recently seemed to be resigned to the view that not only was it inevitable that the civilians should be governed by a military dictator but that, in a space of two square miles the Military themselves should be free from the civilian side of the Administration and independent of the legislation and directions that the Governor should think fit to introduce in respect of civilians.

"Dead letter"

He had in the course of the interview with the Secretary of State referred to the Press Ordinance of 1869 for Gibraltar which enacts:

"It should not be lawful for any any person to print or publish or assist in the printing or publishing of any newspaper or periodical within Gibraltar unless the printing and publication of such newspaper or periodical shall be authorised by a licence in writing for that purpose under the hand of the Colonial Secretary, which licence he is authorised and empowered at his discretion, to grant, refuse, or revoke. Every such licence shall, unless revoked, continue in force for a period of 12 months."

Where was the freedom of the Press in Gibraltar: Mr. Triay asked. He had read this ordinance to the Secretary of State who had commented that he "could not believe that this was in existence and surely it was a dead letter." (laughter).

The A.A.C.R. had applied for a licence in Gibraltar to publish a weekly but up to the present no reply had been received, added Mr. Triay.

Powers to Council

Referring to repatriation Mr. Triay said there was already existing machinery that would put the responsibility for the solution of this problem squarely on the shoulders of Gibraltarians.

"Give the City Council of Gibraltar all the powers now exercised by the Colonial Secretary in respect of housing, health and repatriation and let them do the rest," he said.

We feel that there is no good reason for not permitting the people of Gibraltar to solve their own problems affecting their own people and their own comforts.

"We have no doubt that eventually ways and means will be found for giving us this long delayed right, but in the meantime it is urgent that action should be taken to solve pressing problems and it seems to us that any solution that is agreeable to the majority of the people of Gibraltar would be better than the solution imposed upon them by persons whose sympathy and love for the people, whom they autocratically govern, are very much in doubt."

Visit to camps

Mr. Albert Risso described the visit paid by members of the deputation to the Northern Ireland camps.

They had stayed for three days and three nights in the camps with their fellow countrymen to experience for themselves the conditions under which the evacuees were living.

They had had many talks with General Mason MacFarlane M.P. and Mr. D. N. Pritt M.P,

General MacFarlane had requested him, added Mr. Risso, to bring to the people of Gibraltar his best wishes.

"He promised to help us with our problems and offered his assistance and cooperation." (applause).

"We also visited the five Gibraltarian ladies now in Croydon Hospital continuing their training in nursing," said Mr. Risso. All of them had passed recent examinations.

"System of privileges"

Mr. Risso said the A.A.C.R, policy was "not to attack or victimise anyone but to remove the present system of privileges and favouritism and to ask and establish legality, identical rights and obligations for all. We detest abuses of power, which are typical at present in Gibraltar.

"We protest against the appointments to the Executive Committee of Gibraltar of persons who are not of the people's liking and persons who need a licence to reside in the Colony and who have never taken any interest in the welfare of the Colony."

Mr. Risso announced that the total amount of donations received towards the deputation's expenses was £798.5.6. The total expenses had been £539.19.3, which left a balance of £258.6.3. He wished on behalf of the A.A.C.R. to thank all contributors.

From the above press report it can be seen that the AACR delegation was seeking the power and responsibility to administer matters like housing and medical facilities. They were also seeking to obtain the right to decide how to solve problems affecting the repatriation of the evacuees.

In order to speed up the repatriation process 62 dwellings were constructed in an area of reclaimed land by the Glacis Road where about 300 people had been accommodated. Three weeks later a spell of severe weather in December 1945 blew away many of the roofs of these newly constructed bungalows.

GALE PLUCKS ROOFS FROM HOUSE

16 Gibraltar families without homes

STORM PLAYS HAVOC WITH SHIPPING

A 48-hour battering by a gale that at times reached hurricane intensity left in its wake a long trail of damage and desruction in Gibraltar. Roofs stripped from houses, ships blown ashore, dwellings flooded by heavy rains and waves that swept over the sea wall were the outstanding features of extensive material damage.

One man lost his life when seven workmen on Detached Mole were swept into the sea by a breaker.

This is the story of one of the fiercest gales — and the longest—in living memory:

On Land

SIXTEEN families were rendered homeless when the uralite roofing was blown off the newly occupied Glacis road tenements.

A man in bed in one of the houses had a narrow escape when a section of the roof missed his head by inches.

Resettlement Board officials were quickly on the scene, and three taxis battled for four hours between Glacis Road and the Cecil Hotel centre conveying the 70 people from their stricken homes to various hotels, the Welcome and Seamen's Institute, where they were given shelter for the night.

Half uninhabitable

On Saturday morning the gale was still so fierce that the remaining 200 occupants of the 62 dwellings on the site were taken to the town for safety. Facilities were given for the safe storage of personal beongings and furniture.

Nearly half the dwellings, which have only been occupied for three weeks, have been rendered temporarily uninhabitable by the gale, but it is hoped that the occupants of the remainder will be able to return as soon as it abates.

His Excellency the Governor, the Colonial Secretary, the chairman and members of the City Council were early visitors to the site on Saturday morning.

Swept off mole

At Catalan Bay heavy seas came over the sea wall and flooded the lower rooms of many houses.

Thrughout the week-end military transport stood by in readiness to evacuate the residents.

Whilst working on Detached Mole during height of the gale seven workmen were swept into the sea by a wave. All except one were rescued and were able to go home after treatment, but Alexander Neish, a Gibraltarian labourer, was drowned.

Trees at Alameda were uprooted and traffic had to be diverted from Casemates Road on Saturday night whist a tree in danger of falling was pulled down and removed.

District evacuated

The whole of the La Atunara and El Castillo district in La Linea was evacuated, mountainous seas from the Eastern Beach causing serious floods in the area. Occupants of these houses were placed in hospitals and schools while others were given shelter by relatives and friends.

The main road between La Linea and San Roque suffered extensive damage, and at one time a long stretch of it was under water.

Despite the ferocity of the wind on Saturday BOAC aircraft arrived and left on schedule.

At Sea

LAST night two watchmen who on Friday went aboard the forward half of the 12,000-ton Norwegian tanker "Thorshovdi" (she was salved in two sections after being hit by a torpedo three years ago) were still marooned on their "ship", off Algeciras.

The two men had only a few sandwiches with them and up to last night heavy weather had prevented any attempt being made to rescue them.

Also blown ashore on the other side of the bay are the French

The damages to the roof caused a significant set back in the allocation of houses for those still in transit centres in Gibraltar and consequently for those who were due to repatriated.

One of the dwellings showing most of the uralite roofing blown away.

In January 1946 the Secretary of State for the Colonies Mr.Hall visited Gibraltar to discuss the issues that were affecting the return of evacuees and to stress that the method of selection was the correct one. As a result of Mr Hall's visit, a public meeting was held by the AACR on the 29th January 1946 at the John Mackintosh Square.

Cabinet Minister visiting Gibraltar

RECEPTION AT CONVENT

THE Right Honourable G. H. Hall M.P., Secretary of State for the Colonies, arrived at Gibraltar yesterday evening by air from Bathurst (Gambia), on a short unofficial visit.

His stay will not exceed two or three days and he will be the guest of His Excellency the Governor at The Convent.

Last night His Excellency the Governor and Lady Eastwood held a reception at The Convent to which the following were invited:

Vice-Admiral and Mrs. Crutchley, Brigadier the Hon. C. S. and Mrs. Vale, Air Commodore and Mrs. Rogers, His Honour the Chief Justice and Mrs McDougall, the Hon. R. C. S. and Mrs. Stanley, the Hon. A. R. and Mrs. Cook, the Hon. A. McKisack, the Hon. Major and Mrs. Patron, the Hon. J. L. Imossi, the Hon. D. and Mrs. Benaim, the Rt. Rev. R. J. Fitzgerald, Mr. and Mrs. Muguiro, Consul and Mrs. Fletcher, Monsieur and Madame Mory, Dr. and Mrs. Procter, Dr. and Mrs. Howes, Captain and Mrs. Gowing, the Very Rev. Dean and Mrs. Nason, Col. F. M. Townsend, Mr. and Mrs. Cottrell, Mr. and Mrs. J. J. Russo, Mr. and Mrs. L. J. Imossi, Rev. E. King C.F., Mr. and Mrs. J. Hassan, Mr. and Mrs. Eccles.

MR. G. H. HALL

Reply to A.A.C.R.

Mr. Hall's arrival coincides with the receipt of a reply to the questions raised by the A.A.C.R. deputation, which went to interview him last November.

This afternoon the A.A.C.R. is holding a public meeting in John Mackintosh Square to protest against the reply — the contents of which have not yet been divulged to the Press — and also to protest against the reply received to a memorial signed by 7,000 people on the subject of repatriation, which was handed to His Excellency the Governor just after the deputation left.

The resolutions passed at today's meeting will be handed in at The Convent after the meeting.

Above report referring to Mr Hall's visit to Gibraltar.

At this meeting, the issue of the evacuees in Northern Ireland was fully debated among other items.

The Gibraltar Chronicle reported that about 5,000 people attended this public meeting. Whilst the meeting was taking place shops were closed and workers stopped as a sign of protest.

5,000 attend AACR's protest meeting

ONE of the biggest crowds—estimated at nearly 5,000—ever to assemble at a public meeting in Gibraltar packed every vantage-point in John Mackintosh Square yesterday afternoon to hear Mr. A. Risso, President of the Association for the Advancement of Civil Rights, read the reply of the Secretary of State for the Colonies to the points raised by the deputation which went to the U.K. in November.

The meeting unanimously adopted two resolutions—one considering the reply unsatisfactory and unacceptable; the other petitioning the Secretary of State to reconsider the acute problem of repatriation and those points that had not been conceded.

Above and on the next page are newspaper cuttings showing the coverage given by the Gibraltar Chronicle about the outcome of the public meeting held on the 29th January 1946.

Newspaper cutting on demonstration. Photo Mrs Bossino.

'Gib' goes on strike: 'Ship our evacuees'

GIBRALTAR, Monday.

SHOPS were shut and all work stopped today while thousands of people protested against the non-return of Gibraltar evacuees from Britain.

Today's trouble began when Mr. G. H Hall, Colonial Secretary, arrived in Gibraltar and said that 1,200 to 1,400 evacuees might return before the end of this year, leaving about 1,700 still in Britain.

Demonstrators quickly assembled in great numbers and passed a resolution saying that failure to revise repatriation plans "will only lead to a complete break between the authorities and the majority in Gibraltar."

Thousands then marched to Government House. They were promised that the matter would be reconsidered.—*Exchange.*

Above cutting referring the work stoppage and shops closure.

GOVT. REPLY TO GRIEVANCE MANIFESTO 'UNACCEPTABLE'

The Central Committee of the Association then led the meeting in procession via Irish Town and Main Street to The Convent to hand in the resolutions for submission to Mr. Hall. All shops were closed while the procession passed and crowds lining the streets applauded.

After the Committee had been absent for only a few moments Mr. Risso was able to tell the crowd assembled outside The Convent that they had been assured that Mr. Hall would give reconsideration to the points raised.

The Secretary of State's reply to the points raised by the November deputation, which is signed by Mr. Luke, head of the Mediterranean Section of the Colonial Office, points out that the policy of the Government in all important respects is adopted after consultation with, and with the concurrence of the Secretary of State.

Better understanding

The letter emphasised the importance of those holding responsible positions in the community playing their part in bringing about a better understanding between the people and the Government.

Mr. Hall is sure that, even if disagreements sometimes occur, a vigorous collaboration with the authorities in such spheres as already exist is possible, and must form the best and most effective preparation for the more representative system of government that will shortly be established.

The following are the main points of the replies given to the questions raised:

CHANGE OF POLICY: "Mr. Hall could not agree that there has been any appreciable change in the nature of the local government's policy. He is "fully satisfied that repatriation and other major problems are being tackled by the Government with energy, resolution and understanding."

CONSTITUTION: Full sympathy with the desire of Gibraltarians to assume greater responsibilities and to this end the establishment of a Legislative Council had been approved. Mr. Hall is convinced that Gibraltarians will be able to play a vital part in shaping the policy of civil administration whatever provisions are made in the interests of the Colony's security.

SUBORDINATION OF CIVIL INTERESTS: Operation of the Press Ordinance and Supreme Court Order being examined. It is not the case that the reply to an application by the A.A.C.R. to publish a newspaper was delayed three months.. Mr. Hall understands that the application was first received in incomplete form on October 12, returned for completion on November 10 and resubmitted by the association on December 3, one week after which a licence was issued.

REPATRIATION: Mr. Hall is fully aware of the hardship caused by delay but is not prepared to override the opinion of medical advisers on the spot.

It is impossible to avoid the conclusion that there can be no satisfactory solution to the problem until permanent housing can be provided.

The public meeting as mentioned in the press cuttings shown on this page passed two motions unanimously.

The first motion dealt with the repatriation process described by the AACR as unsatisfactory and unacceptable.

"Hard as the period of waiting must be Mr. Hall is convinced that the policy adopted will in the long run be in the best interests of the community as a whole."

So far as the City Council's being empowered to deal with repatriation, Mr. Hall expresses the opinion that the problem is properly the responsibility of the Colonial Government. Extended system of billeting not favoured.

LAND HELD BY MILITARY: Mr. Hall is assured that the War Department keeps its requirements continually under review and that it is alive to the desirability of releasing as much as possible. A reminder is given of the generous assistance already extended by the military in medicine, education, transport etc.

RESETTLEMENT: The statement that nothing is done for repatriated persons cannot be accepted and Mr. Hall is satisfied that close attention is given to their needs.

LABOUR & SOCIAL LEGISLATION: Preliminary consideration already given to these problems. Further progress awaits the appointment of a Labour Commissioner.

DAMAGED PREMISES & POSSESSIONS: Deputation's points under enquiry.

RENT RESTRICTIONS: The question of the extension of rent restrictions legislation to business premises is being examined in consultation with the Governor.

NORTHERN IRELAND: Camp conditions being further examined and the deputation's observations borne in mind. Concrete suggestions for improvement welcomed.

"Unsatisfactory"

THE following is the full text of of the resolutions passed at the A.A.C.R.'s meeting:

1 That this meeting considers that the answers given by the Secretary of State for the Colonies to the Repatriation Memorial and to the representations made by the A.A.C.R. deputation are most unsatisfactory and unacceptable as they reject the just aspirations of the majority of the people of Gibraltar.

2 That this meeting avails itself of the stay in Gibraltar of the Secretary of of State for the Colonies to reaffirm our representations and to make to him the petition to reconsider the acute problem of repatriation and the other petitions which have not received his acceptance. A continuation of the present state of affairs cannot be allowed to continue and can only result in the complete break between the authorities and the majority of the people of Gibraltar.

The other motion referred to the idea of availing the AACR with the mandate to petition the Secretary of State for the Colonies during his stay in Gibraltar and to put across to him that the present situation could not continue as it was bound to result in a complete split between the authorities and majority of the people of Gibraltar.

Protesters in demonstration held on 29th January 1946. Photo Mr P.Davis

By the end of 1945 there were nearly 3,000 evacuees still living in the camps. Meanwhile the controversy with regard to the repatriation of evacuees in Northern Ireland was to continue for a long time.
The first party repatriated in 1946 consisted of a group of 250 evacuees who arrived on the troopship **Devonshire** on the 3rd March 1946.

The troopship Devonshire. Photo Old Ship Gallery

During April 1946 two officials from the Colonial Office in the UK visited some of the camps and reported that the evacuees were well looked after in terms of food, clothing and health and that their only complaint was their wish to be returned to Gibraltar. The report which was considered very critical about the attitudes of the evacuees was completely opposite to views expressed by the AACR delegates.
The second party of 259 evacuees arrived on board the **City of Paris** on the 17th April 1946.

The City of Paris. Photo Old Ship Gallery

A few months later the AACR carried out an exercise to find out whether the evacuees would be willing to be repatriated even if it meant living in Nissen huts when they returned to Gibraltar.
The Colonial office in the UK also carried out a similar exercise at the request of the Gibraltar Government but apparently the question whether they wanted to return to Gibraltar by putting up with living in Nissen huts again had not been included in the questionnaire by the official authorities.
In the meantime a third party consisting of 175 evacuees arrived on board the **Ascania** on the 29th June 1946. According to the feedback received from the questionnaires, the majority of the evacuees opted to be returned to Gibraltar despite knowing that they were going to continue to live in Nissen huts. Rumours were then reaching the camps that the Nissen huts were in fact intended for those families who were still in transit centres in Gibraltar and not for those in Northern Ireland. The Resettlement Board stated that the rumours were unfounded and that the ultimate objective was to speed up the return of the evacuees in the camps.

Nissen huts at North Front near the cemetery. Photo Royal Gibraltar Police.

The fourth and last group repatriated during 1946 consisted of about 180 evacuees who arrived on board the **SS Cheshire** on the 24th September 1946.

The Cheshire. Photo Old Ship Gallery.

In October 1946 the Secretary of State for the Colonies stated in the House of Commons that it could take up to two years before the whole repatriation was completed. This statement led to angry reactions both at the camps and in Gibraltar. At this stage there were also conflicting points of view between the Secretary of State for the Colonies and the Ministry of Health in UK in relation to the decision to close some of the camps which were working satisfactorily

Fully aware of the remote prospects of an early return to Gibraltar, some evacuees were thinking of returning to London of their own accord to seek employment. At the AACR annual general meeting the issues affecting the repatriation were fully aired. The first motion carried at the meeting was the rejection of the statement made by the Secretary of State for the Colonies that the evacuees might have to wait two years to be repatriated.

Copy of extracts from the Gibraltar Chronicle Dated 12th November 1946 reporting on the outcome of the AACR Annual Meeting where the housing situation was fully debated.

GIBRALTAR HOUSING

NEW PERMANENT SCHEME SUGGESTED

A.A.C.R. Plans Before Colonial Government

A SCHEME TO BUILD 286 PERMANENT FLATS AND FOUR SHOPS AT THE ESTIMATED COST OF £607,342, PLUS DEPARTMENTAL EXPENSES, AT FLAT BASTION ROAD, GIBRALTAR, HAS BEEN PREPARED BY THE ASSOCIATION FOR THE ADVANCEMENT OF CIVIL RIGHTS IN GIBRALTAR.

At the Association's annual general meeting at the Theatre Royal on Tuesday night, presided over by Mr. Albert Risso, President, Mr. J. H. Hassan, Chairman of the City Council of Gibraltar and Vice-President of the Association, said the flats would have the latest kitchen equipment and facilities. The scheme had already been submitted to the Colonial Government, who were carefully considering it.

Mr. Hassan reported that, in the Temporary Housing Scheme, 303 houses had been completed up to the end of October, 1946, and had been handed over by the Council to the Colonial Government. It was hoped that another 61 would be ready before Christmas.

The Gas Service, said Mr. Hassan, had been improved by extending a high pressure main, bettering the calorific value of the gas.

It was proposed, in the near future, to modernise the generating station supply system and to acquire machinery valued at £50,000 to meet future demands on the electricity supply.

A new refuse destructor, to substitute the old one at North Front, removed by the War Dept. for defence reasons, would cope with all the town's refuse.

Reacting to the above meeting the Gibraltar Government stated that the situation in Northern Ireland was being monitored very closely but it was impossible to repatriate the evacuees as was being suggested by the AACR.

NEW TELEPHONE EXCHANGE

In the near future a new telephone exchange, with modern equipment, was to be erected.

The Council intended to appoint a civilian full-time medical officer of health and a pathologist-analyst to the Council's laboratory.

These resolutions, proposed by Mr. Risso, were carried:—

(a) "That this meeting cannot under any circumstances accept as good the recent statement by the Secretary of State for the Colonies that at least two years must elapse before all the Gibraltarian Evacuees can be repatriated.

(b) "That this meeting is firmly of the opinion that, if the Colonial Government decides to make use of all accommodation and to obtain the help of the Military Authorities in handing over a limited number of buildings, the necessary accommodation can be found for the return of all the evacuees.

(c) "That, much as this meeting would regret it, it is their firm conviction that if the evacuees are not repatriated immediately, as suggested in (b) above, the only course open to Gibraltarians here and in Northern Ireland is to act in such a manner as to bring home to the Government once and for all the dreadful plight to which our evacuees have been put purely for war reasons, but for which there is no justification in lasting one more day."

Press cutting about AACR meeting continued from previous column.

A group of evacuees getting ready to leave the camps for London. Photo Mrs Balban

By early 1947 some evacuees had already left the camps of their own will to live in private accommodation in London whilst others continued being repatriated. At that point it was estimated that there were about 2,000 still living in the camps and about 1,500 were already living in private accommodation in London.

The ex-Army Nissen huts refurbished at Devil's Tower Road near to what was the Laguna.
This photo was taken during the Queen's visit in May 1954. Photo Mr L Young

The whole aspect of accommodation in Gibraltar was under very careful consideration to try as much as possible to find ways to tackle the repatriation of evacuees in the camps. In October 1946 most of the families living in transit centres were moved to the Nissen huts which had been erected in many areas of Gibraltar but mainly in the North Front area. As well as medical services and accommodation there was a need to look into schooling matters as the evacuees of school age began to be repatriated. In line with the schooling requirements, premises were being made available for schools. Owing to the many Nissen huts built in the North Front area a school was also built at the Glacis to cater for many of the children living nearby.

As can be seen from the press report below emergency schooling arrangements had been made during the first year of the repatriation.

NEW SCHOOL FOR GIBRALTAR

A GOVERNMENT secondary school is to be opened at Loreto Convent South in the new year. During the past year an emergency school for girls of secondary school age has been conducted at Plata Villa.

The Director of Education (Dr. Howes) told the *Chronicle* that the Loreto nuns woud be here before Christmas. There would be eight teaching nuns who would conduct the secondary school under an arrangement between the Government and the Mother-General. Another nun would conduct a small private school for children under eleven and a half years.

Entrance tests

The new school would accommodate the secondary girls already at Plata Villa, and those who proved successful in the recently advertised secondary entrance examination. In future, the test for entrance would be one jointly devised by the headmistress and himself, but as the school year opened in January only special cases would be examined until December 1946.

No fees said Dr. Howes, would be charged, and the Government would maintain the school in the way of books and school equipment. The arrangements were to last for three years, after which they would be reviewed.

Ultimately, the Convent (Town), at present a transit centre, would become the Girls' Secondary School for Gibraltar on a grant-aided basis, while the Convent (South) would revert to its former status as a private school.

Newspaper cutting reporting the arrangements being made with regard to schooling.

Before the war very few children were taught in Government aided schools and local teachers were trained in Gibraltar. The majority of the teachers in Gibraltar were Christian brothers or nuns. Consequent on this, there were very few experienced qualified local teachers when the evacuees returned. During the first post war years help had to be sought from the military authorities to provide teaching.

Dockyard School 1945-46. Photo Mr H Alecio.
Back: E.Cohen, E.Azopardi, A.Soiza, V.Schembri, M.Apap, J.Bonifacio, Soiza, J.Revagliatte, Sanchez, Brooks, H.Danino, G.Galliano, A.Pulham, A.Gaeto, Penalver, A.Barea, Gomez, P.Del Rio.
3rd Row: A.Ferro, J.Abudarham,…?.... Montero, M.Perera, Noguera, H.Alecio, A.Alecio, V.Figueras, F.Parody, J.Harrison, V.Alecio, W.Wood, H.Edmonds, Gonzalez, V.Bossano, G.De La Paz, F.Chincota.
2nd Row: Lima, R.Gingell, J.Keating, J.L.Rodriguez, J.Martinez, J.Zayas, L.Catania, N.Olivero, Guerrero, ….?......, A.Hardy, J.Pardo, Canessa, H.Noble, F.Cheesewright, W.De La Paz,..?.., J.Lara.
Front Row:…?…. A.Gingell, J.Good,…?…., Captain of the Dockyard, Lt Hill, Commodore Marrack, M.Bonilla, Chief Engineer, Chief Constructor, Benvenuto, S.Martinez, H.Danino

Many of those who were caught in the prime of their school age had their schooling severely interrupted. On their return some of the boys in their early teens took up the opportunity of starting an apprenticeship which also offered day release to attend classes at the Dockyard School run by the Royal Navy. During their apprenticeship those who were keen students were also given the opportunity of being able to catch up with their academic studies in order to better their career prospects.

Sgt Fenner and another serviceman with pupils who had recently been repatriated
In the photo are Galliano, J.Chincotta, Smith, C.Cid de La Paz
C.Galliano, Segui, S.Orciel, Lavarello, Tonna, M.Garcia, Johnston.
Photo donated by Mr A Traverso

Back in the camps the evacuees continued to press for an early return to Gibraltar.

Above evacuees in Ballymena expressing to officials their strong desire to be repatriated. Photo Gibraltar Museum

Below is cutting from an unknown Northern Ireland newspaper referring to a statement made by a Northern Ireland Government official with regard to the treatment of the Gibraltar evacuees.

Complaints By

"Better Fed Than Many Of Our Own People"

—STORMONT OFFICIAL

Evacuees Reiterate Their Grievances

"In my opinion the evacuees are being better fed than many of our own people, an official from Stormont told Press representatives on Friday when interviewed in regard to a report in that day's "Derry Journal" setting out grievances voiced by a committee representative of the Gibraltar evacuees accommodated at four hutments convenient to Derry City.

"The authorities have nothing to hide concerning the treatment of the evacuees; in fact they have reason to be proud," he added.

Since the publication of this statement the Gibraltarians, through the chairman of the committee at each camp, have reiterated their complaints.

It is learned that an official of the Ministry visited the camps at the week-end and, having had the grievances placed in detail before him, promised to have them investigated fully.

Cutting from Mr V Gonzalez.

The official remarks were rejected by the camp representatives in a letter written to the same newspaper as shown in the next column.

A Letter From The Evacuees

We have received the following letter from Mr. A. L. Bellotti, on behalf of the Chairman of the Welfare Committee at each of the four camps:

"Dear Sir—It has come to our knowledge that the general opinion in Derry and, presumably the rest of 'Northern' Ireland, is, that the Gibraltar evacuees are living in luxury, that they are very well looked after, and that they are getting financial support from the Government.

"As this is far from the truth, and so as to clarify matters we are writing this letter so that everyone may know what our real position is.

"We were compulsorily evacuated from Gibraltar on military grounds, brought to London where, whilst the English children were evacuated, our women and children were exposed to the 1940-41 blitz. The treatment accorded to us in England and the food supplies were far from good, but our people were able to put up with these conditions because they were working and earning money and could, therefore, obtain the essentials and food most necessary for living.

"When we were told we were coming to Ireland our minds were relieved because we knew the Irish character and habits were similar to ours, and we are glad to state that we have not been disappointed in this connection. The Irish people we have met have been very sympathetic, their hospitality is marvellous, and the general support received from them will be remembered and appreciated by present and future generations in Gibraltar.

"As regards the official support we unfortunately cannot say the same. We are living in Nissen huts which, though suitable for billeting soldiers, are far from being comfortable and adequate for family life. We do not possess ration books, and we are fed by communal kitchens, and the food supplied is scarce and in many occasions uneatable. We are even deprived of having a cup of tea when we feel like it.

"As to financial means, we have not received any, neither has anything been done in the welfare line. The unemployment benefit to which some of our men and women are entitled from the English Ministry of Labour, is still under discussion; salaries for men who were working in our own centres in London under the Ministry of Health have not yet been received.

"Since our arrival in Ireland we have been forced to spend our small savings in supplementing the deficient and scanty food supplied at the camp, and we do not want to think what will happen if the food question is not remedied.

We have been told that the proper authorities are trying to remedy this state of affairs, but nothing has transpired up to the moment of writing.

"Yours faithfully,
A. L. BELLOTTI,
Chairman, Warbleshinney Camp Committee
J. de SOISA,
Chairman, Molenan Camp Committee.
A. DALLY,
No 16, Tagherina Camp.
F. ALECIO,
Chairman, Ballyarnett Camp Committee.

Above copy of letter sent to a Northern Ireland newspaper by Mr V Gonzalez.

A group of 246 evacuees arrived on the 18th January 1947 on board the **SS Samaria.**

A second group of 115 evacuees arrived at Gibraltar on board the **SS Ascania on** the 20th March 1947. On board with these repatriates were the new Governor Sir Kenneth Noel Anderson and his wife.

A few months after his arrival, the new Governor delivered his first personal speech. In the opening of this speech he said that his duty as Commander in Chief was to ensure the defence and security of the fortress. He then referred to the principal problem of repatriation, the overcrowding and the appalling conditions in which some families were living. Then he mentioned the idea of an emigration scheme as a measure to deal with the overcrowding situation. Among other things he also mentioned in his speech that on completion of the repatriation, the civilian population was likely to be in the order of 24,000.

GOVERNMENT LOTTERY, NEW TAXATION

Disclosed In Governor's First Personal Broadcast

THE announcement of the Secretary of State's approval of the institution of a Government lottery; the introduction of further taxation measures to lessen the gap between the Colony's revenue and expenditure; and a warning that income tax is being seriously considered but he thought its introduction undesirable until the matter can be discussed by the people's elected representatives, were three of the principal points made by His Excellency the Governor in his broadcast on Saturday evening.

HIS EXCELLENCY ALSO SAID THAT HE AND LADY ANDERSON WERE APPALLED BY THE CONDITIONS THEY SAW DURING THEIR RECENT VISIT TO SOME OF GIBRALTAR'S HOMES AND THOUGHT THESE CONDITIONS WERE ONLY MADE BEARABLE BY THE "HOUSE PRIDE" AND CHEERFULNESS OF THE INHABITANTS.

HIS EXCELLENCY COMMENCED HIS BROADCAST BY REFERRING TO HIS VISIT TO GIBRALTAR IN 1942, WHEN ON HIS WAY TO COMMAND THE FIRST ARMY IN NORTH AFRICA, SAYING THAT HE THEN HAD LITTLE IDEA THAT HE WOULD RETURN TO FACE QUITE A DIFFERENT TASK.

"I am of course a soldier still," he continued, "and as Commander-in-Chief I have the duty of ensuring that all steps necessary for the security and defence of the fortress are taken. That is quite vital,

"But though I have only so very recently come to join you I realise already from what I have seen and from the discussions which I have been able to have with many of you that it is the problem of civilian development and welfare that will form the most urgent and difficult part of my task. To that problem I intend to devote myself to the best of my ability. What success my labours will meet I cannot tell.

"Times are hard, money is scarce and many people feel frustrated and despondent. The problems of Gibraltar will not be solved in a day or in a year and in some respects conditions will probably be worse before they are better. This is not a platitude to excuse myself in advance, but is a real possibility we must face.

"It is better to face our facts because in that way we avoid disappointment. I make you no promises but as far as it is in my power to do I shall give you a square deal.

PRINCIPAL PROBLEM

"I do not need you to tell me that your principal problem is repatriation and rehousing. I mention them in the same breath because they are in fact indissoluble parts of one problem.

"We are pretty well at saturation point under existing accommodation conditions. After our visit to some of your worst over-crowded homes my wife and I are appalled at the conditions we saw, made bearable only by the splendid 'house pride' and cheerfulness of the inhabitants.

"Don't think for a moment that the members of my Administration **are satisfied or complacent with what** has been done: they certainly are NOT. We are all profoundly dissatisfied that despite all the efforts which have been made (and they are great) so much more remains to be done.

"It may be possible to add a little more here and there to the temporary housing plan, but taking it by and large we have gone just about as far as space, and at the moment money, will permit. There are at present over 1,700 persons housed in temporary accommodation completed since the end of the war.

"That is a very remarkable achievement in relation to the area and total population of Gibraltar, and compares very favourably with the results achieved anywhere else in the world, and credit for what has been done must go to my predecessor by whose direction this work was planned and to the City Council with whose willing and energetic assistance it has been so speedily carried out.

COLD COMFORT

"Reference to past achievements however is cold comfort for those who are still waiting to come back to Gibraltar and cannot do so because there is no room for them. I am afraid we must all recognise the fact that for a substantial number of those persons it will be impossible to find accommodation until our present permanent building scheme is completed.

"That scheme is now well under way and the date for the completion of the contract is 2nd April, 1949. Some of the blocks should, however, become available considerably before that date unless some unexpected difficulty should arise. The permanent building scheme when complete will enable us to repatriate all Gibraltarians now in camps in Northern Ireland who desire to return, and provide a small margin of flats in addition for Gibraltarians elsewhere who may be awaiting repatriation.

"It will not however offer any solution to our permanent housing needs as a whole, for there are over 1,700 people at present occupying temporary accommodation, more than 2,300 persons who are without houses of their own living with friends and relatives, and about 800 persons in transit centres.

"Many of these persons, if not all of them, require homes of their own, and it is clear a great deal of building will have to take place in Gibraltar before their needs can be fully and finally satisfied. That building, by whatever means it may be undertaken — and that is a problem which needs early and earnest consideration — cannot be carried out until there are sites available, and whether sites can be made available not only for housing purposes but for schools, clinics, recreation and other essential public needs, depends on the approval of schemes for the replanning of Gibraltar which have now been under consideration for a long time.

EARLY DECISIONS

"I hope that I shall be able to obtain very early decisions **on these** matters, for it is clear that unless we take advantage of every possible space saving device we can never hope to provide satisfactorily for the needs of our civilian population. That population, including statutory aliens and those resident aliens performing essential service in the Colony, was 20,400 before the war, but now amounts to over 21,500, and our potential population when repatriation is complete will be something like 24,000 civilians.

"This is a very high figure indeed for such a small area, and we must remember also the natural increase in the population, which must be expected to grow as better health and housing facilities become available.

"There is a limit to the number of persons who can live together in a small area with decency, comfort, and mutual respect and in the enjoyment of those social facilities which we demand as a minimum. When the population exceeds that limit there must either be emigration or a **falling away from** proper standards.

"This problem of emigration is one which in my opinion must be faced as a possibility looming ahead and must be most carefully examined: and I shall welcome any suggestions on the sort of schemes that might be attractive to those who feel that they would like to try their fortunes in other parts of His Majesty's dominions.

"Building and planning are the essence of our problem. But building, as some of you have forcibly pointed out, is costly. I do not think anything will be gained by discussing once again why our permanent scheme is costing us so much. There has already been a very full statement by the Government on the subject, and the question which I think will interest you most at the present time is how we propose to pay for it.

"It was announced in that statement that an assurance had been given to the Gibraltar Government that His Majesty's Treasury would return the sum of £850,000 loaned by this Government free of interest to His Majesty's Government. That sum has now been handed back and is available for the immediate financing of the scheme.

GOVERNMENT LOTTERY APPROVED

"Approval has also been given to raise a loan, and details of the amount to be raised and the conditions of the loan are now under consideration and will be published as soon as possible.

"You will also be glad to learn that a suggestion, made in many quarters, that a Government lottery should be instituted has also been approved by the Secretary of State and I am seeking advice as to the way in which this lottery can be most satisfactorily operated. I have heard some very optimistic estimates of the amount of money that the lottery might be expected to bring in, but my native caution warns me not to count our chickens before they are hatched. However, the lottery will I hope at least provide interest and sinking fund on all the money we want to borrow. Whether it does more than that remains to be seen. I shall be very pleased if it does: the more the better.

In the second part of his speech, the Governor made specific reference to a series of revenue raising measures through indirect taxation. He also said that by means of a sponsored lottery scheme ,the Government hoped to raise funds to meet the Government of Gibraltar's expected expenditures on housing, education, medical services and other related services. He also gave advance notice of the introduction of direct taxation.

"I cannot go further at the moment into the possibilities of obtaining more capital for future requirements. I would however say a few words on the subject of our recurrent expenditure and revenue.

"As you were warned in the statement issued on the 2nd of November, 1946, there will be a serious gap between revenue and expenditure this year. That gap is caused by the serious falling away of the revenue from customs duties and the high cost of maintaining our expanded social services.

"Despite additional taxation imposed last year the revenue from tobacco has seriously declined and it is estimated that in 1947 it will be £68,000 less than in 1945.

"I am advised that there is little prospect of any early recovery, and it is quite clear that if we are to maintain our present standards of social services more money has got to be found by new taxation. That I know is an unwelcome subject, but the plain fact of the matter is that we cannot have social services, and by that I mean such things as free education, improved hospital facilities, infant welfare clinics, and schemes of assistance for aged and disabled persons, unless we are prepared to put our hands in our pockets and pay for them. It is the people who have to find the money.

COST OF CENTRES

"In 1938, the last normal year before the war, the total amount spent by this Government on education, health and welfare amounted to £36,000 or some 17% of the actual revenue for the year. In 1947 the total estimated expenditure on health, education, public assistance and upkeep of welfare centres is no less than £212,000 or some 42% of the total estimated revenue of £498,000.

"Some of this expenditure, namely, that disbursed on the maintenance of centres, will in due course I hope be reduced. These centres, essential as they are, are a great drain on the resources of the administration and proposals designed to reduce the cost of maintaining the centres are being urgently examined

"The scheme of public assistance includes financial aid and grants in kind to those destitute through old age, sickness or disablement, and in certain circumstances to widows with young children, and to unemployed persons with dependents. Special grants are also made to persons who relinquish paid employment in order to undergo treatment for pulmonary tuberculosis.

"These facts, I know, are well known to you, but it is necessary to mention them in order to make clear why we have got to find more money.

NEW MEASURES OF TAXATION

"Without fresh taxation we estimate that our revenue would fall short by some £64,000 of the sum required to cover our total disbursements this year on essential recurrent services alone.

The Government therefore sought, and I have now received, the Secretary of State's approval to introduce a number of measures of taxation which will be brought into effect as early as possible.

"They include increaes of duty on spirits except brandy. These are effected by an amendment to the Revenue Ordinance published today. Then there are proposed duties on selected items of a luxury type which will be notified shortly. Shipping dues, which have remained unchanged since 1939, are to be increased by 50%. There will be certain increases in fees for licences to sell tobacco and perfumery, particulars of which are published to-day. Under the head of Stamp Duties it is intended that Bills of Exchange payable on demand or at sight should carry a duty of 2d. instead of 1d. as at present. Estate duties will be increased by raising the rate of the existing sliding scale, which is now from ¼% to 4%, to a sliding scale of from 1% to 10%. The exemption of estates not exceeding £100 in value will remain. A 50% increase in bonded store rents will be introduced. Finally it is intended to put a small tax on all but the cheapest seats in theatres and cinemas.

"I regret the need for this taxation, but you will understand how necessary it is when I tell you that even with this enhanced revenue there will still be a deficit of something like £24,000 between ordinary revenue and expenditure, without taking account of any items of a special or extraordinary nature for which some provision is necessary in any budget to meet the unexpected.

"It is clear therefore that not only must we increase our income, but we must exercise scrupulous care to ensure that our spending is restricted to what is really essential in the interests of the community and that every possible economy consistent with efficiency is made. It is very certain that we cannot afford to waste money anywhere.

DIRECT TAXATION

"This brings me to what I know is a highly controversial question, the matter of direct taxation. You will probably not have failed to observe that the Secretary of State for the Colonies recently said in reply to a question in Parliament that proposals for the introduction of income tax have been under consideration in Gibraltar but final decisions have been delayed by impending constitutional changes.

"In my view it is not desirable that any step should be taken to introduce income tax until it has been possible for such a measure to be discussed by the elected representatives of the people. I am sure however that such a measure must be seriously considered, and since some time must necessarily elapse before the Legislative Council is in being I see no reason why, whatever the final decision may be, preliminary examination of the question should not proceed in the meantime.

"I therefore propose, as soon as it can be arranged, to place before representative interests in Gibraltar proposals which will enable them to learn exactly how income tax legislation, if introduced, would operate, and the sort of liabilities which would be imposed on individuals in receipt of different incomes.

"It may be that some of you will not agree that income tax is in any circumstances desirable. If so you can say so, and state your reasons. It may be that others, while prepared to accept it in principle, will have constructive suggestions to make as to the manner in which legislation might operate. If so we shall be glad to receive them.

"In any case I believe that no harm and much good will be done by ventilating the whole subject so that when and if the time comes to place measures before the Legislative Council we shall then have a good idea of public feeling on this question.

"UNPLEASANT SUBJECT"

"I have dwelt at length upon this problem of finance because it is important that we should realise that we are spending more than our income, and we must either cut down some of our expenses or find fresh taxation to pay for the services we regard as essential. Whether or not we obtain outside assistance towards our capital enterprises it is abundantly clear that the financing of our day to day needs is the first duty of a responsible community.

"I am sorry that in my first talk to you this unpleasant subject of finance has had to predominate, but I should not be doing my duty, and you would have just grounds for complaint, if I confined myself to easy platitudes, or failed to show you the dark as well as the bright side of the picture.

"Democracy does not mean that we sit down and just wait to have things done for us: it means that we do things for ourselves. Differences of opinion as to method of course there will be, and I welcome them as long as the spirit enlivening them is based on a sense of service and a desire for the common good.

"I feel strongly that people w... only give their best and offer help or constructive criticism if they know the facts and each feels he or she is an essential part of the whole, and all see clearly the objective to be reached. Faith and works can accomplish much, sometimes even miracles. Let us therefore have faith in our power to solve our problems here and let each of us work as part of the team. Then, despite setbacks and difficulties, which will probably be legion, we will continue steadfastly to press ahead. Good night."

In May 1947 the Colonial Office in Gibraltar stated that consideration was being given to the possibility of transferring the evacuees from Northern Ireland to London depending on accommodation available but it would not consist of hotels, as was the case during the war. Those who wanted to find work and accommodation in London were being encouraged to proceed at their own accord and expense. Those who were not interested in this idea had no other option but to stay in the camps in Northern Ireland. A scheme designed to encourage evacuees in the camps to find jobs in the UK was announced as reproduced below and in the next columns.

eme to Help Gibraltarians in N. Ireland to Get U.K. Jobs

A scheme, sponsored by the Colonial Office Welfare Department, to assist Gibraltarians in Northern Ireland to find work in the United Kingdom, is announced in an official communique issued last night.

Details of the scheme include:—

Free travel vouchers to London for workers, and for their families to join them after they have found work;

The grant of financial assistance, according to individual circumstances, whilst looking for work, provided the individual reports regularly to an employment exchange;

A warning that, owing to England's housing shortage, it will not be possible to provide hostels similar to those supplied by the Ministry of Health during the war.

The communique also says that the possibility of providing camp accommodation near a place where work is available is being explored, but if a number of evacuees do not succeed in finding work, there may be no alternative but another winter in Northern Ireland.

The following is the full text of the communique:

The AACR was full of condemnation when it got to know about the above scheme. It described the whole idea as lacking foresight and shameful on the part of the Colonial Office in the UK.

It also proclaimed that the evacuees had a legitimate right to live and reside in preference to others living in Gibraltar.

The Colonial Office announce that consideration has been given to the possibility of bringing back to England the Gibraltarian evacuees at present in Northern Ireland. The Secretary of State is fully aware that, with the exception of those whose repatriation may be expected in the next few months, the Gibraltarians would prefer to come over together and, in particular, that they attach importance to maintaining family units intact.

He is, however, sure that the evacuees will understand that it is impossible to make arrangements at short notice for the removal of so large a number of people, particularly in view of the housing position in this country.

In any case, it will not be possible to provide the evacuees with hostel accommodation such as that provided by the Ministry of Health during the war years. The possibility is being explored of providing, before next winter, camp accommodation within reach of a centre offering opportunities for the Gibraltarians to engage in work; but considerable difficulties are being encountered and no definite promise can be made.

Meanwhile the Secretary of State feels that it would be to the advantage of the evacuees themselves if as many as were able could take up work in this country, and find accommodation for themselves and their families, as soon as possible and ahead of the opening of any camp that may be found.

For one thing it may well be impracticable to find accommodation in this country for all the evacuees who wish to come here; and if a number have not succeeded in making their own arrangements before a camp can be opened, there would appear to be no alternative to remaining in Northern Ireland.

The Secretary of State is well aware that, in order to do this, the Gibraltarians will need some assistance. He realises that they would prefer to come over to this country in family units, but hopes that they will consider very carefully the desirability of the wage-earner coming over first and making arrangements, when he is in a position to do so, to bring his family over at a later date.

He, therefore, proposes that the following scheme should be put into operation under the auspices of the Colonial Office Welfare Department:—

(a) Men who wish to travel to England in search of employment, or to resume the employment which they left in 1944, will be provided with one free travel voucher from the Camps to London.

Free travel vouchers will also be issued to families travelling from Northern Ireland to join men who have left Northern Ireland and taken up employment in London. It must be understood, however, that free travel vouchers will not be issued for journeys back to Northern Ireland or to a second destination.

(b) Limited accommodation is available in a London hostel for working men and it will be possible for Gibratarians to be granted purely temporary residence in this hostel in order that they may secure for themselves private lodgings. The hostel is not administered by the Colonial Office.

(c) A special officer has been appointed to deal with the welfare problems of Gibraltarians in England, and this officer will give every facility to all men travelling to England with the aim of helping them to find suitable employment.

(d) On arrival in London, men will be referred to either the local Employment Exchange or the Assistance Board in order that they may receive financial assistance.

The amount of assistance granted would depend on the individual circumstances of each applicant, and if he had any resources of his own these would have to be taken into consideration, but it may be stated that the amount received would be sufficient to cover board and lodging charges up to 35/-d. a week, plus a pocket money allowance of 5/-d. weekly.

Payment of these allowances would depend on applicants regularly reporting to the Employment Exchange and making every effort to obtain employment. This arrangement would apply equally to men living in private accommodation. It is not possible to state precisely the amount of financial assistance each man would receive as all cases would have to be considered separately and in accordance with the regulations governing Unemployment Assistance generally. A man paying 30/-d. weekly for full board and lodging would probably receive an allowance of 35/-d. weekly. If he were renting a room the amount of assistance would be 18/-d. plus the rent paid, e.g.

rent 10/- allowance 28/-
rent 15/- allowance 33/-

It is hoped that these arrangements will enable many men to travel to England, and application in the first instance should be made to the Camp Warden.

The scheme apparently did not attract many evacuees wishing to leave the camp as it turned out that just about 200 had decided to move to London. One of the remarks made in the notice referred to the shortage of housing in England. It also recommended that the evacuees should leave behind their families. It seems that these remarks alone dissuaded many from taking up the offer. By that time there were still 8 camps remaining – 4 in Co.Antrim and 4 Co.Down.

The third and last contingent to be repatriated during 1947 consisted of 179 evacuees who arrived also on the **Ascania** on the 24th July 1947.

On board the SS Ascania. Photo Gibraltar Museum.

During 1947 officials from the welfare department of the Colonial Office visited some of the camps to assess the conditions in which the evacuees were living. The report when finalised was full of adverse remarks about the living conditions of the evacuees. In summing up their findings, they said that camps were totally inadequate for human habitation and consequently they recommended that the camps should be closed as soon as possible as any further delay would only serve to exacerbate the issue.

The SS Samaria. Photo Old Ship Gallery.

They also recommended that the evacuees should be given every opportunity available to be transferred to London. At that time Mr Lucas, an official from the Gibraltar Resettlement Board also visited the camps and found the people very demoralised. He practically came to the same conclusion as the officials from the Colonial Office. In view of these developments, the Governor of Gibraltar urged the authorities in the UK to make every possible effort to close the camps before the winter of 1947. At the same time the Governor was trying to obtain help for accommodation from the military authorities in Gibraltar and insisting that no more evacuees could be repatriated during 1947.

By then the Colonial office in the UK examined the possibility of obtaining two hostels in London to accommodate the remaining 1,300 evacuees in Northern Ireland. In mainland Britain there were already over 1,200 evacuees who had moved privately but were also waiting the chance to be repatriated.

Belfast News-Letter

FRIDAY, OCTOBER 31, 1947.

The Gibraltarians

Before many weeks have passed the last of the Gibraltarians who found refuge here during the war, will say farewell to Ulster. They had been removed from "The Rock" at a critical stage of the war and for a period lived in London. Then Hitler's flying bombs began to make things unpleasant, and the Government, anxious for their safety, asked the Ulster Government to provide accommodation for them. Camps built in Co. Antrim and Co. Down as emergency centres for people who might have to leave Belfast in consequence of the fury of the Luftwaffe were placed at their disposal. For a time camp life seemed to be agreeable enough, but when the novelty had worn off most of the Gibraltarians longed to go home, and many urgent representations were made to Whitehall on their behalf. Some 4,975 have left since the war ended, and the 1,525 who remain are going [illegible] London, where work can be found for them. A long time must elapse, however, before all of them can return to [illegible] where, it appears, houses [illegible] as scarce as they are in Belfast. May good luck attend them.

Cutting from the Belfast News commenting about the departure of the Gibraltar evacuees. Mr V Gonzalez

Sketch showing evacuees desperately waiting to be repatriated. Sketch and prayer by Mr D Jezzard

Below a prayers imploring for the return to Gibraltar

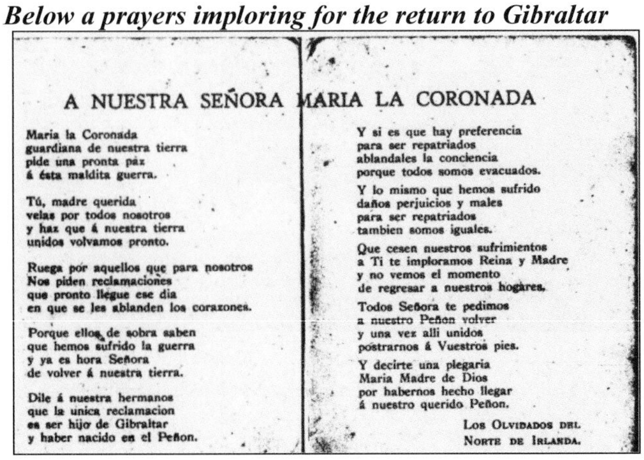

A NUESTRA SEÑORA MARIA LA CORONADA

Maria la Coronada
guardiana de nuestra tierra
pide una pronta páz
á ésta maldita guerra.

Tú, madre querida
velas por todos nosotros
y haz que á nuestra tierra
unidos volvamos pronto.

Ruega por aquellos que para nosotros
Nos piden reclamaciones
que pronto llegue ese dia
en que se les ablanden los corazones.

Porque ellos de sobra saben
que hemos sufrido la guerra
y ya es hora Señora
de volver á nuestra tierra.

Dile á nuestra hermanos
que la unica reclamacion
es ser hijo de Gibraltar
y haber nacido en el Peñon.

Y si es que hay preferencia
para ser repatriados
ablandales la conciencia
porque todos somos evacuados.

Y lo mismo que hemos sufrido
daños perjuicios y males
para ser repatriados
tambien somos iguales.

Que cesen nuestros sufrimientos
a Ti te imploramos Reina y Madre
y no vemos el momento
de regresar a nuestros hogares.

Todos Señora te pedimos
a nuestro Peñon volver
y una vez alli unidos
postrarnos á Vuestros pies.

Y decirte una plegaria
Maria Madre de Dios
por habernos hecho llegar
á nuestro querido Peñon.

Los Olvidados del
Norte de Irlanda.

In the midst of all the foregoing, an official communiqué was issued in October 1947 stating that two buildings had been obtained in London to accommodate the evacuees in the camps. The Gibraltar Chronicle carried a full story about this announcement.

ort to close N. Ireland camps before winter: Evacuees will go to London

TWO large buildings, capable of accommodating nearly 1,000 people, are being secured in London to take evacuees from Northern Ireland and every effort is being made to close the camps before winter.

The evacuees will start coming over to one hostel early in November, but their transfer will have to be gradual as conversions must be made to the building.

THEY WILL COME OVER UNDER A SYSTEM OF PRIORITIES LEAVING THE NON-GIBRALTARIANS TO THE LAST.

This is the news behind an official notice, printed on page 2, issued simultaneously today by the Colonial Office in North Ireland and here in Gibraltar.

These are the priorities under which the evacuees will come to England:

1ST: Dependents of men who have travelled to England under the Employment scheme;

2ND: Applicants who have been approved under the Employment Scheme, but who have been unable to travel owing to lack of accommodation;

3RD: Dependents of applicants under category 2;

4TH: All other Gibraltarians in the camps after categories 1, 2 and 3 have been dealt with;

5TH: Non-Gibraltarians.

The larger of the two buildings, already secured by the Colonial Office, is the Fulham Road Hostel, owned by the London County Council. This is the one which will be ready first and will accommodate up to 600 evacuees in family groups.

The other, still being negotiated, is the Sussex Square Club, which has been used by the War Department as a forces leave hostel.

This will accommodate nearly 400 evacuees.

Won fine battle

This hostel may not be quite so commodious as the one in Fulham Road, but it is infinitely more comfortable than the Camps which the Welfare Department and H.E. the Governor—who have won a fine battle with a host of other Ministries and Departments—realise too well are rapidly deteriorating and need constant repair to be barely habitable for another winter.

Sussex Square is in west London, close to the Bayswater Road and a few minutes from Hyde Park on the north side. Fulham Road is in south-west London and not far from Chelsea Park.

Many lessons learned from the first stage of the evacuees' stay in London and from administration of the Irish Camps are to be incorporated in the arrangements to be made for what is anticipated will be about a year's stay in London.

They are:—

1. **Staff.** The majority of the staff at the two hostels will be Gibraltarians, thus removing one of the great Northern Ireland grievances;

2. **Education.** Children will be sent to existing London County Council Schools unless the numbers involved exceed the capacity of the schools in the vicinity of the hostels. In the case of Fulham Road difficulties in this respect are believed to have been overcome.

The Welfare Department believes that this will be a great step forward for the young evacuee children who will, for the first time, be educated together with English children of their own age and standard.

3. **Employment.** It is thought that all employable evacuees will have no difficulty in finding work and every assistance and encouragement will be given to them to do so.

Special attention will be given to those who have grown up in exile and are taking a job for the first time.

On entry into insurable employment evacuees will qualify for medical benefits under the National Health Insurance Scheme;

4. **Settlement in the U.K.** Every assistance is to be given to families who wish to leave the scheme and, having found employment, to fend for themselves;

5. **Sickness.** Sick bays will be maintained in the hostels and accommodation kept for nurseries. Fulham Road Hostel is close to St. Stephen's Hospital and it is hoped that medical treatment and hospitalisation will be provided by arrangement with the London County Council.

The latest figures of evacuees still entitled to repatriation are given by our London correspondent as follows:

In Northern Ireland Camps—1,375;

Living in England outside the scheme—1,000;

Arrived in London under last May's employment scheme—150.

Total, 2,525

OFFICIAL GAZETTE

11th OCTOBER, 1947

GOVERNMENT NOTICE No: 188.

The following official announcement by the Colonial Office is published for general information:—

"The Colonial Office announce that a limited amount of accommodation has been obtained in England for the housing of the Gibraltar Evacuees and it is now hoped that a number of people will be transferred to England before next Winter.

It is not yet possible to indicate when the transfer will commence, or the number of evacuees likely to be involved, but a further announcement will be made as soon as possible. The Secretary of State is anxious that the maximum number of evacuees should be transferred to England, and further efforts are being made to find sufficient accommodation to enable the Camps in Northern Ireland to be closed.

The return to England will be governed by the following system of priorities:—

(1) Dependents of men who have travelled to England under the provisions of the Employment Scheme.

(2) (a) Applicants who have been approved under the Employment Scheme, but who have been unable to travel owing to lack of accommodation.

(b) Dependents of applicants in this category.

(3) All other Gibraltarians in the Camps after categories (1) and (2) have been dealt with.

(4) Non-Gibraltarians.

It is understood that there may be evacuees who desire to remain in Northern Ireland until repatriation can be arranged, and it would be helpful if any evacuees who may wish to take this course would notify the Wardens of their Camps."

This announcement was also released for publication in Northern Ireland today.

2. It has been ascertained, subsequent to the receipt of the above announcement, that the transfer of evacuees from Northern Ireland to England is likely to begin early in November and that a hostel in Fulham Road, London, has been secured for this purpose. The maximum capacity of this hostel is 600, but as transfer will be gradual and partially dependent on adaptations to the building, full ocupation may not be achieved for some months. It is also learnt that negotiations are proceeding for taking over another hostel in London with a capacity of 400.

By Command,

A. E. Cook,
Colonial Secretary (Ag.).

Colonial Secretariat,
Gibraltar, 11th October 1947

Copy of official notice about buildings for evacuees in London.

It was envisaged that if all the plans to accommodate evacuees in London and Gibraltar went ahead it could mean that the camps could be closed shortly.

Evacuees at camp No.1 urging the prompt return to Gibraltar. In the photo are Clive Coom, Carlos Harrison, Walter Feetham, his wife and son Michael. Photo Mr C Coom

According to information emanating from the Colonial Welfare Department discussions on the details of a transfer to London were high on the agenda. The arrangements to convert the Fulham Road Hostel into a communal dwelling were being looked into with some work already being undertaken. An official who visited Gibraltar in connection the Fulham Road Hostel did not foresee many difficulties with the transfer operation. Despite all these arrangements to house all the remaining evacuees in the camps by December 1947, the move still had not taken place. By then those who had hoped for the transfer to materialise were becoming disappointed and restless. Some of the newspapers in Gibraltar and the AACR were highly critical of the way the whole affair was being handled. The delay in transferring the evacuees from the camps to London gave motive for a deputation of evacuees in the camps to travel to London to seek an audience with the Secretary of State for the Colonies in December 1947.

A correspondent in London picked the story and wrote following story in the Gibraltar Chronicle on the 6th December 1947.

EVACUEES MAY STAGE MASS DEMONSTRATION

Ulster evacuees are discussing plans for a Gibraltarian protest beside those Government Offices responsible for the transfer hold-up.

Mr. Jones, of the Camp Executive Committee, went to Belfast yesterday and addressed a meeting at Camp 17 this afternoon. He is suggesting that the largest possible deputation from the Camps makes an all-Gibraltarian protest early next week outside the offices of the Government departments – presumably the Ministry of Works and the Treasury – responsible for the present impasse.
Sir Walter Smiles, MP County Down, is considering making a direct question in Parliament to the Minister of Works. He is at Ulster tonight so that he will be able to put his question until he returns on Wednesday.

GOING BACK TO LONDON

Gibraltarians in Ulster

(From our own correspondent)
LONDON, Friday.

THE 1,625 Gibraltarian evacuees now living in seven camps in Ulster are to be transferred to London. Hostels are being provided for them by the Colonial Office. In London they will find plenty of work. That is the main reason for the move.

So far it has not been possible to get accommodation for all the evacuees, nor can the date of the commencement of the transfer be stated. The Colonial Secretary hopes, however, that it will be possible to close all the camps in Northern Ireland before the winter.

PRIORITIES

Notices giving details of the scheme will be posted in the camps to-morrow morning. The following system of priorities has been arranged for the transfer:—

1—Dependents of men already in England under an employment scheme arranged some time ago.

2—Applicants approved under the employment scheme who have been unable to travel owing to lack of accommodation, and dependents of applicants in this category.

3—All other Gibraltarians in the camps after categories 1 and 2 have been dealt with.

4—Non - Gibraltarians. These are a small number of Spanish refugees who were evacuated from Gibraltar.

It is understood that some evacuees wish to remain in Northern Ireland until repatriated, and if they notify the wardens of their camps this will be arranged. These are evacuees who have found work.

Four of the camps, which were built in 1942 for expected air raid victims, are in County Antrim, and three in County Down.

PRESSED FOR CHANGE

About 6,500 evacuees went to Ulster from London in July, 1944, but the rest have been repatriated. The date of return of the remainder depends on the housing situation in Gibraltar. The Gibraltarians themselves have been pressing for a transfer to London for some time because of the opportunities of work here. The Northern Government has also made representations from time to time.

An official of the Colonial Office said to-night:—"We appreciate [illegible] much the efforts the Northern [illegible] made for the [illegible] a difficult job, involving all manner of problems—the housing of people from a warmer climate, keeping them for a long time and trying to fight the spirit of boredom and despair which inevitably arose when the evacuees could not get work and had to bring up and educate their children. Northern Ireland has really done a most splendid job in most difficult circumstanc[illegible]

Above report by a Gibraltar Chronicle correspondent in Northern Ireland. Copy Mr V Gonzalez

At that precise moment the Governor in Gibraltar was being told by the Secretary of State for the Colonies that some ministers had objected to the idea of transferring the evacuees to London. Because of the poor conditions in the camps, it had been agreed by the ministries responsible that both the civilian and the military authorities in Gibraltar should explore the possibility of finding alternative accommodation in Gibraltar.

The Governor protested to London in the strongest possible terms for this change in policy. Not aware of this, the planned meeting by a delegation from the camps went ahead. The delegation had the backing of both the Governor and the AACR. When the meeting was taking place the decision had already been taken to cancel completely all the plans to transfer the evacuees from the camps in Northern Ireland to the hostels in London. The delegation was told that alternative arrangements were being made to hasten the repatriation and the evacuees would be accommodated in buildings released by the military authorities in Gibraltar. They were also told that the authorities concerned were in the, meantime, looking for alternative accommodation outside London.

Below cutting from the Gibraltar Chronicle of Saturday 13th December 1947 referring to the cancellation of the London Hostels plans.

London hostels plan is abandoned— evacuees

must stay in Ireland camps

FROM OUR OWN CORRESPONDENT

LONDON, Friday — The scheme to transfer the Gibraltar evacuees from North Ireland to hostels in Fulham Road and Sussex Gardens has been abandoned.

This was decided by the Cabinet Committee which met this morning on the grounds that "London is overcrowded and unable to assimilate further inhabitants."

The above announcement came as a severe blow to the evacuees who by then were experiencing yet another winter in the camps of Northern Ireland.

In Gibraltar representation was being made by an AACR delegation to the Governor as they felt that the British Government had broken their promise to the evacuees in the camps. The Governor was also informed of the indignation being expressed by many of the people in Gibraltar.

Mr Rees Williams.

Copy of main article in the Gibraltar Chronicle of Saturday 13th December 1947.

Mr. Rees Williams, Colonial Under-Secretary, told the deputation from the Ulster Camps which went to see him this afternoon that they proposed to accelerate repatriation, "towards which end Service Departments, notably the War Office, were releasing accommodation in Gibraltar."

Mr. Williams added that he understood that "every effort was being made to give priority to Gibraltar's building requirements."

He had instructed the Welfare Department to make every effort to find the evacuees accommodation in Great Britain outside London.

Until that happens, the evacuees must stay in the North Ireland Camps which, Mr. Williams added, "they would try and patch up."

The evacuee deputation assured him that this was impossible.

Bitterly disappointed at the result of this afternoon's meeting with Mr. Williams, the 22-man deputation is considering the most effective method of protesting against H.M Government's "breach of faith and sustained inhumanity in this matter."

Mr. Jones, of the Camp Executive, was engaged, up to a late hour tonight, conferring with other Gibraltarians at the Prince's Gate Hostel.

When the evacuees in the camps got to know about the cancellation they were obviously full of condemnation. Those who had already moved to London challenged the authorities concerned by organising a sit in.

Below cutting from the Gibraltar Chronicle of the 12th December 1947.

ass movement to quit Ulster camps tc reinforce Fulham "squatters'

FROM OUR OWN CORRESPONDENT

A mass movement is taking place in the Gibraltar evacuees camps in Northern Ireland to obtain travel certificates for England to reinforce the Fulham squatters.

Though it was earlier considered that the Ulster Government would stop the movement of these reinforcements, it was later learned that the Government has no power to prevent people travelling within the limits of Great Britain.

There is every prospect of early arrivals at Fulham Road Hostel, including women and young children, whose husbands or fathers are already living in the hostel.

The attitude of the evacuees at Fulham, far from despair, shows absolute determination, and they have no confidence in the Commons assurances that something is going to be done.

Creech-Jones' question time

Meanwhile in the Commons today Sir W. Smiles (Ulster Unionist, County Down) asked the Colonial Secretary, Mr. Creech-Jones: "What steps is he taking to implement the pledges given to the Gibraltarians, still living in camps in Ulster, to transfer them to London this winter."

Creech-Jones replied: "His Majesty's Government is deeply concerned about the Gibraltarians still living in camps in Ulster, and is doing everything possible to restore to Gibraltar the 1,340 Gibraltarians left out of a total of 17,000 evacuated, as soon as accommodation can be made available in the Colony; but it is evident that at least 700 must remain in the U.K. for some time yet, and every effort was being made to secure accommodation for these people in London.

"Owing to practical difficulties, I regret our hopes have not been fulfilled, and my officers are exploring, with all expedition, with the Ministeries concerned, arrangements for settling them in other parts of Great Britain outside the London area."

Squeezed to limit

"The military are still in ocupation of half the vacated accommodation, and they are squeezed to the limit of their capacity.

Replying to another question Creech-Jones said: "The London premises could not have been made available for Gibraltarians until April next year.

"Captain C. G. P. Smith (Labour, Colchester) asked Creech-Jones whether he will place, in the library of the House, copies of reports which he has received in the last six months on conditions in the camps in Ulster occupied by Gibraltarian evacuees.

Creech-Jones: "The only report which I have received was by an official in my Department who visited the camps on the 4th of July 1947.

"A copy of this report will be placed in the library of the House."

"Broke his word"

Smiles asked Creech Jones a supplementary question: "Is he aware that the Gibraltar people feel he has let them down, broken his word, and that the Ministry of Works is responsible for this "

Creech-Jones: "There are various difficulties in the way of settling these people in London. We did hope they could be overcome.

"Unfortunately that is not the case, but we have started trying to discover accommodation outside London."

Mrs. Manning, (Labour, Epping) asked what had happened to the accommodation in Gibraltar wherefrom these people were taken?

"Why could they not go directly back there?"

Creech-Jones: "It is impossible to get these people back. Gibraltar accommodation is crowded to unhealthy limits.

Further reinforcements cross from Ulster

From our own Correspondent

LONDON, Saturday—More evacuee "reinforcements" crossed from Ulster tonight.

At Fulham Road the ban on visi tors is still being enforced. Th Committee has asked Captain Nay lor, L.C.C. representative, to ap preach the L.C.C. for a relaxatio of the ban on the grounds of unne cessary hardship. He has promise to make representations.

The evacuees have had an answe from Mr. Ernest Bevin, the Foreig Secretary, whom they asked to in tervene on the grounds that th matter had a Spanish angle, sayin that it is more an affair for the C lonial Office than the Foreign Office He has forwarded the correspond ence to the Colonial Office.

Friday's Irish edition of th "Daily Mail" carries a big articl on the evacuees with a headlin across three columns reading: "De spair grips men of Britain's lost c lony. Eighth Christmas in exile."

Written by their reporter fro Clough, County Down, the artic describes how the evacuees sit i dreary corrugated huts lit by o lamps.

"They feel bitter, hopeless an tired. I saw a score of boys an girls wearing clothes made fro blankets taken off their parent beds. The children wear clogs an many of the parents are near barefooted.

"The pocket money of 8/6d. week allowed by the Colonial Office does not run to luxuries. They live on the poverty line.

"The biggest grumble was about the food, on which the evacuees say it is only just possible to live. The children are pasty-faced and listless and there are not enough plates to go round.

"Men and women from many walks of life make up the colony—shopkeepers, commission agents, waiters, skilled tradesmen, a boxer, and a ballerina.

"Six-hundred able-bodied men in the seven camps are bored, restless and frustrated — there is no work for them.

"Mr. B. Martinez said: 'It is painful living on charity. I am able to work. I want work. There is no education and no future for the children here'."

Above extract from the Gibraltar Chronicle dated 19th December 1947 reporting the story about the evacuees in the camps.

Evacuees from camps were arriving in London to support the action being taken by those who were already living in the hostel at Fulham Road.

Consequently, the AACR organised a public demonstration on the 18th December 1947. The outcome of this meeting was reported by the Gibraltar Chronicle as shown below and on the next column.

A.A.C.R. meeting calls on Governor and gives him a cheer

PROTEST SENT TO CREECH-JONES

A public demonstration, organised by the A.A.C.R., of sympathisers with the plight of the North Ireland evacuees, which passed a unanimous resolution recording energetic protest and resentment at the action of H.M. Government in breaking its promise to the evacuees, and urged that all available accommodation in Gibraltar should be used for repatriation, ended dramatically yesterday with loud applause for H.E. the Governor as he appeared unexpectedly on the portico of The Convent.

WHILST MR. A. J. RISSO, PRESIDENT OF THE A.A.C.R., WAS TELLING HIS SUPPORTERS, MASSED OUTSIDE THE CONVENT, THAT H.E. WOULD IMMEDIATELY TRANSMIT THEIR RESOLUTION TO THE SECRETARY OF STATE, BUT REGRETTED HE COULD NOT APPEAR TO ADDRESS THEM PUBLICLY, LOUD CHEERS DROWNED HIS VOICE AS THE GOVERNOR CAME ON TO THE PORCH AND SMILED AND WAVED TO THE CROWD.

With all shops closed and foregoing an hour's Xmas shopping, a large crowd assembled in John Mackintosh Square, listened quietly to four speakers who gave them the story of the transfer impasse, and then marched in an orderly manner to present their unanimous resolution, which read:—

1 **This meeting records its most energetic protest and deep resentment at the action of the British Government in breaking its promise to the Gibraltarian evacuees to remove them from the inhuman camps in Northern Ireland and bring them over to London this winter.**

2 **This meeting supports the action already taken by His Excellency the Governor on behalf of the evacuees, and urges His Excellency to take drastic measures to ensure that in addition to the efforts already made all accommodation in Gibraltar which can be procured and made available be used for the earliest repatriation of all our evacuees.**

We beg to request that resolution No. 1 be transmitted to the Secretary of State for the Colonies.

enough room in Gibraltar for total repatriation. Three thousand, he added, had come back, thanks to the help of those of modest means.

Mr. Risso's points were supported by Mr. Ellicott who, after enumerating the obstacles that had been overcome—lack of nurses, lack of hospital accommodation, lack of building sites, and pointing out that the combined efforts of the Government, City Council and the Services, had brought 15,000 back, said that in this crisis the people of Gibraltar were lucky enough to have someone else who was willing to help—H.E. the Governor—who, he said, was doing much more than many other people to secure the prompt return of the evacuees to Gibraltar.

THREE CHEERS

He called on the meeting to follow the deputation to The Convent and there give H.E. three hearty cheers for his interest and zeal.

Mr. L. Bruzon, the next speaker said he would like to condemn all the Ministers responsible — first Oliver Stanley, then George Hall and now Creech-Jones—to the seven years' sentence endured by the evacuees.

At the end of December 1947 the British Government informed the evacuees in London that the Colonial Office had obtained responsibility for the running of the premises. However, there were many aspects, which still needed to be prepared and settled before the moves took place. The first stumbling block was the actual transfer of the evacuees from the camps to London.

The British Government maintained that the evacuees were responsible for arranging and paying their own transfer.

A few moments after entering The Convent, the deputation announced that part 1 of the resolution would be transmitted to Mr. Creech-Jones immediately.

The first of the four speakers at John Mackintosh Square was Mr. A. J. Risso, who pointed out that the Colonial Office has now admitted what the A.A.C.R. deputation to London had said two years ago—that the conditions in North Ireland camps were "inhuman."

He referred to the interview with H.E. the Governor over the week-end, confirming that H.E. had sent such energetic cables on the matter that the Executive Committee of the A.A.C.R. had nothing to add.

Mr. Risso said it was not correct to say that Gibraltar was so overcrowded as to be a danger to public health, as Mr. Creech-Jones had stated in Wednesday's debate in the Commons.

Mr. Risso knew, as a member of the accommodation committee, that while there were many families living in deplorable conditions, there were others occupying more than they ought to in the present crisis.

VIEWS OPPOSED

The reason why the A.A.C.R. and City Council representatives on the Resettlement Board had not gone to the meeting of the Unofficial Representatives, was that their views on repatriation were opposed to those who had signed the letter in yesterday's "Chronicle".

The A.A.C.R. had always maintained, he said, that there was

He could not believe that a city like London, with 10-million inhabitants, was incapable of absorbing 1,500 Gibraltarians. Are there not 1,500 strangers in a small place like Gibraltar?, he asked.

He called upon those in Gibraltar who "get a lot and give nothing to think of their brethren in North Ireland."

Concluding the addresses, and moving the resolution, Mr. J. A Hassan said that he felt he must comment that if such a muddle could come out of the Colonial Office, Gibraltar was entitled to ask whether it was competent to decide whether or not Gibraltar should have a majority on the Legislative Council.

The evacuees who had opted, in the circumstances, to move to London started making their own arrangements with many difficulties in terms of the actual payment for their fares and having to leave behind some of their belongings which were put in heavy luggage.
The year started with the repatriation of just 46 evacuees on the **SS Oribita**, which arrived in Gibraltar on the 15th January 1948.

The SS Orbita. Photo Old Ship Gallery

At the hostel in Fulham Road there were still many construction works that had not been completed to make the place fit for human habitation. Other essential arrangements like education, medical facilities, which should have been looked into, had not been sorted out. As the evacuees arrived the place became increasingly overcrowded. The AACR, which no doubt was monitoring the whole matter, informed the Governor of the feelings being expressed by the evacuees who were facing many problems at the different stages of their move. The Governor in turn made very strong representations and reminded the British Government of their moral and legal obligation to the evacuees in the UK and that they should be treated as any other British subject.
On the 4th February 1948 the Gibraltar Chronicle reported the latest problems regarding the fees being charged by the Treasury for the use of Fulham Road Hostel. By then there were about 660 evacuees living in the hostel. The levy charged was eventually reduced considerably after many arguments.
In Gibraltar the availability of accommodation continued to be at a critical level. The military services were requisitioned to convert a few buildings to accommodate the evacuees that were being repatriated from both Northern Ireland and London. Many, since their arrival in 1944 were still living in transit accommodation like the Cecil Hotel, the Little Sisters of the Poor, Gavino's Dwelling, the Hebrew School, etc.
After much debate, the Royal Naval Air Station at the North Front was specially adapted to accommodate families who were due to arrive shortly from both Northern Ireland and London. They were repatriated on the **SS Franconia** that brought 102 and 144 evacuees on the 25th February and 27th March 1948 respectively.

Below extract from a report by the Gibraltar Chronicle correspondent in London.

150 evacuees bound for home on Monday

From our own Correspondent

LONDON, Friday — Approximately 150 repatriates leave Liverpool on Monday in the Franconia with a Gibraltarian as assistant supervisor — Mr. Luiz Castro, who was evacuated as a boy of 14 in 1940.

Most of the party will be accommodated at the ex-R.N.A.S. station, North Front.

It is Castro's first visit back to the Rock and he was the first member of the Ulster camp staff to be appointed to assist Mr. Thomas in the Colonial Office Welfare Department. He will return to England as soon as possible.

A complete block of the Fulham Road hostel has now been partitioned and it is hoped to complete the other block next week. About 200 Fulham evacuees are now employed in diverse occupations.

It is believed that a 16 millimetre projector from Ulster, now redundant as film shows in the camps have come to an end, may, if a recommendation of Mr. Jones and his committee is adopted, be sent to Gibraltar for use by the Director of Education in schools.

If this comes about, Gibraltar will be the first colony to be given one for such use.

There is a mild rebellion in Fulham about boarding charges and developments are possible.

A scheme in connection with the Lord Mayor of London's grant of £5,000 has now been prepared, and details will be available shortly.

The name of the second boy to receive training under Messrs. Lipton's scheme is Thomas Estella.

Both he and Peter Alecio have already commenced their course at suburban shops.

A further repatriation party, over 125 strong, is expected to leave on April 22nd—also in the Franconia.

SS Franconia. Photo Old Ship Gallery

Returned evacuees are living in converted Air Station at N. Front

THE majority of the 140 Gibraltarian repatriates who arrived at Gibraltar on Saturday from Liverpool by the Cunard White Star liner "Franconia" have been taken to the Royal Naval Air Station, North Front, which has been specially converted.

The repatriates, of whom about 100 came from Northern Ireland camps, had not seen Gibraltar since July 27th, 1940, when they were evacuated. They all expressed their satisfaction and happiness on their return to their native town, to a *Chronicle* representative who visited them yesterday.

There are about 40 children in the party, a number of whom had been born in the United Kingdom.

Families are allotted in two or three rooms according to the size of the family.

The rooms are well ventilated and recently painted, and fitted with beds, chairs, tables, mattresses, blankets and pillows. There is also a spacious patio which the children use as a playground.

The feeding arrangements are in the hands of the contractor, Mr. P. Montegriffo.

A motor-van arrives three times a day. At about 8.30 a.m. to distribute breakfast. At midday to serve a hot meal and for supper at 6.30 p.m.

The head of the family goes to the kitchen and is issued with food according to the number of coupons. The food is taken away in caseroles and the repatriates eat together in their own apartments.

Another party of about 150 from Northern Ireland and Fulham will arrive here on or about April 27th.

Meanwhile the number of evacuees at Fulham is about 640, and there are still 487 in Ulster. After the departure of the next repatriation party on the Orbita on the 22nd, in the charge of Miss E. M. Seabright, and the population falls to below 400, one of the three remaining camps will close.

Fuham atmosphere is extremely happy. The charges for boarding still cause indignation but protests though simmering, are rather hanging fire.

Fulham evacuees are delighted at the release of a furthr repatriation priority list of 300 names. The April party will exhaust the original list.

The evacuees are also pleased now they are getting certain individual rations, including sugar, tea, jam, butter and margarine from the Colonial Office.

They anticipate the release of the Lord Mayor's £5,000 resettlement scheme on April 1.

The Gibraltar Chronicle reported favourably the conditions in which the repatriates had been accommodated at the RNAS. The Governor visited these families to see how they were living and found that they were quite happy with the assistance being provided.

He also took the opportunity of seeing the extra Nissen huts that were being constructed in the area of North Front for the next contingent of repatriates. By mid April 1948 consideration was given to the idea of assisting financially and socially those evacuees who did not want to return to Gibraltar but wanted to stay in London.

Photo of Main Street near to what was the Cecil Hotel in the late forties. Photo Mr M Bruzon

There were many evacuees still in Northern Ireland, who like Victor Gonzalez (at the time in hospital) were telling officials of their desperate need to get back to Gibraltar. It seems that this official was very impressed at Victor's request since only a few days later he received the following official letter:

GOVERNMENT OF NORTHERN IRELAND

Telegraphic Address: "VitaMin," Belfast.
Telephone No.—Belfast 63210.
Any reply to this communication should be addressed to: "THE SECRETARY" and the following reference quoted—
Ref. No. ....

MINISTRY OF HEALTH AND LOCAL GOVERNMENT,
STORMONT,
BELFAST,
NORTHERN IRELAND.

15th April, 1948.

Dear Victor,

This is just a note to let you know that after I saw you on Friday last, I discussed your case with the Colonial Office in London, and arrangements are being made for you and your family to travel to Gibraltar privately as soon as a passage can be secured for you and it will not be necessary for you to remain here until the next party is sailing from Northern Ireland.

As soon as I hear from the Colonial Office I shall let you know immediately so cheer up.

Yours sincerely,

Mr. Victor Gonzalez,
Emergency Hospital,
Musgrave Park,
BELFAST.

/JHC

Copy of letter Mr V Gonzalez.

At the hostel in Fulham Road there were administrative problems with regard to the distribution of food and the fees charged which were considered to be excessive for the type of board and lodging provided. After some assessment, these issues were resolved amicably by June 1948 when the closing of the camps was being decided.

Another 190 evacuees arrived on the **SS Orbita** on the 27th April 1948 as reported in the Gibraltar Chronicle.

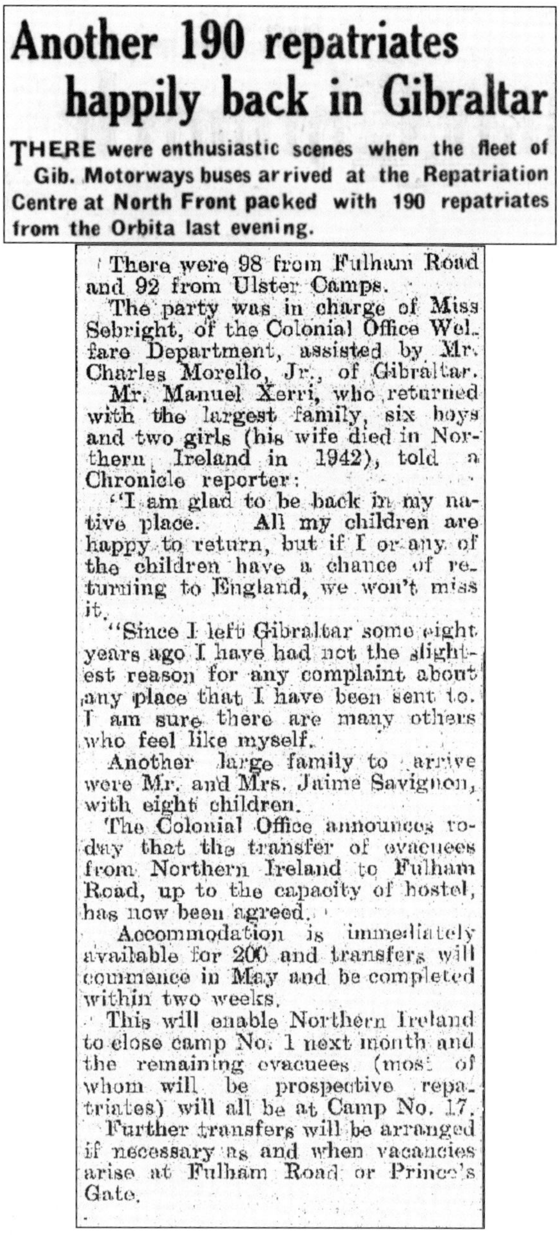

Another 190 repatriates happily back in Gibraltar

THERE were enthusiastic scenes when the fleet of Gib. Motorways buses arrived at the Repatriation Centre at North Front packed with 190 repatriates from the Orbita last evening.

There were 98 from Fulham Road and 92 from Ulster Camps.

The party was in charge of Miss Sebright, of the Colonial Office Welfare Department, assisted by Mr. Charles Morello, Jr., of Gibraltar.

Mr. Manuel Xerri, who returned with the largest family, six boys and two girls (his wife died in Northern Ireland in 1942), told a Chronicle reporter:

"I am glad to be back in my native place. All my children are happy to return, but if I or any of the children have a chance of returning to England, we won't miss it.

"Since I left Gibraltar some eight years ago I have had not the slightest reason for any complaint about any place that I have been sent to. I am sure there are many others who feel like myself.

Another large family to arrive were Mr. and Mrs. Jaime Savignon, with eight children.

The Colonial Office announces today that the transfer of evacuees from Northern Ireland to Fulham Road, up to the capacity of hostel, has now been agreed.

Accommodation is immediately available for 200 and transfers will commence in May and be completed within two weeks.

This will enable Northern Ireland to close camp No. 1 next month and the remaining evacuees (most of whom will be prospective repatriates) will all be at Camp No. 17.

Further transfers will be arranged if necessary as and when vacancies arise at Fulham Road or Prince's Gate.

71 evacuees arrived on board the troopship **Empress of Australia** on 11th June 1948.

The troopship Empress of Australia. Photo Old Ship Gallery

The month of June saw the arrival of another group of 130 more evacuees on board the **SS Scythia.**

The SS Scythia. Photo Old Ship Gallery

From then on very small groups of evacuees were being repatriated. On the 9th July 1948 34 evacuees arrived on the troopship **Asturias**. At the time there were less than 80 evacuees remaining in the camps which were officially closed on the 21st July 1948.

The troopship Asturias. Photo Old Ship Gallery

A small group of about 20 evacuees from among those who had been living in the camps arrived on the **SS Orbita** on the 28th July. Another two small groups evacuees arrived during the rest of 1948 in separate troopships shown at the bottom of this page and the next.

13 on the **Empire Deben** on 18th September 1948.

The Troopship Empire Deben. Photo Old Ship Gallery

At the end of September 1948 Mr Thomas from Welfare Department of the Colonial Office in the UK visited Gibraltar to discuss the planning and arrangements for the repatriation of evacuees for the year 1949 and also inform the Gibraltar authorities that the hostel in London had to be vacated by the end of September 1949. In some places in London like the Prince's Gate Hostel it seems that there was a consensus of opinion that the evacuees wanted to stay in the UK although evacuees continued arriving in Gibraltar during the next two and half years, albeit in small groups. By September 1948 there were still over 2,200 evacuees in the UK made up of over 700 living in official hostels and about 1,500 living in private accommodation in different parts of the UK. The official line was that those living in the hostels had to be repatriated but it was being pointed out by the Gibraltar Government that the accommodation situation in Gibraltar was as acute, as ever, even though there were blocks of flats (the then Humphrey's buildings now the Alameda Estate) being constructed that could accommodate 2,500 altogether between early 1949 and early 1950. The only way to alleviate this problem in the meantime was for the Military authorities to agree to the extension of accommodating civilians in services buildings.

The hostel at Fulham Road. Copy Gibraltar Chronicle.

Only 5 evacuees arrived on the **Empire Test** on the 24th November 1948.

The troopship Empire Test. Photo Old Ship Gallery

Towards the end of 1948 the Secretary of State for the Colonies was insisting that the repatriation of every evacuee had to be completed by 1949.

In response to this the Governor explained that the flats under construction would definitely not solve the problem of overcrowding that still existed. In order to alleviate the problem it was suggested by the Governor that in the meantime the military authorities in Gibraltar be requested to extend by nine months the use of the RN Air Station for the purpose of accommodating the Gibraltar families until March 1950 –the completion date of the blocks of flats.

The policies of the UK and that of the Gibraltar administrations were diametrically opposed. During all this time London was pressing for those who wished to be repatriated to be allowed to do so but the military authorities in Gibraltar were struggling in wanting to help with the huge accommodation problem in Gibraltar. In early 1949 after considering all the alternatives the Secretary of State for the Colonies again put it to the Gibraltar Government that those evacuees living in the Fulham Road Hostel who wished to be repatriated should be allowed to return to Gibraltar before September 1949. The Governor insisted that Gibraltar could not absorb these evacuees from the Hostel until there was assurance from the Air Ministry that they could release the RN Air Station until May 1950. 20 repatriates left from Southampton arriving in Gibraltar on the 2nd February 1949 on the troopship **Empire Trooper.**

The Empire Trooper. Photo Old Ship Gallery

In March 1949 the Air Ministry agreed to extend the lease of the RN Air Station but only until December 1949. However, with reference to the repatriation of the 400 evacuees in the Hostel, the Secretary of State for the Colonies stood his ground and said that if necessary the Gibraltar Government should consider building Nissen huts in Gibraltar at its own expense as the British Government could not afford to contribute. The Governor then stated that in view of this he would authorize the building of Nissen huts at the local government's expense but that the remaining evacuees could not be brought back to Gibraltar until the end of September 1949.

Nissen huts continued being built to cater for the acute accommodation requirements.

Nissen huts near the newly built flats.
Photo Mrs C Cavill

The **Empress of Australia** brought to Gibraltar 8 evacuees on the 25th March, some 20 evacuees on the 30th May and nearly 100 evacuees in July 1949.

The Cordoba. Photo Old Ship Gallery

A party of 139 evacuees boarded the Argentinian ship **SS Cordoba** at Southampton and sailed to Bilbao from where they travelled by train to Algeciras. They then crossed the bay to Gibraltar on the Smith Imossi ferry, the **Mary Claire** on the 31st July 1949.

SOMEWHAT tired and weary after a long journey, 139 'overlander' repatriates arrived at Waterport in the Mary Claire just after 10 a.m. on Sunday morning to find their beloved "Peñon" looking much the same as when they left it nine years ago—wrapped in a misty levanter.

The party travelled by the Argentine ship Cordova as far as Bilbao, and were then taken in two special railway coaches to Miranda del Ebro.

Here their coaches were hitched on to the Morocco Express for Algeciras, but in Madrid four coaches were made available to them instead of two.

They were given meals in Bilbao whilst waiting to entrain, and 110 pesetas each to buy food or eat in the dining car on the long train journey.

The party travelled from Bilbao in charge of Mr. J. Bruzon, of the Welfare Department, who took with him Miss Lawson, Health Visitor, Miss Baker, Nursing Sister, and Mr. Osborne, with Mr. Luis Castro, from the Colonial Office, himself repatriated, assisting.

Gibraltar Chronicle reporting the arrival on the Mary Claire.

The Mary Claire. Photo Smith Imossi

Evacuees coming down the gangway of the Mary Claire.

After this group another small party of 25 evacuees were the last to be repatriated in 1949. They left from Liverpool and arrived on the 17th October on the troopship **Oxfordshire.**

The troopship Oxfordshire. Photo Old Ship Gallery

By the end of 1949 it was estimated that there were still about 2000 evacuees living in the UK.

In connection with the hostels it was announced in October 1949 that the evacuation scheme would end officially on the 31st December 1949 and that free passage would be given for those who wished to be repatriated within a period of two years starting as from 1st January 1950.

Cutting from the Gibraltar Chronicle report the arrival of 29 evacuees who arrived overland and through the land frontier.

JOURNEY'S END FOR LAST EVACUEES CLOSES CHAPTER IN GIBRALTAR HISTORY

A chapter in the history of Gibraltar will close tomorrow afternoon, when the gates at Four Corners open to allow in a green Leyland bus of Gibraltar Motorways—in the bus will be 29 evacuees, the last to come back of the 17,000 who left their homes 10½ years ago.

THIS LAST SMALL PARTY ARE THE FEW WHO REMAINED AND WHO APPLIED TO BE RETURNED WHEN THE GOVERNMENT, IN THE AUTUMN OF 1949, ANNOUNCED THAT AT THE END OF THAT YEAR, NO MORE APPLICATIONS TO BE OFFICIALLY REPATRIATED WOULD BE ENTERTAINED.

The party, comprising five complete families including children born on evacuation, and a few individuals, have had to wait over a year for their chance to come back, which was dependent upon accommodation being available for them. They will go to the Little Sisters of the Poor Centre, pending resettlement.

One of the families, named Rocca, broke up at Victoria Station when the train steamed out.

Frank and Thomas Rocca were on the train. On the platform was father Antonio Rocca and a younger brother and sister. Mrs. Rocca was at home in Kentish Town.

Rocca told why the family split up. "There is no accommodation for people going back to Gibraltar. All this party will go into rest homes when they get there. As we have a house in London there is no point in giving it up.

"After six or seven months the boys will get a place out there. If they can't, they will come back here."

The party has made the journey overland by train, in charge of two Colonial Office welfare officers, one of them being Mr. J. E. Thomas, and are due at Algeciras just after one p.m.

There they will be met by Mr. P. Fernandes, Welfare Officer and acting Executive Officer, Resettlement Board, and other representatives of the Labour & Welfare Dept., and put into the bus for their journey's end. The luggage will come with them in a lorry.

Altogether some 17,000 of Gibraltar's population were evacuated, some 12,000 of them to the U.K. Others went to Jamaica, Madeira and Tangier.

Tomorrow's party brings the total brought back to 16,360. Allowing for deaths and births during evacuation, the difference approximates the number of Gibraltarians who found work and a new life in England.

The first evacuees arrived back on April 7, 1944. By the end of 1945 nearly 13,000 were back.

Any evacuee who declined to be repatriated when offered to do so would be seen as having forfeited their right to be repatriated at public expense. By early January 1950 about 130 people had applied to be repatriated and preparation was made to bring them back to Gibraltar at the earliest opportunity. However, the Governor in Gibraltar was not in agreement with this move as there were no place available to accommodate these evacuees.

In view of this, it was agreed to postpone the repatriation for another six months resulting in only 28 being repatriated during 1950. The British Government raised the matter again after seven months with the idea of completing the whole matter of repatriation by end of March 1951. A small party of 29 evacuees who travelled overland arrived in Gibraltar on the 11th February 1951 as reported by the Gibraltar Chronicle.

On the 27th April 1951 the naval armament vessel **Bedenham** exploded killing 13 people and destroying many buildings some of which were badly needed to accommodate the civilian population that had been recently repatriated.

It also halted for sometime the necessary works that had to be carried out on existing buildings to make them habitable.

The ammunition store ship Bedenham. Photo Old Ship Gallery

The recently constructed flats at the Alameda Estate despite being so near the source of the explosion were able to withstand the brunt of the blast with very minor damages.

Damaged buildings. Photo Mr G Cano

The very last group of evacuees consisting of only 6 members of the same family arrived from London in August 1951 on board the **SS Batory.** This ended the official repatriation process, which had taken more than seven years to complete. In the end about 2,000 evacuees had, for varying reasons and circumstances, decided to remain in the UK- mostly in the district of Fulham in London.

“We Thank God and England..”

When the evacuees began to the return to Gibraltar the health services was in a precarious state owing mainly to the shortage of nursing staff. In view of this and as recommended then by Dr Proctor by 1948 about 40 nursing assistants ,as can been seen in the photograph below,had already been recruited. Some were also undergoing training in the UK.

Colonial Hospital Nursing Staff 1948.
***Back Row:** Mrs. Faulkner, Mrs Josele, Nurses M..Eddings, Z.Hermida, A.Bossano, V.Sacramento, M.Azzopardi*
***FourthRow:**Misses:M Psaila,V.Laguea,T.Olivero,L.Hewitt,M.Fortunato,F.Bensusan,T.Zammitt,M.Panayotti,E.Boulton,A.Ever, L.Copello, L.Valle*
***ThirdRow:** Mrs Bradley, Messrs O .Bossano, V.Hemmi, A.Hermida, J.Gonzalez, W.King, A.Ramagge, J.Azzopardi, C.Colombo, J.Montero, A.Trinidad, B.Durrell, Mrs McIntosh*
***Second Row:**Mr H Bottaro,Miss H De La Rosa,Mrs B.Clark,Miss M.Brook,Mr I Ressa,Matron Miss J.Reilly,Mr S.Fortunato Misses M.Bear, T.Morillo, J.Milan, I.De Torres,A.Azzopardi, Peliza*
***Front Row:** Misses P.Banda, O.Candeas, M.Valverde, C.Bottaro, I.Sheriff, M.Gomez,M.Schembri, M.Silva.*

Towards the end of the repatriation period, a ceremony took place in London on the 21st June 1949 attended by King George VI and Queen Elizabeth to inaugurate the Colonial Month exhibition at Church House, Westminster. Mr John Martinez, in recognition for the help he afforded to the evacuees in London and Northern Ireland was invited to attend.

There were other Gibraltarians, who like Mr Martinez, were residing at the Fulham Road Hostel. These were W Coelho, son of the Commissioner of Lands and Works in the Gibraltar Colonial Government. The guards of honour at the entrance of the exhibition were Sea Scout Joseph Lara and qualified Nurse Pauline Edwards who was undergoing a training course in midwifery at the Queen Charlotte’s Hospital.

King George VI and Queen Elizabeth speaking to Mr John Martinez from Gibraltar. Photo Mr C Martinez

John Martinez meets the King and Queen

From our own Correspondent

HE King and Queen both talked with John Martinez, from Fulham Road, at the opening of ''Co-ial Month'' today.

JOHN, RATHER MYSTIFIED WHEN THE KING ASKED IM HOW LONG HE HAD BEEN IN GIBRALTAR, RE-IED: "I WAS BORN THERE, YOUR MAJESTY."

Heading from the Gibraltar Chronicle correspondent in the UK.

CHAPTER FOURTEEN

EVACUEES IN TANGIER AND SPAIN

When the evacuation order was given in May 1940, those families who could afford it, decided to leave for what was known as the International Zone of Tangier, following an agreement between Spain, Britain and France in 1923.

In June 1940 when France capitulated and Italy declared war on Britain, Spain changed its policy from strict neutrality to non-belligerency. Two days later Franco ordered the military occupation of Tangier in order, as he put it, to maintain the strict neutrality of the zone.

Moroccans in the Spanish Cavalry Regiment entering Tangier on the 14th June 1940. Photographs above and below donated by Moroccan historian.

Dr Manuel Amieva, Spanish Minister taking charge of Tangier's Administration.

Britain protested but kept a low profile on the issue so as not to push Spain into an allegiance with Germany and Italy. At that time there were already about 400 Gibraltar evacuees in Tangier.

There were some cases of Gibraltarians who were employed in British businesses and establishments and therefore took their families to live with them. One of the families affected in this way was the Beanlands.

The Beanlands in Tangier.
Photos above and below Mr C Beanland

Mrs Hortensia Beanland with her son Charles in their house in Tangier.

From 1940 until early 1942 there was no ferry service from Gibraltar to Tangier. During that period, too, there was a strong German influence in Vichy French Morocco and Spanish sympathy for the Axis powers. Some evacuees who were in Tangier during the war gave accounts of the many instances that showed that there were very close links between German and Spanish personnel. These were mainly the occasions when they were seen together at official and social functions. Military ceremonies like the hoisting or lowering of flags and salutes were held jointly between the Spanish and German military authorities.

The ferry service between Tangier and Gibraltar was resumed in January 1942. It was very convenient for the Gibraltar evacuees living in Tangier. On the 6th February 1942, a few weeks after its resumption, there was an explosion on the quay in Tangier shortly after the arrival of the Bland Ferry/Tug **Rescue**. The incident happened when members of the Gibraltar Security Police were about to get into a taxi. The Gibraltar Chronicle reported the incident as described in the cutting below.

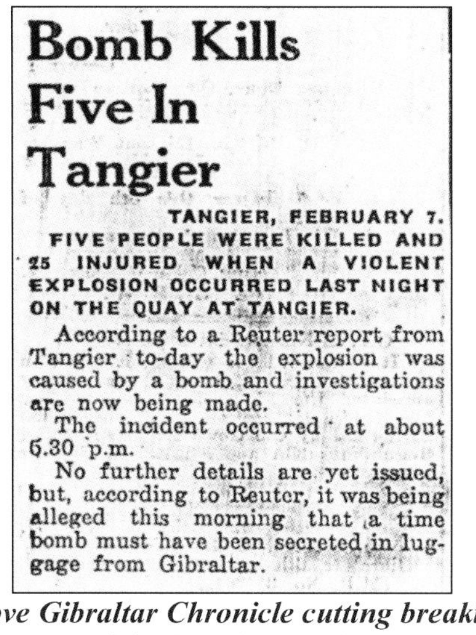

Bomb Kills Five In Tangier

TANGIER, FEBRUARY 7.

FIVE PEOPLE WERE KILLED AND 25 INJURED WHEN A VIOLENT EXPLOSION OCCURRED LAST NIGHT ON THE QUAY AT TANGIER.

According to a Reuter report from Tangier to-day the explosion was caused by a bomb and investigations are now being made.

The incident occurred at about 6.30 p.m.

No further details are yet issued, but, according to Reuter, it was being alleged this morning that a time bomb must have been secreted in luggage from Gibraltar.

Above Gibraltar Chronicle cutting breaking the news of the Tangier bombing incident.

TANGIER BOMB: BRITISH PROTEST

London, February 10.

The British Consul-General in Tangier, Mr. A. Gascoigne, has lodged a strong protest with the commander of the Spanish forces, General Uriate, regarding the Axis-inspired riots which occurred in Tangier on Saturday.

The protest was made immediately following the riots. Spanish troops were sent to the scene and order and quiet were restored.

It was stated in London yesterday that the Spanish Government's attention will probably be drawn to these Axis attempts to embitter Anglo-Spanish relations, and the question of compensation for damage done would no doubt be raised—Reuter.

Another Gibraltar Chronicle cutting referring to the bombing incident.

Many years later it was revealed that the explosion which occurred at Tangier was caused by an SOE Limpet Mine destined for a French dredger in North Africa and that it exploded prematurely. As a result 39 civilians died including the British Diplomatic Courier who had been carrying the mine in the official pouch.

The following four Gibraltar Security Police Officers were also killed.

P.Sgt. Terence Henning
PC Abraham Attias
PC Charles Samuel Curtis
PC Stephen McKillop

PC Curtis in August 1941. Photo Mr FCurtis.

Also in a way attached to the Gibraltar Security Services was Mr Stanley (Chico) Flower who received multiple injuries, some serious. Photos by Mrs Teuma (nee Flower)

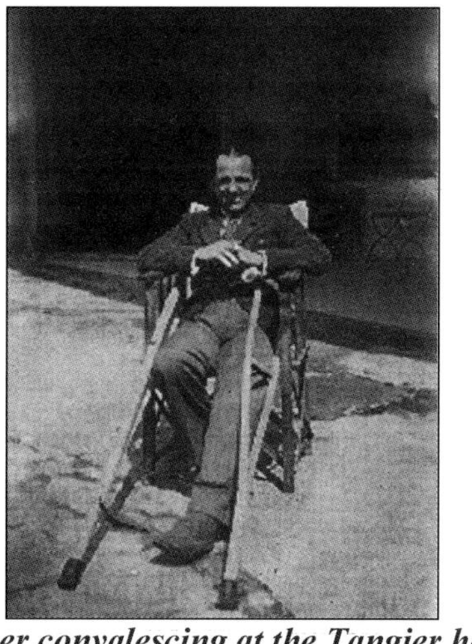

Mr Flower convalescing at the Tangier hospital.

Mr Flower leaving hospital at Tangier.

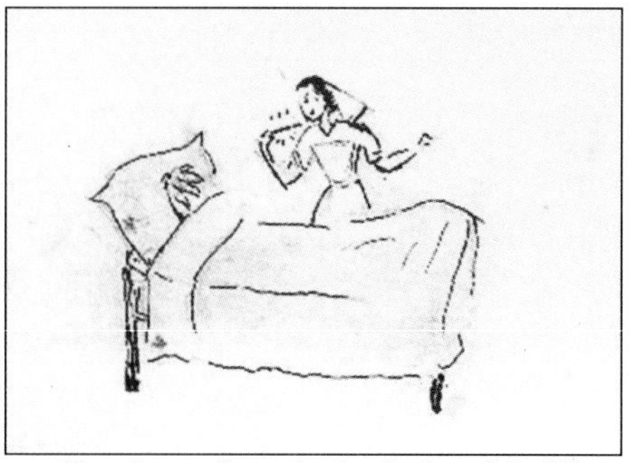

One of a collection of cards depicting Mr Flower's stay in hospital.

Below a more detailed report by the Gibraltar Chronicle about the bombing incident in Tangier.

RELIABLE information from Tangier indicates that the bomb which exploded on the quay on Friday evening was timed for the arrival of the tug Rescue carrying British subjects and diplomatic bags.

The explosion occurred 15 minutes after the Rescue had left the quayside earlier than usual after disembarking her passengers.

Reports as to the number of casualties vary, but authoritative circles give the number of British subjects as six killed and eight injured. Their next-of-kin have been informed. Reuter reports from Tangier say that 25 were killed and 60 injured, six of the killed and 20 of the injured being British.

An EFE message to Madrid gives the figure as 11 killed and 36 injured, saying that six of the killed were Moors of whom three were employed by the British Consulate.

EFE adds that the explosion occurred as a British subject was placing a diplomatic bag in a taxi-cab. The surroundings were enveloped in smoke and a number of propaganda leaflets were scattered about.

DEMONSTRATIONS

Rioting broke out in the town after the explosion. Irresponsible elements, possibly inspired by Axis agents, demonstrated against British business concerns.

The British post office was damaged and several shops, and all the windows of the Minzah Hotel were broken. The rioting, however, did not last long, and the situation is now quiet.

It is announced that as a result of these demonstrations General Orgaz, the Spanish High Commissioner, has proclaimed Martial Law.

CONSUL GENERAL'S DENIAL

His Majesty's Consul General at Tangier has formally denied the accusation made by the Spanish newspaper "España" of February 8 in an article entitled "The Catastrophe of Friday" that the bomb was enclosed in one of the packets carried by the British diplomatic messenger.

Mr. Gascoigne declares that in accordance with information received from His Excellency the Governor of Gibraltar no explosive of any kind whatever was carried in the Rescue and this is proved by the fact that all the passengers and baggage as well as the Rescue herself had been thoroughly searched before leaving Gibraltar in accordance with the usual custom.

The bombing was followed by the distribution of hundreds of anti-German pamphlets in Arabic in the areas about the port and its waters. Based on official records the Special Operation Executive (SOE) at Gibraltar had admitted blame for this unfortunate incident as a result of which sailings were stopped.

Below is a copy of an official record of the incident provided by Mr F Curtis.

6.2.42. - A bomb exploded at Tangiers as the Gibraltar Bland Line Tug/Ferry RESCUE was being unloaded. The bomb was an SOE limpet mine destined for a French dredger in North Africa, it exploded prematurely. 39 civilians died including the British Diplomatic Courier who had been carrying the mine in the official pouch. Also 4 GSP (Gibraltar Security Police) officers were killed :-

P Sgt. Terence HENNING
PC Abraham ATTIAS
PC Charles Samuel CURTIS
PC Stephen McKILLOP

Attias and Curtis (Roman Catholics) are buried in the local cemetery in Tangiers, Henning and McKillop (Church of England) are buried in the Anglican Church of St.Andrews.

The bomb also caused hundreds of anti-German pamphlets in Arabic to be distributed about the port and its waters. SOE at Gibraltar had admitted blame for this unfortunate incident, as a result of which sailings were stopped. There was talk about sabotage having taken place as the explosion blew the mail van up, ~~was~~ the bomb in the van after all. Many casualties who were Moroccans were piled into the ambulances just as if they were logs of wood. Word spread around that it had been the fault of the British (One can guess who may have spread the rumour !) and as a result of this a big mob of Moroccans gathered and went on the rampage against anything which smacked British. Many Gibraltarian families who were living in Tangiers at the time, had to literally flee through windows and rooftops to reach the safety of the British Embassy. Many British properties were vandalised and eventually the disturbance was brought under control when Spanish troops with drawn bayonets were deployed and posted outside these premises.

PC Curtis resting place in Tangier. Photo Mr F Curtis

Mrs Beanland who at the time of the explosion was nearby with her two-year-old son Charles had a miraculous escape. She suffered injuries to her legs from pieces of shrapnel that required hospital admission. In recent years a plaque was placed at the King's Chapel in memory of those who died during the incident. The plaque reads as follows:

Gibraltar Security Police
RIP
In Memoriam
The following departed this life
In the execution of their duty at
Tangier 6th February 1942

Sgt. T. Fenning
P.C. S.M.McKillop
P.C. C.Curtis
P.C. A.Attias

Their duties done to the last
Until they fell by bombs foul blast
They now parade a heaven beat
Until the day we all shall meet

During the war there were, undoubtedly, many spying activities in Tangier which were very noticeable in places like the hotels, bars etc. Below is an advert of the Cecil Hotel in Tangier where it was believed that spies from both sides used to meet to exchange information.

Hotel Cecil in Tangier
advert in the Gibraltar Chronicle.

During their stay in Tangier the Gibraltar evacuee children attended school at a building at the 139 Rue de Hollande. The building had been obtained by Christian Brothers O'Toole and Ryan at the request of the Roman Catholic Bishop of Gibraltar Dr Richard Fitzgerald. The school was called the Christian Brothers' School for Gibraltar boys and opened in September 1940. It was really a substitute for the Line Wall School, which had been closed together with all the schools in Gibraltar. It was financed from the fees paid by the pupils whose parents could afford it. The Roman Catholic Bishop of Gibraltar paid the fees for those children whose parents who could not afford it. There were also regular contributions from ex-pupils and other voluntary sponsors.

Pupils with Brother Healey outside the school building in Tangier
In the photograph from Left to Right are:
At the back Labrador,...?..., A.Massias, J.Manito, Bro.Healy
Middle row: A.Harper, A.Lavarello..,..?..,...?....M.Massias, G.Gomez. In Front: H.Bossano, Sacarello, H.Gomez, M.Mifsud.
Photo by Mr A Harper

In 1942 seven Gibraltarian teenagers sat for their exams at the British Consulate centre in Tangier and obtained the Senior Cambridge School Certificate. They were also pupils of the Christian Brothers' School for Gibraltar boys shown in the photo below.

From left to right Charles Stagnetto, Louis Vasquez, Wilfred Gordon, Paco Galliano, Tony Cottrell, Alfred Vasquez, Charles Gareze. Photo by Mr W Gordon.

Below is a Gibraltar Chronicle cutting reporting other Gibraltar children's school success in Tangier.

GIB. CHILDREN'S SUCCESSES

GIBRALTAR children have had successes in the Cambridge University School Certificate and Overseas Junior Examination at the Tangier centre sponsored by the British Consul-General.

Four boys—M. Cosquieri, M. Massias, E. Mahtani and C. J. Stagnetto—and two girls—M. T. Cabedo and M. L. Gaggero — have passed the School Certificate, with the results of the Haynes Junior Examination yet to follow.

Sixteen boys and girls have now passed the School Certificate since they were evacuated from their homes and five have passed the Junior examination.

They are: L. Stagnetto, C. J. Gareze, W. Gordon, F. L. Galliano, A. J. Vasquez, L. J. Vasquez, M. Massias, E. Mahtani, A. J. Cottrell, C. J. Stagnetto, M. Cosquieri, A. Stagnetto, C. Paron, M. T. Cabedo, E. M. Haynes, M. L. Gaggero, C. Gaggero, A. L. Stagnetto, A. Benzaquen, C. Rugeroni, A. R. Patron.

Below copy of petition prayers by the evacuees in Tangier by Mrs Linares

Petición al Sagrado Corazón de Jesús

Los hijos de Gibraltar
te pedimos con fervor,
que nos vuelvas a nuestro hogar
y libres nuestro Peñón.

Recuerdo del solemne culto celebrado en la Iglesia del Sagrado Corazón de Jesús de Tánger el 30 de Junio de 1941.

As can be seen from above prayers, there was among the evacuees a constant desire to return safely to Gibraltar.

I understand from my research that there was a shortage of essential commodities in Tangier. This, apparently, was despite the fact that there was a regular supply of basic commodities by the Allied countries of which Britain was the main supplier. Below is a cutting from the Gibraltar Chronicle about life in Tangier during the time of Spanish occupation.

How Tangier fared under Spain

LONDON, Thursday.—Spain's temporary usurpation of Tangier produced a negligible effect on that city, says *The Times* special correspondent summing up his impressions from a recent visit.

Stating that in the five years' occupation buildings were planned, but only a school and a hospital were improved, the correspondent quoted the resident Spaniards as saying: "It's a pity we managed things badly as usual."

Her mistake

After saying that Spain could argue after the fall of France that in the interest of her own security she saw no choice but to step in, the correspondent goes on:

"Spanish propagandists now assert the provisional nature of the 1941 coup de force. If so, Spain's mistake surely lay in not avoiding humiliation by expeditious withdrawal instead of waiting until she received the curtest possible notice to quit."

It was a painless extraction and "one could no more begrudge the French the triumph of their return in state with the Mendoub under the wing of the protecting Power than one would seek to belittle the preponderant part they may be expected to play in the international administration of the zone."

Still supplies food

The correspondent reviews the evil effects of the Vichy regime and the German artistice commission on the region which has temporarily reversed the comparative prosperity between the French and the Spanish parts of Morocco.

He pays tribute to the fact that Spain left food behind and still continues to supply food for the zone despite drought and her own difficulties.—"It must be acknowledged that this large gesture of conciliation does her credit."

Mixed feelings

With reference to the expected Soviet participation in the administration he sums up: "Tangier is content to have been readopted internationally but its inhabitants are swayed by mixed feelings about embracing the ideals of the 'internationale'."

The shortage was thought to be mostly attributed to the incompetence and corruption that was alleged to have existed within the Spanish administration of the city since its occupation. At that time Spain was also going through a period of extreme poverty as a result of the devastating effects of the Spanish Civil War.

View of Tangier in 1942. Photos by Mr C Beanland.

When French Morocco became part of the Vichy Government, the only British and American presence in the region was limited to Tangier and Gibraltar. By the time America entered the war there were already intelligence operations from the American consul in Tangier. Later in the war the diplomatic offices of Britain and America became very essential in gathering intelligence information for the planned invasion of North Africa. When the Allies invaded French Morocco in November 8, 1942, the Moroccan national defenders soon sided with the American and the British troops. Shortly after, the whole of French Morocco surrendered and from then on it was used as a supply base by the Allies to defeat the German and Italian forces in the whole of North Africa up to Egypt. In January 1943 a very crucial meeting took place at Casablanca where Roosevelt, Churchill and De Gaulle agreed the plans ahead to achieve "the unconditional surrender" of the Axis forces.

By 1944 Spain was compelled to order the closure of the German consular office in Tangier and by 1945 Spain was also ordered by the victorious powers to return Tangier to its former International Zone status.

Being so near Gibraltar did not mean that the evacuees in Tangier could be repatriated in anticipation of evacuees in much distant places. Although there were about 700 evacuees in Tangier they too had to go through the same process of priority that applied to the rest of evacuees, primarily due to lack of accommodation. The last remaining evacuees returned from Tangier to Gibraltar in July 1948, at the same time as the closure of the camps in Northern Ireland.

During my research I found out that there were about 100 Gibraltar evacuees living in Spain. According to various sources of information it seems that most of them were living in the nearby towns of La Linea, Campamento, San Roque, Los Barrios and Algeciras. The reasons given by some as to why they managed to stay in Spain were because they had families in these places and therefore they could afford to stay with them during the time of the war but could not cross over to Gibraltar. When the order for repatriation was given most of these evacuees returned after they had found accommodation in Gibraltar. The return of these evacuees was very slow and gradual. It took almost up to 1950 for most of the evacuees in Spain to be repatriated.

However, there were cases of some evacuees who continued living in Spain because they were able to obtain accommodation, which in those days was extremely scarce and very expensive in Gibraltar. There were also some Gibraltarian children who were orphans and were taken to a monastery in Granada where the picture on this page was taken. From the source of this picture, I was given to understand by a relative of one of the children that the children's stay in this monastery was not a happy one. There were alleged accounts of child molesting and abuse by those who were in charge of their welfare.

The photo shows a view of the Rock from Algeciras about the time of the evacuation.
Photos above and below by Mr M Bruzon

La Linea city centre with the Rock in the background in the 40s.

Gibraltarian Orphan children in a monastery in Granada.
Photo by Mr J Dalli

CHAPTER FIFTEEN

AFTERMATH

In Gibraltar as well as in the rest of the World many families had lost their loved ones and/or had been separated as a consequence of the Second World War.

Photo taken by J.Gingell.

As a result of their experiences gathered by mixing with other cultures the Gibraltarians had inevitably widened their horizons. Those evacuated to London, acquired courage by remaining steadfast under massive relentless bombing which impacted on them then and even to this day. They brought with them new ideas and methods of how to go about to achieve the social standards which they had not enjoyed since before the evacuation. The knowledge they gained also gave them the necessary impetus for wanting to have a greater say in the running of their own affairs. Many internal matters were badly in need of much attention during the post war years. The lack of accommodation, as mentioned in the chapter on the repatriation lingered on for many years and became undoubtedly the most challenging task facing the then and future administrators in order to achieve social advancements required for the people of Gibraltar.

Many dwellings in the form of Nissen huts were built in the late forties to accommodate the repatriated civilian population for what was to be a temporary period of about six months or at the most a year. Despite this, the fact was that the majority of those who had been allocated in the Nissen huts resided in them up to the late fifties and early sixties. It was not until then that the Nissen huts were demolished to be replaced with more modern blocks of flats.

Army built Nissen huts near the Isolation Hospital which remained in use up to the early sixties. It can be seen that by then most of what was La Laguna had been reclaimed. Photo Mr E Vallejo

Flats built in the 60s at the Laguna Estate to replace the Nissen huts built in the 40s. Photo Mr J Chiara.

In the meantime owing to the very serious accommodation problem, many young couples who had been repatriated tended to go back to the UK and some even decided to emigrate to places like Australia or Canada to look for better opportunities.
Up until the late 80s, there were still many families living in very overcrowded conditions using communal toilets, without proper bathroom facilities and even without internal fresh water supply.

Another area of fundamental pressing importance was that of the education system. After the war some buildings were converted into schools. In the North Front there were many repatriates who had been temporarily accommodated. Adjoining huts were built to be used as a school in the late 40s and which continued to be used as a school until about the early sixties. The purpose-built school at the Glacis Estate was named St Anne's. Below is one of the first groups of children to attend the St Anne's School.

Back row L to R: Henry Enriles, Francis Santos, Antonio Agius, Joseph Martinez, Henry King, Joseph Felices, Eulogio Barea, Antonio Dalli, Joseph Reyes, Luis Caballero, Ernesto Lopez, Alfred Sene, Andrew Gonzalez, Lionel Desoiza.
Second row L to R:Anne Asquez,Pili Cortes,Olga Morello,Iris Correa,Nevada Neale,Angelina Runde,Miss Concesa Rugeroni(Teacher),Lourdes Enrile,Emilia Victory,Elena Torres,Lilian Lima,Lourdes Cheesewright.
Front row L to R:Aida Perera,Matilde Wilding,Concepcion Cornelio,Sonia Barbara,Julia Garcia,Minerva Serra,Margot Masa, Lourdes de La Paz,Berta Cano,Elizabeth Masa. Photo Mrs L Agius (nee Enrile).

Above the newly built Gibraltar Dockyard and Technical School in Queensway. Photo Mr J Chiara.

As part of the ongoing task of providing adequate education facilities since the repatriation, the Government of Gibraltar in conjunction with the Ministry of Defence agreed to the build a technical school for school boys and Dockyard apprentices. The building for this project was inaugurated in February 1949. It was named the Gibraltar Technical and Dockyard School. By 1950 a start was made with the introduction of the Education Ordinance in order to start to bring the education system in line with that of the UK.

Teachers were required to achieve the necessary academic qualifications and undergo formal training in the UK.

Aftermath

When the evacuees returned, Gibraltar had still all the physical hallmarks of a fully-fledged fortress. Some areas remained enclosed and surrounded with barbed wires making them out of bounds for civilians. Because of the large military presence there were many uniformed personnel in the streets. It was very common in those days to watch the odd scuffle outside the bars. I remember while still residing at the Cecil Hotel, seeing soldiers of different Commonwealth countries involved in fight resulting in many of them being injured. I also remember that on a few occasions the residents at the Cecil Hotel had to call the military police to take away sailors who had occupied the residents' rooms in the hotel. Like in the UK there were many basic commodities that had to be obtained with ration books up to about 1950. After years of separation many marriages took place during the early stages of the repatriation.

Marriage of evacuees after their arrival from Northern Ireland. By their Nissen hut in Devil's Tower Road are the married couples Juani Hosken and Joseph Debono. Photo Mr H Hosken

Mr and Mrs Saltariche, newly wedded couples by their Nissen hut near the Slaughter House. Photo Mr L Saltariche

After the Second World War, the World soon entered the atomic age and the start of the Cold War era affecting Gibraltar significantly as a military base.

During the cold war era, Gibraltar in addition to its British national defence role was also a vital NATO base and vulnerable to be attacked, including with nuclear weapons by the Warsaw Pact forces. Many exercises were carried within Gibraltar and its approaches by the NATO maritime forces to prepare Gibraltar for a possible conflict between East and West. These military activities de facto conditioned the life of the civilian population in that there was very little scope for diversification. Most of the commercial activities were directly or indirectly connected with the requirements of Gibraltar as a fortress. 50% of Gibraltar's prime land including most of the recreational areas was for the exclusive use of military personnel and the UK civilians attached to the Ministry of Defence. The local civilians, including even those working for the military authorities, were not allowed to enter these areas except on duty.

The economy of Gibraltar up to 1984, date of the Dockyard closure, was around 60% dependant on defence spending. In this fortress scenario there was little or no scope for commercial developments that could bring about a diversified business oriented economy. In fact many potential developers were invariably discouraged from investing in projects on the grounds that they would conflict with the military requirements. In a sense the economic and social relationship between the military interests and that of the civilians had not, seemingly, changed much since the mid 19th century.

CHAPTER SIXTEEN

EVERLASTING LINKS

After more than sixty years the memories of the evacuation still linger in the minds and hearts of many ex-evacuees. As a way of recording those trying moments in the history of Gibraltar, special links have been established in recent years between the Gibraltar community and those who gave them sanctuary during the Second World War. One of the ways of maintaining these links for future generations has been achieved with the presentation of replicas of Our Lady of Europe. The idea of donating a statue of Our Lady of Europe first came about when Mrs Lillian Ramagge visited the village of Cowie in 1995 for the first time since the evacuation. Mrs Ramagge explained that the people of Cowie had been so good to the Gibraltar families that they had never forgotten the kindness shown to them during their stay. As a way of saying thank you to the village of Cowie, these families decided to commission a replica of the statue of Our Lady of Europe and to take it to Cowie as a gift for the village's Sacred Heart Church.

The idea was fully accomplished in April 1999 when the statue of Our Lady of Europe was solemnly blessed at the Sacred Heart Church by Bishop Charles Caruana. At the opening of the ceremony Mrs Ramagge gave the following talk when she addressed the congregation at the Sacred Heart Church.

My lord Bishop Caruana, Father Kerr, distinguished congregation.
Today marks for me the fulfilment of a dream.
Some fifty-eight years ago, my family and I, along with four other Gibraltarian families, arrived in Cowie having been evacuated from Gibraltar.

We were welcomed with open arms and shown a kindness by all which we will never forget.

I have many happy memories of the village school which I, along with the other Gibraltarian children, attended and of the late Father Bracelin who did so much to make us feel at home, which indeed we did.

We were to be in Cowie for a good four years before returning home to Gibraltar. My family often recalled fond memories of our time in Scotland.

In 1995, I made a long overdue return visit to Cowie and realised that the gratitude felt by our parents towards the village of Cowie could soon be forgotten.

Upon my return to Gibraltar, I spoke with members of the other families. Together we agreed that on behalf of our late parents, we wanted to cement the link between our towns, so that our children and grandchildren will remember and pass on our connection -- as indeed I hope my grandson Stefan who is here with me today, will.

I hope you will find room in your hearts for this statue of Our Lady of Europe as I will always carry fond memories of the people of Cowie in my heart.

Our Lady of Europe (Early 16th Century) Patroness of Gibraltar

Photo of the replica of Our Lady of Europe donated to the Sacred Heart Church in Cowie.

Cowie ties with Gibraltar are celebrated by statue

A LASTING bond between the village of Cowie and Gibraltar has been formed thanks to the arrival of a special statue.

The statue of Our Lady of Europe was presented to the Sacred Heart Church in Cowie by residents of Gibraltar who were evacuated to the village during the Second World War.

During a recent Mass at the Church, Bishop Charles Caruana, Bishop of Gibraltar, solemnly blessed the statue.

Gibraltar resident Lillian Ramajje who was one of the evacuees, flew to Scotland with her grandson Stefan to attend the service.

• **RIGHT:** Pictured are (left to right) Sister May Lewis from the Sacred Heart Church; Stefan Ramajje; Lillian Ramajje; Sacred Heart parish priest Father Philip Kerr; local residents Alfy McAllister, Molly Forshaw and Rebecca Morgan and Bishop Charles Caruana, Bishop of Gibraltar.

Copy of article in the Stirling Observer.

As can be seen from the newspaper cuttings on this page, the event of the donation of the statue of Our Lady of Europe received a very wide coverage both in Stirlingshire and Gibraltar.

Mrs Ramagge grandson Stefan at the entrance to the Sacred Heart Church in Cowie.

The Gibraltar Chronicle reported the event in May 1999 as shown below and in the next column.

RETURN TO COWIE

58 years ago six Gibraltarian families lived in Cowie - Ellul, Gonzalez, Facio, Stagno, Cavilla and Nuza - they were evacuated along with all the other Gibraltarians at the start of World War II. They first went to London as part of the evacuation but when the bombs came several families moved out - five went to Scotland, and Cowie became their home for four years.

The Bishop of Gibraltar Bishop Charles Caruana pictured with Frances Cornelious(nee Stagno) far left, Stefan and Lillian Ramagge, and the replica of the statue of Our Lady of Europe in its new resting place in Cowie.

Bishop Caruana blessing the statue of Our Lady of Europe at a special ceremony.

"I was just a child then but I remember we were welcomed with open arms. Everyone in the village showed us a great kindness. I along with the other Gibraltarian children went to the village school St Margaret's. I recall that the Catholic parish priest at the time Father Bracelin took the families under his wing and helped them out as much as he could," explained Lillian Ramagge.

Mrs Ramagge returned to Cowie in 1995. "it was a long overdue visit and I soon realised that the gratitude felt by our parents towards the village of Cowie could soon be forgotten."

Mrs Ramagge together with the other families evacuated to Cowie then set out to 'cement the link' between Gibraltar and Cowie.

"On behalf of our parents we wanted to establish a link that will not be forgotten so that our children and grandchildren will remember and pass on the connection," she said.

It was then arranged for a replica of the statue of Our Lady of Europe to be sent to Cowie.

A special ceremony and meeting was set up for the Gibraltar delegation and the Bishop of Gibraltar Bishop Charles Caruana also attended. He blessed the statue of Our Lady of Europe at a special ceremony last month in a joint service with the local Parish Priest Father Philip Kerr. Lillian Ramagge and her grandson Stefan were also present. And there was a surprise in store as another of the evacuees Frances Cornelius (nee Stagno) also made the trip with her daughter Carla. The reunion of old friends brought with it many good memories of the time they had spent in Cowie with old photographs as proof of the happy times.

The statue which today sits in the Sacred Heart Church in Cowie just outside Edinburgh is one of a number of replicas made by the Catholic Church in Gibraltar to spread the devotion of Our Lady of Europe to other parts of the world.

Bishop Caruana again pictured with Frances (far left) and Lilian (far right) together with two childhood playmates Molly and Maria Laikin.

"We Thank God and England.."

The news of the presentation of Our Lady of Europe was also reported in the widely circulated Catholic newspaper the Universe when Bishop Charles Caruana visited London for the European Bishops' Conference in 1999.

- Bishop who spent Blitz in London tube station thanks people of Britain -

Memories – Fr Philip Kerr of Cowie accepts a statue of Our Lady of Europe from Bishop of Gibraltar Charles Caruana, who fled to Britain in World War II

I'll never forget your kind hearts

Hugh Farmer

BISHOP Charles Caruana took his place at the European Bishop's Conference in London this week. – after a stroll down Memory Lane.

And as he walked through the posh streets of Kensington, memories came flooding back of the dark days of World War II.

This is where he was evacuated to with his parents and brother and sister, from his happy home on Gibraltar via Casablanca in 1940.

Information gathered by the Secret Service suggested Hitler's war plan was to capture the island then march through Spain and France to invade Britain. All non-essential islanders were moved as quickly as possible from Gibraltar to various parts of the world.

The Caruana family were among those brought to Britain and given a room in the Kensington Palace Hotel – just in time for the Blitz.

Bishop Charles recalls: "I watched the Battle of Britain being fought in the sky above. I will never forget the sight of the Spitfires battling against all the odds to beat back the German planes, to stop them dropping their bombs of death. and destruction."

Like other terrified Londoners, the Caruanas prayed in the local church, Our Lady of Victories, in Kensington High Street before it was bombed.

By then the war on London was taking a deadly twist as the Germans launched wave after wave of their VI and VII rockets. The Doodle Bugs, as the Londoners called them, came flying in almost 24 hours a day.

Bishop Charles recalled: "It became too dangerous to continue living in Kensington so the authorities moved us to a hostel in Notting Hill.

"The bombing continued and along with hundreds of Londoners we went underground during the raids. Home for our family for six months became Notting Hill Gate Tube station.

"We couldn't sleep until the last train had left the station. We sat together, children played and people sang. We did what we could to keep our minds off the war.

War

"I remember mum used to send me for fish and chips during the 'All Clear".

"I made many young friends when I was living in the station and I will always remember the kindness and hospitality.

" Without any hesitation, these big-hearted Londoners would give up their bunk for a child, for a young mother or an elderly person. The charity they showed at such a hard time for everyone was quite remarkable."

As the bombing continued, Bishop Charles and his family were evacuated again, this time to Londonderry where they remained for the duration of the war.

On this visit, the 66-year-old bishop was accompanied by Mrs Lillian Ramaage and her little grandson as they made a special pilgrimage to the parish of The Sacred Heart in Cowie Stirlingshire.

It was here some of his fellow evacuees came when Bishop Charles and his family went to Ireland.

They came, so that Lillian could present, on behalf of those families a statue of Our Lady of Europe in gratitude for the kindness they were shown when they needed it most in their lives.

Above The Universe report on the Bishop's visit to London.

The idea of donating statues of Our Lady of Europe in recognition for the gratitude felt by the people of Gibraltar began to gather popularity among ex-evacuees soon after the successful presentation ceremony at Cowie. The connections that have always existed between the people of Madeira and Gibraltar were being strengthened by means of ceremonies celebrated by both communities. In view of these links those who were evacuated to Madeira also felt that it would be a very moving gesture on their part if they could do the same for the people of Madeira. The necessary enquiries and administrative arrangements were made in conjunction with the Bishop of Funchal who approved the idea of a pilgrimage from Gibraltar to travel to Madeira carrying a replica statue of Our Lady of Europe. The statue was received at the Cathedral of Funchal where the enthronement and crowning ceremonies took place in a concelebrated mass presided by the Bishop of Funchal on the 16th August 2004.

Picture of the enthronement and crowing ceremonies at the Cathedral of Funchal.
Photo Gibraltar Chronicle

Pilgrimage that attended the ceremonies of the Statue of Our Lady of Europe in Madeira. Photo Mrs M Lima.

Bishop Charles Caruana leading the Consecration Ceremony at the Church of Our Lady of Dolours in Fulham. Photo Mr J Grech

Many of those who had been evacuated to the UK also shared the thought of taking a replica of Our Lady of Europe to be presented to the people in London. Based on this information it was thought that the Church of Our Lady of Dolours in Fulham Road would be the ideal place to symbolize a gesture of unity between both communities. The Concelebrated Mass in which the statue of Our Lady of Europe was enthroned and crowned took place on the 14th October 2006. The Church which was packed to capacity with Londoners and Gibraltarians, ended with an act of Consecration by all those attending the service. The majority of the evacuees who were concentrated in the areas of Kensington and Fulham went to pray at the Church of Our Lady of Dolours. It is also the Church where many Gibraltarians go to pray when sponsored for treatment at the major hospitals in London.

Johnny Grech with friends by the Statue of Our Lady of Europe. Photo Mr J Grech

During the ceremony, Bishop Charles Caruana made a special mention of the women in the Royal Women Volunteer Service who dedicated much of their time and effort in attending the needs of the evacuees during their stay in London.

INDEX TO CHAPTER ONE TO FOUR

INDEX TO CHAPTERS ONE TO FOUR (CONTINUED)

INDEX TO CHAPTER FIVE AND SIX

INDEX

INDEX TO CHAPTERS FIVE AND SIX CONTINUED

INDEX TO CHAPTER SEVEN

INDEX TO CHAPTER SEVEN CONTINUED

INDEX TO CHAPTER EIGHT

A

B

INDEX TO CHAPTER EIGHT CONTINUED

INDEX TO CHAPTER EIGHT CONTINUED

INDEX TO CHAPTER EIGHT CONTINUED

INDEX TO CHAPTER EIGHT CONTINUED

INDEX TO CHAPTER EIGHT CONTINUED.

INDEX TO CHAPTER EIGHT CONTINUED

INDEX TO CHAPTER EIGHT CONTINUED

INDEX TO PAGE EIGHT CONTINUED

INDEX TO CHAPTER EIGHT CONTINUED

INDEX TO CHAPTER NINE

INDEX TO CHAPTER NINE CONTINUED

INDEX TO CHAPTER TEN

INDEX TO CHAPTER ELEVEN

INDEX TO CHAPTER ELEVEN CONTINUED

INDEX TO CHAPTER TWELVE

INDEX TO CHAPTER TWELVE CONTINUED

INDEX TO CHAPTER TWELVE CONTINUED

INDEX TO CHAPTER THIRTEEN

INDEX TO CHAPTER THIRTEEN CONTINUED

INDEXES TO CHAPTERS FOURTEEN AND FIFTEEN

INDEXES TO CHAPTERS FOURTEEN AND FIFTEEN

INDEX TO THE SHIPS REQUISITIONED FOR THE EVACUATION TO THE UNITED KINGDOM, MADEIRA AND JAMAICA

CODE LETTER	NAME OF SHIP	YEAR BUILT	GROSS TONNAGE	DATE LEAVING GIBRALTAR	NUMBER OF EVACUEES	DESTINATION
	ROYAL ULSTERMAN	1936	3244	19 JULY 1940	449	MADEIRA
	ULSTER MONARCH	1929	3791	21 JULY 1940	282	MADEIRA
A B C	AVOCETA, BACTRIA CLAN MACBEAN	1923 1918 1923	3442 5000 2407	21 JULY 1940	499	U.K
D	ATHLONE CASTLE	1936	25564	26 JULY 1940	1,597	U.K
E F G	ULSTER MONARCH, ROYAL SCOTSMAN AND ROYAL ULSTERMAN	 1936	 3244	27 JULY 1940	1923	U.K,
	CONVOY OF THE FOLLOWING SHIPS:			30 JULY 1940	5010	U.K
H	BRITTANY	1928	4772		718	
I	STRATEGIST	1937	6255		501	
K	CITY OF EVANSVILLE	1922	6528		496	
J	EURYADES	1913	5713		481	
P	CITY OF WINDSOR	1923	7218		467	
S	BALFE	1920	5369		413	
O	BECKENHAM	1937	4636		391	
M	DROMORE CASTLE	1919	5242		364	
R	BELGRAVIAN	1937	3136		363	
N	BAHARISTAN	1928	5479		303	
T	CALUMET	1923	7268		259	
L	SWINBURNE	1917	4659		250	
	NEURALIA	1912	9182	10 AUGUST 1940	1,248	MADEIRA
	NEURALIA	1912	9182	20 AUGUST 1940	1,786	U.K
	NEURALIA	1912	9182	9 OCTOBER 1 940	1,093	JAMAICA
	THYSVILLE	1922	8176	31 OCTOBER 1940	393	JAMAICA
	ARUNDEL CASTLE	1921	19023	22 MAY 1941	349	U.K.
	NEA HELLAS	1922	16991	30 MAY 1941	500	U.K.
	PASTEUR	1938	29253	4 JULY 1941	152	U.K.
	SOBIESKI	1939	11030	APRIL 1942	?	U.K.

INDEX TO THE SHIPS REQUISITIONED FOR THE REPATRIATION OF EVACUEES FROM THE UNITED KINGDOM AND NORTHERN IRELAND

NAME OF SHIP	DATE OF ARRIVAL	NUMBER OF EVACUEES
DUCHESS OF RICHMOND		
AND ANTENOR	6TH April 1944	1367
STIRLING CASTLE	2nd August 1944	3161
HIGHLAND BRIGADE	2ND September 1944	488
ALMANZORA	5th October 1944	437
ELIZABETHVILLE	25TH October 1944	150
CAP TOURANE	15TH January 1945	170
CARTHAGE	23RD April 1945	285
HIGHLAND MONARCH	11th May 1945	287
BATORY	22nd June 1945	778
BERGENSFORD	23rd July 1945	40
ASCANIA	28TH July 1945	423
EASTERN PRINCE	September 1945	236
CILICIA	22ND November 1945	503
DEVONSHIRE	3rd March 1946	250
CITY OF PARIS	17th April 1946	259
ASCANIA	29th June 1946	175
CHESHIRE	24th September 1946	177
SAMARIA	18th January 1947	246
ASCANIA *	20th March 1947	115
ASCANIA	24th July 1947	179
ORBITA	15th January 1948	46
FRANCONIA	25th February 1948	102
FRANCONIA	27th March 1948	144
ORBITA	27th April 1948	190
EMPRESS OF AUSTRALIA	11th May 1948	71
SCYTHIA	June 1948	130
ASTURIA	28th July 1948	20
EMPIRE DEBEN	18th September 1948	13
EMPIRE TEST	24th November 1948	5
EMPIRE TROOPER	2nd February 1949	20
EMPRESS OF AUSTRALIA	March 1949	8
EMPRESS OF AUSTRALIA	June 1949	20
EMPRESS OF AUSTRALIA	July 1949	100
CORDOBA from Southampton to Bilbao then overland to Algeciras and across bay to Gibraltar	31st July 1949	140
OXFORDSHIRE	17th October 1949	49
BATORY	August 1951	6

* Governor Sir Kenneth Noel Anderson arrived on the SS Ascania to relief Governor Sir Ralf Eastwood